Joe Quinn
Among the Rowdies

Joe Quinn Among the Rowdies
The Life of Baseball's Honest Australian

Rochelle Llewelyn Nicholls

McFarland & Company, Inc., Publishers
Jefferson, North Carolina

ISBN 978-0-7864-7980-1 (softcover : acid free paper) ∞
ISBN 978-1-4766-1531-8 (ebook)

LIBRARY OF CONGRESS CATALOGUING DATA ARE AVAILABLE

BRITISH LIBRARY CATALOGUING DATA ARE AVAILABLE

© 2014 Rochelle Llewelyn Nicholls. All rights reserved

No part of this book may be reproduced or transmitted in any form or by any means, electronic or mechanical, including photocopying or recording, or by any information storage and retrieval system, without permission in writing from the publisher.

Cover Image: Joe Quinn in the uniform of the 1890 Boston Player's League club (Mike Motto)

Printed in the United States of America

*McFarland & Company, Inc., Publishers
Box 611, Jefferson, North Carolina 28640
www.mcfarlandpub.com*

For AB and Zee

Acknowledgments

This book has been a twelve-year labor of love—admittedly with a seven-year hiatus in the middle—but it is a work that, without the support of a network of family and colleagues, would still be a box of brittle microfilm and semi-legible notes in the bottom of my closet.

To Don Kyle, who introduced me to the game of baseball during my first graduate posting—my thanks. The key ingredient in any book about baseball, be it technical, analytical, or biographical, is a sincere infatuation with the game. Thank you for the hours of discussion and debate which instilled in me that obsession, and for your patience with my very Australian interpretation of the game.

Writing about events which occurred across three continents calls for a unique combination of research skills—largely, hypertext hunting, database rummaging, and a Ph.D. in coaxing favors. My gratitude to Oisin Mason, Helen Ryan, Linda Rau, Cindy Neilsen, Joan Thomas, Dennis Northcott, Joseph T. Hetrick, Graeme Haigh, Greg Hallam, Michael Gibson, Jane Winton, John Horne, Andrew Allen, Bob Bailey, Kay Hayes and John White—without your skill and persistence, this work could not have been completed. My thanks also to the Society for American Baseball Research (SABR)—you are a wealth of resources and knowledge. And to Craig Shipley and Australian baseball historian Joe Clark, both trailblazers in whose giant footsteps I can only hope to flounder.

To the extended family of the late Joe Quinn, in particular Michael E. Motto, Mary Catherine Butler, June and Tom Hesemann, Dick Quinn, and Jan Quinn Martinez—it's been a long time in production, but I hope this work offers you a permanent record of Joe's extraordinary life. Thank you for your generosity in sharing your memories and memorabilia.

And to my own wonderful family, Bob, Vicki and Andrew, who set me free to write even when the ironing piled up and I mystified you all with distracted mutterings about OBPs, SLGs and HBPs. Your belief in my ability to finish what I start is what led this undertaking home.

Table of Contents

Acknowledgments   vii
Introduction   1

Part I • Australia: 1862–1872
1. Queen's County to Queensland   7
2. Waltzing Matilda   27

Part II • Iowa: 1872–1884
3. A Special Class of Slaves   37

Part III • The Rookie Years: 1884–1888
4. Union and Liberty   49
5. The Black Diamonds in the National League   61
6. The Price of Honor   76

Part IV • Boston: 1888–1892
7. Back on the Big Stage   89
8. Rebellion!—The Players' League   114
9. Mateship   122

Part V • The Good Fight: 1893–1898
10. The Flea-Bitten Gray and the Bald-Faced Nag   135
11. The Stone of Sisyphus   152
12. Angry Birds   164

Part VI • The Grand Old Man: 1898–1903
13. The Great Player Swap   179
14. Last Days of the Dingo   190

Part VII • The Afterlife: 1904–1940
15. A Very Private Tragedy   209

Epilogue	217
Appendix A: Joe Quinn, Career Statistics	222
Appendix B: Sabermetric Comparison of Nineteenth-Century Second Basemen	226
Appendix C: Australian-Born Major League Baseball Players, 1884–2013	228
Chapter Notes	229
Bibliography	261
Index	281

When window-lamps had dwindled, then I rose
and left the town behind me; and on my way
passing a certain door I stopt, remembering
how I had once stood on its threshold, and my life
was offered to me....

All night I have walk'd and my heart was deep awake,
remembering ways I dream'd and that I chose,...
being brimm'd with all the liquid and clear dark....
O, what horrible dawn
will bare me the way and crude lumps of the hills
and the homeless concave of the day....

—Christopher Brennan,
"The Wanderer," 1897

Introduction

"Their names will endure as long as the game is played. Quinn's will be among them, although he makes no claim for himself. He need not. The printed record and memory of his admirers will do that for him."
—W.J. Monaghan, *St. Louis Globe-Democrat*,
November 26, 1933[1]

Australia, almost by law, reveres sporting heroes. Its champions are lauded in song and fable, and the physical manifestations of adulation are everywhere—there are multiple museums dedicated to cricket supremo Sir Don Bradman; a giant tennis racquet in the country town of Barellan honors indigenous tennis Grand Slam winner Evonne Goolagong; and the heart and hide of Depression-era racehorse Phar Lap remain coveted national relics. But such exaltation is not the exclusive domain of the gold-medal winner or world record holder—Australians love an underdog as much as they love a champion. Steven Bradbury, the outsider who won a speed-skating gold medal at the 2002 Winter Olympics after everyone else in the final fell over, is upheld as an example of that uniquely Australian tradition of "having a go."[2] After all, as broadcaster Phillip Adams neatly put it, "Unless you're willing to have a go, fail miserably, and have another go, success won't happen."[3]

Support for the underdog runs deep through Australian folklore, where success is often characterized by the desire to win rather than the actual result. From the doomed last stand of bushranger Ned Kelly to the disastrous World War I battle at Gallipoli, courage in the face of insurmountable odds remains a commodity valued highly in the Australian consciousness. To the outsider, Kelly was little more than an outlaw—a horse thief, bank robber, and murderer—yet as a symbol of resistance against the ruling classes, he reigns supreme. The Gallipoli campaign was a military catastrophe, but is celebrated every year with a national holiday to remember the unstinting sacrifice of the servicemen who "fell with their faces to the foe."[4]

So in a nation whose coat of arms should probably include the byline "have a go," which celebrates its sporting stars alongside (or even above) its politicians, academics, and cultural icons, how is it that an Australian lauded for seventeen years on one of the world's most glamorous sporting stages remains virtually unknown? Joseph James Quinn, Australia's first major league baseball player and still the only Australian to manage in the major leagues, remains persona non grata in the land of his birth. There is no Joe Quinn statue outside any Australian ballpark, no Quinn Award for an aspiring young Australian player, no Quinn museum with his first pair of spikes and his old battered fielding glove preserved in a glass case. It was only in 2013 that Quinn was inducted into the Australian Baseball Hall of Fame[5]—even then, without a public voting process, and an honor conferred a lengthy 112 years after Quinn walked from a major league diamond for the final time.

In *Total Baseball*, Bill Deane lists 317 foreign-born players as appearing in the American major leagues for the period 1871–1993.[6] In the entries for Australia, there stands a solitary "one" in the pre–1900 column. That "one" is followed by zero after zero until 1986, when Australia got its next look in, with 22-year-old Craig Shipley making his first appearance in the infield for the Los Angeles Dodgers.[7] That is a staggering hiatus—in fact, Joe Quinn was almost exactly one hundred years older than Shipley and had made his own debut one hundred and two years earlier.[8] In the twenty-first century, when the fence-busting glamor of pro baseball is brought to Australia in digital flat-screen and streaming video on-demand, there is perhaps little wonder a lone figure from the sepia years faded from public consciousness.

I am a proud Australian and, having a college education in sports science and a serious infatuation with baseball, should have fulfilled all the criteria for knowing about the achievements of Joe Quinn. However, I am the first to confess I had not heard of Quinn until a cold July night in 1999 when I received the newly-released Society for American Baseball Research (SABR) biography of Baltimore catcher Wilbert Robinson. And there it was, a snippet on page 31: "The 1897 Baltimore Orioles added to their roster Joe Quinn, the first Australian-born big leaguer, and he hit over .300."[9]

So simple.

So astonishing.

Surely *everybody* knew that Shipley was the first Australian to play in the Major Leagues? *Didn't they...?* I asked around among friends who were trivia buffs, sports nuts, college and pro ball players, but Quinn's name didn't come up once among the list of twentieth-century Australian pro players they threw at me: Shipley, Lloyd, Ettles, Nilsson, Durrington. Even Craig Shipley himself admitted it was not until the day after his own major league debut in 1986 that he heard Quinn's name for the first time, in a media interview. "I was really surprised and intrigued," he said. "This was an unknown story to almost all of us in Australian baseball at the time, and I really wanted to know: who was Joe Quinn, where did he come from, and how did he get to where he was?"[10] And so that insignificant line on page 31 of Wilbert Robinson's autobiography became a jemmy in the basement door of Australian baseball history—one clearly shut so tight for so long it was very nearly a tomb.

In 1884, the year of Quinn's major league debut, the world was a far younger place. The first volume of the Oxford English Dictionary had just been compiled. War was raging in the Sudan, Alaska was annexed by the United States, and Dr. John Harvey Kellogg patented flaked cereal. The Statue of Liberty was just a cornerstone on Staten Island. In Australia, the British practice of penal transportation to New South Wales finally ended after almost a century of harsh oppression, and the cities of Sydney and Melbourne were first connected by telephone.[11] Airplanes, cars, refrigeration, electric lights, and television were distant dreams—even radio was still three years away, and legislators were struggling to regulate the speed of newfangled bicycles on city streets.[12] This was the year in which Joe Quinn donned the blue and gray uniform of the St. Louis Unions and, on April 26, became the first Australian to wield a professional baseball bat in the United States major leagues. Yet Australian periodicals and newspapers of the era yield absolutely no mention of this achievement. Perhaps it was all too far away, too exotic and otherworldly, to filter the ten thousand miles back to correspondents' pens in Quinn's homeland, instead evaporating like a wisp of sea mist somewhere over the Pacific.

After all, the sport of baseball was barely newsworthy in Australia in 1884. As residents of a British colony, Australians had taken in the game of cricket with their mothers' milk, and with intercity competition and boards of control firmly in place by 1884 and a fourth tour of England underway,[13] cricket was by far the dominant sport in the settlement. While there are reports of organized baseball on the Australian goldfields as early as 1857,[14] the game was not widely supported until after the World Tour by the Chicago White Stockings and a National League All-Star team in 1888. That tour was big-league excitement, with marching bands, dancing Negroes and balloon flights in addition to the on-field entertainment, and attracted thousands of curious spectators to the twelve matches played in Australia. In the United States, baseball players had been professionals since 1868, with the game carefully regulated by the National League of Professional Baseball Clubs. The color and standard of play brought to Australia by Al Spalding's tourists—including Hall of Famers Cap Anson, Charlie Comiskey, Buck Ewing, and "Ol' Hoss" Radbourn—created a powerful first impression for the game. Spalding also assured the Australian press that the games popular in Australia and the United States were "not really different," that cricket and baseball "both required skill and patience, and above all, discipline."[15] Within a year of the tour, enthusiastic proponents of the new sport had established baseball clubs and regular competitions in Australian east coast cities, and by 1897, an ambitious return tour was organized. That scheme, however, was a financial and sporting disaster, with the Australian team losing 19 of their 26 matches in the United States and their manager absconding with the tour funds. But for all the potential tabloid fodder it provided, the exercise still received scant coverage in the Australian press. And while there is now a well-established relationship between Australian and American baseball, with U.S. teams scouting Australian players in the domestic Claxton Shield competition and a cohort of Australians on college and professional rosters,[16] the profile of the game in Australia remains low, as historian Bruce Mitchell notes: "These first ten years of baseball in Australia (1887–1897) raised problems that have dominated the sport ever since. For baseball to attempt to rival or supplant cricket continues to be perceived as an attack on 'the national game.' ... Baseball began as, and largely remains as, a supplement to cricket and continues to struggle for extensive press coverage or popular following."[17]

So it is no fault of Quinn's that the tale of his pioneering and colorful stint in the major leagues has eluded most Australian sports fans—which is a shame, because behind the headlines Quinn attracted in his adopted country is an underdog story which will appeal to the core of many Australians. Born in a dusty squatter's camp outside Ipswich in the northern state of Queensland in 1862, Quinn was the son of an illiterate, restless Irishman who had fled poverty and famine and married a venturesome Irish orphan who had made her own way to Australia alone. Quinn spent his early years wandering in his father's footsteps as drought ravaged eastern Australia and forced many laborers into an itinerant waltz from job to job (which practice, incidentally, spawned the unofficial Australian national anthem of "Waltzing Matilda"[18]). It was his father's decision during Quinn's adolescence to relocate his family halfway around the world, to the backwoods of rural Iowa, which set the scene for young Joe's entry into the world of professional baseball. But the simple act of relocation to a ball-playing nation was no guarantee of success: Quinn, unlike American boys of his own age, had not grown up playing sandlot ball on weekends or hurling rocks at anything in sight to strengthen his arm. Games had played no part in his short, hard life. But young Joe was equipped with the tools to escape life on the pioneer homesteads or down a mine shaft: an incisive intelligence, good willing hands like his father's, and what he called "an iron arm and steel nerves."[19]

In 1884, after just three years playing amateur ball in Dubuque, Iowa, Quinn was signed by the mutinous professional outfit the St. Louis Unions, for the extravagant sum of $2,000. He became a member of baseball's first rebel league, a cohort of cynical stars and wannabes determined to break the unholy grip of unscrupulous team owners and iniquitous contractual conditions which often characterized early professional leagues. By the mid-'90s, he had played on three different championship-winning teams and the clean-cut Quinn was a public darling, as much for his refusal to indulge in the beer-swilling, brawling loutishness of many of his compatriots as for his agility around second base and willingness to speak out if his friends were being bullied. "Big league teams took Joe Quinn very seriously," declared the *St. Louis Globe-Democrat*, "so much so that sports writers always found something in his prowess or in his personality which was good for anything from a scintillating 'stick' of type to a full column."[20]

But baseball is as much a game about failure as it is about glory—even a Hall of Fame batter fails in over 60 percent of appearances at the plate[21]—and Quinn had his share of struggles. His reputation for honesty and clean living ensured he remained a valuable commodity in the game until he was over forty years of age, but in the latter part of his career the "grand old man" was shunted between teams ranging from the unruly to the outright shameful in an attempt to drag them out of the mire. Having played for baseball's most successful team ever during his debut year of 1884, Quinn found himself at the opposite end of the ledger in 1899, exiled from his home in St. Louis to captain and manage what still stands as professional baseball's most deplorable outfit, the notorious Cleveland Spiders. He seemed ideal managerial material: *The Sporting News* gushed, "Quinn never broke a contract or went back on his word ... he is honest and upright and commands the respect of the fraternity at large, and can always be depended on to do anything honorable in advancing the interest of the club."[22] But Leo Durocher may have been referring to men like Quinn when he declared "nice guys finish last": Quinn's Spiders set a major league record for futility with 134 losses against just 20 wins, a record which stands unbroken more than 110 years later.[23]

Joe Quinn, however, didn't need to play for a winning team or produce Hall of Fame career numbers to be adored by the fans. During his worst season, in which he batted a miserable .230 and made a career-worst 44 errors for the 1893 St. Louis Browns, his dignity in the face of extreme provocation from fickle fans, the erratic team owner, and the press earned him an unexpected reward. He was voted "America's Most Popular Ball-player" by readers of *The Sporting News*, that Bible of baseball fans with its readership of over 80,000. The award carries none of the eternal cachet of an MVP, batting crown, or Gold Glove, and was never recorded on any gilded board in the Hall of Fame, but it was a pure indication of public affection, and Quinn wore the gold watch presented to him as a tribute for the rest of his life.

How easy it is to forget a gentleman in a ruffian's era. While many of his cohorts were setting records for boozing, brawling, and squandering their fortunes, Joe Quinn was saving, investing and engaging in one of baseball's most peculiar off-season practices: he became an undertaker. The choice may have been motivated by love—Quinn married his employer's eldest daughter in 1887 and later inherited Thomas McGrath's funeral-home business—but was also a reflection of plain good business sense. Many revered and beloved nineteenth century baseballers ended their days penniless and forgotten, their huge salaries misspent, deserted by friends and fans. In an interview with *The Sporting News* in 1936, Quinn explained how he had realized the transience of fame early in his career when teammates such as superstar infielder Fred Dunlap and his own good friend King Kelly frittered their fortunes away and died as paupers. Quinn worked in his off-seasons to afford himself a comfortable retirement through a job he figured would always have customers: after all, the dear departed of his adopted home town of St. Louis would always need to be buried. It was a sentiment which, tragically, would return to haunt him in later life.

While Quinn never returned to Australia, having married, fathered twelve children, and established a successful business in St. Louis, he did not forget his roots. The July 23, 1897, edition of the Australian *Argus* carries the only mention of Joe Quinn by an Australian broadsheet of the nineteenth century. During their unhappy sojourn in the United States, characterized by humiliation on the diamond and financial ruin off it, the touring Australian baseball squad arrived in Chicago on July 16 to watch the White Stockings play the visiting Baltimore Orioles. Although there were no surprises when Baltimore lived up to their reputation for arguing, cheating, and fighting, the visitors *were* astonished to be met after the game by Orioles third baseman Quinn, who was "anxious to hear something of Australia."[24] Although he became a naturalized American in 1898—possibly to combat U.S. immigration laws which forbade "imported aliens" from undertaking professional work, including baseball[25]—until his last interview in 1936, Joe Quinn referred often and proudly to Australia as the land of his birth.

Albert Spalding, writing in *The National Game* in 1911, proclaimed baseball "the exponent of American courage, confidence, combativeness ... American pluck, persistence, performance ... American spirit, sagacity, success."[26] The American public evidently perceived these qualities strongly in the immigrant Joe Quinn, with his creamy Irish-Australian accent and clear steady gaze. But perhaps Quinn's hands indicated the truth: during that final interview with *The Sporting News* in 1936, he exhibited his gnarled fists, indicating not only the toll of many seasons fielding without a glove, bearing the brunt of rough base-running and attending the wild swift throwing of the catcher—but also that even Quinn had had occasion to assert himself with those very fists. "You had to be good to stay in fast company," Joe recounted. "It took a good two-fisted fellow to make his own breaks."[27]

Part I
Australia: 1862–1872

1. Queen's County to Queensland

They sailed away in the ships that sailed ere science controlled the main,
When the strong, brave heart of a man prevailed as 'twill never prevail again;
They knew not whither, nor much they cared—let Fate or the winds decide—
The worst of the Great Unknown they dared in the days when the world was wide.
　　—Henry Lawson, "In the Days when the World was Wide," 1896

North Ipswich, Queensland, Australia
Wednesday, December 24, 1862

It could not be further from his sensuous evergreen homeland, this ancient realm of time-worn stone and desolate thirsty trees.

He had wandered half a world away from crystalline rivers to this place of meditative brown water which slid silently, inexorably away into the heart of an unmapped continent. This was Australia. Here was not the heartbreaking beauty of the Irish landscape. There were no "fingers of green land pushing out against the sea, meadows of yellow gorse and slate blue rock, brown boglands, ruined Norman keeps, and medieval monasteries."[1] Here the ring of steel horseshoe on stone evaporated away into a big empty sky, small and insignificant as a bird. Strange creatures bobbed and weaved and muttered through the dark scrub. And heat, merciless December heat, poured over stockmen, cattle, horses, and creatures with no exceptions.

But here, although hot and vast and inconceivably strange, it was quiet. There were no flaming centuries-old religious wars, no wealthy Protestant landlords, no judges or sheriffs or tax collectors. The stink and slime of rotting potatoes was replaced by the wafting pungency of eucalyptus leaves crushed beneath the meandering hooves of fat cattle. This infant nation was not yet one hundred years old and still clinging to the skirts of the British Empire, but the hard work and hunger here had a purity not found in the decay of the old kingdom. Hard labor here meant building a new nation from the ground up, not struggling to claim back an old one stolen by barons and religious zealots. Here, hunger was not imposed as means of oppression but was a natural part of the battle of wits with these strange new elements of heat and dust and drought.

Today was no ordinary day. Patrick Quinn was a father again.

A son—his second son—born in this primordial place, where an ambitious small town had grown out of the gray-green trees, clambering up the banks of the Bremer River and spreading its streets like fingers across the limestone plateau. Today was Christmas Eve, and behind their velvet curtains, the Ipswich wealthy were preparing for festive "magic-lantern" shows and performances by the local Philharmonic Orchestra (described in *Punch* as "a good cure for insomnia"[2]). The *Queensland Courier* of December 24, 1862—had Patrick Quinn been able to read it—was heavy with advertisements for stoutly British Christmas delicacies: currants, chili walnuts, real York ham and Wiltshire bacon, Royal Arms cheddar, lobsters, and Barclay claret to wash the dust from parched throats at nine shillings a bottle.[3] The uninitiated, however, sweltered in canvas tents on the fringes of town, where the hot wind howled like a mournful ghost and melted their last memories of snow. Laboring on five shillings a day,[4] with a two-hundred-pound bag of flour alone worth twenty-two,[5] Patrick Quinn partook of a Christmas dinner most likely based (ironically) on potatoes, supplemented by feral goat shot on Limestone Hill outside the town. He'd bleed it, strip the hide, and give to the dogs what scraps his family could not use. But this year in his canvas tent, far from waterproof and prone to visits from snakes as thick as a man's arm, the uniform grayness of another Christmas in deprivation was unheeded in the bawling of a new life. They named him Joseph, for like the great Catholic saint, the baby was the son of a working man of humble means.[6]

The attending doctor, Kevin Izod O'Doherty, paused to shake Patrick's hand as he stepped into his sulky. The Irish surgeon was, for the Quinns, one of few living links with their faraway homeland. During the *An Gorta Mor*, the Great Hunger of 1845–52, and its attendant social unrest, the young O'Doherty had edited a subversive Dublin journal which called on its readership to "exterminate the English despots."[7] His work earned him a charge of treason and transportation to Van Diemen's Land (now Tasmania) in 1849. Granted clemency in 1854 on the condition he did not return to Britain, the young rebel of course immediately did so, marrying poet Eva Kelly and secretly completing his medical education before returning to Australia to practice and prosper in Ipswich, itself a settlement founded entirely on convict labor.[8]

Australia is an ancient land, with indigenous inhabitation thought to stretch back at least 40,000, and perhaps 60,000, years.[9] It was not until the seventeenth century that Dutch explorers first glanced around the edges of the continent they dubbed "New Holland," but it was the British who first settled the Great South Land in 1788.[10] Contrary to the popular belief that the Brits sought little more than a dumping ground for convicts from their own overcrowded prisons, the colony was rather an ambitious foray into the Pacific, seeking new territory following the loss of the American colonies in the Revolutionary War.[11] Convicts were indeed transported to the far-flung settlement, but they were not slaves—many men were, in fact, skilled tradesmen and women of optimal child-bearing age, and they could earn pardons from which to build independent futures within a new European society. But in the meantime, there were great tracts of seemingly impenetrable bush to push back, and factories, docks, roads, and public buildings to carve from the ageless sandstone continent.

Since their arrival at the port of Sydney in 1788, the British had pressed rapidly up the Australian east coast, shipping convicts to further the reach of the new colony as it ebbed outward from the progenitor settlement. At the head of navigable waters on the Bremer River, almost six hundred miles north of Sydney, the Ipswich area was home to convict miners by 1827.[12] Captain Patrick Logan, commandant of the nearby Moreton Bay penal settlement, had discovered hills of limestone along the banks of the Bremer during one of his many inland expeditionary forays in 1826. The following year, he dispatched an overseer and five convicts upriver to quarry amongst the three-billion-year-old rocks and erect a lime-burning kiln to manufacture mortar for Moreton Bay and Brisbane construction sites.[13]

Despite his exploration prowess and decorated military career, the Scotsman was a merciless despot and bully. Logan had served in the Peninsular War with Wellington's Army of Occupation in Paris before sailing with the 57th Foot Regiment for Australia in 1825 to reinforce the convict guard. Shortly afterward, he took command of the Moreton Bay colony, established for convicts who had committed a further offence after their arrival in Sydney, and Logan ensured their conditions were unremittingly harsh. While he embarked on an ambitious building program which realized a hospital, a farm, and the notorious Windmill of Wickham Terrace (still standing as the oldest building in Queensland),[14] Logan also forced the convicts to labor with little but primitive hand-tools from sunrise to sunset each day, and meted out savage punishments to transgressors with the cat-o'-nine-tails and, ultimately, the noose.[15]

Top: Irish physician Dr. Kevin Izod O'Doherty attended the birth of Joe Quinn in Ipswich in 1862. The former dissident and convict later became one of Queensland's most prominent parliamentarians and philanthropists (John Oxley Library, State Library of Queensland, neg. 65511). *Bottom:* Accommodation for itinerant workers in colonial Queensland was rudimentary, dwellings usually constructed from simple materials including bush timber and canvas, with little privacy or security. Such dwellings were common in the Ipswich area when Joe Quinn was born in 1862, and he may well have been born within one (John Oxley Library, State Library of Queensland neg. 18247).

If the convicts sent up the Bremer saw their assignment as an escape from the reign of terror under which they had lived on the coast, they were mistaken. While the restrictions on the use of ox and plow were relaxed and there were far fewer floggings, the group received a hostile reception from the local indigenous inhabitants at the newly-christened Limestone Station.[16] The convicts' tenancy was characterized by mistrust, theft, and mutual suspicion, with a delegation of soldiers required to guard the interlopers and their lime kilns and stock. Logan himself was killed in a native ambush in 1830. He disappeared in the upper Brisbane River area while on a final expedition before his planned departure for India with the 57th Regiment. When his body was discovered, with his skull crushed and his corpse partially eaten by dingoes,[17] the Moreton Bay convicts "manifested insane joy at the news ... and sang and hoorayed all night, in defiance of the warders."[18]

Relations between the Europeans and the Australian Aborigines—now recognized as the oldest continuous culture on earth—had not always been so prejudicial. In October 1823, the Surveyor-General John Oxley sailed north from Sydney seeking a site for a remote settlement of convicts who reoffended while serving their original sentences. At Moreton Bay, he encountered a trio of ex-convicts whose skiff had been blown northwards from Sydney in a severe storm and landed on what would become the coast of Queensland. They had spent eight months in the area subsisting on fish and fern root, mostly provided by the hospitable local Aborigines. One of the men, Thomas Pamphlett, declared that their "behavior to me and my companions had been so invariably kind and generous, that, notwithstanding the delight I felt at the idea of once more returning to my home, I did not leave them without sincere regret."[19] But with natural resources such as lime, coal, and fertile agricultural land firmly in British sights, and Aboriginal culture based on custody of the land rather than ownership, conflict was inevitable. Justice Blacklock recommended to the British Parliament in 1837 that reserves be created for Aboriginal people in colonized areas following the model used in the United States and Canada, to reduce conflict over land and resources.[20] But the recommendation went unheeded, and bloody clashes between settlers and the indigenes were an ongoing feature of the British push into the interior of Queensland, with up to 300 Aborigines taking part in one battle in 1854.[21] There may have been up to 500,000 Aboriginal people in Queensland prior to white settlement; as many as 30,000 were killed in the "wars of extermination" during the nineteenth century.[22]

The convict era at Moreton Bay ended in 1839, twelve years after it began, with the area opened for free settlement and most of Queensland's felons sent back to Sydney. However, a small group remained upriver at Limestone Station to tend the crops and stock under the command of ex-soldier George Thorn (whose son, George Jr., became premier of Queensland in 1876).[23] Establishment of a farm beside the kilns had been a priority in order to provide fresh food at the new frontier of European expansion. But on the stony ridges punctuated by ancient grass trees,[24] their potatoes and maize refused to thrive and their lean-bodied sheep to fatten, so the convicts shifted operations down onto the fertile river flats beside Bundamba Creek (albeit with one eye continually abroad for the mythical *bunyip* which haunted the billabongs after dark[25]). Free settlers and small businesses sprang up like seedlings around the farm. When the last convicts were finally withdrawn from the site in 1842, the Plough Station operated for a further five years until residents of the surrounding village—now named Ipswich—complained the government farm was unfair competition for local graziers, as it occupied the only area close to town where stock could graze. The site was sold in February 1848 and the convict epoch in Queensland finally ended.[26]

Like Jules Verne's Passepartout, who had been "a sort of vagrant in his earlier years,"[27]

The British push into the interior of Queensland often resulted in conflict with local indigenous peoples, with as many as 30,000 Aborigines killed in "wars of extermination." The first convicts sent to settle the Ipswich area required armed soldiers to guard against Aboriginal attack (S.T. Gill, 1853–1874/State Library of New South Wales, call no. PX*D 384/31a).

Joe Quinn's father Patrick had already traveled half the globe in an enforced quest for work, food, and security by the time he'd graduated from adolescence. He was born in 1838 near Arles in Queen's County[28] (now County Laois) in southeastern Ireland, a landlocked region largely bounded by the Barrow and Nore Rivers and the Slieve Bloom mountains. According to *Lewis' Topographical Dictionary of Ireland* (1837), Arles was a village of about two hundred inhabitants on the road from Carlow to Maryborough, of "neat and pleasing appearance" although in threat of decline as the manufacture of "excellent" floor and roof tiles by the cottagers was being superseded by commercial production of slates.[29] There was, paradoxically, also a considerable effort devoted to limestone quarrying in the area, as evidenced today in many roads and buildings around County Laois.[30]

Quinn's parents, farm laborer Thomas and his wife Mary, lived half a mile outside Arles on the Killabban parish boundary, on one of nine lots owned by Protestant brothers Hugh and Patrick Governy.[31] The Quinns' circumstances were truly grim. *Griffith's Valuation*, the first full-scale valuation of property in Ireland undertaken between 1847 and 1864, assessed the Governy land and buildings as collectively worth a respectable 21 pounds and 10 shillings. But Thomas Quinn's dwelling was the meanest of the group—it had no yard, garden, or outbuildings, and was valued at a lowly 5 shillings, half the value of its eight compatriots.[32] Its location at the edge of the parish, and the very meanness of the Quinns' lives, meant young Patrick had little schooling and seemed condemned to a life of servitude.[33]

The Governy land was soft and green and hedged, as pretty a piece of provincial paradise as was to be found, but no more immune to the fungus *Phytophthora infestans* than any other holding in Ireland. The "potato blight" first appeared in Irish potato crops in 1845, and by the following year, had decimated the national harvest. One third of the Irish population was entirely dependent on the potato for food, and in the subsequent six years, two million had died or fled to the United States, England, and Australia. For more than 120 years after what is still Western Europe's greatest peacetime catastrophe, Ireland's chief export was its people.[34] When talk in the smoky local taverns turned to the Assisted Immigrant scheme, a form of subsidized passage from the United Kingdom to the Australian colony which was crying out for trades and labor,[35] the imagination of the adolescent Patrick Quinn caught fire. He could earn 30 to 40 pounds a year, with rations, as a farm laborer, far outweighing his present desperate privation.[36] His decision to choose a long and hazardous voyage south instead of the relatively swift trip across the Atlantic to the United States or Canada may have also been influenced by the prominence of the Know-Nothing movement in the United States in 1855. The group, so named for their members' tradition of denying all knowledge of the society's activities if questioned, sought to purge American politics and public life of the influence of Irish Catholics and other immigrants, driven by popular fears that the country was being overwhelmed by foreigners hostile to the republican values of liberty and unalienable rights.[37] Saving the one pound necessary to secure passage was no small feat for a teenage farm laborer earning only a shilling a day,[38] but on February 21, 1855, seventeen-year-old Quinn sailed on a one-way ticket from Liverpool on the *Matoaka*,[39] his face turned to the thunderous Irish Sea and beyond to the hammering southern waters of Australia.

The safe arrival of the *Matoaka* in Botany Bay with 402 assisted immigrants and a cargo of soda ash, iron pots, coal, and British mail, was noted by the *Sydney Morning Herald* of Friday, May 18, 1855.[40] The paper also carried reports of Crimean troops dying of cold for want of stoves and candles, and of Turkish soldiers eating the ears of dead horses to ward off scurvy and dysentery. But the *Matoaka* log indicated hardy Patrick Quinn had no need of horse's ears after twelve weeks on board, listing him in "good condition" on arrival. The ship was only two years old at the time, and the New Zealand *Lyttelton Times* described it as a "fine vessel ... in a condition to serve almost as a model of what an emigrant ship ought to be. Capacious, clean, a fast sailer and well victualled, she has transported her living freight from one side of the world to the other with the least possible inconvenience to themselves."[41]

By the mid–1850s, Sydney was as bustling a Victorian seaport as its British masters could wish. With the local population exceeding fifty thousand and fine shops and houses lining Pitt Street and Wynyard Square, there were "marble tables, files of *Punch* and *The Times*, dominoes, sherry cobblers, and strawberry ices"[42] to be had for the Bucks and Brummels of the colony.[43] Museums and zoos, banks, theaters and even a university rose in sandstone splendor around the rim of the magnificent deepwater harbor. But at The Rocks, where many of the mail-ships arrived, a motley collection of wharves and tenements intermingled in such anarchic privation that English social commentator W.S. Jevons was moved to exclaim: "I am acquainted with most of the notorious parts of London ... but in none of these places perhaps, would lower forms of vice and misery be seen than Sydney can produce. Nowhere too is there a more complete abandonment of all the requirements of health and decency than in a few parts of Sydney."[44]

There was no time, however, for Patrick Quinn to reflect on the paradoxical world into which he had sailed, or his absolute lack of an exit strategy. The day after the ship docked, voracious Sydney labor agents swarmed on board, eager to fill an undersupply of "good useful farm servants."[45] But Assisted Immigrants were under no obligation to accede to the blandishments of these agents, and many joined the surge west over the Blue Mountains, infected by the wild fever for gold driving the boldest to the teeming diggings at Ophir, Turon, and the appropriately christened World's End.[46] Patrick Quinn, however, elected to follow the route taken by many of his Irish predecessors in turning south, the sea on his left hand, to the coastal hamlet of Broulee. One hundred and eighty miles from Sydney, the area had been surveyed and gazetted in 1837, with Irishman Henry Clarke carving the first farm from the hinterland in 1839. Shortly after, Irish settlers also built the district's first inn, the *Erin-go-Bragh* ("Ireland Forever"), at the northern end of the headland on which the village perched.[47] But despite the cheapness and wide availability of land, the coastal ranges were notoriously difficult for farming. One visitor complained to the *Sydney Gazette* in 1841, "The township is an isolated promontory of wretched land, surrounded by deep sand in all directions.... Harbour for anything larger than 100 tons, there is none.... It is utterly worthless for any purpose whatever, unless it may be a few small spots here and there about 5 miles from Broulee, under cultivation by small settlers."[48]

But the main attractions at Broulee were not in the pitiful village or struggling farms: gold was discovered in the Araluen Valley inland of the hamlet in 1851, and within months, 15,000 men had landed in Broulee and walked the thirty miles to the goldfield, where some

Sydney in the 1850s was an immigrant town, new arrivals pouring in from Asia and the Americas to seek their fortune on the goldfields and many Europeans taking advantage of the Assisted Passage scheme to start a new life in the Australian colony. It was under this system of subsidized migration that both Joe Quinn's parents arrived in Australia from Ireland (O.W. Brierly, 1853/Dixson Galleries, State Library of New South Wales—call no. DG 1/7).

100,000 ounces (2,830 kg) of gold was taken in the first year alone.[49] With no local newspapers, electoral rolls, or directories surviving from those early settlement years, there are very few records of itinerant workers in the area—that is, unless a birth, death or occasional marriage was recorded.[50] And in 1857, the birth of Patrick Francis Quinn, Jr., was registered at Braidwood, the nearest town to the Araluen goldfields,[51] one of 178 births in the town for the year.[52] In the previous year, Patrick had married a fellow Irish immigrant, Catherine McCaffrey, in Broulee,[53] and the adventurous pair made their way inland from the bitter environment of struggle on the coast to the perilous clamor of the goldfields, presuming to find their fortune.

The diggings were no place for a woman. However, Catherine McCaffrey was no stranger to risk, particularly to the type of desperate actions undertaken by the destitute when the very question of survival is at hand. If her new husband's circumstances in Ireland had been dire, her own had been positively calamitous. Born in Derryvullan, County Fermanagh, in what is now Northern Ireland, in about 1830, Catherine was the daughter of Edward and Mary McCaffrey,[54] servants in the house of farmer John Ramsey. Ramsey was reasonably prosperous, with thirteen acres in the townland of Ballindullagh and a family of four children.[55] But by the age of fifteen, "Caddie" had fallen on hard times as the full horror of the Potato Famine razed northern Ireland. Historian Cecil Woodham-Smith recalled the dreadful impact of the famine on small landholders such as the Ramseys as the merciless Irish winter set in: "Farmers were reported to be actually consuming the seed which should be sown for next year's crop ... [and] owing to the total loss of his potato crop, [have] no means to feed and pay the servants [they] once kept."[56] The fate of Caddie's parents is unclear, but with so many farm servants set adrift to face starvation and destitution amid the iron cold of Ireland's winter, it is likely they succumbed to hunger, disease, or both. When Caddie McCaffrey crept on dread feet through the gates of the notorious workhouse in the large provincial town of Enniskillen, some ten miles from Ramsey's farm, in the winter of December 1846, she was alone.[57]

An undated photograph of Joe Quinn's mother, Catherine Quinn, *née* McCaffrey. "Caddie" was a great survivor, journeying alone to Australia after losing both parents to the Irish potato famine, and bearing two sons in deprived circumstances before undertaking her second great journey across the globe to the United States (courtesy Michael E. Motto, great-grandson of Joe Quinn).

The options for waifs of low parentage amid the chaos and desperation of the *An Gorta Mor* were bleak, particularly for those averse to a life of exploitation and misuse in the bawdyhouses and back lanes. The workhouse offered a desolate kind of refuge from the dangers of street life, but conditions within were deliberately designed to deter any able-bodied pauper: the towering gray edifice on the north bank of the River Erne housed one thousand inmates in the most forlorn of conditions, with repugnant food, overcrowded sleeping quarters, familial segregation, unpaid and often backbreaking work. The majority of those forced into the workhouse were the old and the infirm, orphans, unmarried

Orphaned as a teenager by the ravages of Great Hunger, and with no other family to care for her, Catherine McCaffrey was forced into the Enniskillen workhouse in County Fermanagh, Ireland. She was the only person admitted on December 7, 1846; this evocative engraving demonstrates the despair and misery of Ireland's destitute generation (Mary Evans Picture Library).

mothers, and the physically or mentally ill—those, like Caddie McCaffrey, with nowhere else to go.[58]

The government-sponsored "home for the impotent pauper" at Enniskillen had been in operation for a year when the teenage Caddie arrived.[59] In that year alone, the inmates' diets had been badly affected by the nationwide famine, disintegrating from milk and potatoes three times a day to meager helpings of buttermilk and "stirabout" (maize mixed with water or milk) whenever it could be procured. Luxuries such as tea and sugar were often sold off by workhouse officials for their own gain, and by May of 1847, conditions were so dire around that around 15 percent of the inmates had died of starvation and neglect, their bodies piling up in unmarked mass graves.[60]

Despite the appalling conditions, the workhouse was not a prison. Residents could, in principle, leave whenever they wished, for example if outside work became available. Caddie had arrived at Enniskillen with all limbs accounted for but "dirty," according to the Workhouse Register. The admissions procedure (which included an arduous interview with the Relieving Officer in which the applicant justified his or her reasons for wishing to enter), involved bathing and delousing, shingling the hair, and donning workhouse-issue garb to prepare for labor.[61] As a young able-bodied female, Caddie may well have been assigned to dreary manual tasks such as sweeping out kitchens, scrubbing, or *oakum-picking*—teasing out the fibers from old hemp ropes, with the resulting material used for making string or stuffing mattresses, or to be sold to shipbuilders to be mixed with tar and applied as a lining to wooden ships.[62] But in addition to her youth and health, young Caddie had advantages many of her co-residents did not—she could read and write,[63] and had presumably been schooled in the ways of a domestic servant. She was able to leave the workhouse in 1847 after a stay of just months, and when she boarded the *Telegraph* to sail for Australia six years

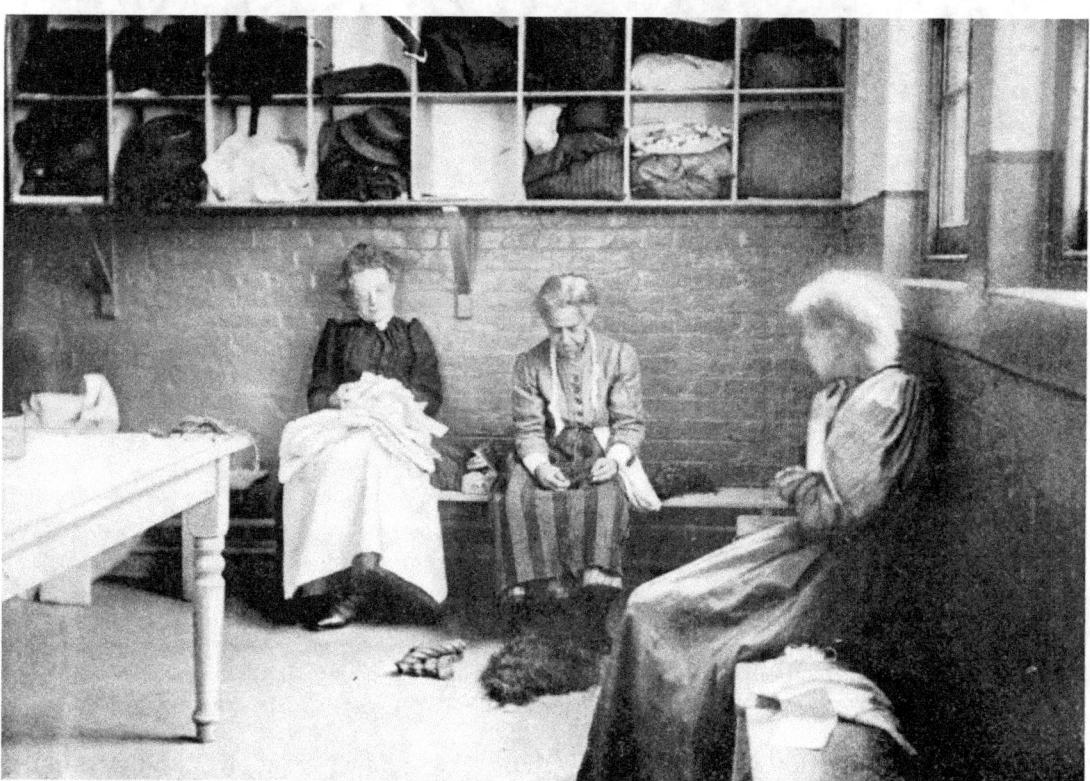

Sewing and oakum picking were among the many drear tasks assigned to female inmates of British and Irish workhouses. This photograph, thought to have been taken at Lambeth in south London, shows three women in workhouse uniform: one is picking oakum, with a heap of picked oakum at her feet. The overhead racks show the limited storage space available for personal possessions (Mary Evans Picture Library/Peter Higginbotham Collection).

later, the ship's passenger list indicated she had been employed as a farmhouse servant in Newtownbutler, a small village surrounded by boglands seventeen miles south of Enniskillen.[64]

Caddie McCaffrey, now twenty-three years old, was nothing if not resourceful. She, like her future husband, saved the necessary one pound from her paltry servant's income to embark for Australia on an Assisted Immigration ship. But while she sailed alongside 442 other government immigrants on the Willis, Merry & Co. chartered *Telegraph*, departing Liverpool on June 21, 1853, Caddie was very much alone, with no relations in the new colony, sailing to a destination and future of which she could know very little. She arrived in Sydney on September 18 after four months at sea with her renowned health still unbroken,[65] but was plunged into chaos before she had even disembarked. An anonymous letter to the *Empire* on September 26, 1853 spoke of "indescribable confusion" on board the *Telegraph* as the captain, mate, and ship's surgeon left the immigrants to fend for themselves amid voracious Immigration Department agents seeking to swoop on the best of the available labor before private employers—whose taxes subsidized the voyage—arrived.[66] The unmarried women not immediately hired (about 146 in number) were relocated to the Hyde Park military barracks, where they were "open for engagement" like cattle at a sale over a period of two days.[67] While little is known of Caddie's fate through her first three years in Australia, she married Patrick Quinn at Broulee in 1856, by which time she was twenty-six years old and presumably wise to the ways of this new land. Her new husband was eight years her junior and had been in the colony less than nine months and their eldest son, Patrick Francis, was born soon after the marriage, in 1857.

The name Araluen derives from the Australian Aboriginal word for "a place of water lilies."[68] However, in 1857, the Araluen area was far from a place of sweet flowers floating on tranquil ponds. The gently sloping valley and the Araluen Creek winding across its floor were gutted by uncontrolled gold mining sparked by a first strike made in 1851 by Alexander Waddell and Henry Hicken.[69] During the desperate rush for riches that followed, thousands of European and Chinese fortune-seekers crowded the valley, tearing up the watercourses searching for shallow alluvial gold. The goldfields at Araluen were second only to the huge operation at Ophir in terms of productivity, yielding in excess of 11 million pounds of gold over their 88-year lifetime.[70] There were reports of diggers making a staggering £160 per week, four times the amount a farm laborer would earn in an entire year.[71] By 1856, there was such an enormous demand for workers in the goldfields that even humble laborers engaged to work another man's claim could earn £3–5s. (or 65 shillings) per week,[72] compared to a farm worker's average takings of between 10 and 14 shillings.

The fortunes yielded by the colorfully named fields—"Big and Little Fenians"; "Good Enough"; "Beardy's"; and "Perseverance"—were enough to keep multiple local hotels in business, with many more "sly grog" shops dispensing wicked concoctions from their stills as the hopefuls either celebrated good fortune or sought to drown their ill luck.[73] Many public houses also had an attached dance hall, with girls imported from Sydney (a fresh batch each month), earning £3 per week in return for entertaining: the "indescribable saturnalias" on Saturday nights were said to "equal at least [those of] the Greek and Romans." But this mixture of riches and revelry also attracted the criminal element. Bushrangers roamed the hills surrounding Araluen, greedily eyeing the gold coaches crawling their laborious route up the escarpment to banks in Braidwood. The Clarke brothers, Tom and John, were frequent visitors to the dance halls in the boom days and were quite popular with the locals (and especially the girls).[74] It was to this decadent and debauched valley that Patrick took his new bride, and into which their first son entered the world.

Top: The hamlet of Broulee, 180 miles south of Sydney, was an attractive area for Irish immigrants in the 1850s as a gateway to the Araluen goldfields. It was also where Joe Quinn's parents, Patrick and Catherine, were married in 1856 (S. Prout, T. Heawood, ca. 1857–1910/Mitchell Library, State Library of New South Wales, call no. PXD 993/145). *Bottom:* The Araluen goldfields were primarily alluvial, with the precious metal obtained by panning in shallow creeks and pools (Mitchell Library, State Library of New South Wales, call no. ON2/604).

Broulee was little more than a hamlet on the New South Wales south coast until the discovery of gold inland at Araluen in 1851, whereupon more than 15,000 men landed in the village to walk the thirty miles inland seeking their fortunes. Patrick Quinn and his new wife Catherine were among them (S.T. Gill, 1853–1874/Mitchell Library, State Library of New South Wales, call no. PX*D 384/33a).

It took an event of almost biblical proportions to cleanse the Araluen valley of the social and environmental turmoil of the Rush. On February 8, 1860, the valley was swamped by unseasonal summer flooding, a disaster that left 24 people dead and the town of Araluen in ruins. Floods were not unknown in the area—in June 1857, the area was hit by a deluge which swept "tools of every description and large masses of earth" away in its headlong course,[75] and the diggers had spent much of the month preceding the 1860 disaster repairing damage from an unseasonal summer inundation.[76] The lead-up to the February flood had all the hallmarks of impending catastrophe: the days were unnaturally hot—hot enough to drive pigs and chickens mad and cause the deaths of a number of infants[77]—and when the threatening skies finally opened, the thunder, lightning, and ferocious southerly winds persisted for three days and nights, with "gales of unabated fury and hailstones as large as duck eggs."[78] The result left "many an industrious poor man ruined, and many rich families on the brink of poverty."[79]

Such was the power of the debris-laden waters tumbling down the valley that a fully loaded bullock team was washed away at Lower Araluen,[80] and the public houses belonging to Mr. Barrett and Mr. Carney were both destroyed, with their families all carried away save for Carney and one boy.[81] Also lost were the boarding house, the butcher, Eaton's general store, and the library. Upper Araluen was one vast sheet of water from the foot of one range to the other and the floor of the valley was leveled, with wheels, pumps and tools all gone.

Shovels, tubs, casks, furniture and human bodies were seen floating in the floodwaters. Among the dead were six Chinese miners who had worked upstream on Bell's Creek, a treacherous cleft running between two narrow ranges and subject to flash flooding: reports from nearby Irish Corner said "people were being washed over Bell's Creek Mountain in dozens."[82]

It was more than a week before news of the devastation reached the outside world, when a telegram received in Sydney on February 17 pleaded: "Come or send to Braidwood at once. Destruction of life and property very great. Dreadful destruction of property in all directions, 20 or 25 lives known to be lost. People without food and shelter at Araluen."[83] The people were by then in a "starving state," the surviving stores unprepared for the extra demand and the roads to Braidwood impassable. Poultry and market gardens had been washed away, cattle swept to their deaths or disappeared into the ranges, oats and hay and wine casks carried off like flotsam. The price of bread leapt from 1 shilling to 3 shillings a loaf, and beef from 4 pence to 9 pence a pound.[84] Most tragically for the great population of Irish in the valley, their staple potato crop were "very seriously injured, if not wholly destroyed,"[85] and with the wheat ruined by the previous month's heavy rains and the farms covered with such a depth of sand that all hopes of tillage was destroyed, prospects were very grim indeed. And to compound the misery of the survivors, the gold sinkings were also filled with sand and mud, their months of labor rendered valueless.[86]

Many prospectors and fortune-hunters left the devastated area in the aftermath, with Patrick and Caddie Quinn amongst them. The obvious option would have been to return either to familiar territory at Broulee, or to Sydney and one of its many Irish enclaves such as that at Campbelltown on its western fringes. But the two had already proved themselves both great travelers and restless but able seekers of independence. They eschewed a life crowded with much of the Australian population into the narrow coastal strip around Sydney, instead starting a journey of more than one thousand miles north toward the farthest axe marks of the fledgling nation, to Queensland. Exactly why is not clear. Some aspects of the Irish character, it is said, are attributable to centuries of British oppression—a taste for the fantastic, delusions of the escape of the powerless. Playwright George Bernard Shaw bewailed the tendency: "Oh, the dreaming! The torturing, heart-scalding, never satisfying dreaming, dreaming, dreaming...!"[87]

Perhaps it was a simple desire to exercise their new freedom to make choices—why not go as far as possible simply because it *was* possible? It may have been merely a question of economics: rumors of the imminent construction of a railway in Queensland—the first in that newly christened colony[88]—may have reached the southern Irish communities and, with the prospect of guaranteed long-term work, the long march north began.

In 1842, the first hardy free settlers at Logan's Limestone Station were confounded by a visit from the colonial governor Sir George Gipps, who cast an eye over the surveyors' plans and ordered them to change the village name from Limestone to Ipswich in what transpired as a bizarre act of self-promotion. The grimy sprawling community bore no resemblance to the quaint British town of Ipswich, but Gipps, an Englishman himself, was well aware that that particular Suffolk village had originally been christened "Gippeswic"—literally, *Gippe's Village*.[89] Perhaps he hoped Limestone would grow into its new name, following the same logic that drives a parent to buy boots two sizes too big for a gangling adolescent. But when the Quinns arrived around 1860, there were no shaven lawns or topiary hedges, no walled English gardens or swans coasting serenely on stately ponds. With three thousand residents and the town jockeying to be named capital of the new Queensland colony,[90] Ipswich was ferociously matter-of-fact, with blacksmiths and carpenters, tailors and tin-

Founded as a convict outpost in 1827, the town of Ipswich, some 20 miles upriver of the Queensland capital Brisbane, grew as improved river and rail services linked the town to inland and coastal centers. This photograph was taken in 1872, the year the Quinn family left Australia for the United States, and shows the historic rail bridge spanning the Bremer River (John Oxley Library, State Library of Queensland, neg. 4884).

smiths, and an apothecary stocking Holloway's pills for everything from chilblains to elephantiasis and "bad breasts."[91]

That Australian institution, Cobb & Co. Coaches, had reached Ipswich by the 1850s. The advent of side-wheeling steamers in 1846 also reduced the upriver trip time from Brisbane from twelve hours in a whaleboat to around four. By 1860, small steamers crowded "The Basin" at the end of Nicholas and East Streets, beyond which rocks and shoals prevented further progress. At the other end of East Street, the market resounded with livestock sales, and stalls were piled with produce dusted in both grit from the unsealed roads and the ever-present brown flies. The *Queensland Courier* recommended discouraging flies from food by planting *Apocynum androsaeomifolium*, a fly-trapping shrub apparently capable of 100,000 kills.[92] The six hotels in Ipswich included the Caledonian, with its illegal rum-still built into the chimney, and One Mile Hotel, outside which bullock teams camped amid the scraggly gums on Hungry Flats. Road transport using these teams was torturously slow and inefficient: a bullock dray covered around 7 miles a day at a cost of 25s.–5d. per ton. Although railway track cost £7,000 per mile to lay, the cities of Sydney and Melbourne both had established lines by 1855, and the burgeoning settlement at Brisbane was eager to follow. But if the prospect of work on an inland rail line had lured the Quinns to Ipswich in the early 1860s, they met with disappointment. A line from Ipswich to Toowoomba was surveyed by the Moreton Bay Tramway Co. in 1861,[93] but lack of public support bankrupted the proposal ere a clod had been turned.[94]

However, there were plenty of other options for a working man, with an experienced laborer like Patrick able to find employment on one of the many squatters' runs pegged out

The early rail workshops at North Ipswich, constructed not far from where Joe Quinn was born in 1862 (John Oxley Library, State Library of Queensland, neg. 196832).

around Ipswich, building fences, felling trees, or jousting with the scrub bulls. Dairy cattle, pigs, sugar cane, corn and wine grapes were all in production, and timber-getting was profitable while the supplies of hoop pine and hardwood lasted. Cotton was the area's crop of choice in the 1860s due to the international shortage induced by the American Civil War,[95] and the *Sydney Morning Herald* of July 12, 1864, described girls picking cotton in crinolines and earning a shilling a day amidst the caterpillars and weeds.[96]

It was the push west into the fertile blacksoil expanses of Queensland's Darling Downs which saw wool boom and pressure again increase in the early 1860s to build an inland rail line to bring the wool to Ipswich, from where it could be floated by barge to Brisbane. In 1864, British firm Peto, Brassey & Betts won tender for the Ipswich-Grandchester line, and the North Ipswich Railways workshops became the starting point for the first railway in Queensland.[97] Although no employment records remain for itinerant workers during the period, the fact Joe Quinn's birth certificate gives his place of birth as North Ipswich, which

Opposite, top: When the Ipswich area was opened to free settlers in 1839, pastoral leases and early industries including mining, timber-getting, and later cotton and dairying grew around the burgeoning town. Arriving in the area two years prior to the commencement of construction of the Ipswich-Grandchester Railway, Patrick Quinn likely found employment in one of these early industries as a stockman, laborer or timber-cutter (John Oxley Library, State Library of Queensland, neg. 57554). *Bottom:* Typical quarters for married men working on the Ipswich-Grandchester railway, this one near Murphy's Creek on Section Five of the line (1865–67) (Queensland Rail Historical Collection).

The appropriately christened "Faugh a Ballagh" (Gaelic for "clear the way") makes the first trial run of a locomotive and carriages out of the Ipswich rail workshops on January 11, 1865 (Queensland Rail Historical Collection).

soon after became the site of a large camp accommodating laborers for the rail line, suggests his father may have joined one of the laboring "gangs" living at Wide Gully alongside the new railway workshops. With men flocking to the town to take advantage of employment opportunities on the rail line, this hastily-erected canvas settlement drew vigorous complaints from the local alderman Pettigrew, who claimed it was "filled with the sort of people likely to do all the stealing in the neighborhood."[98]

Within a year, a short line had been laid between the Bremer River wharf and railway workshops to carry in materials shipped from England. There was a notorious sharp bend in the line and, rather cruelly, during an inspection visit by Governor Sir George Bowen, one of the wagons tumbled off the line into the river.[99] It was from here, however, that the workers turned west and the hard slog toward Toowoomba began. Working conditions were extremely difficult—the first unions to protect the interests of rail workers were not formed until 1914, and on the Grandchester line, there were few facilities for the workers to eat or wash, and no sick pay, so laborers had to contribute to their own fund to support ill or

Opposite, top: Toiling against an unforgiving ancient continent, railway workers excavate a cutting on the Ipswich-Grandchester rail line. After initially dynamiting the site, they removed much of the detritus using hand-tools and horses (John Oxley Library, State Library of Queensland, neg. 193617). *Bottom:* Fettlers laying sleepers and rails in Queensland. This photograph, taken in the early twentieth century, illustrates a technique unchanged in decades, where wooden sleepers are driven using "dog spikes" and overlaid with steel rails (Queensland Rail Historical Collection).

injured colleagues.[100] Lunch was a hunk of rough brown bread hung in a canvas sack on a tree until the sun was overhead and the men could find a nook in the shade for a brief respite. The *Courier* of August 19, 1864, reported the first death in the tunneling operations, with laborer James Edwards crushed under two tons of raw geology and big sandstone rock-knuckles, and a second man, Davis, lucky to escape.[101] To compound the workers' miseries, Queensland was sliding into the grip of a memorable drought and the earth was baked hard as flint. The skinny sheep looking down from the wind-bitten ridges, they knew it—and the men with sweat stinging their eyes and shirts sticking to their backs, they knew it. But they had to swallow their thirsts and dig until dark each day, showered with stinging splinters of lime and granite, snorting dust out of their noses and carving yet another gash in the limestone hills.

The main Ipswich-Grandchester line was opened on July 31, 1865, with the day declared a national holiday.[102] Four trains imported from Avonside Engine Co., in Bristol, UK, made the grand journey at an average of nine miles per hour up the line from central Ipswich through the workshops site, and west for twenty miles over Ironpot Creek to Bigge's Camp (now Grandchester).[103] It seemed in 1865 that Brisbane would be next to be connected to Ipswich by rail (a distance of only twenty-four miles)—but eleven years would pass before that line became a reality.[104]

2. Waltzing Matilda

Dear dreamy earth, receding flickering lamp,
Dear dust wherein I found this night a home,
Still for a memory's sake I turn and cling,
Then take the road for many a distant camp,
Among what hills, by what pale whispering foam,
With eager faith forever wandering.
   —John Le Gay Brereton, "Swags up!," 1928

It was "swags up"[1] again for the Quinns in 1866, when the west wind pouring in from the baked interior of the continent consolidated the drought afflicting much of eastern Australia. Under the Bureau of Meteorology's definition—acute water shortage and 5 percent probability of rainfall over three consecutive months[2]—this was the first major drought recorded in colonial Australia. The lack of moisture, and limited water storage infrastructure such as dams and reservoirs, hit introduced crops and stock hard. Cropping around Ipswich, particularly cotton growing, was dependent on regular summer rain aided by significant winter falls, failure of which extended through the summer of 1865 into the following autumn.[3] Stores of wheat and fleece dwindled, meat and vegetables became scarce, and the Ipswich rail line ground to a standstill as the locomotive water supply at Grandchester failed.[4] Jobs dried up and blew away on the scalding wind. In September 1866, a group of unemployed railway *navvies*[5] seized a train at Helidon and traveled to Ipswich to protest the lack of government aid for the hungry and unemployed, begging, "All we want is work, little children are crying for bread."[6] It was time to leave. Young Joseph was now three years old and Patrick Jr. nearly nine—clearly old enough, in the view of their resilient parents, to withstand the rigors of the road.

The folk song "Waltzing Matilda," penned by poet Banjo Paterson in 1895, has long been recognized as Australia's unofficial national anthem behind the grandiose "Advance Australia Fair."[7] With its rollicking tale of an itinerant worker caught stealing a sheep and jumping into a waterhole to escape police, "Waltzing Matilda" cemented in folklore the long-standing Australian tradition of walking the back roads in search of employment during times of economic hardship. The title is thought to derive from the medieval German *auf der Walz*, or "on the road," the practice of newly-qualified apprentices leaving their craft-masters to go in search of their own niche. And as a "swagman's" only companion on the road, his bedroll or *swag* came to be personified as a woman—his "Matilda."[8] While often identified with the crushing economic downturn of the Great Depression preceding World

War II, the practice of Waltzing Matilda in Australia was in fact born in the nineteenth century,[9] and the severe financial privations induced by the 1866 drought saw hordes of the unemployed stirring the dust of outback roads.

There was also plenty of "stirring" in metropolitan centers: on September 20, 1866, hundreds of jobless Queensland rail workers descended on Government House in Brisbane, crying foul over cuts in wages of up to 50 percent. In response, the colonial secretary tendered free passage for thirty married couples to Gayndah and one hundred single men to Rockhampton, where there was a greater demand for labor, and granted £3,000 per month to rail contractors Peto, Brassey & Betts to employ extra hands. These terms, favorable as they were, did not meet the demands of the desperate crowds of unemployed, and with drunken rowdies now mixing with the restive mob, tempers flared. Amid the clashes with police that followed, stones were hurled and store windows smashed. This "Bread or Blood" riot saw the three ringleaders—Eaves, Parker and Murray—jailed with hard labor for up to twelve months each.[10]

As was their wont, Patrick and Caddie Quinn were not content to simply relocate a short way down the road in search of their next opportunity. Their 1866 journey took them right back to where it all began, six hundred miles south to Sydney. The wild rocks and skeletal white trees of Queensland's thirsty outreaches gave way once more to the drab sandy plains of the original convict coast. Sydney city was, in 1866, a teeming sprawl on the shores

Now a sprawling part of the western suburbs of Sydney, in the late nineteenth century, the village of Campbelltown was still separated from the state capital by rolling virgin farmland. This photograph shows one of the main streets in Campbelltown, Queen Street, with the early incarnation of Public Park (later Mawson Park) in the foreground, c. 1890 (Campbelltown and Airds Historical Society).

The celebrated humanitarian Caroline Chisholm assisted over 14,000 Europeans to settle in colonial New South Wales, including many of the Irish Catholics who populated the area around Campbelltown in the 1850s and '60s (Angelo Collen Hayter, 1852/Dixson Galleries, State Library of New South Wales, call no. DG 459).

of Botany Bay, replete with whores, ex-cons, sly grog, and the aggressively ambitious. The satellite settlement of Campbelltown, however, remained separated from the main metropolis by tracts of bush and virgin farmland, and was a popular stronghold for Irish ex-convicts, their colonial-born offspring, and free immigrants who gravitated toward their entrenched countrymen.[11] Many of the original inhabitants had been settled by altruists Caroline Chisholm and Father James Goold, both instrumental in raising Australian awareness of the widespread distress in Ireland during the Great Hunger. Chisholm's support for migrants, women, and families saw her assist over 14,000 people to settle in New South Wales,[12] and by 1856, one-third of Campbelltown's thousand residents were Gaelic-speaking Irish Catholics.[13] While sectarian differences were rare, Campbelltown's Presbyterians often raised a fuss about Catholics carrying arms on Sundays for sporting, opportunities for which were plentiful as wallabies, pigeons, and rabbits abounded along the Georges River.[14] On the back of good works done during his eight years in Campbelltown and an outstanding reputation for piety and compassion, Fr. Goold was appointed the first bishop of Melbourne in 1847.[15] His successor in Campbelltown was another Irishman, Fr. John Roche, who served as the town's parish priest for thirty years, until 1877.[16]

Despite being born in Ipswich, Joe Quinn was often described as "a native of Campbelltown,"[17] for it was here that he spent his formative childhood years, although few details of that time are documented. The settlement of Campbelltown had had a promising beginning, christened in 1820 by the great New South Wales Governor Lachlan Macquarie himself, in honor of his wife, Elizabeth Campbell. Surveyor-General John Oxley—the same John Oxley who had discovered the site of the Moreton Bay penal colony in Queensland—named the village's first streets.[18] While the settlement consisted primarily of weatherboard and slab cottages with bark or shingled roofs, there were exceptions, such as the residence of the Ray family, who operated the Three Brothers Inn and lived in a two-story home richly furnished with pianos, carpets, cedar tables, and birdcages. Gilchrist's main street store was stocked to the rafters with rice and barley, starch and soap powder, gloves, flannel shirts, and queer bitter quince jam stewed up in equal parts of sugar and fruit.[19] Doctors William Bell and Arthur Scouler set broken bones, pulled teeth, and prescribed powders, charging £1 1s. for a visit and 10s. for medicines (which, recollecting an average farm laborer earned around 30s. a week, was often as painful as the illness itself).[20]

And while the town's reputation was largely one of bucolic godliness and convict rehabilitation, Campbelltown was also well known for a far more supernatural event. In 1827, local grazier William George Worrall was hanged after being found guilty of the murder of his neighbor, former convict Frederick Fisher. Fisher had mysteriously disappeared the previous year, and his body lay undiscovered in a field for months until a wealthy and respectable farmer, John Farley, stumbled into a local hotel one night in a state of shock, proclaiming he'd been accosted by "Fisher's ghost." Farley insisted the ghost had been sitting on the rail of a bridge and had pointed to the paddock where Fisher's body was later found by police. At the subsequent trial, Worrall revealed he had been appointed temporary guardian by Fisher of all his property when he was incarcerated over a knife fight in 1825. And while he only ever admitted to killing Fisher by mistake after his release—believing him to be a stray horse in his wheat crop—he was found guilty of murder and put to death.[21] Despite the inadmissibility of Farley's supernatural claims in court, the Fisher's Ghost legend is still celebrated in Campbelltown, with festivals, creeks, and bridges all named in honor of the local spook.[22]

As the Quinn family resided in Campbelltown until 1872, it was probably where Joe, now ten years old, and Patrick Jr. (15) first attended school. While few school records from the time survive, the town was renowned for its high proportion of educated residents: in 1856, two-thirds of the Campbelltown population could read and write, and several small church-run schools and private academies gave "mathematical and classical education with accomplishments of music and drawing if required."[23] The gabled Gothic-style Catholic primary school on the Old Menangle Road, which the Quinn brothers would have attended, was one of three schools in the town. An 1861 inspection found the discipline at St. Patrick's was good and the attainments of the students, on the whole, satisfactory, although the cleanliness of the boys was "only moderate." Three years later, the school was taken over by Patrick Newman and his wife Eliza, who taught at Menangle for fifteen years (in between caring for a large family), and they were so beloved as to be followed by many pupils when they moved to the Campbelltown Public School in 1880.[24]

However, despite the popularity of educators such as the Newmans, attendance at school was by no means a given for the children of Campbelltown. The 1870s were a decade of peculiar significance with respect to the number and proportion of children active in the New South Wales workforce. With the loss of convict labor and eager movement of many families into primary production through the Free Selection Acts of the 1860s,[25] child workers had become particularly critical to farmers and new industrialists. There were few legal impediments to the use of children in the workforce,[26] and schooling was not yet compulsory: the 1871 census indicated there were over 37,000 children aged between 5 and 15 years who were not in school but working as trade apprentices, shepherds, harvest hands, milkers or domestic servants. Such labor was desperately cheap—boys aged between 11 and 15 commanded as little as 5 shillings per week—and the hazards were many: children were often swallowed up by the unforgiving bushland, trampled by stock or wagons, scalded, underpaid, or simply overfaced with tasks unsuited to their strength or physique.[27] The problem of child labor was regularly mentioned in Council of Education inspectors' reports bemoaning non-enrolments and absences at school: Menangle district inspectors of the early 1870s frequently mentioned children "being kept at home to work," or arriving late at school having milked dairy cows from 5 a.m. to 9 a.m. (an average of 14 cows per child, morning and evening) before walking a "fair distance" to school.[28]

Even among those children lucky enough to have families who could afford school fees,[29] seasonal absenteeism was extremely high. With as many as 54 pupils crammed into one very small building at St. Patrick's, the 1863 school inspection report bemoaned that the heat was stifling in summertime and contributed to the elevated rate of nonattendance.[30] Young Joe Quinn's birthday came in summer, in December—a time still so strange to the Irish community forlornly expecting snow for Christmas. In Australia, summer was being woken by the shriek and swoop of galah parrots and the tinkle of bell-birds chiming in bowers. Gumnuts were perfect for shying at uneasy loads of silver hay yawing past in the dry

Children outside St. Patrick's Catholic School on Old Menangle Road, Campbelltown, ca. 1870–1889, the school most likely attended by the Quinn brothers. Schooling was not compulsory in the late nineteenth century and was often undertaken around children's employment as domestic or farm labor (Campbelltown and Airds Historical Society).

rutted tracks. Cricket was also popular for those with an overactive throwing arm, although the town reserve was not fenced until 1878 and straying stock often impeded the matches.[31] But for the working children of struggling or impoverished families, there was little time for such games, particularly in summer, when the backbreaking tasks of shearing, haymaking, and harvesting demanded many hands, big and small. The giant ratchet-operated wool presses took two men to manage, and two more were needed to strain and hoist the giant bales of wool by pulley onto the drays. An old hand kept the tally, scrawling like a broker amid the scything sweep of shears, the panting of the tight-packed sheep, and the bleating as blade nicked flesh. Boys yelled and whistled to pen up the flocks, the fingers of classers and sorters flew over the greasy matted fleeces to tease and comb out the pasture stains and burrs and flattened thistles. And all of this in a scorching tin shed hot enough to fry eggs upon. Outside, wheat was the crop of choice among the lower classes and small landowners, and was sown and reaped by hand, as horse-drawn threshers were rarely affordable. Boys plodded along endlessly scooping straw into stands, stumbing on tussocks with the sun beating hard on hatless heads and crows circling high like distant vultures, waiting for the first man to fall.

◆ ◆ ◆

"Around the world in eighty days? I should like nothing better."
—Jules Verne, *Around the World in Eighty Days*, 1872

The world was obsessed with travel in 1872. Stanley had unearthed Livingstone in Africa, Jules Verne wrote *Around the World in Eighty Days*, and the ill-fated "ghost ship" *Mary Celeste* gathered sail for a voyage from New York to Genoa which would launch her deep into the annals of both maritime and paranormal legend.[32] Ten years before, the redoubtable Scotsman John McDouall Stuart became the first explorer to traverse Australia from south to north from a starting point in South Australia[33]; the next challenge for Australian adventurers was to negotiate the two thousand miles of uncharted desert between Stuart's route and the arid western coast, and the first attempt was made by Ernest Giles in 1872. Lack of water forced him to turn back, although not before he had discovered the Finke River and the stupendous natural wonder of Mount Olga (Kata Tjuta) in central Australia.[34]

As the Australian nation and its new territories unfurled, Campbelltown was struggling to keep its head above a tide of labor exodus and the environmental catastrophes which Australia's harsh climate could so swiftly inflict on unsuspecting European settlers. Construction of the Great Southern Railway had attracted new residents to the town in 1857,[35] but as locomotives replaced the coaches and bullock-drays which had traditionally patronized the village, one resident observed in 1863, "Our town presents a rather quiet appearance and I regret to see so many houses let.... There are no buildings or public works going on in the town, consequently the laboring class have to seek some other spot where work can be obtained."[36] A further mass departure of workers to the enticements of the goldfields in the 1850s ensured the burgeoning town grew little beyond a stunted sapling, with the population static at around one thousand from 1840 to 1870.[37] Crops were hard hit by hailstorms and drought in the mid–1860s,[38] and an outbreak of fungoid stem rust in 1864[39] cut local wheat production by 75 percent, from 16,000 bushels in 1861 to a mere 30 bushels in 1873. By 1884, the three mighty flourmills which had dominated the Campbelltown landscape since 1842 all stood silent.[40] One of the few industries really thriving when the Quinns arrived in 1866 were the tanneries, which made leather for harness, saddlery, and boots, brewing wicked concoctions from bark, water, and dung, and fouling the clean air and rivers in the process.[41]

Sheep carcasses were also boiled down for candles and a kind of vile soap, and while the foul stench ensured the practice was banned in the Sydney metropolitan area in 1848,[42] three tanneries operated in Campbelltown until 1870.

Despite the unremitting environmental challenges, the town's economic struggles were also partially self-inflicted. The residents had been slow to take advantage of both coal reserves and the plentiful water of the Georges River so suitable for irrigation of crops. The town didn't get its first bank until 1875, and in 1880, the main street remained nameless, the clock in St. Peter's tower was stuck at ten-to-two, and wild roses were growing rampant over the graves in the churchyard.[43] The Irish-Catholic families who farmed around the local villages of Minto, Airds, and Appin became disillusioned struggling against the fickle coastal climate and, as per their wandering custom, began to leave.

By 1872, Patrick Quinn too was itchy-footed again. He was still a young man, only thirty-four years of age, with a wife who knew how to travel, and two robust sons. He had come to Australia to escape destitution in Ireland, but the fledgling nation was not the promised land it had seemed, with its own litany of struggles against a seemingly pitiless environment. Although the little he owned was barely a haul enough for a mouse, their few dregs of savings afforded the Quinn family passage on one of the twelve ships to sail from Sydney to America in 1872.[44] These ships departed each month from Botany Bay and sailed via Auckland and Honolulu to San Francisco in a flickering and flapping of canvas, with salty cormorants posing on the poop and their plunging wooden hulls all encrusted in limpets like ancient crustaceans.

Traveling in steerage, the Quinns were far removed from what Australian poet Henry Lawson called the "the idle and careless aft passengers."[45] These resided in cushioned saloons,

The early village of Campbelltown struggled to thrive against a tide of workforce and environmental challenges. After decades as a stopping-point for bullock drays *en route* to the New South Wales inland, the Great Southern Railway bypassed the town and a series of droughts and storms saw many residents leaving by the 1870s, among them the Quinn family (John Oxley Library, State Library of Queensland, neg. APE-019-01-0009).

replete with such delicacies as steaks, oyster sauce, coffee, and claret, and were comforted from the buffetings of the sea by a haze of cigar smoke and laudanum. Below decks, the walls were damp and smelled of pickled seaweed, and the passengers could sleep only in snatches, mocked by the swinging barometer and the thunderous whip of the sails.

◆ ◆ ◆

> SHOELESS JOE JACKSON: *"Is this Heaven?"*
> RAY KINSELLA: *"No—it's Iowa."*
> —Field of Dreams, Universal Pictures, 1989

Despite the extreme discomfort of the voyage, Patrick Quinn barely paused for breath when his feet struck land on the golden docks of San Francisco. After all, why would a hardy Irish journeyman unencumbered by poor health, debt, or politics stop here when he could be buffeted further eastward like a tumbleweed across the Rocky Mountains to the great unexplored territories? Fearing not the wilds of Utah, the Quinns traversed the old Pony Express route through Salt Lake City, across the vast Kansas plains, all the way across the 91st meridian to Iowa. It was a journey of more than eleven thousand miles when Patrick finally called a halt in the village of Dubuque. Here, perhaps, he felt at home in a way he never had in Australia. Irish settlers had flocked to the area in escaping the *An Gorta Mor*, and for years afterward, they continued to settle the southern part of the town, which became known as "Little Dublin."[46] For the first time in his independent life, Patrick unshouldered his swag and never picked it up again.

Iowa lacks the harsh angularity of Australia's ancient landscape. It is subtly curvaceous, with soils enriched by endless cycles of flood and fire, growth and decay, and from whose famous deep loam has sprung American legends including Buffalo Bill, John Wayne, Glenn Miller, and Herbert Hoover.[47] In 1803, the U.S. acquired the area which is the modern Hawkeye State from France as part of the Louisiana Purchase, and when the 1832 Blackhawk Wars forced the local Mesquakie Indians to cede the area to the federal government, settlers armed with John Deere's new sharp-bladed steel plow swiftly carved the prairie into pastures and lanes and trails and plots. With their own homeland ravaged by famine, Iowa's Irish population boomed from around 5,000 in 1850 to more than 28,000 a decade later, many immigrants choosing to avoid the overcrowded eastern cities in favor of cheap land and plentiful laboring and mining jobs.[48]

Perched on wooded limestone bluffs above the Mississippi River at Iowa's eastern fringe, Dubuque is the oldest of Iowa's cities. In 1860, 14 percent or some 1,800 of its residents were Irish-born, many of them day laborers or tradesmen living in the First Ward around "Little Dublin." They were carpenters, plasterers, painters and stonecutters, dockhands, boatmen and baggagemen; just 15 were classed as professionals: lawyers, teachers, architects, or engineers.[49] But while the *Dubuque Herald* claimed nearly all who lived in "Little Dublin" were guilty of the crime of being poor, with whiskey as their greatest enemy,[50] some of its Irish inhabitants were also significant citizens: Patrick Quigley was the town's first justice of the peace, and F.K. O'Farrell served as mayor between 1844 and 1846.[51]

Among the blue-collar element of the First Ward in 1860 were 56 miners. Lead mining was the oldest industry in the town, established by French-Canadian fur trader Julien Dubuque, the first white man to settle the area in the early 1780s. From his hut on the west bank of Mississippi opposite the present-day Illinois-Wisconsin border, Dubuque befriended the local Mesquakie Indians, and established such rapport with them that in 1788, the Indians signed over the right to mine their lead-rich lands with a contract that read, "He shall work

Mining is the oldest industry in Dubuque, Iowa, with town founder Julien Dubuque establishing the first lead mining operation in 1788. By 1860, zinc was the primary metal mined at Dubuque and the main site of exploration, the Avenue Top Mine, opened in 1875. This image shows the timber structure enclosing the top of the vertical mine shaft in Julien Avenue (courtesy Loras College Center for Dubuque History, Dubuque, Iowa).

at the mine as long as he shall please ... no white man or Indian shall make any pretension to it without the consent of Mr. Julien Dubuque ... he shall be free to search wherever he may think proper to do so, and to work peaceably without anyone hurting him."[52]

There was still Spanish title on the land, so Dubuque named his operation the "Mines of Spain." The mines flourished, shipping up to one thousand pounds of lead per month by canoe to St. Louis.[53] When white settlement was authorized in 1833, ten thousand settlers swarmed in to make their fortunes in the miasma of cold underground darkness and ominously creaking timbers: ten thousand pounds of lead were now being extracted every day, keeping twenty smelting furnaces busy, making the area the most productive in the nation. However, the boom was not to last—by the late 1840s, miners had tunneled so deep into the bluffs that many shafts filled with water and there was no way to drain them.[54] But the Shot Tower on the Dubuque riverfront still stands as a monument to the early days of a munitions industry which produced lead shot during the Civil War and brought manufacturing to the pastoral quietude of eastern Iowa.

And the Quinns, from their cottage on Grandview Avenue near Pear's West Hill,[55] were at the heart of it.

Part II
Iowa: 1872–1884

3. A Special Class of Slaves

"For oh," say the children, "we are weary,
And we cannot run or leap—
If we cared for any meadows, it were merely
To drop down in them and sleep.
Our knees tremble sorely in the stooping—
We fall upon our faces, trying to go;
And, underneath our heavy eyelids drooping,
The reddest flower would look as pale as snow.
For, all day, we drag our burden tiring,
Through the coal-dark, underground—
Or, all day, we drive the wheels of iron
In the factories, round and round."
—Elizabeth Barrett Browning, *The Cry of the Children*, 1842

In 1880, Joe Quinn, at seventeen years old, got his first job.[1] The technical term for it was "dead work."

When Julien Dubuque died in 1810, riddled with debt and suffering from suspected lead poisoning,[2] Iowa's heavy metals bonanza could easily have died with him. However, the quest for the valuable ores secreted beneath the lush topsoil continued, spurred by the need for lead shot as white settlement probed further into the interior of the U.S. With the California gold rush drawing many miners away to the west, lead production in the upper Mississippi peaked in 1848, and by 1860 was superseded by the commercial production of zinc.[3] Around the same time, post–Civil War, Iowa's population grew by over 77 percent in a single decade, from 674,000 in 1860 to 1.12 million in 1870,[4] increasing demand for both natural resources and state revenue to drive development. In 1872, impetus was added to the burgeoning zinc mining industry by the new General Mining Act, which allowed unlimited claims to be staked over mineral resources in almost any public, recreational, agricultural, or wildlife area across the United States.[5] The Upper Mississippi valley was set for a dramatic transition from a "corn and hogs" economy to leadership of eastern states zinc production.[6]

Zinc has been mined since before the time of Christ, when the Romans first used extracts from the soft gray metal for both healing wounds and making brass.[7] By the twelfth century, brass-making and the use of zinc for medicinal purposes had spread as far as the Middle East and South Asia. It was 1743 before the first zinc smelters were developed in England and another one hundred years before such technology reached the United States, but it did so at a time of growing industrial demand for zinc as an anti-corrosion coating, construction material, and micronutrient.[8]

In Dubuque, the main site of zinc exploration—the Avenue Top Mine, located on the aptly named Julien Avenue—was opened in 1875. McNulty, Burt & Company had discovered a large body of lead ore, or galena, 60 feet below the surface, then extended their Avenue Top operation down a further 140 feet to reach a strike of zinc sulphide ("Black Jack"),[9] from which over ninety-five percent of the world's zinc is refined.[10] The boost to the mining sector by Avenue Top and other zinc sourcing operations, including the Goosehorn, Alpine, Beadle and Brugh mines[11] in the mid–1870s, was extremely timely for the Iowa economy: the collapse of the Northern Pacific Railway company in 1873, just a year after the Quinn family arrived, saw financial panic erupt across the northeast, and, coupled with a locust plague,[12] lynchings, and frontier violence[13]—Jesse James was operating in Iowa in the early '70s—the bucolic Hawkeye State was perhaps no more the promised land than was colonial Australia in the 1850s.

Ever ready to get their hands dirty, Patrick Quinn and his two sons shouldered their picks and descended the depths of Dubuque's new zinc mines in the early 1880s, those deep dank shafts from which 100 to 200 tons of ore would be extracted every day, mostly by the sweat of man and mule.[14] It was not uncommon for a child to lie about his age to find employment in the nineteenth century. Baltimore Hall of Fame shortstop Hugh Jennings worked in a Pennsylvania coal mine alongside his father from the age of 12, claiming he was actually 14, and the discrepancy in his date of birth followed him throughout his baseball career. It may have been so too with Joe Quinn, whose death certificate and his 1940 obituary in *The Sporting News*[15] both cite his date of birth as December 25, 1864, while his Australian birth certificate attests that he was, in fact, born on December 24, 1862, making him two years and one day older.

The zinc ore at Dubuque was located almost entirely in vertical crevices found within the city limits, extending down through "top," "middle," and "third" layers: the first was worked at West Dubuque, the middle was forty or fifty feet further down, and the third another thirty feet below.[16] The sphalerite,[17] or lower level of the Avenue Top mine, was reached only by a handful of vertical shafts[18]—and so few entry points meant few exit points if trouble struck. Rock falls were common, and even if a miner survived such an accident, nineteenth-century company owners rarely offered any form of compensation or support.[19] With all three of her men descending the perilous 200 feet into darkness every day, Caddie Quinn faced the very real threat of losing her entire family to a cave-in, underground flood, or dynamite accident. Thankfully, major disasters in Iowa's nineteenth-century mines were rare—the worst accident occurred on February 14, 1893, when a gunpowder charge ignited dust in the "Chicago and Iowa" mine near Albia, the resulting explosion leaving eight men dead.[20]

The limited number of shafts accessing the lower levels also made air quality a real issue in the mine. Modern underground operations typically use multiple shafts to create a convection current of fresh air throughout the mine, along with electric fans and pumps to drive heat and pollutants out of underground work areas. But in the nineteenth century, air conditioning, if any, was often provided only by a simple coal brazier which stimulated hot underground air to rise—with the choking accompaniment of fumes and smoke. The close conditions meant exposure to zinc oxide dust was also unavoidable, and while little is known about the long-term effects of chronic zinc exposure, acute contact with the dust is linked to chest pain, respiratory distress, skin eruptions, and the severe flu-like symptoms of "metal fume fever."[21]

The livelihood of a nineteenth-century miner was a meager one, paying between $1.25 and $2.50 per twelve-hour underground shift, with credit rarely extended.[22] Many late nineteenth-century company mining operations also required employees to lease company tools, rent company-owned homes, or shop at company stores. Boys such as the teenage Joe Quinn, just 13 years old when Avenue Top sank its first shaft in 1875, often accompanied their fathers into the mines to perform the "dead work" for which an adult was not paid—work which included shifting rubble and materials for laying track, and dangerous tasks such as shoring up unstable roofs and walls[23]; for such labors, boys earned a trifling 50 to 74 cents a day.[24]

✦ ✦ ✦

When the world contracted to a dark tunnel of creaking rock, lit only by the flickering shadow of uncertain torches, there remained one place in Dubuque where a dirty, grimy boy could feel free—where the air was pure and clear, the grass flawlessly green, and the sky a great open dome of blue. That place, described by poet May Swenson as that where "ball hits bat, or it hits mitt," or "sails to a place where mitt has to quit in disgrace"[25]—the baseball field.

By 1880, Joe's older brother Patrick had married Dubuque-born Mary Flynn and fathered a son, William.[26] He had also found his own recreational niche by forming "Patrick F. Quinn's Social Quadrille Band," a quartet whose dance cards exclaimed, "On with the dance—let joy be unconfined!"[27] While young Joe, now eighteen, also loved music,[28] his thoughts were far from marriage or settling down—he had discovered the game of baseball. It really was inevitable, Quinn remembering simply in his last interview in 1936, "All of the lads were playing the game."[29]

It was perhaps the first occasion in Quinn's life when he had the time, money, and family stability to allow for recreation. And sporting opportunities were now available in a way they never had been during his nomadic, impoverished childhood—in Australia during the 1860s and '70s, the game of baseball barely existed, a shadowy and mysterious pastime undertaken only among American expatriates in faraway Victoria or on the goldfields. It was 1878 before the first organized game was played in Sydney,[30] some six years after Joe Quinn's departure. But in the United States during the year 1880, recreational sports were numerous and well-organized. It is ironic that in the northeast of the United States, the teenage Joe Quinn could just as well have been a cricketer—the very sport that modern baseball competes with, largely unsuccessfully, for notice in Australia. Cricket was played in New York as early as 1751, and by the late 1840s, when baseball was just emerging in the United States, some 400 cricket clubs were already flourishing across 125 cities.[31] But baseball spread on the tide of the Civil War, and the increasingly independent and assertive American society of the 1870s sounded a death knell for cricket as an irrelevant symbol of English culture and identity. In *Diamonds in the Rough*, Zoss and Bowman attribute the burgeoning popularity of baseball to the fact Americans saw themselves as "not so brutal" as the English and "more fond of excitement associated with novelty and change" in their games.[32] But the Brits hit back in their way in March 1889, when the Chicago White Stockings and a touring team of All-Stars played an exhibition baseball game at England's Old Trafford Cricket Stadium. The *Manchester Guardian* sniffed that the American game was "slow" and "wanting in variety," and when M.P. Betts launched the National Baseball League of Great Britain with four Americans imported as instructors the following year, needless to say, the venture was short-lived.[33]

Baseball in Dubuque in the mid–1870s was of the strictly provincial and amateur variety.

The *Dubuque Herald* described the local boys as reporting for spring training a mere three weeks before the 1880 season commenced.[34] Nonetheless, spring games pitting veterans against rookies or married men against singles often drew large crowds. In the season proper, there was often no fixed schedule: games were organized by written invitation from the host club, and the prize to the victorious team was usually the match ball, inscribed with the date and score, to be nobly retired into a cabinet in the clubrooms. Following this ritual, the clubs partook of a communal meal, toasts, speeches and songs, at a local hotel.[35]

However, in 1878, such bucolic amusements were on the cusp of a revolution. Dubuque's merchants raised a purse to form a semi-professional team, with the revered Timothy Paul "Ted" Sullivan placed at the head of operations. With "a face that beamed intelligence and a great fund of Irish wit," Sullivan came to Dubuque from Milwaukee in 1874, having secured the contract for selling newspapers and convenience foods on the Illinois Central railway.[36] Sports journalist Alfred Spink, writing in *The National Game* in 1911, described Sullivan as "one of the real builders of baseball, a man of widest vision and the best judge of a ball player in America."[37] In 1879, Sullivan formed the Northwestern Baseball League, incorporating his Dubuque club with those from Peoria, Davenport, and Rockford: it was the first so-called "minor league" formed outside the east coast, and Sullivan took steps to establish it as a minion to the National League, which to some further established the operation as baseball's first legitimate minor league.[38] And when a pretty park was built on 26th and 24th streets in Dubuque, a diminutive field surrounded by family homes almost exclusively painted white, the famously flawless surface sown in six-inch deep Iowa black loam[39]—the newly christened Rabbits were ready to play.

When the Northwestern League commenced in 1879, Sullivan himself managed the Dubuque team, for which he had secured finance from Iowa Senator William B. Allison and

Dubuque's first semi-professional baseball team, the Rabbits, made their home at 26th Street Field. The field was later rechristened Comiskey Park after Hall of Famer Charlie Comiskey, who played with the inaugural Rabbits team in 1879 (undated photograph, courtesy Loras College Center for Dubuque History, Dubuque, Iowa).

The Dubuque Rabbits, with Hall of Famers Charlie Comiskey and Hoss Radbourn on their roster, were the inaugural champions of the Northwestern League in 1879. Joe Quinn joined the Rabbits in 1881 and was then recruited by the St. Louis Union Association team, where he made his major league debut in 1884 (courtesy Loras College Center for Dubuque History, Dubuque, Iowa).

future Congressman and House Speaker David Henderson, both prominent Dubuque citizens.[40] But before the season proper began, the Milwaukee National League team folded and their players relocated *en masse* to Rockford. Anxious to avoid a top-heavy competition, Sullivan shuffled many of the Peoria players across the border to Dubuque, describing his new team as one "made up of stalwarts ... a lot of witty kindred spirits."[41] Sullivan also recruited Tom Loftus from Peoria as captain and manager. Born and educated in St. Louis, Loftus had played for one of St. Louis's first professional outfits, the Reds, as a twenty-year-old in the late 1870s. Sullivan described him as "one of the kindliest, jovial and best-natured spirits ever connected to the game, of which he is twenty years ahead," and when he died in Dubuque in 1910, Al Spink praised him as having done much to "bring the game into its proper sphere ... and win it lasting and influential friends."[42]

Also among the Peoria arrivals were future St. Louis Browns major league stars William and Jack Gleason, and a twenty-four-year-old underhand pitcher named Charles Radbourn. He was to prove a fine slugger, hitting .337 from 47 games in 1879, but his ticket to the Hall of Fame was guaranteed by his iron right arm. In his debut season for Dubuque, during which the club ran away with the Northwest League pennant, Radbourn came to immediate attention with his astonishing underhand curveball. When Sullivan took his team on a barnstorming tour through Wisconsin in 1879, the schedule included an exhibition game in the village of Prairie du Chien. The villagers could not believe Radbourn's pitches could change course so dramatically on their transit from the pitcher's hand to the catcher, but Radbourn, ever the showman, bent the ball up and down, out and in—and was promptly accused by the locals of having a "crooked baseball."[43] Talk of young Radbourn's abilities attracted the National League's Chicago White Stockings (today's Chicago Cubs) to visit little Dubuque in 1879 for a pair of post-season exhibition matches, and the young pitcher promptly shut them out 1–0 in the second game[44]—clearly not intimidated by the blond colossus of the Chicago captain, Adrian "Cap" Anson, and his brilliant white soldiers.

And Anson was certainly not to be underestimated: he was one of the largest players of the nineteenth century, and arguably the best. He was an Iowa farm boy, described approvingly by the *Louisville Courier-Journal* of 1894 as a "wholesome example to young ballplayers ... he smokes three cigars a day."[45] He was the first professional ball player to achieve three thousand hits, and Anson hit over .300 for fifteen seasons in a row, captaining the Whites to five consecutive National League pennants in the 1880s.[46] Anson batted under .300 only twice in his twenty-two-year major league career, still hitting .303 at age forty-five, and his lifetime .339 average saw him inducted into the Hall of Fame in 1939. But after being shut out by Radbourn in 1879, Anson marveled, "In my fifteen years as a premier batsman of the game, I never faced a pitcher who baffled me more completely with his curves than did Radbourn on the occasion of that memorable game in Dubuque."[47]

Despite serious interest from the White Stockings, Radbourn signed with the Providence National League club in 1882, winning over one hundred games for the Grays in the next four seasons. In their pennant year of 1884, Radbourn made an unrivaled 72 appearances in the pitcher's box, hurling a total of 678 innings. He won 60 of these starts, including a League record 26 consecutive decisions, striking out a record 441 hitters at a miserly ERA of 1.38. He acquired his moniker of "Ol' Hoss" that year when he pitched 30 of the last 32 games and won 26, as well as playing first base, second base, and outfield.[48] But no arm could stand such strain. By this time, Hoss could no longer raise his arm to brush his hair with his right hand, and warmed up by rolling the ball to his catcher before getting a horse-liniment rub: it would be half an hour before he could throw across the diamond.[49]

Despite his heroics on the field, Hoss Radbourn remains one of the most tragic figures in the game's history, littered as it is with the famous and the fallen. Accidentally shot in the face during a hunting accident in 1894,[50] the great pitcher was left disfigured and partially blind, and withdrew from the baseball world to relieve the mental and physical anguish of his injuries in a haze of alcohol. Just five years later, penniless and racked by the convulsions which ultimately claimed his life, Hoss Radbourn died; he was 42 years old. In 1939, he was posthumously elected to the National Baseball Hall of Fame among the first group of inductees—which also included both Anson and Comiskey—a .253 career hitter who had pitched 309 winning games.[51]

According to Al Spink, the "real material" on the ballfields of the early 1880s was as scarce as hen's teeth.[52] But the Dubuque Rabbits were a breeding ground for genuine talent. In late 1879, Ted Sullivan scored his second coup when he scouted a former schoolmate from St. Mary's Kansas College to play for the Rabbits.[53] Charlie Comiskey was a gawky hitter but a promising hurler, and Sullivan promised the teenager a job selling peanuts on the trains for the Western News Company if he played for the Rabbits. Comiskey joined the Dubuque squad on a "prairie tour" to St. Louis in early 1880, but pitched just five innings before retiring with heat stroke, the score standing at 2–1. The Rabbits disintegrated after his retirement into a 9–1 loss, but Al Spink (who was the Browns' secretary at the time) was still moved to invite Comiskey to play for the American Association club in 1882.[54] He wrote Comiskey saying, "They are paying players $90 to $125 per month. Make your terms as low as possible so I can clinch one of the jobs for you." Thus commenced one of the most notorious careers in major league baseball history.[55]

George McGinnis, the St. Louis Browns' star twirler, remembered Comiskey's first game for the Association debutants: "He was put in centerfield, but was unable to judge fly balls and asked [manager] Sullivan to shift him to first base. There he played deep and was the first man to field the position as it should be."[56] While only an average hitter, Comiskey revolutionized first base play by positioning himself away from the bag to stop base hits, and forcing the pitcher to cover the bag. By 1884, Comiskey was captain of the Browns and led them to American Association pennants in every year between 1885 and 1888, and World Series titles in 1885 and 1886.[57] He had climbed from newsboy on the Iowa trains to become president and manager of the Chicago White Sox between 1900 and 1931, winning a further five flags. In 1929, the Dubuque baseball park was rechristened Comiskey Field in his honor. But Comiskey, like Radbourn, is as much enshrined for his tragedies as his triumphs—despite his election to the Hall of Fame in 1939, Comiskey is probably best remembered for his miserly ill-treatment of his players and the resulting 1919 Black Sox scandal as for his contribution to the style of both modern play and managership.[58]

Exhibition game or no, the Rabbits' famous 1879 victory over Anson's White Stockings no doubt stirred the *Dubuque Herald* of March 7, 1880, to proclaim, "Dubuque is favored to be one of the best clubs in the country. A fine team which will not permit the championship of the northwest to be taken from it."[59] After all, the 1879 Rabbits were so far ahead of their Northwestern League rivals that the league itself had folded in August,[60] forcing the club to revert to its former informal playing arrangements against nearby towns.[61] But with future Hall of Famers and one of baseball's greatest talent scouts and managers all present in the organization, Sullivan and his minions were undeterred—and a teenage Joe Quinn was invited to join them in 1881, playing first base as backup for the highly fancied Comiskey.[62]

The decision to have Quinn play first base was intriguing—for he was small, made of sinew and light bones and springy tendons, and at 150 pounds, about half the mass of a Cap Anson, who stood that bag for the White Stockings. Writing in *The National Game* in 1911, Charlie Comiskey noted, "A first baseman must be a tall rangy fellow who can cover ground, but more especially, one who has a reach to catch throws a trifle wild. Many a first baseman who understands his position robs batsmen of hits merely by stretching out and meeting the ball."[63] Quinn, at 5'7" and 150 pounds, looked about as durable as a creampuff, but in reality was sturdy as a young tree. Hall of Famer Hugh Jennings also contributed to Comiskey's treatise on playing the infield, adding, "A first baseman must have natural talent for taking all kinds of pickups. He must not be afraid of a runner coming into the bag, and he must be a sure catch with either hand." This latter is a timely reminder that baseball gloves had not yet been invented and all catches were made with bare palms, keeping the body right behind the catch for the one that fizzed through the fingers and put the structural integrity of nose, eyes, and teeth all in jeopardy. And so it was Joe Quinn began his baseball career, small but bold, on the far right side of the diamond.

• • •

> "I call to mind ... a few great thoroughbreds who were with us from the time the first gun was fired in 1883 until the association was gobbled up by the National League two years later. Among these fine fellows were ... Fred Dunlap, perhaps the greatest second baseman that ever lived; Joe Quinn, George Shaffer and Dave Rowe, all great players...."—Alfred Spink, *The National Game*, 1911

Baseball prior to 1876 was very much a frontier affair. While professional clubs were loosely governed by the National Association of Professional Base Ball Players, gambling was rife, with bookmaking booths at parks through which both fans and players openly placed bets with professional gamblers. Liquor sold freely and the stands swarmed with pickpockets; fist fights and wholesale brawls took place both in the seats and on the field; and if a man happened to let out a cheer for the wrong team, he stood a good chance of having his skull laid open by some pugnacious opposition rooter.[64] The Association lacked the authority to police its own ranks and bring order to the parks. Most owners were old-time players with no business experience, and as a result of the slipshod way they ran things, attendance fell away everywhere, clubs folded, and the game very nearly disappeared as a professional sport.

It was saved by the 1876 efforts of two men—William A. Hulbert, president of the Chicago club, and Albert G. Spalding, star twirler for the Bostons. Hulbert was a businessman who had never stepped onto a diamond in his life, but he could see the need for baseball to clean out its house to ensure its survival. He convinced Spalding, a noted non-drinker and opponent of gambling, to jump from Boston to Chicago so they could lay plans to form a new circuit (and so Spalding could, incidentally, pitch for Hulbert's White Stockings). Hulbert called a meeting of four western clubs—Louisville, St. Louis, Cincinnati, and Chicago—and persuaded the owners to fall in with his plans. The new agreement included abolition of gambling and liquor sales on the grounds, written contracts for players to be respected by all owners, no city of less than 75,000 population to be given a franchise, no Sunday baseball, and the league to receive $100 in annual dues from each club. The eastern magnates also agreed to this new regime—all except Boston owner N.T. Apolonio, who was understandably enraged after the poaching of Spalding and three of his other top players by Hulbert. Nonetheless, in February 1876, the National League—America's first major league— was born.

But this era of temperance and good intentions was short-lived. By 1882, Hulbert had died (one of his final acts being to expel ten of the League's hardest-drinking players), and a new league, the American Association, sprang up in direct competition with the National League. The upstart Association not only permitted Sunday games, but openly sold alcohol at their parks and charged half the National League admission price at a mere 25 cents per ticket.[65] War—both on and off the diamond—seemed inevitable. Such disastrous conflict was only averted when, in the latter part of 1882, delegates from the National League, American Association, and Northwestern League adopted the tripartite National Agreement to "furnish a central government for all professional baseball clubs and players, and to settle disputes which may arise between two associations or leagues, or between clubs of different organizations."[66] But there were plenty of dirty tricks still afoot and many loopholes through which a crafty player or club could wriggle. While in 1882, "compensation" (payment) of players was still prohibited, many clubs did pay clandestine salaries or give their players a percentage of gate takings, and this in turn gave birth to the practice of "revolving": players wantonly deserting clubs in search of better pay and conditions, often jumping from one club to another and back again within a single season. The National League instituted an anti-revolving policy requiring thirty days' membership of a club before a player could play,[67] but this policy had little impact on the practice or the spiraling player salaries which resulted.

In 1879, the League also adopted the reserve clause, which gave each club the right, at the end of every playing season, to name the five players with whom that club alone could negotiate for services the following year. Its purpose was, according to *The National Game*, to "preserve teams intact from year to year after they had been brought up to a degree of efficiency worth preservation, and to make impossible the destructive practices of tempting good players by offers of fabulous salaries to desert cities where they had made reputations and friends. It also kept salaries within money-making bounds and checked the tendency among the players to demand such sums as could not be taken in at the gate."[68] At that time, professional players usually signed one-year contracts. The reserve clause enabled clubs to reserve a player's services for each subsequent year until it sold the contract or released the player. If a player was released, he did not become a free agent but had to sign with another club within ten days. Any club who signed a player in defiance of the clause faced expulsion from the League. Beginning as a secret gentleman's agreement permitting teams to reserve five players each, the clause remained the foundation of a team owner's control over players until it was overturned in 1975 as a restraint of trade, leading to the modern free agent system. The major aims of the reserve clause were to decrease the advantage of wealthy clubs in obtaining player services, and to reduce a player's ability to bargain. However, the irony of the regulation was it was created by clubs wanting to hold onto their players while also wanting players to have the freedom to move to their club and bolster their own stocks.[69]

The limitations imposed by the reserve clause were a significant millstone about the necks of nineteenth-century players, and as professionalism, the desire to win, and the need to attract the paying public all increased in importance, club control over players only tightened. Albert Spalding was a prime mover of the reserve clause, insisting, "Baseball depends on two interdependent divisions: the one (the clubs) to have absolute control and direction of the system, the other (the players) to engage—always under the executive branch—on the actual work of production."[70] John Montgomery Ward, president of the first players' union formed in 1885, parodied the sentiment when he referred to the reserve clause as creating "a special class of slaves."[71]

Unrest was heightened by an 1880 National League "Address to Players" that instituted a new code of conduct under which players could be suspended for offenses including insubordination, gambling, "stupid" plays on the field, loss of equipment, and illness, with penalties enforceable under the code expanded in 1881 to include the blacklist.[72] The only avenue of appeal was the winter meetings of the National League, at which players stood little chance of regaining back pay even if they were reinstated.

Player grievances peaked, loudly and publicly, in 1883, as the number of players allowed to be reserved each year by a club was hiked from five to eleven.[73] Such incidents provided impetus for a group of zealous, wealthy and well-connected entrepreneurs to lay down a plan to "deliver the professional players from bondage"[74] by establishing a rival league which endorsed neither the reserve clause nor the blacklist. The rebels were led by an opportunistic young millionaire from St. Louis, Henry V. Lucas, who had inherited a fortune from his grandfather's real estate investments and had gotten interested in baseball after his uncle, J.B.C. Lucas, bought part-ownership of the Browns. Lucas became so passionate about baseball that he installed a diamond on his own estate for the pleasure of himself and his many guests. But despite his frivolities, Lucas was a fierce critic of the reserve clause, insisting it only reserved what was good for team owners. His plans for a breakaway league were backed by additional financial might in the form of St. Louis brewers Ellis Wainwright and Adolphus Busch, and A.H. Henderson, a Baltimore mattress manufacturer. Lucas also surrounded himself with notables from the baseball world: he lured baseball pioneer George Wright out of retirement to head the Boston franchise, promising Wright's sporting goods firm would have the same monopoly on equipment as that of Al Reach in the American Association and Albert Spalding in the National League.[75] Guided by local newspaperman Al Spink, Lucas also enlisted Ted Sullivan to entice players to the breakaway league (and to St. Louis in particular), luring him away from his position managing the St. Louis Browns in the American Association for the princely sum of $8,000.[76]

Lucas's "Union Association" was formed on September 12, 1883, with eight teams on the books: St. Louis, Chicago, Cincinnati, Philadelphia, Baltimore, Boston, Washington and Altoona. The organization was promptly banned from the National Agreement for its audacity in placing Union clubs in League cities, and League clubs which played Union clubs were expelled. The National League attempted to discredit the Union Association by publicly decrying it as "financed by beer money" and "a haven for deadbeats and played-out bums who cannot find employment in respectable clubs," but the Union Association retaliated by placing a similar ban on their own clubs from playing National Agreement teams, and enlisting small-town clubs as "alliance members" to boost their depth.[77]

Baseball was turned on its head, with players jumping back and forth between leagues and using the fierce competition for their services to lever their salaries to exorbitant heights. Providence pitcher Charlie Sweeney deliberately got himself suspended so he could jump to the Union.[78] The entire Delaware team deserted the Eastern League, despite having just won the 1883 pennant, for Lucas's rebel circuit.[79] The adroit Sullivan had rounded up about fifty players for the Union prior to the 1884 season, although many, including controversial pitcher Tony Mullane, repented and withdrew as the National Agreement leagues dipped into a secret cash pool to lure them back.[80] The National League also tried to stop players from jumping to the Union Association by threatening to blacklist them if they didn't sign League contracts within thirty days of receiving them: clubs who employed any "jumpers" thereafter were expelled from the National Agreement. But Lucas was willing to pay whatever it took to get the best players—and some stars did come. By December 26, 1883, Sullivan had brought to St. Louis Dave Rowe from Baltimore, brothers Jack and William Gleason from Lucas's cross-town rivals the Browns, and a coup in the form of Fred Dunlap from Cleveland.

Sullivan's approach came at a judicious time for Dunlap, the leading second baseman of the time, who was maddened by Cleveland's plunge from two games clear at the top of the National League on August 25, to finishing fourth in the 1883 pennant race. When Dunlap laughed at the proposition to switch his allegiance to the Union, Sullivan was undeterred—he quietly pulled a roll of money from his pocketbook and asked how much a year Dunlap could make playing ball. Dunlap named the top salary of the time, $1,750. Sullivan countered, "There's fifty thousand in this roll, and you can have any part of it if you sign this contract." He then proffered a contract for two years at $5,000 a year, but Dunlap still demurred.

"Some say your league won't last two years, and then where would I be?" he challenged.

Sullivan calmly counted off ten one-thousand dollar bills. "Here's your money," he said. "Just sign." Dunlap signed on the spot.[81]

There were no professional talent scouts in baseball in 1884. Owners and club presidents relied on hearsay and word of mouth to draw their attentions and open their pocketbooks to potentially valuable new players. And skill on the diamond was just one component of the package owners sought: manners, habits, and attitudes were considered almost as important.[82] Well aware of the record of the Rabbits in producing outstanding players, and with the Gleason brothers already secure on the Union books, Ted Sullivan returned to Dubuque in late 1883 to follow up word from Tom Loftus about a youngster the Union might interest themselves in. The *St. Louis Globe–Democrat* reported on December 30, 1883, "T.P. Sullivan, manager of the Lucas Union Base Ball Club of St. Louis, to-day, engaged Joe Quinn, formerly of the Dubuques, as a member of the reserve nine of the above club. Mr. Quinn is a remarkably active and ambitious player, and will undoubtedly fill his position with credit."[83]

It was an indication of both skill and temperament that the lightly built Quinn was not only holding down the cornerstone sack for the Rabbits, but doing enough to attract the attention—and checkbook—of Henry Lucas. Sullivan showed the twenty-one-year-old zinc miner the same roll of cash he'd shown to Dunlap, and offered him $2,000[84]—a sum which would buy passage from Sydney to San Francisco more than fifty times over, and a permanent escape from the yawing darkness of the Dubuque pits. Zinc prices had slid more than 25 percent since the previous year, with "great dullness" and "a disposition to fall off further" looming.[85] This was Quinn's chance to live in the sun, away from the slag heaps and the boisterous winter wind and the uncertainty of life underground.

However, this ephemeral chance almost blew away in the cold Iowa wind before it even took root. Just weeks before his departure for St. Louis, Quinn took a nighttime walk which very nearly ended his baseball career: a rotten section of wooden sidewalk gave way beneath his feet, sending him crashing and tumbling down a long embankment. Among his many serious injuries was a broken arm—a potential physical and financial catastrophe for the young ball player. With his career in jeopardy, Quinn filed suit against the city of Dubuque for $5,000 damages. It was March of 1885 before the case was tried, and Quinn received a payout of $2,500[86]; by that time, however, his arm had completely healed.

Part III
The Rookie Years: 1884–1888

4. Union and Liberty

Union and Liberty!
Sons of the free,
Shall e'er our motto be....
—Civil War anthem, 1861

St. Louis, Missouri, stands a day's steamboat ride south from Dubuque, the two cities linked by the great brown artery of the Mississippi River. As the Iowa docks and boatyards fell away, the river slid south out of deep bluffs and left behind otter and heron, muskrat and trout, to wind a new path through rattling cobblestone streets speckled with potholes and mud-puddles. In St. Louis, the steamers trailed their dark oily snatch of water in the shadow of the Eads Bridge, calling like mournful ghosts across the brown water to greedy wharves and factories awaiting their cargoes of cotton and coal, wool and wheat. In 1849, fire had destroyed almost half of the city when the steamboat *White Cloud* exploded on the riverfront,[1] but thirty years on, punts and paddle-steamers were still the primary source of freight and passengers to St. Louis from both the upper and lower reaches of the Mississippi. Almost thirty million tons of freight are still moved via the river every year,[2] with little change to the demands on the men who pilot the ships: satellite navigation and depth soundings aside, a boat captain must still know the character and size of every crossing, rip, and sandbar, often over a range extending from northwest Minnesota to the Gulf of Mexico. As Mark Twain, a steamboat pilot himself, mused, "One cannot easily realize what a tremendous thing it is to know every trivial detail of twelve hundred miles of river and know it with absolute exactness...."[3]

By 1880, St. Louis was the sixth largest city in the United States, and with a population of over 350,000, was more than 15 times the size of little Dubuque.[4] Since Laclede and Choteau selected the site near the confluence of the Mississippi and Missouri Rivers as a fur trading post in 1764, naming it for their sponsor, King Louis IX of France, the city had been an important center of trade and commerce, aided by its proximity to water, and later rail, for transportation. Thousands of immigrants eager for a new life on the edge of the frontier poured into the city, particularly between 1840 and 1860, as German and Irish immigrants fled famine and revolution in Europe. As affluence grew, so too did the range of sporting and recreational pursuits available to the residents. Horse racing, boxing and swordplay at Mr. J. Roper's "Sparring and Fencing Academy," bowling and bearbaiting all absorbed the leisure hours, and by 1860, the inventory of pleasure pursuits also included baseball.[5]

At the time of Quinn's arrival in 1884, organized baseball in St. Louis had amassed

With the Mississippi River flowing right past their doors, steamboats were a way of life for Dubuque residents in the latter half of the nineteenth century, connecting the town to large centers such as St. Louis downriver (courtesy Loras College Center for Dubuque History, Dubuque, Iowa).

some 25 years of history. The city's first club, the Empires, was founded in 1860, and was revolutionized by the arrival shortly after of a great tall boy from Brooklyn, Jeremiah Fruin, who brought the eastern styles and techniques of baseball with him. Shepard Barclay, who went on to become a judge in the Supreme Court of Missouri, recalled the impression Fruin made on the game: "I was a little fellow and played all sorts of games on a field located right where Lafayette Park is now. I remember while playing there one day Jere Fruin came among us. He was a stranger who had come from somewhere in the East and on our field he laid out a diamond and showed us how to play the modern game of baseball."[6] Speaking at the turn of the century, Fruin admitted his St. Louis teammates were "a rough and ready set, ready at any time to call a halt to the regular proceedings to engage in a game of fisticuffs."[7] However, standing over six feet tall and straight and imposing as an arrow, Fruin quickly put a stop to their unruliness and turned the attention of the St. Louis boys to the plays in vogue on the eastern seaboard. Fruin was as resolute off the field as on it, and was still working at the head of his Fruin-Colnon Construction Company into his eighties.[8]

Fruin's intervention energized the game to such an extent that the St. Louis Unions and Red Stockings teams were formed to play against the existing Empires club, and in 1865, the nines began to venture out to Iowa and Chicago seeking wider competition. But Fruin's Empires, with a team of savvy businessmen as directors and plenty of skillful players on the roster, dominated the St. Louis scene. In 1867, they obtained permanent grounds on Grand Avenue at the site of what would become Sportsman's Park; and by 1875, there was such enthusiasm for the game that a drive for a professional team was put on and the St. Louis Brown Stockings—the forerunners to the modern St. Louis Cardinals—were born. Henry Lucas's uncle and reportedly the richest man in St. Louis, J.B.C. Lucas II,[9] was president of this club and secured a place for the team in the National League, where they finished fourth in their debut season. They moved up to third behind Chicago the following year, but resigned their membership in 1877 after the blacklisting of four Louisville players they had engaged.[10]

Undeterred, the baseball-loving public resurrected a professional nine from the ashes of the old Browns in time for the 1881 season, the park on Grand Avenue was refitted, and millionaire German saloon-keeper Chris Von der Ahe was anointed as president. The Gleason brothers, Trick McSorley, George Baker were all amongst the old Browns who swore an oath "to be prompt, to do their level best at all times and take for [their] pay just as small a percentage as the welfare of the park and its owners would allow, to dispel the black eye that the blacklisting affair had given St. Louis in the baseball world since 1877."[11] But the unforgiving National League ignored these blandishments and the born-again Browns remained barred from the 1881 competition. Local fans were forced onto on a diet of games against "prairie nines" until 1882, when Captain Comiskey's boys were admitted to the American Association and finished fifth.[12]

But the glory and financial rewards of the Browns' monopoly on baseball in St. Louis were short-lived. By December 1883, the upstart Union Association had 47 players on the books and had held their first official meeting in Philadelphia, eagerly laying their plans to claim a share of both public affection and cash.[13] However, there were early concerns that the St. Louis nine, already featuring such luminaries as Fred Dunlap, George "Orator" Shafer, Jack Gleason, and Tony Mullane, would dominate and decimate the other Union teams,[14] and Lucas's acquisitions were not without complications. Tony Mullane was no less than the Browns' number one pitching ace, and his audacious signing by the cross-town Unions made him the first player to violate the National Agreement's reserve clause.[15] To further complicate the situation, Mullane promptly jumped back to the American Association, but not to the Browns—he went to Toledo, who offered him the same $2,500 salary Lucas had dangled before him. A livid Henry Lucas threatened to sue the great pitcher, even attempting to gain a restraining order against him in the District Court.[16]

With ambitious business tycoons and talented players aplenty, St. Louis was also home to some of nineteenth-century baseball's most influential journalists. The Spink family was of Scottish stock but their ten children, including three sons, were all born in Quebec, Canada. The thirteen Spinks immigrated during the Civil War to Chicago, where third son Alfred Henry, and his older brothers Frederick and William, played on a prominent amateur baseball team known as the Mutuals and developed an interest in baseball writing. Young Al followed William (Billy) to St. Louis in the late 1860s, where Billy working for the *Globe-Democrat* as "St. Louis' first real baseball editor."[17] Determined, collected, and farsighted, the youngest Spink entered a similar profession across town with the *Post-Dispatch*, but the brothers were far from being rivals, instead working together to popularize baseball in St. Louis by arranging "prairie tours" such as that of the Dubuque Rabbits in 1881.

Ted Sullivan, the new manager of the 1884 St. Louis Unions, was a great friend of Al Spink, and in his kindly fashion, arranged for the young Joe Quinn to board with Spink during his first sojourn to the city. Quinn recalled in a 1936 interview with *The Sporting News*, "I stayed at Al's house that year and he was very good to me as I was still only a boy."[18] The modest house at 1813 California Avenue was shared with Spink's wife Bertha, two-year-old Alfred Henry, Jr., and newborn baby Charlie, and from its windows, the young man from Dubuque could watch offices and stores opening expectant eyes to the day's business, and in the evenings, ladies parading in silver fox wraps. He perhaps wondered if they could see him, a boy from out of town, or hear what he heard in every hoofbeat passing: the happy tap of bat on ball!

• • •

Despite assurances the Union Association competition would be an even one, there was no doubt St. Louis gained a flying start on its rivals. As early as December 1883, the Lucas-Sullivan combination were already playing practice games in New Orleans and Pensacola, and by February 1884, the "Maroons" were working out at a brand-new purpose-built clubhouse on Jefferson and Cass Avenue. A pioneering development in professional baseball, the Unions' clubhouse was a grandiose three-story building with reading and lecture rooms for the players, billiard rooms, dressing closets, and a washroom with nine bathtubs.[19] It wasn't until 1892 that most League clubs had such facilities to obviate the need for players to travel to the park in uniform; in 1884, such luxuries were indeed the envy of the other start-up Union clubs, who were hastily assembling what facilities they could before the start of the season.

Lucas also spared no expense on his Union Association Park alongside the ostentatious clubhouse. Proclaimed by Sullivan as "the palace park of America,"[20] Lucas's field was the smallest and most pretentious in the country,[21] with right field only 179.5 feet and left-center a mere 250 feet, but it was purpose-designed to facilitate the excitement of long hitting and fast fielding. Bordered by Cass Avenue on the south and Jefferson Avenue to the west, it was a mile and a quarter nearer the city than the Browns' Sportsman's Park, and resplendent with "opera chairs" in the stands (which could seat 2,000 fans), bleachers for 8,000 more, and an infield rolled flat as a marble slab. Bluegrass and clover brightened the outfield, which was encompassed by a cinder track for sprinting and bicycling. A large bulletin board at the southeast corner of the field provided game scores not only for the Maroons, but telegraphed tallies from other Union Association games,[22] and the carriage yard along Cass Avenue was large enough to accommodate over a hundred vehicles.[23]

Quinn was the one of five players aged 21 or younger on the St. Louis list, but he lacked the imposing stature of his 6'2", 220-pound counterpart Perry "Moose" Werden, and he was a full 30 pounds lighter than either Charlie Sweeney or John Cattanach.[24] Quinn's were unfashionably clean-shaven features when the handlebar moustache was king; he looked every bit as young as he was, and it immediately landed him in trouble. There were no callow boys here in the big-city league: his teammates were men—broad-faced and lantern-jawed, with arms hard as blocks of wood. Fighting, drinking, and gambling were a way of life among professional ball players. Browns catcher "Pat" Deasley was arrested for drunkenness and offensive behavior in May 1884, and just six days later was seriously injured in a vicious brawl with his own teammates, Joe Quest and Tom Dolan. Browns management was forced to draft his wife to travel with the team and keep him on his best behavior for the rest of the season.[25] Rum-addled Richmond pitcher Frank Larkin was jailed twice in 1884, first for terrorizing his wife and shooting at a policeman, and just months later, for threatening his own father with a shotgun.[26] And pitcher "Gid" Gardner was forced to retreat to the Union Association after being fired by his Baltimore American Association club for savagely beating both his lady friend and a woman who came to her aid.[27] For young Joe Quinn, here was not the family-like atmosphere of the village green and the Rabbits: this was the reality of professional baseball in 1884. Some of the veterans—Dunlap and utility Dave Rowe in particular—took an immediate dislike to the youngster and his active, energetic work, and subjected him to a merciless hazing the likes of which Quinn had never experienced. They would pitch beanballs at him, refuse to back up balls hit to his area, tear his uniforms, and lock him out of the clubroom. The pair complained loudly to Sullivan that Joe was too small to play first base—Rowe being anxious to appropriate that position for himself—and would curse him when his sprightliness in the field showed up their own slowness or indifference.[28]

Unaware or uncaring of such antics, Lucas remained supremely confident about the form of his men as the season opener neared, despite gloomy predictions of an early death for the Association. His threats of retribution to Mullane had turned to cold contempt, assuring the press he "had another pitcher anyway, and you bet he is a dandy."[29] He also laid down the law to his own outfit, making an example of the unfortunate Jimmy Woulfe—the outfielder had asked for a $300 raise above his $1,800 sign-on fee, to which Lucas responded by sacking him. The extravagant young millionaire then boldly offered a cash prize to any local amateur nine who could beat his fancy team, but the sweeping gesture very nearly backfired as the Maroons just scraped past champion St. Louis amateur club Prickly Ash with a score of 9–8 on April 13, the amateurs scoring six runs in the last inning on three errors by Maroons second baseman Dunlap. As a final spring warm-up, Lucas Park hosted a free-entry game between the first and reserve Union sides on April 15, which the firsts won 11–2, Dunlap atoning with five doubles and a single. Playing first base for the reserves and resplendent in his new gray uniform and blue stockings, Quinn's pair of doubles at the plate and twelve putouts at first base earned him widespread praise in the St. Louis press as "the promising young Dubuque player."[30]

• • •

> *And one was there, a stripling ... a small and weedy beast,*
> *He was something like a racehorse undersized,*
> *With a touch of Timor pony—three parts Thoroughbred at least—*
> *And such as are by mountain horsemen prized.*
> *He was hard and tough and wiry—just the sort that won't say die—*
> *There was courage in his quick impatient tread;*
> *And he bore the badge of gameness in his bright and fiery eye,*
> *And the proud and lofty carriage of his head.*
> —A.B. "Banjo" Paterson, *The Man from Snowy River*, 1890

On a freezing, windswept April Sunday in St. Louis, the curtain was raised on the Union Association's inaugural game. Lucas chose the date deliberately, openly flouting National League disapproval of both games on Sundays and beer at ballparks, with all their connotations of disrespectability.[31] It was April 20, 1884, and 10,000 eager fans turned their coat collars up to the rain and tugged on gloves and mufflers as the thermometer sank relentlessly toward zero, cheering as slipping and sliding cost the visiting Chicago six errors and a 7–2 loss, with the game called after six innings due to the appalling weather. Captain Fred Dunlap set a high standard for his own season, taking a walk, going to second on a Shafer sacrifice, stealing third and galloping home on a passed ball, later scoring two more runs and making three assists and two putouts at second base. In an eerie portent of complacencies to come, St. Louis first baseman Billy "Bollicky Bill" Taylor, all 227 pounds of him,[32] made the worst play of the day in the second inning when, with two out and men on base, he popped up a high ball but didn't bother to run, although Captain Dunlap screamed at him to leg it and actually ran from the dugout to shove him out of the batter's box. Chicago pitcher Hugh "One Arm" Daily got under the ball and dropped it, but still threw Taylor out at first.[33] Quinn watched this rigmarole from the bench, no doubt hoping the fiasco would be enough to get him a start at first bag.

Three games later, on April 26, 1884, Quinn strode onto Union Park for the first time in an official capacity to face the men from Altoona. With the circus, theater matinees, and the Wild West show at the fairgrounds competing for notice, a crowd of just 1,000 fans was on hand to witness the professional debut of the youngster from Down Under. Batting last in the lineup, Quinn got his first swing at the Altoona boys in the second dig. Milt Whitehead had got to third, and twirler Jim Brown served up a big fat pitch on the outside corner that Quinn banged right back, sending it sailing right over the shortstop's head for a base hit. Dunlap followed him in the lineup, and Joe found himself on third as Dunlap lined one out to bounce off the right field wall. Although Altoona catcher George Noftsker tried to throw Dunlap out when Orator Shafer bunted foul, the inimitable captain stole second and Shafer's drive into right field scored them both to set up a 9–3 victory.[34]

Quinn secured his place in the first team with an errorless series at first base. While his debut was meritorious in its own right, it was almost impossible to fail in such a stacked and dominant outfit. St. Louis decimated the Altoonas in their four-game series, averaging over 14 runs per game while the Pennsylvania boys scored just 12 for the entire series,[35] and the *Missouri Republican* was already describing the victories by "the invincible" St. Louis as "the usual defeats."[36]

Quinn's first road trip was, ironically, a return visit to Altoona, but he had a nervous time of it. Rain made the ball as elusive as a greased pig in the first game on April 30 and Quinn made three errors, although St. Louis won easily, 16–3. With the shadow of Bollicky Bill Taylor looming large, Quinn grabbed the bit between his teeth and slammed three doubles off pitcher Joe Connors in game two, and once more the St. Louis nine trounced their opponents, scoring 42 runs to Altoona's 10 over the four-game series. The Pennsylvania outfit would take 11 straight losses before winning its first Union Association game, and win only five further games before being replaced in the league by Kansas City at the end of May.[37]

The Unions stayed home in May, with series wins against Washington, Baltimore, Boston, and Philadelphia. Their streak of 20 consecutive victories is a major league record which still stands,[38] but such a mauling of their fellow outlaws had already destroyed any hopes of a meaningful pennant race. Quinn found himself "riding the lonesome pine"[39] again after the Washington series, an ignominious 0-for-4 appearance in the last game on May 11 probably the catalyst. Taylor returned to first base in the subsequent 7–5 defeat of Baltimore, but when the big man was called to pitch the following day, Quinn returned for a 20–6 rout of the "Monumentals," accumulating a grand total of four hits and four runs.[40] May 1884 was itself an extravagant and record-breaking month in professional baseball. On May 10, Washington catcher Alex Gardner played his first game in the American Association and allowed 12 passed balls, a record still unbroken, as his team was rolled 11–3 by the New York Mets. Gardiner never played again.[41] Three days later, Quinn's old Dubuque teammate Hoss Radbourn grabbed five hits to lead his Providence Grays to a 25–3 thumping of Detroit in the National League, the most decisive victory in the league that year: Detroit's staggering total of 18 errors, including five alone by right fielder Fred Wood, was a forerunner of failures to come, with the Wolverines finishing the season in a miserable last place.[42] Detroit was on the receiving end of another hammering on May 30, when Chicago's Ned Williamson belted three home runs and the Colts overwhelmed the Wolverines 12–2. Williamson's home runs were the first of 27 for the season, a feat which survived until Babe Ruth hit 29 in 1919.[43]

Those were gala days for the undefeated St. Louis Unions. Henry Lucas's generosity extended beyond his *carte blanche* on salaries: he ordered Sullivan to permit the players to come and go as they pleased, and to discipline themselves. Sullivan later confessed to Al Spink he "did not have the heart to tap a player's pocket" anyway,[44] and as a result, the days were easygoing and loose, with the men playing cards to pass the time, lounging on the sunny grass at Lucas Park while chewing great wads of leaf tobacco and spitting to drown as many ants as possible (a pursuit considerably more challenging than any opponent they had faced thus far). Quinn had a lifelong penchant for tobacco, which ball players widely chewed in the nineteenth century to keep the mouth moist and to produce saliva to lubricate both glove leather and spitballs (until they were banned in the 1920s[45]). His granddaughter, Mary Catherine Butler (the daughter of Joe's oldest child, Catherine Marie Becherer), lived with Quinn for a year as a small child, in 1936, as her own family struggled to recover from the Great Depression. He affectionately christened the twelve-year-old child "Caddie," in memory of his own mother. Mary Catherine recalled that, even into his old age, Joe had silver spittoons in nearly every room of the house, even the hall, and that she once asked if she could try some of "Grandpa's chew," to which Joe responded by handing her a piece of fudge so she could have a "chew" alongside him.[46] After 1900, it was discovered spitting could spread tuberculosis, and the practice of tobacco chewing became far less socially acceptable, although most ball players continued chewing well into the 1940s.[47] However, chewing did have some benefits: in 1899, the *Worcester Gazette* reported gum saved Providence's Charlie Nyce's jaw from being broken after his teammate Pete Cassidy's bat flew out of his hand and struck Nyce in the face as he sat in the dugout.[48]

St. Louis had routed Boston 13–3 and 16–4 on May 21 and 22, the second game showcasing the remarkable talents of Fred Dunlap as he scored five runs, hit three doubles and a triple, and had eight putouts and six assists at second base.[49] Although Dunlap had what Spink described as "the finest features, the nose of an Indian chief and the brown eyes of a beautiful woman,"[50] Fred Dunlap ruled his teammates and opponents with fists of iron. His tormenting of young Joe Quinn was public knowledge, and almost expected, given the reputation with which he had arrived in St. Louis. During his Cleveland days of the early 1880s, one of his teammates had abused him in the clubhouse after a game and threatened to beat him to death for an error on the field, to which Dunlap responded that would do little good, as neither would be able to play the next day. He then gave his much-bigger opponent "the worst beating a man ever received."[51]

But for all his pugnacious character, the tragic Dunlap was a champion born, not made. Orphaned as a child, he had grown up wild on the prairies outside Philadelphia, unable to read or write but learning every letter of the baseball game. Spink marveled his arm was "as accurate as the best rifle shot and speedy as lightning," and his disproportionate strength made him a wonderful hitter, with a lifetime .292 average. He was also ambidextrous, a great advantage for a middle infielder in the days before gloves were worn. Dunlap led the National League in 1885 and 1889 at second base, and although Spink watched all the greats, including Bid McPhee of Cincinnati, Chicago's Fred Pfeffer from Chicago, the great Nap Lajoie, and Joe Quinn himself, he still rated Dunlap as "the greatest ever" and unlikely to be surpassed.[52] But by 1891, a broken-down Dunlap was out of the game, and upon his enforced retirement, sank into a morbid depression. The $100,000 fortune he had accumulated soon disappeared in a haze of drink and ill-thrift. When Spink last saw him in 1896, Dunlap boasted of how he had taken care of his money and owned valuable property in Philadelphia. But in the winter of 1902, a message was received at the newspaper office in that town, that a man supposed to have once been a great ball player had died in the Alms House and was to be buried next day in the Potter's Field. The editor went to investigate, and sure enough, it was Dunlap, without friends or money enough to have his body carried to a decent grave. The hack drivers made up the pallbearers at his funeral.[53]

The sustained success of the St. Louis nine inevitably bred complacency, and on May 24, the wheels first wobbled on the runaway Unions train. A home crowd of 5,000 saw St. Louis accumulate eight hits but only one run, narrowly escaping being shut out by the Boston battery of Tommy Bond and Ed Crane. In contrast, Boston played errorless ball and scored four of their eight runs on St. Louis mistakes, including three passed balls. Maroons switch-hitter Milt Whitehead got his hit batting left-handed against the curve ball that struck out nine of his teammates, including Bollicky Bill Taylor three times. Quinn again watched the debacle from the bench. And the local followers of the game proved themselves a fickle lot, ready to go into ecstasies when the team won or to lynch the whole nine when it lost: the *Missouri Republican* sneered on May 25, "The home crowd appeared to enjoy the downfall of the local club, and from the start the visitors received nearly all the applause."[54] Barbed, the Unions surged back with a succession of monstrous wins, including a 17–1 annihilation of the struggling Philadelphia Keystoners on May 30, Quinn being one of four St. Louis players to hit two or more doubles. It was a nasty precedent for the June return series, which St. Louis won 15–1, 6–4, 12–0 and 6–0: in one game alone, Philadelphia contributed a wretched 15 errors to guarantee their own demise.[55] Cincinnati was the only semi-threat to the St. Louis steamroller, defeating the Unions 3–1 in an errorless performance on June 11, but when pitchers Taylor and Bradley faced off again two days later, St. Louis won 16–11.[56]

Meanwhile, the war between the Union and the existing major leagues again flared to life like embers before a strong wind—this time with Joe Quinn front and center. Quinn had played in all but six games, settling into a pattern of consistent, if light, hitting. He retained his spot at first base where, grudgingly assisted by Dunlap, he often made ten or more putouts per match (gloveless, it must be remembered). But on June 22, his burgeoning career took a sinister twist when the young first baseman was allegedly approached by "persons unknown" with an offer to abandon his Union contract and join Washington in the American Association.[57] Rumors abounded that Ted Sullivan, now managing at Kansas City,[58] was actively encouraging his former protégée to break his contract, but Sullivan emphatically denied the story and Quinn remained firmly entrenched in St. Louis. Given Sullivan's recent reassignment by Lucas to take over as manager of the struggling Kansas City outfit, it is unlikely "Ted" would have repaid the favor by attempting to lure one of Lucas's own stars out of St. Louis. Nonetheless, the rumors prompted a furious outburst from Henry Lucas, who declared that, having until now withstood the attacks of the League and American Association without retaliating, the Union Association would "enter vigorously into the contract-breaking business."[59]

The Fourth of July series in Baltimore finally put a brake on the cavalier Maroons. At Belair Lot, the only major league park ever to be located in East Baltimore (although it was never used again after 1884),[60] a free-swinging Baltimore lay in wait for Lucas's stars. Having never scored more than eight runs against their southern rivals, Baltimore made 13 runs from their 12 hits, while the St. Louis boys appeared completely lost on the Belair basepaths—Dunlap was too ill to line up, and "Orator" Shafer's move to from the outfield to second base upset his equilibrium so much that he managed only one hit from five at-bats. Quinn mirrored that effort, rubbing salt into the wound by making two errors at first base.[61] The loss was compounded by the Maroons' having to immediately catch a train south to Washington to play again the same day. The trip clearly disagreed with the already disconcerted crew, who were promptly hammered 12–1 by the one of the league's worst teams, one who would finish the season 47 wins adrift of their Missourian counterparts.[62]

New pitcher "Handsome" Henry Boyle exploded into the St. Louis lineup on July 9, holding the Baltimore Monumentals to seven hits and slamming a triple and a home run of his own in the 7–4 win. He was forced to start again three days later after Billy Taylor, having compiled a 25–4 record, deserted the Unions for the American Association's Philadelphia Athletics, for whom he would win a further 17 games.[63] But Boyle was a more than valuable replacement, for in addition to his 15–3 pitching record at a miserly 1.74 ERA, he appeared in 51 further games playing at almost any position, including first, second, and third base, shortstop, and in the outfield, making just 19 errors and hitting a respectable .260.[64]

Quinn was elevated in the lineup to face "the seceder from Detroit,"[65] National League deserter Frederick Shaw, on July 19 in Boston. The first game of the series had been lost 12–10 without Dunlap and Taylor on the park, Boyle and Quinn both grabbing three hits and leading the charge for six runs in the final three innings.[66] They had their first look at the portsider Shaw two days later, and look was about all they did as the wily left-hander fanned fourteen. Shaw had whiffed ten by the fifth inning before Quinn collected the first safe hit of the day. He whacked a bounding groundball hard past Murnan on first and dashed to the bag like a hound after a hare, beating Crane's throw. While no run was scored, the ferocious "Dupee" did not appreciate his no-hitter being spoiled, and when Quinn re-entered the box in the seventh with Gleason sweating on third base, Shaw had steam bursting from all vents. The pitch was so wild it was lucky the sole umpire stood well behind the catcher or it would've taken his head off. A whooping Jack Gleason scored on the error with an Indian's yell, and while there was one moment of trepidation in the eighth when Boston's Tommy McCarthy belted a left-field triple, Milt Whitehead's cutoff throw busted him at the plate and St. Louis had won the game of the season. Henry Boyle was in disbelief at grabbing a 1–0 win when Shaw had claimed 14 scalps. Dupee pitched all three games of the series on July 19, 20 and 21, amassing a staggering 48 strikeouts, a major league record for three consecutive games (as was his record of 34 strikeouts for two games on July 19 and 21).[67] Quinn, in the meantime, was the darling of the St. Louis papers for being the only one to hit The Seceder safe.[68]

• • •

With a jaw-dropping 28–3 record, by mid–June St. Louis had destroyed their struggling opponents and, despite Lucas's best efforts, the Union Association was serious in danger of implosion. In August, the Chicago franchise transferred to Pittsburgh, and in its first game, defeated the front-running St. Louis 3–2—then promptly disbanded and was replaced by St. Paul, who had the shortest-ever season of a club in a major league, dropping out after losing six of their first eight games.[69] The Philadelphia franchise also collapsed, replaced by Wilmington from the Eastern League, who only lasted a month before being replaced by Milwaukee—that club also crumbled after just twelve games. Washington defected to the American Association and Cincinnati was clamoring to follow a similar course. *Spalding's Guide* blamed alcoholism for the failure of about one-third of the professional clubs in 1884,[70] but the real reason was the weighty total of 34 major league clubs: poor gate receipts were primarily responsible for the massive rate of club mortality, and the Union suffered additionally because of its unbalanced competition.

The threat of annihilation by bottom line was obviously no deterrent to the high-flying St. Louis team. So far ahead they needed binoculars to see the opposition,[71] St. Louis set themselves for another series sweep when the third-placed Outlaw Reds from Cincinnati came to town on August 5. They immediately shut out the visitors 8–0 on Charlie Sweeney's one-hitter. The acquisition of Sweeney was one of Lucas's greatest triumphs over his National League rivals. On June 7, while still pitching for Providence in the National League, Sweeney had struck out 19 Boston hitters, a major league record for a nine-inning game which remained unbroken until Roger Clemens fanned 20 in 1986.[72] Ten days later, Sweeney pitched his second one-hitter of the year, then was promptly suspended without pay after refusing to be substituted, despite holding a safe lead over Philadelphia with one inning remaining. While the hot-tempered Sweeney was eventually persuaded to leave the field, his foresight was clearly justified—replacement pitcher Joseph "Cyclone" Miller immediately surrendered eight runs and handed the A's a 10–6 win.[73] Outraged, Sweeney accepted Lucas's offer to jump to the Unions, breaking up one of the most powerful and belligerent pitching twosomes in the National League: he and Hoss Radbourn had shared the Grays' pitching duties and despised one another in equal measure, Radbourn furiously jealous of his younger rival and Sweeney drinking, carousing, and taunting Old Hoss on his way from win to win. His departure left Radbourn to pitch the final 38 games of the year in Providence, but the aging hurler was more than equal to the task. He won the last 18 games straight to tally an astonishing 59 wins for the season, clinching both the National League pennant for Providence and the World Series in three straight games.[74]

With clubs falling like bowling pins around him, Lucas's final bold quest to bolster the Union with National League stars was his most desperate—coming, as it did, to the immediate detriment of his own team. Needing only to win on August 10 to take the series against Cincinnati, the St. Louis Maroons were astonished to be confronted by a Reds lineup heavily stacked with National Leaguers from Cleveland! And these weren't just any garden-variety ball-players, but the heavy battery of catcher Charlie "Fatty" Briody and "Big Jim" McCormick (who had already pitched 19 winning games), and star shortstop Jack Glasscock, a five-time National League leader.[75] Lucas had coolly enticed them to Cincinnati with his bottomless checkbook, leaving the Cleveland National League outfit in tatters and his own boys absolutely shell-shocked. Cincinnati piled on six runs in the second inning and downed the Maroons 7–4, although Charlie Sweeney held the visitors to one hit after the disastrous second inning and Quinn contributed two hits and two double plays with Dunlap at second base.

It took an eight-game winning streak for St. Louis to regain their equilibrium. In the final game on August 30, Quinn gave another of the season's most entertaining clutch hitting performances: with the score locked at 3–3 in the top of the eleventh against Chicago and Rowe and Boyle on base, Quinn lined pitcher "One Arm" Daily into centerfield and Rowe scored the winning run, again much to Daily's displeasure.[76] The Chicago hurler's moniker was entirely appropriate—he had lost his left arm in a explosion at the Front Street Theatre in Baltimore, where he worked as a lighting technician as a young man,[77] and to compensate for the injury, he fixed a pad over the affected limb and caught the baseball by trapping it between the pad and his right hand. Daily was as well known for his vile temper as for his disability, showering umpires, opponents, and fans alike with curses and profanity. He once even knocked out his own catcher for not throwing balls back to him more softly so as to protect his arm stump.[78] But for all his vitriol, by the end of the season, Daily had become the first major league pitcher to hurl consecutive one-hitters, throwing four for the season to set a major league record only equaled by Grover Alexander in 1915.[79]

While displays of temper between players were common, the advent of professionalism, the increasing complexity of the game, and high stakes to win in the 1880s also led to a rise in vilification of umpires. Umpires were frequently hit with bats or other missiles, mobbed, beaten and required police escorts to leave both the park and the town. On-field rowdiness was thought to attract bigger crowds, so team owners often actively encouraged disrespect and outright physical violence among their players, and happily paid any fines incurred by their unruly charges.[80] Teams were also not above forfeiting if they couldn't work with an umpire. On August 22 at Kansas City, down 6–3 in the ninth, St. Louis seemed doomed to lose to the lowliest of lowlies, even with Brennan and Werden on base. Milt Whitehead hit a terrific blast to right field and Brennan bolted like a dog off a string. There was a great stir in the dugout and it was hard to see just what went on, but from where the St. Louis boys sat, it seemed that Cowboys catcher Baldwin came along the baseline to receive the throw and stopped Brennan from making a dive. Umpire Seward was of the same mind and called "safe," which caused instant consternation among the Kansas nine. They surrounded the unfortunate arbiter and demanded a reversal of the decision, but Seward refused, in spite of Kansas President McKim's threatening all sorts of retribution and the St. Louis team running to shove their rivals back so the game could go on. Kansas forfeited the game in disgust,[81] and per the rules at the time, the official final score was registered as a 9–0 victory for St. Louis.

The inevitable complacency that had stalked St. Louis for most of their season of devastating dominance finally became public late in the year. As the season drew to a close in October, the *Missouri Republican* commented bitterly, "For some time, the St. Louis Unions have [been] careless and indifferent and not batted with anything like their old-time vim. At the opening of the season, every man in the nine used to hit the ball, and from the time play was started until the last man was out, they never quit playing. They all took an interest in coaching each other and encouraging the batsman ... now they sit around on the benches and let the batsmen and base runners take care of themselves."[82] Five of the Maroons' six games after their trip to Kansas City were decided by a margin of one run, and it was a trip to rainy Boston which finally rusted out the wheels of the mighty St. Louis machine. They lost 8–4 on September 20 in seven innings, were crushed 16–3 without Dunlap on the 22nd with Quinn in unfamiliar territory in right field, and lost again 6–4 in spite of Sweeney's three-hit, 16-strikeout performance in the box in the final game. Gleason's fumbling at third base cost five runs in the third inning, and five Dolan muffs at the plate were the cherry on top of a distinctly stale cake.[83]

Eight thousand forgiving fans still greeted them home on September 28 and were rewarded with a 12–1 thumping of Baltimore, and the Unions didn't lose again until Sunday, October 19, the final game of the year. Ten thousand fans packed tiny Palace Park for the showdown with Boston. They were first entertained with a 135-yard footrace between Messrs. Murphy, Saunders and Taylor, and an attempt by Ed Crane to beat John Hatfield's record for maximum distance thrown: a strong headwind meant Crane threw only 134 yards 5 inches, almost a foot short, and Lucas lost the fifty dollars he had bet on him.[84] It proved a bad omen. St. Louis was humiliated in a 5–0 shutout at the hands of The Seceder, Dupee Shaw; not only did he strike out 12 Maroons, but Shaw also had three RBIs when his bases-loaded double was mishandled by Dunlap. Sweeney was batted hard and Baker behind the plate again made three errors. According to the *Republican*, Quinn made an error in the first dig by going too far down the baseline and muffing a dropped-strike out, but he made up for it with a fine double-play in the fifth. In the fourth, Sweeney hit a double, got to third on Quinn's sacrifice, but was out at the plate trying to score on Dolan's infield dribbler; St. Louis didn't pass second base again.[85]

The public embarrassment continued during the two-game post-season series played against American Association outfit Louisville on October 24–25, again at the Palace Park. The visitors crushed the Unions 7–2 in the first game, with the press pouring scorn on the home side and criticizing the Union Association as pretenders to major league status. Stung, the locals hit back with a 15–1 trouncing of their guests the next day—a farcical end to a ludicrous season.[86]

St. Louis had decimated the Union Association with their 91–16 record, distantly followed by Cincinnati (69–36) and Baltimore (58–47). Never before or again would a team win with such carefree ease or merciless regularity. Dunlap hit a ferocious .420 with 13 home runs and a .926 fielding average to sweep the honors in almost every category,[87] the most dominant season by any non-pitcher of the nineteenth century. Also leading the league in their positions were Dave Rowe (centerfield) and George Baker catching (in spite of his 63 errors).[88] The remarkable Charlie Sweeney hit .416 in addition to his heroics in the pitcher's box, in which he won 24 games and lost just 7 at a miserly ERA of 1.83; Henry Boyle was a good second with a 15–3 record at 1.74.[89] And despite his mid-season defection to the American Association, Bollicky Bill Taylor's 25 wins and four saves at an ERA of 1.68 were second across the three major leagues behind only Cincinnati's "Big Jim" McCormick (1.54).[90]

The Sporting Life of November 19, 1884, mused that "players of the caliber of O'Rourke, Radbourn, Brouthers, Anson, White and Richardson are not made in a year. It takes the suns of many summers and the snows of many winters to toughen their hides and give them the necessary experience with ball and bat."[91] As the youngest player on the Maroons roster, Joe Quinn had just had his first summer in the sun. He hit .270 for the season, and made over eight hundred (gloveless) putouts at first base, with a league-leading 33 assists and 55 double plays. He also posted a similar lead in the errors column for first basemen, with 62. He was one of only three players (the other two being Dunlap and Shafer) to hit over 100 singles, and also contributed 22 doubles and 3 triples, finishing the year ranked fortieth of 114 Union men in hitting. He ranked twelfth as a first baseman, with a .938 fielding average, but ten of those preceding him played fewer than 35 games, while Quinn played 82 of the season's 112. And of all the St. Louis Maroons, Quinn went on to have the longest major league career (17 years), significantly ahead of his closest counterparts in Orator Shafer (13 years) and Fred Dunlap (12).[92]

But for all his glories, salary, and new comforts—with all his money, he now had all he could desire in books, pillows, clean socks, and blankets—reality awaited Joe Quinn as the season ebbed away. When snow began to fall in St. Louis, Quinn returned to Dubuque and his job laboring in the mines alongside his father—underground in the dark, away from the sun, the sky and the new-mown grass.[93]

5. The Black Diamonds in the National League

"A startling story: Mr. Lucas to desert Union Association!"
—*The Sporting Life*, December 17, 1884

The banner headline was akin to that of a modern tabloid screeching scandal over a celebrity or political indignity. After spending much of his fortune on the breakaway Union Association in 1884, Henry Lucas was not only abandoning his post at its head, but tethering his much-vaunted and gilded ship firmly to the stern of the detested opposition, the National League. In the stroke of a sportswriter's pen, the breakaway association was publicly and officially decapitated.

A friend of Lucas's, A.L. Bird, had written to *The Sporting Life* on December 17, 1884, explaining Lucas realized his Unions had "won everything possible," and the only way forward was to "join the established leagues." Bird's claim was allegedly verified by an unnamed source in New York—Lucas had agreed to withdraw his opposition to the reserve clause and amalgamate the Union Association with the National League, acknowledging the clause was painfully necessary to maintain internal competition and public interest in both the game and the fate of its players.[1]

Lucas's desertion was "startling" because both he and Ted Sullivan had made bold public claims about the bright future of the Association in late 1884, even hosting a meeting on October 20 to discuss the formation of a new Western League as an ally.[2] And the perceived strength of the Union was obviously worrying the established leagues: *The Sporting Life* of November 19, 1884, leaked the story that the National League and American Association were in cahoots to overthrow Lucas's growing influence, working together with Secretary Harry Diddlebock of the Eastern League to tempt the Boston and Washington Union outfits to strengthen their own ranks.[3] The newly reelected President Lucas and Sullivan counter-attacked by traveling to Indianapolis in December to persuade owner John T. Brush to jump from the American Association, claiming the league was cutting back to eight clubs and Indianapolis would be the first to go.[4]

Lucas had also opportunistically purchased the Cleveland franchise (which he had, of course, already helped to ruin with mid-season player raids) in January 1885. But instead of refitting it to sail in the Union Association, Lucas initiated secret negotiations with President Mills of the National League in December to admit a combined Cleveland-St. Louis franchise, to be based out of St. Louis. Mills, however, was no supporter of Lucas or his schemes—

he bitterly contested St. Louis's admission to the National League, aiming to punish Lucas for his adoption of perceived "anti National League" tactics, including Sunday baseball and cheap admission to Union parks. But the League overrode Mills's decision to blacklist the players who had jumped to the Union, and Mills resigned in protest when they were readmitted after paying nominal fines.[5] League secretary Nicholas Young was elevated to the top job, and while he persuaded Lucas to accept the reserve clause and to give up Sunday baseball and liquor sales at his park as part of the deal to admit his new team to the National League, obtaining consent from the owner of the St. Louis American Association club for establishment of a second club in the city was not so straightforward.[6]

For all his many eccentricities, "Der Poss President" of the St. Louis Browns, German saloonkeeper Chris Von der Ahe, was no fool when it came to spotting a business opportunity. He quickly recognized advantages in having an additional club in the city, including gate takings from exhibition matches between the two teams, a large block of stock in the new club, and the fact his own league permitted Sunday games, beer sales, and 25-cent admission, while Lucas would be debarred from such luxuries. But when the National League formally admitted St. Louis on January 10, 1885, Von der Ahe's graciousness toward his rival evaporated. With all the pain of the old cross-town conflict with the Union burning to the surface, he demanded $10,000 in compensation from Lucas and the blacklisting of every player who had broken a contract to join the Union Association.[7]

Amazingly, Lucas, his eyes on a bigger prize, agreed—despite having already lost somewhere between $50,000 and $250,000 of his personal fortune on the Union venture.[8] Many of his champions—Dunlap, Shafer, Rowe, Sweeney, Gleason, Boyle and Dolan—were all subsequently barred, although Dunlap and Shafer had refused to be reserved and therefore never actually signed National League contracts. The group demanded to know how Lucas expected to make even a half decent showing without them, but the protest went virtually unheard.

The place of the defunct Union Association in baseball history remains a controversial one. Was the Association ever a "major league?" In the *New Historical Baseball Abstract*, Bill James describes a lengthy criterion for the achievement of major league status, including overall league stability, player quality, geographical reach, media coverage, and a structure to attract talent. While the Union plainly viewed itself as a professional league through its determined acquisition of players from competing leagues, and its geographical reach was extensive, with clubs across the northeast from Pennsylvania to St. Louis, perhaps only the St. Louis club could claim a quality of play and players demonstrably greater than that of the existing minor leagues. In James's assessment of the 272 players on Union rosters, none were considered major league "stars," and just 14 (including Charlie Sweeney, Jack Glasscock, Fred Dunlap, and Joe Quinn) were legitimate major league players; two-thirds of the remainder had either no major league career after 1884 or brief but failed stints at the top level.[9] Without any kind of minor league feeder system and three teams folding during the first season, the Association can be remembered for little more than the rampaging success of its St. Louis franchise, whose 91–16 record still remains unrivaled in professional baseball history, though achieved against opposition chiefly composed of has-beens and never-weres. But as baseball's first attempt to argue for the rights of professional players, the Union Association remains a milestone in the evolution of baseball's modern industrial structure. And for young Joe Quinn, the experience had been a life-shaping one, awakening a desire for fairness and player's rights which would shape many choices in his future.

• • •

Despite Lucas's agreeing to compensate Von der Ahe, the National Agreement meeting of January 24, 1885, declared Von der Ahe ineligible for any damages. The obstreperous German did, however, have one of his wishes granted: a March 3 meeting of the National League Arbitration Committee refused to reinstate the blacklisted players. This move ought to have been a serious blow to the new St. Louis Maroons, to have the likes of Sweeney and Dunlap sitting around, wasting their good arms. But with typically brash conviction in himself and his financial resources, Lucas plowed ahead, preparing what remained of his new franchise for the 1885 season. He had luxurious new uniforms commissioned, with shirts and trousers of white English flannel and the buttonholes and St. Louis logo embroidered with maroon silk. The caps were also of maroon, the belts featured silver-plated buckles, and the playing shoes were crafted from the best available deerskin.[10] Lucas also had a new park constructed at the intersection of Vandeventer and Natural Bridge Avenues: the site was a strategic choice, lying as it did at the intersection of two streetcar lines operated by his own Mound City Transportation Company.[11] Horse-drawn trams such as Lucas's had by now overtaken the omnibus (a type of large stagecoach) as the dominant form of urban public transport in St. Louis. While steam-powered cable cars were introduced to the city in 1876, the initiative was largely unsuccessful as the vehicles were noisy and frightened the working horses, and by 1881, St. Louis had 500 trams pulled by a staff of 2,200 horses and operating on some 120 miles of track, carrying a staggering 19.6 million passengers every year.[12]

The newly christened Maroons again finalized their preparations for the season by defeating their local pre-summer rivals Prickly Ash 9–0 on April 1. The blacklisted Sweeney played and contributed a double and two triples; Quinn watched from the sidelines. Confidence was further boosted by a second clean defensive slate when free admission drew a huge crowd to the new Lucas Park to see the Maroons beat another local amateur side, St. Gotthards, 6–0, on April 4.[13] Quinn again did not play; however, in defiance of all injunctions, every one of the blacklisted Maroons did. A series of nine pre-season games against the Browns was then arranged, but the opener on April 10 saw the pretenders shut out 7–0 on a Dave Foutz one-hitter. The Maroons slunk out of the Browns' den on Grand Avenue with their tails firmly between their legs, but rallied two days later to reverse the result at home, 6–4. There was clear hope the blacklisted players would be officially reinstated, for Henry Boyle lined up for the Maroons and pitched a classy two-hitter. Joe Quinn also played his first official practice game, taking a walk, scoring once, and playing errorless ball at first base. The Browns had their revenge on April 16, shutting the Maroons out again 8–0 and going on to win six of the nine games, apparently through "the personal supervision of Chris Von der Ahe," *The Sporting Life* sneered.[14]

Lucas's campaign for the reinstatement of Dunlap et al. was finally realized on April 22, just a week before the 1885 season opener, when Lucas persuaded the National League that attendance in St. Louis would suffer if they were seen to punish players for actions instigated by league officials. The League finally acquiesced, fining the jumpers $1,000 each, and Dunlap was hastily appointed manager of the Maroons. They celebrated the return of the "Black Diamonds" by thrashing Tom Loftus's Milwaukee outfit 13–0, Joe Quinn grabbing three hits (with a double) and making fourteen errorless putouts at first base.[15] The Maroons were back, once more riding the crest of expectation generated by their tearaway 1884 season, anticipating instant success in the National League.

◆ ◆ ◆

A rainy Opening Day failed to daunt the 7,000 fans who packed Lucas Park on April 30 to cheer the Maroons' 3–2 defeat of Cap Anson's Chicago in their first official League appearance. The result was indeed as close as the scoreboard suggests. The home side got off to the perfect start with two runs in the first inning off wild pitches by White Stockings pitcher Larry Corcoran and smart purloining of bases by Dunlap. But new rules introduced in 1885 saw the visitors equalize when two balks by home pitcher Charlie Sweeney walked George Gore home, then a triple that bounced over the fence was ruled a home run as it was considered a "hit over 210 feet."[16] Still a run behind, the visitors loaded the bases in the final inning and Mike "King" Kelly started for home on a third base error, but Jack Glasscock was the hero of the day, swooping from shortstop to throw Kelly out at the plate and end the game. Quinn made the starting lineup but was hitless (although errorless) at first base.[17] Cap Anson's White Stockings, destined to sweep the league with 87 victories, were avenged 9–5 the next day as the Maroons disintegrated under five walks from a skittish Henry Boyle and 15 errors by his equally jumpy defense. The third game was an even greater debacle for the home outfit as pitcher Charlie Sweeney, already Anson-bait with a visibly sore arm, conceded six runs in the first two innings and was replaced by Boyle, who immediately gave up seven more in a 16–1 trouncing. Sweeney had to pitch again two days later, and the strain of three starts in five days told as he again conceded four runs in the first inning of a 7–2 loss, although he did partly redeem himself with a two-hit, two-run performance at the plate. In this fourth game, Joe Quinn had his first hit of the season, a double, but at least had yet to make an error in the field.[18]

The Maroons were on the road for the remainder of May. Their trip north to Detroit drew blood on May 8, inflicting Detroit's first loss, 10–3, in wet and freezing conditions that contributed to a staggering 27 errors; it was only Boyle's six-hitter that kept the Maroons in front. They faced League heavyweights Boston two days later, winning the opener courageously 5–4 before 3,000 fans. Joe Quinn gamely led the final-inning charge with a long shot to centerfield; the catch was fumbled by Charlie Buffinton, and Henry Boyle scored the winning run from second base.[19] The Maroons backed it up the following day, winning 8–6 on Dunlap's three-hit, three-run, no-error performance ("a most agreeable surprise," according to *The Sporting Life*[20]). But they were unable to carry the winning feeling to Providence, who had captured the National League title in 1884: Henry Boyle was belted out of the box in a 10–2 defeat on the 19th, and Charlie Sweeney suffered the same fate the following day.[21]

St. Louis failed to win another game until May 30, when they shocked league leaders New York 4–1 in the last of a doubleheader; they had previously lost three times to the Giants during May, including the humiliation of an 11–0 shutout in which even the woeful-hitting New York pitcher Tim Keefe got two hits.[22] But the future prospects were not good. Sweeney and Boyle both had sore arms, Fred Dunlap was ill, and Fred Lewis had a hamstring problem. Batting .170 for the month, Quinn found himself shunted to right field to make way for .294-hitting Alex McKinnon at first base. However, this was not the absolute demotion it might appear. Nineteenth-century managers paid more attention

Joe Quinn as he appeared while playing for the St. Louis Maroons of 1885–86 (courtesy Rogers Photograph Archive, Arkansas, Texas).

to right field than at the present day, and in the 1870s and '80s, the fleetest fielders were placed here and were expected to throw runners out at first base. Such a play is seldom successful now, but in the early days, it was pulled off regularly by exponents such as Quinn's teammate George Shafer. An .861 career fielder over 13 seasons, Shafer was known as "the Orator," as Al Spink recounted in the *National Game*, "for the reason that he was a great stickler for his rights, and talked constantly to himself when he was not talking to the umpire."[23]

Quinn also took a turn in left field, and was praised by *The Sporting Life* for his work there in the 5–2 win over Buffalo on June 2, in which he made five barehanded catches.[24] On June 4, the Maroons defeated Buffalo again in the last game ever played at the "Palace Park of America." Two days later, the Maroons moved into their new home at Vandeventer Lot (which was later rechristened as Robison Field and would house St. Louis baseball until 1920[25]). Despite the presence of 10,000 expectant local fans, Chicago unkindly christened the park with a 9–2 thrashing of the Maroons: "Gorgeous George" Gore and "Silver" Flint accumulated seven hits off their old teammate One-Arm Daily as he made his debut for the Maroons, and the remainder of the series was swept 9–8, 6–1, and 13–1.[26] The White Stockings were a team of superstars, managed by A.G. Spalding, himself a celebrated underhand pitcher who guided Chicago to five pennants in the 1880s. His captain, Adrian Constantine "Cap" Anson, was the first pro ball player to reach the milestone of 3,000 hits, and remains the all-time leader in hits, runs scored, doubles, and runs batted in for the Chicago franchise.[27] Regrettably, Anson was also one of the most virulent racists of the period, which was already one not favoring black rights: between 1889 and 1903, around a dozen African Americans were lynched, burned, or mutilated every week in the United States.[28] The city of St. Louis was divided by the 1847 Dred Scott trials in which Scott, a slave who accompanied his owners to the free states of Illinois and Wisconsin, sued his owner's widow, claiming traveling to a free state made him free. It was another fifty years before the Supreme Court passed a statute requiring railroads to provide equal (albeit separate) accommodation for whites and blacks; notwithstanding, other laws continued to restrict black access to hospitals, theaters, hotels, libraries, and ballfields.[29] An 1867 resolution banning black ball players and the teams they played for from joining the National Agreement was never formally adopted, but a "gentleman's agreement" ensured non-whites were almost totally excluded from organized baseball.[30] Only 55 are known to have played prior to 1900, and it was not uncommon for white players to deliberately slide into or pitch beanballs at African American opponents. In 1883, Fleet Walker became the first black player to appear in the professional leagues, catching for Toledo in the American Association. When Toledo met the White Stockings, Anson allegedly bellowed, "Get that nigger off the field!" Although he was forced to retract under threat of forfeiture, it was an act he repeated often.[31] On the White Stockings' World Tour of 1888, Spalding and Anson defied the Emancipation Proclamation by taking along Clarence Duval, a black youth they called their "mascot" but who, in reality, was little more than an indentured servant. Before each game, he was decked out in white trousers and a red coat edged with gold lace, and he would lead the team onto the field with an exhibition of plantation dancing.[32]

While the sore-armed Maroons were hanging on in sixth place with their ten wins, Chicago and New York, with 24 wins apiece, seemed intent on clearing out on the field. Quinn had been errorless and hit safely in every game of the Chicago debacle, but was dropped for the first time in five weeks on June 12 as the Maroons were shut out 2–0 by the 1884 third-place getters, Buffalo. Their uncertain and often ignominious form was drawing little sympathy: *The Sporting Life* scoffed on June 17, "St. Louis at least found somebody they could beat," when they entertained last-placed Detroit and won 7–1.[33]

With an average home attendance of only 800 mildly-interested fans, the Maroons' cause was not helped by a visit from champions Boston on June 23, who swept them cleaner than a parlor floor in all four games of the series. Fred Dunlap was still sick and struggling to assemble the Maroons into a winning combination, trying George Baker at third to replace the error-ridden Ed Caskin, and Henry Boyle variously at second, in centerfield, and pinch-hitting. The team was thrown into further turmoil by the expulsion of Fred Lewis, who allegedly struck out against both Buffalo and Detroit just to spite Dunlap.[34] But they finished June with a three-game winning streak, knocking over Philadelphia (who were fresh from a sweep of Chicago), with Henry Boyle winning twice in three days and Dunlap at last returning to the lineup. But Joe Quinn's batting average had slipped into serious danger territory at .162: he had hit safely in just 34 of 122 at-bats, and scored only seven runs.[35]

He rallied for the Fourth of July home series against Providence with two hits in the 4–0 shutout. The occasion was altogether a grand one for the Maroons, the stands at last filled, and among the fans, large numbers of women. In spite of a derisive reference in *New York World* to female spectators as "charming deadheads," *The Spirit of the Times* of September 22, 1855, noted women in the stands "manifested the utmost excitement, brandishing parasols, ecstatically waving handkerchiefs and studiously applying themselves to their scorecards."[36] By the 1880s, most parks provided separate restrooms and entrances for women, and often hosted Ladies' Days with free admission to the fairer sex. Although many men complained of freeloading women taking the best seats, the fact they "kept an admirable order" also meant women were desirable attendees—it was hoped their presence could save their game from its own self-destruction at the hands of gambling, profanity, prejudice, and hooliganism.[37]

Crowd behavior was often bad, regardless of the presence or absence of the parasol-brandishing ladies, but in the late 1880s, the rowdies and drunks were more often *on* the field than off it. Players turned up intoxicated, fought, cheated and abused the umpires—and such behavior only incited the crowd to copy and amplify it. There were furious objections, both on and off the field, during the home series with New York in July when the Maroons lost the final game 3–2 after lack of an umpire saw Giants pitcher "Smiling" Mickey Welch don the blue jacket. The close result drew howls of protest from visitors' dugout, with scuffles and furious insults exchanged between the teams and spreading like wildfire to the stands. In this highly charged final game, Joe Quinn was not exempted from the action, running from his post in left field to add voice and body to the hullaballoo.[38]

The Maroons had won just 26 games to Chicago's 56 and New York's 53, and the St. Louis correspondent in *The Sporting Life* of July 23 scathingly diagnosed the problem as "'slack fever': a highly-contagious condition whose symptoms included "sore arms, stiff knees which precluded running, bleared vision, general nervousness of fly balls, aversion to hitting balls with sticks, and sulkiness." Apparently, treatments such as *finum frequentum* and *without payum* could be applied with some expectation of success, but the correspondent recommended *expelum blacklistum* and *non-reinstatum* for particularly difficult cases.[39] Stung by such vicious criticism, the Maroons defeated Philadelphia 6–1 and 6–3 behind a still-sore Sweeney in late July, but encountered a fire-breathing Hoss Radbourn at Providence on the 30th and 31st, losing both games, including a heartbreaking 4–2 defeat in which Henry Boyle conceded all four runs in the final two innings.[40]

August was the Maroons' most ignominious month. They had only one pitcher in the overworked Henry Boyle—Sweeney was being rested with chronic arm pain, and in his only appearance, on August 15, he conceded 23 hits to Buffalo.[41] The Maroons lost 16 games and won just two, one of which was behind the new recruit John Kirby, who pitched them to a 13–7 win over Buffalo on the 23rd. In between, they were swept by Providence, Buffalo, and Chicago, conceding 129 runs in 18 games.[42] To add insult to injury, across town Von der Ahe's Browns had racked up 70 wins and were galloping off with the American Association pennant while the Maroons were dead last in the National League, 47 wins out of first place.[43]

To Lucas's fury, his former Union Association stars had completely failed to adapt to life in the "real" major leagues, despite the expensive acquisitions from Cleveland. Brennan, Gleason, Dolan, and Rowe managed only 24 games between them. The catchers were struggling: Briody was "taking on weight fast"[44] and hitting a terrible .195, and Baker's season average was an even more abysmal .122. Redoubtable rightfielder Orator Shafer, who had been the second-best hitter in the Union and "won many friends for his fearless, aggressive and always earnest and effective work,"[45] now couldn't hit the side of a barn with a shovel, batting only .195 from 257 appearances. Dunlap had plummeted from hitting .412 to a less-than-convincing .267, and although he would lead the league in fielding at second base,[46] he bore the brunt of Lucas's chagrin when he was replaced as manager by Alex McKinnon. McKinnon was one of the few Maroons to distinguish himself in 1885, hitting .294 and leading the League at first base, but was reported as "unusually thin and delicate looking."[47] He later contracted typhoid while playing for the Pittsburgh Alleghenies in 1887—tragically, McKinnon had been having his best season, hitting .365, but was dead within two weeks.[48]

By late 1885, Dunlap's unpredictability and uncertain health ensured that the rumors about his imminent departure grew more insistent.[49] As if sensing his impending demise, the mercurial second baseman inspired the Maroons to spring a surprise on the league-leading White Stockings, drawing 1–1 in 11 innings behind Kirby on September 8 and winning 7–2 the next day in their best performance of the year, Boyle pitching a three-hitter and Quinn with two hits at third base. Even the subsequent 2–0 shutout had its silver lining, with new Maroons pitcher John "Egyptian" Healy (so named because he hailed from Cairo, Illinois[50]), conceding just five hits.[51]

But after their 1884 cakewalk, the frustrations of season 1885 finally told for the Maroons on September 10. With his fallen stars languishing in last place, a humiliated and furious Henry Lucas relinquished daily control of the team to Mr. B.J. Fine, a St. Louis railroad man whose first action was to give notice to half a dozen of the worst-performing players.[52] Quinn survived the cull, despite batting a tenuous .213 from his 97 games. He had contributed just 10 extra-base hits for the year and crossed the plate only 27 times, compared to 74 in the previous season. This fall in offensive production was common throughout the entire Maroons outfit, though, and is a clear reflection of the higher standard of both opposition pitching and defense. On the field, Quinn had been shunted from the outfield (57 games) to third base (31) and first base (11) as McKinnon mirrored Dunlap's struggle to position his men effectively, but his error count had fallen dramatically from 64 in 1884 to just 35, which may have saved him from Fine's axe.[53]

The Maroons responded by shutting out Providence 7–0 on the 19th, Sweeney fresh from three weeks' rest, and finishing the month with a home series win over Boston.[54] Although his record was a somewhat tragic 11–21 with an ERA of 3.93, Charlie Sweeney was easily the most valuable of the Maroons' pitching staff as they stumbled through the season. He hit a respectable .206 with seven doubles and 24 RBIs, and picked up 81 outfield putouts. Henry Boyle, too, hit .202 with nine doubles, and was semi-economical at an ERA of 2.75 for his 16–24 record. But neither was in the league of New York fireballers Tim Keefe (who won 32 games at an ERA of 1.58) and "Smiling Mickey" Welch (44 wins at

1.66). The iron-hearted Chicago twirler John Clarkson won 53 of that team's 87 victories at a miserly 1.85 ERA, and pitched 68 complete games with 10 shutouts to ensure Chicago took the flag.[55] New York was two games behind after losing three of their last four fixtures. The Maroons never climbed out of the National League cellar, winning only 36 games, and were forced to endure the cross-town celebrations of the Browns, who had lifted their first of four consecutive American Association pennants. Browns owner Chris Von der Ahe (who had once bragged he owned the biggest baseball diamond in the country until it was pointed out that all diamonds were the same size), celebrated with a $50,000 week-long champagne binge for his stars—a staggering spend that would have paid the wages of the entire Maroons outfit for the 1885 season.[56]

• • •

"I realized I only had a limited period as a player, and seeing all about me great stars doomed after their playing days to poverty and often starvation, I determined that when my time came, there would be no such story told about me."—Joe Quinn, *The Sporting News*, May 21, 1936

Between 1840 and 1860, more than four million immigrants flooded into the United States, including 1.7 million Gaelic-speaking Irish Catholics who, by 1850, comprised over 40 percent of the foreign-born population in the United States.[57] With cheap land available and business opportunities in abundance due to the proximity of river and rail transport, many Irish arrivals made their way west to St. Louis, which elected its first foreign-born mayor in 1842, former Dubliner George Maguire.[58] A first generation of Irish had been firmly established in the city since 1803 and was widely admired for their education and generosity, but the new influx of "Harps" flocking across the Atlantic to escape the privations and darkness of Europe in the early 1850s stirred the resentment of "native" Anglo-Americans and prompted the formation of blatantly anti–Irish, anti–Catholic movements such as the Know-Nothings.[59]

Gaelic settlers in St. Louis gravitated toward a section of open common northwest of the city, and the disparaging term "shanty Irish" was born for their makeshift houses and squats. The enclave, bounded by Broadway to the east and 20th Street, Franklin Avenue, and Mullanphy Street (named after the Irish philanthropist who had made his fortune in cotton after the War of 1812[60]) to the north, soon became a great stopping point for the Irish after Ellis Island. The area was rather unromantically titled "Tract 25b" by city officials and "The Bloody Third District" by borough police, but locals preferred the optimistic epithet "Kerry Patch," after the pretty southern county in their homeland.[61] The Patchers were isolates in a predominantly Protestant city, and drew fire for opening their taverns on Sundays to fill their glasses with their traditional warm, dark stouts and ales. But however wretched their existence in their miserable abodes, a city guidebook of 1878 described the inhabitants as "poor but independent ... and they laugh[ed] as lightly as though they were dwellers in marble halls."[62] But the same guidebook also noted disapprovingly that, with colorfully-named gangs such as "Egan's Rats" and "The Green Ones" lurking in Tract 25b, a chief amusement of the residents was also "punching each other's eyes." This culture of fisticuffs even filtered down to the neighborhood children, who specialized in brick-throwing with missiles readily available from Bollman's Brickyard on 19th Street: one resident recalled grimly, "It was a familiar sound to hear the clatter of closing shutters as bricks started to fly."[63]

Few outsiders ventured into the Patch, and few insiders encouraged them. Among the motley collection of residents, according to the guidebook, were "even a few baseball players." "Poor Tom" Dolan and the "Kerry Patch battery" of pitcher James "Pud" Galvin and his receiver Tom Sullivan, were all Patchers. Sullivan was a particularly tragic figure—after playing for the Dubuque Rabbits in 1879, he spent two years catching Pud Galvin's fierce pitching for the St. Louis Reds on the old Compton Avenue grounds near the Missouri Pacific Railway tracks, and Al Spink enthused, "There were few stolen bases when he was doing the receiving."[64] One winter night, however, the young man walked across town from the Patch to the St. Louis Poor House to visit a friend; it was a cold night and during the long walk, Sullivan's hands froze. Within days, gangrene had set in and both had to be amputated, leaving the lad who was one of the first to catch up close to the bat, a hopeless cripple.[65]

Also among those resident ballplayers was Joe Quinn. In 1885, he left the house of his benefactor Al Spink to engage rooms at a boarding house at 2906 Sheridan Avenue, near Mullanphy Street.[66] It was in the hothouse of the Patch that Quinn made acquaintance of Thomas McGrath, a forty-year-old Irishman who had arrived in the U.S. in 1861. It was a meeting that would change his life.

Nineteenth-century players were as colorful off the field as on it. Brooklyn shortstop John Montgomery Ward completed a law degree at Columbia University, brainy Browns catcher Doc Bushong was a dentist, and Baltimore pitcher Arlie "Doc" Pond studied medicine.[67] John McGraw and Wilbert Robinson ran a pool hall, and Chicago's Mike "King" Kelly was a noted vaudeville actor in cahoots with Cap Anson and that well-known clown, Browns third baseman Arlie Latham: the trio tried with mixed success to remember their lines in skits and performances of "Casey at the Bat."[68] But if there were an award for most unusual off-season pursuit, Quinn would be a front-runner: under the wing of Thomas McGrath, 23-year-old Joe Quinn became an undertaker.

McGrath operated a livery stable and undertaking practice at 4821 Easton Avenue in the Patch. In the late nineteenth century, the two businesses were inextricably linked, with embalming and funeral arrangements complemented by transportation services to the church or burial site; in St. Louis alone, there were almost 80 establishments offering combined livery and undertaking services.[69] Livery stables also bought and sold horses, rented buggies and mounts to the public, and, with such a high degree of competition in the industry, offered additional services including watering and grooming, feed sales, and consignment of non-livery items such as books and furniture. The work was as hard as it was varied: the cut and thrust of horse-trading, endless shoeing and grooming and harnessing, hefting and carrying, and all alongside the incongruous delicacy of arranging end-of-life departure for the city's dead.

There was no morbid fascination for Joe Quinn in the mortician's practice. With the foresight and

Undated photograph of Joe Quinn's father-in-law, St. Louis funeral director Thomas McGrath. In 1886, Quinn married McGrath's eldest daughter Mary Ellen, and he would later become a full partner in McGrath's undertaking and livery business (courtesy Michael E. Motto, great-grandson of Joe Quinn).

pragmatism so characteristic of him, Quinn's decision to enter the industry was primarily an economic one. "I realized I only had a limited period as a player, and seeing all about me great stars doomed after their playing days to poverty and often starvation, I determined that when my time came, there would be no such story told about me," he recalled in 1936.[70] Observing the downfall of many ballplayers around him, with no savings and frequent reliance on capricious off-season employment, their fortunes squandered on gambling, drinking, and fast women, Quinn saw the wisdom of entering an industry where demand was not likely to run out: after all, the departed would always need to be appropriately farewelled.

While its origins date back to ancient Egypt, Greece, and Persia, embalming remained a developing science in the United States in the late nineteenth century. The purpose of embalming was to shield the sensibilities of mourners from the progression of putrefaction, to permit burial without unseemly haste, and reduce the spread of infection. The awkward method of packing bodies in ice and laying them on cooling boards (concave ice-filled boxes fitted over the torso and head) was losing favor by 1885, although the display of preserved specimens in mortuary windows was still common.[71] Embalming by arterial injection, a practice begun in England some one hundred years before, was being promoted by an emerging group of undertaker-businessmen in the United States. Resistance to this practice, at first considered mutilation of the body, had decreased during the Civil War, as it was used to prepare the bodies of soldiers for shipment home, and later to embalm the body of no less than President Abraham Lincoln himself.[72]

Thomas McGrath was among these progressive thinkers in the funeral industry, and proceeded to school his new apprentice in these modern techniques. With the body first laid out and washed on a porcelain table, the mouth and eyes were closed in a natural expression, with discreet stitching applied where necessary. The new embalming method then involved draining the blood from a vein, usually in the neck, and replacing it with a 37 percent aqueous solution of formaldehyde and water. Fluid from body cavities was removed with a long hollow needle known as a trocar and replaced with a chemical concoction which rendered the body proteins fibrous, thereby inhibiting the rate of decomposition. The main ingredient in these embalming fluids was an innocuous-looking white powder of which a lethal dose could be as small as a few teaspoons: arsenic. With up to 12 pounds per corpse required to kill the microorganisms responsible for decay, and many embalming fluids also containing toxins such as mercury and creosote,[73] the potential for poisoning was considerable in this era before overalls, gloves, face shields, and showers were *de rigueur*. In 1910, arsenic was banned in embalming for the health of practitioners: it is quickly absorbed through the stomach and intestines into the bloodstream, causing nausea, diarrhea, impaired heart and nerve function, conjunctivitis, and—ironically—death.[74]

The rituals and traditions of the American funeral had also continued to evolve. In the 1840s, young couples considered it a privilege to sit up all night with the corpse before burial, and undertakers habitually cried right alongside mourners at the funeral—the flow of tears directly proportional to the expense of the interment.[75] The trend was now for smaller tombstones and epitaphs, but that didn't stop the *Maysville Daily Evening Bulletin* of October 30, 1885, reporting with awe on the $100,000 mausoleum erected for William H. Vanderbilt upon Staten Island.[76] However, despite the substantive developments in the funeral industry during the nineteenth century—perhaps the most rapid and significant in western history— the implications of burial practices from the late 1800s are still being felt today. Wooden caskets do little to contain non-degradable arsenic and embalming fluids, and percolating groundwater carries these deadly poisons into the surrounding soil to be ingested or inhaled by archaeologists, cemetery workers and others coming into contact with contaminated soil or human remains at old burial sites.[77]

Whatever the risks associated with the funeral industry, a professional association with Thomas McGrath also had one big personal advantage for Joe Quinn. McGrath had four daughters: Mary Ellen, Maggie, Kitty, and Liddy.[78] The eldest, Mary Ellen, was six years Quinn's junior, and her dark hair, level brow, and air of good taste—not to mention her dewy dark-lashed Irish eyes—were an irresistible attraction to 4821 Easton Avenue.

◆ ◆ ◆

Despite the embarrassingly public carnage of the Maroons' 1885 season, baseball in St. Louis had retained one definitive supporter in the local media. Alfred Spink left the *Globe-Democrat* in late 1885 and set up offices on North 8th Street, from where he first published *The Sporting News* on March 17, 1886—St. Patrick's Day.[79] At a weekly cost of five cents, the new paper covered all sports from racing to hunting and even the more genteel pursuits of the theater, but most particularly, *The Sporting News* thrived on the gossip, drama, and intrigue of the ball field, so much so that it became known as "The Bible of Baseball."[80] Spink invited his brother Charles Claude, who had been homesteading in South Dakota, to join the staff as business manager after admitting the paper was initially "having a hard row to hoe": when Charles came on board, the initial total of 3,000 subscribers skyrocketed toward 60,000.[81] Joe Quinn was invited to reminisce about the birth of the paper in a special fiftieth anniversary edition in 1936. He was, by that time, "a straight-shouldered, well-put-up little septuagenarian, his silvery hair arranged just-so," with a well-tailored dark suit and polished demeanor, and he told reporter Dick Farrington, "I remember when the Spinks brought out *The Sporting News*, I remember very well. Let's see—that was in 1886, all right. Yes, and we ball players used to call it our bible even in those days. Fifty years ago! It doesn't seem that long. I was 20 then, and had played league ball in St. Louis two years before the paper was born." He had spent the 1884 season boarding with Al Spink, so it was only natural, he declared, that he was among the first readers of the paper.[82]

The Maroons, meantime, were determined to erase all traces of their 1885 disappointment, appointing a new manager for 1886 in the imposingly-titled Gustavus Heinrich Schmelz. The impressively bearded Schmelz had coached American Association club Columbus to second place in 1884 and was a great favorite with both the players and the German expatriate crowds, who often flocked to baseball to drink beer and yell, "*Kraftjes schlagen* (hard hitting)!"[83] Quinn, too, had signed again with the Lucas outfit, and was exempted from the reserve list after promising to return for the 1886 season at the end of the previous year.[84]

Despite his having been shuffled from infield to out and subsequently struggling for form and consistency amidst the chaos of 1885, this promise marked a significant epoch in Quinn's baseball career. His was a fiercely loyal and devoted nature, and it was not in his makeup to desert a floundering ship once he had signed up for its crew. With the ongoing struggle between the National League and American Association, opportunity abounded for unscrupulous players to profit from breaking a contract with a second-rate club if it meant greater salary or prestige elsewhere. But Quinn's decision to remain with the Maroons, who had been utterly embarrassed in 1885, was the first of several such he would make during his career, handcuffing himself to some of baseball's most inept and dispirited nines when cash and kudos were his for the taking, through a fidelity which earned him respect and admiration across the wider baseball community.

With the likes of Glasscock, Boyle, McKinnon, and Dunlap all still in the Maroons squad, it was amid an atmosphere of general bonhomie and optimism that the 1886 season opened on April 29 with a home series against a well-armed outfit from Detroit. Five thousand forgiving and expectant fans turned out at Vandeventer Lot, only to see the Maroons hammered 9–2 by the Wolverines, whose "Big Four" infielders—Hall of Famers Dan Brouthers on first and Deacon White on third, with Hardie Richardson and Jack Rowe in the middle—gorged on three hits each while the Maroons accumulated only three between them. Quinn started the year in centerfield and was hitless at the plate but accepted two chances and two assists in defense. Many of his high-class compatriots had a similar record: Dunlap, Glasscock, and Dolan all left the plate empty-handed.[85] It was an ugly precedent. The Maroons lost 11 of their opening 20 games, all at home, and, humiliated by their ignominious start to the season, fled the city to spend the next month on the road.[86]

Baseball road trips were predominantly conducted by rail, and after the Civil War, St. Louis had developed into a rail center second only to Chicago. However, for all his riches, Henry Lucas was notoriously stingy with train travel for his team—he would buy the players day seats and only half the required number of sleeper berths, even when railways offered reduced rates to ball clubs.[87] Players were crammed two to a bunk, rejected by many hotels and in others not permitted to mingle with the guests,[88] conditions that may have been the inspiration for incidents such as that which occurred on the Maroons' return trip to Detroit in July 1886. They had been jostling along with crowds at all the stations to see them go through, and as night began to fall, some of the boys had stayed up in the day car amidst a clandestine clink of bottles and slap of cards. Being nimbler than most, Joe Quinn had bagged an upper berth in the sleeper, and had barely dropped into a doze when a terrific squalling jerked him awake. He slithered crossly out of the bunk and stuck his head out of the compartment to the most amazing sight. An ample gent was filling the narrow walkway, blowing steam and smoke and in a fine uproar, threatening to throttle third baseman Jerry Denny and shove him out of the speeding carriage on the very spot. Just beyond the pair, pitcher John Kirby was splitting his sides with laughter. Denny had filled himself to brimming with good Kentucky whiskey and lost most of his pocket-change at cards, and so had taken himself back to his stateroom, where he found a sleeping form ensconced in his bunk. He presumed it was Kirby pulling a prank, so he gave the sleeper a hard slap on the *derriere*, only to find he was in the wrong room and his victim was a teenage girl, who sat up bawling like a dogie who'd lost its mama.[89]

Such indiscretions aside, classy infielder Denny had come from Providence in 1886 to replace the .179-hitting Ed Caskin, making 182 putouts and 270 assists for the season to lead the league in both categories at third base.[90] Freed from the strain of managership, Alex McKinnon also found his bat and hit .301 for the year.[91] But it was shortstop Jack Glasscock who roared to life after his relatively poor .280 season in 1885: he slammed .325 with 29 doubles in 1886 and fielded at .906 to lead the league, having led in 1881 and 1883 at Cleveland and going on to do so again in 1889 and 1894 with two other clubs.[92] But despite the hot bats and classy fielding, the Maroons were sinking back into the mire by the end of July because they just could not find a winning pitcher. Egyptian Healy tried hard for 17 wins at an ERA of 2.88, but he was a terrible hitter, managing just 0.097 from 145 plate appearances. John Kirby struggled to 11 wins and 26 losses at 3.30, and the weary Henry Boyle won a paltry nine games, although he hit .250. Charlie Sweeney's arm had completely given out and he appeared in only 11 games, winning five at an expensive 4.16.[93] On June 12, Detroit hit a new major league record seven home runs off Sweeney, who remains the only pitcher in major league history to give up seven round-trippers in a game.[94] Detroit second baseman

Hardie Richardson later recalled, "Joe Quinn did most of the chasing that day and always maintained that Detroit tried to run his legs off. That was the year that we [the Wolverines] ran 16 straight victories."[95]

In contrast, across town, the Browns' pitching staff not only were twirling the club to another American Association pennant, but *The Sporting Life* of July 7 listed three of their hurlers—Dave Foutz, Bob Caruthers and Guy Hecker—among the top ten hitters in the league.[96] On August 15, Hecker scored seven times in a game (a major league record) and supplemented the achievement with three home runs of his own to tie the existing mark for a pitcher.[97] Two days later, "Parisian" Bob Caruthers (so named after removing to France while holding out at the start of the season) became the first pitcher to make four extra-base hits in a game—but he also allowed ten runs in the eighth inning, lost the game and snapped the Browns' eleven-game winning streak.[98]

But the Browns, despite their enormous financial resources and plumbless depth of talent, were also developing a reputation for evil trickery to notch up their ongoing succession of victories. On May 14, Browns captain Charles Comiskey prevented a ninth-inning double play by running full-tilt into Reds second baseman Bid McPhee, laying him out like a carpet and handing the Browns a 2–1 win. The Cincinnati fans were livid but the umpire stood firm, and "breaking up the double play" is now an accepted part of the modern game.[99] However, the Browns' underhanded tactics attracted enemies with scurrilous ideas of their own—on May 29, the Philadelphia Athletics tried to slow down the Browns' swift baserunners by loading their basepaths with sand. But Comiskey was wise to the ploy and personally helped the ground-crew to shovel away the offending mineral before he would take the field. The Browns went on to win both games with a total of 14 stolen bases. At the next American Association meeting on June 9, Von der Ahe airily paid the many fines Comiskey had accumulated on his devious pathway toward the pennant, and an infuriated Association threatened to ban the pair indefinitely.[100]

By August 8, rumors abounded of the imminent demise of the Maroons after star second baseman Fred Dunlap was sold to Detroit for $4,700 and Lucas announced the venture had cost him more than $250,000 in the past three years.[101] The continuing hapless form of his club, winning just one game in every three they played, saw the St. Louis outfit 37 games behind league leaders Chicago and Detroit in late September. By season's end, the Maroons had clambered from eighth place to sixth, but on October 9, Chicago clinched the pennant by beating Boston 12–3 on the final day of the season while Detroit lost both games of a double-header to the Phillies; the Maroons languished 47 games back.[102] Detroit second baseman Hardie Richardson blamed the loss of the pennant squarely on a Georgia hog. At the start of the year, the Wolverines were midway through a series of practice games in Tallapoosa, Georgia, when rainy weather stranded their train in the countryside for some hours. Richardson, pitcher "Lady" Baldwin, and manager Bill Watkins left the train to forage a meal for the hungry ballplayers; Watkins managed to procure a sack of supplies from a nearby farm, but upon sitting down to rest before returning to the train, the sack was raided by an importunate razorback pig. This cheeky incursion forced all the players to disembark the train and walk through the rain to another farm for food, during which muddy slog so many contracted colds that it was a month or more into the season before the club could field its best nine and Chicago had already stolen a march on the pennant.[103]

The pennant was the White Stockings' fifth of the 1880s. Pitcher John Clarkson won 35 games, "Big Jim" McCormick blazed to 16 straight victories, Cap Anson hit .371, and Mike "King" Kelly slammed .388 to win the league batting crown.[104] Kelly was one of the most charismatic and inventive players of the nineteenth century, and in 1905, the *St. Louis Republic* featured an interview with the retired Joe Quinn, a lifelong friend of the King, in which he discussed the mighty Kelly's unique style: "Kelly always hit between .325 and .350. Nearly all batsmen to-day take a side position at the plate. The deceptive feature of Kelly's stand at the bat was that you could never tell until he swung at a ball where he aimed to place the hit. Anson and Kelly had the same position.... They would stand over the plate with their back to the catcher, and look the pitcher straight in the eye and hold their bat down until the pitcher delivered the ball. Then they would raise their club and swing for the ball. They were the first batsmen to introduce this position at the plate."[105]

Kelly's creativity manifested at a time when the game was becoming increasingly representative of the modern game, with fielders moving in and out with the play, pitchers covering first base, catchers adopting masks and heavy gloves, and bunting increasingly popular (although Anson particularly hated the bunt, calling it a "baby act"[106]). The first restrictions were also placed on ball size and bat dimensions—although bats with one flat side were permitted in 1886.[107] Pennsylvania inventor William Williams also claimed to have invented a paper bat which was more durable and more elastic than wood or rattan.[108] Not surprisingly, the concept never took hold.

Joe Quinn played more positions than anyone else on the Maroons roster in 1886, hitting .232 from 75 games, which included 11 doubles, three triples, and the only home run of his three-year professional career. He made appearances at every infield position except pitcher and catcher, but to his chagrin, spent nine-tenths of the season in the outfield. Lucas had claimed at the outset of the season to have the fastest set of outfielders in the country, with Cahill, Seery, Howard and Quinn all timed running 100 yards in less than 11 seconds during the spring.[109] Quinn didn't enjoy the assignment. Bought as a second baseman by Boston two years later, Quinn was similarly shunted to the outer paddocks and wrote acridly to *The Sporting News*, "I do not care to play the outfield," before adding as a guilty afterthought, "but if they think it best to keep me there, I will do all in my power to bring the club to the front."[110] His gloveless hands, however, may have rejoiced in the move away from first base and having to receive daily dispatches from the hard-throwing Dunlap. But the outfield is a lonesome kingdom where any muff draws howls from the fickle fans, who figure reaction time is clearly proportional to the distance from the hitter. This may be, in part, true[111] ... but there's nothing like a fly ball wobbling and shifting around like a kite and the sun bright in your eyes to bring a quake to the knees and a tremble to the hands. Quinn made 12 errors from his 114 chances in the outfield, fielding at .895.[112]

Despite their horrible on-field performances and ongoing inability to remain competitive in the National League, it was cross town rivalry with the Browns which ultimately sank the Maroons' ship. Fifty cents was the National League's standard admission price, but in 1886, clubs facing inter-city competition from American Association teams such as in St. Louis and Philadelphia were officially permitted to charge 25 cents admission in line with American Association prices.[113] With both low attendances and this reduced admission price, Lucas's bottom line was severely compromised. Salaries too were rising, further extending the financial strain on franchise owners. Although a salary cap of $2,000 per player had been instituted in 1885, it was flagrantly disregarded, the most famous example being King Kelly who was paid an extra $5,000 a season, allegedly for the use of his photograph in "promotional materials."[114] For the average worker earning $900 a year,[115] a day at the baseball game (with cab fares and ferry tickets) would cost as much as $1.25. Decreasing the price of admission, while opening the game up to more people, effectively cut into Lucas's ability to pay salaries that would attract star players, and the temptation of players to accept bribes or rival offers was heightened, as was the need to sell off stars such as Dunlap to keep the team afloat. Lucas's requests to the League for Sunday games were continually rejected, and falling attendances through direct competition with the successful Browns did little to add to the club's coffers. In November 1886, the Maroons withdrew from the National League. Quinn, at the time, was the only player to have put his name to a Maroons contract for 1887—the others were all holding out for more money (as were all the Browns!).[116] They needn't have bothered. Lucas had finished his baseball splurge "financially and spiritually pancaked."[117]

Not that Lucas's mania for entrepreneurship could be quenched for very long. In 1895, he spent vast sums constructing a velodrome in St. Louis and inviting famous cyclists to compete on it. Again, the venture ended badly. Lucas then moved to Chicago, but by 1902 had filed for bankruptcy in that city. The following year, his wife divorced him, citing desertion and non-support, and the last three years of Lucas's life were spent as a street inspector in St. Louis, earning just $75 a month. In 1910, he died.[118]

◆ ◆ ◆

The successful ballplayer—on paper, at least—appeared to be quite a catch for an eligible young lady. There was no sports professional so well paid for his work, and salaries had an encouraging upward tendency in 1886. The young man economical in his habits would not have to wait long before he could amass a snug sum. Yet this was a period when ballplayers also had to work hard for social acceptance. Many players had no business prospects or education, and spent their winters hunting, gambling at poker and horse races, or propping up the bar in a saloon squandering every dollar they had earned during the season. The *Saint Paul Daily Globe* observed sadly, "While players in general were not the low-lives many thought, as many did not drink heavily or smoke and had reputable intellectual and social standing ... few ball tossers have laid by anything."[119] Some, however, like Quinn's former Maroons teammate Bollicky Bill Taylor, were never without cash. "Well, dere's one satisfaction in knowin' dat I always have money wid me," he told *The Sporting Life*. "I swallered a dime when I wiz a kid, an' it hain't never been seen since."[120] Nonetheless, many families did not want ballplayers for son-in-laws, seeing them as uncouth ruffians fit only for "driving beer-trucks in the off-season."[121] Joe Quinn, however, had proven himself with his commitment to Thomas McGrath's undertaking practice and often earned extra cash by shoeing horses[122] or tending the bar at the Maroons' clubhouse.[123] Now for the first time since 1884, Quinn would not take winter quarters in Dubuque. He and Mary Ellen McGrath—his "Molly"[124]—were married on November 17, 1886, at St. Bridget's Catholic Church in St. Louis. They lived at Quinn's Sheridan Avenue residence,[125] and their first child, Catherine Marie, was born there in 1887.

6. The Price of Honor

"He smelt of lamp-oil, straw, orange-peel, horses' provender and sawdust, and he looked the most remarkable sort of centaur, compounded of the stable and the play-house."

—Charles Dickens, *Hard Times*, 1854

Like a hyena circling the stumbling Maroons, Indianapolis department store owner John T. Brush pounced after Henry Lucas left the bones of his St. Louis club to rot in late 1886. Brush had already bought into the new Indianapolis National League franchise—primarily as a vehicle for advertising his business—and saw amidst the wreckage of the Maroons the glint of gold which might add just the right gild to his Hoosiers in their inaugural National League season. On March 8, 1887, Brush picked up the majority of the St. Louis team for the bargain price of $12,000.[1] Quinn, of course, went north alongside Jack Glasscock, Jerry Denny, Henry Boyle, and Egyptian Healy. He was 24 years old and had been married just five months.

The austere Brush was nothing if not a pacesetter, despite the fact he walked with two canes because he suffered from the painful neurological disorder *locomotor ataxia*.[2] With hawk-like eyes and a nose sharp as a hatchet, he'd spotted the opportunity to take the Hoosiers forward with the collapse of the St. Louis franchise: a small investment, he felt, for what could be a sizeable return. Likewise, during 1887–88, he attempted to popularize night baseball with games under lights, although the natural-gas illumination in Indianapolis proved inadequate.[3] For the late 1880s were a time of sporting innovation and risk-taking, and 1887 witnessed further changes to the game of baseball, the most notable of which was the formal definition of the modern strike zone as between the tops of the shoulders and bottom of the knees. The old practice of batters being able to call for a high or low pitch (above or below the waist) was abolished. Making life additionally difficult for pitchers, the number of balls required for a walk was reduced from seven to five, and the practice of taking a run and jump before delivery was outlawed. Base coaches were no longer permitted to roam freely around the diamond, but were restricted to boxes on the baselines; base coach Fred Dunlap had physically chased Billy Taylor out of the batter's box on that memorable occasion in 1884, and Charlie Comiskey had used his previous freedom to stand close to the plate and harass the catcher. Further restricting another of the game's noted tricksters was the ruling that a baserunner hit by the batted ball was out[4]: Chicago's King Kelly had popularized the practice of slyly kicking grounders or deliberately allowing himself get hit in order to impede the fielders.[5]

6. The Price of Honor

Kelly himself was skating on thin ice. The King was born in 1857 on New Year's Eve, and seemed to have spent most his life celebrating (unlike his great friend Joe Quinn, who was born at Christmas but proved of far more sober habits!). Kelly was fashionable, carried a cane, twiddled his moustache at the ladies, and regularly indulged his fondness for strong drink, fine food, betting on horses, and carousing in the Chicago saloons. Asked once if he drank on the field, Kelly replied as quick as a flash, "It depends on the length of the game," and one game was actually held up while Kelly and several fans in the front row toasted each other.[6] Cap Anson bemoaned, "There is not a man alive who can drink Mike Kelly under the table."[7] But Kelly *could* play, and his banner year was 1886, when he hit .388 for the White Stockings to win the National League batting crown.[8] However, the King's bat went cold almost immediately thereafter, and the 1886 World Series went south with Chris Von der Ahe's Browns. Chicago owner Al Spalding, who had once hired a detective to follow Kelly on the town, was fed up with his drinking and his bad example. On February 6, 1887, he gathered the team at Hot Springs, Arkansas, and extracted a pledge of abstinence from each of them. Even the mascot, 11-year-old Willie Hahn, had to sign the contract. "You should have seen the little fellow open his eyes!" recounted a club official when the agreement was read to the boy.[9] Two days later, Spalding met with Kelly, who wanted to claim the $375 bonus for good behavior he had been promised for 1886. Although Kelly had won the batting championship and the White Stockings the regular-season pennant, Spalding both refused him the bonus and withheld $225 from his salary for drinking. But the real punishment was meted out the following week, when Kelly was sold to the Boston Beaneaters for $10,000, twice the price ever previously paid for a player.[10]

The 1887 National League season opened on April 28 with a loss at home for the upstart Indianapolis Hoosiers, dropping a 4–3 thriller to eventual pennant winners Detroit.[11] The Wolverines' star recruit, former Chicago slugger Sam Thompson, would finish the season with 166 RBIs, a nineteenth-century high, and eleven players on the Wolverines' list hit better than .300 for the season, including pitcher Lady Baldwin and the resurrected Fred Dunlap. Thompson and left-handed slugger Dan Brouthers each hit over .400: Brouthers' .419 average was a standout among the fourteen consecutive seasons in which he hit over .300 during his career. Big and heavy-set, with the powerful legs and barrel chest of a true ax-man, Brouthers won five major league batting titles and had a lifetime batting average of .349 for his 19 seasons.[12] Hall of Famer John McGraw would later recount, "When I first went to Baltimore, there were little flags stuck on the fences of the different parks to show where Brouthers had driven balls out."[13]

Also taking full toll of the new strike zone and scoring system were the St. Louis Browns in the American Association. Their Canadian left-fielder Tip O'Neill slammed .492 in 1887, although he nonchalantly dismissed the achievement, saying all pitchers looked alike to him. He was originally a pitcher himself, but when his arm gave out, manager Charlie Comiskey retrained him as an outfielder.[14] In their April 30 home opener, the Browns launched an offensive rampage that would last all season long, setting a St. Louis scoring record that still stands by trouncing Cleveland 28–11. In that four-game sweep of the Blues, the Browns scored 74 runs alone, and Comiskey's men knocked in a staggering 1,132 for the season.[15] The big jump in scoring reflected the ongoing struggle of pitchers with the new strike zone and rules limiting the pitching motion. On May 30, New York pitcher Bill George walked a record sixteen Chicago batters; highly touted California pitcher George Van Haltren would tie that record a month later. In utter frustration, Pittsburgh's Ed Morris refused to pitch on May 9, and was punished with a three-week suspension.[16]

The week of May 16, 1887, was notable in baseball circles for three occurrences. White Stockings rookie Marty Sullivan tied the record for outfield errors in a game, making five blunders as Chicago lost its third straight game to Washington. In the same week, New York's Mike Tiernan tied the record with five errors of his own in a game against Indianapolis.[17] And that game marked Joe Quinn's last appearance on the Hoosiers bench. He'd been in the red and cream uniform[18] two months and, in that time he had not played a game. With Brush's acquisition of the Maroons on top of his own local squad, Indianapolis was top-heavy with five pitchers, three specialist catchers and a glut of infielders: temptation to sell a surplus player for a big profit was high.[19] That opportunity arose—tragically—on May 11.

Infielder John Ake had signed with the Maroons from Boston at the end of the 1886 season, and had been part of the Brush purchase. However, he secured his release from Indianapolis shortly after arriving so he could accept a flattering offer to play for Duluth, Minnesota, in the Northwestern League. On that fateful May day, Ake and teammates Bill Barnes and Billy Earle were boating on the Mississippi near La Crosse, Wisconsin, when their small craft capsized in the rollicking wash of a passing steamboat. While his companions struggled to shore, 24-year-old Ake, who could not swim, clung to the hull of the upturned boat. Earle and Barnes then watched in horror as Ake let go of the craft and, after only a few strokes, disappeared beneath the water. His body was recovered two days later.[20] Milie Bunnell, editor of the *Duluth Herald*, was in La Crosse to see the Duluth boys play and later wrote sadly that Ake's death was "one of those accidents which seem, after they occur, to have been unnecessary."[21] The Duluth club immediately dispatched executive board member Jay Anderson east to secure a replacement for Ake—a challenging task, Bunnell felt, given the team had no fewer than 33 players on its 1887 roster but "there seemed to be some hoodoo that disabled all the good (Duluth) men as soon as they got fairly down to work."[22]

Obviously unaware or unmoved by the alleged Duluth curse, Brush immediately agreed to loan "extra fielder" Quinn to the Freezers, feeling the Hoosiers could "get along without him."[23] The trouble Quinn had experienced with jealous and volatile teammates in St. Louis had followed him north, with persistent rumors of how former Maroons captain Jack Glasscock and several other Hoosiers players resented Quinn's enthusiasm on the field and sober habits off it.[24] The nineteenth century's leading shortstop, Glasscock was a fiery character at the best of times, and he was already disgruntled and unhappy at the move to Indianapolis, far from his West Virginia home.[25] He drank, stomped, and snarled his way through the season, bullying and baiting teammates, fans, and umpires alike, and while he was hitting .360 and had little to fear from Quinn, he clearly needed a scapegoat for his own frustration and homesickness. On the field, second baseman Charley Bassett had plenty of reasons to begrudge Quinn's presence as his own form was wretched; he was batting a cringeworthy .181.[26] Likewise, while Otto Shomberg was leading the team in hitting, his first base play was so dreadful that he committed 55 errors for the season and *The Sporting Life* observed ruefully, "He seems utterly unable to throw a ball across the diamond with any accuracy."[27] And waiting on the sidelines, with defensive skills on both sides of the diamond, was the threat of young Joe Quinn. Perhaps it was fortunate for all concerned that the one-way ticket to Duluth came when it did.

Duluth agreed to pay both Quinn's salary and a $265 fee to Indianapolis for the loan.[28] But importing the experienced big-leaguer drew immediate protest from other Northwestern League clubs, with threats that every game Duluth won with Quinn in the lineup would be vigorously disputed.[29] Duluth manager William Lucas was forced to travel to Indianapolis personally to negotiate an arrangement that would pacify his rivals. While some reports suggested Brush wanted $3,000 to let Quinn go,[30] Lucas's final offer of $850 for undisputed possession was accepted, netting Indianapolis a total of $1,165 profit plus the saving of Quinn's $2,200 salary.[31] The ironies associated with the deal were many. While the 1886 Duluth outfit had captured the Northwestern League pennant at their first attempt, there were clear hopes that Quinn would bolster their hitting stocks still further—despite the fact he had only batted a tenuous .213 and .232 in his two previous seasons. And, with Duluth needing to quickly replace the unfortunate Ake at second base, who better than a player who'd spent most of his professional career playing at first base or in the outfield?

Thrust into this ludicrous situation, trucked 600 miles north like an unwanted beast of burden, Quinn gave a further example of the remarkable strength of character for which he would be best remembered. Perhaps he reveled in the opportunity to fill a specific niche after two years of being used wherever and whenever the need arose. Perhaps nettled by his lack of opportunities in Indianapolis, the ill-feeling of his former teammates, and the indifference with which Brush let him go, Quinn was eager for a chance to prove himself. Or it might simply have been that great Australian trait of looking a challenge straight in the eye and "having a go."

In 1887, both the village of Duluth and its baseball team were in their adolescence. Today a city of some 86,000 residents,[32] Duluth was a village of just thirty years' standing when Quinn arrived in May 1887, perched on a cold bluff at the western end of Lake Superior 150 miles northeast of St. Paul. It was a hamlet of ranchers, hunters, and fishers, their hides toughened by winters in which the temperature averaged around 10 degrees F. and the summers were considered balmy if it reached 60. The winter of 1886-87 had been particularly severe, with the combination of forty-below-zero temperatures and ten-inch snowstorms inflicting a harsh lesson on many ranchers new to these severe northern conditions: as the *St. Paul Globe* mournfully pointed out, "It does not pay to drive in late in the fall huge herds of cattle that have been accustomed to a warmer climate, only to have them freeze to death."[33]

Originally christened the Cardinals, for most of its early existence the Duluth baseball club were known as the White Sox or, for obvious reasons, the Freezers. They joined the Northwestern League in May 1886, largely through the efforts of Clevelander William H. Lucas—it seemed Quinn's destiny was tied to the Lucas moniker!—who had played for St. Paul in the League Alliance, the first minor league, in 1877, then been lured to Duluth in 1885.[34] The local semi-pro outfit lined up against "places where crack times were reputed to exist," including St. Paul and Eau Claire. A serious ankle injury to Lucas in August proved an unexpected boon, as it that gave him the time he needed to garner support for a future professional team in the town.

His efforts were realized on May 12, 1886, when the new team, briefly christened the Jayhawks, made their Northwestern League debut at Minneapolis. A narrow 7–6 loss was avenged next day, Duluth declaring their presence in the reformed league with a 25–14 thrashing of the Flour City outfit. Freezers board member Jay Anderson ensured the whole town was hung with posters, banners, and rosettes in preparation for the home opener on May 14, and a crowd of some 1,200—almost half of the town's 3,000 residents—gathered at the brand-new park on Rice's Point by Duluth Harbor to witness a 9–7 defeat of St. Paul. The excited fans even paid double the usual admission price (50 cents) to help fund the cost of the new park.[35]

The Jayhawks were worth paying to watch, with eight former or future major leaguers on the 1886 roster.[36] They were led by 39-game-winning pitcher Mark "Fido" Baldwin, one of the nineteenth century's hardest-throwing and hardest-living hurlers. Baldwin's fastball was almost unhittable (and uncatchable, with only Llewellyn Legg daring to crouch at the plate with the fireballing Baldwin in the box). Baldwin was signed by Chicago at the end of the 1886 season, and despite his erratic pitching, nervous unpredictability, and fondness for strong liquor, remained amongst professional baseball's most spectacular hurlers over the course of his seven-year professional career.[37] Part-time catcher Bill Traffley was one of the few Jayhawks with major league experience prior to 1886, having made 177 appearances in the American Association, chiefly with Baltimore.[38] However, it was his teammate and fellow catcher George Bignell whose name remains in the baseball record books, despite his playing only four games at the top level. Catching for Milwaukee during the 1884 Union Association season, Bignell accepted 23 chances as Henry Porter struck out 18 Boston batters on October 3; his major career ended two days later when his ungloved hand was struck by a batter. Bignell dabbled in minor league play until late 1886, when he closed his career after winning a pennant with Duluth.[39]

The Jayhawks finished the 1886 season at the top of the standings with a 47–33 record, four games clear of Eau Claire in what was a closely fought competition—even last-placed Milwaukee won 36 games. The league championship pennant was displayed for many years at Anderson's saloon on West Superior Street in downtown Duluth.[40] But by June 1887, much of the luster had rubbed off the triumph. Milwaukee was leading the eight-team Northwestern League with a 22–10 (.687) record, with St. Paul having also won 22 games, although their charge for the lead had been interrupted by rain so they had played two fewer matches. Duluth was a disappointing sixth, already six games out of the lead at 16–34 (.320); only the Eau Claire Badgers stood between them and oblivion.[41]

Quinn swung straight into action—literally. His first appearance for his new team was on June 1 when he led the Freezers to a 17–10 victory over the visiting Badgers—only the second win at home for the Freezers that season. The Duluth park was in sight of Lake Superior, and fully subject to the moods of that vast, temperamental body of water. The diamond on June 1 was extremely foggy and at times sprinkled with rain, keeping the crowd to just 400, but the loyal fans were treated to a monstrous home run by Duluth pitcher Tod Brynan, who slammed the first pitch of the third inning over the centerfielder's head, over the railroad, onto the lake beach. Quinn was in everything—walking in the first and scoring on Kellogg's hit, fumbling an error in the Eau Claire half but atoning with a fine double play. Clearly still finding his feet at the keystone sack, Quinn made two further errors in the second, giving away a base and a run. But in the fifth, he hit a single to short and scored Sexton, and two innings later, he fouled off six pitches, then slammed a double to left field, scoring McMillan and Jones. He then personally scored from third on Kellogg's hit. His tally of three errors was only outdone by that of his teammate, third baseman George McMillan, who made four.[42] Quinn would make 52 errors in his 96 games for the Freezers in 1887—his highest tally for any year in his professional career.[43]

Quinn was better equipped for his new middle infield role than his record might suggest. During his time in St. Louis, Joe had observed Fred Dunlap's playing style, now copying his moves when given a chance around the keystone sack.[44] And he had no difficulty adjusting to the standard of minor league pitching. Having hit only one home run in his three-year professional career and batted no better than .232, Joe slammed 11 home runs and 37 doubles for a .372 season average in 1887.[45] Home runs were comparatively rare in the nineteenth century—most hitters choked up on bats as heavy as 60 ounces and aimed to hit *past* the fielders rather than over them.[46] This hitting-for-average was a hallmark of Quinn's later career, so his home run glut in Minnesota suggests either a life-giving infusion of confidence, smaller parks, or weaker pitching—most likely some combination of all three.

The Fourth of July clash away to third-placed Minneapolis was a grand occasion indeed for the Freezers. The Duluth boys were staying at their traditional downtown haunt at the St. James Hotel, although they might have been wiser to choose the nearby West Hotel, which claimed to be "the only fire-proof hotel in Minneapolis" ("Absolute safety from fire!" trumpeted the advertisement in the *Daily Globe*[47]). Grandiose as it sounded, fire resistance probably took precedence over clean sheets and the quality of the whiskey in Minneapolis, given there had been five fires in downtown stores, hotels, and saloons in the preceding weeks.[48] But the visitors escaped incendiary interference and business was suspended in Minneapolis at noon on July 4 to make way for amusements including races at the Twin Cities Driving Club, rowing and yachting regattas on Lake Calhoun, shooting at the North Star Gun Club (with a worthy $50 prize), cricket on the South Minnesota grounds, and a big baseball double-header. For the less energetic, there were picnics in Lincoln Park with a brass band and choir, fireworks on Minnetonka Beach, and concerts at both the Theater Comique and Pence Opera House.[49] Urban Minneapolis also offered other enticements not to be had in the provincial village of Duluth—for example, the *St. Paul Daily Globe* of July 4 carried an advertisement from Messrs. Sutherland & Ray, Painless Dentists of Minneapolis, claiming to extract "from 1 to 28 teeth in one minute without any pain whatever."[50] It would be worth the journey for that experience alone.

On the field, the trip to Minneapolis was highly beneficial for the Freezers, who for once kept their own tally of errors below that of the opposition to force a win in each game, 4–3 and 8–7. Despite the showery weather, the crowd of 6,000 proved so intent on enjoying themselves it was frequently necessary to shepherd them out of left field back into the overflowing stands. Quinn had his best game for the club in the first part of the double-header, with three hits, two stolen bases, and a flawless performance at second base. The second game went to extra innings, with a wet and heavy ball keeping scoring low until the eighth inning, when a catalogue of errors from the home side saw four Zenith City men, including Quinn, cross the plate on a single hit; a further three errors in the eleventh inning gave Duluth the winning run. The result hauled Duluth to within two games of fifth-placed Des Moines, and was particularly costly for the Twins, as they slid out of the top three.[51]

As the weather warmed to a soaring 74 degrees, so did calls in Duluth for the club to ascend the standings and to do so smartly. After the previous season's pennant win, community expectations were high that the team should easily carry off the Spalding Trophy in 1887. Made from solid silver, standing two feet high and adorned with representations of masks, bats, balls, and a game in progress, the enormous cup cost $500 to manufacture—more than many middle-class workers earned in a year—and the Duluth board were desperate to have it adorn their clubrooms.[52] On July 13, the *Duluth Herald* carried strictures that the former Northwestern League champions, although now in fourth place, should "not be satisfied with anything short of first place, and the builders of the pennant may as well conduct their operations accordingly."[53] The Freezers responded by dropping their next game to mid-table rivals Minneapolis "in a way that made Quinn weary," mourned the *St. Paul Daily Globe*.[54] While Twins pitcher Winkleman walked five batters, the home team trialed a new pitcher in Brewster from California—and he was promptly hammered for 20 hits and seven walks, the result a 12–4 humiliation which set the Freezers up in the worst possible fashion for an away clash with league leaders St. Paul on July 18.

That game was like a walk into the jaws of Hell, conducted in the hottest weather experienced for thirty years as a heat wave slugged the North, 104-degree temperatures claiming 62 lives in Chicago and responsible for four drownings on Wisconsin waterways. In Pittsburg, the Law and Order League[55] insisted every saloon in the city remain closed tight on Sunday, July 17, along with all cigar stores, confectioneries, ice cream parlors, and soda fountains. The result was many deaths from the intense, unrelieved heat.[56] However, more than 5,000 fans (including 150 hardy travelers from Duluth) willingly braved the conditions in St. Paul for what proved to be one of the most hotly contested games of the year (no pun intended), the result in the balance until the last batter. Lucas gamely put "the Californian Phenomenon" Brewster back in the pitcher's box, but with outfielders Jones and McMillan making five catches and the young pitcher limiting himself to seven walks and 16 hits, the Freezers hung doggedly in the contest until the last pitch, when, with Ingraham on second, a simple single would break the 8–8 tie and win them the game. Quiet was the order of the day. Billy Rourke, the strapping youngster from Omaha, advanced to the plate and twice slashed viciously at the ball without touching it. The third one he made contact: the ball struck the ground in front of St. Paul pitcher Lee Viau and bounded high in the air, but the little pitcher jumped for it and sent it to first in time to catch Rourke a step short. Hats and seat-cushions flew in every direction, and the echo of the shout that went up is probably still reverberating around the Saintly City.[57] The victory—and fellow contender Milwaukee's fourth consecutive loss—kept St. Paul in equal first place in the league standings (although the *St. Paul Daily Globe* predicted an immediate demotion, as the team was forced to hurriedly catch a night train to play at Oshkosh in Wisconsin, a painful 275-mile overland journey).[58] Twelve games behind, Duluth was lagging painfully in fifth place, tied with Minneapolis at 26–56.

The close loss to the league's leading team did little to endear the Freezers to their expectant and suffering fans, and a 14–4 thrashing from third-place Des Moines on July 24 sent howls for change ringing through the village. Despite a considerable dose of bad luck for the team, including a season-ending arm injury to pitcher Charles Holacher and the drowning of John Ake, calls for revolution were both loud and unremitting. Most particularly sought was the overthrow of the club directors (whose "niggardly" management had almost cost the club the services of pitcher Frank Foulkrod from Williamsport), and supplanting of manager Lucas with Joe Quinn.[59] Praised in the press as "the mainstay of the struggling club,"[60] Quinn had not played in the Des Moines debacle after wrenching his ankle and being sent home to St. Louis to recuperate. However, he was expected to return in early August, bringing one or two new players from St. Louis and presumably taking the reins of the Freezers.[61]

But to add to the discord, Lucas refused to be displaced, insisting there was no dissension in the team and the arrival of new players would turn the tide of victory in favor of the club.[62] He did rally his troops to push league-leaders Milwaukee to eleven innings in a gallant 8–7 home loss on August 2, but the revival was short-lived.[63] Quinn returned for the rematch with Des Moines on Saturday, August 6, but failed to bring any new recruits with him, and the result was all too predictable: despite a much-improved performance by Brewster (with only five hits made from him), five costly wild throws and endless fumbling in the field handed the game to the visitors.[64] And it could all have but one outcome: on August 18, Lucas was deposed, and despite his total lack of management experience, Quinn was installed as captain and manager of the strife-torn club.[65]

In the early decades of professional baseball, the responsibilities of the captain extended beyond on-field duties to full accountability for discipline among the players, supervising daily practice, and reporting absentees and misconduct to club directors, who then administered fines or expulsions. Miscreant players could even be the subject of police action—

during one riotous American Association game on June 16, 1887, St. Louis Browns baserunner Curt Welch flattened Orioles second baseman Bill Greenwood to prevent a double play and was promptly arrested for assault by a policeman on duty at the park (and later fined $4.50 by a local magistrate).[66] Even team owners were not safe from the long arm of the law: St. Louis police stopped the home game on July 16 and arrested Browns owner Chris Von der Ahe for violating a new civic law barring the conduct of all business on Sundays.[67]

The change at the top had come far too late for the Freezers. With the millstone of local expectations heavy around their necks, Duluth was anchored in sixth place in the league, 12 wins behind their nearest rival, Minneapolis. Their disgusted fans didn't bother to turn up for Manager Quinn's home debut against Minneapolis on August 23—and with good reason, for season-long habits were not easy to break: Brewster was thrashed for seven runs and taken off in the fifth inning, and although Quinn grabbed two extra-base hits and was flawless in the field, the toll of eight team errors was as costly as ever in the 11–5 drubbing.[68] And the follow-up match looked equally dire when Duluth failed to score until the sixth inning. Quinn himself contributed two errors, perhaps feeling the pressure, but equally likely just slipping and sliding in the drizzling rain—however, he atoned with two timely doubles as the home team piled on five runs in the seventh and eighth innings to win the game 6–5.[69]

The triumph was extremely short-lived. Just three days later, Minneapolis inflicted a heartless 19–4 hammering on the woebegone Freezers; pitcher George Winkleman, even with a damaged arm, shut out Duluth for eight innings, and it was only his exhaustion in the final inning that allowed four runs. In contrast, Freezers hurlers Morkin and Scheibeck both hurt their own arms trying to stem the riptide of 21 singles, three doubles, two triples and a home run from Flour City bats. Quinn, with six outs in the field and a home run, battled gamely, but like the penny whistle amongst the brass band, his efforts were in vain, and it was a mercy when the fourth game of the series was rained out.[70]

There was plenty of incentive to start September with a rush—Duluth was just two wins ahead of the lowly Eau Claire Badgers and in danger of slipping to last place in the league. While their September 1 contest against St. Paul was described as "the prettiest contest this season," with neither pitcher granting a walk and even Brewster restricting himself to giving away only six hits, the result was still a 2–1 loss.[71] St. Paul was leading the league standings for the first time since July 18, but they had a series against third-placed Des Moines to look forward to, whereas title rivals Milwaukee were next set to "toy with Duluth" (which they indeed did).[72]

But it was the surprise packet Oshkosh, the Wisconsin outfit who had lingered mid-table for most of the season, who burst to the top of the standings on September 13, going two wins clear of both Milwaukee and St. Paul with a dual humiliation of the Duluth men. At over 330 miles each way, the road to Oshkosh was the longest in the league for the Freezers, and this particular trip was vilely unprofitable. In game one, Brewster was hammered for 18 runs in the first five innings, although he was not aided by what the *St. Paul Daily Globe* sneered at as "eight of the most laughable errors" and his teammates' inability to cross the plate more than three times.[73] The second game was closer, but the Duluth fans wanted a win, not a narrow 5–3 loss. But Duluth saved the farce for the final encounter: Jay Anderson protested the 1–0 shutout and in particular the antics of Oshkosh pitcher Con Murphy. The *St. Paul Daily Globe* called Murphy "as good a representative of the monkey family as can be found,"[74] and his gyrations in coaching and captaining the team so infuriated Anderson that he officially protested both Murphy's behavior and his very presence (he was lately arrived from the International League) at the conclusion of the game. The Oshkosh Base

Ball Association retaliated with an action for slander against Anderson, claiming he'd publicly accused Oshkosh of bribing the Duluth pitchers with liquor to increase the chances of Oshkosh winning the pennant. Both actions failed.[75]

Quinn missed the Oshkosh series, but with good reason—Molly had given birth to their first child on September 10, and he was given permission to return to 2906 Sheridan Avenue for a short visit. The child was a girl and christened Catherine for Quinn's mother and Marie for his wife, although she would be known as Mira.[76] But such distractions, and a loss to cellar-dwellers La Crosse on September 16, saw Duluth slip to seventh place, a pitiful 26 wins behind the three teams now vying for the pennant: Milwaukee, Oshkosh, and St. Paul.[77] Quinn finally returned for the home rematch against La Crosse on October 2, and his running single-handed catch of a fly ball to right field was lauded as "the best ever seen." His boys finally found their bats and pounded La Crosse for 15 runs in the first five innings, their efforts assisted by four errors from visiting shortstop Joe Miller and the monstrous home run hit by Frank Foulkrod that cleared the railroad tracks and landed in the lake beyond, sending the Freezers fans into paroxysms of delight and numerous small boys scrambling after the coveted floating sphere.[78]

The pennant race was down to two by October 5, with St. Paul's chances evaporating after a 6–3 loss to Oshkosh. The *St. Paul Daily Globe* blamed the result entirely on St. Paul shortstop Nate Kellogg, mocking him as a "towering form who shrank from the opportunity to do brilliant work at the hour when magnificent fielding and batting might have brought the pennant to St. Paul."[79] The luckless Kellogg made three errors which all resulted in runs, and twice came to bat with loaded bases but failed to make either appearance count. Milwaukee, too, had plenty of help from their opponents in advancing their argument for the pennant—four Duluth errors in the eighth inning amid sub-zero conditions handed the game to them 7–1 on a silver platter, and the Freezers meekly succumbed to a further 13–2 thrashing the following day.[80]

To compound the misery, while their team was suffering in Milwaukee, their so-called fans called a public meeting in Duluth to consider whether the village ought to have a baseball club at all in 1888. The meeting, however, was a failure. Five newspaper reporters, six or eight small boys, and about twenty men met at the opera house and waited for someone to start the thing going. After half an hour, the gas was turned off and the people dispersed without a useful exchange made.[81] This outcome was indicative of the malaise into which the mistreated fans had sunk, given the fact at least five other towns were clamoring for admittance to the Northwestern League, including Davenport, Iowa, which had already raised $750 for that purpose.[82] However, Jay Anderson insisted on October 16 that not only would Duluth remain in the league, but expectations for capturing the 1888 pennant were already high as the services of Quinn, Scheibeck, Brynan, and Earle had been reserved.[83] While the directors quickly raised a purse of $5,000 to pay the reserved players a cash advance, they needed at least twice that amount to keep the club afloat. Within 24 hours the Duluth club—after its brief, blinding grandeur and equally dismal slide into oblivion—was no more. And with Des Moines, Milwaukee, Minneapolis, and St. Paul all departing to join the Western Association, the Northwestern League died with the Freezers.

The collapse of the Duluth Freezers could hardly be blamed on Quinn, who hit .372, put 11 over the fence, and stole 46 bases—but his departure from the cold north was chilly. His relationship with director Jay Anderson was particularly cool. In a last-ditch bid to save the Freezers from, well, the freezer, Anderson had proposed selling Quinn to the highest big-league bidder, but Quinn refused to be sold, determined to go down with his bullet-riddled ship, and this infuriated Anderson. Speaking in response to reports that Anderson was publicly abusing him, Quinn was typically diplomatic: "Mr. Anderson lost considerable money by the Duluth club, and as I would not allow him to sell me to any league club, this gentleman must feel aggrieved. Jay Anderson is a genuine good fellow, and no matter what any Duluth scribe could or would say would ever make me think otherwise."[84]

❖ ❖ ❖

> *"The town of Des Moines is entirely daft on base ball. When a game is played, not only the whole team, but the whole country, turns out."*—St. Paul Daily Globe, August 25, 1887

Joe Quinn was jobless for only three short weeks following the demise of the Freezers. In October, Manager Charlie Morton of the Des Moines Western Association club signed Quinn to captain the "Prohibitionists" back in his adopted home state of Iowa. His decision to accept Morton's offer raised eyebrows back in St. Louis, but Quinn told *The Sporting Life*, "My reasons are the best in the world. My refusal to sign with either the League or Association was not because I was afraid that I could not hold up my end, but because I would prefer to play in a minor organization. I have been in the League, and, to use a common expression, have been through the mill. I feel satisfied that I will like Des Moines. It is a live town and the people up there are quite enthusiastic over the team that is to represent them next season. I am well satisfied with the salary I am to receive, and the club people were not a particle close with their advance money. They mean to treat us right." And with his own tough initiation into the world of professional baseball still a recent and painful memory, he had this wry recommendation for aspiring youngsters: "I would not advise any young player to go to the League or American Association unless they were first-class in every particular. A man may be a corker in one of the minor leagues, but when he gets into real fast company his name is just as liable to be Dennis as it is to be success."[85]

Nineteen-year-old Duluth catcher Billy Earle, who had been alongside John Ake on that fateful boat trip and had also hit .331 for Quinn's Freezers, now expressed a desire to play in Des Moines under his former captain. Des Moines was equally interested in him, and advanced the young man a sum of money he claimed to want to send home to his family in Pittsburgh. Management was clearly unaware Earle—who was not known as "The Little Globetrotter" for nothing[86]—had already promised his services to St. Paul (who had also made him a financial advance), and also to Duluth, should they be able to raise a team! Earle's professed dream to continue his career alongside Quinn never eventuated, however—he chose to uphold his contract with St. Paul, perhaps after reading this warning in the *St. Paul Globe*: "The young man had better look a leedle out ... one or the other [of the clubs] may give him a rattle before the thing is over."[87]

Despite losing their manager, captain, and most of their players, Duluth had not given up on having a minor league team in the 1888 season. As late as January 19, the *St. Paul Daily Globe* was reporting the Zenith City as "anxious to get into the Western Association and willing to put up a large roll."[88] Rumors abounded that Kansas City would vacate the Western Association to join the American Association, and Duluth was so confident of snaring their position that, despite strong competition from Denver, Jay Anderson traveled to Chicago to meet with Western Association directors, replete with $7,500 of the $10,000 necessary to secure the franchise.[89] But even while he was *en route*, Kansas City president Edward Menges was emphatically denying the withdrawal of his team, and the Duluth bid was derailed, condemning the village to four years in the baseball wilderness before a combined Duluth/St. Paul team was admitted to the Western Association in 1891.[90]

Winter snows rarely freeze the fluid world of baseball, and the off-season of 1887-88 was no exception—players, managers and whole organizations were on the move. On January 2, 1888, Fred Dunlap signed with Pittsburgh out of Detroit, agreeing to a staggering $5,000 salary—plus a $2,000 sign-on bonus that itself equaled most regular players' annual income.[91] Three months later, that deal was eclipsed when iron-armed Chicago pitcher John Clarkson was sold to Boston for $10,000. With the previous year's deal for King Kelly, Boston had acquired a $20,000 battery from the White Stockings, and rumors now ran hot that they next planned to splash their cash in the Western Association—with Joe Quinn firmly in their crosshairs.

Ironically, while Quinn was still with St. Louis in 1886, Manager Schmelz had offered Quinn to Boston in exchange for an outfielder, but Boston would not contemplate the deal.[92] Now the *St. Paul Daily Globe* reported on January 7, 1888, that Boston had made a lavish approach to the Des Moines club for their new second baseman, but the Prohibitionists' management flatly refused the offer.[93] Given the obvious temptations of Boston's limitless financial resources for their infant organization, it is difficult to believe the Iowa club would reject outright a fulsome check for Quinn's services. Quinn's own influence seems to have been at work, just as three months before when he had refused to desert the sinking ship Duluth for the safe haven of a National League contract. Quinn's reputation for integrity and honor had, if anything, been enhanced by the debacle in Duluth and his insistence on seeing the 1887 season out with his struggling team: just after the New Year in 1888, the *Boston Globe* reported Quinn had grown significantly since his Union Association days— both in physical stature and as a ballplayer.[94] He had filled out to 17 pounds, and his refusal to break a contract, despite the sumptuous rewards dangled before him which had tempted so many others, was now an established reality.

Amid all this cash-splashing and backroom-dealing, life did go on. Quinn returned to his father-in-law's mortuary practice in St. Louis to continue his education in the funeral industry over the winter. Beyond the stark and occasionally grisly reality of embalming, there were more subtle arts to learn: the judicious application of cosmetics to the corpse, preparation of the black-edged mourning cards which were as much of a souvenir as they were a notification of death, with their original verse and condolences.[95] There were also commercial considerations; metal caskets such as the cast-iron Fisk Burial Case were becoming popular as they were elaborately custom-formed to the body—creating an unnervingly mummy-like effect—and included a glass viewing-window to provide a glimpse of the departed while protecting mourners from odor or disease. Such a quantity of metal also acted as a serious deterrent to grave-robbers and was thus highly attractive to the affluent sector of society, coming at a cost of up to $40, compared to $2 for a standard pine coffin. The nineteenth century was a coffin-inventor's bonanza, yielding the papier-mâché coffin, the wicker casket, and perhaps weirdest of all—the rubber burial case.[96]

Life for a 19-year-old wife with an infant daughter, separated from her husband for six months of the year, cannot have been easy. Molly Quinn may have hoped that, with the demise of the Duluth club, Joe could secure a place with Chris Von der Ahe's St. Louis Browns and remain alongside her in the Patch. But the contract with Des Moines was signed and there was no changing his mind. And all too soon, the appointed season approached, when Quinn's fingers itched toward the brass-studded trunk in the attic and he swung an imaginary bat in his hands as he moved about the house and yard, his eyes dreamy with far-away visions of green turf and chalk lines and bleachers.

Iowa's undulating plains have always been synonymous with corn, and the Hawkeye

State remains the leading producer of the golden grain in the United States, garnering a staggering 2.2 billion bushels in 2008.[97] Why corn? According to Crawford County farmer Jake Jacobsen, "There's no reason to waste good Iowa land and rainfall on wheat, which can grow fine in drier areas. Corn'll give you two to four times more bushels per acre than wheat. Iowa's big in pork and beef, of course, because this is where the corn is. Nothing matches corn-fed stock for quality.... So you see, it all comes back to corn."[98] And in the center of this rolling sea of green and gold, Des Moines stands proud as the unofficial capital of America's grain empire. The site was originally a military fort, but after that settlement was destroyed in the floods of 1851, the town was rebuilt and grew vigorously as gold rush travelers decided to stay put rather than face the rigors of the western trails.[99] For a young ballplayer with his nerves perhaps a little rattled by the fruitless struggle in Duluth, where better than this fertile Middle Earth to re-root his ambitions?

With their home state among the strongest supporters of the temperance movement in the Union, it is hardly surprising the Des Moines baseball nine was known as the Prohibitionists in 1888. After the team's third-place finish in the defunct Northwestern League in 1887, the *Omaha Bee* of April 16, 1888, bravely proclaimed the team had "no weak spots" and would attract even larger attendances and enthusiasm in this, just the second year of professional baseball in Des Moines. Of particular interest was the addition of Quinn, "the Dunlap of the Western Association."[100] Quinn himself told the *St. Paul Daily Globe* he thought the team would be a "hummer": "Stearns will play first, I will cover second and Alvord third base. Macullar will go to short field, Whitely to left, Holliday to center and Van Dyke to right. You know all about the batteries. I think our team will be a great one." He also modestly insisted he had not signed for the privilege of captaining the team, but if Manager Morton offered him that office, he would most likely give it consideration.[101] There was obviously no argument that Quinn would be Des Moines captain in 1888.

The pitcher's box was filled by Frank Wells and Ted Kennedy, returning from the 1887 nine, and new acquisitions in Fred Smith, a winner from the Southern League, and the left-handed Ed Cushman.[102] The Cushman acquisition was an acrimonious one, with Des Moines, Minneapolis, and Milwaukee all squabbling over his services. Cushman came into prominence with Milwaukee in the 1884 American Association with his phenomenal average of 15 strikeouts per game. However, he then mysteriously vanished from the baseball scene until the final week of the 1887 season, when, aged 35, he won two games for Milwaukee in the Northwestern League, and that club claimed to have secured his services for 1888 just days before Manager Morton's announcement he would be joining Des Moines.[103] Nonetheless, the team was an impressive outfit, with 15 of their 18 rostered players former or future major leaguers,[104] including the legendary Cincinnati hitter Bug Holliday, Quinn's former Maroons teammate Dick Phelan, and Ted Kennedy, who had learned the art of pitching as a young boy by studying the curve ball of none other than Hoss Radbourn, himself a young fireballer with the Peoria outfit. Completing the lineup was another of Quinn's old Maroons sidekicks and "the oldest man in the world," according to the *Omaha Daily Bee*: Orator Shafer, who despite his 36 years, made more hits than any other Western Association player for the season.[105]

Despite its beautiful setting at the junction of the Des Moines and Raccoon Rivers, a site which has attracted human occupation for over 7,000 years,[106] the city of Des Moines is also at the mercy of those rivers. The first settlement had been destroyed by flood in 1851, and in 1993 and 2008, flooding caused significant damage and disruption to the city.[107] Baseball was not exempt from such natural phenomena. In early 1888, Athletic Park, located on the old Polk County Fairgrounds fronting the Raccoon River, was inundated by a spring flood, spoiling the chance for Quinn's Prohibitionists to profit from any preseason exhibition games.[108] But this was the only black spot as the Prohibitionists prepared for what seemed set to be a successful season.

And a gala it was. Quinn helped himself to another .300-plus year, grabbing 105 hits in 77 games and swiping 40 bases for good measure at the head of a Des Moines outfit hurtling like a dinghy with the wind abeam toward a pennant. It seemed a return to the open skies and nurture of this black-earth country agreed wholeheartedly with Quinn, for the *Wichita Daily Eagle* exclaimed, "He developed so rapidly he was considered the best second baseman in the northwest."[109] But by August 12, St. Paul had wrested—and extended—the championship lead from Des Moines, and with eight weeks of the season remaining, Omaha was also in touch with the leaders, equal with Des Moines at 43 wins and three games back from St. Paul.[110]

On that same day, August 12, as Des Moines management plotted their strategy to rein in the importunate Apostles, a visitor arrived in the town and disrupted all their plans. Despite their capitulation in negotiations over possession of Joe Quinn back in January, Boston's National League team had continued to shadow the Des Moines captain. In August, they used Omaha manager Frank Selee (himself destined to become Boston manager in 1890[111]) as a stalking horse to tempt Quinn with $3,000 for his release plus a handsome bonus and a considerable raise in salary should he consent to the move.[112] The free-spending tendencies of the mighty northeastern club had paid off in the past, with 12,000 fans flocking to see their "$10,000 beauty" Mike Kelly play in 1887, presenting the great catcher with "more flowers than a favorite prima donna on an opening night or a young girl at her first party."[113] And as early as June 1887, the *St. Paul Globe* had marveled, "Boston is to have the champion base ball team next year, regardless of expense, the management having made up its mind that the niggardly policy it formerly pursued was penny wise, and that money spent on good players was profitably invested.... A majority of players could not be replaced with better ones, but the acquisition of two or three really big men would render the nine unapproachable. If such men can be obtained, Boston will bid heavily for them."[114] But for the second time, Quinn looked the big-spending club right in the eye and responded that he would not consent to the sale, even if the Des Moines management was willing—which they were not.[115] Selee reluctantly left Des Moines empty-handed.

In August 1888, Joe Quinn was undoubtedly one of the hottest commodities in baseball, and his staunch attachment to the Prohibitionists did nothing to cool the ardor of other clubs, among them 1887 National League champions Detroit, who now entered bidding for his services. Boston, however, had it distinctly understood that in the event of Quinn's release, they would outbid any rival offer for him.[116] Des Moines management continued to reject all overtures, although they did let it slip that the only circumstance under which they would consider Quinn's release was "if compelled to do so through financial reasons."[117]

By August 28, national dailies were muttering nervously of war in both Europe and Asia, with German Chancellor Bismarck and his Italian allies pursuing provocative policies against France, and Russian agents stirring Tibetan unrest of the borders of British India.[118] There was unrest of another kind in the cornfields of central Iowa, with Boston launching a final decisive assault on Fortress Des Moines for their ultimate prize—acquisition of Joe Quinn.

And this time, they succeeded.

Part IV
Boston: 1888–1892

7. Back on the Big Stage

"But there are times in this harum-scarum world when figuring out the right thing to do is quite simple, but doing the right thing is simply impossible...."
—Lemony Snicket, *Horseradish: Bitter Truths You Can't Avoid*, 2007

Despite their seemingly limitless financial resources—they had, after all, made over $35,000 profit in 1886[1]—there was a gaping rent in the Boston infield.

The 1888 National League team ought to have been as tightly competitive as a Roman phalanx, replete with future Hall of Famers including catcher King Kelly, man-mountain Dan Brouthers wielding a bat, and John Clarkson and Hoss Radbourn sharing the pitching duties. The roster also boasted two of the nineteenth century's fastest outfielders in Tom "Sprinter" Brown and Dick Johnston.[2] But at the hub of this impressive legion was a hole, a hole so deep in 1888 that it had already swallowed three men before mercilessly disgorging them into minor league obscurity. Billy Klusman (28 games), Jack Burdock (22), and Bill Higgins (14) had all stood at the seemingly cursed second sack. Klusman fielded at a respectable enough .914, but he was an erratic hitter, averaging just .168 from 112 appearances at the plate.[3] Despite being the first National League player to hit two inside-the-park home runs in one game,[4] Klusman secured only one further stint in the major leagues after his 1888 struggles—a four-week cameo with St. Louis in the 1890 American Association.[5] Higgins' 14 games were almost a carbon copy of Klusman's: the 28-year-old journeyman from Delaware fielded at .906 but hit a dreadful .185, and he was released to Syracuse in the International Association.[6] Although "Black Jack" Burdock had been named as second baseman in an 1885 *Harper's Weekly* American all-star team,[7] his remarkable abilities were tragically clouded by his addiction to the bottle. Being thrown from a tram in 1883 and spending several days in a coma seemed to exacerbate both his habitual binge drinking and the effects of numerous concussions he had suffered during courageous plays made on the field. After his accident, Burdock's alcohol consumption became chronic, and his behavior on and off the diamond increasingly fractious, and he was finally sacked by the Beans in June 1888, his sixteen-year major league career in ruins.[8]

Beaneaters management had a simple solution to this crisis on the right side of the diamond—*spend*. Four thousand dollars on August 15, 1888, did the trick.[9] Deny it as they might, the Des Moines Prohibitionists were in financial trouble.[10] They were charging toward the 1888 Western Association pennant, but despite their dominance of the fledgling minor league, attendances were waning. While other clubs played as many as 12 home games on Sundays, Des Moines was the only city in the league where Sunday baseball was not permitted, and the Prohibitionists had lost further revenue when their park was again flooded just two weeks into the season.[11] But the Western Association itself was reportedly on shaky ground,[12] with some teams "forced to do a good deal of financial jugglery to keep alive," under pressure from unrealistic salaries and too-low admission prices.[13] With a salary outlay of $24,000 and $10,000 in costs such as league dues to cover, Des Moines needed to clear $1,550 per game just to break even, and by August they were deep in the red.[14] And circling the Des Moines outfit like a hungry wolf, jaws dripping with cash, was the might of the Boston National League conglomerate. A sacrifice was demanded—the Prohibitionists' best player, their second baseman, captain, and number-one hitter,[15] in exchange for funds to keep the Prohibitionists' heads above water. They had resisted twice, but this time, with their backs to the wall and their very survival in question, there was no option but capitulation.[16]

There is little doubt Quinn had no love for the plan. His refusal to be sold from either struggling Duluth or the more successful but equally doomed Des Moines was testament to a loyalty transcending both flattery and financial incentive.[17] As late as August 12, he was still keeping Boston at bay, unmoved by the weighty inducement of $3,000 plus a handsome bonus and significant increase in salary.[18] It went against all Quinn's principles to leave midseason a team to whose mast he had pinned his colors. But there were forces at work which exceeded even his own considerable willpower, as he had learned after being shunted from Indianapolis to Duluth in 1887—as a player, he was merely a commodity to be traded, sold like a sheep at a market and fed to the vultures who now circled his stumbling club until it collapsed. On August 15, he was given ten days to be in Boston and ready to play.[19]

The timing of Frank Selee's second trip to Des Moines suggests the raid coincided with a much-anticipated return series against National League leaders New York scheduled for August 27, a fact confirmed by the *Boston Globe*.[20] The previous series on August 2 had been disastrous. Not only had the Giants swept all three games in front of the Beans' home fans, but Boston had been badly let down by their "twenty thousand dollar battery" of pitcher John Clarkson and his catcher Mike "King" Kelly.[21] The team were relying on the pair, acquired from the Chicago White Stockings for that unprecedented five-figure sum,[22] to drag them up from fifth place, but Kelly sat out the first two games of the series in protest against a fine for drinking,[23] and Clarkson was knocked out of the box both by powerful Giants hitting and a succession of errors by his defense.[24] The Beans' desperation to find a winner at second base was evident when captain John Morrill—best known as a first baseman—started the first game on the right side of the diamond, where he fumbled about so badly[25] that Klusman had to be brought back for the remainder, and he was, typically, hitless.[26] But worst of all, the trio of losses ensured Boston had lost 23 of their last 24 games and were 15 games behind the Giants, in sixth place.[27]

While Boston had shaken themselves back into some kind of order and won 12 of the 14 games leading into the return series,[28] their middle-infield woes could no longer be ignored, and there was an air of hope in the *Boston Globe*'s proclamation of August 27: "Quinn ought to pan out well."[29]

The report was matter-of-fact, but as the Beaneaters barely dared to hope, Quinn exploded to public notice on his debut three days later—and unlike his hapless predecessors, it was for all the right reasons. The rivalry between the Beaneaters and New York Giants was one of the most powerful of the 1880s, the Giants countering the strength of the Boston lineup with their own champion hurler in Tim Keefe,[30] classic shortstop John Montgomery Ward, and perhaps the nineteenth century's greatest catcher in the fearless Buck Ewing, of whom Quinn recalled, "King Kelly could throw a ball to second without moving out of his tracks, but Buck Ewing could throw like chained lightning without taking a step backward."[31]

Naturally, the feats of one of these greats were expected to determine the outcome of the game in New York on August 29, the day of Quinn's debut. But the *New York Times* marveled, "An unexpected hit by a new player does the work."[32] Quinn, like rightfielder Tom Brown, who had won the first game of the series for Boston with a seventh-inning bases-loaded home run,[33] was not renowned for his hitting power. His new clubmates even told the *Times* before the series that they "did not look for anything remarkable from him in the way of batting," and Captain John Morrill declared, "He's a lightning fielder but a weak batter."[34] But while spending two seasons in the minors is an affront to any young professional player, Quinn's relegation had had benefits, particularly as an opportunity to renew the confidence which had waned during two years in the National League with the struggling St. Louis nine. He had hit for average and knocked out only one home run in those early seasons, but during his exile he'd launched fourteen over the fence, feasting on the lighter pitching and smaller grounds.[35] So while his new club looked to him chiefly for his prowess on the right side of the diamond, Quinn now had extra tricks up his sleeve.

He watched the first two games of the series from the bench, both won by Boston in tight contests, and was slotted into the nine for the third after Bill Higgins made bad errors at second base in both.[36] Facing Quinn was a Giants outfit stung by vicious criticism in the *Times* of their "stupid and indifferent work ... despite looking pretty in their new suits of tight-fitting white Jersey cloth with maroon trimmings,"[37] and four thousand New York rooters determined to holler their team home. But it was the Beans who took the lead in the third inning as speedy Dick Johnston hit safely, stole second, and came home on another timely Tom Brown hit, which Giants outfielder Mike Slattery allowed to bounce. Although they had had men on base in almost every inning, it was the top of the final inning before, by sheer dour struggle, the Giants scored an equalizing run: shortstop Monte Ward hefted a double to left field and scored on a close call when Roger Connor hit a fly ball out to Brown. The effort sent the home crowd into a frenzy of hope—they were "shouting so loudly the cheering could be heard for a radius of a quarter of a mile."[38] It was a terrible blow to Boston pitcher Bill Sowders. The humble journeyman from Kentucky had struck out just two batters to Keefe's ten, but had battled grimly all day to defend the precious run

In the nineteenth century, cigarette companies such as Old Judge produced collectible "cabinet cards" of leading sportsmen posed against studio backdrops. This card from the N-173 series features Joe Quinn taking a bare-handed catch in the uniform of the 1888 Boston Beaneaters (National Baseball Hall of Fame Library, Cooperstown, New York).

Boston scored in the third, sending fourteen batters back to the bench on fly catches. Now, perhaps, that herculean effort had been in vain.

Before the wild shouts of the Giants' fans had died away, out of the dugout walked "little Quinn"[39] to face Tim Keefe. He didn't wait, like a pampered tennis player, for the stadium to fall silent. He didn't watch a pitch or two across the plate to get a feel for Keefe's notorious curving deliveries.[40] Whether he simply got "his" pitch, whether Keefe underestimated him (as had almost everyone else), or whether his swing was one for all the injustices of his sale by Des Moines, we shall never know—but Quinn sent the first ball he faced sailing high over Slattery's head to land amongst the overflow of carriages parked in centerfield.[41] In the nineteenth century, when the ball was less lively and major league parks generally had very large outfields, most home runs were of the inside-the-park variety[42]—such as in this case—and therefore despite being entangled amongst the carriage wheels, the ball was still live. A collective gasp ... then a shout erupted as though a dam had let go, and, like sunflowers, every upturned face followed the white orb—every face but that of Quinn, who was off like a greyhound. The ball was hurtled back to shortstop Ward, who was screaming for the throw, seemingly in time to catch the speeding Quinn at the plate—but with one eye on the runner, Ward put out only one hand to catch it and the sphere bounded out of his reach, drawing howls of dismay and derision from the crowd as Quinn slid in for the winning run.[43] Kelly burst from the dugout; the Bostons were all charging and sweeping the little fellow up onto a sea of shoulders, carousing delightedly and still finding breath to taunt the disconsolate Giants with oaths and raised fists.

There were so few Boston enthusiasts present, there was almost nobody to cheer this unexpected feat—but what they lacked in numbers, the Bostonians made up in exultation. "You're a daisy, you're a daisy!" yelled "General" Arthur Dixwell, the wealthy eccentric and number one supporter of the Beans. "Boston is yours; you can have the Bunker Hill monument; the State House will be your residence!"[44] And this refrain became a mocking echo across the Polo Grounds as the sullen home crowd filed out: three straight defeats at the hands of the Bostons were too much for the admirers of the Giants.

And the trio of losses became a clean sweep the following day when ten thousand exultant fans welcomed the Bostons home for the final game of the series,[45] all anxious to witness a fourth humiliation of the Giants and the home debut of their intriguing acquisition from Des Moines. Again, the New York offense broke down, Clarkson holding their feared batters to just five scattered hits and the dominant quartet of Richardson, Tiernan, O'Rourke, and Ward all failing to lay bat on ball.[46] The *Times* reported Quinn was "overanxious in the field" and made an unprepossessing trio of errors[47]—perhaps understandably, as he was the focal point for the biggest crowd he had yet played before. But he again surprised with his performance at the bat, hitting two doubles, scoring a run, and striking out just once in the 7–3 victory.[48]

The Boston public was now clamoring to know and claim the serious, steady-minded young man. "Joe Quinn has caught on big with the Boston ball public," enthused the *Omaha Daily Bee*. "As a batter he is up with the top-notchers of the National league, and his second base play has been of the phenomenal order."[49] So who better to take Quinn under his wing and guide him through the minefield of life in the spotlight than a true celebrity of the game—a star as much for his on-field prowess as for his blithe, boisterous adoration of public attention? Many of the Boston players lived together in apartments on Huntington Avenue,[50] and in 1888, Quinn became fast friends with his new teammate, Mike "King" Kelly, whom he described as "like a brother to me."[51]

This was a deserved reward for Quinn's perseverance, befriended now by the greats of the day rather than bullied and vilified by them. But it was certainly an incongruous pairing—the sober, temperate apprentice undertaker in cahoots with one of the game's most dynamic personalities and most committed imbibers. Kelly had made his debut as a 20-year-old with Cincinnati in 1878, but it was with Cap Anson's Chicago White Stockings he won five National League pennants in the 1880s and individual batting crowns in 1884 and 1886. However, 1886 also brought his downfall, with an untimely post-season hitting slump squarely blamed for the shock World Series loss to St. Louis. It was too much for the Chicago owners, who had tried for seven seasons to curb Kelly's joyous carousing—the offer of ten thousand dollars from Boston for their disgraced hitter was instantly accepted.[52]

Hall of Fame catcher Mike "King" Kelly, that irrepressible Irish rascal who was as much adored by his fans as he was despaired of by team managers, was a great friend of Joe Quinn's. The pair met when Quinn joined the Boston Beaneaters in 1888, and while their friendship was tested in the wake of the 1890 Players' League upheaval, Quinn always spoke highly of the King's shrewdness and talent (National Baseball Hall of Fame Library, Cooperstown, New York).

But there *were* commonalities between the disparate pair. Kelly's parents, like Quinn's, were Irish immigrants who had fled famine and deprivation for a better life in the New World.[53] Perhaps the same craving for love and attention fostered by the death of both parents while he was a child[54] that drove Kelly to give the public something to remember every time he stepped on the diamond, also drew the King toward Quinn, with his quiet steadfast nature the perfect foil for Kelly's exuberance. Such was Kelly's passion for melodrama that he once objected to an umpire's call by standing on his hands and braying like a donkey.[55] He worked the vaudeville circuit in the off-season, and was adored as much for his wit, charm, and willingness to buy the next round as for his astonishing inventiveness and talent on the diamond.[56] And he was quick to turn that very wit toward his new protégée in Quinn. The same year of their meeting, 1888, Frances Hodgson Burnett's classic tale *Little Lord Fauntleroy* was dramatized on Broadway,[57] and Joe Quinn's granddaughter Mary Catherine Butler recalled Kelly cheekily christened Quinn after the little protagonist, with his ruffled lace collar and long golden curls[58]: "He had a strong, lithe, graceful little body and a manly face," went Burnett's fable, "he held his head up, and carried himself with a brave air ... innocently fearless, he looked as if he had never feared or doubted anything in his life...."[59]

While it was a more than apt description, much to the chagrin of the new arrival, the epithet stuck. But it was utterly typical of the dazzling, hearty Kelly, who captivated all with his Irish wit and his wholly guileless and irresponsible bonhomie. But for all his love of the limelight, Kelly was no fly-by-night on the diamond. Tom McCarthy, crack outfielder with the St. Louis Browns of the 1880s, recalled, "Kelly was far and away the brainiest player I ever saw.... Not that his ball playing was dirty ... he simply did lots of things for the first time."[60] Quinn agreed, recalling in 1905, "Kelly was chock full of baseball brains and a more headier player never walked on the field than the only Mike. A great trick of Kelly's when catching was to fool a runner on first with a fake wild throw. He would signal the right fielder to come up and then throw the ball over first base into the right fielder's hand. The baserunner, thinking it was a wild throw, would start for second only to be met by the ball. Kelly pulled this play off for quite awhile, then everybody 'got on' to it and he had to invent something new."[61]

That proved simple enough: Kelly was the first catcher to balk base-runners sliding for home by dropping his mask—quite innocently, of course—on the plate.[62] Kelly himself was a famous slider, eliciting roars of "Slide, Kelly, slide!" from the crowd whenever the King was on base.[63] Quinn learned not only the finer arts of base-running from the King, but also the risks of standing the second sack against such tactics, remembering, "Kelly taught me how to slide into second. He would jump into the air ten feet from the sack, dive directly for it, dig one of his spiked shoes into the bag and then swerve clear over on his side. Few second basemen in those days had the nerve to stand their ground and block his hurricane dives for the bag."[64]

This hook slide allowed Kelly to evade tags, and he often simultaneously kicked the ball out of the infielder's glove—when called out once on a close play, he picked up the loose ball from underneath him and addressed the umpire with a grin, "If I'm out, what's this?"[65] Such was the speed of the Kelly wit that Quinn never saw his friend "feased" but once:

King Kelly was one of the great innovators in nineteenth-century baseball, often employing dramatic and cunning tactics to fool opponents and umpires. His friend Joe Quinn often recalled in admiring terms Kelly's unequaled talent for baserunning and sliding, and it was common for crowds to yell "Slide, Kelly, slide!" while the King was on base (McGreevey Collection, courtesy the Trustees of the Boston Public Library).

The Boston team was entering the field at Indianapolis one day when an old Irishman in the bleachers yelled to Kelly, "You're a fine lookin' tin-thousand-dollar beauty, ain't you now?"

"Well, I got the best of you, old man," replied Mike. "I'm eating strawberries and ice cream off the salary I earn performing for suckers like you."

"Yes, and the bartenders get yours all right," was the response hurled back by the wily old Turk. The reply was so literally true that Kelly shut up like a clam.[66]

In the heady presence of the King and his cohorts, Quinn thrived in his return to the big time. He collected 47 hits at an average of .301 in Boston's final 38 games of the year, stealing 12 bases and having a hand in over 200 outs at second base. He also slammed four home runs, a record he only exceeded twice in the remaining 16 years of his career, in 1890 and 1894.[67] Quinn was lauded by the *Wichita Daily Eagle* on October 16 as "one of the best second basemen in the profession, as quick as a cat, covers a great deal of ground ... going for everything, a good batter and a splendid base runner."[68]

On December 20, despite finishing only fourth in the league after all their extravagant outlay, Boston renewed Quinn's contract for 1889 with a generous $2,500 salary.[69] Back in Des Moines, his former colleagues captured their own pennant by a mere half a game (or 0.006 percent) to Kansas City, who protested that the Prohibitionists never played three

The Des Moines Prohibitionists captured the 1888 Western Association pennant by 0.006 percent over Kansas City. Despite leaving the team to join the Boston National League outfit in August, Quinn (middle row, far left) was still included in a photographic montage of the Des Moines champions at the end of the season (National Baseball Hall of Fame Library, Cooperstown, New York).

additional games to make up for those forfeited to them mid-season by Sioux City.[70] But despite the cash injection from Quinn's sale and their on-field success, the club was in a terminal financial tailspin, losing between twelve and fifteen thousand dollars for the season.[71] Des Moines finished last in the Western Association the following year, and in August 1890, the franchise was transferred to Lincoln, Nebraska.[72] Professional baseball would not return to Des Moines until it joined the Western League in 1894, with the club still known as the Prohibitionists (although one newspaper jeered, "Gambling syndicates are numerous and the players are heavy drinkers"[73]). But by 1896 the club had again become such a powerhouse, with a .718 win-loss percentage, that the Western League collapsed under the cavernous inequality of the competition.[74]

• • •

> *"I could have told you a lot of this before, but I wanted to get all the facts so you could depend on anything I told you.... No matter what happens, do not mention my name in connection with this letter."*—Correspondence from Joe Quinn to Al Spink, September 21, 1889[75]

Historian Daniel Pearson called 1889 "the culmination of baseball's first real decade of growth."[76] On the field, the game was rollicking, urgent, and violent, its rules and equipment and tactics growing more sophisticated each season—evolving in step with a rapidly urbanizing nation, with its changing demographics, economy, diplomacy, and industry. Baseball's first industrial relationships were similarly evolving alongside those of their trade counterparts. The "Brotherhood of Base Ball Players"—professional baseball's first players' association—was formed in 1885 as conflict between players and owners over the reserve clause and abuse of the blacklist became increasingly frequent and acrimonious.[77] But it was in 1889 that industrial discontent among ballplayers erupted into outright rebellion.

The year began so innocuously for Joe Quinn. His greatest concerns were supervising his burgeoning collection of investment properties in northwestern St. Louis,[78] and protecting his pretty young wife from the wiles of "Jack the Kisser," a crank with a mania for pestering attractive women after dark in the downtown. The Kisser was known to leave his victims with a sheaf of love poetry and a ticket entitling the holder to "eternal happiness." While the press wrung its hands over the "unwonted disturbance to the slumberous atmosphere of St. Louis"[79] by this artist of osculation, many of his victims were, in fact, quite agreeable to the seduction, one gushing, "I wish I could meet him again. He is certainly the best looking and most courageous gentleman I ever met, and he kisses as I never knew a man to kiss before. Besides, his breath was not tainted with nasty beer or vile tobacco smoke."[80] But his activities inevitably attracted scrutiny from the more muscular sex, and on February 19, Quinn found the following placard pinned to a tree near his home:

> To the Ladies:
> You need not expect to meet me again in this place.
>   My time in St. Louis is limited. I must
> change my field of action to another part of the city.
> I cannot leave the dear West End
> Without a pang of pain,
> For the dear lips that I have kissed,
> I shall ne'er kiss again.
> But when other lips are pressed to yours,
> And other arms entwine,

7. Back on the Big Stage

> I know your thoughts will then turn back
> To these poor lips of mine.
> —Jack, the Kisser.[81]

Despite the location of the note, there was no indication of whether Molly Quinn had been amongst the victims of the sassy smoocher.

Also occupying the interest of the baseball fraternity at large, Quinn no doubt among them, was the progress of a party of Chicago White Stockings and National League "All-star" players who had embarked on a world promotional tour for the game on October 20, 1888. First port of call and top of the tour billing was Australia.[82] The tour, destined to bedazzle northern Africa, Asia, Europe and Quinn's own homeland, was organized by Chicago owner Al Spalding, and the two traveling teams were replete with the greats, including Quinn's great friend King Kelly, Cap Anson, middle infielders Fred Pfeffer, Bid McPhee, and Monte Ward, and future Hall of Famers Charlie Comiskey, Ned Hanlon, Buck Ewing, and Hoss Radbourn.[83] The coterie were feted by President Grover Cleveland at the White House before departing: Kelly gleefully squeezed Cleveland's fat, soft hand so hard the President winced, setting a precedent for all the others to follow, and Kelly later noted cheekily, "The President didn't shake hands when we left."[84] Soon after, though, Kelly backed out of the tour, citing myriad reasons, each more creative than the last—that his wife was sick, that he planned to open a saloon in New York, that a fortune had been left to him. Spalding did extract a promise that Kelly could attend to his business interests, then meet the teams in Denver as they barnstormed west across America before their departure for Australia, but Kelly simply never turned up.[85]

The tour itinerary included twelve games played in Australia. Baseball had been played on the Australian goldfields as early as 1857,[86] but the Spalding tour was the first formal contact of most Australians with the American national pastime. The party arrived in Sydney on December 14, 1888, where the All-Stars won all three of the opening games, played before curious crowds numbering more than 5,000. Chicago struck back when the tour moved on to Melbourne and Adelaide—in fact, the White Stockings lost only one of the last six tour matches on Australian parks, which drew as many as 12,000 sports-mad Australian spectators.[87] The tour then barnstormed across Europe and Northern Africa: when the All-Stars beat Chicago 10–6 in the shadow of the Egyptian pyramids on February 9, 1889, Cap Anson felt compelled to make a public and very funny apology to the Sphinx for his team's poor play.[88] The jaunt formally concluded on April 20 when the two teams played for the final time in Chicago prior to the start of the 1889 season. The tour's legacy in Australia was a partial fulfillment of Spalding's objectives—new baseball clubs were established in major cities, and some, such as those in East Melbourne and Goodwood in South Australia, still survive today.[89] Spalding's tour secretary Harry Simpson remained in Australia and established the Victorian Baseball League in 1889, and with the South Australian Baseball League formed around the same time, intercolonial matches were soon underway. However, in 1891, Simpson contracted typhoid and died, aged just 27. His death marked the passing of a true baseball visionary who helped the sport gain its first organized toehold in Australia.[90]

For those not offered a place on tour, spring training was underway in April 1889, and it was a drying-out period for many players, endured so the "players would not look like aldermen after a winter of lushing," wrote Ted Sullivan in despair.[91] Drinking was a serious issue amongst major league players, so much so that in 1888, Louisville had signed Pete Browning only after extracting an oath of abstinence from him in front of a local judge,[92]

A.G. Spalding's 1889 worldwide jaunt to promote the game of baseball was actually advertised as "Spalding's Australian Base Ball Tour." In addition to portraits of the participating Chicago and All-American team members, this poster features the Australian coat of arms, with its kangaroo and emu motifs (National Baseball Hall of Fame Library, Cooperstown, New York).

and Chicago owner Al Spalding had hired detectives to shadow the White Stocking players and report back on their drinking habits.[93] Most northern clubs spent at least part of the spring detoxing in the warmth of the Deep South, and a typical day meant rising at 6 a.m. and dousing each other with buckets of sea water, a hike over the sandhills before breakfast, followed by working out with dumbbells, batting, sliding, throwing, playing handball, and scrimmaging; after supper, the players would "swap lies" until lights out.[94] Joe Quinn prided himself on maintaining peak physical condition throughout the year, and fretted that these southern trips were an unnecessary waste of his valuable business time. He told *The Sporting News* in 1895, "I take good care of myself at all times and do not need the preparation which the idle players who accumulate flesh while dissipating wealth find indispensible. About all I have to do to get in the game is work my throwing arm into shape. There is no necessity for my [going south] and I will not leave my business more than ten days before the season opens."[95]

But in 1889, Quinn did (reluctantly) report as required on March 29, and despite a glowing report in the *New York Sun* that the Bostons, particularly Kelly, Brouthers, and Quinn, were "lively as kittens" and "speeding around the gymnasium,"[96] Quinn wrote crossly to *The Sporting News* on April 12, "As the championship season is about to start, and the much-abused Boston Club is here for practice, I thought I would write you a few lines,

Hiking (in full baseball uniform) was a typical part of the Boston baseball spring training program as early as the nineteenth century. This photograph shows the Boston Red Sox hiking at their regular spring training base in Hot Springs, Arkansas, c. 1906 (McGreevey Collection, courtesy the Trustees of the Boston Public Library).

stating that nearly all the members of the Boston Club are out of condition. But it is too late now and it will be a case of 'charley horse' with the players. It would make a man think of home and mother to play in some of these practice games."[97]

But in that spring of 1889, a flabby and poorly conditioned roster was the least of Boston's problems. The feud which had simmered for two years between King Kelly and manager John Morrill had boiled over, and their back-stabbing and jealous sniping erupting into open conflict. Handsome, black-haired "Honest John" had managed the team since 1882, but when Kelly arrived from Chicago in 1887 and was immediately awarded the prestigious field captain's position, the first schism arose.[98] Morrill ferociously disapproved of Kelly's lifestyle, and the resultant year of infighting and sniping between the disparate pair saw the team rise no higher than a mediocre fifth place. Morrill was reinstated to the captaincy for 1888, and he and Kelly settled on an uneasy truce until Boston played an exhibition game against a local semipro team in the spring of 1889, with the Braves led by Kelly. The decision to "lend" Morrill to bolster the locals was a fatal affront to a pride already battered by the public attention lavished on his rival. An outstanding player in his own right,[99] Morrill protested furiously at his debasement, so the Boston owners' triumvirate of Conant, Billings, and Soden instituted an immediate solution: they sold him to the abysmal Washington.[100]

James Aristotle Hart of Louisville was drafted in as replacement manager and Kelly retained the captaincy, but the King was the subject of considerable ill-feeling in the press: Chicago owner Al Spalding publicly described the King as "bad goods,"[101] implying he was unable to stay on the wagon without Cap Anson's steadying hand. Hart immediately jumped to the King's defense, retorting, "Mike Kelly was a big-hearted, open-handed, kindly chap.... A man who could hold any ill-feeling against Mike would have had ice water in his veins instead of blood."[102] But in the great Australian tradition of standing by your mate, Kelly's staunchest defender was his friend Joe Quinn, even when his support of the King saw him similarly vilified in the press. "It seems as though Kelly ... and myself are targets for some of the Boston scribes," Quinn wrote on April 12. "Some of my friends are sore on me for upholding Kelly. Well, Kelly acted like a gentleman when I first went to Boston. He could not do any more for his brother than he did for me. He would not harm a child, but he likes to keep at the reporters, but still, if they wanted a friend, Kelly would do almost anything for them. I also wish to say that Morrill ... is a gentleman in every respect."[103]

In this atmosphere of bickering, upheaval, and general agitation, it was anticlimactic that the first two games of the 1889 season—supposed to pit the year's two front-running teams, New York and Boston, against one another—were washed out on April 22 and 23. The four-game series was scheduled for the old St. George's Ground on Staten Island, New York City Council having relocated a street through the center of the Polo Grounds and left the Giants homeless.[104] The American Association Mets had played at St. George's in 1886–87, and from its stands, fans could look across New York harbor to see the Statue of Liberty being assembled (that is, when the fog that perpetually haunted the ground actually lifted).[105] The Giants now shared the park with a production of the play *Nero*—literally: the right fielders were obliged to play on part of the stage platform, necessitating the use of rubber-soled shoes. Two years earlier, the presence of another theater set cost the Philadelphia Athletics a game when Gus Weyhing hit an apparent triple that Mets rightfielder Bob Hogan kicked onto the stage of the play *The Fall of Babylon*. Any ball hit into the set was supposed to be ruled a double and Weyhing was directed back to second base, prompting furious protests that the triple had resulted from Hogan's error. Neither Umpire Sullivan nor the Athletics would back down, prompting the arbiter to forfeit the game to the Mets.[106]

The remaining two games in that first series were each decided by a single run, with Boston pitcher John Clarkson defeating "Smiling Mickey" Welch 8–7 in the first game. Welch had set an all-time major league mark in 1884 by striking out the first nine batters faced in a game,[107] but in 1889, John Clarkson was the most dominant hurler in the National League. He had been a teammate of Kelly's at Chicago before being purloined by Boston for a cool ten thousand dollars; he was a handsome figure who wore a white silk kerchief when he pitched, and many ladies would wave theirs adoringly at him.[108] As overhand pitching grew in popularity, an increasing variety of pitches were thrown, from the incurve, outcurve and reversing curve, to the inshoot, jump ball, change of pace, and the lethal beanball aimed squarely at the hitter's unprotected head.[109] Clarkson was an exponent of many of these, with a devastating change of pace and sinker, but it was his work in conjunction with his old battery mate King Kelly that made him so effective: as a catcher, Kelly had almost single-handedly turned the pitchers' emphasis from strikeouts to throwing to their defense, and Joe Quinn remembered, "The only Mickey [Kelly] taught John Clarkson [was] how to signal the men behind him so that the infield knew what he was going to pitch—a curve ball, slow one, or fast straight one. This knowledge helped a player wonderfully."[110]

Although purchased by the Boston triumvirate as a second baseman, Quinn started the season "putting some grass in his hat"[111] in the outfield. The arrival of infield specialist Hardie Richardson in 1889 saw him shunted out to the green paddocks to replace the aging Joe Hornung.[112] Thirty-four-year-old Richardson had missed most of last season with a bad ankle injury, and was anxious to return to where he'd left off with the heavy-hitting Detroit Wolverines[113]—he had hit over .300 for the previous five seasons and fielded at no less than .925.[114] But Quinn had declared that he would "pack up and go home before playing in the outfield,"[115] and wrote Al Spink grudgingly on April 12, "The understanding was that I was to play second base, but it looks as though they are going to keep me in left field. I do not care to play the outfield, but if they think it best to keep me there I will do all in my power to bring the club to the front."[116]

May proved an opportunity for Boston to gain early breathing space over New York. Behind Clarkson and Radbourn, Boston won twenty games and lost only six, taking advantage of New York star pitcher Tim Keefe's absence as he held out against the Giants' owners for a higher salary.[117] His stand left the Giants so short on pitching staff they were forced to start catcher Buck Ewing in the box for the May 9 series against Boston, and although the game was won 10–9, Quinn remembered, "Ewing threw his arm out of gear pitching a winning game against the champion Bostons, and was never of any account again."[118]

Horrified by the injury to his good friend, Keefe hurriedly signed a $4,250 contract[119] and pitched on May 8 to punish the Bostons 7–0.[120] However, it was a long road back for the Giants: Boston had doubled New York's attendances for May,[121] and when the two teams faced off again on June 6–7 in Boston, Clarkson defeated Keefe 10–7 and Hoss Radbourn consolidated with a 9–4 win amidst much arguing with umpire George Barnum, to the delight of the record Thursday crowd of 4,500 fans.[122] But Keefe and Welch turned the tables on the Boston starters on June 10–11 in Manhattan: Keefe defeated Clarkson 5–1 in a twelve-strikeout, rain-soaked demolition, and Welch followed up with a two-hitter of his own to defeat Radbourn 2–1. Kelly moved himself to right field, and his place behind the plate was taken by big handsome Charlie Bennett. Even Buck Ewing acknowledged, "If I could catch as well as Bennett was catching for Boston, we would win the championship."[123] Bennett was the leading catcher in the National League for five seasons with those powerhouses of the 1880s, the Detroit Wolverines, before they were disbanded in 1888. The Boston owners

The Boston National League team at the South End Grounds, c. 1889. In this illustration, the fielders are gloveless and the catcher wears no mask or mitt. The umpire is positioned to his right to avoid being struck by passed balls. A difficult location from which to call pitches on left-handed hitters such as that shown in this picture (McGreevey Collection, courtesy the Trustees of the Boston Public Library).

swooped on the Wolverines' "heavy hitters" in Dan Brouthers, Ned Hanlon, Jack Rowe, and Bennett himself, who had hit over .300 for three consecutive seasons between 1881 and 1883. Unlike Ewing, who caught splendidly equipped with the weapons of defense including glove, mask, and chest protector, Bennett never wore a catcher's mitt. The only glove he wore while catching was an ordinary kid glove—and that with the fingers and thumb cut off. Lon Knight, the famous old Athletics player, told how Bennett's thumb was once split open from the hand to the tip, "clear to the bone." Bennett courageously persisted in catching day after day, sponging the gash between innings "to remove the corruption which was continually flowing from the wound," heedless of warnings he must either stop playing until the thumb had entirely healed, or lose his thumb or even his arm.[124] Years of such abuse left Bennett's hands more like claws, but it was in January 1894 that the courageous catcher fell victim to a far more horrific fate—he slipped while boarding a train in Wellsville, Kansas, falling between

Opposite, top: The Boston Beaneaters (c. 1888) in front of the Grand Pavilion at the South End Grounds, Boston. The pavilion was one of the most magnificent of the nineteenth century until the wooden structure was destroyed by fire in 1894 (National Baseball Hall of Fame Library, Cooperstown, New York). *Bottom:* The view from the Grand Pavilion at Boston's South End Grounds. Note the immaculate dress of the patrons, with top hats and fancy millinery abundant. This photograph was obviously taken before catchers' masks and mitts came into common usage: the catcher and umpire can be seen in their typical positions, a long way behind the batter's box (National Baseball Hall of Fame Library, Cooperstown, New York).

the carriages and being pinned beneath the moving steel wheels. The accident cost him both legs.[125] Bennett somehow survived his terrible injuries, and until his death in 1927, made a living painting china from his home in Detroit, which named its park in his honor: for almost three decades, Bennett threw out the first pitch on home openers while balanced bravely on a pair of artificial legs.[126]

In late June, the Boston bubble burst spectacularly. They were ahead by five and a half games on June 22, but both Hoss Radbourn and Kid Madden had sore arms and the team dropped three of four games to lowly Indianapolis, including two bad losses for their only fit pitcher, John Clarkson. They also lost three games in Chicago, primarily through the struggles of their $20,000 battery, Kelly and Clarkson. While back in his former hometown, Kelly went on a wild drinking binge in his old haunts, and to make matters worse, Clarkson's famous control totally deserted him: Boston was rapidly discovering the handsome pitcher went to pieces under any kind of sniping, and Clarkson did exactly that as he was mercilessly taunted across the diamond by his former captain in Cap Anson. When Clarkson died in 1909, Anson remembered, "Clarkson was one of the greatest pitchers that ever lived ... but not many know what an amount of encouragement it took to keep him going. Scold him, find fault with him, and he could not pitch at all."[127]

The wreckage prompted wholesale changes in the Boston lineup in an effort to find a winning combination. Quinn was reassigned to shortstop, a position he had only ever appeared briefly at, during the 1886 season. The shortstop was not considered important by early professional teams until Dickey Pearce of the Atlantics played that position in the 1860s and was the first to study the batsman, fielding close for weak batters and very deep when the hard hitters came up.[128] Quinn was not happy with the move, and it showed. The *Omaha Bee* declared stoutly, "If his work at Boston's short-field has not been satisfactory he can hardly be blamed, as he never made any pretensions to being a short-stop, but always contended that his home position was second base."[129] And although longtime Boston correspondent to the *Pittsburg Dispatch* Charles Foley concurred on June 16, "Quinn's fielding of late has been out of sight, while his timely batting has brought many a run across the plate,"[130] the beauties of the left side of the diamond were wasted on Quinn, who declared bluntly to *The Sporting News*, "I am not in love with my new position, but it is a case of necessity."[131]

In 1882, a ballplayer traveled an average of 45,650 miles during the regular season.[132] The traveling part was little more than an endless litany of waiting: waiting to board, waiting to disembark, waiting for a cab, waiting to check in, waiting to check out ... so much time wasted in a vacuum of just doing nothing. By 1895, the travel demand was up to 113,637 miles,[133] and Quinn's burden of unhappiness was compounded by homesickness in June. "I would sooner play in some place nearer home, so I could take a trip to dear old 'Kerry Patch,'"[134] he told Spink on June 22, and closed with this disparaging observation about life in Boston: "Oblige me by telling all your St. Louis friends that if they ever visit the Hub, never stop on a corner to think which way you will go or they will be arrested. Pretty soon they will arrest you in Boston for thinking."[135]

This was an uncharacteristically trenchant period for the normally optimistic and gentlemanly Quinn. Despite the prestige associated with his move to the pennant front-runners, he had struggled to settle into a regular playing position or to adapt to a life so isolated from his young family. To compound his misery, he fell seriously ill with malarial fever in July. He had played in what he called "very yellow fashion" for several weeks without being able to account for it, his eyesight poor and beset by dizzy spells.[136] The enforced lay-off grated hard on him[137]: while playing, his mind could not wander homeward, but now, confined to a cold and impersonal hotel bed, he longed for the warmth and vitality of the Patch, his young wife, and the daughter he barely knew. He was granted leave to return home to visit his wife and baby, but only for a few short days.[138]

His superstitious teammates, meanwhile, were searching the Boston skies for a white pigeon and its streets for a wagonload of empty barrels—both apparently symbols of an upcoming change in fortune.[139] While six thousand forgiving fans had welcomed the Beaneaters home after the Chicago debacle on July 8, *The Sporting Life* was not so cordial, scoffing, "Boston require another good pitcher, less good times after games, more ginger on the field, and a captain who will be up and hustling and coaching instead of sitting on the bench."[140] Hoss Radbourn was still sidelined with a sore arm, and while Dan Brouthers was leading the league hitting .395 and Kelly had managed a below-average (for him) .287, Billy Nash, Dick Johnston, and Charlie Bennett all had batting averages below .230.[141] Quinn had missed a lot of playing time during his illness and struggled to an average of .261[142]: it was fully ten weeks before he was back playing "class A ball."[143]

• • •

While Boston's troubles persisted on the diamond, a revolution was brewing off it. On May 19, player representatives from all eight National League teams had met secretly at New York's Fifth Avenue Hotel, and the single item on the agenda was the possibility of staging a strike in early July to protest the ongoing aggravation and restrictions of the reserve clause.[144] That hated contractual proviso had been a long-running grievance for the Brotherhood of Base Ball Players, whose ninety or so members had struggled over the last four seasons to elicit any kind of modification to the clause by the National League.[145] The players described it as "a fugitive slave law ... [which] denies a man a harbor or a livelihood and carries him back, bound and shackled, to the club from which he attempted to escape...."[146] The negotiators were headed by New York shortstop John Montgomery Ward, who, with Keefe, Ewing, and six of their teammates, had formed the Brotherhood in 1885. Ward was well qualified to lead the association, earning a law degree at Columbia University in New York the same year.[147] Al Spink described in *The National Game* how Ward wrote many articles and studied the game in depth, showing both the "fine education of the man and the keen relish he took in the pastime."[148] Joe Quinn, with his own finely developed sense of justice, was a great admirer of "Monte." The *Omaha Sunday Bee* even reported in early 1890, "It is said that Joe Quinn is thinking about studying law in imitation of Johnny Ward."[149]

Quinn had joined the Brotherhood while with St. Louis back in 1886, attending a meeting held at the Old Polo Grounds on May 29 in New York.[150] The Brotherhood had moved swiftly, forming chapters in eight cities in their first year and attracting future Hall of Famers Connie Mack, Charlie Comiskey, King Kelly, Hugh Duffy, Ed Delahanty, Ned Hanlon, Hoss Radbourn and Dan Brouthers as subscribers. At first, anxious to develop a working relationship with the leagues, Ward diplomatically described the reserve clause as "made necessary by the peculiar nature of the baseball business."[151] The Brotherhood also accepted a system of fines for "dissipation" and even agreed to use of the blacklist, although only after a fourth disciplinary offense.[152] But this state of semi-harmony was blown apart when the National League owners passed the Brush Classification Rule in November 1888 (conveniently, while Ward was away playing on Spalding's World Tour). Indianapolis owner John T. Brush introduced the rule to place a ceiling on skyrocketing player salaries, with players paid according to a classification ranging from A ($2,500 per year) to E ($1,500). Each player's salary level was determined by owners and managers according to a player's "habits, earnestness and special qualifications."[153] Al Spalding was a wholehearted supporter of this new system, asserting "baseball depends on two interdependent divisions, the one to have absolute control and direction over the system, and the other to engage—always under the executive branch—in the actual work of production...."[154] On Ward's return in April 1889, the players, some of whom were accustomed to earning $4,000 or more per season,[155] appealed to the league—but to no avail. And Ward had come home to problems of his own, having been sold to Washington in his absence for the record price of $12,000.[156] The sale, however, collapsed when Ward abjectly refused to go: it was the end, as he saw it, of the battle to maintain diplomatic relations with the league. A bold and audacious plan was taking shape in his mind, and when Ward met Spalding privately in June and the Chicago owner dismissed the unrest as unworthy of immediate action, Ward declared ominously, "The League will not classify as many as they think."[157]

Thereafter, he wasted no time enacting his plans. Two of the decade's leading players, Jack Rowe and Deacon White, had threatened to take the League to court after being sold to Pittsburgh despite investing heavily in the Buffalo club. White declared ferociously, "No man can sell my carcass—unless I get at least half,"[158] but Ward persuaded the pair to instead lie low in Pittsburgh and continue the clandestine maneuverings, now squarely aimed at forming a breakaway league. Al Spink described these machinations as the beginning of "the most important fight ever made on the National Agreement ... a most desperate war against the injustice of the reserve rule."[159] The players were preparing not only to bite the hand that both fed and restrained them, but to give it a significant mauling.

• • •

Boston won four of their next five games at home on an infield heavily rutted by rain, but their lead over the Giants was down to one and a half games by July 15. The press was still riding Kelly hard for his indifferent leadership: *The Sporting Life* of July 17 noted coldly, "Kelly says Boston will not land better than fourth. That is pretty talk for the captain of a team thought to be a pennant winner."[160] *The Sporting Life* also noted Joe Quinn was still not fully fit and not playing well, but Hoss Radbourn was enough recovered from his lingering arm injury to defeat Chicago on July 17 in his first start in two weeks. Newly signed Jersey City pitcher Bill Daley won the other half of the double-header, and Boston won nine of fourteen games at home at the end of July to ratchet their lead back out to four and a half games.[161]

Although still in the shadows, the clandestine plot for the breakaway "Players' League" continued to gain momentum. An important break came on July 22 when Pittsburgh manager and Brotherhood foundation member Ned Hanlon approached Cleveland streetcar magnate Albert Johnson to both finance the rebel league and recruit as many National League players as were within his reach. Johnson agreed enthusiastically amid visions of new parks positioned along his tramlines, and organized meetings with National League players from Indianapolis, Philadelphia, New York, and Boston as they came to play in Cleveland.[162]

By August 12, Boston's wildly seesawing season saw the Beans drop five of eight games to the hopelessly inept Washington and Indianapolis before being humiliated 19–8 by Cleveland on August 15: Spiders' outfielder Larry Twitchell had a 6-for-6 day at the plate, with a single, a double, three triples and a home run, and Cleveland became the first National League team in history to score in all nine innings.[163] Before the Beaneaters moved on to Chicago, Boston part-owner James B. Billings telegraphed Hart, "What is the matter with this team? You are disgracing the Boston public!" Billings urged him to dispose of Madden, Johnston, Radbourn and new shortstop Pop Smith.[164] Hart further demoralized his players by publicly describing young pitcher Daley as a quitter and Madden a drunk.[165] But such public humiliation, particularly during the sojourn in the secessionist hothouse of Cleveland, did little but fuel the fire of the Players League rebels to escape their bondage.

Despite winning their final two games in Cleveland, the Beans' lead at the top of the standings had shrunk to one game, and with Kelly in a hitting slump and Clarkson severely overworked, Hardie Richardson was shifted to left field and Joe Quinn back to shortstop in desperation before the New York series on August 19. More than thirty-three thousand fans crammed the Old Polo Grounds to watch Boston draw the first game, then win the next two 12–2 and 10–4 behind Radbourn and Clarkson while their own boys hobbled about the diamond. The season was growing long and star Giants outfielder "Gorgeous George" Gore was lame, both Mickey Welch and Tim Keefe had sore arms, and a weary Ewing made two bad errors in each of the three games.[166] The result saw Boston draw two games ahead of New York with 59 wins; the two teams were clearing out on the field, Philadelphia their nearest challenger in third place on 51 victories.[167]

The most fiery series of the year came on August 26 in Philadelphia. On July 29, Kelly had infuriated Phillies captain Sid Farrar when, with two Phillies runners on base, home-run king Sam Thompson drove a ball to right field, a hit assumed to be a home run. But Kelly claimed the ball hit the top of the fence and bounced back; he threw it to the catcher and held all runners. A furious Farrar accused him of secreting a ball—a favored tactic of the King's—and Boston journalist Charles Foley reported disapprovingly, "Farrar's profanity [was] something awful when his Cuban blood was aroused."[168] But the charge was never proven and the result stood.[169] Farrer was obviously well aware of the King's reputation as a specialist in outfield trickery: once, with a game tied in extra innings, two men out and darkness falling, Kelly took off after an opposition hit, jumped and simulated the catch, then ran off the field. The umpire called the game for darkness. Later, a teammate asked Kelly how far the ball was hit. "How the hell would I know?" came the reply. "It was a mile over my head."[170] The return game between the Phillies and the Beans went to twelve innings before Dick Johnston singled Kelly in for the winning run, but *en route* Johnston failed to touch first base. First baseman Farrar went for the ball to tag Johnston, but Kelly got to the ball first "and the two big men fought for it in a tremendous row," Quinn observed from his post at shortstop.[171] Although Philadelphia fans mobbed Kelly, attacking him with canes, beer mugs, and fists, neither umpire had seen Johnston miss the base and the run scored.[172]

Ten thousand fans crowded into the new Polo Grounds stadium for the final New York–Boston series on August 30—under which duress the new grandstand shifted and nearly caused a stampede.[173] In 25 games in exile on Staten Island and Jersey City, the Giants had drawn a paltry 57,260 fans—in their next 38 games at their new central Manhattan home, they drew over 144,000.[174] Hundreds also made the journey down from Boston, including "General" Arthur Dixwell, whose piercing chant of "Hi, hi, hi" was imitated by the New York fans with sardonic roars of "Hey, hey, hey!" The travelers were rewarded when Clarkson defeated "Smilin' Mickey" Welch 6–4 on a Kelly sacrifice that redeemed an earlier base-running error.[175] Hardie Richardson gave them more to cheer for when he used a bat to smash Buck Ewing's mask to pieces after the big catcher dropped it on the plate in an attempt to impede Richardson from scoring. But it was Quinn who made a play "fit for a gold frame" in the ninth inning when he gloved Tiernan's high ball—the *Globe* praised him, "It made the little second baseman look as big as a Chinese giant."[176] Now three games behind, Keefe rallied New York and they defeated Radbourn 7–2 in the second game: although New York made nine errors, Hoss gave up fourteen hits and Boston managed only three. In the final game, fifteen thousand fans saw Clarkson give Boston a 6–0 lead after two innings, but a Kelly error in the third set off a New York rally and the Giants had tied it on the back of thirteen hits when the game was called for darkness.[177]

By the Labor Day double-header on September 1, Boston still had their noses in front by two wins, and celebrated the holiday with a pair of wins over Jack Glasscock and his "uncontrollable band of Hoosier Hottentots" at home in front of 19,000 ecstatic fans.[178] But the Indianapolis crew had their revenge in the third game, charging back from 7–2 down in the ninth inning to beat the Beans: Kid Madden, suffering with a chronic undiagnosed illness, was hammered for five hits and six runs, and even Foley was forced to concede that "a more disgruntled crowd of spectators never left the Boston grounds."[179] Quinn was back in the outfield—to his disgust—although correspondent Charles Foley praised him, "Joe Quinn is playing class A ball, so it looks as if Sprinter Brown will hold down the bench during the rest of the season."[180]

The Boston public obviously agreed. On September 11, Quinn was presented with a gold-inlaid bat as a tribute by the Bachelors' Club of Jamaica Plain.[181] While he promised the Bachelors he would try to hit a home run with it in the double-header against Cleveland the next day, the best he could do with a solitary hard-hit single past shortstop.[182] He was, however, involved in the most physical play of the day in the first inning of the second game. His own fumble had seen Patsy Tebeau make first base, and when the follow-up hitter, Bob Gilks, hit a high one out to Kelly in right field, the King's own tangle with the ball saw Gilks speeding for second by the time the ball was *en route* to Quinn. Joe snared the throw but lost sight of Gilks as he did so, stumbling backwards over the runner and ending up sitting squarely astride Gilks' back as he sprawled on the basepath. The *Globe* reported Quinn "triumphantly hit [Gilks] with the ball and grinned from ear to ear" as the runner was called out.[183] However, it was John Clarkson's heroics that day which truly placated the unhappy Boston rooters, when the iron-armed twirler won both games of the double-header using what the *Herald* called a "changeup big as an ice-wagon,"[184] allowing just ten hits in the 3–2 and 5–0 victories.[185] Clarkson, who had already won 38 games for the year, challenged Radbourn to repeat the feat next day: but Hoss lost the first game 3–0 and was forced to hit a ninth-inning home run himself to salvage a 4–4 draw in the nightcap game.[186] Clarkson won again on the 14th, but lost two days later in another savage confrontation with Philadelphia when Charlie Bennett was picked off in the ninth inning with clutch hitter Hardie Richardson at bat; the exhausted Clarkson had shut out the Phillies until the eighth inning on his fifth start in six days. It was a game characterized by squabbling, squalling, and fracas, with Mike Kelly exclaiming afterward, "I'm lucky to be alive! There may be a deal of motherly love in Philadelphia, but can't see where the 'brotherly' love comes in. It should be named the city of Cowardly Love."[187]

New York was now in front of the Beans by a mere 0.006 percent, each having 74 wins and 14 games clear of third-placed Philadelphia.[188] With two weeks remaining in the season, the atmosphere in Boston was desperate. On September 17, the *Boston Globe* offered the Beaneaters $1,000 to win the pennant,[189] and when the Beans went on the road two days later, the Music Hall downtown opened its doors so anxious fans could receive "live telegrams" with updates on their team's progress.[190] The overworked John Clarkson was still battling gamely toward the ultimate prize, defeating Washington on both September 19 and 20 but only managing a draw on the 21st in a twelve-inning marathon—his reward, New

York went ahead by one game. Hart finally rested Clarkson on September 22, but only reluctantly, damning his other pitchers—Madden and Daly–as "useless," and Radbourn "unable to be depended upon."[191]

• • •

"The flywheel is the anarchist of mechanics. It is always engaged in revolutions."
—Peppermint Drops, *Omaha Daily Bee*, July 28, 1889[192]

The deceptive innocence in Joe Quinn's gray eyes, his quiet dignity and detachment from the bad behavior of many of his associates, belied the headfirst manner in which he both played and watched the game. Thrust straight into the public spotlight from the moment of his arrival in the Hub, Quinn delivered lively and often acerbic media commentary during the 1889 season that gave a candid glimpse into the realities of life as a professional ball player—the release of Boston veteran Joe Hornung in January for his "unruly tongue" obviously no deterrent.[193] But Quinn's literary *coup de grace* exploded in *The Sporting News* on September 21, 1889. Whisperings and hints of a possible player breakaway, including an indiscreet slip from Al Johnson's brother Will,[194] had been ignored by National League owners as merely another ploy for increased salaries. But they could no longer turn a blind eye when *TSN* published a letter from a "leading Boston player" fully disclosing the Players League plan: "In the spring I wrote you that we contemplated a strike.... To strike then would be to break our contracts and rob us of the sympathy of the public. We concluded to start an association of our own and ask no more favor from the directors of the league. It will not only give the public good ball playing, but every player will work with a will knowing that he is directly interested in the gate receipts. I could have told you a lot of this before but I wanted to get all the facts so you could depend on anything I told you ... no matter what happens, do not mention my name in connection with this letter."[195]

The dispatch was anonymous, but Quinn's closeness and ongoing correspondence with editor Al Spink made him a plumb candidate for authorship—and he was later identified as having penned the letter.[196] While this premature leak may have exposed the underbelly of the Players League and gave the National League owners sufficient time to counterattack, Boston Hall of Famer George Wright[197] was quick to defend the announcement: "[The scheme] is too far gone to be affected.... League clubs have no claim on their players after their contracts run out in October. Yes, it will mean the present Boston Club will have the fine ball grounds and no team to play on it."[198]

Quinn had correctly gauged the level of public sympathy behind the players and wrote Spink purely to garner extra support; in turn, Spink, who Quinn described as "always a friend to professional baseball players,"[199] was heartily delighted and splashed his front page with the headline: "The greatest move in the history of the national game. The players to start an organization of their own,"[200] lauding the players at the head of the scheme as "the brainiest in America."[201] Spink also marveled the National League owners appeared to have had no inkling of just what was going to happen next season (or else they would have been "shaking in their shoes"[202]). Al Spalding was furious at the report, and was quick to rebuke the rebels, "Tell [the dissidents] if they were thinking of it, to get capital of at least half a million dollars, as the National League will outdraw them two to one and they will get sick of it before the season was half over."[203] He did offer to meet Ward for mediation talks on September 29, but Ward gleefully declined and no Brotherhood members signed National League contracts in September.[204]

The Brotherhood formally announced their intention to withdraw their members from the National League on November 6, 1889, after which Secretary Tim Keefe wrote, "Heroic treatment was necessary to rid the game of its most disagreeable features—selling, buying and clumsy transferring of players, the reserve rule and classification system.... In the day when the National League had a chance to show it cared for the game when not associated with its own profit, the National League's exhibition was a mean and miserable one."[205]

• • •

The courageous arm of John Clarkson was now almost the only thing keeping Boston in the pennant race. He and Radbourn beat off the visiting Chicago on September 23, but Clarkson lost the following day and New York drew level at the top of the standings.[206] Team owner William Conant now traveled with the Boston team to enforce discipline, particularly where Kelly was concerned, pulling out all stops to ensure an indiscretion did not cost the team its greatest prize. Boston scored four runs in the seventh inning to beat Cleveland 6–3 on the 26th, again behind Clarkson, who had won seven of nine starts since the 18th—but New York remained ahead by 0.003 percent by tying 3–3 with Pittsburgh.[207] New York's record was 80–43 to Boston's 79–42, each having five games left. Clarkson reinstated Boston in the lead on October 1, beating off Cleveland 8–5 in spite of three Kelly errors in right field. The King celebrated by slipping the Conant leash and guzzling whiskey at a party held by Al Johnson, and although the Clevelanders vehemently denied Boston's accusation of a deliberate play on Kelly's weakness for drink, the next day Kelly was both hung over and in disgrace.[208] It was a horrible day. Kelly derided his own team from the bench when they fell three runs behind. "You never win when I don't play," he boomed. "Kelly is King. I am a king." He even had the Cleveland crowd stamping and booing and chanting along with him until he was thrown out of the park after he attacked plate umpire John McQuaid for calling Hardie Richardson out on a close slide at the plate. The Beans lost the game 7–1.[209]

Clarkson was utterly demoralized by Kelly's bizarre antics, and his exhausted arm now hung like a limp rag after every pitch. He was ill with a bad chest cold in Pittsburgh two days later, but Kid Madden won 4–3 to close the gap to one game behind New York.[210] Boston wanted to schedule a double-header at Pittsburgh on October 5, the last day of the season. New York had one game in hand—if Boston won two, the pennant would be theirs. In desperation, James Hart offered Cleveland pitcher Henry Gruber and catcher Cy Sutcliffe $500 each to keep New York at bay, while Giants manager Jim Mutrie promised the Pittsburgh boys new suits if they could beat Boston, and caught an overnight train to Pittsburgh to watch the game, ready to wire to Cleveland if Boston were going to play an extra game so the Giants could also play one.[211]

Gruber and Sutcliffe never got their thousand dollars, with Cleveland beaten 6–3 on a Tim Keefe six-hit performance. So fittingly, the season came down to John Clarkson. Six thousand breathless fans packed the Boston Music Hall to "watch" the Pirates game, almost roaring the roof off when incoming telegrams proclaimed each of King Kelly's three hits. But greater was the despair as Boston made five errors behind a coughing, laboring Clarkson. He had won a staggering 49 games for the year but this, his nineteenth loss, was the game fans would most remember: the 6–1 defeat handed the pennant on a platter to New York.[212]

The Globe gave Boston their $1,000 anyway,[213] for there was much to like about their season despite the disappointing finale. The Braves had averaged 4,400 fans at each of their 67 home games, outdrawing New York almost two to one,[214] and had also won 48 of these games, the most of any club.[215] John Clarkson led the league in almost every category: wins

7. Back on the Big Stage

Despite paying almost $25,000 for the services of King Kelly, John Clarkson, and Joe Quinn, the Boston Beaneaters fell two games short of the National League pennant in 1889, losing out to the New York Giants. Joe Quinn stands at the far left of the back row. Also featured are Hall of Famers Dan Brouthers (back row, fourth left), Hoss Radbourn (middle row, second left), John Clarkson (middle row, third left), and King Kelly (middle row, third right) (National Baseball Hall of Fame Library, Cooperstown, New York).

(49), win-loss percentage (.721), ERA (2.73), strikeouts (284), complete games (68), shutouts (8), and innings pitched (620, a staggering 200 more than his nearest rival, Harry Staley of Pittsburgh).[216] Dan Brouthers won the league batting crown with a .373 average, from Jack Glasscock (Indianapolis; .359) and Cap Anson (Chicago; .341).[217] Quinn finished 34th in the league batting rankings on .261, hitting 13 doubles (Kelly led the league with 41), 5 triples and 2 home runs.[218] He was ranked seventh of ten second basemen in the league (.925 fielding average), but played only 47 games there, as opposed to his rivals, many of whom played 120 or more. Most of his season (63 games) had been spent at shortstop, but his clear dislike for that appointment evidenced in his ninth-placed league ranking and paltry .860 fielding average, well below the league median of .888.[219]

Despite their team's many individual heroics, the Boston public demanded a scapegoat for the loss of the pennant. Clarkson (who had quite literally shouldered the most significant workload in the league), Hardie Richardson, and Charlie Bennett were all absolved, but Kelly, Kid Madden, Dick Johnston, Hoss Radbourn and even Joe Quinn were ridiculed in the *New York Sun* as "lushers" and frequently in no condition to play.[220] *The Sporting Life* dismissed these claims as "rot,"[221] with no evidence linking Quinn to the habitual dissipation of his teammates, despite his close friendship with Kelly. But amid accusations Hart had no

The debonair John Clarkson, who would win 49 of his 68 starts for Boston in 1889—worth every penny of the $10,000 Boston paid to secure his services from the Chicago White Stockings. Despite his election to the Hall of Fame, Clarkson was a tragic figure who would end his days in an asylum in 1909, aged just 33 (National Baseball Hall of Fame Library, Cooperstown, New York).

Charles Radbourn's moniker of "Old Hoss" was eminently suitable. Another product of the Dubuque Rabbits, he was the workhorse of the National League. He won the 1884 National League pitching triple crown and was renowned for his ability to regularly pitch two games in a day. Radbourn was one of baseball's last great underarm hurlers, and was elected to the Baseball Hall of Fame in 1939. He is pictured here in 1889 while a teammate of Joe Quinn's in Boston (National Baseball Hall of Fame Library, Cooperstown, New York).

control over the players and their *savoir-vivre*, Boston owner William Conant declared the real problem was the players' preoccupation with unionism and the Players' League, that thorn in the owners' sides which refused to go away[222]; Conant brought out the whetstone to sharpen his axe.

As it turned out, the Brotherhood did his job for him. Many of his stars—including all of the "lushers," Kelly, Madden, Johnston, Radbourn and the apparently blameless Quinn—refused to re-sign with the National League, and on November 24, Ward telegraphed Quinn and his St. Louis–based colleagues to say he would be in town in two days with Brotherhood contracts in his inside pocket. Despite being detained by other business,

Ward deputized Columbus pitcher Mark Baldwin—that old Duluth stager—to call on the rebel sympathizers and obtain the signatures of Quinn, "Bug" Halliday, and Baldwin's own catcher Jack O'Connor.[223] "I have signed a Brotherhood contract," Baldwin told the *Pittsburg Dispatch*, "because I believe it's going to be the greatest and squarest baseball organization ever established."[224] But Quinn, despite his long allegiance to the Brotherhood and being "pretty sore" over the loss of the pennant,[225] hesitated at the last moment in following the lead of his friends and conspirators. With most of his savings invested in St. Louis property, he was suddenly extremely nervous about the threat of the litigation from the National League,[226] and it took much of Baldwin's persuasive power to convince him to proceed. And while he did sign on the dotted line, at least he could be sure of one thing: he had been offered only a one-year National League contract back at the start of the season and therefore, despite his defection to the Players, his reputation for never having broken a contract remained intact.[227]

8. Rebellion!—The Players' League

> *"Undismayed by opposition, undaunted by desertions, unmoved by all the bluff and bluster a powerful enemy could devise, in the face of obstacles which might have crushed a less just or weaker cause, the new movement and its men went fearlessly on, turning neither to the right nor left, stooping to no dishonorable action, until today the Players' League stands brightly forth as the strongest group of eight clubs in playing talent and general personnel ever gathered together, and the representation of all that is manly and honest in baseball."*
> —John Montgomery Ward, 1890

It was part industrial revolution, part barefaced public popularity contest.

By February 25, 1890, the Players' League had materialized from a pipe dream into bricks-and-mortar reality. The secessionists had invaded seven of the National League's most important cities—Boston, New York, Brooklyn, Philadelphia, Pittsburgh, Cleveland, and Chicago—and had also set up a new franchise in Buffalo. They purloined 78 players from the National League and 24 from the American Association, and while the National League still had 40 more players on its books, more than half of their 153 men were drawn from the ranks of minor leaguers and untested hopefuls, whereas the Brotherhood claimed only one in ten of their men were no-names.[1]

The Players were well aware the only way they would outdraw the National League in 1890 was with star power, being at such a disadvantage in weight of numbers, infrastructure, and governance experience. While the pro–League papers sneered, "Only five of the 78 pilfered National Leaguers are genuine stars and the entire lot could have been dropped out of the League this year and their places filled with other men in minor leagues without disturbing to any appreciable extent the quality of League ball playing,"[2] this was little more than propaganda. Among those to sign with the Players were future Hall of Famers King Kelly, Dan Brouthers, Hoss Radbourn, Buck Ewing, Roger Connor, Tim Keefe, Charlie Comiskey, Connie Mack, and Ned Hanlon. In addition, crowd favorites Joe Quinn, Arlie Latham, Dummy Hoy, and Fred Dunlap had all put pen to paper, further bolstering the popular appeal of the rebel competition.[3]

However, amongst this glut of stars was a notable absentee in Cap Anson. Ted Sullivan later recalled, "The players of the League ship were deserting it in this terrible storm by getting onboard the Brotherhood craft, but the form of big Anson was still seen on the National League ship, refusing to leave her, ready to sink with her if she went down."[4] The batting champion had a significant stock holding in the Chicago White Stockings, and despite the

Left: "Smiling Tim" Keefe was the National League's leading hurler in 1888, winning 35 games at a miserly ERA of 1.74. He still ranks in the top ten all-time pitchers for lifetime victories. Keefe was also a leading advocate for player rights and a key figure in the 1890 Players' League revolt (National Baseball Hall of Fame Library, Cooperstown, New York). *Right:* As well remembered for his staunch opposition to the reserve clause as for his prowess as a pitcher and shortstop, John "Monte" Ward was as astute off the field as he was on it, having earned a law degree at Columbia University in 1885 (National Baseball Hall of Fame Library, Cooperstown, New York).

fact all but two of his men left to join the Players, he refused to betray the National League as they, he felt, had betrayed their old employer. But while Anson stood on the burning deck, wealthy and influential men were lining up to back the secessionists. On January 16, 1890, Samuel Gompers, president of the American Federation of Labor, and three other union leaders all pledged support for the rebels at a meeting in Philadelphia. Albert Johnson, the Cleveland transport magnate, had lost none of his own enthusiasm for the scheme, with visions of revenue dancing before his eyes and a Players' League park to be built right alongside one of his major streetcar lines.[5] Millionaire St. Louis Browns owner Chris Von der Ahe also favored the Players' League after Al Spink convinced him of its potential profitability, but Ward would have nothing to do with the obstreperous German, whom he dismissed as "talking too much."[6] Even politicians, it seemed, were siding with the rebels: on May 4, 1890, a Boston newspaper canvassed the Massachusetts House of Representatives about the struggle for superiority on the city's ballfields, and of its 106 members, 100 publicly declared support for the Brotherhood.[7]

By late December 1889, eight rebel clubs were formally organized and new parks hastily constructed on vacant lots. Each club had an eight-member board (four men elected by the players and four by their backers), and the new League was governed by a sixteen-man senate headed by realtor Edwin A. McAlpin. The gate was split equally between teams (with the home team keeping profits from concessions), and a profit-sharing arrangement agreed upon, in which the first $10,000 profit to went to players on the top four teams, the next $10,000 to the owners, the third $80,000 to remaining players, and anything further split between players and owners. There was no reserve clause or classification rule, and simple oaths of good behavior replaced the blacklist.[8]

With such generous employment conditions laid out before them, the defectors were mostly loyal to the rebel league and refused huge inducements from the National League and American Association to return. Al Spalding tempted Kelly with $10,000 to jump back to the White Stockings, an offer the King took great delight in refusing.[9] But such a flow of ready money was too great a temptation for some—a number of players changed sides up to three times, with the National League offering three-year contracts, inflated salaries, and hints at abolition of the classification rule.[10] The Brotherhood barred the jumpers and also punished those original union members who had backed out at the last minute, as Quinn had considered doing. On December 18, 1889, John Clarkson, Kid Gleason, and Jack Glasscock were expelled, and while Jake Beckley and Ed Delahanty were also debarred, the pair eventually jumped back to the Players' League and were reinstated, despite vehement protests from the "Brothers" who had remained loyal. A written remonstration urging non-reinstatement of any deserters was tendered on March 28, 1890, and it was signed by twelve Brotherhood stalwarts, including Joe Quinn, whose faith in the outfit was clearly restored.[11]

As the season opening approached, these internal problems were compounded by ongoing legal action from the National League, determined to reclaim what it felt was its rightful property, despite already being denied three times in the courts.[12] And while the rebels had the advantage of popular players on its books, Al Spink pointed out the National League "had the best of the battle in leaders and experienced generals,"[13] and it was these battle-scarred campaigners who shifted the inter-league war into the press. The breakaway competition, and Ward in particular, were publicly criticized by such heavyweights as Henry Chadwick and Al Spalding as secretive, ungrateful, and secessionist. The National League also sneered at the mutineers' reliance on gate-takings to pay salaries, deliberately scheduling games to clash with the Players' League: Pittsburgh president William A. Nimick threatened on February 1, 1890, "If I had my way, I would duplicate all the home games of the Brotherhood clubs."[14] When the official National League schedule was released on March 6, it was, startlingly, a *ten*-team schedule that included the Brooklyn and Cincinnati franchises from the American Association. This proved to be a ruse to divert the Players, as the National League fielded but eight teams when the season commenced, but the rebels hit back by bidding to use National League grounds to force up the opposition rent. They also adopted a two-umpire system (despite the added cost), introduced a livelier ball, and increased the pitching distance from 55½' to 57' to add to the spectacle and excitement of their games.[15] And Joe Quinn, fiercely loyal to the Brotherhood, struck back at the League with his own personal campaign: on May 27, 1890, the *Boston Globe* complained, "The Globe would like to see Joe Quinn stop singing 'Tommy, Bring Your Wages Home,'" a provocative tune favored by unionists which Quinn would sing at the top of his marvelous tenor whenever in earshot of reporters.[16]

• • •

In the northeast, the "Outlaw Boston Reds" had placed Kelly at the helm of the breakaway club, and he was joined by many of the old Beaneaters—Tom Brown (arguably the best right fielder and baserunner of the time), the timeless Hoss Radbourn, club stalwarts Billy Nash and Dick Johnston, and public favorite Joe Quinn. Accompanied by the New York rebels, the Reds sailed south to Savannah, Georgia, in March 1890 for a series of barnstorming exhibition games. The weather was summer-like and the atmosphere festive as they booked into the fancy De Soto Hotel in preparation for their triumphal march. Even the *New York World* admitted that the two squads, led by Kelly and Ewing, "looked a lot like the powerhouse National League teams of old."[17] But that very same day, March 18, back in a gray and wintry Boston, the National League loyalists were reporting to manager Selee at the YMCA gymnasium to prepare for the upcoming struggle for public affection. And the League partisans had retained plenty of stars of their own, including the eschewed John Clarkson, rising pitcher Kid Nichols, catcher Charlie Bennett, and young second baseman Bobby "Link" Lowe[18]—a man Joe Quinn would come to know rather too well in ensuing years.

The southern exhibition tour, however, proved so profitable for the Reds that they were able to pay for a brand-new park to be built on Congress Street, on a piece of reclaimed land not far from the Fort Point Channel on Boston Harbor.[19] And so, a-brim with confidence, the outlaws relocated from the South End Grounds to their new and distinctive home, with even the veterans kicking up their heels like colts, overjoyed at freedom from the harness of the oppressor. Hoss Radbourn, now 35 years of age and with his arm as worn as a soldier's boot, declared to Kelly he was ready to pitch at least three times a week.[20] The only hitch for the outlaws came three days before their opening series against Brooklyn, when Joe Quinn had his nose broken at practice by a bad throw from catcher Morg' Murphy.[21] It would be six years before Louisville's Pete Cassidy became the first player in major league history to be X-rayed,[22] so Quinn had to endure the pain of having his nose reset manually. Despite looking more like a groggy prizefighter than a ballplayer, with blotches of bruise surrounding both his eyes, Quinn played in a practice match at Fall River the following day, April 17, and had little choice but to line up against Brooklyn on April 19, half-sighted as he was: while there were many advantages to signing on with the Players' League, his contract decreed he had no claim to wages if he was injured or ill.[23] The pain proved worthwhile, however, with a Quinn sacrifice over first base bringing Billy Nash home for the winning run in a ninth inning 3–2 victory.[24]

Two weeks into the season and the Brotherhood had had by far the best attendances of the four big leagues. Boston had won eight of their eleven games and Chicago six of nine; while there was already talk of the Reds and Chicago clearing out on the field,[25] Boston had taken the lead in the pennant race at the end of April and Chicago quickly fell away. Apart from brief periods tied with New York during June, the Reds were never headed, charging away to finish the season six games in front of their nearest rivals, Ward's Brooklyn Wonders. For the Reds' second baseman, it was a glory year: 1890 was Joe Quinn's first .300 season in a major league, in which he hit seven home runs, scored 87 times, and drove in 82 RBIs at an average of .301 (the league average was .274).[26] He crossed the hallowed 100-hit mark on August 9,[27] making 153 for the season (second only to teammate Hardie Richardson, who clubbed 181), and stealing a career-high 29 bases for good measure.[28] With almost all players now wearing gloves, Joe also led the league in fielding average from his 130 games at second base. Charlie Comiskey, by now a noted authority on infield play, later wrote, "Only players with a natural aptitude for baseball can become successful infielders. A good mechanical player, who can hit at a fair clip, may make good and hold a position in the outfield, but when he comes into the diamond, he must be a quick thinker, a fast fielder and a natural player as well."[29] It was Quinn's 431 putouts and 395 assists at an average of .942, well above

The 1890 Boston Players' League "Outlaw Reds." While the League only lasted one year, it was an aggregation of some of the nineteenth century's great players. The Boston team alone featured Hall of Famers King Kelly, Hoss Radbourn, and Dan Brouthers. Joe Quinn (middle row, second from right) led the league in fielding average at second base (National Baseball Hall of Fame Library, Cooperstown, New York).

the league average of .913 and ahead of such luminaries as Fred Pfeffer and Lou Bierbauer, which earned the little fellow praise as the greatest middle-infielder among the seditious crew. The *Globe* had forgiven Quinn his choice of tune and lavished him with praise on October 11: "Joe Quinn, aged 26 years, 5'8", 160 lb, is the most valuable second base man in the Players' League. His sacrificing won many a game, he is among the leaders in batting, has the highest fielding average of the Players' League and tries for everything. He has been a gold find." In addition to these individual honors, Quinn's contribution to the pennant-winning Boston team was generously acknowledged by the *Globe*, when it described him as "first, last and always for the success of the team."[30]

It was a year in which individual brilliance was *de rigueur* in the struggle for column inches and public pennies, and the Players carved out plenty of monuments to their short-lived venture. The rebel hitters were clearly relishing the new lively ball, for on June 2, Cleveland's Ed Delahanty went six-for-six with five runs scored in a 20–7 thumping of Chicago,[31] and on July 23, Boston's leading slugger Harry Stovey hit the one hundredth home run of his career, the first major league player to achieve this milestone.[32] On the mound, Hoss Radbourn had found a career second wind and both pitched and fielded in wonderful style, several times making half a dozen assists in a game and making some timely hits of his own.

His 27–12 record, at a respectable ERA of 3.13, was third in the League.[33] On May 8, Cleveland's Willie McGill hurled a complete-game 14–5 victory over Buffalo. Aged just 16, he was the youngest pitcher ever to perform the feat, and against an impressive Buffalo lineup including Connie Mack, Dummy Hoy, and the redoubtable Deacon White. At 42, White was the oldest player in the major leagues and destined, with Mack, for the Hall of Fame.[34] But with the increased pitching distance and ball lively as a rabbit, pitchers generally had a bad time of it in 1890. On July 26, Buffalo hurler Charles "Lady" Baldwin gave up 14 runs in the sixth inning to Philadelphia, yet remained in the game to concede a whopping total of 28 hits and lose 30 runs to 12.[35] Buffalo was on the wrong end of another walloping when a youngster whom history records only as Lewis showed up at the Brooklyn park on July 12, and was given a tryout by the Bisons. He was battered for 13 hits and walked seven in his three innings, and left the game with 20 runs marked down beside his name. Buffalo rallied after his departure, but were still humiliated 28–16.[36]

◆ ◆ ◆

Such entertainment aside, all three major leagues were suffering declining attendances by mid–July. Each league falsified attendance figures as part of the ongoing propaganda war—the Players' League claimed to have drawn 980,887 fans for the season, over the National League's 813,678, with the American Association trailing with approximately 500,000 fans passing through its gates.[37] But Spalding would send his spies to count real Players' League attendances and he gleefully published them against the inflated figures, and it was public disgust at such constant public wrangling which saw attendances in all leagues plummet.[38] National League New York owner John B. Day was forced to go cap in hand to the League in July, pleading for $80,000 to enable him not to sell out to the Players' League. Spalding, Anson, and John T. Brush came to the rescue, but not before Cincinnati owner Aaron Stern was also forced to sell out to the Players' League for just $40,000.[39]

In a final attempt to mediate the schism between the major leagues, three Players' League owners and Albert C. Johnson met Spalding and John B. Day on October 9 as the season concluded. But the National League had no intention of negotiating with the rebels. While they had publicly and commercially undermined the rebels during the season, they saved their killing blow for the capitalist flank of the breakaway league. Spalding tricked the Brotherhood into believing consolidation could happen on a three-way equal footing, and many of the Players' backers eagerly tried to make deals with the National League, but all without consulting the players.[40] Infuriated at such disloyalty, the Brotherhood met on October 20, with Ward making a long, spirited plea for the players' participation in the negotiations. But he was shouted down by Al Spalding, and the three league committees voted 2–1 against the players' involvement in any future negotiations.[41]

It was the bottom line which finally determined the fate of the Players' League. The venture had lost around $340,000,[42] a deficit from which most backers were unable or unwilling to recover. In November, the league was officially dissolved. Each backer left to make his own deal to escape the financial wreckage: the better-resourced National League swept the Players cleaner than a spinster's parlor. Pittsburgh joined Allegheny of the National League. The rival New York clubs were consolidated, and the rebel Chicago outfit was sold to Spalding's White Stockings; many of these players were never paid.[43] The National League and American Association proceeded to scrap the remaining Players' League clubs, with the powerhouse Boston first on their radar.

Blame for the failure of this brief excursion into self-management by ballplayers was apportioned in many directions. Al Spink identified problems with both the leadership and business plan of the league, particularly the "absence of a strong leader in a crisis, and dependency on anticipated profit."[44] An angry and humiliated Ward struck back, claiming "stupidity, avarice and treachery" had undone his grand scheme.[45] But Chicago sportswriter and Players' League secretary F.H. Brunell admitted major business mistakes had undermined the rebel scheme, with clubs needing at least $50,000 in stock at commencement, rather than the average $20,000 each outfit had raised. They should, Brunell confessed, have also fought the National League on their own terms by vigorously retrieving players who were tempted back.[46] And in the adoption of a purist philosophy, banning Sunday ball and beer in Players' League parks and charging fifty cents admission, the rebels effectively precluded the blue-collar fans whose grassroots support (and quarters) may well have ensured their survival.[47]

In December 1890, Joe Quinn wrote a friend in Boston (with tongue firmly in cheek) that he deserved a raise in salary for 1891. *The Sporting Life*, however, noted sadly, "Wonder if Joe reads the papers? Salaries will take a drop all round next year."[48] The war had done little to further the case of player rights, and in some cases had hurt it badly. The collapse of the Players League and consolidation or elimination of its franchises left many players unemployed, and those lucky enough to sign League contracts were in a poor position to bargain over salaries. The final humiliation was the introduction of a new National Agreement in late 1890, which introduced only the mildest of industrial reforms: the two established major leagues would be joined by the Western Association, a three-member board was instated to approve all player contracts and hear disputes, and, as a last kick at the downed rebels, the reserve clause was retained.[49]

It was left to Al Spink to record this melancholy footnote to the affair in *The National Game*: "Their names will go down in history as those of a lot of brave fellows who believed in standing by one another and who lost out in the battle—not because their hearts were not in the right place."[50]

Unionism in Australian Baseball

While Joe Quinn was a participant in one of sport's earliest industrial revolutions, and the Brotherhood of Professional Base Ball Players holds the distinction of being the first attempt by sportspersons worldwide to act collectively in defense of their employment rights,[51] Quinn's homeland of Australia has its own history of attempts at player unionism.

After an excursion into interstate competition post–World War II through the long-running Claxton Shield tournament, the Australian Baseball League (ABL) was formed in 1989, almost 150 years after the sport made its first appearance on the Victorian goldfields.[52] In 1989, no Australian player had succeeded Joe Quinn in securing a place on an American major league roster, and the new ABL took on a primarily amateur mantle, despite logistic, financial, and player support from Major League Baseball in the U.S.[53] Domestic governance by the Australian Baseball Federation (ABF) permitted some forms of player payments, but these were heavily constrained by the ABF's membership of the International Baseball Federation, the governing body of amateur baseball. It was this ambiguity of mission and organization that prompted the first attempt at unionization by Australian baseball players, five years after the inauguration of the ABL.

The League played a 42-game season in its opening year of 1989, with 20 rostered players in each club sharing payments totaling A$1,000 per game. But by 1993, despite increases in both the cost of living and the number of games per season to 64, this salary cap remained unchanged and the financial burden on ABL players was significant. Clause 6b of the standard ABL contract required players to make themselves available for road trips throughout Australia during the summer, often necessitating taking unpaid leave from their employers. The clause also demanded players fund their own medical insurance, relocation expenses, gym memberships and physiotherapy, and precluded players from individual promotion or sponsorship deals. Player payments were not made during the eight-week spring training period, and the standard contract featured a version of the reserve rule, a one-year one-way renewal clause which gave clubs perpetual ownership of players.[54] As a consequence, most players earned less than $1,000 for the entire six-month season; at the time, the average income of an Australian family was between $890 and $1,090 per week, or $391 for single-person households,[55] and the median cost of renting in a major city such as Sydney was between $180 and $320 per week alone.[56]

During the 1990s, most professional sports in Australia had formed player associations, including the professional codes of Australian Football, cricket, and soccer. In addition, the popular amateur game of netball—with one of the highest participation rates in Australia—had also formed an organization to represent players in the National Netball League.[57] In 1994, Sydney Blues utility player and law student David Hynes, together with teammate Mark Shipley and Ronald Finley of legal firm Corrs Chambers Westgarth, announced the formation of the Australian Baseball Players Association (ABPA)—the twenty-seventh attempt at unionism to protect the employment rights of sportspersons in Australia.

The ABPA described the $42,000 salary cap a "most pressing concern for all players,"[58] as was the fight for free agency (which had been introduced into Major League Baseball in 1976), abolition of the reserve clause, funding for medical insurance and ancillary costs, and distribution of royalties from marketing and promotion. Stefan Kamasz, president of the Australian Baseball League, welcomed the creation of the APBA and said "the league would be happy to work with a Players Association which acted responsibly, and was more than pleased to negotiate with it in seeking to further the league's development."[59] However, it was without entering into formal negotiations with the ABPA that the ABL increased the salary cap over the subsequent three seasons to $50,000.

The ABPA adopted an unwieldy 22-member executive, constituting around ten percent of all ABL players, a very high proportion of rank and file participation in decision-making processes. However, it was not player participation but player apathy which most threatened the organizational viability of the ABPA. Most members were "too busy to attend to the needs of the organisation."[60] Lack of capital was also a fatal blow as players balked at the $25 joining fee and $50 in annual dues. By 1996, the APBA collapsed—a not-unprecedented event in Australian sports union history. At the time, only four of the preceding 26 attempts at player associations were still in existence.[61]

A second attempt to form a baseball player's union in 1997, led by Adelaide lawyer Timothy Charles White, also foundered on player apathy.[62] According to industrial relations historian Braham Dabscheck, the competing demands of playing, employment, and family often precluded voluntary involvement by amateur athletes in further commitments. Membership subscriptions were far too low to provide working capital or employ staff to work for the members, and in addition, the geographical dispersal of association members in large countries such Australia exacerbated the difficulty of meetings.[63]

There have been no further attempts to form player associations in Australian baseball to date (up to and including 2013).

9. Mateship

"You know, I'm Australian, and we've got the worst sense of humor. We're cruel to each other."
—Steve Irwin

The chaos and acrimony that accompanied the collapse of the Players' League hung like smoke after a great fire across the baseball world into 1891. The ash crept relentlessly into every crack and cranny, choking off the smoothly triumphal march of the National League machine and setting it to spewing smoke and bile at its remaining rival, the American Association. And it infected the players, grinding into the gears of old friendships and alliances as men struggled to realign themselves in the disorder and uncertainty.

The legacy of the Players' League was anything but peace. After putting the last of the Players' League clubs to the sword, the American Association and National League went immediately to war, invading each other's cities and stealing players with abandon as they fought like titans for public supremacy. The National League went toe to toe with the Association on their own terms by finally permitting "quarter ball" (25-cent admission), and assigned their clubs to openly target certain players for acquisition: Pittsburgh earned its present nickname of Pirates by spiriting Pete Browning and Scott Stratton away from American Association strugglers Louisville.[1] The Association had its revenge by establishing a franchise in Boston and stocking it with former Brotherhood players from both Boston and Philadelphia, despite a previous agreement to return all Brotherhood players to their former clubs.[2] For some players, particularly among the St. Louis Browns, the strife was the perfect excuse to escape domestic torment—many took advantage of high-salary offers from the National League simply to escape the volatile owner, Chris Von der Ahe.[3] In February, the American Association withdrew from the National Agreement in protest against the League's destructive campaign against it.[4]

Joe Quinn rejoined the Boston National League outfit, and his inclusion made the front page of the *Boston Globe* on February 20: "Joe Quinn, Boston's famous second baseman, has finally decided to cast his lot with the Boston league team for the season of 1891. The following telegram explains itself: 'T.H. Murnane, Boston Globe: I have kept my word with J.B. Billings and signed a Boston league contract tonight. JOE QUINN.'"[5] It was a decision that elevated eyebrows. "Quinn, it is said, will only receive $2,000 from the local club, and could have signed for $3,300 with the St. Louis Browns!" marveled *The Sporting Life*. "What magnate would have acted likewise under similar circumstances?" But the choice was self-evident, even to the popular press. "He had given his word," *The Sporting Life* concluded rather gloomily, "and that settled it. This does more credit to Quinn's heart than to his head."[6]

The St. Louis Browns did not provide the sole test of Quinn's heart and loyalty. The *Boston Globe* mused, "Quinn was a warm Brotherhood man and a good friend of Mike Kelly, so many expected him to go back to the Congress St. grounds,[7] but he was a man of his word." After his defection to the Players' League, King Kelly had received a very cool reception from Frank Selee at the Boston National League club in 1891. In typically insouciant fashion, Kelly packed his kit for Cincinnati, where he spent the first half of 1891 defiantly captaining "Kelly's Killers" in the American Association. Kelly also openly acted as an agent for the Association, signing Dan Brouthers, Hardie Richardson, Billy Nash, and Bill Daley to AA contracts with Boston in February,[8] and turning to St. Louis next to hunt down Joe Quinn to play second base.[9] It was the first time Quinn had ever refused Kelly anything. He had promised his services to Selee's outfit, and even the famous cajoling and inveigling of his greatest friend would not change his mind. Joe Quinn was that rarest of commodities in nineteenth-century baseball—a player who placed principle before pay, and now, it seemed, even before friendship.

Quinn was not the only one to rebuff the King, however. Former Players' League heavyweight and new Pittsburgh National League manager Ned Hanlon dismissed Kelly's actions contemptuously. "Kelly is mad simply because Ward has been so much noticed lately, while nobody has apparently been aware of Kelly's existence," he told the *Pittsburg Dispatch* on February 19. "Kelly is killing himself. He likes to be looked up to as the king, and since he has been treated as an ordinary being he has become mad at himself."[10] But the shenanigans did not end there. When the Killers went bankrupt mid-season, Kelly signed with none other than Boston—but for its American Association franchise, perhaps the ultimate nose-thumbing gesture to his detractors. It was August before the National League made him an offer he could no longer refuse—and, perhaps unsurprisingly, the staggering offer came out of the seemingly infinite coffers at Boston. On a two-year $25,000 contract, Kelly returned to the Braves, chortling, "The National League can no longer think small beer of me!"[11] Although Kelly's hard-living lifestyle had taken a toll and he looked portly and bloated, his impact was immediate. Late in his first game back, with opposition runners on base, a high fly ball was popped up near the Boston dugout. Kelly leapt off the bench, snatched catcher Morg' Murphy's mitt and yelled, "Kelly now catching for Boston!" Kelly took the catch to make third out and squelch a comeback.[12] The League was quick to amend the rules so no changes in the lineup were valid unless formally announced by the umpire.

While war continued to rage around them, many of the fallen Boston Players' Leaguers returned to the South End Grounds.[13] The Beaneaters' manager, Hall of Famer Frank Selee, handled the team for nine years and led them to five National League pennants between 1891 and 1898. Selee's scientific approach to coaching was quite revolutionary in the late nineteenth century: he had the players practice their swings in front of mirrors and took still photographs to improve their technique. He also bought a pitching machine, a fearsome contraption that fired out balls by exploding a cartridge. But just as important as his methods was his nature. Al Spink said, "Few men were ever more popular.... Frank Selee was a gentleman by birth and breeding. His methods were of the quiet kind. He ruled his players gently, yet firmly. He believed the best results could be secured by bestowing confidence in his men, and it was rare indeed that his confidence was misplaced."[14]

One of Selee's most valuable contributions to the Bostons in 1891 was to recruit a young pitcher to bear the burden previously shouldered by the tragic duo of Clarkson and Rad-

Joe Quinn won his first National League pennant with the Boston Beaneaters in 1891. New manager Frank Selee's scientific training methods and introduction of powerful young pitchers saw the Beans finish the season nine games clear of title rivals Cleveland (McGreevey Collection, courtesy the Trustees of the Boston Public Library).

bourn. Ol' Hoss had notched up a 27–12 record in the Players' League, but as observers sadly noted, "By 1891, only his uniform was pitching."[15] He struggled to an 11–13 record with Kelly's Killers in Cincinnati, and upon their demise, he withdrew completely from the game to manage a saloon in his home town of Bloomington, Illinois. His peaceful retirement, however, was short-lived. On April 13, 1894, Hoss was accidentally shot in the face during a hunting trip. He lost his left eye, his face was partially paralyzed, and he suffered permanent brain injuries. He was no longer a big, strong, good-looking athlete, and took refuge in both solitude and alcohol as his powers of speech, feeling, and locomotion all drained away. On February 3, 1897, Radbourn suffered a convulsion from which he never awoke; he was just 42 years old. In 1939, he was elected to the National Baseball Hall of Fame among the first group of inductees.[16]

The 1891 campaign was also John Clarkson's last full season. He had, unsurprisingly, developed arm trouble and was shunted to Cleveland in 1892, where he coached the youthful pitcher and future Hall of Famer Denton "Cy" Young. But his career with the Spiders was marked by clashes with the former Brotherhood members among his teammates, and by 1894, Clarkson was out of the game. He suffered a breakdown in 1905, and, beset by a paranoia undoubtedly exacerbated by his heavy drinking, he was committed to an insane asylum in Michigan, where double pneumonia claimed his life in 1909.[17] Selee's replacement for the ill-starred pair was a diminutive right-hander who pitched with no windup and scorned the curveball. Charles Augustus "Kid" Nichols was an immediate sensation in Boston, winning 27 games in his inaugural season. Despite his slight build and baby face, Nichols was a workhorse who was relieved in only 24 of 501 career starts; he would have seven 30-win seasons between 1891 and 1898, lead Boston to five pre–1900 pennants, and become the youngest pitcher to win 300 games, at 30 years of age.[18]

National League Opening Day on April 22 was, as ever, sumptuous, riotous, extravagant and expectant. Over 17,000 fans crowded the Polo Grounds in New York, breathlessly anticipating the renewal of rivalry between those 1889 greats, Boston and the Giants. And the game lived up to their every hope and wish. The Giants lost to Boston 4–3, only through a ninth-inning outfield error by the Giants' "Gorgeous" George Gore.[19] It set the tone for a pennant race largely fought out between these two teams, with the addition of a Chicago White Stockings outfit still led by the stalwart and ageless Cap Anson (now 39 years of age and having hit over .300 in each of the last 20 seasons[20]). Indeed, "Old Man" Anson showed up for the game against the Beans on September 4 wearing a wig and a long white beard, sending the home crowd into ecstasies when he maintained the costume throughout the game. His men somehow won 5–3 to stretch Chicago's lead over Boston at the top of the table to seven games.[21] The win also avenged the June 11 rout in which Boston thrashed the White Stockings 14–6, with star shortstop Herman Long going six-for-six at the plate. The two clubs met again on August 7 in one of the best games of the season. A run-scoring wild pitch by John Clarkson allowed Chicago to beat Boston 6–5 in 10 innings, the fourth consecutive encounter in which Chicago beat the Beans in extra digs.[22]

• • •

> "I'd like to write you a policy in our non-forfeitable, non-assessable, double-jointed security company," observed an insurance agent to a stranger.
> "Well, I don't know," replied the latter.
> "But you should think of your wife and family. If anything should hap—"
> "All right; go ahead, with your policy."

> *"Thanks! Your name, business and age, please."*
> *"Dickson Jones, base ball umpire, age thirty-one."*
> *"O. Excuse me—I'm sorry, but I'm afraid I can't stay any longer just now. Goodby."*
>
> —"The Risk Was Too Great," *Pittsburg Chronicle*, July 24, 1887

For Joe Quinn and many of his colleagues, 1891 was a time of strained and strange friendships. In the same year as he'd fallen out with Kelly, Quinn's proclivity for odd alliances led him to befriend one of the most unlikely men to appear on the radar of a man renowned for his steadiness and honesty—a boxer and brawler, and an umpire to boot. Ted Sullivan once declared, "The umpire with a butterfly personality will never do, though his brain is an encyclopedia of all the rules. He must be decisive and earnest in his verdict: when the sheep are in the meadow or the cows in the corn, he must blow the horn."[23] But even in this, his debut National League season, umpire Timothy Carroll Hurst was no Little Boy Blue. He was an arrogant braggart who, if a player disputed a call, either punched him in the face or slugged him over the head with his mask. He would often then track down the offending player at his hotel and thrash him some more. "If players persist in being pugilistic, the umpires should be allowed to carry a bat during a game," Hurst once declared, "and if a bat won't preserve order, then an ax would probably keep the scrappy players at arm's length."[24]

Hurst was as quick with his wit as he was with his fists. When Cincinnati first baseman Jake Beckley dared petition Hurst that a ball hit along the first-base line was foul, urging Hurst, "Come here and look at the line, you can see where the ball struck," Hurst responded coolly, "My feet are tired—bring the line back here and I'll look at it." He gave the same short shrift to St. Louis' Mike Donlin, who once rushed at him shouting, "You're blind, that ball was foul by four feet!"

"No, you fresh ballplayer," retorted Hurst, "only two feet foul."[25]

Despite his former career as a boxer and his love of a good scrap, Hurst's belligerent behavior was, in part, self-defense. Umpires were—and remain—a scapegoat for all the frustrations with authority in the daily life of the populace, and the many failures of the players. Professional umpires were introduced by the American Association and National League in 1882. National League rules stated they were to be addressed as "Mr. Umpire," but that was the extent of official protection and recognition accorded them. Umpiring was a dangerous game: frequent revisions of the rules and developing playing techniques meant the turnover rate was huge as the men in blue were subject to vile abuse and missiles thrown from the crowd, and being spiked, kicked, cursed, and spat upon by the players. Hurst himself was expelled from the National League on August 4, 1897, following an incident in which a fan threw a beer mug at him: Hurst hurled it back, but hit the wrong fan and knocked him out cold. The crowd exploded onto the field, and although the former professional sprinter and boxer managed to fight them off until law enforcement arrived, he was fined $100 and fired.[26] Twelve years to the day later, on August 4, 1909, Hurst was sacked again, this time from the American League after he spat in the face of brilliant young Philadelphia second baseman and Columbia graduate Eddie Collins, merely because he "didn't like college boys."[27]

Quinn himself made appearances as a substitute umpire in three National League seasons (1889, 1894, and 1896); it was relatively commonplace for a player to stand in when the umpire was indisposed or both teams agreed he was either biased or incompetent.[28] It is unlikely Quinn adopted the pugnacious style of his friend Tim Hurst, whom Quinn described as "quick and handy with curses, quips and fists, and often gave me the gate for so much as a cross-eyed look."[29] So where was the common ground between the disparate pair?

After baseball and family, there was little Quinn loved better than singing. The *Omaha Daily Bee* chortled in 1892, "Joe Quinn is often taken for a song and dance man. Heavens!"[30] Quinn recalled to *The Sporting News* Hurst had heard him singing one day, and the pair often got together to share their love of music thereafter: "Hurst used to like Irish ballads and we would often get together at night and I'd warble for him. But our friendship made no difference when it came to the ballfield. He pitched me just as quickly as the next man, and how Tim loved to battle."[31]

◆ ◆ ◆

The Boston bats were far from hot in 1891. Not one of the Beans hit over .300 for the season, shortstop Herman Long leading Selee's crew on a somewhat tenuous .282.[32] Outfielder Harry Stovey, a .308 hitter in 1889, found his nemesis in Brooklyn twirler George Hemming: the Bridegrooms' wonder struck Stovey out five times on June 30, and in the August 21 rematch, fanned him a further four times in the Beans' 8–1 loss.[33] Even Quinn was far from impressive, hitting just .240,[34] but he had the day of his life on September 20 when, in front of a home crowd in a double-header against Pittsburgh, Quinn slammed a home run in each game (the second with bases loaded), sending seven runs across the plate for his team in the 11–3, 11–2 victories. As the *Pittsburg Dispatch* mourned, "There were two nice plums hanging upon the South End grounds this afternoon, each labeled 'Game won,' and the Beaneaters gathered both, wanting them for dessert."[35]

In late September, Chicago was clinging to the pennant lead with 76 wins, ably led by pitcher "Wild Bill" Hutchinson, who posted his fortieth win of the season on September 14, beating Boston 7–1. Boston, after a sweep of Pittsburgh, also had 76 wins but had played two more games than the Colts. The two teams were clearing out in the race, third-placed New York now eleven wins behind.[36] Quinn spent time on the sidelines after being struck in the head by a pitch from New York's Amos Rusie, the man whose blinding fastball so terrified batters that League and Association officials moved the pitcher's box back to sixty feet, six inches, where it has stayed ever since. At 6'1" and 200 pounds, the "Hoosier Thunderbolt" was just 20 years of age but would lead the league with 337 strikeouts in 1891, and his catcher Dick Buckley caught with a sheet of lead inside his glove to protect his hand from the impact of receiving the Rusie delivery.[37] The pitch that felled Quinn on August 17 was a devil. *The Sporting Life* recounted in awe, "Rusie, the New York pitcher, drove the ball toward the plate with all his strength. When fifteen feet distant, it broke in the air and made directly for Joe. He saw the 'break' and dropped to his knees to allow it to pass over his head. He had no time, however, to take in the fact that with all its speed the ball had, in addition to the 'jump,' a heavy, unnatural 'drop.' It followed Quinn down and hit him with terrific force squarely on the side of the head and knocked him silly for a few moments."[38] With his skull unprotected save for a felt cap, Quinn was fortunate not to join the three other known fatalities among batters struck in the head by a pitched ball prior to 1900.[39]

But momentum remained with the Braves—Chicago had been hammered in their three-game series with New York, and by September 25, Boston was on a ten-game winning streak and within half a game of the lead. New York, though, refused to give up hope of the flag, despite there being less than one week remaining in the season and the Giants' arriving in Boston on September 28 without 32-game-winning pitcher Amos Rusie or their best hitter in Roger Connor. They even arranged to cram five games into three days in a last desperate charge at the pennant—and promptly lost each one of them to catapult Boston to the top of the league with just three days to go. New Chicago president (and former Boston manager) James Hart protested furiously at the extra games played in that series and the advantage it handed to Boston: there was open speculation amongst sportswriters about the validity of the series, particularly when four Giants were conveniently retired at home plate in the final game.[40]

Nonetheless, with a National League enquiry clearing the clubs of collusion, the result stood, and on October 1, Boston clinched the National League pennant with its seventeenth consecutive victory, a 6–1 win over Philadelphia. Chicago lost to Cincinnati by the same score. The following day, the streak extended to 18 as Kid Nichols won his thirtieth game on the mound—a feat he would replicate another six times in his career.[41]

With their cross-town rivals also winning their league title, the prospect of an all–Boston World Championship playoff was mouth-watering—but was unfortunately thwarted by the collapse of the American Association late in 1891.[42] The National League now stood to claim the entire public purse, and to add insult to injury, the four strongest American Association clubs—St. Louis, Washington, Baltimore, and Louisville—were absorbed into the National League to form a 12-team mega-league.

Despite the rather sad conclusion to the season, Frank Selee's stable of rising stars was a worthy winner of the National League title. Harry Stovey led the league with 16 home runs. Kid Nichols broke the magic 30-win barrier, and Joe Quinn was feted again as "pretty nifty" and "right at the tops."[43] His Boston admirers presented him with a tribute in the form of a life-sized oil painting of poet-journalist John Boyle O'Reilly.[44] The gift was a most appropriate one, given both Quinn and O'Reilly's Irish and Australian connections: O'Reilly was an Irish seditionist whose "treasonable songs and ballads" earned him transport to a remote Western Australian convict outpost in 1868, after he had only narrowly avoided execution in Dublin. O'Reilly did not go without a fight, and within a year he had escaped the convict settlement aboard an American whaling ship (again barely evading capture). Settling in Boston, O'Reilly continued his advocacy of Home Rule in Ireland, but he didn't forget his miserable colleagues back in Australia—in 1875, he carried off a daring rescue of Irish political prisoners still incarcerated in Fremantle, complete with storms at sea and skirmishes with the British navy.[45] A granite monument to O'Reilly still stands at Australind in the south of Western Australia.[46]

◆ ◆ ◆

> "I believe baseball is a homeopathic cure for lunacy. It is a kind of craze in itself, and gives the lunatics a new kind of crazing to relieve them of the malady which affects their minds."—Dr. S.B. Talcott, superintendent of the New York State Lunatic Asylum, April 30, 1892

In 1892, the National League, unencumbered by competition or external rivals, got creative. They experimented with a split-season format in which the winner of the first half of the year (ending on July 15) would meet the winner of the second half in the World Series. The united National League met in New York on March 1 to induct the four teams from the collapsed 1891 American Association into a new twelve-team competition.[47] Boston stocks were boosted by a pair of ex–St. Louis stars in Hall of Fame outfielder Tommy McCarthy and pitcher Jack Stivetts. McCarthy was a native Bostonian and relished the opportunity to rejoin his lifelong friend, Hugh Duffy, in the Beans' outfield ranks after six seasons away. The two robust Irish-Catholics, aggressive, creative, and fleet of foot, used both the hit-and-run and the feigned outfield fumble to devastating effect, and soon became known as "Boston's Heavenly Twins."[48] King Kelly and Charlie Ganzel would share catching duties "until the weather gets warmer," when 37-year-old Charlie Bennett's arthritic joints permitted him to join the fray; Kelly himself was reported as in fine shape that spring, perhaps a little off with the stick but catching and throwing well. The *Pittsburg Dispatch* admitted the infield duo of Nash and Quinn "have no equals playing ball in their respective positions."[49] With an exciting stable of young pitchers in Nichols, Stivetts and Harry Staley (all under 25 years old), things looked bright for Selee's men—although the players blushed at management's new stipulation that, as reigning pennant winners, they travel to the ball grounds in open horse-cars instead of the traditional closed carriage.[50]

The season began splendidly on the field for the 1891 title holders, who opened their account on April 12 with a 14–4 thrashing of the Washington Senators in the nation's capital. But it was almost immediately followed by a disastrous excursion on April 14: the team were still in Washington, but there was no game scheduled for that day, so Manager Selee gave permission for the team to go on a bicycle tour to the Smithsonian after practice. Harry Stovey and Kid Nichols were apparently experts on the newfangled machines and promised to teach the other members of the team the intricacies of two-wheeled perambulation. While Quinn and Mike Kelly rode off successfully enough after a few early wobbles, Tommy McCarthy crashed repeatedly because his legs were too short to reach the pedals, and Herman Long took a terrible tumble at speed, sliding head-first into a hitching post. Billy Nash and Charley Bennett had elected for safety in numbers aboard a tandem bike, but as they came down a hill, a carriage emerged from a cross-street and Bennett instinctively wrenched the bike sideways, hurling Nash over his head and bending the front wheel of the machine. The battered and dejected procession, with torn clothes and bleeding heads, turned back after that.[51]

Quinn, despite rumors that he would sign with or be dispatched to St. Louis persisting well into the season,[52] had started the season brightly. In late June, he was second in the league in fielding average at .961 and sixth in chances accepted per game (6.20).[53] *The Sporting News* enthused, "Where could Boston get a better man than Joe Quinn?"[54] In 1892, another Australian was also making rare headlines on the U.S. sporting stage. Boxer George Dawson, hailing from the ominous-sounding Dark Corner in New South Wales, lined up against Pacific lightweight champion Jack Gallagher in San Francisco on April 19. Dawson was one of a cohort of Australian boxers trying their luck in the United States, including Jim Hall, Paddy Gorman, Abe Willis and Billy Maher. Despite his moniker of "Gentleman George," Dawson is remembered largely for invention of the kidney punch: he would retreat from a left lead and, with his own left, turn aside his opponent's offensive hand to expose the kidneys to his devastating right.[55] The evenly matched pair fought to a marathon finish, Gallagher pounding Dawson's mouth and neck with his heavy right fist until the thirtieth round, when, as exhaustion told, Dawson struggled to the lead by splitting Gallagher's lip nearly in two. But it took twelve further rounds to separate the pair, the shattered Gallagher finally falling to Dawson's knockout blow in round forty-two.[56]

Boston clinched the championship of the first half of the season, and celebrated with an outlandish display at Chicago on July 11, in which the entire Beans outfit appeared on the field in costume. The scheme, naturally, was Kelly's, designed to override Cap Anson's publicity for three new players Chicago had acquired that week. The King first suggested his men mimic Anson by dressing up as old men, but the stunt went even further, as a visit to a local costume store had them outfitted in "calico and gingham suits of the loudest color," guffawed the *Boston Globe*. "Mike Kelly was made up as an English dude. Hugh Duffy wore Red Galway sluggers and a red nose. Tommy McCarthy was made up as the one fireman.

Jack Stivetts had a heavy beard, also a red nose. Kid Nichols wore white whiskers. Joe Quinn sported a handsome pair of whiskers, of the reddish hue, a white necktie and blue cap, looking very Fourth of July. Tom Tucker wore a full beard. Herman Long was made up as the three ball merchant Frank Bush. Bobby Lowe wore black whiskers, a red nose and one black eye. Charley Bennett wore gray whiskers."[57]

The crowd, some 2,000 strong, was enchanted by the tomfoolery, particularly when all but catcher Bennett and pitcher Nichols proceeded to play the entire game in their hideous garb. And the game was none the worse for it: needing two runs to win in the ninth inning, Anson himself came to bat with runners on second and third and one out. The Beans' ploy of a deliberate walk was spoiled when Anson flung his bat at a wide Nichols pitch for the second strike. Trying for a Hollywood finish and a grand strikeout of the old master, Nichols switched gears and sent his best fastball right over the plate. Anson was not to be denied, and sent it scorching back past him for what looked like the game-winning hit. But he had not reckoned upon Joe Quinn. Whiskers flying, Quinn hurled himself at the smoking sphere and brought it down, tumbled over, and still got the ball to second base in time to make the double play that ended the match in a 3–2 Boston victory.[58] The party mood was quickly dissipated, however: three days later, the Beans were humiliated in front of their home fans with a 20–3 hiding from the lowly St. Louis Browns.

The departure of aging hurler John Clarkson to Cleveland left the gate open for youngsters Jack Stivetts and Kid Nichols to stamp their authority on the 1892 season. Hall of Famer Nichols was in just his third year in the major leagues but would win a staggering 35 games at an ERA of just 2.84.[59] And despite often being mistaken for a batboy because of his diminutive appearance, Nichols could also hit when required—on September 19, he slugged a grand slam, then a bases-loaded triple to give Boston a 14–0 lead over Baltimore. However, in the following inning, he was forced out of the game after being felled by a line drive. The Orioles then knocked in 11 unanswered runs, but Boston hung on to win 14–11.[60]

A Pennsylvania native who won the American Association pitching crown in 1889, his first year as a professional, Jack Stivetts had a year that included tossing an 11–0 no-hitter against Brooklyn on August 6, and on September 5, winning two complete games in a single day over Louisville, 5–2 and 2–1, this last in 11 innings. Like Nichols, he was a more than handy hitter—on three occasions throughout his career, he hit two home runs and struck out ten batters in a game.[61] Stivetts was also an unusually open-minded character amid the chronic paternalism of nineteenth-century baseball. In 1892, a bill before the New York State Assembly sought to prohibit the employment of females as baseball players, but six years later, Lizzie Arlington made the first appearance by a woman in organized baseball when she pitched the closing inning for Reading in an Atlantic League game against Allentown. She gave up two hits but no runs, and while the Reading papers concluded, "She hasn't the strength to get much speed on and has poor control," her talent had clearly been recognized by Stivetts, who had spent 1897 playing in Fall River and taken time to teach her to pitch.[62]

By September 29, Boston was the tearaway league leader, having spent 178 days of the season in first place, their 91–46 record four wins clear of Cleveland (87–50) and Brooklyn (87–55).[63] A visit to tenth-placed Washington was hardly a frightening prospect, but the result was what the *Evening Star* decried as "The worst game in years!" A total of 25 errors, including fourteen by Boston and five alone by Joe Quinn, completely eclipsed the 12–8 win by the visitors.[64] However, despite the damage inflicted on his fielding average by such carnage, Quinn still led the league at .951, a point ahead of Pittsburgh's Lou Bierbaeur, Cincinnati Hall of Famer Bid McPhee a breath behind at .948. Incidentally, the Beans' return visit to Washington for the final series of the year on October 14 was postponed because the Washington field was double-booked for a football game between Columbia and Princeton.[65] When the players did take the field the next day, Jack Stivetts closed out the year for Boston with, appropriately, a 4–0 no-hitter.[66]

Joe Quinn lined up in his first post-season championship in 1892. During the 1880s, nearly every major league club played a couple of weeks of post-season games, generally against major- and minor-league teams they hadn't faced during the regular season. Informal series were arranged by clubs without league sanction, varying in the number of games played according to the wishes of involved clubs. The World Series began in 1884 with a three-game series between the Providence Grays (National League) and the Metropolitans of New York (American Association). In the following six seasons, the National League and American Association pennant-winners played in series ranging from 6 to 15 games, but the World Series was canceled in 1891 with the demise of the American Association. The twelve-team National League revived the concept in 1892, in which the winner of the first half of the season, Boston, played second-half winner, Cleveland, in a seven-game series.[67]

Stivetts was given the honor of starting the first game against the league's leading hurler, 36-game winner Cy Young, and the two battered each other to an eleven-inning scoreless tie. Once again, it was Joe Quinn who saved the game. With runners on and two out in the ninth inning, Jesse Burkett rose up to bat for the Spiders. The left-handed Hall of Famer Burkett hit over .400 three times in his career, boasting he could bunt .300 alone. He won three National League batting crowns, but Burkett was universally detested for his surly disposition. Appropriately christened "The Crab," he was complaining and griping when he wasn't arguing and protesting; he was hopeless in the outfield and a league leader in errors, and only his .338 lifetime batting average made his personality tolerable.[68] When Burkett slammed a line drive back past Stivetts, it seemed for all the world the game was up. But with a dramatic dive, Quinn pulled the ball down and threw The Crab out at first; the game was then called for darkness.[69]

Boston drew first blood on October 18 in Cleveland, with 7,000 rowdy fans retiring disappointed after Boston snuck home 4–3, Harry Staley (himself a 22-game winner) beating his old mentor John Clarkson. Boston centerfielder Hugh Duffy starred, driving in three of Boston's four runs and scoring the fourth himself after belting his second triple off Clarkson. In the bottom of the ninth, he also brilliantly caught a leadoff line drive, preventing a tie or a Cleveland win.[70] Earlier that season, Duffy had saved another game against Cleveland, albeit in rather different circumstances: the Boston left field fence backed onto a railroad track, and empty cans and debris had piled up against the palings. Cleveland's Jimmy McAleer knocked a long hit to left field, and the ball rolled under the fence into an empty tomato can. Duffy grabbed the can and tried wildly to dig the ball out while McAleer, the fastest runner then playing, was tearing around the bases. Finally, in desperation, Duffy threw the ball—can and all—to third, the third baseman hurled it to the catcher, and he touched McAleer out with it. There was an enraged protest from Cleveland and the umpire finally declared McAleer safe and the run legitimate—after all, the rules stated the runner must be touched "with the ball" to be called out.[71]

Stivetts, too, proved his worth in game 3 of the series with a 3–2 win over the great Cy Young. Shut out in Boston on October 21 by a merciless Kid Nichols with 6,500 fans at his back, the Cleveland nine were very nearly on their knees. In 1905, Quinn, who had contributed a two-RBI single in this game, remembered the role King Kelly had played in that win: "He was behind the plate with two out and Burkett on third. The hitter grounded to shortstop, who threw to first. Burkett saw Kelly drop his mitt, apparently signaling the end of the inning, and he slowed—but the runner at first was safe, the first baseman threw to Kelly, who caught barehanded and tagged Burkett for the third out.... It took some rapid mental calculating for Kelly to think that play out, but he knew every angle of baseball and always did the right thing at the right time on the ball field."[72]

The death blow was delivered after a Sunday's rest. The freezing Boston weather meant only 1,800 fans showed up to see Boston's fourth and deciding victory, but victory it was.[73] The $1,000 prize was divided among Boston's thirteen players with each receiving $76.92.[74] The split-season format was never used again.

Quinn finished the series hitting 0.286, with four RBIs and no errors. But his year with the bat had been lean, to say the best. He hit only .218 from 143 games in the regular season and struck out a rather ignominious 40 times, the most by far in any year of his career.[75] His season had also been restricted by a lame ankle,[76] with the papers at one stage bawling that he was accumulating so much flesh he could barely raise a gallop at second base.[77]

He had remained a part of Selee's championship-winning outfit primarily on the

The 1892 Boston Beaneaters. Joe Quinn (middle row, second right) led the league at second base and helped the Beans to a second consecutive National League pennant, but was released at the end of the year in favor of young utility Bobby "Link" Lowe (seated, front center) (McGreevey Collection, courtesy the Trustees of the Boston Public Library).

strength of his league-leading defense. But on October 19, the *Pittsburg Dispatch* reported Quinn's "hat had been chalked,"[78] and despite a semi-creditable performance in the World Series, the signs were not in his favor. On December 5, St. Louis manager Bill Watkins came to Boston aiming to trade outfielder Cliff Carroll for Quinn, with "little doubt the trade can be made, with Lowe put on second base and Carroll in left field."[79] Bobby "Link" Lowe was four years younger than Quinn and had played most of the year in the outfield, where he was more than useful, playing 90 games at .928. But despite batting just .242 in 1892, Lowe would go on to become the first player in history to slam four home runs in one game, in 1896, and be recognized as one of baseball's great utility players.[80] Quinn had famously told the papers in 1892 he cared little about what the fans thought of his work, and if the bosses found fault with his playing they could give him a release, as he had sufficient capital in St. Louis to keep his family and himself without his baseball salary. "Well, Joe will have a chance to do that next season," concluded *The Sporting Life* in October, "for he is on the slate to go."[81]

Part V
The Good Fight: 1893–1898

10. The Flea-Bitten Gray and the Bald-Faced Nag

"Man is so made that he can only find relaxation from one kind of labor by taking up another."
Anatole France, *The Crime of Sylvestre Bonnard*, 1881

In 1866, one hundred million bison roamed the wide plains of Missouri and Kansas, providing food and raw materials for the indigenous tribes of the region and a powerful spiritual totem. Nearly three decades later, in 1893, only one ten-thousandth that number remained, slaughtered by the advancing military to force an Indian surrender, then pushed further toward the margins of existence by encroaching western civilization, with their accompaniments of concrete and celluloid, barbed wire and telephones and typewriters.[1]

Likewise, by 1893, the glorious "frontier" days of the St. Louis Browns were also dead. Charlie Comiskey had led the club to four consecutive American Association pennants between 1885 and 1888, and his Browns were on such a rampage in the mid-'80s that the Philadelphia Athletics had tried to slow them down—quite literally—by loading their home basepaths with sand.[2] According to Ted Sullivan, Comiskey had a volcano burning inside him to make himself famous. "As a captain, he outclassed any man who ever gave orders to ball players," he said. "He is the only ball player in the entire history of baseball who has attained the heights of success by legitimate ball playing and the strength and magnetism of his personality."[3] Quinn called him "the craftiest of all managers."[4] But Albert Spalding noted the three all-time greatest evils in baseball were whiskey, gambling, and the owners of the 1890s (of which, ironically, he was one)[5]; and all of Comiskey's magnetism proved as effective a buffer against Browns owner Chris Von der Ahe as a penny whistle in a brass band. By 1893, Comiskey was gone, overwhelmed by von der Ahe's chaotic despotism, and the team was floundering like a rowboat in the wake of an ocean liner.

When baseball struggled for a foothold in St. Louis in the early 1880s, German shopkeeper Chris Von der Ahe was one of the first to come forward as a promoter and financier for a professional league. At the time, he was a modest shopkeeper on Sullivan and Spring Avenue in the west end of St. Louis, but noting that many of his patrons were also baseball-goers, he spotted an immediate commercial opportunity. During 1882, when the American Association was born, Von der Ahe personally saw to it that none of its clubs fell by the wayside, and as co-founder and first president of the Browns—which he named for no other reason than that their stockings were brown—he spent liberally to ensure the success of his own team, declaring, "Nothing is too goot for my poys!"⁶ Mac Davis, in *The Lore and Legends of Baseball*, described how, when Von der Ahe once could not buy a talented bush-league player for the Browns, he bought the whole team instead.⁷ The Browns won the American Association championship in 1888 and were to play New York for the World Series, so Von der Ahe organized a special train to carry the St. Louis party to New York, hung with banners and conveying all the friends, associates, and hangers-on as could cram aboard. The round trip cost Von der Ahe more than $20,000—ten times the annual salary of most players. And upon clinching the first game of the series, Von der Ahe not only splurged on champagne but ordered each player to buy a new suit of clothes at the club's expense, and every man who had accompanied them on the trip was likewise instructed to visit the New York tailors and send Von der Ahe the bill.⁸

Such lavish spending brought with it an intense sense of possession—Von der Ahe did not merely finance the team, he *owned* it and everyone connected with it. He named apartment blocks after his stars, and would parade the players to the park in the open carriages, then have them march single-file behind him onto the field.⁹ And with his bottomless checkbook, the concept of a losing team was as alien to Von der Ahe as that of temperance. When the Browns began to struggle in the '90s, he first concluded the problem must be at managerial level. The proud Charles Comiskey, winner of four pennants, shared the fate of his friend Ted Sullivan, who had managed the Browns ten years earlier until he incurred Von der Ahe's displeas-

"Der Poss President" of the St. Louis Browns, Chris Von der Ahe. The German saloon-keeper's colorful reign over the Browns lasted from 1882 until 1898, during which time he appointed himself as manager on three occasions and turned his playing field into an amusement park. It was during one of his legendary fits of temper in 1896 that he sold Joe Quinn, his long-suffering captain, to Baltimore, sparking a national outcry (National Baseball Hall of Fame Library, Cooperstown, New York).

ure: "Commy" departed for Cincinnati at the end of 1891. The American Association, too, folded in that chaotic year, and the Browns joined the new twelve-team National League.¹⁰

Absolutely undaunted by the sacrifice of his great manager, Von der Ahe squeezed his feet into Comiskey's shoes and ran the Browns show alone in 1892. Former Browns secretary Al Spink described his managership as a "reign of terror."¹¹ The volatile Von der Ahe watched every move of the players through binoculars, blew whistles at them from the stands, and stormed into the rooms after games to berate players for hitting the ball to the opposition. He hated fly balls as much as he hated teetotalers, and would scream from the dugout, "Stop hitting them high fliers! Keep them on the floor! Don't you know them fielders can catch de high vuns?"¹² Such was his iron grip on his men that Von der Ahe even banned all pockets in their uniforms after an 1889 incident in which centerfielder Cliff Carroll went after a slow groundball which hit a tussock, bounded up and hit him in the chest, and somehow, in the ensuing tangle, lodged in his pocket. The opposition runner had gone to second, turned to check where the ball was, and set off for third, so Carroll ran after him, still trying to tug the ball free—but to no avail: the run scored and the game was lost. Von der Ahe nearly had a fit. He fined Carroll $50 for putting the ball in his pocket, suspended him for the rest of the year, and decreed that all uniform pockets were to be sewn up.¹³

Von der Ahe recruited a new manager for the 1893 season in W.H. (Bill) Watkins, who had managed American Association club Detroit to a pennant in 1887 with eleven .300-plus hitters on his roster, including Sam Thompson and Dan Brouthers, Ned Hanlon, Fred Dunlap, Hardie Richardson, and Charlie Bennett. Watkins was not a young man—white of hair, a small tidy figure with bowler hat and round spectacles—but despite his mild-mannered mien, he was short-tempered and not well-liked by his players. In 1888, it had taken more than three months of coercion to persuade Deacon White to sign with Detroit, the famous infielder swearing he would never play under Watkins.[14] Von der Ahe warned the Browns, however, that Watkins's word would be law, from which there would be no appeal.[15] He had no time to give the players his personal attention, he blustered, so from now on they must look to Manager Watkins for "fatherly advice."[16] It was indeed an unhappy prospect. Von der Ahe's final gesture in preparing the team for the 1893 season was to release last season's captain, dead-armed pitcher Bob Caruthers.[17]

With an already unpopular Watkins on the coaching line, the Browns needed a youthful, capable on-field chief to lead the disgruntled players by example, and serve as a go-between with both the capricious owner and the new manager they regarded with such a dubious eye. This alone was a task requiring such a level of tact, diplomacy and sheer bloody-mindedness that few would voluntarily assume it. And the job came coupled with the need to drag the team out of the mire of eleventh place, to which it had sunk after Comiskey's exit. However, to his credit, Von der Ahe was "in the habit of selecting talent which he considered the best available,"[18] and *The Sporting News* of February 11, 1893, reported Joe Quinn had signed to captain and play second base for St. Louis.

Quinn had put a good face on his ditching from Boston for the dashing young Link Lowe. He returned to his home on Dickson Street in St. Louis and accepted the captaincy of the chaos-ridden Browns with such grace the St. Louis cranks were charmed. *The Sporting News* gushed, "The selection is a wise one. It means that St. Louis now has a man in every way capable of filling the great void left by the departure of Comiskey.... Quinn will add greatly to the team's popularity and in fact bring back to it hundreds of friends. No professional baseball player ever making St. Louis his home has a larger circle of friends than Quinn.... Unlike many other professionals, he has never broken a contract or been charged with double-dealing of any kind. In all his dealings with this club, that, and the other, he has been honest and upright and this is why today he commands the respect of the fraternity at large."[19]

In the same week in February, the first recorded musical version of "Casey at the Bat," probably baseball's best loved folk poem, hit the popular music charts.[20] But, fond as he was of singing and song, Joe Quinn had far more on his mind than catchy new tunes. He was as quietly ambitious about his career off the field as on it, and in early 1893, his well-known temperance and thrift paid a handsome dividend. In partnership with his friend Patrick Gorry, a Kerry Patch coal merchant, Quinn was able to buy his first business, a livery stable at 1804 N. Grand Avenue in St. Louis.[21] The nineteenth century was not an easy period for professional players, particularly those with families, to manage their finances. They were paid on a six- or seven-month basis and players frequently ran short over winter; although clubs would advance sums between $100 and $500 against future earnings, many were reluctant to do so in case players then jumped to rival leagues and absconded with the cash. But an anonymous letter to *The Sporting News* described Quinn as "always very thrifty and putting aside a good proportion of his salary every year."[22] He now had two children, with a third set to arrive in August, and for the conservative young man, love was a verb, a doing word—he was doubtless eager to impress his father-in-law with his business acumen and ability to provide.

Despite the almost endless salary disputes and industrial wrangles, even a major league rookie on $1,500 was wealthy—during the playing season at least—compared to his blue-collar cousins, who earned around one-third that sum each year. So it was rare for players to undertake anything except baseball—and bacchanalia—in spring and summer. Quinn, on the other hand, threw himself into his new business with the same verve he showed on the ball field: buying, selling, and stabling horses, renting buggies, transporting every man from politicians to doctors to tourists, and all in between his now-numerous and complex duties on the diamond.

Quinn first led his men on a tour of southern towns on March 17, with Chattanooga, Nashville, and Memphis all on the itinerary, before returning to play a Sunday exhibition game against the Browns' own reserves, the Whites.[23] In his "stable" were former Maroons Perry Werden and Quinn's old adversary Jack Glasscock, who, despite injuring his hand in 1891 which thereafter restricted his ability to throw, still remained one of the League's most dangerous hitters and fielders, leading the League at shortstop in 1893 and hitting .320.[24] The Browns had also acquired a pair of talented youngsters of German extraction, popular catcher Henry "Heinie" Peitz, bought from the Southern League for the bargain price of $500,[25] and a young left-handed pitcher called Theodore Breitenstein whom Von der Ahe had bought, also cheaply, from Grand Rapids. "Breit" promptly tossed a no-hitter in his major league debut in 1891, but the following year was very nearly released for his 9–19 record.[26] However, Von der Ahe thought a great deal of the young man—possibly because he could swear at both him and Peitz in German and the pair would understand his obscenities. The two players became known as the "Pretzel Battery"[27] for their habit of drinking beer and eating pretzels after games, and there was much excitement about their potential impact on the cellar-dwelling team as the season opener drew near.

The first three weeks of the season were a dream for Joe Quinn's Browns. The *New York Sun* had boldly proclaimed the Boston champions would "outdo themselves" and that the Giants were in fine fettle,[28] but by Monday, May 15, "Captain Quinn and his gingery young Browns"[29] were actually leading the league, both Quinn and Watkins "tickled as babies with rubber rings."[30] The weather was magnificent and home stands packed with the curious and cynical St. Louis cranks. Old Sportsman's Park, the oldest diamond in the country,[31] had been laid to rest on April 23 after 27 years of faithful service, and its successor sported seating for ten thousand, fancy iron columns, and a railway loop outside the grandstand. The park was formally opened on the first day of the season, April 27, and in declaring the diamond open, Lieutenant Governor O'Meara described it as "a monument to the grand old national game that calls for our heartiest admiration."[32,33] But for Chris Von der Ahe, the ideal running mate for a baseball team was *beer*. To celebrate the opening of the new edifice, he ran up a golden ball inscribed "Game Today" over his nearby Golden Lion saloon and laid on drinks at the park, whose turnstiles admitted 12,230 persons to sip Anheuser Busch ale and draw luxuriously on Schottmueller cigars while witnessing the Browns defeating Louisville 4–2.[34]

But the high-flying Browns, perhaps dizzy with the heights of their unaccustomed success, were brought back to earth by an ugly incident during the May 15 contest with the Cincinnati Reds. After tagging Browns outfielder Steve Brodie in a collision at the plate, Reds catcher Harry "Farmer" Vaughn retaliated for the heavy contact, hurling a bat at Brodie and hitting him on the shoulder. Vaughn was one of the hardest throwers in the League, having hurled a record 402′7½″ in a throwing contest in 1890, and for his grievous attack on Brodie, he was ejected and fined $25—the same amount he had won in the throwing contest. Brodie did not get off so lightly, missing nearly a month of game time while nursing his various hurts.[35] But such trifles aside, Von der Ahe reveled in the team's early success and the positive influence of his new captain, with the press trumpeting, "Joe Quinn and Chris Von der Ahe are the warmest kind of friends at present."[36]

It couldn't last. Despite winning four straight games at the beginning of the month—their longest winning streak of the season—the Browns won only three further games for the remainder of May.[37] Slipping downward with the inevitability of water down a slide, St. Louis continued to provide only a kind of nuisance value to their opponents, defeating the high-flying Cleveland Spiders 3–2 on May 27 to send Cincinnati to the top of the table despite their own 4–1 home loss. The other league front-runners were Quinn's old team, Boston, and when the two met on June 14, the Browns were demoralized by the performance of Braves outfielder Cliff Carroll, the man for whom Boston had traded Quinn. Said to be playing better than ever in his life, Carroll made a phenomenal outfield catch to rob St. Louis of a home run; then, in the bottom of the ninth, he knocked in two runs and scored a third to propel Boston to an 11–10 win.[38] By June 23, the Braves were in first place; however, the Phillies' victory the next day brought them back into a tie at the top of the standings. It was a 12–5 thrashing of the eighth-placed Browns on July 1 which allowed Boston to forge back into the lead as Cleveland similarly spanked fellow contenders Philadelphia 13–6, the Spiders staging their second eight-run ninth inning rally in a month.[39]

It was a year of strange player proclivities. On July 14, right-handed Baltimore pitcher Tony Mullane, on the end of a 7–2 deficit against Chicago, pitched the final inning left-handed in a vain attempt to bamboozle the hard-swinging Whites. The experiment was not a success—the Colts whacked him for a further three runs and won 10–2.[40] Not to be outdone, on August 7, facing a left-handed Brooklyn pitcher, New York's Roger Connor batted right-handed for the first time in his career, but he miraculously slugged a single and two home runs in the 10–3 victory.[41] St. Louis' Hall of Fame left-fielder Jesse Burkett was heavily criticized after making three errors in a loss to Cleveland on August 12, but the public censure was not for his technique, timing, or glovework—it was for his failure to follow Pittsburgh outfielder Elmer Smith's example and wear that marvelous new invention, sunglasses.[42] Equally resistant to such newfangled devices was Cincinnati Reds star second baseman, Bid McPhee, except McPhee's resistance was directed toward wearing what is now a standard item of fielding attire—a glove. It was a concession that had already been made by most other players, but

Quinn was very proud of his forty-year friendship with Hall of Fame manager Connie Mack, whom he met while Mack was catching for Pittsburgh in 1893. Mack would later lead the Philadelphia Athletics to five World Series titles and seven pennants in his 50 consecutive years at the helm between 1901 and 1950, before retiring at the age of 87 (National Baseball Hall of Fame Library, Cooperstown, New York).

McPhee, almost alone in the National League, still preferred to play bare-handed. Bid was persuaded to don the dread device for a stint on September 21, 1893, but by the end of the year he had discarded it again.[43] The *Omaha Daily Bee* called it ridiculous to see the shortstop or second baseman hiding behind a glove. "They might as well contrive a hand catapult for pitchers and a spring bat for the batter," the paper scoffed.[44] The other vocal opponent of the practice was Cap Anson, who opined scornfully, "Nobody likes to see a play made with the aid of gloves."[45]

While Quinn demonstrated no such odd tricks or travesties, it was for him a year in which another significant lifelong friendship was forged. In a 1933 interview, Quinn recounted with pride his forty-year camaraderie with the legendary Cornelius McGillicuddy—"Connie Mack"—who in their playing days was a "skinny, brainy fellow catching for Pittsburgh."[46] Over his eleven-year playing career, begun in 1886 with Washington, Mack would lead the National League in putouts, assists, and double plays as a catcher; he was also the Players' League's number one catcher in 1890, and renowned for his creativity behind the plate.[47] "I will not tolerate profanity, obscene language or personal insults from my bench," he regularly declared, but his righteousness did not prevent him from frequently substituting an old dead ball with a lively one which had been kept on ice overnight.[48] But it was for his managerial career that Mack—"The Tall Tactician"—was inducted into the Baseball Hall of Fame in 1939. He would manage the inaugural Philadelphia Athletics for an American League record 50 consecutive seasons between 1901 and 1951, capturing nine pennants and five World Series championships.[49] Quinn and Mack had both played in the rebel league of 1890 (into which Mack had poured his entire life savings[50]), and they came face to face on the field again on May 24, 1893. Mack almost single-handedly routed the Browns, starting a triple play in the fourth inning, then driving in the winning run to lead Pittsburgh to an 8–7 victory. The result, and the soft-spoken man who didn't drink, smoke, or swear, so impressed Quinn that a bond was immediately formed between the two. Born on December 22, 1862, Mack was just two days older than Quinn, but they certainly were an odd pair: the tall erect catcher with his starched collars and talent for trickery, and the athletic Quinn as plainly honest off the field as he was on it.

But by late summer, the competing demands of home, business, and ball were taking a toll on Quinn. With visions of broken buggy wheels and empty feed bins dancing before his eyes, and a new baby in the Dickson Street nursery,[51] Quinn was on the slippery slope toward fulfilling the prophecy of the anonymous crank who had warned *The Sporting News*, "Ball players who also engage in business during the playing season always have an off year."[52] His batting average was the worst of the regular nine, hovering between .220 and .240, and only the fumbling Jack Crooks made more errors in the field.[53] *The Sporting News* fretted, "Quinn was at the stables early and late, only getting to new Sportsman's Park in time to get into uniform before practice. He'd bustle out as soon as the game finished, but if the bald-faced nag did not have the colic, the flea-bitten gray would pick up a nail or the sorrel mare would cast a shoe or go lame. Little Joe was kept in hot water all the time."[54]

Von der Ahe did little to support him. In fact, the presence of the German owner only made matters worse. The deteriorating relationship between Von der Ahe and Watkins meant the volatile owner regularly bypassed his manager to personally persecute his players as the Browns continued their inexorable downward slide. He insisted the fielders must have been misplaced if any hit happened to pierce the defense—an infraction incurring a fine in the Browns' camp—and the local fans picked up on his ongoing colorful tirades, stamping and booing and hissing like wild geese at every flub or fumble.

Patrick Gorry did all he could to shoulder the cares of 1804 N. Grand Avenue, but with Quinn hastily hobbling the pair and bounding up the steps, still in his street clothes, ten minutes before the first pitch, and Von der Ahe berating him audibly as the Browns ran onto the field, Quinn was far from doing himself justice—and by September, he was very nearly on his knees like one of Napoleon's own horses. The Browns were in no-man's land in ninth place with a 47–61 record, light years behind the runaway Boston, whose 75 wins had them eleven clear of second-placed Pittsburgh. And Quinn was not the only man fraught and miserable. *The Sporting Life* reported Kid Gleason was sullen and discouraged, Dad Clarkson forlorn, Glasscock "constantly had the gloves on" as he was fed up with playing for a losing team, Breitenstein sick of working for a "ribbon tearer's wages," and Jack Crooks was a specter of his former merry, joshing self.[55]

The one bright spot in the year came on September 30, when the Browns, having lost their previous ten games, faced a rampaging Boston just a week away from their third consecutive National League pennant. The Browns somehow crushed the league leaders in both games of the double-header, 17–6 and 16–4. And the star of the show was Joe Quinn, who amassed eight hits against his old team—eight sharp reminders of what they had so cheaply given away.[56] However, it was no coincidence that Quinn's return to form coincided with his decision to sell 1804 N. Grand Avenue. He knew that shutting up the shop would not make him bat .300, but a cold bat was not his primary problem: it was the fact the sun rose and set every day with only an obstinate ten hours in between to get everything done, and this selfish propensity of the day to refuse him extra hours was hurting both his baseball and his business. Despite his obvious affection for the McGrath family, Quinn's pride was no doubt wounded at having to admit defeat and return to working for his father-in-law. But Al Spink was right when he said, "One of the most earnest and effective players of the profession, [Quinn] can always be depended on to do anything honorable in advancing the interests of the club with which he may be connected"[57]—even if this meant putting his club ahead of the business which so crucially defined him as a provider for his family.[58]

The decision to sell out, painful as it was, really came far too late. Quinn batted a dreadful .240 for the season. He played every game for the year and, amazingly, struck out just seven times in 547 at-bats, but he also found new and unique ways to appear at the wrong end of the statistician's ledger. As a *bona fide* leader to the dismal St. Louis outfit, he hit no home runs and knocked only 71 across the plate. His harried cohorts faithfully followed his example. Perry Werden made a league-leading 43 errors at first base. Third baseman Jack Crooks batted a sickly .237 and made a stunning 53 errors.[59] But Quinn's 1893 season was especially poor in light of the hitting explosion set off by the change in pitching distance made at the start of the year. In one of the most significant rule changes in major league history, the National League had eliminated the pitching box and installed a pitcher's rubber at the modern distance of sixty feet, six inches from the plate. Since 1875, there had been a steady evolution from the original pitching distance of 45 feet: in 1881, a pitcher's box with the front line 50 feet from home plate was created, with a hop and skip by the pitcher permitted as long as it occurred inside the box. This motion was outlawed in 1889 and the pitcher had to keep one foot on a line set 55'6" from the plate. The mound from which pitchers now deliver developed in the late 1890s to counter the hitting explosion set off by the 1893 rule change: with that much more time to see the incoming sphere, Jesse Burkett hit over .400 for three seasons and Ed Delahanty two, Hugh Duffy hit .438 in 1894 and Willie Keeler .437 in 1897.[60] The 1893 rule change was immediately devastating to the struggling St. Louis hurlers. Arthur "Dad" Clarkson, brother of John, was the Browns' only winning pitcher in 1893, with a 12–9 record. William "Kid" Gleason and Ted Breitenstein, who by the late 1890s would be considered one of the nation's greatest left-handed pitchers, lost 45 games between them.[61]

Quinn resigned the captaincy of the Browns in September, sick of the thankless job and fully admitting his incompetence as captain: according to *The Sporting Life*, by now, Quinn was "making scarce an effort to shown an authority he didn't care to possess."[62] "The laurels that were tossed at him at the opening of the season have turned to cabbages and cauliflowers, which the cranks have nurtured with pitchers of ice water," the paper mourned. However, his honesty in admitting his failings was praised. Quinn had voluntarily offered his resignation as captain on several occasions, but the offer had been rejected in the face of his earnestness and conscientiousness before his disgruntled and often difficult charges.[63] And in a delicious subplot to Quinn's gloomy year, the fickle public either didn't notice or didn't care for the statistics usually so prized by baseball cranks. Although Joe's presence was not enough to lift the ignoble Browns above tenth place, his own inopportune slump received an unexpected reward when Quinn was voted by readers of *The Sporting News* as the "Most Popular Ball-player in America." He was presented with a heavy gold watch inscribed inside the back cover, "First prize. Presented by *The Sporting News* in the 'Most Popular Ball Player' contest. Capt. Joe Quinn, St. Louis Browns, 1893."[64]

The whole tableau was an acute embarrassment to Quinn, but confirmed that, whether batting .240 or .440, his refusal to become clouded by the heavy boozing of the day or provoked into undignified outbursts despite incalculable provocation, had greatly endeared him to the public. While he generally allowed his actions to speak for themselves, Quinn gave rare voice to his philosophy when he told *The Sterling Advocate* in 1894:

> The players who use vulgar or profane language or act the rowdy or bully during a game have not sense enough to see that such practices affect the patronage and consequently their own reputation. There is no penalty too severe for such offenses, and if the clubs won't discipline players who make these breaks, the manager should. The better class of players condemns hoodlumism. The umpire should be instructed to promptly fine any player who swears or uses vile language during the game, and if the offense is repeated the tough who persists should be run out of the game. The foul-mouthed player does the profession as much if not more harm as the dirty ball player. People will not patronize the sport if they are compelled to listen to the language of swell-headed toughs.[65]

It was over forty years before Quinn admitted to being pleased by *The Sporting News* award, although his characteristic modesty moved him to protest the gold watch would not suit his sober image as an undertaker. He was finally enticed to show the watch to *The Sporting News* reporter Dick Harrington in 1936 as part of the paper's fiftieth anniversary celebrations, and he fondled it carefully, the engraved ornamentation on the gold hunting case almost completely worn away. "You know, there was a big diamond set in the back of that watch. But I had it taken out some years ago, because the case had worn to the point where I was afraid I might lose the stone. I've got the diamond put away, because it doesn't look good to wear any frills like that in my business. But," he divulged modestly, "I have always been proud of it."[66]

• • •

> "Joe Quinn expects to play better ball next season than was the case last, as he will be freed from the entanglements of his livery business, which he has sold out. Quinn's play was also hampered by his captaincy. He was never cut out for a leader."—The Sporting Life, January 13, 1894

10. The Flea-Bitten Gray and the Bald-Faced Nag

Joe Quinn's professional baseball career was very nearly amputated at the neck on March 14, 1894, thanks to a vigilant United States Immigration inspector.

The Alien Contract Labor Law (Sess. II Chap. 164; 23 Stat. 332) was ratified in 1885 to prevent the importation of foreigners to work in the United States. Manufacturing and industrialization had grown at an extraordinary rate in the late nineteenth century, and with the accompanying demand for labor, immigrants had flooded into the U.S., particularly from Europe and Asia. The first incarnation of the Act in 1864 actually encouraged employers to recruit migrants, but as the torrent of cheap labor drove down wages, an 1885 revision forbade almost any foreign labor being imported into the United States. An 1887 amendment made provision, however, for "persons belonging to any recognized profession" to be exempt from the contract labor law.[67] The question was: was the relatively recent phenomenon of professional baseball a "recognized profession?" The aforenamed inspector, De Barry, was tipped off that Buffalo had signed two Canadian players for the 1894 season, and he went straight to the Treasury Department to determine if a violation of alien labor laws had been committed. In St. Louis, Joe Quinn had never renounced his Australian citizenship, and there was a collective holding of breath in the Mound City. Buffalo, meantime, didn't wait for the outcome of De Barry's enquiries—the Canadians were quickly dispatched back across the border and only "bona fide Americans" appeared on their 1894 roster.[68] The only public comment from St. Louis was a casual, "Joe Quinn has got out of the livery business and hopes to cover second base in his old style this season."[69] There was no mention of the dread stamp in his passport, and, mercifully, no visit from Inspector De Barry.

That danger averted, there were still ominous overtones in the Browns camp following the departure in high dudgeon of manager Bill Watkins. In a disturbing echo of 1892, Von der Ahe, having been unable to hire either Hall of Fame manager Harry Wright from Philadelphia or New Yorker Pat Powers to replace Watkins, announced on March 5 he would again manage the club himself. His governorship was thankfully short-lived, as within weeks, former Pittsburgh captain George "Doggie" Miller arrived to both manage and captain the Browns. Von der Ahe told *The Sporting Life* on March 27, "Last year we had a manager who did not suit some of the players, and in Baltimore was chased out of the hotel. George Miller, former Pittsburgh captain and first class player, is to take over. Regular practice is to be held. Miller has a reputation as shrewd, calculating, modest, wise and with plenty of 'snappy' ideas. If that does not work, I will take full responsibility."[70]

Miller's impact was immediate. He believed rifle shooting would hone the eye and reflexes of his players, and had the Browns practice at a local range every morning.[71] And St. Louis won all three pre-season games they played: the 26–8 trouncing of Toledo, with Werden hitting two home runs and Quinn and shortstop William "Bones" Ely one each, had Von der Ahe already boasting about his "unexcelled" staff.[72] The Browns also beat a Minneapolis outfit 13–3 on April 9, with Joe Quinn, freed of all leadership responsibilities, helping himself to five hits (including two doubles) and turning two fine double plays.[73]

Opening Day on April 19 brought Miller's former team, Pittsburgh, to town. But Doggie's rejuvenated Browns brushed last season's runners-up contemptuously aside, racking up eleven runs to three in front of 5,000 adoring fans. Breitenstein defeated the league's leading left-handed pitcher in Frank Killen, who had won a convincing 36 games in 1893. Quinn, too, relished Killen's deliveries, belting him for three hits, including a triple. And in a further sign that Miller's "daily practice" had paid off, St. Louis made only one error (ironically, by Miller himself at third base), while Pittsburgh fielded very raggedly.[74] The triumph was rather short-lived, though, when the Pirates took advantage next day of cold, rainy conditions and a small and subdued home crowd to avenge themselves with a 7–2 win. *The Sporting Life* reported the Browns lost heart by the sixth inning after a series of questionable decisions by Umpire McQuaid, and the Pirates, trailing 1–2, gleefully whacked them for six runs thereafter. On April 23, the Browns turned the tables back on their more fancied opponents, the 4–3 victory featuring a series of dazzling plays and a game-winning Ely home run in the ninth inning.[75]

The new middle-infield pairing of Bill Ely and Joe Quinn was already attracting the right kind of attention to the Browns. Far from being downcast at his axing from the captaincy and the loss of his business, Quinn showed celebratory form. *The Sporting Life* trumpeted on April 21, "Joe Quinn, whose form last season was unfortunate, is now playing second base as skillfully and artistically as any guardian of that bag, and hitting the ball with marked frequency and with a bat that seems fairly electrified with base hits."[76]

Shortstop Bill "Bones" Ely was the perfect foil for the revitalized Quinn. He had made his professional debut with the Buffalo Bisons in the same year as Quinn, 1884, and journeyed between Louisville, Syracuse, and Brooklyn before being picked up by the Browns in 1893. His first season was a modest one, hitting .253 and fielding at .905 in his 44 games,[77] but *The Sporting Life* boldly predicted bigger things for the pair: "The two men, Ely and Quinn, who were thought so strikingly deficient in the manner of batting, now lead the team in hitting."[78]

The flying start to the season had given the Browns a kind of "Jack and the Beanstalk" giant-killing confidence. While the Chicago Colts had been much below par in 1893, finishing just one rung above the Browns in ninth place, their roster still boasted credentialed hitters including the likes of Cap Anson (who would bat .388 this year), shortstop Bill Dahlen (.359), and outfielders Jimmy Ryan (.357) and Walt Wilmot (.329).[79] Such a fearsome lineup was no deterrent to the Browns on April 25—they thrashed the Colts at home 16–8 and 10–4, Quinn with a four-for-four outing in the first game.[80] Last year's third-place Cleveland was next in the Browns' sights. Down 4–0 on April 28, the Spiders were very nearly shut out but scored on a Bones Ely error in the sixth inning. Ely immediately atoned with a triple and another of his specialty ninth-inning homers, and Breitenstein grabbed a huge scalp with his defeat of Hall of Famer and 1893 34-game winner Cy Young. *The Sporting Life* crowed, "The Browns are now strong where the critics howled they were weak last season: smashing the ball, doing it when it is most needed, cutting off base hits, backing up, and hard earnest effort." The transformation was attributed solely to the influence of Miller, who gave the Browns what they were lacking last season: "a leader who will do himself what he wants his men to do."[81] This was a sad indictment on Quinn, but nonetheless true and one Quinn himself was quick to admit—the overburdened second baseman certainly had not done himself, or his team, justice in 1893.

May did not get off to such a bright beginning for the Browns. Two defeats by Cleveland (including a Cy Young two-hitter) were followed by a series whitewash in Pittsburgh, the third game of which included an all-in brawl after Pirates shortstop Jack Glasscock accused Pink Hawley of deliberately pitching at him, and hurled his bat in retaliation. Every player rushed in to separate the tussling pair and the scrap was monumental. Von der Ahe later complained of the Pirates' dirty play, especially that of Glasscock and catcher Connie Mack.[82] He clearly had an upset constitution during that road trip, because he also fined four of his own players $25 each for drinking after the game. On Opening Day in St. Louis, Von der Ahe had gifted each player a new suit of clothes—made, of course, in the same style as his own. Now while in Pittsburgh, the motive behind such unusual generosity became clear: he hired a private eye and instructed the gumshoe to "tail all players dressed like himself." Gleason and Breitenstein were among those sprung at 3 a.m. in the atrium of the team hotel on Seventh Avenue. Gleason protested, "What are you trying to do, get back the price of the suit by soaking us enough to pay for it?" Fortunately for the guilty ones, this remonstration amused the capricious Von der Ahe so much that the fines were forgotten.[83]

The Pirates themselves were on the end of two of baseball's most bizarre and unsavory incidents in 1894. On May 26, they led Cleveland 12–3 in the eighth, and disgruntled Spiders fans started a seat-cushion fight that spilled onto the diamond, forcing the Clevelanders to forfeit the game. Then on July 20, Cincinnati benefitted from two bottom-of-the-tenth inside-the-park home runs by "Farmer" Vaughn and "Germany" Smith, the latter with two outs, to squeak past Pittsburgh 7–6—but only after Reds fans physically manhandled Pirates outfielder Elmer Smith (of sunglasses fame) to prevent him from retrieving the game-winning hit from the left-field bleachers, one even drawing a revolver on Smith after he hit several spectators in a desperate scramble for the ball.[84]

The tone for the Browns' season was confirmed on May 10. The game started so well: for the first time in major league history, teammates combined for three straight home runs, the Browns' Frank Shugart, "Doggie" Miller, and Heinie Peitz hitting consecutive round-trippers in the seventh inning against Cincinnati. In all, Shugart hit three home runs for the game and Heinie Peitz two—but all their heroics were in vain as St. Louis fell 18–9 to the middle-of-the-table Reds on the back of eight dreadful fielding errors.[85] The Browns were shut out 5–0 by the Reds two days later thanks to seven Breitenstein walks, and their subsequent trip to Cleveland was equally depressing. With Cy Young on the mound and heavy hitters Cupid Childs (.353) and Jesse "The Crab" Burkett (.358) in the lineup, Breitenstein needed to be on his mettle and he was not, granting them seven runs in two innings for a 7–2 loss. To compound the misery, the Browns equaled the Spiders' hit total the next day with seven, but could get none of them across the plate and were comprehensively shut out, 7–0.[86]

The Boston Beaneaters, meantime, were on target for yet another record season, with Quinn's old rival Link Lowe leading the charge. On May 11, they edged Brooklyn 9–8 with the aid of Lowe's fifth-inning grand slam, but the *piece de resistance* came on May 30 in the afternoon game of a double-header with the Reds. Lowe hit four home runs in four consecutive at-bats, including two in the third inning, leading his team to a 20–11 conquest of Cincinnati and a sweep of the double-header. The homers all came off Icebox Chamberlain pitches, and Lowe also added a cheeky single to amass 17 bases for the game, a record only bested by the Brewers' Joe Adcock in 1954.[87] After Lowe's fourth homer, the crowd immersed him in $160 worth of coins and he was fortunate not be injured by their shower of generosity.[88] In the first game, Lowe's teammate Herman Long also set a major-league record by scoring nine times; Long had taken dinner at the North Boston Railroad Station that day and he tried eating the same meal the following day, hoping no doubt for equal luck at the bat—but he went hitless.[89]

By June, the Browns had slid back to a more familiar eighth place and Von der Ahe was forced on to a mid-season shopping expedition to inject some new talent into his lineup. The Browns were struggling at first base: Perry Werden had been released, and although Bill Brown was signed from Louisville, he was a weak hitter and played just three games. Heinie Peitz had been "making do" at first, but he was needed to relieve Dick Buckley catching. Von der Ahe offered Cleveland his pitcher Kid Gleason in a direct swap for first baseman Jake Virtue, but the deal was heavily skewed in Von der Ahe's favor: despite winning twenty or more games in the past four seasons, Gleason had started 1894 poorly, losing six of his eight outings, and Cleveland rejected the proposal. Gleason had also fallen badly foul of Von der Ahe, both for his habit of wearing a rueful grin when being hit hard, and for confronting the owner when he had withheld $100 from his pay for a misdemeanor. Kid crashed into Von der Ahe's office and bellowed, "Look here, you big fat Dutch slob, if you don't open that safe and get me the $100 you fined me, I'm going to knock your block off." Gleason got his refund—accompanied by a one-way ticket out of St. Louis.[90] He was sold to Baltimore at the end of June for $2,400 and would win them fifteen games before the year was out, but Gleason reached his greatest fame much later, as a manager of the infamous 1919 Chicago "Black Sox."[91]

By some miracle, and with their first base problem still unsolved, the Browns managed to finish the second half of May by winning more games than they lost. Fourteen thousand fans packed Sportsman's Park on May 20 for the double-header with Cincinnati, of which St. Louis won the first game 4–3. Joe Quinn contributed two doubles, including the winning blow in the tenth inning, which, with bases loaded and two men out, sailed gloriously over the centerfielder's head. The second game was a typical Browns farce, however: a 7–1 loss on four Bones Ely errors. It was fortunate the game was called for rain in the seventh inning before the humiliation could get any worse. But things looked up with gutsy one-run wins over Chicago and Brooklyn in the final week of the month. Brooklyn did, unfortunately, rebound to win the May 30 double-header 6–2 (after Dad Clarkson walked eight batters) and 5–2 on the back of some wild Pink Hawley pitching.[92]

It was only undisciplined opposition pitching that granted St. Louis a rare series win over seventh-placed New York in June. Huyler Westervelt walked seven Browns and added three wild pitches for good measure on May 31 to gift the Browns with a 6–2 victory, and the great Amos Rusie gave up eleven hits to Arthur Clarkson's four the following day in a 4–1 result. With such generous assistance, St. Louis had now reached the dizzying heights of seventh place on the league standings with 16 wins and 18 losses, although they were four wins behind leaders Pittsburgh.[93] Aware of the danger of losing touch with the top teams, St. Louis turned in an inspired effort on June 4 and 5 to defeat the second-placed Phillies twice in Philadelphia, 3–2 (on a ninth-inning Tommy Dowd double), and 7–3 (despite three errors between Quinn and Ely).[94] The Browns, by some further miracle, defeated Boston on June 6, but were swiftly brought back to earth the following day. In rainy conditions, Breitenstein walked thirteen men as Boston avenged the previous day's humiliation with a 19–8 rout (and even then, most of St. Louis's runs were scored in the bottom of the eighth after Kid Nichols took his foot off the gas). It was part of a three-game rout in which the old champions scored 42 runs to the Browns' 21, and Hawley had to be sent home "poultice in plaster" after slipping on the wet ground and straining his ribs. Quinn matched up twice against his old adversary Link Lowe, the first on June 7 in which Lowe took the honors with three hits to Quinn's one, but with the pair slamming three each the next day.[95]

Von der Ahe's quest for a quality first baseman finally paid dividends on June 16 when, to both his and everyone else's surprise, he snared the legendary Roger Connor from New York. He offered mediocre outfielders Dowd and Goodenough for the thirty-six-year-old future Hall of Famer, but "nearly dropped dead" when told he could have Connor if he simply maintained the salary Connor had earned with the Giants.[96] The .316 career hitter was greatly needed, as Dick Buckley had been concussed by a Pink Hawley "erratic downshoot," and both Tommy Dowd and Duff Cooley could barely hobble with injured ankles. Hawley's own ribs were still hurt, Miller was forced to catch game after game and soon had split fingers and sore hands, and while Cooley and Shugart were tried as replacements at third base, both struggled.

On top of this litany of hurts came a series of woeful pitching performances from the Browns' hurlers, still unable to adjust to the 60'6" pitching distance. On June 13, St. Louis was humiliated 12–3 by tenth-placed Washington as Kid Gleason gave up an astonishing 19 hits; Von der Ahe's resulting fury was probably justified, given he'd just granted the pitcher three weeks' leave to get in better shape.[97] It was Gleason's final appearance in the dark blue uniform with its crimson trim and brown stockings: Von der Ahe suspended him for "intentional disloyalty" (i.e., not trying) and shipped him straight to Baltimore.[98] Two days later came an even worse thrashing for the Browns at the hands of that very outfit when the heavy-hitting Orioles took Arthur Clarkson for 23 hits while St. Louis garnered just six off Hawke. One of those was a Joe Quinn drive to left field which was called a home run because it rolled under the fence—ironically, in the previous day's contest, the Orioles' Hugh Jennings hit one to the left-field bleachers, but the ball bounced back and Frank got it to Quinn in time to hold Jennings at second base. But Jennings was awarded a home run, to the fury of Doggie Miller, who railed at Umpire Stage throughout the game and afterwards filed a (futile) written protest.[99] Perhaps it was poetic justice that in the next day's 17–3 hiding, Jennings was the only hitless Baltimore player. The rout was finally completed on June 16 when the Birds hammered Breitenstein for twelve runs while Sadie McMahon held the Browns to just two hits. McMahon was rested after the seventh inning and replaced by the dapper Inks: while only two of his first 25 pitches were strikes and St. Louis pinched five runs off him, the Birds were never seriously threatened.[100]

These disasters can probably be as much attributed to light hitting and lax fielding as to the quality of hurlers on the mound, but Quinn, in a fit of public asperity, blamed a higher authority in Doggie Miller and his management methods. He told *The Sporting Life* crossly, "The trip would have been better if our pitchers were in shape—we would have won five more games. This idea of alternating pitchers is a mistake. A pitcher worked three times a week is overworked. Old-time pitchers could do it, modern pitchers do not have the stamina."[101]

Whoever was to blame, declining attendances were hurting Von der Ahe where it hurt most—the hip pocket. It was the club treasurer, Von der Ahe's own son Eddie, who stepped in with decisive action. Von der Ahe junior was detested by players and fans alike for his tyrannical manner and clear distaste for the game beyond the profits it generated. His first move was to get Dick Buckley released by loudly insisting his arm was gone (which it wasn't). Then he publicly announced the imminent sale of Breitenstein to New York, which was also a fairy tale. All salaries were cut and the club placed on the market for $45,000—a price that included the players, the new park, and the National League franchise. The team was now almost as demoralized off the field as they were on it, coldly assured by young Eddie that their individual and collective days could be very limited indeed.[102]

To make matters even more unprofitable, rain continued to dog the Browns' home season, making the traditionally profitable Fourth of July double-header a decidedly soggy affair. As a result, St. Louis drew the smallest crowd in the league, just 6,500 compared to the 15,000 who packed the Pirates' park in Pittsburgh. The Browns divided the honors with lowly Washington after what the *St. Louis Globe–Democrat* called "two miserable struggles,"[103] the first game particularly exasperating for the home fans. Pink Hawley hit three batters in succession in the first inning and was therefore largely responsible for four runs. The contagion spread through the team. The Browns tried minor leaguer John Ricks from the Belleville Clerks at third base to rest the sore-handed Captain Miller, but by the third inning Miller was called in to replacement the inept amateur—and ironically, he only made matters worse, with a wild throw letting in three runs. He was then forced to catch after the fifth inning as Peitz was hurt at the plate, and the result was a 10–5 loss. The second game was, thankfully, a complete reversal of fortunes, with a 15–8 win for the Browns. Quinn, whom *The Sporting Life* approvingly christened "the liveliest colt in Von der Ahe's stables," made three hits, scored two runs, and swiped two bases. He also had an errorless afternoon in the field, turning three double plays. It was all going so well—until he was hit on the hand by an Esper wild pitch and forced out of the game.[104]

It was July 27 before Quinn's hand healed. The enforced layoff was probably more painful than the injury, for he had been in singular form in the preceding weeks. He and Miller had pulled off a rare triple play against Boston on June 29, and the following day he and his faithful ally Bones Ely dismantled the Braves in a 10–9 win as they stole bases, hit doubles and made a brilliant saving play in the eighth inning to stop Boston from tying the score. Now, forced to watch Miller, of all men, standing in his place near the second sack, Quinn told *The Sporting Life* on July 14, "When I see Ely going for a ground, it gives me a pain to know I won't be on second base to receive it…. He is the best man I ever played alongside, we work together like pieces of machinery. There is no shortstop in the country with a better arm, which enables him to play deeper yet still make beautiful throws to first base—and how much did St. Louis pay for him when he was released to the Southern League by Brooklyn for being no good? Just 200 simoleons."[105]

Quinn did find brief alternative employment on July 13 when umpire Hartley went down with heat stroke during the game against Baltimore and Joe took over at the plate. He probably should have been retained for the July 15 match, which Baltimore won 9–8 in 11 innings: Umpire John "Mr. Alcohol" Gaffney was clearly drunk on the field, according to the protest filed by Von der Ahe to the National League.[106] While unable to practice or play, Quinn also had plenty of time for reading the papers, which, on July 19, were filled with news of the arrest of his old St. Louis Maroons friend and teammate, pitcher Charlie Sweeney. After a saloon brawl in San Francisco in which local ruffian Con McManus was shot dead, Sweeney was charged with murder. Sweeney pleaded self-defense, claiming McManus had repeatedly menaced him without provocation, but he was convicted of manslaughter in November. He was released from prison in 1902 but was dead within months from chronic tuberculosis.[107]

Despite their lowly status as league cellar-dwellers, the Browns were having a remarkable impact on the 1893 pennant race. By July 13, Boston had claimed first place in the league with a 22–7 bombardment of Cincinnati, while nearest rivals Baltimore tripped up against the Browns 11–10. Boston lost and the Orioles won the following day, giving both teams a winning percentage of .667 and equal share of first place; this only lasted a day, as Baltimore snatched the lead on July 15 with a 9–8 eleven-inning victory over a gutsy St. Louis. But the powerful Boston outfit inflicted a three-game sweep on the upstart Orioles at the end of the month to take a four-game lead to teach them who was boss in the competition.[108]

Champing at the bit, Quinn literally threw himself back into the game when he was finally given the all-clear to play again on July 27. He made two spectacular errors at second base but atoned with a three-hit performance at the plate to lead the Browns to a 6–4 win over Louisville in front of an adoring home crowd. The effort clearly took an emotional toll—and possibly a physical one—for the following day, he was very flat, hitless and committing an error at the bottom of the ninth which scored the Colonels' two winning runs.[109]

He and Ely took some time to rekindle their middle-infield magic as the pair of them were responsible for four errors in the final game of the series, allowing Louisville to make nine runs from their nine hits while the Browns could only score twice from their own ten. And to compound the misery, Quinn reinjured his hand. He could not catch, bat, or throw, but as a positive and steadying influence he had few equals, so he still traveled with the team as they left for Chicago. The Browns had slipped to a miserable tenth place (35–50), trailed only by Louisville (27–55) and Washington (24–57), and Quinn's support around the benches would be invaluable given Miller's commitments out on the field. But the Browns needed nothing short of divine intervention to save them from themselves: on August 1, the White Stockings turned the game into a burlesque by walking the bases in the last two innings and refusing to come home on wild pitches by young Ernie Mason as he was belted for 27 hits in a 26–8 mortification.[110]

While Quinn rode alongside his dispirited teammates, not traveling to Chicago were Bones Ely, Tim O'Rourke and Charlie Frank. Ely's wife was gravely ill with typhoid pneumonia and he was given leave to care for her, but O'Rourke and Frank were given a different kind of leave by Von der Ahe—the permanent kind. Such was his pique at the team's poor performances that, in addition to the sackings, Chris also suspended Arthur Clarkson indefinitely for his indifferent work, leaving only Breitenstein and Hawley to pitch, both of whom were sadly used up. His hand still half-healed, Quinn speedily reinstated himself at second base and Miller returned to more familiar territory at third, but the team was still unsettled, anxious, and discouraged. *The Sporting Life* tried to put a positive spin on the situation on August 4: "The return of Joe Quinn to his position will greatly strengthen the club. He has been badly missed both at bat and in the field. When he was injured, he had just gotten his eye on the ball and was lining them out with great regularity. Second base has been a weak spot since his enforced retirement."[111]

Miller bravely defended the team's poor showing, telling *The Sporting Life*, "With the exception of two weeks, I have not been able to put a team of sound men on the field: Buckley's leg injuries, Peitz was catching until he got hurt as well, so I went behind the bat; Shugart and Cooley filled in at third base and three of us played first until Connor arrived after Werden's release."[112] But the sackings and suspensions infuriated the aching and demoralized Browns, and by August 11, *The Sporting Life* reported the team were "ripe for rebellion," with players claiming not to have been paid for six months but still fined and suspended for errors. No one, it seemed, except Miller cared whether they won or lost, and the Browns threatened to strike while in Pittsburgh. But Von der Ahe telegraphed Miller coldly, "You tell those boys to play better ball or I'll send fifteen amateurs to take their place, and if I can't find amateurs, they'll play for amateur wages."[113] It was no idle threat. When results failed to improve, Miller himself—that former favorite son—was briefly stood down by Von der Ahe, who accused him of being "too easy with the men."[114] But Browns secretary George Munson talked Von der Ahe into giving Miller a second chance. It was Munson's own parting gesture—soon after, he abandoned the Browns' sinking ship for a more sedate career managing musicals at the St. Louis Grand Opera House, including directing the play *Derby Winner*, written by none other than Al Spink.[115]

Von der Ahe denied withholding player salaries as an incentive for his men to play better. "They are paid every 15 days when at home," he blustered to *The Sporting Life*. "$1,700 is due to them, as league contracts stipulate they are not paid when on the road."[116] But it was $1,700 Chris very likely did not have, for he now had trouble on the home front as well. He had always indulged his son Eddie, but now Eddie refused to return the favor, despite his father's numerous and growing financial challenges, and Chris was forced to take the boy to court to recover some of the money he had loaned him to finance his own debts, which grew like weeds in the night as gate receipts continued to wither.[117] By August 15, Von der Ahe had fled St. Louis to join his team in New York to escape his son's assertions of refusal to pay wages, new allegations of infidelity, and now rumors the Browns would have to be sold. A local syndicate had offered Von der Ahe $20,000 for the outfit but the old stager refused, stubbornly clinging to his old asking price of $45,000.[118]

Quinn and Ely both returned for the series with the Giants who, with 61 wins, were in third place and some 20 wins ahead of the tenth-placed Browns. The pair tried hard, making only one error each for the whole three-game series, but the fact the Browns had only two starting pitchers, both of whom were exhausted, saw the visitors win just one game, and that by only one run. Their deficiencies were most cruelly exposed by Brooklyn on August 20 and 21. The sixth-placed Bridegrooms spanked St. Louis 20–4 (scoring 18 of those runs in the first five innings off Clarkson) and 20–11 (as the Browns made nine errors and Breitenstein gave up 24 hits).[119]

There were few highlights in the remainder of the season for the Browns. Two, however, came in the final week of August when St. Louis first defeated eventual pennant winners Baltimore 10–6, Hawley keeping his former teammate Kid Gleason at bay by restricting the Birds to seven hits and hitting a double himself as part of a six-run binge in the eighth inning. Three days later, the Browns defeated league front-runners Boston 9–5. Boston knocked in five runs and tied the score in the sixth inning, but St. Louis struck back with four runs of their own to hold the pretenders at bay.[120] But the team descended to an unprecedented level of farce in September, losing their series to eleventh-placed Washington in the worst possible way: tied 4–4 at the top of the ninth on September 5, St. Louis employed every known delaying tactic hoping the game would be called for darkness—and Umpire Reitz did indeed call the game: as a 9–0 forfeit to Washington for the Browns' time-wasting.[121] On September 9, the team had a 7–5 win over Brooklyn in the first of a double-header (Joe Quinn with two hits including a triple), but the second game started very badly indeed, Clarkson giving away four runs in the first inning and Hawley six in the second. Breitenstein was summoned to take over, but refused to pitch again, having thrown the entire first game and pitched the previous day as well.

The St. Louis correspondent for *The Sporting Life* gave this eyewitness account of the ensuing incident:

> Von der Ahe stormed into the rooms as Breitenstein was changing into his street clothes after the first game, bellowing, "Vhy you take off your uniform, huh?"
> "I tort I was tru."
> "Did I tell you you were tru?" Breitenstein nervously removed his hat. "Vell den, get back to your tressing-room, right away, undt get your suit on. You godt to pitch dis game out."
> "But Mr. Von der Ahe, I've pitched my game and won it. Don't you think that's enough for one day? I pitched yest..."
> "Not if I vant you to pitch two games."

But Breitenstein didn't pitch, and was suspended indefinitely and fined $100.[122]

On September 25, Baltimore clinched the National League pennant, beating Cleveland 14–9. Such were the celebrations of the hard-drinking Orioles that they were promptly thrashed seven games to nil by second-placed New York in the post-season Temple Cup series, including a 16–3 humiliation in the final game on October 8.[123] St. Louis finished the season in ninth place with a 56–76 record. The Browns made the lowest profit in the league,

10. The Flea-Bitten Gray and the Bald-Faced Nag

with just $5,000 to show for their season compared to New York's $75,000 and Baltimore's $40,000. It could have been worse—after all, last-placed Louisville made a $10,000 loss—but a good proportion of the Brown's meager proceeds immediately disappeared into the St. Louis courthouse coffers on October 8 when Von der Ahe was arrested for assaulting the owner of Johnson's saloon, convicted, and fined $500.[124]

Despite his injured hand and all the stresses of the season, Quinn finished the year second in fielding at second base only to Baltimore second-sacker Heinie Reitz. From his 106 games, he made just 33 errors for a fielding percentage of .954, ahead of Bid McPhee (Cincinnati, .949) and Fred Pfeffer (Louisville, .931), both among the nineteenth century's premier second basemen.[125]

• • •

> "Satisfaction with the present and careless of the future, a heart as big as an ox, tricky but never dishonest, his faults injured none but himself, he has made his last home run."—*The Sporting Life*, November 17, 1894

November 1894 saw two incidents occur of personal significance to Joe Quinn. The first was the birth of his third son and fourth child, Clarence Patrick, on November 13. Just four days after this happy event, the death was announced of Mike "King" Kelly.

Kelly was just 35 years of age in 1894, but he looked twice that. In the nineteenth century, it was a common belief that meat over-stimulated the gut, as did alcohol, tobacco and coffee. Spices, butter, sugar, and white bread all produced dyspepsia—but Kelly loved them all, and despite still playing for the New York Giants in the 1893 season, the King was badly overweight. Cigarettes, in particular, were viewed as highly effeminate during the 1890s, and many managers saw smoking as an indication of weakness and loss of confidence. It was widely publicized that this additional vice also killed Kelly's batting eye and further hastened his downfall. On November 10, 1894, Kelly contracted pneumonia on his way to Boston to appear at the Palace Theatre, and a week later, he was dead. Quinn later gave an account of his passing to the *St. Louis Republic*: "Kelly died penniless after earning $90,000 in salaries while playing baseball. The day he died he slipped off a stretcher while being conveyed into a hospital and his last words were, 'This is my last slide.'"[126]

Quinn had lost one of his greatest friends, who had "acted like a gentleman when I first went to Boston, [and] could not do any more for his brother than he did for me."[127] Kelly's obituary in a Boston paper declared he had "taken the decision of the Great Umpire from which there is no appeal."[128] In his 16-year professional career, he earned a .307 lifetime average and won a batting crown in 1887. But Kelly was remembered as much for the man he was as for his on-field genius. As his old manager James Aristotle Hart recalled, "His earnings belonged to everybody and anybody but himself.... He was dubbed King Kelly, and if there was a king of good fellows, it was His Royal Highness. There will, in my opinion, never exist a player who will be so sincerely loved by the entire baseball public ... who in life never had an enemy but himself."[129]

> Slide, Kelly, slide!
> Your running's a disgrace!
> Slide, Kelly, slide!
> Stay there and hold your base!
> If someone doesn't steal ya
> And your batting doesn't fail ya
> They'll take you to Australia!
> Slide, Kelly, slide![130]

11. The Stone of Sisyphus

"There was the din and clangour of war about Sportsman's Park last Sunday, and when Chris Von der Ahe paused to wipe the blood off his battleax and mop his scarlet face, the ground was strewn with heads."
—*The Sporting Life*, June 29, 1895

Greek legend holds that Sisyphus, the king of ancient Corinth, was condemned for his life's misdemeanors to forever roll an immense boulder up a hill in the Underworld, only to have it roll back down each time he neared the summit—damned to an eternity of fruitless effort and unremitting frustration.[1] There was an air of Sisyphean tragedy about the St. Louis Browns of 1895, damned as both the most- and the worst-managed ball club of the era.[2] The league had twelve teams, and in the three seasons between 1895 and 1898, the Browns had as many managers. As the seasons proceeded, the procession degenerated from the sublime to the ridiculous, and the team's performances correspondingly declined from mediocre to downright comatose.

The 1895 season was just eight weeks old when the yoke of managership landed—uninvited—on the shoulders of Joe Quinn.

His predecessor, Al Buckenberger, came to the Browns from Pittsburgh on January 26, 1895, with scandal hanging about his own neck like an albatross. Buckenberger and Louisville manager Bill Barnie had been expelled by the National League the previous year for allegedly plotting to resurrect the rival American Association.[3] While the twelve-team National League had a monopoly on professional players, no realistic competitor, and booming attendances, there were trolls such as Buckenberger and his allies lurking under the bridge, aware of the ease of destabilizing this happy situation, with franchise owners having a too-heavy hand in league affairs and Nick Young more of a figurehead than a president. The gap between the best and worst league clubs was also widening: the winning average of pennant-winners Baltimore was .695 in 1894 compared to .277 of the twelfth-placed Louisville.[4] Although their plot to revive the American Association failed and the blacklist was lifted from both Barnie and Buckenberger by year's end, Buckenberger was out of a job, Connie Mack now entrenched as player-manager with the Pirates. Von der Ahe quickly swooped to bring "Buck" to St. Louis.

Despite his off-field proclivities, Buckenberger had managed the Pirates to second place in 1893 with an 81–48 record, but 1894 had not been so kind, Pittsburgh struggling to 53–55 before Buck's suspension. His record in St. Louis was just as unflattering. From 50 games, the Browns won just 16.[5] They had made their usual fine showing in the spring of 1895, winning all six exhibition matches on their Southern tour in late March, and despite several players getting hurt and unusually bad weather keeping profits down, Von der Ahe "had not felt so encouraged in years."[6] A further happy omen came on April 18, when for the first time since 1892, the Browns lost their opening series to Chicago. A strange occurrence to celebrate, indeed! The wildness of pitchers Breitenstein and Ehret literally force-fed the Chicago hitters with walks, and the Colts won both opening games 10–7 and 11–5. The Browns, however, were determined to put a positive spin on the loss: previous seasons had gone on to a bad end after a flying start, so an early disappointment might signal a change in their long-term fortune.[7]

Such hopes were, naturally, extinguished instantly. St. Louis lost six of its first nine home games, and with morale fragile as spun glass after the turmoil of the 1894 season, it took very little to dishearten the Browns. Von der Ahe was unhappy as attendances were already poor, and he blamed weak hitting by his aging stars: Dowd and Connor were threatened with the "yellow envelope" (ten days' notice of release) unless they improved. To complicate matters, Bones Ely was sick after the rainy trip south, and Duff Cooley was forced from the outfield to try to cover his position at shortstop. Quinn was almost the only Brown holding his own—notwithstanding the loss of his infield partner, in five games he accepted 30 of 31 chances, and his play was described by *The Sporting Life* as "great."[8] To rub salt into their many wounds, the first visit of Buckenberger's old club, Pittsburgh, was particularly astringent for the Browns, shut out 6–0 on April 26 by their former teammate Pink Hawley, then losing the following day 5–4 by allowing a run at the bottom of the ninth. But this time, Von der Ahe held accountable not the manager or players, but a pair of geese which had nested in the St. Louis outfield—"goose eggs" was the slang term for zeroes on the scoreboard, and the volatile German had both birds roasted.[9]

The offensive upsurge which had worried league officials into potentially changing the pitching distance back to 55 feet at the start of the season, showed no signs of abating. On May 3, Link Lowe registered five hits and scored six runs in Boston's 27–11 rout of Washington.[10] Browns catcher Heinie Peitz attempted to emulate the feat two days later, going five-for-five with three extra-base hits against Cincinnati—but Peitz somehow failed to score a single run himself; St. Louis did win the game, however, 11–4. And on May 10, in the course of a 14–4 win over the Browns, Philadelphia slugger Sam Thompson became the third man in National League history to hit 100 career home runs.[11] The Browns were at last in the mood to do some slugging of their own—on June 1, aging first baseman Roger Connor grabbed six of his team's 30 hits in a 23–2 thrashing of New York. Connor became the league's all-time home run leader two days later, passing Harry Stovey with his fourth of the season and one hundred-and-twelfth of his career, but the day was still a dismal one, that historic hit driving in St. Louis' only runs in a 5–2 loss to Brooklyn.[12]

Despite these occasional flashes of brilliance, the Browns fans—the few they had left—had lost patience by June, hounding the players unmercifully from the bleachers and whistling "the Dead March" anytime their former favorites fell behind. But *The Sporting Life* of June 8 argued that while the pitching had been poor, the fielding and baserunning were first class, and the cranks did not seem to realize the players felt ten times worse over losses than they.[13] Nonetheless, the eleventh-placed Browns continued to mortify themselves on the diamond. On May 8, leading Boston 7–4 in the eighth inning, Red Ehret split his fingers and was replaced in the pitcher's box by Ted Breitenstein—who immediately gave up eight runs for an 11–7 loss.[14] Two weeks later, on the back of a loss to last-placed Washington in which he made five errors behind the bat, Doggie Miller resigned as Browns captain to try to improve his own form, the reins now presented to Heinie Peitz. The 24-year-old catcher had held out for a raise until the very end of March before giving in, signing a contract and heading south with the Browns. But he had not been idle in the off-season—*The Sporting Life* reported he had doubled his size, strength and armspeed, and that Quinn and Ely would have a warm time stopping his throws.[15] Now Peitz's method of inspiring his men was a fighting-cock's aggression on the coaching line and sliding into base spikes first to show the boys how it was done. It seemed to work, briefly—Washington was trounced 23–7 and New York 23–2, Breitenstein restricting himself to ten hits and his defense plundering 30 hits, five stolen bases, and four walks off a sore-armed Jouett Meekin. Quinn and Ely could almost have won the game alone with six hits and six runs between them. The Browns' crowning achievement was a three-game sweep of Philadelphia in the Brotherly city on June 5–7, one of only two occasions on which the Browns won three consecutive games that season.[16]

Such a feat was—unsurprisingly—followed by eight excruciating losses, and the final straw came on June 21–22, when the Browns lost the first two games in their series against Buck Ewing's eighth-placed Cincinnati Reds. While reports vary as to whether Buckenberger resigned[17] or was forced to quit,[18] by June 24 the manager had fled St. Louis for his home back in Pittsburgh. Von der Ahe complained to the *Washington Times* that the ex–Pirate had tried to govern the Browns with kindness and friendship, and as a result, was double-crossed by them.[19] This was, in a measure, true. Von der Ahe allowed the players to go to the races at the Fairgrounds across from Sportsman's Park on their days off, and the party was usually headed by Buckenberger. He drank with them and defended their dissipations and errors, their vices and carousings, to a man. But it was Buckenberger's relationship—or lack thereof—with Chris Von der Ahe that finally sank the boat. The pair had clashed repeatedly over the handling of the players. When, on June 6, Von der Ahe telegraphed Buckenberger and demanded Clarkson's suspension for his poor form on the trip East, Buck refused—so Von der Ahe had Clarkson traded to Baltimore.[20] And on June 22, a furious confrontation erupted between the pair after Buckenberger refused to fine Ely $25 for dropping a fly ball which let in three winning runs. When Von der Ahe threatened to fire him unless the team made progress, Buckenberger never wavered.

"Why not do it now?" he challenged.

So the next day, Von der Ahe did—and for good measure, also dispatched a gate-keeper, a score of program sellers, and a couple of park policemen, just to make himself feel better. Von der Ahe told the press, "I must give the people good ball or go out of the business. Buck did his best for the players ... and he is too good a fellow to be associated with such ingrates. I will govern by the power of the purse rather than by love. Men do not play ball for love—they want hard money for their services."[21]

Von der Ahe himself managed the third game of the Reds series on June 23, sitting on the bench with binoculars to better espy and hound his own men, and remonstrating with Umpire Keefe when that man refused to eject a Cincinnati player who was sledging him. By some miracle, the Browns won the contest 9–3, largely on the back of Roger Connor's unassisted double play and two home runs.[22] Meanwhile, the Browns directors were meeting to formulate an offer sufficiently tempting to entice a new manager into the den of the chaos-racked Browns. It would cost them $200 a month (the average public servant earned around half that), plus $2,000 playing salary, to secure the signature of Joe Quinn in late June.[23] It was unlikely the money tempted Quinn. His sense of duty to his disordered comrades was powerful, despite his clear distaste for leadership and limelight, and he was the obvious choice as a role model to the dispirited Browns: not only was he playing the game of his life, batting .362 and fielding .913, but the *Washington Times* stated simply, "Steady and reliable, Joe is one of the most respected players in the profession."[24]

Quinn remains the only Australian ever to manage in the major leagues. He seemed ideal managerial material, in spite of his early career failure in Duluth: *The Sporting News* gushed, "Quinn never broke a contract or went back on his word ... he is honest and upright and commands the respect of the fraternity at large, and can always be depended on to do anything honorable in advancing the interest of the club."[25]

But would being a "nice guy" alone be enough? Leo Durocher may have been referring to men like Quinn when he declared "nice guys finish last."[26]

Quinn was in a much better personal position to assume control of the Browns than he had been during his captaincy in 1893. While he was still in business at McGrath & Quinn, livery and undertakers of 4821 Easton Avenue, the bulk of the in-season work was now assumed by his father-in-law. But Von der Ahe had another motive for the choice, made even in the face of an offer from former New York Giants president John B. Day, to take over the team.[27] At the close of the 1894 season, Von der Ahe had told *The Sporting Life*, "Miller is a foxy fellow. He only uses his wits to keep me from knowing his scrapes and shield Shugart and the rest of his companions in midnight carousels. But Quinn is an easy man to handle."[28]

As in his previous foray into managership in Duluth, Joe captained the eleventh-placed Browns the only way he knew how—by leading from the front on the field, and through his impeccable behavior off it. It was by no means a romantic transition for the team. The Browns lost their first seven matches under Quinn's stewardship, including a 15–3 thrashing from Pittsburgh which was only stalled when the game was called in the eighth inning so St. Louis could catch their train. It was July 2 before their first win; the Browns scored 11 runs in the first inning on the way to a 15–9 victory over Chicago, Quinn grabbing two of these and three hits for the day.[29] On July 25, Quinn slammed four singles and a double against the visiting Brooklyn to drag the Browns out of a six-game losing slump. It was the only time he got five hits in a National League game.[30] By August 25, the *Omaha Daily Bee* buzzed excitedly that Quinn had struck out but three times in 89 games, reflecting he had come a long way since his days with Des Moines in 1888, when Omaha ace Bill Burdick once struck him out four times in a single match.[31]

Determined not to repeat either Buckenberger's mistakes or his own from 1893, Quinn also took his players in hand off the field. *The Sporting Life* publicly warned Quinn on July 13, "Manager Quinn should see that the coach lines are occupied all the time, and try to fill the boys with some of the earnestness which distinguishes his own work on the diamond. Give the men to understand that they must play ball, and winning ball too, or stand the consequences." Ted Breitenstein was first in Quinn's crosshairs. The young pitcher was caught on a drinking binge, allegedly consuming four beers *during* a game amid the July 7 trip to Baltimore, and despite the extravagant offers he had fended off for his star hurler, Von der Ahe was ready to simply shovel him out of the team on the spot.[32] Where Buckenberger might have excused him, through friendship or simply to spite the team owner, Quinn instead extracted a promise for reform, despite Breit's insisting the drinks were only soda water and the episode had been a prank to aggravate Von der Ahe.[33] Nonetheless, Quinn told Breit, "If you are caught drinking, I will take off your uniform. The St. Louis team is in a crippled condition; certain members of it have taken too many liberties, have kept bad hours, and have done things they should not have done. I want you to know, Breit, that so long as I am manager of this team, you will have to play or sit on the bench. If you ever take one glass of beer in business hours, or if you leave the field without my consent, you will quit playing ball for all time."[34]

Quinn's new approach was certainly noted in the press, *The Sporting Life* observing with approval on July 27, "The Browns are doing better, much better, under the direction of Manager Quinn than they did while directed, or rather misdirected, by their ex-manager. There is more harmony in the club, less chance for jealous differences, and when a few broken fingers and wrecked joints have got into normal condition, still better results may be looked for."[35] But the ghost of Al Buckenberger was not easy to exorcise. Fred Ely, for one, had had enough of the Browns. Despite the Browns' winning two of their three games against Louisville on July 4 and 5, Ely came to Quinn's rooms on the night of the 4th in an agitated and emotional state, vowing to quit on the spot and go home the very next morning. While he divulged the source of his unhappiness to Quinn at the time, the problem was not revealed officially until the December meeting of the National League—Ely had been compelled to play with the Browns in 1895 as a punishment for "use of contemptuous and disrespectful language when speaking of his employer, Mr. Von der Ahe." If he had refused, he would have been blacklisted. Von der Ahe had originally planned to trade Ely to Pittsburgh, but Ely's alleged utterances caused him to reconsider: the wiry shortstop would now play for St. Louis or not at all. Ely had earned $300 a month in 1894 and Von der Ahe also threatened that if he didn't hold his tongue, his salary would be reduced to $50 a month. Rumors were now rife that Buckenberger was trying to persuade him to jump to the Pirates—mainly as a swipe against Von der Ahe—and it took all of Quinn's diplomacy to persuade Ely to remain, at least until a replacement could be found.[36]

In between playing and placating, Quinn also had to patch up the holes left by the many crippled members of his squad. Miller and Peitz could barely catch with their injured hands, and Denny Lyons was at three-quarter pace with a swollen knee. So the Fourth of July was no celebration for Quinn as he played two hard games, interceded with Ely, then spent most of his remaining free hours at the city telegraph office, hustling to secure a brace of new fit players. Twenty-four-year-old John Otten from Murphysboro, Illinois, answered the call. Otten had just caught a game at Springfield but came straight on to St. Louis without sleep and caught against Louisville, putting out five stealers at second base and getting two hits. Quinn immediately signed him ahead of interest from a number of Southern League clubs—but two weeks later, Otten had a broken finger and joined the Browns' legion of sore-handed backstops.[37] The young man was the major leagues' first Dutch-born player, and caught a further twenty-five games for the Browns before being farmed out to the San Antonio Missionaries of the Texas Association in 1896; he would spend the remaining three years of his career in the minor leagues.[38]

While *The Sporting Life* was fulsome in its praise of Quinn on July 20, trumpeting, "Manager Quinn is making a good showing and no player in the profession deserves success more. Von der Ahe is a lucky man,"[39] Quinn's dwindling staff of fit and willing players was a dead weight upon his back. Red Ehret had lost 11 of his 14 appearances, and of the team's meager 17 wins, 11 had come behind the overworked Breitenstein. In July, the Browns lost series to Philadelphia and New York, the latter after two bad starts by Red Ehret. However, light hitting was as much to blame, with St. Louis scoring only 13 runs in the New York series to the Giants' 25. Veterans such as Roger Connor, himself a former Giant, were the target of strident media criticism: "Mr. Connor needs to wake up and hit the ball harder," bellowed *The Sporting Life* on July 20.[40] The very next day, Connor quit. The Hall of Fame left-hander towered over his teammates at 6'3" and 220 pounds, but was quiet and introspective by nature, and, although he was hitting .327, he was terribly dispirited by the performance of the Browns and his own public vilification. Tim "Biff" Sheehan was drafted in from Little Rock as his replacement.

Such was the poor form of the Browns that, after being swept in their three-game series against Boston on July 22–24, their 20–3 defeat of ninth-placed Brooklyn on July 25 was extravagantly described by *The Sporting News* as "a winning spurt." Breitenstein barely gave away a hit, Ely slammed two doubles and Quinn one, Ely and Cooley both hit triples, and Quinn stole two bases. The paper crowed, "Joe Quinn Exalted: The recent winning spurt of the Browns has aroused a lot of enthusiasm. Manager Joe Quinn has been so overwhelmed with congratulations that he is liable to go into the prediction business if success keeps up. He said today: 'I am not claiming anything, I said some time ago that Mr. Von der Ahe had a good club but it was playing in hard luck.'"[41]

It was almost the last good thing said about the Browns during Quinn's reign—for they won only one of their remaining 11 games under his managership, a 7–4 defeat of second-placed Pittsburgh on August 5; in the meantime, they had lost series to lowly Brooklyn and Louisville (the only team beneath them in the standings).[42] The series against the Colonels was the most disastrous—the first game was a close 1–0 loss, but on July 30, they were annihilated 18–2 thanks to eight St. Louis errors (Brown, Ely, and Quinn all making two each), and their former teammate, shortstop Frank Shugart, punished them with three triples. Their humiliation was completed in the third game when Breitenstein walked nine batters and Louisville scored ten runs in the final inning to win 15–7.[43] Quinn was now physically ill and managed just half a game in the series in Chicago. His problems were becoming farcical indeed, with 17-year-old Denver infielder Billy Kinloch tried at third base[44]: Quinn's account of Kinloch's debut had Chicago's "Big Bill" Lange making one of his famous bunts— "one of those bunts which go through stone walls." Kinloch bobbled it anxiously and it bounded out of his glove, almost jolting his teeth loose with the impact. That was more than enough for Kinloch—he crossed the diamond to Quinn at second base and demanded his release; despite all Quinn's reassurances that he was fielding fairly, Kinloch insisted he "had a little girl in Denver that wouldn't look well in black," and he was gone, barely waiting for the game to conclude and vowing never to darken the door of a National League club again.[45] It was here, with the boisterous wind whistling across Lake Michigan, that the stone of Sisyphus finally rolled backward over its bonded servant. Quinn watched the remainder of the series from the coaching lines as his men were overwhelmed by the mysteries of the Chicago pitchers. The three pitiful losses, including a 6–0 shutout, turned his feet in the direction of the hotel clerk and his telegraph. He cabled his notice to Von der Ahe on the night of August 4.

The reaction was not what he expected. Winning just 10 games from 36 should have guaranteed the axe across his neck—instead, Von der Ahe sent an instant reply rejecting his resignation. He would personally join the team in Cincinnati on August 7, and would have Manager Quinn maintain charge of the Browns until then. However, that was the extent of his support for both Quinn and his team: Von der Ahe sent a second cable ordering the immediate release of Harry Staley—leaving the Browns with only three pitchers—deposition of the hustling Peitz as captain and reinstatement of an unhappy Miller, and ordering the team to travel with only eleven men to save money.[46]

Still not completely recovered, Quinn led the disordered crew into battle against second-placed Pittsburgh on August 5. Despite illness, interruptions, and the heavy responsibility of managership, he was still batting .347, and made two glorious hits in the 7–4 victory. But the discarded Pink Hawley pitched the Pirates to an 11–2 revenge the following day, and they rubbed salt into the wound with an 18–1 mortification of the Browns on August 7, thrashing Red Ehret for 11 runs in the third inning, with Quinn 0–4 at the plate.[47] When the team arrived in Cincinnati late the same night, they were met at their hotel by Von der Ahe himself. What followed was a stormy confrontation between Quinn and the Browns' owner, during which Quinn insisted the best way he could serve the battling club was to focus on his playing alone. Von der Ahe's response was to withdraw all support for his beleaguered second baseman and reappoint himself as manager to take the Browns on the road for their toughest challenge of the season: a three-game series against league-leading Cleveland. It was never going to be a contest. The sacking of Staley forced both Ehret and Breitenstein to pitch five games between them within a week, and their sore-handed catchers could do little to support them: the Spiders swiped six bases in a single game on August 13 against the weary St. Louis batteries, and carried away the series unchallenged.[48]

Even after this litany of the pitiful, the tragic, and the just plain weird, the bizarreness was not over. On arriving back in St. Louis on August 15, Von der Ahe unveiled his choice as a new permanent manager for the Browns. While John B. Day, founder of the New York Giants who had carried off National League pennants in 1888 and 1889, had repeatedly indicated interest in the job, Von der Ahe instead installed a local businessman with no record of involvement in the game, even as a fan. Very little is known about Lew Phelan, the Browns' third manager for 1895 and seventeenth in six years. He was a shadowy figure whose sporting involvement extended little further than partnership with the Australian middleweight fighter Dan Creedon in the St. Louis saloon business.[49] He appears nowhere in the annals of baseball history or folklore, and just where he got his credentials to manage the Browns is anyone's guess. He was simply another example of Von der Ahe's desire for a puppet at the helm of the Browns, with himself firmly grasping the strings.

The Browns' owner was, however, a man on the brink of implosion. With gate receipts non-existent, and his team was publicly disintegrating, so too was Chris Von der Ahe's personal and professional life. In January, his wife had filed for divorce, citing infidelity and neglect, and on March 30, Von der Ahe was arrested in St. Louis for allegedly shooting a Negro in the foot. He was also being sued by released third baseman Denny Lyons for refusing to pay Lyons' salary while he was suspended in June.[50] Von der Ahe was in serious financial trouble, having never really recovered from his investment in keeping the American Association afloat amid the Players' League revolt and the subsequent war with the National League. But, ever the entrepreneur, he unveiled his solution in August—to attract the public back to Sportsman's Park by transforming the once hallowed turf into an amusement park-cum-shooting gallery-cum-racetrack. With sales of tickets and beer declining, the establishment was now rented out for clay pigeon shooting, "Red Indian" shows, and balloon ascensions—many of which took place around or during ball games—and the place became known as "The Coney Island of the West."[51] Al Spink slammed it as "prostitution of a ballpark,"[52] and *The Sporting Life* called on the League to prevent the consolidation of gambling around baseball and horse racing. Betting on baseball was already legal in Pittsburgh, and the paper warned, "Nothing makes a sport so dishonest as to have bets made on it. There are ball players who are not above accepting bribes, and there are betting men who would not hesitate to give a portion of their winnings to one or two players in order that they may rake off a big profit.... Ball players are not above temptation."[53] However, the League took no action, ruling it was Von der Ahe's park and he could do with it what he wanted. And the players loved it: the *Omaha Daily Bee* reported Breitenstein, Miller, Dowd, and Peitz were all daily visitors to the Sportsman's Park track, hinting Von der Ahe would soon get back all the salary he paid them.[54]

Meanwhile, with Phelan nominally in charge, by September 1, St. Louis was still in eleventh place with a 32–69 record. Cleveland was the clear leader at 68–39 with Baltimore making a run at them at 59–35.[55] The Browns celebrated their departure for their final away run against the Eastern teams on August 18 with three straight victories over Louisville, disposing the latter of their hopes of dispossessing the Browns of eleventh place. Despite his financial straits, Von der Ahe went east with the team to search out young players in order to "build the team up from the bottom" in the manner of Ned Hanlon at Baltimore, clearly undeterred by the Billy Kinloch fiasco. He had already released veteran outfielder Tom Brown and warned more older players would follow as "dead limbs were lopped."[56] Nonetheless, he also approached Cincinnati about buying back aging former Brown Arlie Latham, as much for his huge popularity as his wealth of experience: after all, his oldest player—Joe Quinn, aged 33—remained the only Brown among the top twenty hitters in the league, with .345. The *Wichita Daily Eagle* paid him the following rather unusual compliment: "Joe Quinn, at second, with Samuels, Connor, and Miller, shines out like the rich jewel in an Ethiop's ear. That being the case, Samuels, Connor and Miller must be the ear."[57]

After August 20, the Browns won only seven further games for the season, closing out the year with an inglorious 18–2 loss to the Pirates on September 28—the visitors hit two home runs, three triples, and four doubles, and stole 11 bases in their wild rampage around Sportsman's Park,[58] after which Lew Phelan and his 11–30 managership record disappeared forever into the fog of forgettable folklore.

It was with extraordinary relief that Quinn escaped the hothouse of the Browns and Sportsman's Park for his self-imposed solitude in the cool and quiet of the mortuary during the winter. But even during the season, Quinn took time to further his knowledge in his chosen profession. On September 23, the *St. Louis Globe–Democrat* reported somewhat dubiously, "For a ball player, Joe Quinn is a man of curious tastes. While the team was in New York the other players made daily trips to the seaside. Joe spent his days in the swell undertaking establishments on Broadway. He is in the business in St. Louis, and takes more interest in the latest things in funeral fashions and furnishings than in the best trick ever turned on a ball field."[59]

Such diligence paid dividends, however. In 1895, Quinn was made a full partner in his father-in-law's undertaking business, and was reported to have already saved a staggering $30,000 during his baseball career.[60] "I am keeping on the boys and the game, but I seldom see any of my fellow-players," he told *The Sporting News* in November.

> I am in the stable from early in the morning until 9 o'clock at night, except at meal-time when I report with regularity to Mrs. Quinn. I don't propose to go South to play exhibition games in the spring another year. There is no necessity for my doing so and I will not leave my business more than ten days before the season opens. I take good care of myself at all times and do not need the preparation which the idle players who accumulate flesh while dissipating wealth find indispensible. About all I have to do to get in the game is work my throwing arm into shape. I have no intention of quitting the diamond, not for several years to come at least. I like the game and I have yet to be accused of being a "has been." I suppose that talk has its origin in the fact that I am in business. I have not signed for next season, but expect to be back in harness. It's a business matter with me and while I receive the money I estimate my services to be worth, I'll play ball. But you can bet that I am always consulted about figures, which go into the body of my contract.[61]

His renowned singing voice and love of skits and plays had not escaped the notice of his old friend, Ted Sullivan, who liked writing them as much as Quinn enjoyed performing them. In the late winter of 1895, Sullivan wrote a play especially for Quinn called *Biddy Moriarty*. Biddy was a historic character who lived in Dublin in the time of Daniel O'Connell, and was oft-claimed as the wittiest woman in Ireland. The emancipator O'Connell himself once engaged in verbal jousting with her across her stall at the Dublin markets, although the identity of the great statesman was only revealed after he retired, vanquished.[62] This was the premise of the play, which was apparently very clever and funny. Quinn was also known to sing publicly during the Browns' spring training trips: he had received a "big time" in Savannah, Georgia, after delivering clever songs for the Irish regiment the Jasper Greens,[63] amongst which were his all-time favorite ballad "The Old Red Shawl My Mother Wore"[64] and, daringly, "a grand oration on Von der Ahe."[65] His granddaughter, Mary Catherine Butler, remembered Quinn as playful and "jokeful" even into his old age, and very popular in St. Louis, constantly called upon to emcee local events and parties because of his great sense of humor and storytelling abilities.[66]

• • •

Anti-utopia: an imaginary place or society characterized by human misery and oppression.—American Heritage Dictionary of the English language, third edition, 1996

After the exhaustion and turmoil of the 1895 season, changes were afoot at Sportsman's Park in the winter—both within and without the Browns team.

The *Omaha Daily Bee* of November 17, 1895, stated bluntly, "What St. Louis needs is a manager who knows his business and can get along with Chris. There is some good material in St. Louis, like Breitenstein, Peitz, Ely and Quinn; not much building up would be required to make a winner out of that team, which, however, can only be done by a capable manager."[67] But through that winter of 1895–96, Chris Von der Ahe was happily occupied in digging up the far portion of the Sportsman's Park outfield to create a lake suitable for skating. He also had visions of creating a "Shoot the Chutes" ride in the summer, complete with ramps and sliding hollow logs.[68] He *had*, however, torn himself away from these dreams of pleasure and profit for just long enough to recruit a new manager for his team.

This one had at least some baseball experience. Harry Diddlebock had been sports editor of the *Philadelphia Times* and *Philadelphia Inquirer* and also served as secretary, treasurer, and president of the Eastern League.[69] Von der Ahe gave him a typically extravagant reception when he arrived in St. Louis on February 8, 1896: Diddlebock was greeted by a reception committee at the station and conducted to a *soirée* at the Planters Hotel attended by Von der Ahe, Browns board members, the media, and even Police Commissioner Forster.[70]

Such excesses aside, Von der Ahe also made good on his threat to cull his older players in favor of younger (and possibly more naïve) talent. While he had reserved many of the aging stars in November—including Miller, Peitz, Ely, and Quinn himself—by the time Diddlebock arrived in February, most of them were gone. Miller had been sold to cellar-dwellers Louisville (the ultimate insult for his loyalty and service), and Ehret and Peitz traded to Cincinnati, ironically for the 36-year-old Arlie Latham, pitcher Tom Parrott, and catchers Morg Murphy and Ed McFarland. Von der Ahe had also attempted to buy high-class sluggers Ed Delahanty (who hit .404 in 1895) and Sam Thompson (.392) from Philadelphia for the staggering sum of $30,000, but the offer was rejected.[71] The most notable departure from the Browns was that of disgruntled Fred Ely. Just after Christmas, Connie Mack arrived in

St. Louis for his second attempt in eight weeks to buy the star shortstop for Pittsburgh, and this time added a $1,000 cash bonus on top of his offer to trade pitcher Bill Hart and shortstop Monte Cross for Ely.[72] Von der Ahe now snatched the bait like a greedy trout: with a mutinous crowd of Browns beating down his door for raised salaries, he needed every penny he could raise.

These insurgents were suitably led by Ted Breitenstein. Breit worked as a guard at the Illinois Penitentiary in Chester, Illinois, during the winter, and had visited St. Louis while searching for an escaped prisoner on February 6. While Von der Ahe had reserved his services for 1896, Breitenstein was adamant he would not play until paid a salary more proportionate to his work. He had thrown 47 complete games and faced 1,936 batters in 1895, more than any other pitcher in the League, for which he had earned just $2,000.[73] Von der Ahe had already offered him $2,400, the limit imposed by the League, for the 1896 season—but Breit and almost everyone else knew that this limit was arbitrary and regularly flouted. He had grown still more physically imposing over the winter, at 5'7" and 165 pounds (with most of it above the belt), but when he called upon Von der Ahe at Sportsman's Park, the equally burly German merely waved him out of the office and referred him to the new manager. Diddlebock tried to get Breit to sign a contract at the limit, but Breit just smiled, said he'd been promised $2,500 by the Chester club, and walked out.[74]

A month later, Breitenstein was still holding out and was now accompanied by Dick Cooley, who wanted $2,400 (double his 1895 salary), Tommy Dowd demanding $2,200 (a $500 raise), and young catcher McFarland wanting $2,000, $500 above his minor league salary with Indianapolis.[75] It took a special trip by Browns secretary Benjamin Muckenfuss to the team's spring base in Dallas to negotiate with the recalcitrant quartet, Von der Ahe authorizing him to sign Breit "at all hazards," which in this case cost him $2,400 plus a $200 bonus and $30 for a new uniform.[76] Quinn had, meantime, quietly signed his contract and, as promised, foregone the southern trip to focus firmly on his livery and undertaking business, only joining the team on April 1.

In 1896, the National League encountered a significant financial business depression. There was growing competition for the summer sporting limelight from cycling and horseracing, and public interest in sports was also captured by the first modern Olympic Games, held in Athens between April 6 and 15, with the remarkable American Robert Garrett bringing home four athletics medals for the United States.[77] Australians, too, were captivated by early success at the Games: their sole representative, runner Edwin Flack, fought off severe travel sickness to win the 800m and 1500m races, and was leading the marathon with just two miles to go (despite having never run further than ten miles in his life) when he collapsed and was tended to by none other than Games patron Prince Nicholas of Greece.[78]

In the nineteenth century, the young nation of Australia lacked a true national sporting identity. It had no flag of its own and its national anthem was still Britain's "God Save the Queen." Aside from the national cricket team, examples of international sporting representation were scarce, and Australia was ripe for a new hero in 1896. Edwin Flack, like Quinn, was an Australian sporting pioneer, as the first to compete at the Olympic Games and the first to win a gold medal. Like Joe Quinn, he had independently taken himself to the Games, which at the time, very few Australians were even aware of[79]—rather like major league baseball, as evidenced by the complete lack of coverage of Joe Quinn's achievements in the Australian press. And like Quinn, Flack's "have a go" spirit was on show as he entered both the tennis competition and the marathon at the Games, despite having little or no experience with either event. But unlike Quinn, Flack's bold accomplishments in Athens—playing

Olympic tennis on the morning of the 800m race, and his dual gold medals on the track—endeared him immediately to the Australian public, who christened him "The Lion of Athens."[80] Flack is now a member of the Australian Sports Hall of Fame, and a bronze statue commemorating his achievements (unveiled by fellow Australian running legend John Landy) stands in his home town of Berwick. His alma mater, Melbourne Grammar, awards the E.H. Flack Scholarship, and parks and streets have been named in his honor, including Edwin Flack Avenue adjacent to the Sydney Olympic Stadium.[81] No statue to Joe Quinn stands in any Australian street, and it was not until 2013—some one hundred and ten years after his baseball career ended—that he was inducted into the Australian Baseball Hall of Fame, and even then, only by special dispensation of the Australian Baseball Federation Heritage Committee.[82]

In addition to these external challenges, the National League had plenty of problems closer to home in 1896. Gambling was an increasing conundrum, with parks such as Von der Ahe's only encouraging the habits of many players and owners in openly betting on the pennant race. There were still complex religious difficulties associated with Sunday baseball, with Protestants strongly objecting and Catholics generally supporting the concept so long as alcohol was not sold. But their greatest fear of all was the prospect of competition from another league. On February 29, 1896, Western League president Ban Johnson asserted, "The Western League has passed the stage where it should be considered a minor league.... It is a first-class organization, and should have the consideration that such an organization warrants."[83] It would be four years before Johnson would act upon this belief, renaming his operation the American League in 1900 and achieving major league status through widespread establishment of clubs and acquisition of players, but the National League could clearly scent the storm on the horizon.

The 1896 season opened on April 16 with the twelve franchises unchanged from last year. The largest Opening Day crowd in nineteenth-century history of 24,500 witnessed the year's first game in Philadelphia against visiting Boston.[84] Cincinnati second baseman Bid McPhee commenced the season wearing a glove, amid much good-natured ribbing from his opponents; he was the final player to make the transition from the bare-handed days.[85] St. Louis hosted Cleveland and recorded a 5–2 victory,[86] but as was the traditional pattern for the Browns, it didn't take long for the season to descend into a circus. The year was just 17 games old when new manager Harry Diddlebock was sacked after being discovered, intoxicated and bloodied, in a St. Louis alley at 3 a.m. on May 8.[87] He claimed to have been assaulted, but with the Browns' poor 7–10 record, the axe was quick to fall. Third baseman Walter Arlington "Arlie" Latham was thrust briefly into the breach—which seemed an odd move on Von der Ahe's part, as the puckish humor of the "The Clown" was often directed straight at the owner. Historian Daniel Pearson joked that Latham did not play baseball, he *performed* it: he would cartwheel home after hitting a home run, do backflips to celebrate a good play, pretend to faint on bad calls, and constantly banter with the crowd. He was so popular he was the first player invited on Spalding's World tour of 1888, and given the honor of explaining the game to the King of England.[88] While Latham did have some credentials befitting a manager—including great intelligence, resourcefulness, and knowledge of the game, having been a member of the mighty four-time pennant-winning Browns of the 1880s—his career as a major league manager was short, losing all three games of which he was in charge.[89] Von der Ahe himself managed (and lost) the following two games before electing reinstated first baseman Roger Connor to the managership. His record of 8–37, and that of his successor Tommy Dowd (25–38), were just as depressing.[90]

The behavior of Chris Von der Ahe was increasingly erratic. The *St. Paul Globe* of May 17, 1896, marveled, "St. Louis has a new captain each day, but Von der Ahe, like the brook, babbles on forever."[91] The previous week, he had suspended catcher Ed McFarland, but the young man took his place, unchallenged, behind the plate the next day. Likewise, rumors abounded that Duff Cooley's neck was next on Der Poss President's block, notwithstanding the fact his fielding percentage was perfect at 1.000 and he was batting over .300.[92] The revolving door of players and managers and a long spell of bad weather had ill-feeling boiling into a witch's brew for the Browns, both on and off the field. But the *St. Paul Globe* concluded sadly, "Several thousand fans and all the newspapers of that city cannot move Von der Ahe one whit in his ideas of what a ball team should be."[93]

The bad weather stalking St. Louis reached a peak on May 27, when the city was devastated by a massive supercell tornado. In just 13 minutes, 80 mile per hour winds and torrential rain damaged or destroyed more than 8,000 buildings in a one-mile-wide swath through the city, from Lafayette Park through the downtown area for more than two miles northeast. Both the City Hospital and Eads Bridge were severely damaged. Palatial homes and hovels alike were destroyed, trees and fountains uprooted, business houses, factories and smokestacks torn apart, and streetcars flung around like toys. The storm never hesitated as it reached the Mississippi River but flung itself upon steamboats, sailboats, and barges, splintering them like kindling and sending crew and passengers alike to the bottom as it sped on to wreak havoc on the Illinois side. The death toll was estimated at 255 with almost 200 missing, presumed killed by flying bricks, falling walls, fire, or drowning. It was the single deadliest natural event to ever hit St. Louis.[94] The Browns were away in Baltimore at the time and thereby escaped any harm; Joe's family and business likewise were unscathed. But a cyclone of a different sort hit his team on July 1.

The Browns had had a series of long losing streaks in 1896—six to May 6, a further five to May 12, ten straight losses between May 26 and June 5, followed by two wins, then another eight losses. And by July 1, the Browns were midway through what would be their worst losing streak—fourteen straight.[95] Von der Ahe was already strapped for cash after being sued by his wife the year before, and from a series of heavily mortgaged real estate investments which had gone sour.[96] On July 1, in a fit of furious temper after the Browns' seventh straight loss, a 7–2 defeat by Pittsburgh, he flung about for the nearest scapegoat—and lit upon Joe Quinn. Von der Ahe cared little for Quinn's steadying presence around the team. His second baseman was having a poor season, hitting just .209 from his 48 games,[97] and a high-profile head had to roll as a warning to the rest of the motley crew, dangerous and half-savage as they were, like a pack of starving dogs.

Quinn was given ten days' notice and a one-way ticket to Baltimore. The national media were aghast, headlines shrieking, "'Der Poss President' is considered to be headed for the foolish farm!" and "'Der Cherman Pand' must be playing madhouse airs!"[98] The decision had absolutely no effect on the team's performances—the Browns lost a further seven games before stumbling to a 9–7 win over Boston on July 9, but Quinn played in none of these games.[99] And as he packed his bags for Baltimore, his replacement Roger Connor was fired and replaced as player-manager by Tommy Dowd: he was the Browns' fifth manager of the season, which was still only three months old. The crowning insult to Quinn in this entire debacle: the man with the cleanest reputation in baseball was sold to its dirtiest team.

12. Angry Birds

*"McGraw eats gunpowder for breakfast
and washes it down with warm blood."*
—Arlie Latham

Joe Quinn arrived out of the St. Louis frying pan into the Baltimore crematorium midway through the 1896 season, joining the hothouse of Oriole baseball and an outfit hurtling—in the wickedest possible fashion—toward their third consecutive pennant. Baltimore was a hustling, tumultuous town, a coarse and potent sprawl at the mouth of the dirty Patapasco River, where the rattle and clatter of rambunctious life echoed through the cobbled streets, circus parades jostling with hollering newspaper boys, barking dogs, roosters, horns and firecrackers. And at the heart of this commotion and cacophony stood the equally raucous and rowdy Orioles.

Quinn reflected many years later, "Every game was a dog-fight and each team made the going as tough as possible for the other."[1] And he wasn't kidding. Despite winning consecutive National League championships in 1894 and '95, the Baltimore Birds were better known for craftiness, fighting, and outright cheating than for their many achievements on the diamond. Their escapades came mainly at the behest of their wily manager Ned Hanlon. A champion outfielder who had captained the 1887 Detroit Wolverines to a World Series crown, Hanlon had been a conspirator in the 1890 Players' League before taking over as player-manager in Baltimore in 1892. Quinn praised Hanlon as "one of the brainiest men ever connected with the national game,"[2] and although his Oriole stable was replete with future Hall of Famers including John McGraw, "Wee Willie" Keeler, Hugh Jennings, Joe Kelley, and Dan Brouthers, the success of the outfit was a product of far more than mere talent. Hanlon brewed within the squad a wicked combination of dirty tricks and outright crimes, laying the groundwork during spring training for his ugly, dishonest style of baseball: the strategic knee or elbow, open and vicious sledging, stealing bases as though they were a rare and valuable commodity, and blatantly cutting across the diamond. This latest ploy, popularized by the bad Birds, became a common transgression in the late 1890s, particularly with only one umpire to stand guard over proceedings. In response to a reader's question about a baserunner's right to employ such a tactic, the *Omaha Daily Bee* sniffed, "He has no such right, but if the umpire does not see him cut a base, what are you going to do about it?"[3]

Refining such a malicious and piratical game required hard work, and the Orioles were often out on the field at eight in the morning before a late afternoon game. And after game and dinner, they bent their versatile and sassy heads together to plan for more. Quinn remembered, "We had elaborate systems of signals and there was a constant flashing of signs. We spent many an evening scheming what to do about this fellow and that on the opposition."[4]

Amid these confabulations sat Birds groundskeeper Thomas J. Murphy, usually smoking and nursing a strong ale, and grinning ghoulishly from under one of baseball's most impressive moustaches. He was the Jekyll to Hanlon's Hyde, an evil genius who built up the baselines so bunts would roll fair and kept the outfield lawn long to conceal hidden balls.[5] In spite of such knavery, the Orioles did have one of the greatest sets of outfielders in history. Walter (Steve) Brodie was the league's leading centerfielder on three occasions in the '90s, and regularly showed off by catching fly balls behind his back.[6] Brodie had been a teammate of Quinn's at the 1893 St. Louis Browns before being controversially released for his acrimonious relationship with Manager Watkins[7]; he was continually singing and chattering under his breath—until he made an error, whereupon he would often not speak to himself for the remainder of the game.

Brodie was flanked by rightfielder "Wee Willie" Keeler, who didn't fight, drink or swear, but had, during a Fourth of July game, gleefully fired blanks into the air from a pistol in his pocket.[8] Keeler was the runt of Lucifer's litter at just 5'4" and 140 pounds wringing wet, but he was also one of the nineteenth century's great left-handed hitters, a two-time National League batting champion and a three-time leader in hits. He insisted the secret of his success was a simple one: "Keep your eye clear, then hit them where they ain't."[9] This simple philosophy helped Keeler to a place in the Hall of Fame, with eight straight years of 200 or more hits, 13 consecutive seasons batting over .300, and a career average of .341.[10]

Leftfielder "Handsome Joe" Kelley made his National League debut in 1891 with the pennant-winning Boston Beaneaters as a teammate of both Brodie and Quinn, and was renowned for both his lithe athleticism and rugged good looks (his habit of carrying a mirror for mid-game grooming was exposed when it fell from his pocket one day while he was making a dive at a fly ball).[11] Left field was one of the hardest positions to play in the early days of the professional game, when the pitching was slower and the ball contained more rubber, distributing long hits in that direction with great frequency. So the fleetest men were stationed here, and Al Spink described Kelley as of "heroic build and figure, a man of great nerve and strength,"[12] whose place in the Hall of Fame was guaranteed by his lifetime .317 batting average.

But John McGraw and Hughie Jennings were Hanlon's star pupils. They were also the most reviled players in the league, reeking of profanity, spitting and snarling and grinding their spikes into their

John "Muggsy" McGraw was the poster boy of the Baltimore Orioles in the 1890s. Fiery and aggressive, he was a chief strategist (and brawler) on Ned Hanlon's infamous roster as they won three consecutive pennants between 1894 and 1896. During his later career as manager of the New York Giants, he offered a trial to Joe Quinn's son Scotty in 1920, but the boy died in the Spanish Influenza epidemic before playing a game (National Baseball Hall of Fame Library, Cooperstown, New York).

opponents' feet. Shortstop Jennings, red-headed, freckled, and destined to hit .401 in 1896, was one of the game's most accomplished intimidators, both through his poisonous tongue and his habit of crowding the plate, literally daring pitchers to throw inside.[13] His partner on the left side of the diamond, the volatile McGraw, was a square young man with such short arms he had to have his suits specially tailored. He prowled like a predator around the inside corner of his bag: Connie Mack recalled the horror of passing second only to confront "Muggsy" snarling and stomping and scuffing a rabbit-hole in the basepath.[14] Aggressive as a starving bull terrier, in May 1894 McGraw got into a fierce brawl with Boston third baseman Tommy Tucker, and the resulting fracas spread to both benches and the grandstands. Amidst the melee, the only double-decked wooden stand in Boston baseball history was set ablaze and destroyed—along with 170 downtown buildings.[15]

Completing the Birds' lineup was an equally colorful staff of pitchers headed by the burly, hard-drinking pitcher "Sadie" McMahon; Arlie "Doc" Pond, who shipped out of the game in 1898 to serve as a medico in the Spanish-American War; and George Hemming, who learned to pitch (in self-defense?) while working in an insane asylum.[16]

As if it weren't enough to bend the rules, Hanlon also bred an atmosphere of swagger and surliness among his players, which meant the Orioles were often to be found brawling in local hotels, or squabbling, snarling and cussing at umpires, fans, and each other. The dugout was awash with vile tempers and conceit, often punctuated by scuffles, pushing, and the clatter of bats across the concrete floor. The Orioles' Union Park was built next door to an amusement park and beer garden, which was such a magnet to the players that in 1899 a rule was instituted that players must remain on their bench—and nowhere else—during their half of each inning. Quinn recounted to the *St. Louis Globe–Democrat* almost forty years later, "If a man didn't get out and do battle, he didn't last long ... you had to be good to stay in fast company. The players were a rip-snorting lot and it took a good two-fisted fellow to make his own breaks. No quarter was asked or given."[17]

When Quinn arrived in August 1896, Jennings was hitting .401 and had taken 49 hit-by-pitches (HBPs) to force in runners with bases loaded: Jennings was as belligerent and detested as McGraw, so most pitchers were delighted to oblige with a fastball to the body. But he was well prepared—he would stand up against the batting cage during spring training, and McGraw would pitch at him until he overcame his old habit of pulling his head away from the ball and instead strode boldly toward it.[18] As a result, Jennings set a major league record for HBPs on May 11, 1894, taking three from Philadelphia's Kid Carsey in a single game.[19] McGraw's own nemesis Tommy Tucker actually had the most career HBPs until 1899, with 272—but by 1903, Jennings had 287, a record that still stands above the marks of Craig Biggio (285) and Ron Hunt (243), who famously donated his battered body to baseball instead of science.[20] Batters were far more likely to get hit by a pitch in the nineteenth century than in modern baseball. After the 1887 ruling that an HBP granted automatic passage to first base, "taking one for the team" became a legitimate offensive strategy. The 1920 death of Ray Chapman, his unprotected head struck by a pitch, is thought to have made modern pitchers reluctant to brush hitters back from the plate—but Hanlon's Orioles openly goaded pitchers into throwing inside, using the HBP as a weapon to get runners on base and unleash their devastating base-stealing strategies.[21]

Bred as they were in the fervency of "Mob City," the Orioles' fans were equally tricky and nasty, using mirrors to reflect the sun into enemy hitters' eyes, or surging onto the field to manhandle the umpire if a decision went against their boys—as a result, Baltimore management surrounded the field with a barbed wire fence (presumably to keep both the fans off the diamond and the players on it).[22] In 1896, Washington catcher Malachi Kittridge wrote, "In Baltimore, the cranks are impetuous, hot-headed, devoted to their team and never sore upon their players. They forgive all errors with cheers and cries of 'Better luck next time— can't get them all!' and they lionize the player who does anything worthy of mention. Visiting clubs are treated with courtesy, but in a sort of patronizing, 'sorry-you've-got-to-lose' manner." This he compared contemptuously to the fans in St. Louis, dismissing them as caring more for their beer than for the playing of Von der Ahe's men.[23]

What place, then, was Baltimore for a man like Quinn, even-tempered, straight, and honest, amongst this crew that played like the devil in an atmosphere that was like hell with the lid knocked off? He was not possessed of what Mark Twain called "natural cussedness": in fact, *The Sporting Life* reported on July 18 that "few men would act in such a manly fashion as Joe Quinn in the face of his release from St. Louis."[24] But after years of abuse from Von der Ahe, shunted to the front of the hapless Browns locomotive to become the primary target for the disgruntled fans and press, Quinn was no pushover. In fact, he bloomed in the Oriole hothouse: the *St. Louis Globe–Democrat* later noted Quinn had a "pair of gnarled fingers attesting to that fact."[25] His batting average skyrocketed from .245 to .329 as he caught the spirit of the Baltimore Birds, recalling in 1905, "The success of the champion Baltimore team was due to the fact that we kept our opponents guessing all the time. With two men out and the bases filled, the Orioles had a habit of bunting when everybody thought the play would be to hit the ball out." Then, grinning, Quinn recounted that, when the opposite field would come in anticipating a bunt, the Orioles would respond with a ferocious "bumping hit" to "tear their shins off."[26]

Even when they didn't invent their trademark dirty and cunning plays, the Orioles still executed them with precision. They once worked the hit-and-run play[27] thirteen times in succession and were widely credited with inventing the classic offensive maneuver, although Quinn himself disputed this: "The Chicago White Stockings pulled off that play as perfectly as the Orioles long before McGraw, Keeler, Kelley and Jennings were heard of. Ned Hanlon saw this play perfected by Chicago and drilled McGraw, Kelley, Keeler and Jennings into it when he assumed charge of the Orioles. The modern style of baseball, supposed to have been introduced by the champion Baltimores under Hanlon's management, was nothing more than old tricks revamped and perfected by modern experts."[28]

By June 3, 1896, the Orioles were atop the standings and on a ten-game winning tear, their latest a bottom-of-the-ninth victory over Pittsburgh courtesy of Hugh Jennings taking an HBP from Frank Killen with bases loaded. But two days later, they were thumped 10–4 by title rivals Cleveland and gave up first place to the Spiders.[29] The situation was barely changed when Quinn arrived in early July, the two teams tied at the top and Cleveland now on their own six-game winning streak. Baltimore snatched the lead back on July 3 as the New York Giants wasted a triple play and two double plays to be shut out by the Birds, 6–0. And the Giants further helped the Orioles' cause by beating Cleveland 5–2 on July 13.[30] The Spiders' Jesse Burkett led the league batting averages at .429, but Jennings was snapping at his heels at .417 as both teams swung for the fence in an effort to tip the win-loss percentage in their favor.[31] League president Nick Young marveled that Jennings "could have been bought for 50 cents when Louisville signed him in 1891," but Hanlon now wouldn't sell him for $5,000.[32]

Quinn's arrival as a new utility infielder in early July was expected only to strengthen the Orioles pack. "Jimmy Reitz had better look out or 'Gentleman Joe' will succeed him as the regular baseman," crowed the *Washington Morning Times*. "Quinn is too fast a player to warm the bench as a member of any club."[33] However, despite the healthy addition to his batting average, the move to the northeast did not sit entirely comfortably with Quinn's Irish-Catholic roots. The orange trim of the Birds' uniform was rather too reminiscent of the Protestant loyalists who fought to maintain political and religious ascendancy in the face of agitation for Catholic emancipation, stories of which were no doubt oft-told around Quinn firesides. The *St. Louis Republic* reported, tongue-in-cheek, that Quinn even threatened not to play with Baltimore unless the colors of the club were changed from orange to green.[34] But such blandishments aside, Quinn's Irish heritage stood him in good stead with the Orioles, providing a point of commonality where little existed. Hugh Jennings' parents were both Irish, and Keeler, Kelley, McGraw, Hanlon, and McMahon were all of Gaelic descent. Jennings's father, in fact, paid a visit to his son in Baltimore in late 1897, and while watching the team practice, was enraged by the presence of a man in a red sweater in the infield. "Who's that?" Jennings Senior bellowed from the bleachers. "He looks like an Irishman—but he's flashing the wrong color!" And he marched onto the field to eyeball Joe Quinn, accusing him of being a "turncoat" and "a disgrace to his country." A much-amused Quinn obligingly exchanged his sweater for a green one in the face of the old man's extreme distress.[35]

But despite the jarring shift in team culture from St. Louis to the rampaging Birds, Quinn's escape from the Von der Ahe regime and the mire into which the Browns had sunk was undoubtedly a relief. Winning was a half-forgotten habit, but a pleasant one to revive. Quinn's first game against his old side was on July 24 when the Browns came to Baltimore midway through a humiliating 14-game losing streak under the care of new player-manager Tommy Dowd, their fifth manager of the season. Dowd had started his managerial career well enough, winning three of his first four games in charge before a 14–1 thrashing by Washington on July 13 brought him solidly down to earth.[36] The third-placed Orioles may have underestimated the league's bottom team on July 24, however; with night falling over a thirteen-inning 8–8 tie, there was undoubtedly cause for concern. But one thing the Birds could depend on was the Browns' unique ability to lose the unlosable: the Browns flagrantly delayed at the bottom of the thirteenth inning, hoping for the game to be called for darkness, but Umpire Bob Emslie didn't see it their way and simply forfeited the game to the Birds.[37]

Baseball fever was running high in Baltimore by August. The town's saloons installed telegraph wires to receive scores directly from the parks, and staff would write these on big blackboards[38]—the Birds pioneering an early version of a Twitter feed. John McGraw had been sidelined almost all season with a different kind of fever—typhoid—but he made his reappearance on August 8, replacing the unlucky Jim Donnelly, who had hit .328 in Muggsy's absence. The 21–16 defeat of Washington was remarkable for the 37 singles hit, each team making the same number as its run total. Quinn replaced Reitz in the ninth after Heinie, from his own four appearances at the plate, made no hits or runs. Quinn managed a putout and an error at second base, and the *Washington Morning Times* reported Quinn fell down on a double play but was "full of ginger all the same."[39] His new free-swinging style had not gone unnoticed because the very same day, the Boston club tried to buy his contract from Baltimore. The Orioles were apparently willing to sell, but true to form, Quinn would not consent. A cynical report in *The Sporting Life* alleged Quinn "wanted a whack at the Temple Cup money,"[40] but given Quinn's comfortable financial circumstances and dismissive attitude toward salary, this is unlikely, and an Oriole he remained.

Late in the season, the pennant was down to a three-way wrestle between Cleveland, Cincinnati, and Baltimore. The Cleveland Spiders' promising young pitcher Denton "Cyclone" Young had pitched no-hit ball for 8⅔ innings on July 23 in a 2–0 win over

Philadelphia to give them a sixth straight win and haul them to within a game of the Orioles. Five days later, Cincinnati's 9–8 win over Cleveland was the Reds' eighth straight; the Spiders were still within grasping distance of the league lead when, upset by the umpiring, Cleveland player-manager Pat Tebeau came in to pitch in the ninth with Reds runners on second and third, no outs, and an 8–8 tie. He promptly gave up the game-winning hit to Germany Smith. It was Tebeau's only major league pitching appearance, and a very expensive one at that.[41]

An 11–4 conquest of the Senators on August 11—their tenth straight win—handed the Birds sole possession of top spot for the first time since July 4. But their form was inconsistent for the remainder of the month: they dropped two games to Brooklyn before pounding the Bridegrooms 19–3, squeaking home 3–2 and 16–15 against Philadelphia (courtesy of an eight-run ninth inning), then losing 9–7 to the hapless Browns.[42] It was a 7–0 shutout of St. Louis on the 21st, coupled with Cincinnati's 10–9 loss to Boston, which saw Baltimore finish the month still in top spot, now four wins clear of the Reds, with a 76–34 record; scribes at the *Washington Evening Times* predicted that even if Cincinnati won all 17 of its remaining games, Baltimore could lose seven of the 19 games to be played and still win the pennant.[43] St. Louis had managed to scramble off the bottom of the ladder into eleventh place, but with only 35 wins, they were so far behind the Orioles they needed a telescope to see their distant rivals. The batting race between Burkett and Jennings was now too close to call, Jennings shading Burkett .393 to .392 and willing to do anything to increase his edge: he had even laid aside the old "holy" glove with which so many brilliant plays have been made and was now using one loaned him by Joe Quinn.[44]

September gave Quinn a chance to renew his acquaintance with another of baseball's renowned raconteurs. Tim Hurst was in town on September 14, scheduled to umpire the upcoming series against Boston. But soon after his arrival, the *Baltimore News* reported Hurst was bedridden at the Carrollton Hotel, laid low by both chills and fevers and the effects of a visit paid to him by Joe Quinn. Hearing that his old sparring partner was ill, Quinn had gone with a friend to visit Hurst and take him a powder. After he had gravely mixed his concoction and Tim had swallowed it, Joe said, "Allow me to introduce my friend, Undertaker Mears, of this city." Tim turned pale at the evident reasoning conveyed by the double visit. Either the medicine or the appearance of the undertakers had its effect, for Hurst was at his post the next day.[45]

The Birds opened September with five wins in two days over last-placed Louisville, and by September 12, had clinched their third consecutive pennant.[46] However, even this the last-minute flurry wasn't enough for Hughie Jennings to win the batting title, with Jesse Burkett grabbing three hits in Cleveland's final game on September 26 to finish the year at .410, the first major leaguer to hit .400 in consecutive seasons (a feat later duplicated by Ty Cobb and Rogers Hornsby).[47] But the 1896 Orioles were the most successful Baltimore team ever, with a 90–39 record and a team batting average of 0.328 supplemented by a jaw-dropping 441 stolen bases.[48]

Cleveland had overtaken Cincinnati for second place, and faced off with the triumphant Orioles in the seven-game Temple Cup post-season series. The cup itself was a grandiose gold and onyx structure, fully thirty inches high and worth $800, and had been offered to the league in 1894 by entrepreneur William C. Temple.[49] In the previous two years, the Orioles had been embarrassed in the post-season, too hung-over from celebrating their pennant successes to bother with further efforts. This year, however, promised to be a competitive and bitter series: Cleveland had beaten Baltimore in eight of 11 encounters in the regular season, and sported a clutch of mean and nasty dispositions to rival the best of the Birds, with police often called in to ensure the peaceful progress of what should be a friendly contest of athletic skill. And such behavior had a terrible effect on the popularity and viability of the sport as a whole. In 1898, baseball writer Ren Mulford warned that rowdiness was killing the game in both Baltimore and Cleveland, with barely enough revenue drawn "as to even keep up stock in a banana stand" and the League liable to drop both teams if it continued.[50]

Even Tim Hurst acknowledged the hardest decision he ever made was in an 1896 game between Baltimore and Cleveland. It had been a brutal and spiteful struggle, with no quarter given until the ninth inning. With scores tied, Spiders captain Pat Tebeau came to bat against Bill Hoffer, whose out-curve had already bamboozled Tebeau for much of the day. Such was his frustration that by the ninth, he was walking right out of the batter's box to swing at it before it broke, a practice Hurst repeatedly cautioned him against. But with Cupid Childs on second base and darkness gathering, there was nothing for it; Tebeau ran fully ten feet to meet the pitch and belted it to centerfield to score the go-ahead run. Catcher Wilbert Robinson led the immediate protest from the Birds and, during the tumult, Hurst called Tebeau out and sent Childs back. The home crowd was stunned; Tebeau came running in from second, bawling, "You didn't call me out for *that!*"

> "You knew you stepped out of the box and you got what was coming to you," was Hurst's cool rejoinder.
> "Well, I might have stepped out a few feet," Tebeau expostulated, "but you ought not to give a decision like that in the presence of this home crowd!"

But Hurst's will was a steely one, the game went on to a twelfth inning, and Baltimore won. Hurst needed a police escort to get out of Cleveland that night.[51]

The first Temple Cup game, on October 1, was rained out, but the following day, Baltimore hammered Cy Young out of the game to win 7–1 behind their own 35-game-winning pitcher Bill Hoffer.[52] The 5'9" right-hander from Iowa had also won 35 games in 1895, and while he was the leading pitcher in the National League (on paper) in both years, he was described by Al Spink as "not remarkable," the support of his teammates contributing greatly to his success.[53] Baltimore took the second game 7–2 on October 3. Cleveland's losing pitcher was Bobby Wallace, who would be moved to shortstop in 1898 and there build a Hall of Fame career. But neither he, nor 28-game-winning pitcher Cy Young, nor the .410-hitting Jesse Burkett, could save the Spiders—by October 8, the Orioles had swept the series.[54] Joe Quinn appeared in one game *in locum tenens* for Heinie Reitz at second base, but had no hits in three at-bats. The games were poorly attended, and the rowdy behavior of both teams did nothing to endear the public toward the troubled series. The players received $200 each (less than half of what Cleveland had received the previous year), and a further $80 each for playing a few exhibition games and two theater benefits in Baltimore. Despite his arrival midway through the season, Quinn received a full share as promised by Hanlon when his contract was signed,[55] which the *Evening Times* described as "a very liberal arrangement."[56] However, the same sports editor mused, "When players are treated this way, no wonder they play ball for Baltimore," perhaps recalling those celebrated words of Thomas Jefferson, "That government is best, which governs least."[57]

When it was finally all over, the Birds celebrated the victory in style with a gala feast at Ganzhorn's city hotel, where the tables were laid out in the shape of a diamond and the team toasted by Cardinal Gibbons. "Much credit is due the Baltimore club," he solemnly proclaimed, "not only for their professional skill, but for their personal and moral rectitude."[58] The mind boggles.

12. Angry Birds

❖ ❖ ❖

"[Quinn] is a native of Campbelltown and anxious to hear something of Australia."—Melbourne Argus, July 23, 1897

Physical fitness was a priority to most players in the late nineteenth century. Many wrote letters to their managers and the papers in the off-season, assuring clubs and the world at large that they were walking, hunting, working out, and keeping their arms in good shape. It was during spring training with St. Louis during the early part of Quinn's career that he got into one of his few documented fist-fights: he shared a room with catcher Dick Buckley, who kept him awake once too often lifting dumbbells at one in the morning.[59] But Quinn's first spring training with the Orioles was somewhat more standard: the usual throwing and batting plus a daily mile run around the field, during which Steve Brodie would carry a load of bats and "Dirty Jack" Doyle would slide headfirst into every base.[60] If players reported overweight, they were ridiculed in the press: the light-framed Quinn was never the subject of such derision, but his captain, the hearty and substantial catcher Wilbert Robinson, suffered this fate every year he played in the majors. He and McGraw had opened a bar at 519 N. Howard Street in 1895, and life at the Diamond Café, with its oak and maple trimmings, reading rooms and bowling alleys, beer and whiskey laid on, suited Robinson utterly.[61] The League's leading catcher in 1895, "Robbie" never took his public humiliation personally, and he would jog from the hotel to the park each day to shed the accumulated winter baggage. Although Hanlon would rarely give the time of day to a player without a black streak in his character, Quinn remembered Robinson as genial, lighthearted and "a friend to all."[62]

Meanwhile Quinn, as was his wont, had both kept himself in shape and immersed himself in his business concerns over the winter of 1896-97, *The Sporting Life* slyly noting his winter was "brightened by reading of obituary notices" and that Quinn skipped the Orioles' post-season tour of England to pursue his morbid trade.[63] But beneath this humdrum façade brewed a growing resentment at the lack of field time he had been granted in 1896. Quinn's hopes were fueled by rumors in November that the imminent sale of utility Jim Donnelly would open the way for him to join the starting nine—rumors Ned Hanlon immediately denied, much to Quinn's disappointment.[64] Added to the mix was open interest in Quinn from the Louisville Colonels, and, while such a move would mean a tumble from the tower to the cellar, Quinn told the press quite openly in March, "I prefer playing regularly to bench duty, and am willing to go to Louisville should my release be bought by President Pulliam. I don't like the idea of waiting to fill another man's shoes."[65]

But an offer from the southern club never eventuated, denying Quinn the opportunity of playing under the fiery young manager, 24-year-old Fred Clarke. That youthful tyro would eventually claim a place in the Hall of Fame, but in 1897 he lived up to his reputation for never backing away from a fight, allegedly drawing a revolver on New York's Bill Joyce and George Davis in a hotel lobby after an on-field altercation.[66] Quinn's contract instead was renewed by the Orioles for 1897, although tension remained between the now 34-year-old Quinn and Hanlon. He forwarded his signed contract to the club on March 12 but wrote that business would prevent his joining the Orioles at Macon, Georgia, until March 25.[67] Hanlon's telegraphed response was terse: "Report March 18 or stay in St. Louis until October 16."[68]

Quinn reported, but was neither happy nor secure. Hanlon had sacrificed several veteran pitchers over the winter, including Sadie McMahon, George Hemming, and Duke Esper, promoting 20-year-olds Jerry Nops and Joe Corbett to the starting ranks. *The Sporting Life*'s

Baltimore correspondent Albert Mott described the move as a "doubtful experiment caused by no lack of confidence."[69] Mott speculated that Heinie Reitz, who, at 30, was the oldest of the regular infielders, might be the next neck on the block, and that his successor in Joe Quinn had just the set of skills to fill the breach: "If little Henny Reitz gets the pip, Joe Quinn will get a job to sass the umpires," he said. "You know Joe can talk from way back. His particular profession is talking people to death so as to make business good. Anything Joe 'undertakes' he does successfully. If he plays second base through one series and Bob Emslie umpires, there will be a job of embalming in Baltimore and Joe will get paid the usual commission."[70]

The Orioles were, after all, collectively renowned for their verbal gymnastics—well, almost all of them. "You wouldn't know Willie Keeler was on the lot at all except for a man going out now and then and for two or three or four or five base hits," was Mott's further observation. "If you bought Willie and paid his price in so much a noise, you would get him for about three coins and a half." Keeler preferred to let his bat do the talking: his Opening Day single and double began a record streak of safe hits in 44 consecutive games that would remain unbroken until Joe DiMaggio extended it to 56 in 1941.[71] And in front of 13,000 parochial witnesses, amid the noise of drum corps and parade floats and every known racket-maker, Joe Quinn replaced a sick John McGraw at third base after one inning and hit safely for three bases, the best of the Baltimore sluggers in the 10–5 win over Boston.[72] Promoted to lead-off hitter as McGraw continued his struggle with ill health, Quinn kept pace with the Baltimore big hitters in their home series victories over both Boston and Brooklyn, with a rash of triples, sacrifice flies, and errorless performances ensuring his place in the starting lineup as the team left for a month on the road on May 3. The sardonic Mott went so far as to concede, "Quinn hardly leaves anything to be desired at third base, but still there is always a general desire to see McGraw on the team. That young bundle of nerves puts a whole lot of life into the team that is not there when he is absent."[73]

The May 10–11 series with perennial cellar-dwellers Washington would ordinarily have little to recommend it, but kept spectators interested with a freakish hit by Birds first baseman Jack Doyle—the ball bounced near the outfield wall where a ladder had been left, then astonishingly rolled *up* the ladder and disappeared over the fence, and was scored as a home run.[74] The other extraordinary aspect to the match was the result—a 13–5 Orioles loss on the back of some very lax Jerry Nops pitching. The following day, Washington catcher Duke Farrell set a major league record by throwing out eight Orioles trying to steal second base—but the Birds still gained a 6–3 revenge.[75] The bizarre and fantastic continued to fascinate the public throughout the year: on the field on May 18, Bill "Scrappy" Joyce's four triples sent the New York Giants to an 11–5 win over the Pirates at Pittsburgh, a feat only previously achieved by George Strief in 1885 and never replicated since.[76] Off the field, Chris Von der Ahe's eccentricities reached new heights in May when his long-planned "Shoot the Chutes" water slide finally opened at Sportsman's Park, his final throw of the dice in his desperation to attract paying customers.[77] But he did not, by any means, hold the monopoly on bizarre and fantastic marketing strategies. Using mechanical dummies, an electrical baseball machine reproduced interstate action for punters at Philadelphia's McCauley Theater, which had been fitted out like a ballpark. Messages transmitted from the field were translated by manipulation of the machine's keyboard into a life-sized re-enactment in this earliest forerunner to real-time baseball coverage.[78]

On a roll of eight consecutive victories, the Orioles landed in Cincinnati on May 20 to face the second-placed Reds, who were two games back on 17 wins. "Two hacks and a hearse" was the good-humored greeting reserved for Quinn by his old Browns teammates Red Ehret and Heinie Peitz, now in battery for the Reds.[79] A whole fleet of sarcophagi would be required to carry the Birds back out of town, however, as Cincinnati dismantled the visitors in three straight games, taking Hoffer for 18 hits in the first. McGraw was twice ejected by Umpire Sheridan; both times, Undertaker Quinn took his place at third base, where he played an errorless series.[80]

A long month of travel, in which the O's played 23 games in nine different cities and traveled more than 2,200 railway miles, was taking a toll by early June. "Doc" Pond diagnosed bronchitis in both Quinn and outfielder Jake Stenzel, and there was much hobbling and wringing of split fingers and sore arms among their cohorts.[81] However, *The Sporting Life* of June 5 was philosophical: "The Orioles have temporarily fallen on evil days, the team being badly broken up by accident. This was something of a compensation in stopping the Orioles making a runaway charge for the pennant and giving up to six other teams a fair chance."[82] Quinn dragged himself back onto the field on May 31 for a double-header in Chicago, but, weakened by the severe attack of cold, was hitless in nine appearances at the plate. Even on the long-awaited return home on June 2 for a gala game against Cincinnati in which the Birds "took very kindly" to Joe's old teammates, pitchers Breitenstein and Ehret, Quinn could only struggle to a single walk.[83]

Despite their many maladies and physical woes, the Orioles were still somehow leading the pack in mid–June, but within two days, they suffered two major disappointments. On June 19, Keeler's 44-game hitting streak was finally broken on a Frank Killen five-hit loss to Pittsburgh.[84] The loss proved costly, as two days later, Boston moved into first place, posting its seventeenth straight victory by beating Brooklyn 11–6. The Orioles regrouped, and the following day beat off New York to regain first place when the Bostons went down to lowly Brooklyn.[85] Stung, Boston charged back to the top of pennant race with a 13–2 rout of the Bridegrooms on June 23. The Orioles' cause was helped when 20-game winner Cy Seymour walked eleven batters in the Birds' victory over New York on June 30. But Boston was still in the lead, and their win on July 6 gave them a record of 28 wins from the last 30 games. Baltimore was still close behind, but lost to the Reds, who won ten of 11 and passed the Orioles into second place.[86]

Willie Keeler, for one, was not giving up. On July 17, he grabbed five hits and scored five runs in a 20–2 rout of Chicago. Cap Anson made his 3,000th career hit in the subsequent game as the Colts defeated Baltimore 6–3, but Quinn missed the game entirely—the previous day he had incurred a bad spike wound to his left leg while sliding into base, and the injury became infected with dye from his uniform. He was confined to his room at the Leland Hotel, attendant physicians working to prevent the blood poisoning from spreading.[87] He joined an illustrious although unwelcome group for the 1897 season: the *Washington Evening Times* reported 59 of the 214 listed National League players had been disabled so far that year. For Baltimore, McGraw, Keeler, Jennings, Kelley, Doyle, Clarke, Robinson and Quinn had all been severely injured or laid up by sickness. As the paper remarked morosely, "Baseball is a really good business for accident insurance policies."[88]

The month of July brought a personal revelation to Joe Quinn, the likes of which he had not experienced since arriving in the United States 25 years before. The Australian *Argus* newspaper had been following the progress of a party of Australian baseball players touring the United States, playing matches against semi-professional nines from Hawaii all the way to New York.[89] The gusto with which Australia had received Al Spalding's touring party back in 1888 prompted local sporting and political officials to immediately dream of a reciprocal tour. Leading the push was Harry Musgrove, who had managed the Australian cricket team in the 1896 cricket tour of England and had, as did many Australian cricketers, played baseball himself, for a club in East Melbourne.[90] In 1897, less than ten years after Spalding's triumphal march, Musgrove formed a representative baseball team to return the visit, comprised mainly of Victorian and South Australian cricketers. But the tour was beset with difficulty from the outset, struggling both for finance and to finalize any sort of itinerary before they even sailed. Most of the players paid their own way, and it was only after Adelaide cricketer and patron A.J. Roberts stepped in and personally backed the team that they could set sail from Sydney in March 1897. Their stopover jaunts in New Zealand, Samoa, and Hawaii were as carefree as any summer vacation, but the utter naivety of the party was revealed almost the moment they landed on the California docks, when the *San Francisco Examiner* marveled, "Customs inspectors revealed the curious fact that there was not a ball or bat in their possession."[91]

National League President Nick Young encouraged his twelve National League teams to arrange exhibition games with the visitors as a courtesy for their long journey, and "exhibition" was the right word. While much store was set by their arrival, with the *Washington Morning Times* gravely proclaiming, "If the Judgment of many who claim to know is correct, [they] will give American players a hard battle for first place in the baseball world,"[92] the expected contest rarely eventuated. The team was regularly humiliated by their American counterparts, even the amateur sides as they mostly were, and savagely caricatured as "kangaroosters" in the California press.[93] They were thrashed 20–9 by the Californian Olympics, 21–11 by Omaha University, and 24–4 by Council Bluffs.[94] The *Examiner* sneered, "They played baseball like cricket, and stopped to think too often. They are nimble and quick but butter-fingered and don't seem to know what teamwork is."[95] But despite their dismal showing, the tourists remained objects of enormous fascination to their hosts. When they squeaked past Denver 18–17 on May 23, the *Denver Daily News* reported generously, "A party of very gentlemanly fellows from the Antipodes ... have all the marks of good cricket players — run well and field well, either hand or both.... In fact, they did most of their fielding one-handed, which created intense wonder in the base ball audience."[96]

With poor gate receipts and most expenses unmet, Musgrove considered ending the farce after the western leg of the tour, but decided to continue east in the hope of attracting better crowds with improved advance publicity.[97] But by the time the team reached Chicago in July, their embarrassing inexperience and the poorly planned itinerary had seen them battered both on the field (where they lost 19 of their 26 matches) and in the press. In fact, their only allies appeared to be Cap Anson and A.G. Spalding, who supported them in their darkest hour — when Harry Musgrove abandoned the team and ran off with the tour takings (meager as they were).[98] The Australian press had shown scant interest in either the tour or its many failings — despite the banquet of tabloid fodder it generated — and even Musgrove's treachery gained barely a mention. The *Argus* conceded succinctly that "the tour was a failure," but even that was harsh criticism considering the players were self-financed and literally blew their own money, as well as falling victims to Harry Musgrove's deceit.

The visit to Chicago in July marked the most significant breakdown in team organization and morale. Only one game was played in ten days, with much more money spent than was earned.[99] Musgrove was nowhere to be found and the players were too broke or dispirited to do much, on or off the field. But during their sojourn in the Windy City, the Australian squad sought to allay their miseries by treating themselves to possibly their last visit to a major league park, scraping together the cash to visit the West Side Grounds to watch the Colts entertain the visiting Orioles on July 16. And entertainment it was, with the game

12. Angry Birds 175

decided only by Hugh Jennings's heroics in the last inning, as described by Johnny Evers in *Touching Second*: "The crowd drew closer and closer to the field as the contest hotted up. Scores were tied in the ninth, one out, Bill Everett on third. A foul ball was hit into crowd behind third where they were ten deep. Jennings tore from second, hurled himself over the spectators and caught it and fell among them. Everett had tagged up and bolted, but Jennings still threw him out at the plate and Baltimore won the game (2–1) in the next inning."[100]

The *Argus* of July 23, 1897, contains the only mention of Joe Quinn by a nineteenth-century Australian broadsheet. Their correspondent, a player known only by the odd nom-de-plume of "Twister," wrote excitedly, "In Chicago, we had a most hearty welcome.... We were fortunate in striking the visit of the crack Baltimores. The Baltimores have the reputation of being great 'kickers,' which in America means wrangling with the umpire, and they lived up to it, for the captain and vice-captain were at different stages ordered off the ground by the umpire. We found that Quinn, who plays third base for the champions, is a native of Campbelltown, NSW, and he was anxious to hear something of Australia."[101]

For our purposes, it was a sadly underreported meeting. What did those brown men from Down Under, in the midst of their vexing jaunt, tell Quinn of matters in his homeland? We may never know. But those bereft men, barely surviving on the rattle of brass and vilified

A rare photograph of nineteenth-century Australian baseball players, in this case a team from South Australia, c. 1889. Baseball in any organized form was uncommon while Joe Quinn lived in Australia (prior to 1872). It was only after the 1888 Spalding world tour that national enthusiasm for the game saw clubs and state-based leagues truly emerge (Ernest Gall, State Library of South Australia, image no.: B1730-A).

by the world's press, may have found a kindred spirit in the Baltimore third baseman. The *Omaha World Herald* mused on July 15, "It's been many a long and weary year since a more gentlemanly lot of baseballers have been here than the Australians. Not once during the game did they find fault ... throughout the game the visitors preserved an unruffled exterior and demeanor."[102] These were many characteristics they shared with Quinn, despite his quarter of a century in the United States and most recent sojourn among the cantankerous and ornery Orioles.

The jaded Australians closed their tour with visits to Boston and New York, where they were graciously escorted by Cap Anson; he had himself visited Australia on the Spalding tour and was eager to return the hospitality he had enjoyed there. Cheered by his attentions (and his funds), the "Dingo Land-ers" managed to beat a combined Chicago-Brooklyn nine, 11–4. The visitors were, however, mystified when the Chicago men all surrounded the umpire and proceeded to "kick" loudly at a decision he'd made, one that appeared quite correct. It was only after the game that Anson affirmed, "Didn't you notice our pitcher was rattled? We just wanted to give him an opportunity to recover himself!" Such tactics were almost incomprehensible to the Australians. *Argus* correspondent Frank Laver marveled, "Baseballers try to mislead an umpire to gain an advantage, whereas cricketers—in first-class cricket at least—endeavor to assist the umpire to give a fair decision. Baseball is really more of a business than a sport in America."[103]

While in New York, Anson also treated his guests to a visit to the veriscope (an early variety of cinema) to watch the famed 1897 James Corbett–Bob Fitzsimmons boxing encounter—the world's first feature film. Corbett's younger brother, incidentally, was Joe Corbett—Baltimore's own 24-game-winning pitcher. He would leave the Birds at the end of the 1897 season in a dispute over salary with Hanlon, who also allegedly reneged on a promise to buy him a new suit for winning 20 games.[104] But meanwhile, even the backing of two of baseball's most influential figures in Anson and Spalding was not enough to dig the ill-fated Australian tour out of the mire. With gross receipts of just 400 Australian pounds and expenses of nearly £3,000, the penniless tourists were forced to work their way home via England, burdened by a financial liability that took some of them years to recover from.[105]

In *Time and Game,* Australian baseball historian Joe Clark links the progress and fortunes of baseball in Australia directly to the interest Americans display in the game Down Under. The disastrous 1897 tour saw the game languish in Australia, struggling for notice against the entrenched "Empire" sports of cricket and football, and scrabbling for a foothold as a series of isolated state and city leagues until the formation of the first semi-professional national competition, the Australian Baseball League (ABL) almost a century later in the summer of 1989. The ABL began with eight teams in a 42-game season, and derived most of its income from merchandising and sponsorship (for example, Pepsi-Cola paid A$500,000 for naming rights to the competition). Attendances are generally comparable with those of minor league games in the U.S., averaging 2,300–3,500 in the 1993-94 season,[106] and each ABL club has a formal link to a U.S.-based major league club with provision to include a number of minor leaguers on its roster. Australia is now both a popular destination for developing American players, with its high standard of living and safe environment, and is a recognized source of college and major league talent. But with an ongoing struggle for television air-time and governance by the International Baseball Federation constraining players to an effectively amateur status,[107] the game still faces significant hurdles in competing for notice and participation among Australia's comparatively small population.

12. Angry Birds

On August 2, Baltimore retook second place from the Reds with their twenty-second straight win.[108] But, perhaps understandably complacent while on such a tearaway winning binge, their guard slipped and they lost to Philadelphia for the first time in nearly two years the following day. The Orioles went to first-placed Boston needing to win on August 6, but were edged out 6–5 in a fiery contest—in the 8th inning, Umpire Lynch lost his temper and hit argumentative Baltimore first baseman Jack Doyle in the face, and police had to be called to restore order on the diamond and in the stands. Leftfielder Hugh Duffy saved the game for the league leaders by throwing a Baltimore runner out at home in the bottom of the ninth inning.[109] The gutted Orioles proceeded to lose again to Boston the following day, and the defeat saw them slide back to third on the ladder. They went on a nine-game winning streak, only to be shut out twice in a day by Cleveland on August 19, recovering to sweep a double-header from Boston and grab back first place (only by a percentage of .683 to .679) on August 27. Quinn was still playing his part, despite limited opportunities and ongoing trouble with his leg: he had been sent home to recuperate after the Chicago series in July,[110] but if he was ever to consolidate a place in the starting nine, he would both have to play and play well whenever offered the chance. And this he did, as the *Washington Times* reported admiringly on September 5: "When Chris Von der Ahe, in a fit of angry pique which quickly passed away, shoved a notice of release into Joe Quinn's hands, he did not know that he was throwing into Ned Hanlon's hands the player destined to save Baltimore from many a slump. It is all right to dump laurel branches at the feet of Hughey Jennings, Muggsy McGraw and Henry Reitz, but without Quinn the chances are one pennant already won would have been lost and he has done his share toward putting the champs where they are now."[111]

What the O's needed to give them the impetus for a final push toward the pennant was an easy-beat opponent, and a new record was set on September 3 when, for the first time ever, two players (Keeler, who was batting .424, and Jack Doyle) each went six-for-six at the plate as Baltimore crushed St. Louis 22–1.[112] The Browns' punishment continued on September 8, as debutant pitcher Rube Waddell lost his first appearance 5–1 on the back of eleven hits, four walks and just two strikeouts. Waddell would eventually register 2,316 career Ks for a place in the Hall of Fame, despite his untimely death from tuberculosis, aged just 37, in 1914.[113]

Since the Birds had won the last three pennants, there was still good money, even amongst their rivals, on Baltimore's momentum to carry them over the line for a fourth. "I don't see how they are going to beat out Baltimore this year," Chicago's Jimmy Ryan told the press. "Right now is the time the Orioles will play their hardest. They will not allow the slightest chance out of their fingers. They will win by playing together on everything that comes up. They are the greatest fighters in the business, although I do not think they have the best team."[114]

"Of course the Orioles will win the pennant, and there is no reason why they shouldn't," was the analysis of Cleveland's Pat Tebeau. "They have a team that is better equipped all around, on the bases, in the field, and at the bat, and I think that there are a few mere ounces of brains in that Oriole rank than the Beaneating aggregation carry under their tiles."[115]

But the Birds' run was dramatically slowed when league-leading shortstop Hughie Jennings suffered a fractured skull from a fastball hurled by the "young Hoosier giant," 37-game winner Amos Rusie. Jennings missed the entire last month of the season, and would suffer the same injury on two subsequent occasions, first by driving a car off a cliff, and then by diving into an empty swimming pool.[116] And while Joe Quinn was "playing the banner ball of his life in short field" during Jennings's absence,[117] the pressure of the nail-biting pennant race was telling. With the O's now three games behind Boston, bursts of furious bad temper between Baltimore players and officials, and infighting and bickering among the Orioles stars, was attracting lascivious media attention, the *New York Times* of September 3 describing the players as "degenerates."[118]

A narrow 3–2 squeak over bottom-placed Louisville on September 10—largely thanks to four hits from Willie Keeler and continuous arguing and intimidation of Umpire Kelly[119]—was sufficient to boost the Birds back into first place. The season came down to a three-game series between the front-running Orioles and Boston, who trailed by just one-thousandth of one percent, .707 to .706. On September 24 at Baltimore, 13,000 fans saw the local heroes beaten by Kid Nichols 6–4 and first place handed back to the visitors. But the Birds struck back the next day with a 6–3 win.[120] On September 27, a record 28,000 fans crammed Union Park to witness Boston overwhelming the Orioles 19–10.[121] The overflowing stands put fans within 20 feet of the plate, while 15 ground-rule doubles fell among outfield overflow. The Beans put the game away with nine runs and eleven hits in the seventh inning, while Kid Nichols went the distance and was nicknamed "Nervy Nick" for beating Baltimore twice in three days.[122] The disheartened Orioles seemed to lose the will to battle thereafter, and within three days, Boston had clinched the pennant—Selee's fourth—with a 12–3 win over Brooklyn, as Baltimore lost miserably to lowly Washington.[123] Boston finished the season with a 93–39 record, and their winning percentage of .705 is the highest in Boston history.[124]

The Orioles swallowed the loss as gladly as if it had been a draught of wormwood. Although the Temple Cup was now virtually meaningless, they gained revenge in four of the five games against Boston in front of crowds so small that management refused to release exact numbers; these efforts netted the players just $300 each. It was Baltimore's second consecutive Temple Cup, but was so dismally unpopular that the competition was never held again.

A week later, Quinn was back in St. Louis for the birth of his fourth son, John Richard. From limited opportunities, he had finished the season with the highest fielding average in the league at both third base (.952, with just six errors) and shortstop (.967, four errors), albeit having played just 34 and 21 games in each position, respectively.[125] His nearest rival at shortstop, Hugh Jennings, had played 115 games for a .933 average, but as Quinn told the *St. Paul Daily Globe* on October 25, the redheaded tearaway seemed destined for a more permanent move to the right. "Rumors regarding Jennings becoming a first baseman for the Orioles are no product of the pipe," Quinn said, "as the famous shortstop [is] suffering with arm trouble and Hanlon is actively looking for a good youngster."[126]

Prophetic remarks indeed, as it was not the only change afoot in the Baltimore infield.

Part VI
The Grand Old Man: 1898–1903

13. The Great Player Swap

"It is a shame to keep such a grand player tied up with such a combination. The old man is very much the whole team."
—*The Sporting News*, October 14, 1899

The year 1897 was bitter, both for the Orioles collectively and for Joe Quinn personally.

The team had lost the unlosable pennant and gained no professional or financial consolation from winning the post-season Temple Cup in front of apathetic crowds. While Ned Hanlon assured the press he would retain Quinn as a utility man for 1898,[1] the arrival of .341-hitting second baseman Gene DeMontreville from Washington was the final nail in the coffin of Quinn's quest for a permanent posting in the middle-infield. Hanlon was clearly excited at the potential of the 25-year-old native of St. Paul, who had enjoyed a 36-game hitting streak during 1896-97, still the tenth-longest stretch in major league history.[2] "DeMontreville at second will strengthen the team very much in batting, base running, and even in fielding," Hanlon proclaimed. "While he will make more errors than Reitz, he will cover more ground and is faster, especially in making double plays."[3]

Now effectively third in line for his preferred position, Quinn's frustration and ongoing homesickness were palpable. Playing Quinn in just 12 games during the first two months of the 1898 season, Hanlon soon had the material excuse he needed to rid himself of an increasingly awkward conundrum: when the Orioles lost five games in a row in late May and slipped alarmingly from second to fifth in the standings, Hanlon's immediate response was to trade Quinn and Jake Stenzel to St. Louis.[4]

The trip south was akin to sliding down the biggest reptile on a "Snakes and Ladders" board—from the top of the standings straight to the National League cellar. Quinn would take captaincy of the Browns, and there were plenty of homely advantages in returning to 2623 Dickson Street, which the eight Quinns shared with Thomas and Margaret McGrath and Molly's four siblings[5]: Joe could return to his beloved business, his profitable sideline in real-estate speculation, and his place in the choir at St. Bridget's Church.[6] But also waiting was his old tormentor in the form of Chris Von der Ahe. Kerry poet and anthologist Brendan Kenny speculated that the strength of the Irish was drawn from "our consciousness of suffering, our ability to turn suffering into music."[7] The musical Quinn's strength, had he known it, was about to severely tested—again.

The Browns finished the 1897 season a whopping 64 games out of first place, and a predictably apoplectic Von der Ahe had taken over once more as manager on October 1,

1897—the team's twelfth manager since joining National League in 1892. His reign, thankfully, barely lasted until spring, but in keeping with his habit of making bizarre and inexplicable managerial appointments, in March of 1898 he handed the reins of the Browns to none other than the league's most hated umpire, Tim Hurst.[8] Detested by almost every player—except Joe Quinn—Hurst's management style was not unlike his umpiring mien: colorful and cantankerous. However, even "Timmy" had to put a brake on his dubious reign on April 16: the season was only one inning old when the Sportsman's Park grandstand began to burn with the Browns at bat against Chicago. Dozens of fans were trampled as the crowd of 6,000 stampeded to escape. The grandstand and half of the bleachers were destroyed, as was Von der Ahe's saloon, club office, correspondence, and extensive wardrobe. The incident was the fifth such fire at Sportsman's Park in the 1890s, and this time, Von der Ahe was up to his ears in lawsuits.[9]

With Hurst nominally in charge, the Browns were soon in equally bad shape on the field as off it. In fact, it took a bad case of *hari-kiri* by the opposing team for them to win a game, as occurred on May 18 when Chicago pitcher Walter Thornton hit three consecutive batters in the Browns' 11–4 victory. Thornton's three HBPs in a row is still a major league record for lack of skill and control.[10] Further depths were plumbed on August 15, when only 200 fans watched the eleventh-placed Washington Senators defeat the cellar-dweller Browns 10–2. Captain Quinn was forced to endure this humiliation on the sidelines, having suffered a gruesome wrist injury when struck by a ball on August 7—the limb swelled to twice its natural size and pundits feared he would not play again that season. On reporting Quinn's mishap, the *Washington Times* observed slyly, "Joe Quinn's wrist is swollen twice its natural size; he was hit with a ball recently. That is nothing. We have a player on our team whose head is twice its natural size, and he was hit only by a little egotism."[11]

Two weeks later, however, Quinn returned—or tried to: he was hit in the eye by a batted ball during practice on August 27 and forced to watch the series against the Orioles from the sideline (with his remaining good eye). It was a mortifying experience: Hugh Jennings was a true magnet for the ball, grabbing 10 assists in the first game as the Birds strode to a 6–2 win. Hurst was called on to leave his managerial duties and officiate over the second when scheduled umpire Bob Emslie was too ill with heat-stroke to work. Orioles manager Ned Hanlon approved Hurst's taking over, and although the Birds won 6–2, Hurst was wildly cheered by the home crowd.[12] But the butchery continued, as on September 10, Chicago reeled off three double plays in a 4–2 win against St. Louis, the White Stockings *en route* to a season total of 149 double plays. That record would stand until 1917, when the achievements of infield trio Dahlen, Connor, and Everett were subsumed by the famous "Tinker to Evers to Chance."[13]

The Browns' final loss of the year came in typically oddball circumstances on October 9, again facing Chicago, when the White Stockings' Jack Taylor defeated the Browns' Jack Taylor 5–4 in 10 innings. The winner was a newcomer who had won 28 games for Milwaukee in the Western League, the loser a hard-drinking eight-season veteran better known as "Brewery Jack."[14] Hurst had managed the Browns to a club-worst 111 losses and a second consecutive last place in the league, and he was fired for his troubles.[15]

Chris Von der Ahe's comical, tragic tenure as Browns owner was also over. An opportunistic attempt to expel the Browns at a league meeting in New York on March 2, 1899, was defeated by a 7–4 vote: the city was still attractive as it allowed Sunday ball, had loyal (albeit long-suffering) fans, and a large metropolitan population. But the club was bankrupt, and two weeks later was auctioned off, sold for $33,000 to G.A. Gruner, a prominent St.

Louis lumber dealer representing the creditors; Charlie Comiskey and Tom Loftus were at the auction but did not bid. Edward C. Becker, vice-president of the American Baseball and Athletic Exhibition Company of St. Louis, then bought the club from Gruner for $40,000 and entered a partnership with Cleveland street railway magnate Frank de Haas Robison, who was also the owner of the Cleveland club. Robison anointed himself president, and his brother, M. Stanley Robison, took over terms at the Cleveland club.[16] Chris Von der Ahe, forced to watch all of this from the sidelines, never regained his former extravagant lifestyle, and in later life was reduced to tending the bar at a nondescript saloon. Ironically, many of the players whose lives he had ruled so bizarrely now reached into their own pockets to support him, in particular Charlie Comiskey. In 1908, the St. Louis Cardinals and St. Louis Browns staged a benefit game which raised over $4,000 for their former owner. When Von der Ahe died in 1913, the massive monument he had erected to himself outside Sportsman's Park was moved to his gravesite in Bellefontaine Cemetery—a grandiose gesture of which Chris would have thoroughly approved.[17]

Syndicate baseball—two or more clubs with common ownership—is now illegal in professional baseball in the United States.[18] But in the nineteenth century, it was a common arrangement. In the 1890s, Al Spalding, Boston part-owner Arthur Soden, and John T. Brush all had interests in the New York Giants as well as their own clubs. Prior to the start of the 1899 season, the co-owners of Baltimore and Brooklyn shuffled players between the two teams, Hanlon taking Willie Keeler, Joe Kelley, and Hugh Jennings with him to Brooklyn to form an outfit so powerful they were nicknamed the Superbas, while the old Orioles had their wings so effectively de-feathered they would finish no better than fourth in 1899 and were subsequently dropped by the National League.[19] And the Becker-Robison deal was to yield a farce equally devastating to two of the League's oldest and proudest clubs.

The Robisons immediately stamped out all memories of Von der Ahe's Browns by renaming Sportsman's Park to League Park, and adding bright red trim and red socks to the St. Louis uniform. But the major change came on April 3, 1899. After winning the 1895 Temple Cup, the Cleveland Spiders (having garnered the nickname in 1887 after showing off a uniform featuring dark blue stripes in a web-like pattern[20]), had struggled. In 1898, they were already known as the Exiles, having played 83 of their final 87 games on the road and having the poorest attendance in the league.[21] Their aging lineup did include stars such as pitcher Cy Young, .400 hitter Jesse Burkett, and shortstop Bobby Wallace, but the trio, along with eight others, were packed off to St. Louis before the start of the 1899 season to bolster the lineup of the Robisons' latest acquisition.

The rejuvenated St. Louis club was rechristened the "Perfectos"—the Cleveland imports refusing to play under the old Browns moniker, with all its negative connotations—and former Spiders player-manager Oliver Wendell "Patsy" Tebeau was placed at the helm. Tebeau and his brother George were actually St. Louis born and bred, having learned to play on a lot near the old water tower on Grand Avenue and starting for the local "Peach Pie" amateur team before Patsy signed with Chicago in 1887.[22] His somewhat genteel nickname aside, the impetuous Tebeau was not to be trifled with. Usually found prowling at first or third base, Patsy could—and would—throw a hip that would land a baserunner in the bleachers,[23] and he would have his underlings sharpen their spikes with files before every game.[24] He had even caused a full-blown riot in 1896 when, ordered from the field after rejecting a close call at first base, he and Umpire Lynch had squared off in a fistfight that spilled over into both dugouts and the crowd; more than 50 police were needed to disentangle the combatants.[25]

If only they knew... The 1898 Cleveland Spiders before the team was dismantled when Cleveland owners Frank and Matthew Robison also purchased the St. Louis National League franchise. The best Cleveland players were packed off to St. Louis and the Spiders restocked with castoffs and rejects. Joe Quinn captained and managed the Spiders, who finished 1899 with major league baseball's worst-ever record of 20 wins and 134 losses (National Baseball Hall of Fame Library, Cooperstown, New York).

To enable the stripped-out Cleveland to field a team in 1899, the Robisons made an indifferent attempt to restock the Spiders with mediocre minor leaguers and washed-up veterans. St. Louis outfielder Dick Harley had declared in the off-season that he was sick of playing for the mournful Browns and wanted to be traded. He got his wish; he was one of nine Browns dispatched to Cleveland. His carriage-mates included fellow outfielder "Buttermilk" Tommy Dowd, who had managed the Browns in 1896 and 97, left-handed catcher Jack Clements, infielder Lave Cross, and pitchers Kid Carsey, Jim Hughey, and Willie Sudhoff.[26]

Joe Quinn had had a ringside seat to witness the demise of his old oppressor in Chris Von der Ahe, but if he was gloating over Der Poss President's tumble from grace, destiny had a far worse fate in store for him. The ninth one-way ticket to Cleveland had Quinn's name on it.

• • •

I was the conscript sent to hell,
to make in the desert the living well;
I bore the heat, I blazed the track,
furrowed and bloody upon my back...
—Dame Mary Gilmore, "Old Botany Bay," 1918

Although *The Sporting News* reported encouragingly that Cleveland had defeated Indianapolis twice in pre-season games,[27] the tone for the Spiders' 1899 season was set from the very first official National League game, in all its cruel humiliation.

Cleveland's season opener was, callously, scheduled against the heavily stacked St. Louis Perfectos. The game was set to be played at the Spiders' home park, but the Robisons had the game transferred to St. Louis, and a crowd of more than 15,000 braved bitter weather to see the home team crush the Spiders 10–1 on April 15. *The Sporting News* proclaimed sternly the "game [was] not up to National League standards"[28] as Spiders starter "Wee Willie" Sudhoff gave up 13 hits (including five doubles), as well as four walks and a wild pitch. The *Cleveland Plain Dealer*'s mournful (and prophetic) headline declared, "The farce has begun."[29] Former Cleveland pitcher Cy Young was on the mound for St. Louis—he alone would win 26 games in 1899, six more than his old team would manage for the entire season.[30]

Despite the lopsided contest and the mortification of some of their former favorite sons—although Quinn escaped the worst of it, his fielding praised as "masterly"[31]—18,000 enthusiasts crammed the rechristened League Park for the second game of the series. The Spiders acquitted themselves much better, grabbing 12 hits to seven, but they still lost 6–5: Wilfred "Kid" Carsey held St. Louis to one run over five innings, but the Perfectos scored a decisive five in the sixth as Carsey's arm gave out. The Kid had pitched more than 1,500 innings in his preceding five seasons with Philadelphia, and by the time he arrived in Cleveland, his arm was worn like an old shoe and he was good for little more than three or four innings.[32]

Injury to rightfielder Dick Harley forced one of the Spiders' precious few genuine pitchers to step in for the team's first away trip, to Louisville. "Happy Jack" Stivetts, Quinn's old Boston teammate, was anything but happy in Cleveland. Despite a 204–131 career record, Stivetts lost all four of his appearances with the Spiders before being given his marching orders.[33] Stivetts was a .297 career hitter but he drew a blank for the entire Louisville series, and although the Spiders won their first game for the year on the third and final day of the Colonels contest, it was an ugly and miserable game whose crowning shame was the ejecting of Spiders shortstop Harry Lochhead and fiery Fred Clarke for brawling.[34] The result, nonetheless, saw the Spiders soar briefly into a tie for tenth place, the highest ranking they would achieve all year. But their triumph lasted less than an hour, as they were comprehensively thrashed 15–2 in the afternoon half of the double-header.

Downcast in the extreme, the Spiders headed home to Cleveland to play their April 28–29 home opener, but the series was postponed after the sudden death of Frank Robison's eldest daughter.[35] So the Spiders took an overnight train to Cincinnati but immediately wished they hadn't, as they were firmly shut out 9–0.[36] The Spiders ended the first month of the season with a doleful 1–7 record, and their fans were obviously not convinced of their potential for improvement. When they finally did play their home opener against Louisville on May 1, only 500 people paid to watch, barely filling a corner of the 18,000 capacity League Park. Even though the home team split a close double-header 5–4 and 1–2, even fewer fans bothered the ticket-takers the next day. Frank Robison had chosen the site of his park so his streetcars passed the main entrance at the corner of East 66th and Lexington Avenue and patrons could disembark no more than twenty feet from the entrance, but Clevelanders were still furious that their favorite players had been sent away to St. Louis, and even with the incentive of door-to-door public transport, fewer than 1,200 fans turned up to witness the Spiders losing their next three home games.[37]

Fortunately for the Spiders, while their feet were firmly set on the path to record-breaking futility, other National League teams were also suffering from the bizarre and unprecedented. Louisville's future Hall of Famer Honus Wagner, destined to lead the league in stolen bases five times and having already gone 3-for-5 against the Spiders on May 21, gave the game away to the Clevelanders after forgetting how many outs there were and being thrown out at second base in the final inning. And on May 3 in Pittsburgh, the year's most bizarre result ensued when the Pirates' Jack McCarthy slammed a potentially game-winning drive to the wall in the bottom of the ninth, again against Louisville. The ball bounced into the right field corner and through an access door, which a quick-thinking Pittsburgh employee slammed shut before the fielder reached it. With players and umpires alike bewildered as to the appropriate ruling, the League had no choice but to declare the game invalid and order a replay.[38]

The Spiders staggered home on May 9 to host blood brothers the Perfectos in a four-game series. They started in inspired fashion before a "bumper crowd" of 1,500 fans, holding their unwelcome visitors to 1–1 for seven innings before collapsing, in typical Spiders style, to an 8–1 loss. That was enough for the unforgiving public to desert them for all three remaining games, played before virtually empty stands—there really was little to pay to see, as the Spiders lost each of them with great thoroughness.[39] But in fairness to the under-resourced Cleveland outfit, there were other factors surrounding the public's waning interest in baseball in early 1899, including the Spanish-American War, which put a significant brake on public attendance at sports and entertainments.[40] But on May 14, the *St. Paul Globe* stridently declared the "mismanagement of puffed-up managers thinking the public went to the ball park to see them" (naming Von der Ahe, the Robisons, and even Ned Hanlon) was most to blame for the "fatal lack of local enthusiasm," even in cities such as the newly high-flying St. Louis, who had more stars than the Milky Way on their roster.[41] Chris Von der Ahe's 1893 decision to release Charlie Comiskey was squarely blamed as the beginning of the downfall of baseball in St. Louis. "He let them go whenever and wherever they would bring him the cash," raged the *Globe*, citing the sale of the "idol" Brodie, the "dude" Latham, and the pride of St. Louis, the battery of Breitenstein and Peitz, as the straws which broke the diamond-studded Browns' backs. "He even disposed of Joe Quinn, who is a St. Louis boy, when Joe could draw more money to the ball park than any other member of the team!" the paper lamented.[42] But whether undertaker Quinn's drawing power would be sufficient to bring the dead to life in Cleveland remained to be seen.

By May 22, the Spiders were on a roll—of two. Their victories over Philadelphia and Louisville were the only time in 1899 that they won consecutive games, but they were hurriedly brought back to earth with home losses to Washington, a 16–10 romp by Boston—during which rightfielder Chick Stahl went six-for-six against them—and 13–4 and 14–2 hammerings from Ned Hanlon's Brooklyn Superbas, who were one of the few genuine beneficiaries of the syndicate system.[43] Despite a distinct lack of public sympathy or support in the form of gate receipts, the Spiders retained a shred of advocacy in *The Sporting News*, who came out with strong criticism of syndicate baseball in late May, mourning, "Syndicate baseball results: May 17, 1898: Cleveland 16 wins, 8 losses.... May 17, 1899: Cleveland 3 wins, 20 losses."[44] This record had improved to seven wins by the end of the month, but the Spiders were still wallowing hopelessly in last place.[45]

There was a long-held superstition among nineteenth-century baseball teams about starting road trips on a Friday, probably stemming from the ancient maritime practice of never leaving a port on that day,[46] but the Spiders foolishly set sail for Philadelphia on May

28 and paid the ultimate penalty, shut down 7–1. That loss sparked a gut-wrenching ten-game losing streak from which the Spiders did not emerge until June 15 in Pittsburgh.[47] And the Clevelanders were now in trouble off the field too. On May 9, Lou Soxalexis, their graceful Native American outfielder, had returned to the lineup after being sidelined with a long-term ankle injury. He had signed with Cleveland in 1897 after belting a home run off Amos Rusie in an exhibition game against New York for Notre Dame, and hit .413 before his injury, which, incidentally, occurred while Soxalexis was making a quick exit out a hotel window.[48] The enforced inactivity proved the ruin of his career as Soxalexis developed chronic alcoholism during his rehabilitation. But the fans still adored him and before long were referring to the Cleveland team as "the Indians," now the modern club's official moniker. But back in May 1899, just one week after his return to the game, Soxalexis was in a police court facing charges of public intoxication. He avoided jail and, four days later, took the field as the Spiders won their third game of the season against Philadelphia, but Soxalexis played so erratically he was immediately released.[49] Also taking the train out of Cleveland that night was catcher Jack Clements, who had played—or butchered—four games for the club. With his axing, professional baseball lost one of its last regular left-handed catchers, Clements having caught more than 1,000 games in his career.[50]

And where was Quinn amidst this deepening quagmire of misery? On May 16, the *St. Paul Globe* reported: "Joe Quinn, of the Clevelands, is showing some of the league second basemen how to play the base this season."[51] *The Sporting Life*, too, noted Quinn had "never played better or faster ball,"[52] and that he shared with manager Lave Cross the honor of being the most popular man on the Cleveland team.[53] Oscar Wilde wrote his classic satire *The Importance of Being Earnest* in the same year the Spiders' debacle was unfolding. Wilde's "trivial comedy for serious people" was in fact one of western literature's greatest ironies, mocking and discouraging the practice of being serious about anything. Perhaps Joe Quinn should have taken a leaf out of Jack and Algy's book. He was doing his best amidst the undistinguished veterans and no-name kids, but he really shouldn't have bothered: it only drew attention to him, and attracting the spotlight amidst the 1899 Spiders was not a wise career move.

The Spiders' 1899 player-manager Lave Cross has been called everything from a "complete klutz" to the "best third baseman of his generation."[54] He had led the National League at third base on four occasions and was by June 5 doing enough to earn a ticket back to the Perfectos stable. Cross had until then received little attention or assistance from the Robisons, but now the cares were someone else's and Cross couldn't jump the Cleveland ship fast enough. And to add insult to injury, when Cross fled the scene of the crime, he took the Spiders' only reliable pitcher, Willie Sudhoff (3–8), with him. The stone of Sisyphus was once again rolled to the most prominent and best-performing of the hapless Cleveland outfit—Undertaker Joe Quinn, who was fast becoming baseball's patron saint of lost causes.

Quinn was now manager of a doomed team who'd lost five games in a row and would lose another seven before they beat Pittsburgh 6–2 at home before a crowd of 100 on June 15. Given Cross was a Cleveland local, and as such engendered his struggling team with a certain measure of public support, the decision to whisk him away was a near-fatal one for the Spiders.[55] The Robisons did design to provide Quinn with replacement staff in Perfectos castoffs Frank Bates and Ossee Schreckengost, but even these were on short-term loan. "Schreck" would hit .313 for the Spiders before being recalled to St. Louis—his three hits helped Cleveland beat the Perfectos for the only time on June 25, after which the Robisons quickly reclaimed him. Although a shortage of quality pitching was the Spiders' major shortcoming, the Robisons commemorated this rare victory by trading the Spiders' winning pitcher "Still Bill" Hill to Baltimore, swapping Kid Carsey to Washington, and sending Jack Stivetts home to Pennsylvania, where he gave up the game to become a carpenter.[56]

The Spiders were left with Coldwater Hughey, Frank Bates, and three new signings to prop up the pitching staff. Bates had a 2–1 record with Cleveland in 1898 but somehow earned a spot on the St. Louis train in 1899, which he blew spectacularly: in his only two appearances, he gave up seven hits and five walks, so he was gifted back to Cleveland before he could embarrass the Perfectos any further.[57] Charlie Knepper was signed from Youngstown in June, and although his 4–22 record was dismal, he was let down by his teammates right from the start: his debut was a 10–6 loss to Pittsburgh on June 13 on the back of seven Cleveland errors.[58]

The Robisons made two further outrageous signings for the Spiders in June. The team's 7–2 loss to New York on June 24—a game in which Giant Tom O'Brien was walked three times and stole five bases, including home[59]—was enough to embarrass even the blinkered brothers into action. Former Cleveland pitcher Fred "Crazy" Schmit was 33 years old and had been toiling in the minor leagues from Memphis to Mobile for the previous six seasons. He was a vile drunk and had been arrested in 1898 after a fan alleged Schmit had thrown a brick at him. Schmit retorted in his own defense, "I'm a professional pitcher—if I'd thrown a brick, I wouldn't have missed!"[60] The judge was suitably impressed, for he let Schmit go, but Crazy's "accuracy" would only win one game for the Spiders. Thirty-year-old amateur Harry Colliflower was signed from Oswego, New York, only to attract fans to the Washington-Cleveland series on July 17. Amazingly, the ploy worked—the debut of the left-hander drew 2,500 fans and the Spiders defeated Washington 5–4—but naturally, the memorably named new hope of the Clevelanders then lost his next 11 starts and vanished into baseball oblivion.[61]

The fate of the team the *Cleveland Plain Dealer* had christened "the Misfits" was all but sealed on June 26. The appalling home attendance—fewer than 200 fans per game on average—prompted Matthew Robison to banish the Spiders to the road for the remainder of the season.[62] The decision coincided with the infamous Cleveland Streetcar Strike of 1899, which began on June 10 as over 850 employees of the Cleveland Electric Railway Company walked off the job demanding better wages and conditions. The holdout descended into rioting as police and hired strikebreakers clashed with mobs of disgruntled workers; trams and lines were sabotaged across the city and public transport severely disrupted.[63]

But the Spiders did manage a last hurrah for 1,000 of their most patient and long-suffering local fans. On July 1, they defeated title contenders Boston 10–9, coming from 7–0 down at the start of the ninth inning in one of the season's greatest comebacks. Quinn came to bat twice in the ninth inning, scoring once on a McAllister safe hit and reappearing with two men out and two runs needed to win. There might have been ten thousand cranks in the stands, such was the pitch of hysteria raising the roof of the place, and Quinn didn't let them down—he banged out a beauty that scored the tying run and then, in the eleventh inning, stole second base and crossed the plate a winner. The Spiders were mobbed, embraced, and tossed in the air; even President Robison was at the park to shake the hand of each of his players. And the reaction of the local press was equally enthusiastic, the *Cleveland Plain Dealer* gushing, "There were no snarling remarks at the left-field bleacherites, no talking about 'getting down to the Hawley' for supper, no loafing, no grandstand bickering with the umpires. Instead, Quinn's men simply played ball. That is what the people like. And while the Cast Adrifts were thus making the champions look like canceled postage stamps, the ex–

Clevelands were sassing the umpires, quarrelling with the audience and—incidentally—getting a beautiful walloping at the hands of the rejuvenated Orioles down in St. Louis."[64] It was sweet indeed, although ephemeral as a soap bubble: the Spiders then lost 14 wretched games in a row before breaking the drought on July 17 by winning the first half of a doubleheader in Baltimore behind Coldwater Hughey, who was starting every fourth or fifth day and whose 5.41 ERA made him the ace in the Cleveland pack.[65]

Although in *The Lore and Legends of Baseball*, Mac Davis indicated Joe Quinn was "more interested in his gloomy profession (as an undertaker) than in rallying his dejected players,"[66] one facetious Washington writer suggested the Cleveland team had the proper manager in Quinn, as it was "eminently proper that a corpse should be in charge of an undertaker."[67] But, up to his armpits in quicksand and with no means of escape, the 36-year-old second baseman simply did what he did best—hauled himself up to his best season since 1895. He was batting .281, had stolen a dozen bases, and was the team's highest-quality fielder on .958. The *Washington Times* gushed on July 19, "Among the old-timers who are still wearing the spangles of the diamond and playing the game as well as they ever did, is Joe Quinn, captain of the Clevelands. The hand of time has been laid lightly upon him and there seems several more years of usefulness left for this clever player. Notwithstanding he is playing with a losing club, that fact does not appear to handicap his good work. He is batting and fielding as well as he ever did. If not better. He is a credit to the profession, and the game would be better with more of his kind."[68]

Rumor even had it Quinn might have done enough to earn a recall to the Perfectos.[69] However, St. Louis second baseman Clarence "Cupid" Childs would field at .934 from his 125 games in 1899,[70] good enough to avoid the dreaded dispatch to Cleveland and thereby condemning Quinn to remain hog-tied to the mast of the sinking Spiders ship. It is doubtful whether Quinn would have left the miserable outfit anyway, even if he had been given the chance. His reputation for loyalty to struggling teams was unblemished, and it was perhaps a big part of the reason the Robisons had dispatched him to what they knew would be a team of misfits: they could be confident he would stay put.

But while the venomless Spiders were considered the joke of the League, the overindulged Perfectos weren't above some slapstick of their own. The *Washington Evening Times* of August 3 gleefully described one of the queerest plays ever seen on a diamond as worked by St. Louis infielders Patsy Tebeau, Bobby Wallace, and Mike Donlin. Brooklyn's Tom Daly hit a vicious grounder toward third and as Wallace got down to it, it sprang up and struck him clean on the forehead. The ball then speared off toward Tebeau at short, who somehow retained enough poise to throw it to Donlin for the out at first. The *Times* slyly hinted the official scorer should grant Wallace an assist for "such a piece of headwork."[71]

The Spiders split the July 18 double-header with Washington, Quinn putting in what the *Spalding Base Ball Guide of 1899* described as the fielding performance of the season, making eight putouts and 14 assists without a single error.[72] In fact, *The Sporting Life* of August 5 reported Quinn had not made an error in any of the previous 18 games, and only six flubs in his last 43 appearances.[73] But his miserable troops could not follow suit: they didn't win again until August 6, when they fell home 10–9 against Chicago in a game that attracted 14,000 fans, many no doubt fascinated by the novelty value of the hapless Cleveland outfit in the same way a traffic accident draws a morbid crowd of spectators.[74] Clearly overcome by their victory before such an enormous crowd, the Spiders then lost their next 11 games, then returned home after an absence of nearly two months on August 26 for a series with second-placed Boston and grandly lost all four games as part of a 24-game losing streak.[75]

Between August 25 and October 15, Cleveland won just one game—and lost 40. Their one-hundredth loss of the season came on August 31, when Crazy Schmit blew a three-run lead to Brooklyn to lose 9–3.[76] Quinn continued to lead from the front, although *The Sporting News* mourned, "It is a shame to keep such a grand player tied up with such a combination. The old man is very much the whole team."[77] But his struggles, weighed down by the yoke of futility, had not gone unnoticed, and other clubs were already prowling for his services. In late September, the Spiders were front-runners in the jostling to secure Quinn as a utility player for next season,[78] despite one of the team's most dreadful performances against fellow strugglers Washington on September 17: they had a huge lead after scoring eight runs in the second inning, but the Senators were then allowed to score the next 14 to win 15–10.[79]

By September's end, there were rumors the dispirited and disgruntled Arachnids were considering going on strike. They were more than 30 games out of eleventh place and *The Sporting News* reported dolefully that the players had not been paid for "some period."[80] A 15–3 thrashing from the Perfectos on September 26 only added insult to injury, but it was October 7 before the Robisons granted the Spiders $25 each to keep them quiet and keep them playing. Quinn denied rumors of a strike in his typically diplomatic fashion, telling *TSN* the Spiders' long sojourn on the road was solely responsible for the delay in salaries being paid—but his façade slipped when he added as a testy footnote, "Some of the boys blame me for not making a fight to get their money. It was none of my business and I certainly could not be expected to do more for them than I did for myself."[81] It was an aside that reflected Quinn's real limitations as a manager—while on the field he was a rallying point for his players, off it he was a loner and he lacked the genuine empathy with the men that distinguishes the captain from the general.

So the Spiders closed out the season the same way they had started—dismally, thrashed 16–1 and 19–3 by Cincinnati.[82] There was more than a touch of déjà vu about the encounter—Cincinnati had already beaten them 14 times that season. Manager Quinn gave the final start of the year to 19-year-old hotel clerk Eddie Kolb, who had been hanging around, begging for a chance to display his pitching prowess. Quinn finally accepted a box of cigars from Kolb and let him try. Kolb gave up 19 runs, 18 hits, and five walks, and never darkened a major league diamond again.[83] Although the Spiders never received their final paychecks, they were, according to Al Spink, "ecstatic" when the season finally ended. They pooled the last of their funds to present a diamond locket to club secretary George W. Muir, in acknowledgment of his forbearance—he had had to watch every one of their 154 games, including their 134 losses, a major league record destined never to be equaled.[84]

In the 1899 season, National League offensive averages jumped by 11 points and scoring by six percent, attributable to alterations to the balk rule that a pickoff throw may not be faked: any pickoff made without stepping toward a base constituted a balk.[85] As a result, six hundred extra bases were stolen in 1899.[86] But it may also have been simply a statistical phenomenon, with league averages wildly skewed by the inept Cleveland, who gave up 1,252 runs (448 more than the league average), lost 134 games, had no pitcher win more than four games, and finished 84 games out of first.[87] Cleveland's League Park was famed for having very little foul territory—according to Cleveland baseball historian Peter Jedick, "The fans sat on wooden benches so close to the field they could watch the players sweat and hear them cuss."[88] In 1899, the Spiders could hear their few fans doing plenty of cussing as their team finished last in every category that mattered: runs, doubles, triples, homers, batting average, slugging percentage, and stolen bases. They had six losing streaks of 11 or more games, lost 40 of their last 41 games and conceded more than 10 runs 50 times. The Spiders' winning percentage of .130 is still major league baseball's all-time lowest.[89]

At the end of 1899, the distended National League reverted to an eight-team competition. Pennant winners Brooklyn had dominated the season thanks to their Baltimore acquisitions (a rather more successful case of syndicate ball), Boston was second (six games behind), and Baltimore fourth, the unexpected death of John McGraw's young wife Minnie keeping Muggsy on the sidelines in the latter half.[90] St. Louis finished fifth but still garnered a whopping $40,000 profit thanks to 220,000 fans flocking through the gates of League Park—36 times the attendance garnered by the Spiders, who saw only 6,088 (mainly uninterested) fans in their bleachers, the worst attendance record in major league history.[91] Joe Quinn was the last-ever manager of the Cleveland Spiders, who finished with a team batting average of .253 (worst in the league) and ERA 6.37 (equally bad)—for which they were rewarded by being thrown out of the league.

Although the Spiders had won just 12 of the 116 games played under his watch, Quinn was valiant and led the team batting with a .286 average. He hit 24 doubles, scored 73 runs and knocked in 72 RBIs, some of his best career figures. He also stole 22 bases at age 36, his best return since 1895. The ineptitude of his players in the field, with the worst Defensive Efficiency[92] in the league, must have almost turned his hair gray, because the aging second baseman had led the league in fielding at his own position, with a .962 average and just 31 errors from his 147 games.[93]

There was one little ray of sunshine in Quinn's dark year. In November, his seventh child arrived, a girl named Estelle. But a photograph taken of Quinn early in 1901 shows the strain the year in the nest of Spiders had imposed on him—his mild features had hardened and his jaw was set, the skin tightened across his facial bones like one of his own funeral shrouds.

14. Last Days of the Dingo

How steep the stairs within Kings' houses are
For exile-wearied feet as mine to tread.
   —Oscar Wilde, "At Verona," 1881

"Walkabout" is a rite of passage unique to the Australian Aboriginal people. The walker leaves his tribal home alone to undertake a journey unencumbered by clock or calendar, unaided by compass, radio, or companions. The walkabout is no aimless wandering but a deliberate and focused journey in which the walker develops an intimate understanding of his landscape and environment, with all its spiritual interconnections, returning with a sense of oneness with the world in which they live.[1]

Joe Quinn's final three years in professional baseball might be viewed as a type of walkabout—not only in the literal sense, as a time of constant shifting and relocation—but also as a time of consolidation, of his beliefs, values, and his place in the larger scheme.

The year 1900 had not dawned inclusively. Anti-immigrant feelings were swelling across the United States in 1900 as a boom in railroads, mining, and manufacturing attracted a fresh wave of immigrants.[2] The baseball fraternity was not exempt. The *New York Clipper* of February 3, 1901, demanded, "What is baseball coming to? For nearly half a century, things ran smoothly enough until they began to rope in a few ringers such as [Eddie] Abbaticchio, [Louis] Soxalexis, [Ossee] Schreckengost, and now Accorsini."[3] But despite U.S. Immigration's 1894 reservations about baseball as a "recognized profession," the list of foreign-born players in the major leagues was growing. According to the *St. Paul Globe* of April 12, 1901, Australian Joe Quinn now played alongside Russian Jake Gettman, Chicago's Clark Griffith (Welsh), and Englishman Harry Smith. Bob Wood was born in Scotland, Nap Lajoie and Candy LaChance were French Canadians, John Anderson was a Norwegian, and—the paper could obviously not resist the jibe—pitcher and comedian Rube Waddell was simply a monkey.[4]

Quinn had, in fact, renounced his Australian citizenship and become a naturalized American in 1898.[5] Perhaps the encounter with the Australian team in Chicago had set him to serious consideration of where he indeed belonged. With all of his immediate family—parents, siblings, and his own wife and children—in the United States, and international travel a prohibitively expensive, protracted, and often dangerous undertaking, his chances of, and reasons for, returning to Australia were few. While Quinn was always proud of his antipodean heritage, naturalization offered a kind of belonging and certainty that his nomadic early life had always precluded. There were many tangible benefits to the exercise, too—tax exemptions, eligibility for public office, and voting rights.[6] But given Quinn's comfortable circumstances, well-established business, and lack of professed political ambition, his decision may not have been a material one. In any case, the motivation behind the choice may never be truly known.

◆ ◆ ◆

Battered but not wholly embittered by the Spiders debacle, Quinn returned home to St. Louis in late 1899 after his miserable Cleveland outfit was disbanded. He was now 37 years old and there was no certainty he would receive a contract to play on in his home city. With the *retour* of Quinn and fellow Spiders survivors Coldwater Hughey and Jack Harper to St. Louis, competition for a place on the newly renamed Cardinals roster was intense in the spring of 1900. For both the anxious youngsters and many of the aging stars alike, it came down to their performance in a three-game intraclub series between the "Colts" and the "Veterans" in the first week of April 1900. As the oldest man in the squad by some margin,[7] Quinn could not afford to hide his light beneath a bushel. He played the first match on April 5 at second base for the Vets, the old-timers winning 22–8 in cold and wet conditions. The Colts really had no chance as, like front-line conscripts, they stuck their heads up above the trenches straight into the sights of the big guns—the Cardinals' best-conditioned pitchers, Young and Thomas, both lined up for the Vets, as did Jesse Burkett. The loss put glum faces on many of the youngsters as the prospect of release or farming loomed large before them, but Captain Tebeau took pity and gave them a couple of good pitchers for the second game, as well as himself and Quinn to play the infield. St. Louisans had heard of Quinn's third-base play and were excited to see him work that bag, and he didn't let them down: Joe and star shortstop Bobby Wallace pulled off two lightning double plays in the game, and the *St. Louis Republic* reminisced, "It brought back the days when Quinn and Ely led the League in double plays in the year of 1894. Though Joe has had but two days' work, he covered half an acre of ground and his whip is almost as good as Wallace's. The old boy was there with his bingle."[8] Unfortunately, for all his dash in the field, Quinn's game came to an abrupt and bloody end in the batter's box—the little undertaker got under one of Bert Jones' hot pitches and it climbed up his bat like a kitten up a drainpipe, striking him over the right eye and inflicting what doctors diagnosed as a "severe yet not dangerous wound."[9] It would be five years before the A.L. Reach sporting goods company patented a form of protective headgear for batters known as the "Reach Pneumatic Head Protector," but even then, few players would wear the bulbous creation, despite the frequency of accidents such as Quinn's.[10] Quinn himself returned for the third game of the series, bruised and patched up like a pub brawler on a Monday morning but still "looking for blood," the *Republic* declared excitedly.[11] His age was already against him and the Spiders fiasco hung like an albatross around his neck, but there was no question that he would not be out there and playing for his life, even batting one-eyed and sore-headed. And somehow he did enough. Soon after the third game, Sullivan, Harley, McAllister, and Lochhead were all released to Detroit while Quinn and many of the other aging stars, including Tebeau and Cy Young, lived to fight another day.[12]

Quinn's career would probably have continued somewhere, though, even if the Robisons had sent him to Detroit with the unlucky quartet. Rumors abounded that New York, Cincinnati, and Chicago all had lines out for Quinn's services and that "these teams would give a snug chunk of money for the little man who can play all the places alike," reported the *Republic*.[13] The fact the Cardinals held onto Quinn suggested they certainly intended to use him:

after all, the *Republic* affirmed, "The introduction of 'the Dingo' to the game would not weaken the team."

Baseball's last Opening Day of the nineteenth century was a memorable one. April 19 saw the Cardinals open their account with a 3–0 home dismissal of the Pittsburgh Pirates (who would finish a narrow second in the league). Cy Young's five-hit, nine-strikeout performance and a big triple from Bobby Wallace sent 15,000 fans home happy, although there was no sign of their old favorite Joe Quinn: ex–Baltimore shortstop Bill Keister started the game at second base.[14] In Boston, 10,000 fans watched the Phillies win 19–17 in 10 innings, still the highest-scoring season opener in major league history[15] and one of baseball's greatest "almost-comebacks": Boston scored nine runs, including a major-league record three by pinch hitters, in the bottom of the ninth to tie the score at 17 apiece before their ultimate capitulation in the extra inning.[16] Even in Cleveland, baseball fans had something to do on their Thursday afternoon: the new rival to the National League, the upstart American League, played its inaugural game in the Forest City on April 26, drawing 6,500 fans (more than their National League team drew for the entire 1899 season) to see the new Blues beat Indianapolis, 7–6. It was an equally emotional opener in Detroit, where double amputee and former catcher Charlie Bennett threw out the first pitch. However, the Tigers, clearly overcome by the occasion, were no-hit by Buffalo's Doc Amole, 8–0.[17]

Manager Tebeau's Cardinals won two of three games against Pittsburgh, then split an eight-game series with the Chicago Cubs to finish the month.[18] Fresh from their fifth-place finish in 1899, the team had retained the services of Cy Young, Jesse Burkett, Bobby Wallace, and .300-hitting outfielders Emmet Heidrick and Patsy Donovan, and were further strengthened by the arrival on May 8 of John McGraw and Wilbert Robinson from Baltimore.[19] The Birds had been victims of the same syndicate system which decimated Cleveland in 1899. The co-owners again redistributed players between Baltimore and Brooklyn at the start of the 1900 season, but McGraw and Robinson refused to relocate to Brooklyn because of their mutual business interests in Baltimore. The disgruntled owners promptly sold the pair to St. Louis, but they refused to go there either, even when McGraw was offered the manager's job. By May, however, McGraw could no longer refuse the Robisons' unprecedented offer of $100 a game (remembering that the average middle-class worker earned around $75 a month) and removal of the reserve clause from his contract.[20] But despite McGraw's assuring *The Republic*, "Now that we have come here, we will work our finger nails off to win"[21]— and he did bat .344—he and Robinson mostly wasted the season away, often getting ejected from both the baseball diamond and numerous local hotels. With his services conveniently unreserved, McGraw upped stakes as soon as the season ended to return to his beloved Baltimore and play for their American League outfit in 1901.[22]

If the Baltimore pair failed to make an immediate impact on St. Louis fans, they could be partly forgiven—the same day as they arrived, May 8, the Street Railway Employees of America went on strike to protest low pay and long working hours. The streetcar strike paralyzed both business and sporting affairs in St. Louis. On May 9, the baseball game between the Cardinals and Cincinnati was called off. The lack of transportation had seen fewer than 400 people attend the previous day's game, and as the salaries of gatekeepers, ticket-takers and other park attendants amounted to over $100 each day, with player salaries pushing the daily expenditure toward $750, management took the decision on business grounds. "If this strike endures for three weeks," Frank Robison told *The Republic*, "we will lose $15,000."[23] The strike strangled the city far longer than three weeks. While the St. Louis Transit Company initially acceded to the union's demands, they then retracted and brought in strikebreakers who fired into a crowd of activists, leaving three dead and many more hurt. The workers responded with furious demonstrations which degenerated from throwing of rocks, bread, and—oddly—frogs, to cable sabotage, fiery barricades, and dynamiting of the tracks. But early public support for the workers soon palled as the lack of transport services hurt St. Louis residents and businesses. By September, with 14 strikers dead and over 300 injured, the impoverished workers were forced to surrender.[24]

But despite the city-wide chaos, baseball was back at Robison Field by May 12. Police protection on selected streetcar lines saw patrons venture back for the much-anticipated series with second-place Brooklyn, and the debut of the two old Orioles. The contest was all it should be—Brooklyn won the first game 5–4, despite the Cardinals' leading 4–2 with two Brooklyn hitters out in the ninth. Captain McGraw threw McGuire's grounder wild to first before Cy Young walked two batters, enabling Brooklyn to stage a batting rally and win 5–4. The 1899 champions, with Hanlon at the helm, also twice caught the Cardinals napping with a brilliant new play: with Quinn on second, Robinson on first and none out, pitcher Young came to bat and the routine play was for Cy to bunt to advance the runners. Just before the pitcher was ready, Brooklyn shortstop Bill Dahlen ran to second to force Quinn back from his lead. Dahlen remained on the bag and as Quinn was returning, McGinnity pitched. Young made a perfect bunt but McGinnity let him go, instead throwing Quinn out at third by a mile. *The Republic* mourned, "Everybody in the stand wanted Quinn killed for not being on third an hour before. It was the greatest play seen in five years, if not twenty-five—yet not ten people in the 5,000 present saw it for its beauty."[25]

Ironically, the play was repeated in the sixth inning on exactly the same combination: this time Quinn got a fair start, but Young miscued and popped up to the pitcher. Quinn tried to scramble back, but Dahlen was on the bag and the double play was made. The play won the game for Brooklyn, and Hanlon claimed it had already won them four games that season. Despite the loss, both McGraw and Robinson made impressive debuts—McGraw with two walks, a single and a HBP and Robinson three hits, including a drive to left field that was only prevented from being a home run by a fluky rebound off a foul flag.[26] *The Republic* also praised Quinn's two splendid plays in the ninth inning, despite his base-running woes. Jimmy Sheckard drove a vicious grounder at Dan McGann on first, which McGann half blocked: Quinn was behind him, nailed the ball, shouted to McGann to take the base, which he did, and they made the play; Quinn then picked a high ball of DeMontreville's out of the sun and wind in fine style. While the Cardinals indulged in a grand 8–0 sweep of the visitors next day, Brooklyn won the final two games in hard-fought contests, 3–2 and 5–2, to take the series.[27]

Despite his honest workmanship, Quinn mysteriously remained a target for jibes from local fans in early 1900. It was a longstanding peculiarity of St. Louis cranks, observed the *Cincinnati Enquirer*, that nine-tenths of the cheering was regularly for the opposition, that cranks would bellow "Play ball!" when the home team was trying to stall for a victory, and yell "Fine him!" at the least indiscretion by one of their own.[28] In the May 8 win over Cincinnati, Quinn made a wild throw during a gallant effort to turn a double play with Reds runner Jimmy Barrett almost hanging off his neck, setting the bleacher-critics to bawling, "Take him out! Give us Dillard!" *The Republic* was exasperated:

> If Quinn played it safe, made a bluff to catch the spectators and then held the ball as if to say: "No use, he was safe," he would have been cheered. But he took a proper chance, like a good ball player, not like a grand-stand poser. Joe led the team at the bat, took part in two forked-lightning double plays and fielded his position like Lajoie, or like Quinn, who is just as good a fielder as

anybody. The people of Boston and Baltimore, where Quinn played with champions, and of Cleveland, where he played with a tail-ender, think there is no one like him. But in St. Louis, where he lives, of which he is a substantial business man and a first-class ball player, he, like his fellows Sudhoff, O'Connor, Tebeau, Peitz and Breitenstein, is but lightly esteemed. Truly, the ballplayer, like the prophet, is not without honor, save in his own country.[29]

After spending most of May at home and compiling a 12–9 record for the month, the fifth-place Cardinals embarked on a disastrous eastern trip which caused near-fatal injury to any pennant hopes they may have entertained. Despite commencing the journey with a double-header victory over Brooklyn (a result *The Republic* unpatriotically dismissed as "sheer luck"[30]), the boys in red trim then lost 10 of the next 14 games. Their generally poor play was characterized by the June 14 loss to league leaders Philadelphia, after which *The Republic* sneered, "Wretchedly slow and stupid fielding by the St. Louis team gave Philadelphia the game—Keister's awful blunder: the shortstop thought there was a man on first base when there was not, played for a double and missed everyone."[31]

The Robisons' extravagant spending had not brought them a winning team, and bad spring weather and the ongoing streetcar strike had pierced the St. Louis coffers, from which money was now bleeding away into the gutters. The $10,000 profligate McGraw was lame, and Quinn spent much of the trip at shortstop after Bobby Wallace injured his knee in a collision with his own teammate Lave Cross on June 4.[32] Quinn did not have a good time of it—he started well enough, with extra-base hits in both games against Boston, then he piled on four errors in three games against New York.[33] On June 12, while still in Philadelphia, Quinn was given ten days' notice of release.[34] With McGraw, Wallace, Tebeau, and Keister all scrapping for infield positions, Quinn had played only 22 of the Cards' 41 games, hitting .263 with three extra-base hits and four stolen bases.[35] *The Sporting Life* accompanied news of Quinn's release with the odd observation that the Cardinals' infield combination of Dillard and Kiester would now improve as they were freed from the specter of Quinn standing ready to take their places, but *The Republic*, which had firmly defended Quinn throughout the season, simply threw up its hands in frustration. "Quinn is not a shortstop," the broadsheet barked, continuing,

> Keister has been a regular short fielder. Quinn can play a better third base than anything else. Yet Dillard, who is fast and is supposed to be an infielder, is not sent to short. It is plain that Quinn's convenience was not consulted in the matter. He was given the position that was least to his taste and which of all he can play with least effect and ease. Now he is to be released with the idea that Keister and Dillard will be improved when taken from beneath his ominous shadow.[36]

The *Cincinnati Commercial–Tribune* joined the chorus, wondering aloud why Tebeau allowed Quinn to be released at a time when his team was badly crippled, and why indeed Quinn had not been played at second in partnership with Keister.[37] But, even at 37 years of age, the "man who is not good enough for St. Louis"[38] immediately became the subject of a wide-ranging bidding war. The *Cincinnati Enquirer* was quick to point out that Quinn's 1899 fielding average of .969 at second base was behind only that of Reitz and DeMontreville, and in advance of such luminaries as Link Lowe and Nap Lajoie. He had also hit .286 in 1899, the equivalent of Lave Cross. "A man who can field like that and tie such players as Lave Cross in hitting is far from the 'has-been' class," declared the *Enquirer*. "He would strengthen Cincinnati, because he has a head and has learned by experience where to play for batters."[39] And the Reds needed all the help they could get, languishing as they were at the bottom of the National League standings.[40]

14. Last Days of the Dingo

While eight years had passed since Quinn played under Frank Selee, that Boston manager was also quick to express interest in the veteran second baseman. "He takes excellent care of himself and is good for several years," he told the *Boston Globe*. "In case of injury or illness to either Lowe or Long ... Quinn would be just the man to fill any infield gap."[41] Quinn's good friend Connie Mack, managing the Western League outfit in Milwaukee, also put a claim to President Johnson for Quinn's services. An even older associate, Tom Loftus, was now manager in Chicago, and was quickly dispatched by President Hart to meet with Quinn. The Orphans had bought St. Louis second baseman Cupid Childs at the beginning of the year, but the big man had struggled with recurring bouts of malaria in 1899 and was still not playing well[42]; Loftus was granted *carte blanche* to get Quinn as a replacement.[43]

Meanwhile, Patsy Tebeau took over from the discarded Quinn as Cardinals shortstop and was an immediate calamity: his three errors and a wild throw helped Philadelphia to an 11–5 victory over St. Louis on June 15. Even the *Philadelphia Exchange* admitted, "With Joe Quinn in yesterday's game, the chances are that St. Louis would have won."[44] Thankfully, Wallace, who had been rehabilitating at his home in Bennet, Pennsylvania, was set to return within the week.[45]

Quinn was an unemployed ball player for just a few days after his release. On June 17, *The Republic* reported John T. Brush had made "Reliable Joe" the right offer, and he would become a Cincinnati Red Leg on expiration of his ten days' notice.[46] The St. Louis paper remained stubbornly loyal to the little undertaker, farewelling him benevolently, "Leaving St. Louis, [Quinn] takes with him the very best wishes of thousands to whom his clever exhibitions have given a great deal of pleasure and to whom he never has, in thought, word, or deed, given offense."[47]

Ironically, Quinn's final game for the Cardinals, on June 17, was a 9–3 loss to the Reds. With McGraw (lame), Wallace (knee), and Heidrick (bad leg) out of the game, Keister and Dillard out of position, and Quinn out of a job, it was a very sad-looking St. Louis aggregation indeed. In the top of the ninth, trailing 3–1, St. Louis got an immediate double to left field through Donovan, Robinson was walked, and then Quinn came up to bat in his last game. He turned out a timely hit past Beckley on first base to score two runners, an effort bringing applause even from the grudging St. Louis cranks. The Cardinals then got two men on base in the tenth, bringing "Old Reliable" Quinn up again. The crowd was with him, but even Quinn could not deliver the goods twice in succession—he struck out for just the second time in his twenty-two games, and the crippled St. Louis outfit allowed their visitors six runs at the bottom of the eleventh inning. But despite all the sniping and snarling to which he had been subjected in 1900, after the game, Quinn was the subject of a testimonial which no released St. Louis player had ever received. His friends and admirers presented him with a huge horseshoe of flowers, and even the fickle fans rose in their seats to give him a royal salute—as though he were a baseball hero come to strengthen the outfit, instead of a man released because the club saw no use for him.[48]

• • •

In the industrialized northern city of Cincinnati, Quinn played his final 74 games in the National League. Here he was reunited with the old St. Louis "Pretzel Battery" of Ted Breitenstein and Heinie Peitz, and owner John T. Brush of old Indianapolis fame. Despite Cincinnati's genteel moniker of the "Queen City," the Reds were anything but decorous. On July 11, 1886, during only the second-ever Sunday game played in that town, umpire George Bradley was hit by a beer mug hurled from the rowdy crowd and a riot ensued.[49]

With moral and political objections to Sunday baseball never far from the surface, such occurrences only provided further ammunition to the ethical guardians of the sport that games on Sundays attracted mostly "hoodlums" and "foreigners" and should cease immediately.[50] Such trenchant advice was strategically ignored in Cincinnati, where Sunday ball continued to be both popular and unruly.

The Reds played at League Park on Findlay and York, a site notorious as one of only two baseball parks ever to collapse causing loss of life. Hastily erected on the site of an abandoned brickyard, the stand fell down the very first time patrons were admitted, on Opening Day in 1884; one person died and many others were hurt.[51] The park was, however, immediately rebuilt and would serve as the site of Cincinnati baseball for the next 86 years. But despite being rebuilt from concrete and steel, the first ballpark to meet new building codes intended to stem a rash of park fires, the park burned in both 1900 and 1902, and before being closed in 1970, the grandstand was moved, renovated, and redeveloped several times at various locations around the site.[52]

Quinn had been in town just a week when the Cardinals arrived to play ball. The two teams were level-pegging on the league ladder, Cincinnati sixth with a 23–28 record, St. Louis seventh at 21–28. And it was the man not good enough for the fast aggregation from Missouri who "sunk the ungrateful fangs of the viper deep in the bosom of his erstwhile teammates"[53] for a 7–5 victory to the Reds. Young Bert Jones was on the mound for the Cardinals and holding fast until the sixth inning, when Harry Steinfeldt cut him down with a terrific line drive which struck him in the stomach, felling him "like a flower snipped with a pair of shears," marveled *The Republic*.[54] The plucky youngster resumed, but by the eighth inning, his speed and nerve were gone, and he was facing a highly unsympathetic undertaker at the plate. Quinn belted his best pitch so hard that he fell down from the force of his swing: had it not been for that, the blow would have been a left-field stand-up double. Steinfeldt then got another swing at the shell-shocked pitcher and slammed a triple to the right field fence. Peitz walked, Scott singled, and the game was over. The *Cincinnati Commercial-Tribune* jeered, "When Tebeau released Joe Quinn, he gave it out that he took this step because Quinn was too slow to make a double play. However, Quinn has not shown the least weakness in this respect since he joined the Reds. In Sunday's game he figured in three double plays, and today he took part in two. Five double plays in two days certainly does not look as if that was Quinn's weakness."[55] Interestingly, by August 11, *The Sporting Life* was far from complimentary about Quinn's speed around the second sack, calling him Cincinnati's "one weak red spot," despite simultaneously giving him credit for at least half a dozen of the team's victories.[56]

Tebeau himself unexpectedly resigned the managership of the Cardinals on August 18, citing his own inability to make the team play to the level it was capable of.[57] Confusion abounded after his departure, with Frank de Haas Robison announcing McGraw had been appointed as new manager and McGraw flatly denying it, insisting Cardinals business manager Louis Heilbroner was the new boss. *The Republic* speculated McGraw actually *was* in charge, with Heilbroner as a convenient scapegoat all dressed up for use in case Muggsy failed to make the team win. However, the paper conceded McGraw's position was probably a wise one. Given his short term of service in a team not of his choosing, and jealousy of his salary and reputation amongst the players, he wisely declined to assume any sort of official responsibility. But many of the players refused to take orders from the 4'9" Heilbroner, and it was widely accepted that, behind the scenes or no, McGraw really was the driving force.[58]

Meanwhile, July had brought league strugglers New York to Cincinnati League Park.

The Reds won the first three of the four-game series so easily that, perhaps bored by the succession of victories, local fans decided to inject some liveliness into the final match. In the third inning, Giants first baseman Dirty Jack Doyle slugged umpire Robert Emslie after being called out on a steal attempt, and delighted fans jumped from the stands to join the brawling pair; it took all 18 players to untangle the joyful rioters. Doyle was then arrested by two vastly outnumbered park policemen and taken to the York Street lockup, where he was fined for assault. The Giants won the disrupted game 6–3.[59]

Despite the series win, the Reds had no chance to swell their heads—the next day, as legendary posses tend to do, pennant leaders Brooklyn swaggered into town. They were four games in front and toting a carefully crafted reputation for merciless demolition of struggling clubs—after all, the Reds themselves had been on the end of an 11–1 thrashing from the Superbas just three weeks before.[60] Nonetheless, it took a remarkable feat of pitching for Hanlon's nine to put the Cincinnati boys away this time. On Thursday, July 5, Brooklyn won 2–0, but only on the back of a Jerry Nops one-hitter, and the following day, Frank Kitson also had to pitch a one-hitter to beat the Reds.[61] The back-to-back one-hitters added up to a feat which had not occurred since June 17–18, 1884.[62] Incidentally, the Reds enjoyed their own pitching triumphs in July. Frank "Noodles" Hahn twirled a 4–0 no-hitter on July 12 as the Reds won against the Phillies, and followed up the feat with a 9–0 shutout of St. Louis three days later.[63] Reds pitcher Bill Phillips also made a name for himself in 1900, although for a rather less salubrious effort: he king-hit Phillies batter Roy Thomas on August 16 after Thomas fouled off a dozen pitches in the eighth inning. Phillips was thrown out for his troubles, but fortunately for him, the Reds did stagger to a 5–4 extra-innings victory.[64]

The league's favorite blue-coated pugilist, Tim Hurst, was also back in the 1900 season, despite a cohort of team owners' attempting to having him banned for his disruptive influence. The *St. Paul Globe* welcomed his return, declaring Hurst had the best control over the players through his fearless bravado and "the rapid-fire sarcasm that leveled many a wordy assailant." Even Undertaker Quinn fell victim:

> "That ball was six inches outside the plate," Quinn protested one day when Hurst tallied a strike on him.
> "You wouldn't call that six inches if you were selling a coffin," came the immediate reply.[65]

The Reds' inconsistency cost them a higher place on the standings than their eventual seventh-place finish. They threw away a series against Brooklyn in July after clearly outplaying the league leaders in each game. As the *New York Sun* would have it, "Old Lady Fortune hid her grinning face behind a cloudbank,"[66] for at the bottom of the ninth inning of the final match, with two outs and the score tied at 5-all, an intentional walk to the Superbas' Deacon McGuire went embarrassingly awry: McGuire reached out and tapped at Noodles Hahn's pitch, but catcher Wood picked it up and promptly dropped it, allowing the winning run to score. The Reds batters, however, did have their moments, such as on August 20, when they pounded Cy Young out of the box in a fiery 15–7 thrashing of the Cardinals. "The Reds connected with Young's delivery as though he was a schoolboy," marveled *The Republic*. "The big farmer tried hard, used all the things that have made him famous in his profession, but he was helpless.... It was a batting matinee, pure and simple."[67] Quinn grabbed three hard hits (including a triple) and Jimmy Barrett four to lead the Reds' charge. It was a bitter, brutal game, characterized by interminable arguing between umpires, players and even fans. After the game, a fuming Cy Young stormed out of the dressing rooms to even up a score, not with an opponent, but with a spectator who had called him a "rank quitter" while he was being bombarded to all parts of the park: a heckler who happened to be sitting right beside Young's own wife. *The Republic* mocked, "The spectator took Cy's scolding and slunk away without making a reply."[68]

But for all these ephemeral glories, the Reds wasted chance after chance to improve their standing. On September 3, they started a five-game series against New York with a promising 10–4 win at the Polo Grounds. They promptly lost the next four by increasingly embarrassing margins, ending with an 11–3 drubbing on September 5.[69] Their crowning anti-achievement was a jaw-dropping 17 errors in a double-header against Brooklyn on September 12 (naturally, losing both games). The feat remains a record for the most errors committed in a single day by any team since 1900.[70] The Reds would stage an attempt on this record on October 8 but confined themselves to a mere 8 errors while the Chicago Cubs lavished the double-header with 17; fortunately, the Reds won both games.[71]

Soundly beaten thrice more by the Superbas on September 11 and 12, the red-faced Reds rolled away to rainy Philadelphia, where they pushed the Athletics to a creditable 5–6 loss in twelve muddy innings on September 16. The Phils, however, showed little sympathy for the strugglers and won the remaining four games of the series, albeit by three runs or fewer in each. It was Reds captain Tommy Corcoran who quite literally uncovered the secret to the Phils' success, however. In one of early baseball's most sophisticated scams, players in the Phillies locker room would read the opposing catcher's signs and relay them to the third base coach via an electric wire concealed beneath the outfield grass.[72] Had Corcoran's spikes been not been so sharp, the Phils must have finished a lot higher than third in the 1900 season.

During the wind-up of September, the Reds were on the end of yet another loss—this time of a trade deal with the New York Giants. Nineteen-year-old rookie pitcher Christy Mathewson had been given three pitching assignments with the Giants and lost them all, rounding out by blowing a 7–4 lead to Boston on September 26. The Giants shipped him back to his home club in Norfolk rather than paying $1,500 to buy him, and Mathewson was promptly picked up by the Reds for the bargain-basement price of just $100. But Mathewson never played a game in Cincinnati; in December, the Reds traded the raw youngster back to the Giants in exchange for veteran hurler Amos Rusie, who had spent the last two years on the sidelines with arm problems. The deal was an agreement between the two clubs to save $900; the Giants would have had to pay $1,000 to Norfolk if they'd kept Mathewson after the season, and Reds owner John T. Brush was negotiating to purchase the Giants from Andrew Freedman.[73] Although only 30 years old and a candidate for the Hall of Fame, Rusie was well past his prime in 1901 and appeared in just three games for the Reds for an 0–1 record.[74] Mathewson, on the other hand, pitched a no-hitter against the Cardinals on July 15 and won 20 games at a 2.41 ERA for the Giants.[75]

On October 3, Brooklyn clinched the National League pennant by defeating Boston 6–4 and 3–1, capturing Ned Hanlon's fifth pennant in seven seasons. Meanwhile, the Reds rounded out the season with, for Quinn at least, the ultimate humiliation—losing both games of a double-header to the Cardinals in St. Louis and finishing the season in second-last place. It was Quinn's final game in a Reds jersey. *The Sporting Life* called his Cincinnati engagement "bittersweet," acknowledging both his faithfulness and the contribution of his stickwork to many a victory, but insisting he realize "old Rag Time had taken a few springs out of his legs" as his declining ability to turn a double play had helped lose just as many.[76]

Still, it could have been worse. In reaction to the St. Louis team's fifth-place finish, the

Robison brothers withheld the entire final month's pay to the Cardinals, citing ill-discipline, heavy drinking, and gambling as reasons for their poor performance. The club, already financially stretched by the streetcar strike, was then mortgaged on November 20 to clear its debts, which still did not include making the final payment to its players.[77] At least Quinn had no such financial concerns. On the same day as the Cardinals auction, *The Republic* reported Quinn was having his usual busy winter "in his dismal but not unprofitable line," one of the few men of his ilk to make more money in winter than in summer: "When the days of bleak north and sunny south come along in devastating and bewildering alternation, as they have such a cruel, pretty habit of doing along this line of Mason and Dixon, then it is that Undertaker Joe reaps his grim harvest," intoned the paper. "For it is then that the bony claws of King Death fasten themselves upon the throats of the marked ones, and Claypole Quinn gives them swell and decent burial."[78]

• • •

> *"A Cleveland dispatch says that Jimmy McAleer wants Joe Quinn for his American League club. Not unlikely that Jim does, but how is he going to get the National League teams to waive claim to Joe? If Quinn was not wanted in St. Louis—wanted and needed—about four National League clubs can use him. Quinn will not leave the National League these many years, and it is not likely he will leave St. Louis."—The (St. Louis) Republic*, Wednesday, May 9, 1900

Two years earlier, in 1898, *St. Louis Post–Dispatch* sporting editor Al Spink had called for serious attention to the declining public interest in baseball. He boldly called for establishment of a second major league to both rival the monopolistic National League and reset the stage for an annual world's championship.[79] Naturally, National League franchise holders immediately opposed the scheme, and little encouragement came from the baseball identities and journalists Spink wrote to for help—save from the dependable Ted Sullivan, that "man of shrewd mind and long experience in organizing baseball associations," Spink said approvingly.[80] Sullivan came to St. Louis from Chicago in the summer of 1898 and volunteered his assistance in scouting cities for the new league, and by the fall, Spink was sufficiently confident to call a meeting of supporters at an obscure hotel in Chicago. Sullivan, Chris Von der Ahe, Anson and a collective of sportswriters were present, as were Charlie Comiskey and Tom Loftus, both longtime friends of Spink's. Their chief plan was now to resurrect the old American Association, and they invited Western League president Bancroft B. Johnson to head the breakaway group.

Johnson was one of the biggest men in baseball—both physically and influentially. He had been a baseball writer in the 1880s with the *Cincinnati Commercial Gazette*, and there befriended Charlie Comiskey while he had command of the Cincinnati Reds. From that alliance, the defunct Western League was reborn, with Comiskey heading a team in St. Paul and Johnson as league president.[81] The modern-day American League was also born of this friendship. After many evenings of discussion at the Ten Minute Club in Cincinnati, Comiskey and Johnson expanded their Western League into the American League in 1900. As early as 1896, Johnson had proclaimed, "The Western League has passed the stage where it should be considered as a minor league,"[82] and now, four years later, he acted, renaming the Western League and leading the charge toward major league status by expanding into Cleveland and Chicago (where Comiskey took the helm). There were plenty of players to go around after the National League downsized from twelve to eight teams at the end of 1899, and Johnson grabbed many of these "leftovers." The new franchises joined Indianapolis,

Milwaukee, Kansas City, Detroit, Buffalo, and Minneapolis, with Washington, Boston, and Connie Mack's Philadelphia joining in 1901 and St. Louis in 1902.[83] An American League franchise was also established in Baltimore with John McGraw at the helm. Muggsy was so furious the Birds had been dropped from the National League at the end of 1899 that he eagerly joined the American League campaign, and so bitter was the struggle for supremacy in Baltimore that he and former manager Ned Hanlon literally fought for control by setting up rival factions across the Union Park diamond, McGraw's men camped at third base and Hanlon's at first.[84]

The National League initially devoted little energy to fending off Johnson, Spink and their conspirators. They ought, perhaps, have turned greater attention to their own internal dramas. Ten years after the Players' League rebellion, in 1900 the players formed the Protective Association of Professional Baseball Players, with three delegates from each National League team. They were, as the name proclaimed, primarily supportive rather than combative, but the National League continued to reject their requests for revision of the reserve clause, establishment of medical funds, and the right of release if contract conditions were violated. The result was a crowd of unhappy and resentful players. The straw that broke the camel's back came when League owners, suffering from a drop in attendance in 1900, voted to limit salaries to $2,100 and cut rosters to sixteen players, which the Protective Association claimed aimed to pressure players into signing through shrinking the number of available jobs.[85]

Angry at such heavy-handedness, many players took the opportunity to jump to the American League in 1901; of 182 players on American League lists, 60 percent were former National Leaguers. Johnson's American League contracts included provision for dispute arbitration, clubs to pay for treatment of game-related injuries, free agency if a club abandoned the league, and no farming or selling without the player's written consent.[86] The National League tried to restrain the jumpers, but, as during the 1890 war, the courts ruled their contracts lacked mutuality and constituted a restraint of trade. The League appeared to offer a conciliatory hand to Johnson by inviting him to their December 12 meeting—but Johnson was then unceremoniously refused entry and left sitting in a hotel corridor.[87] So Johnson simply never signed the 1900 National Agreement, leaving the National League to threaten a return to 12 teams to counter his American League moves into prime baseball cities.

The future of St. Louis's aging roster was the subject of much speculation in early 1901. After the departure of McGraw and Robinson, *The Republic* of February 3, 1901, called for local men such as Quinn and Ted Breitenstein to be high on the St. Louis recruitment priority list, but mused that the pervasive phenomenon of anti-local sentiment might put paid to the suggestion. "Players who claim St. Louis as a residence have never been any too popular in their home city," the paper complained. "There is no doubt about [their] class and ability. This being so, there exists no reason why [they] should not have a chance with the St. Louis club. For [they] are St. Louisan. But maybe that is against [them].... Of course, the fact that Breitenstein and Quinn are native St. Louisans should not entitle them to positions on a St. Louis team. Neither should it operate against them."[88]

However, Breitenstein had been amicably released by the Reds at the end of 1900, and Quinn, too, was free to sign where he pleased. With the well-known affection of both men for their adopted city, why should they not look there first? *The Republic* speculated Breit might have compromised his reputation by throwing conservatively during his two years with Cincinnati, preserving his arm in the realization the club was never going to win a pennant. However, there were no such doubts about Quinn:

As for Joe Quinn, he needs no commendation. He is not as good a second baseman as Lajoie. But, bar Lajoie, there is not any of them better than Quinn. Ritchie, Gleason, Keister, Daly, McCormick, Childs, not any of them can hit or field better than the undertaker. Quinn was released by the St. Louis club last season, though he was 2 to 1 a better second bagman than Keister, who was chosen for the position. Of course, Keister, being a stranger in a strange land, was given the butt of it by the journalistic critics. Keister sat in the press box and did his own advertising. Quinn all the while was on the field doing his best to play ball. It is much easier, and much more forceful in some ways, to play ball in the press box than on the diamond. The best ball playing Keister did last season was done while he was nursing his injuries in the press box. Quinn was not long picking up a job in Cincinnati. He did well there, clearly outplaying Steinfeldt. But Steinfeldt was another Keister. He did some press-box playing on his own hook.[89]

But while Breitenstein was signed by the Cardinals, by April 8, Quinn was still sitting on the sidelines. *The Republic* of April 8, 1901, reported on an exhibition game between St. Louis and Indianapolis at which Joe Quinn was a spectator, mourning that "it was a crying shame to let such a second baseman go to the minors as he appears to be in splendid condition."[90] Ironically, the paper also reported Breitenstein was given a rousing reception from the fickle St. Louis cranks.

Two days later, Quinn's ticket to minor league oblivion was revoked: he was offered a contract by Ban Johnson's Washington Senators.[91] Some sources describe Quinn as a jumper for his acceptance of an American League contract[92]; however, he did not take the decision of many of his compatriots in the Protective Association and transfer in protest against oppressive labor conditions in the National League. He was free to sign as he pleased and had clearly displayed his inclination to remain within the National League by his long wait in St. Louis through the spring. But he was in shape to play and if it meant a move to the league and a new franchise in Washington, then so be it. As matters stood, he didn't join the Senators until eight days before the opening of the American League season on April 28, lingering in his hometown until the last possible moment, checking and double-checking every detail in his beloved business.[93] But the contract constituted Quinn's appearance in his fourth major league, a rare achievement indeed. He had also played on seven championship teams—one in St. Louis, one in Des Moines, three in Boston, and two in Baltimore,[94] and his experience in that regard is probably a record.

Quinn joined his new Washington teammates at Hampton, Virginia, where they had been getting into condition under the eye of manager Jimmy Manning. Manning, in his days at the head of the Kansas City team, had supplied the major leagues with such notables as pitcher Kid Nichols and shortstop Herman Long, and the Kansas City franchise itself had relocated to Washington to take part in the American League in 1901.[95] The squad were eagerly waiting for their new park to be completed: American League Park, on 14th Street Florida Avenue NE and Bladensberg Avenue NE, seated 10,000 and was a significant improvement on the old National League Capitol Park, which was known as the "Swampdoodle Ground" for its dampness and proximity to the Tiber Creek.[96] Nonetheless, the new park was only used in 1901 and 1902 before the team moved to Boundary Field.[97]

Quinn's arrival was greeted excitedly by the Washington press, with the *Times* proclaiming on April 21, "They say, in local baseball circles, that Joe Quinn, who will hold down the second pillow, has discovered the secret of eternal youth, and that this year he will show the youngsters in the league how they used to play the game in the good old days ... when Henry Chadwick was playing on his grammar school team. Quinn is the best eighty-seven-year-old player in the business, and believes he will be in the game for a score or more of years yet. Just the same, the old man is fielding like a three-year-old and hitting the ball as if he had a grudge against the trademark."[98]

The group enjoyed a thorough trouncing of local teams during their southern sojourn, including an astonishing 68-run shutout of the lads from Phoebus, Virginia,[99] and left for their opening American League battle with Philadelphia on April 26 in high regard of their own prospects. And even with National League defectors Lajoie, Fraser, Bernhart, and Platt in the Quaker lineup and 16,000 roaring fans squeezed into the stands, the Philadelphia party was spoiled as Bill Carrick pitched the Senators to a 5–1 win. Lajoie had three hits for the Athletics on his way to an American League record 0.422 batting average, but the next day, the Senators reinforced the humiliation with an 11–5 follow-up victory.[100]

Their home opener on April 29 was a grand occasion, with a marching band preceding the Senators and the visiting Baltimores into the new park and Spanish-American War hero Admiral George Dewey throwing out the first pitch. And again, the Senators lived up to expectations with another fine Carrick pitching effort, capturing a 5–2 win over McGraw's Birds. With former Kansas City left-hander Wyatt "Watty" Lee beating Roger Bresnahan 12–6 next day, the Senators started the season with four straight wins.[101] However, such a winning streak was "mighty monotonous ... and robbed of the uncertainty that is its chief attraction," complained the *Times* of May 2. The paper reported (tongue firmly in cheek) that Manning sent word to his players to "give the Orioles a chance—they are good fellows, and there was no use discouraging them at the very commencement of the championship." This order was, however, obediently complied with, and Baltimore drew a 6–4 consolation win from their visit to the nation's capital. Quinn, who had started the season brightly, was also brought back to earth with a hitless game and his first error of the season. However, the *Times* was suitably forgiving of its new favorite: "There's one good thing about the undertaker when he makes a bad break; he never stoops to tie his shoe-string, but chases back to his stamping ground at once."[102]

The Orioles left the Senators a parting gift in the form of an 11–4 defeat on the final day of the series on May 2. The home team contributed to their own demise as Manning put another of his promising Kansas City youngsters, Dale Gear, in the pitcher's box, and he was promptly hammered for seven hits and as many runs in the first inning.[103] He was not the only rookie given a harsh lesson that day: Boston whacked rookie Philadelphia hurler Pete Loos for an excruciating 19 runs in two innings and Loos slunk out of the game with an ERA of 27.00; he never pitched in the majors again.[104]

It was left to Carrick again to shunt the Senators back onto a winning track when he led Washington to a 9–4 win over Boston at home on May 3. But Boston unleashed new signer Cy Young to teach the Senators a 10–2 lesson next day, the start of a four-game losing streak that included a further two losses to the Red Sox. However, they were quickly avenged with a four-game sweep of Boston on the road at the Huntingdon Avenue Grounds, Joe Quinn saving the first game with a superb diving save of a Tommy Dowd double in the eighth inning and a ninth-inning double of his own,[105] and the unlikely Dale Gear defeating Hall of Famer Cy Young 3–2 on May 14 in what was the crowning achievement of his short career. Gear had pitched two games for Cleveland in 1896, losing both, and after finishing the 1901 season with a 4–11 record, faded into the baseball ether.[106] The Boston series was closed out with the American League's first shutout, the Senators beating Boston 4–0 on Watty Lee's three-hitter. The Senators were now in fourth place with a 9–6 record, and consolidated by returning home to beat Philadelphia in three of four games.[107]

A visit to Cleveland—who were, naturally, in last place—ought to have been a cinch for the Senators, but it induced the kind of nightmares Joe Quinn had experienced there in 1899. The trip started badly with a 6–5 loss on May 22, but May 23 was worse—the newly christened Blues scored a major-league record nine runs in the ninth inning to defeat Washington 14–13. With the Senators leading 13–5 and two out, the game seemed a foregone conclusion and many fans were leaving, but Case Patten just could not get the final out. Jack McCarthy had one strike on him but Cleveland put the next ten men on base courtesy of six singles, two doubles, a walk, a HBP, and a passed ball which won the game for the Blues. It was probably the first time a pitcher who had given up 13 runs—in this case, Bill Hoffer—was chaired off the field. Perhaps the biggest irony of all was the next day, when Washington reversed the dose—down 5–0 after 8 innings, they scored five runs in the ninth to draw the game.[108]

By May 25, the Senators were flourishing in third place following two defeats of second-placed Detroit. They did waver slightly on their pedestal by losing both games of a doubleheader against seventh-placed Milwaukee in icy conditions on May 30,[109] but their comeback was immediate with four wins from seven games against first-placed Chicago. In the June 9 win, Quinn at second made one of the most spectacular saves yet seen on the local grounds. It occurred in the seventh and the victim was Quinn's former Browns teammate Frank Shugart. He had seized on a waist-high Watty Lee delivery and driven it with such force into the infield that the crowd could barely get a line on it before Quinn was observed making a lunge with an outstretched paw. When the fans spied the little white ball nestling safely in the undertaker's mitt, Quinn was given one of the big rounds of applause of the day. Shugart, the *Times* reported gleefully, looked utterly disgusted and characterized the out as "a mean trick."[110]

However, it couldn't last, and the league leaders rallied to win 13–10 on June 11, the Senators slipping back to third place. Quinn slammed a two-run homer as part of a eight-run rally in the ninth inning, but the Senators pitchers were in trouble and the pressure was on their defense—both Carrick and Patten were struggling for form since their return from the western trip (the first ball Patten pitched on June 9 hit Dummy Hoy squarely on the head) and Win Mercer had a sore arm.[111] Watty Lee was doing his best, winning seven of his nine starts and also hitting a remarkable .313, although this was some way behind the league's leading batter Nap Lajoie (.449). Lajoie also led the second basemen in fielding (.959) with Quinn second at .942.[112] But the slide continued with return visits from Detroit and the Cleveland Blues, who each beat the Senators twice to push them back to fourth (19–18).[113]

It was June 20 before the Senators won again, and even then only by the narrowest margin (an 8–7 defeat of the Tigers led by Dale Gear); Quinn made the star play of the game by taking a fly ball in right field while running with his back to the ball, to which play the occupants of the stands rose *en masse* to applaud the hardworking second baseman.[114] But the Senators were now seven games out of third place and rapidly losing touch with league leaders Chicago (29–18), Boston (25–17), and Detroit (27–20). They stayed at home for the remainder of the month. Their game on June 26 was the greatest farce of the season—while the Senators enjoyed a 5–4 win over the Athletics, a late schedule change meant Boston (and an American League umpire) had arrived in Philadelphia, also for a game against the A's, unaware the calendar had been altered and they were supposed to be in Baltimore. The Orioles and 4,500 fans waited for ninety minutes in triple-digit heat for Boston to arrive before the game was abandoned.[115]

Boston came to the national capital on June 27 to inflict two further defeats on the Senators, pushing them down to fifth in the league with a 25–22 record. In the face of this

Now 38 years old, Joe Quinn (back row, far right) was clearly looking to a future beyond baseball in his last year in the major leagues with the Washington Senators (National Baseball Hall of Fame Library, Cooperstown, New York).

increasingly familiar and depressing record, Quinn could no longer deny the call of home. He sought his release from Manager Manning, citing that his undertaking business in St. Louis had grown to such proportions that it required all of his time and that of his partner.[116] It was the first and only time in his 17-year career he turned his back on a down-sliding club.

The decision did little to help the ailing Senators, as they finished the year in a mediocre sixth place. Only two regulars, outfielders Sam Dungan and Irv Waldron, hit over .300, and Case Patten was their only winning pitcher (18–10 at 3.93). Watty Lee struggled to a 16–16 record at 4.40 ERA, and the remaining hurlers were horrible: promising Bill Carrick fell away to finish the year on 14–22 (3.75), and the losing records of Win Mercer (9–13) and Dale Gear (4–11) ensured Mercer was sold to Detroit and Gear's career was over.[117] Twelve months later, the popular and handsome Mercer was dead, thought to have taken his own life after incurring huge gambling debts while on a barnstorming tour of California.[118]

• • •

"I did not quit because I had lost any love of the game, nor because I was slipping."—Joe Quinn, *The Sporting News*, May 21, 1936

A blunt and decisive departure such as Quinn's from Washington would usually prompt caution in any manager looking to hire a second baseman, particularly a 38-year-old second baseman. But Quinn was a commodity the world of professional baseball could not seem to let go. There were rumors Boston's American League team would be relocated to St. Louis in 1902, with Quinn, Hugh Duffy, or Jake Beckley at the helm.[119] The *Washington Times* insisted Quinn would succeed Al Buckenberger at Rochester,[120] but the *St. Paul Globe* linked him with a move to Colorado Springs in the Western League, where millionaire gold mine owner Thomas F. Burns (who was a friend of Quinn's) was putting together a team, just for fun.[121]

And whether it was the insistence of the gossip or just the sheer force of 17 winters anticipating the *thunk* of ball into glove in the spring, by March 1902, Quinn's attention was again edging away from McGrath & Quinn at 3128 Cass Avenue. An invitation to manage the new Des Moines club in the 1902 Western League was more than he could resist. The eight-team Western League had plenty of familiar faces, with Quinn's ex–Boston teammates Hugh Duffy taking control of the Milwaukee outfit and Kid Nichols in Kansas City, and his former Washington captain Bill Everett managing the Millionaires in Colorado Springs.[122] There were, however, some cynical eyebrows raised when Quinn's decision was announced, with the *St. Paul Globe* noting sarcastically on April 7, "To hear Joe tell of the way his firm buried persons over in St. Louis, one would have thought that the firm required the services of at least a dozen treasurers. And yet Joe is willing to leave this business for the summer, when the burying business is usually active, and tie up with the Des Moines of the Western league. More than likely Joe will have a big embalming contract on his hands in his new berth."[123]

But there was an eerie coincidence in this bit of throwaway scribble. Just three days later, Quinn's father Patrick died suddenly in Dubuque. He was 64 years of age and had been widowed the previous year by his remarkable wife Caddie, who herself had survived famine and destitution to travel the world beside him and bear him two fine sons, living to the grand age of 71. The *Dubuque Telegraph–Herald* called Patrick's death "a sad surprise" and the loss of a "generous-hearted, whole-souled fellow with a ready faculty of making friends."[124] Patrick was appropriately farewelled in the small clapboard church of St. Columbkille—named for one of the three great saints who brought the Catholic faith to Ireland[125]—and buried at Mt. Olivet cemetery beside his wife.

Joe Quinn was now almost 40 years of age, but played more than 120 games in each of his last two seasons of professional baseball with Des Moines.[126] His staff were a colorful bunch, including his former Orioles teammate and Iowa native Bill Hoffer, now 31 years old and hoping to ease into a farmland retirement, and St. Louisan rookie pitcher Tom Barry, who would be drafted by the Phillies in 1904 and throw one inning in relief, giving up five runs and earning an immediate release.[127] Of greater potential was another Mound City native, the younger brother of Pittsburgh Hall of Famer Fred Clarke. Outfielder Josh "Pepper" Clarke grew up in St. Louis and was signed by the Cardinals out of Des Moines on Quinn's recommendation in 1904, playing five seasons in the majors for a .952 career fielding average.[128] Fellow Midgets Charley O'Leary, "Doc" Marshall (because he *was* a doctor), and Lee Fohl all built substantial major league careers after playing under Quinn in Des Moines.[129]

Pennant winners Kansas City and nearest rivals St. Paul had streeted the Western League in 1901, but were brought back to the field in 1902 by a powerful Omaha outfit who just missed out on the pennant, their .600 win-loss percentage just outdone by Kansas City's .603. Des Moines was some way back with their 54–83 record, faring no better in the standings than in 1901, when they had also finished seventh.[130] But Quinn was described by the *Des Moines News* in 1902 as "the bright and shining light of the locals.... The way he landed on the ball was enough to discourage any pitcher that ever served up a sizzler for an unsuspecting mortal to bite at."[131] And despite the mediocre results, there were fond memories for Quinn of his two seasons in central Iowa, including the "scratchiest" home run of his career. As he told the *Salt Lake City Herald*:

> The field at the Iowa metropolis is a narrow boxlike affair with the fences on either side so close that it is easy to knock a ball over them. For convenience, gates were cut in the sides so the ground keeper could go out after balls. The Des Moines team was playing Colorado Springs one day and the home team was at bat. I was at that time manager of the Des Moines team and three of the team had preceded me and were occupying the cushions when I stepped to bat. One or two good ones passed and then I landed on a good one. Straight past third it went, so fast that Granville, the best third baseman in the league, never flagged it. Just as it reached the fence, some power from the outside pushed the gate open and without a slip or a bounce, the ball went through. The attendant was away and all the Springs team could do was to look at the twenty-foot fence and sigh while I, preceded by my three teammates, completed the circuit of the sacks. These were the only scores of the game.
>
> It afterwards developed that a boy on the outside of the fence had heard the crack of the bat and pushed open the gate in time to let the ball go through. A like occurrence will probably never happen again in baseball.[132]

In 1903, the Western League season was declared closed by President Sexton two weeks early owing to unceasing inclement weather, during which Des Moines itself was badly flooded.[133] Hugh Duffy's Milwaukee outfit finished six wins ahead of the Colorado Springs Millionaires (83–43 to 77–52). Des Moines once again collected seventh place with an almost identical record to 1902 of 55–76. However, they led the league in games lost by either one or two runs (34), and also in extra-innings games (14), and the club had the second-highest batting average in the league (.265) behind Colorado.[134] Charley O'Leary batted a creditable .311 from his 129 games (one of only 12 Western Leaguers to hit over .300), and Lee Fohl made .296. Quinn was not far behind with .282. Des Moines also led the league on fielding average (.952), and leading second baseman, 40-year-old Joe Quinn, was a long way ahead of the next best second baseman, McBride of St. Joseph (.976 to .961).[135] The team, which had been known as the Midgets in 1902, even changed its moniker to the Undertakers in 1903 to honor their reliable and decent manager. When Quinn gave notice that he would not return next season on August 28, 1903, the president of the Des Moines club, C.H. Myrick, wrote to August Herrmann of Cincinnati saying he was "at a loss to know where to find such a good man to take his place as Manager."[136] Myrick later recruited Quinn's old middle-infield compatriot from Boston, shortstop Herman Long, to fill the void.

But the world was turning in 1903, and baseball turned with it into the twentieth century. The Wright brothers defied gravity to complete the first powered heavier-than-air flight, and the first transatlantic radio broadcast was made from the United States to England.[137] Al Spink would later recount the devastating effect of modern technology on some ball players: "Boston centerfielder Tris Speaker bought an automobile.... He has learned the mechanism of the machine and now spends his mornings speeding on the suburban roads. And doubtless this same automobile has affected his batting eye. No one can guide an automobile for twenty miles without returning with a kind of squint in the eyes.... Hans Wagner of the Pittsburg Club, who owns and operates an automobile, had to stop riding it because his batting fell off to nothing.... Speaker could easily bat .400 if he would leave the automobile alone."[138]

And, as J.M. Barrie declared wistfully in the 1904 classic *Peter Pan*, "I suppose it's like the ticking crocodile, isn't it? Time is chasing after all of us." The clock, for Joe Quinn, had wound down, in soul if not in body. He was still fit, agile, hard-running and hard-throwing, beloved by public and players alike, but his long walkabout was over.

Joe Quinn was one of those rare players whose grace and dignity allow them to play well into "old age" and choose their own time of retirement. He closed the book on his career on September 17, 1903, resisting the offer to stay on with the Undertakers with the firm declaration that his business now "required his full attention."[139] Quinn's final *adieu* to professional baseball was as definitive, although as was his way, rather less spectacular, than those of some of his counterparts. The same year, Philadelphia slugger and Hall of Famer Ed Delahanty, who had averaged .367 and three times hit over .400 in 12 seasons, ended his career by wandering out of the team hotel after a heavy bout of drinking—and tumbling off a bridge into Niagara Falls.[140]

In 1860, sportswriter Henry Chadwick, "the father of baseball," wrote, "Baseball requires the possession of muscular strength, great agility, quickness of eye, readiness of hand, and many other faculties of mind and body that mark a man of nerve.... Suffice it to say, it is a recreation that anyone might be proud to excel in, as in order to do so, he must possess the characteristics of true manhood to a considerable degree."[141]

And that, Joe Quinn unquestionably did.

Part VII
The Afterlife: 1904–1940

15. A Very Private Tragedy

"Thou detestable maw,
thou womb of death,
gorg'd itself with the dearest morsel of the earth...."
—William Shakespeare, *Romeo and Juliet*

By 1920, indulgence, leisure, and social revolution were bywords for the American way of life. Traumatized by the ravages of the First World War, the nation sought comfort in the simple, the predictable, and the cathartic. The Model T Ford stood alongside the great racehorse Man O' War in the public's affection, Douglas Fairbanks and Theda Bara swooned on silver screens, and jazz, bobby-cuts, and low-waisted dresses with beads and bangles were front and center as part of the nation's liberation and healing.

Despite the Black Sox scandal of 1919,[1] baseball was booming. War hysteria and the emphasis on patriotism and preparedness were subsiding from the ball field: clubs no longer performed drills using bats as rifles during spring training, for which Ban Johnson had even gone so far as to award the Red Sox a $500 prize for outdoing the Browns in the execution of such drills in 1917. The 1918 season had been shortened and attendances plummeted as Provost Marshal General Crowder had decreed men previously excused from the draft by dint of marriage or engagement in "productive activity" were now eligible: actors and singers remained exempt in the interest of public entertainment, but in spite of appeals to the president, Secretary of War Baker, and General Crowder, baseball players were not. Public opinion decreed that a bat and ball game should not be favored over patriotic service, and many players either joined the reserves and played for service teams, or entered war-related work. But the end of the war saw major league baseball attendances more than double, reaching nine million by 1920 as crowds flocked to worship "The Sultan of Swat" Babe Ruth and a gallery of slugging stars including Lou Gehrig, Rogers Hornsby, and Ty Cobb in baseball's new golden age.[2]

Joe Quinn, "still in good physical condition" and father of eight, had settled into his undertaking business and the simpler pleasures of life, including singing in St. Bridget's Church choir every Sunday morning.[3] Despite a vigorous declaration to the *New York Sun* in February 1905 that "he [would] never try to play ball again and does not even care to be a spectator,"[4] Quinn was tempted out of retirement just once, in that same year. He was a member of the Knights of Columbus, the world's largest Catholic organization dedicated to providing charitable services and promoting Catholic education, and on July 5, 1905, the Chicago chapter played a charity match at League Park in St. Louis against the local Knights, defeating the home outfit by 10 runs to 6. Forty-three-year-old Joe Quinn played second base for St. Louis and, according to *The Republic*—always glowing in its praise of the undertaker—"covered himself with glory." However, the commendation *was* justified as Quinn dismantled Chicago pitcher Parker with a single, a double, and a triple, then sent the crowd into ecstasies with a backward running catch of a high, twisting fly ball.[5]

But by 1920, life had settled into a distinctly domestic framework. Quinn moved his family and business to newer, larger premises at 1389 Union Boulevard,[6] and McGrath & Quinn had taken on a distinctly twentieth-century mien through closure of the livery stable once attached to the funeral home.[7] While the business still kept carriages to form part of the funeral cortege, the unremitting advance of the automobile had driven the commercial livery industry to the fringe—truck registrations in the U.S. grew from 10,000 in 1910 to 1.1 million in 1920, and coincided with a drop in employment of livery stable keepers from 35,000 to 11,000 over the same period.[8]

Despite all this cozy familial predictability, the Great War had not left the Quinns untouched. The United States declared war on Germany on April 6, 1917, just five days before the major league baseball season opened, and shortly afterward, the national draft commenced. Joe Quinn's father-in-law and business partner Thomas McGrath had died in 1907, and Quinn now ran the business with the assistance of sons Clarence and Joseph Jr. But with the outbreak of war, Quinn was left to manage the business single-handedly after both young men enlisted on July 15, 1918. Twenty-three-year-old Clarence, the tall, slender, fair-haired and blue-eyed young man who had worked as a carriage driver for his father,[9] served with the 7th Infantry Division.[10] But when Clarence sailed for the Western Front in October 1918, his older brother remained behind: while he had enlisted healthy, Joseph's service record indicates he suffered a "33 percent disablement" while undertaking basic training with the 57th Depot Brigade at Camp Macarthur, Texas, and he remained there as a private with the 57th until he was honorably discharged in 1919.[11]

Clarence, however, saw action at the front during the last bloody days of the conflict. The 7th had come under shellfire, and then, at the village of Saint-Mihiel in northeastern France, withstood the full horror of chemical gas attack as they drove out German forces in a brutal seven-day struggle in late September.[12] Clarence and other reinforcements had sailed for the front on October 8, 1918, as the division was pushing east toward the Moselle River as part of the Second United States Army, preparing for an attack on the Hindenburg Line, the major German defensive position in eastern France. As part of this drive into enemy territory, infantry elements captured Hills 323 and 310 and drove the Germans out of the Bois-du Trou-de-la-Haie salient.[13] Under General Edward Wittenmyer, the 7th surged out onto the Voëvre Plain at the head of the main army on November 10, but the German troops, already in disarray, fled from the impending assault and the main attack was never launched. At eleven-hundred hours on the following day, November 11, the Armistice was declared, making the 7th one of the last units to fight to the very conclusion of hostilities. During its 33 days on the front line, the 7th "Hourglass" Division lost 204 men in action, with more than 1,500 wounded.[14] But peace did not bring an immediate ticket home for the 7th: they remained in western Europe on occupation duties for another year, and Clarence was honorably discharged, uninjured, on August 22, 1919, after eleven months in the European theater of war.[15]

The reunited Undertakers Quinn had little time to rest or recuperate. In 1918, one of the Four Horsemen of the Apocalypse—*Pestilence*—had come to St. Louis, and the city remained under siege from a deadly invisible foe. The origins of the Spanish Influenza are

Joe Quinn's sons Clarence and Joseph Jr. enlisted to fight in World War I during 1918. Both were sent for basic training with the 57th Depot Brigade to Camp Macarthur, Texas, where activities such as bayonet practice were a daily ritual. Joseph was injured during training and never sailed for Europe; his younger brother saw action on the Western Front in the last days of the war (National Archives and Records Administration, image no. 165-WW-146B[16]).

controversial: While some American scientists claim the outbreak first occurred in China in 1918, Chinese bureaucrats deny this, insisting the pandemic originated in Europe and spread eastward from there.[16] But within a year, the virus had spread to every inhabited continent, a plague more insidious and deadly than any historical scourge which preceded it. In the first wave during May–June 1918, the symptoms were comparable to those documented in an 1889 outbreak—highly infectious although seldom fatal, and mainly affecting the very young, the old, and the frail.[17]

The second wave in August, however, was far more lethal, preferentially attacking healthy young adults, ferocious in the rapidity of decline and brutality of symptoms. Doctors initially speculated it could not be flu but instead some strain of typhus, cholera, dengue fever or botulism, so swift and merciless was the tsunami crashing across an already war-weakened world.[18] In the month of October 1918, 200,000 deaths were recorded in the United States alone.[19] Isaac Starr, a third-year medical student at the University of Pennsylvania in 1918, described the symptoms: "As their lungs filled ... patients became short of breath and increasingly cyanotic. After gasping for several hours, they became delirious and incontinent, and many died struggling to clear their airways of a blood-tinged froth that sometimes gushed from their nose and mouth. It was a dreadful business."[20] The two-year pandemic claimed up to 40 million lives, compared to a total worldwide fatality count of nine million in all of World War I.[21] The Spanish flu claimed more victims in less time than all the great plagues of history combined, and gouged an entire generation of child-bearers and wage-earners from society. Among the early casualties was Margaret McGrath, the mother of Joe's wife Molly. She died on December 5, 1918, at 76 years of age too frail to withstand the physical calamities of the disease.[22] But the Spanish Lady had worse in store for Joe Quinn.

In 1919, John McGraw's New York Giants finished second in the National League, nine games behind Cincinnati.[23] Hall of Famer Ross "Pep" Youngs hit .311 and was third in the batting race, in keeping with the .322 average he earned over ten years in the majors before his untimely death from Bright's disease in 1927.[24] Giants third baseman Heinie Zimmerman had won the batting triple-crown back in 1912, but, at 32 years of age, made 1919 his last year in the majors. The Harvard-bred Eddie Grant, who also played third base for the Giants, was killed by shellfire while fighting in France during the war.[25] Thus bereft of the experience and talent he had enjoyed in the infield prewar, McGraw was now looking around for replacements. A scouting report from *St. Louis Republic* sportswriter John B. Sheridan caught his eye—Sheridan fancied a lightly-built fellow playing the Mound City corner lots as a potential Giants infielder: his name was John Richard "Scotty" Quinn, son of the old Oriole, Joe. As pitcher Christy Mathewson averred, "In the selection and retention of players, McGraw's judgment is rarely at fault,"[26] and the champion manager wrote and offered Scotty a trial for the 1920 season.

Margaret McGrath, the mother of Joe Quinn's wife Molly. Margaret died during the Spanish Influenza outbreak of 1918, the first of two tragedies to touch the Quinn family during the pandemic (courtesy Michael E. Motto, great-grandson of Joe Quinn).

Scotty was not the first of Quinn's sons to make an impression on the baseball diamond: Joe's second son Joseph Jr. had played amateur ball with some success, but had given up the game following the death of Thomas McGrath in 1907 to help his father in their growing mortuary practice.[27] Scotty, too, worked with his father,[28] but for the 22-year-old man, there was life beyond the cold parlor and its pervasive stink of formaldehyde, face creams, and funeral bouquets. Scotty was a born ballplayer, and Joe loved him for it. What insights he might have offered his son as he recalled the hustle and aggression of McGraw back in those heady 1890s days of the championship Orioles! And was Scotty himself not born in that grand year of 1897 when the Birds had captured their second Temple Cup with Joe Quinn at third base?

The night of Monday, February 2, 1920, put all those grand plans on hold. Joe's youngest daughter Estelle had come dashing, hysterical, into the funeral parlor and fetched him upstairs, where he found Scotty confined to bed. The rattling cough and the wheezing effort to breathe were unmistakable. Quinn and his sons inhaled it every day, the vapor and miasma of the influenza, as they washed and cleaned and dressed the city's dead. Had it been a moment of haste or carelessness, half-washed hands, or just one unlucky breath? Joe watched his son struggle for life for almost three days. The fine eyes which had once sparkled with intelligence became glassy and unresponsive, blood gargling in his foam-ravaged lungs as bitter as the cud. At 3 p.m. on February 5, a shadow fell across the house, and Scotty was gone.[29]

The Quinns had lost four children, three girls and a boy, to stillbirth or early infant mortality between 1902 and 1909, interspersed by the birth of their fifth son, Richard, in 1904. Only one of the lost babies lived long enough to be named: a girl, Dorothy, in 1905.[30] But this catastrophe was something different. Following a Requiem Mass at St. Alphonsus Rock Church on Grand Avenue, opposite which St. Louis' first-ever baseball games had been played some 60 years before, undertaker Joe Quinn buried his son on February 9, 1920, in the family plot at Calvary Cemetery.[31] Joe's youngest daughter, Estelle, was very close to both Scotty and her father. Estelle's only child June Hesemann said her mother never really recovered from the shock of her brother's death, and that Joe, too, always bore the cross of the tragedy: he never spoke of his beloved son again.[32]

Joe and Molly Quinn's daughter Dorothy, who died in 1905 shortly after this photograph was taken. Of the Quinns' twelve children, four died in infancy (courtesy Michael E. Motto, great-grandson of Joe Quinn).

◆ ◆ ◆

"I am an old man who will live until I die."— Ernest Hemingway, *For Whom the Bell Tolls*, 1940

In the summer of 1936, Joe Quinn gave his final media interview. Reporter Dick Farrington met the now 74-year-old at the premises of Joseph J. Quinn, Funeral Directors, on Union Boulevard, hoping to reminisce with Quinn for the fiftieth anniversary edition of *The Sporting News*, and he was not disappointed. Neat, dapper, and with the gold watch awarded him 43 years before still tucked modestly into his waistcoat, Quinn spoke as unwaveringly as ever about his observations of the game past and present.

He had seen two other former second basemen follow in his footsteps as managers in St. Louis: Rogers Hornsby, replacing Bill Killefer as manager of the American League Browns in 1933; and Frankie Frisch, taking over at the helm of the Cardinals in the National League in the same year. The *St. Louis Globe–Democrat* reflected, "Both new managers were former second basemen, and [Joe] Quinn must have mused over the time, over forty years before, he had managed both those clubs as a second baseman. History does repeat itself."[33]

Ever ready to speak plainly, Quinn refused to concede modern players were any more skilled or better prepared than their nineteenth-century counterparts, just that they had superior equipment and a faster ball. But he was not one to deprecate modern-day baseball: rating old-time players by modern standards, he said, could only produce arguments. "In the '80s and '90s, [we] still had great arms and fast legs, ran bases, hit behind the runner and dragged bunts," he insisted. "It's a good game today, only not so scientific. In my time, we played for one run. We knew inside baseball: we had to know it, because one run was a precious advantage then. Since 1919 when the rabbit ball came in, the managers have gone in for group scoring. It became a case of power overcoming power. Mind you, I don't want to be placed in the light of knocking the modern game. There are stars, just as there have been down through the years, and I still enjoy watching the games at Sportsman's Park."[34] And he was free to watch as often as he chose. In the early 1930s, Quinn had received a lifetime pass from major league baseball in recognition of his "long and meritorious service." The pass was awarded by commissioners Ford C. Frick (National League) and William Harridge (American League), with the hope he would find opportunity to "use it frequently."[35]

Poet Robert Frost once famously stated, "In three words I can sum up everything I've learned about life. It goes on." Even after the terrors and privation of the Great War and the devastating loss of his son, life rolled forward in its inexorable fashion for Joe Quinn. The boy who had once earned a living grubbing in the darkness of Iowa's mines was now one of the most successful funeral directors in St. Louis. By 1936, a second funeral parlor was opened at 1522 N. Grand Boulevard with Clarence in charge; the young man was now married to Ruth Lamar Grassman and the pair were resident above the parlor. Joseph Jr. too was married, to Regina Meehan, and still working with his father at 1389 Union.[36] The old second baseman was showing no signs of slowing down, but the following year, life dealt him another cruel blow—the loss of his wife of 51 years. Molly Quinn had suffered from chronic heart trouble, and died on December 12, 1937.[37] She was 69 years old, and was interred in the Quinn family plot in Calvary Cemetery, St. Louis. Joe and Thomas McGrath had purchased adjacent plots back in 1900, so Molly was buried alongside both of her parents and five of her twelve children.[38]

While Joe continued working,[39] taking comfort in the familiarity of the business despite perhaps realizing the scant equipage it had provided him to deal with personal loss, his own health began to decline. He had heart trouble of his own, and the presence of arterial sclerosis (hardening) was exacerbated by myocarditis, an inflammation of the heart thought to result from either infection or immune dysfunction.[40] He was hospitalized on February 8, 1940, at St. Alexius Catholic Hospital, and never returned to his home on Union Boulevard. He died in the same hospital nine months later, on Tuesday, November 12, aged 77.

Survived by seven of his children, Quinn's funeral at St. Alphonsus Rock Church was arranged by his faithful sons Joseph and Clarence, and attended by many members of the St. Louis Funeral Directors Association. He was buried in the family plot at Calvary Cemetery on November 15, 1940, beside his wife and his beloved Scotty.[41]

◆ ◆ ◆

As an Irish enclave, the Kerry Patch had faded out of St. Louis consciousness by the end of World War I, and by 1940, it seemed the residents were always just one step ahead of the wrecking ball. The clapboard houses, the hitching rails and feed stores, and even great mansions like that at 2433 Dickson Street, once

Joe Quinn was presented with this Lifetime Pass during the 1930s in recognition of his long commitment to professional baseball. He was one of the first to receive this "golden ticket" which entitled him and a guest entry to any major league game (courtesy June Hesemann, granddaughter, and Tom Hesemann, great-grandson of Joe Quinn).

15. A Very Private Tragedy

Joe Quinn's wife Molly (standing, third from left). Joe's three daughters Catherine Marie (standing, right), Marguerite (seated, right) and Estelle (seated, left) are also pictured, with two unidentified women (undated photograph, courtesy Michael E. Motto, great-grandson of Joe Quinn).

Undated photograph of Joe Quinn's daughters and descendants: daughters Marguerite (holding child), Estelle (to Marguerite's right), and Catherine Marie (above Marguerite's left shoulder). Others in the photograph unidentified (courtesy Michael E. Motto, great-grandson of Joe Quinn).

owned by the "King of the Kerry Patch" James Cullinane, were mowed down to make way for the infamous Pruitt-Igoe housing project, factories, and tenements which now lie like stranded ships, wind blowing and weeds growing through their abandoned hulls. Even St. Lawrence O'Toole Catholic Church at 14th and Fallon, once the pride of the Patch, ended its days as a truck repair garage.[42] Gone were the goats and the geraniums, the surreys and the sandlots. Gone too, were the spirits of ordinary men who carried St. Louis out of the horse-and-buggy age into the twentieth century, when it became a powerhouse of American business, industry, and sports. Many of these men, quiet and modest in their habits and steadfast in their duty, are unremarked in history and would have it no differently. Quinn's old home and the site of Joseph J. Quinn, Funeral Directors, at 1389 Union Boulevard is now an overgrown vacant lot. There is no Joe Quinn statue outside the Cardinals ballpark and no Quinn plaque in the Hall of Fame. But material accolades were not Joe Quinn's way.

The one monument to his life, still standing in Calvary Cemetery, is appropriately unpretentious but unutterably poignant, for it is marked only:

Quinn

Epilogue

There is something pathetic in baseball reminiscence—it is like walking through a long dim hall where hang the pictures of the family dead. Every name recalled brings a flood of memories, which, even though they be about a mere ball tosser, have something almost sacred about them. The pathetic part of these memories is the fact that they cannot be shared. They are to be recalled in silence. The old names mean nothing to the new generation, although they are but a dozen years back. The old timer refrains from speaking them because he cannot bear to hear the irreverent comment of the new era that knows them not. As the old theatre-goer at Hamlet sees upon the stage not one ghost, but many, so the old rooter at the ball game sees the phantom forms of the many he was wont to cheer in the old days—all of them a name and nothing more. No class of performers who are applauded by the public passes so soon into oblivion and forgetfulness as the ball players—not even the actor. Today his name is on every tongue, and his praise in big letters in the public print. Tomorrow he is consigned to the gentle resting place of the old fan's memory, where, so long as life lasts, he is held in beautiful remembrance—for the baseball rooter never forgets.
"Baseball heroes of the past," *St. Paul Globe*, December 8, 1901

St. Louis Cardinals outfielder Joe "Ducky" Medwick remains the last National League player to win the elusive Triple Crown—leading the league in batting average, home runs, and runs batted in for the same season.[1] When Medwick captured the coveted prize in 1937, the Cardinals organized a grand testimonial dinner for him, with a score of past and present St. Louis players invited to the big party. As the occasion neared and invitations were issued, the *St. Louis Daily Globe–Democrat* mused, "One name must have brought back memories to old-time fans and must have caused a little wonder among newer followers of the game.... Who was Joe Quinn?[2]"

Since Quinn's time some forty years previous, Hall of Famers Miller Huggins, Rogers Hornsby, and Frankie Frisch had all stood the keystone sack for the Cards, and amidst such reflected brilliance, it was easy for a modest figure from the nineteenth century to be eclipsed. The *Globe-Democrat* hurried to point out, however, that Quinn, now 74 years old, did appear first on the long list of great St. Louis second basemen, and had been a compatriot of such luminaries as King Kelly, John McGraw, Charlie Comiskey, and Cap Anson, all enduring legends of the game. And while the paper acknowledged Quinn may not have been the greatest player of the day, it insisted "he was one of the most popular," recalling vehement protests right across the east when Quinn was released to Baltimore by the erratic Chris Von der Ahe in 1897. The *Globe* also reminded fans that in the old days, Quinn had been honored by enthusiasts much the same way Medwick would be feted at the upcoming testimonial. The gold hunter watch which remained in Quinn's waistcoat all his life was an enduring symbol of the love and respect lavished on the little undertaker.

In May 2013, Joe Quinn was inducted into the Australian Baseball Hall of Fame, 110 years after his baseball career ended. Had he attended his own induction, he would have been 150 years old. But despite this belated honor, Quinn's place in Australian baseball history remains somewhat unresolved, having never played the game in Australia nor ever returned to the land of his birth. However, Craig Shipley, whose own debut with the Los Angeles Dodgers in 1986 marked the first appearance of an Australian-trained player in major league baseball, is quick to point out that Quinn's circumstances were very different from his own, raised as he was on the ballparks around Parramatta in Sydney in the 1970s.[3] A century earlier, Quinn never played the game in Australia through sheer lack of opportunity—baseball did not exist in any organized form until well after his departure for the United States, and given his poverty-stricken family life, time for recreation was in very short supply. A later return to his homeland was not the simple matter of a couple of mouse clicks, a wave of the passport, and the 14 hours on an Airbus that twenty-first century jetsetters enjoy. Travel to Australia in Quinn's time was logistically difficult and prohibitively expensive, and involved a commitment of many months, most of which were spent buffeted by salt-spray and sharing a cabin with at least 3 other snoring and seasick companions.

Despite the lack of a physical connection to the game and its fans in Australia, Joe Quinn's pride in his antipodean heritage remained a constant throughout his baseball career. It set him apart in an era when foreign-born players in the United States were rare and, for a time, illegal. The American press loved to refer to it and Quinn discussed his origins freely, right up until his final interview in 1936. Even despite his naturalization as a U.S. citizen, an enduring affinity with his homeland remained Quinn's trademark and makes him worthy of recognition as Australia's first-born pro ballplayer.

So what place for Joe Quinn in the wider baseball firmament? His will never be a gilded star on the Cooperstown honor boards; in fact, his lifetime Total Player Rating (TPR) of minus-27.4 may be one of the lowest in professional baseball history.[4] But only the greatest of players earn memorials for their career numbers. Even fewer are remembered, or survive for longer than they ought in the game, for being what Australians call "a good bloke." Sabermetrics aside, Quinn's integrity earned him a resounding respect which kept the contracts flowing his way even when his legs were slowing down and his bat failing. In an era characterized by inter-league battles and a constant tug-of-war for player services, men who could be relied upon to remain at their station were almost as valuable as those with a hot bat. Quinn was the glue that held together teams pulled apart by greedy owners, failing finances, or sheer broken spirits. He took the helm when no one would, embodying that unique Australian quality of "having a go," even while admitting his solitary character and unwillingness to throw a punch did not befit him for leadership of men who were often rowdy drunks or overindulged prima donnas.

Quinn's acceptance of others for their worth, be they rookie or superstar, umpire or undertaker, outweighed his self-confessed leadership deficiencies and blue-collar playing style. He never feigned celebrity, never aspired to it, and never depended on it: brought up knowing the value of a crust, he knew baseball was a means to an end, a game to be played while he could be of service to his team and his fans, but always in balance with his commitments to his family and business interests outside the game. He was a man who brought honesty and veracity to the game in an era when so many were famed for deceptions and disloyalty. Perhaps someday those qualities will be memorialized on honor boards on par with hitting streaks and home runs.

The last word shall be reserved for the *St. Louis Globe-Democrat*, that doyen of news in Quinn's adopted home town. "Joe Quinn was not the sort of fellow to talk much, particularly when the opportunity appears to make himself the topic of the dialogue," said the *Globe* in 1933. "But his name will be among those who endure as long as the game is played, although he makes no claim for himself. He need not. The printed record and memory of his admirers will do that for him.[5]"

Joe Quinn: The Facts

- Full name: Joseph James Quinn
- Born: December 24, 1862
- Died: November 12, 1940 (aged 77)
- Bats: Right
- Throws: Right
- Height: 5'7"
- Weight: 155 lbs.
- Position: Second base (also appeared at first base, third base, shortstop, and outfield)
- First Australian-born player in major league baseball
- First (and only) Australian to manage in the major leagues: St. Louis 1895, Cleveland 1899
- Debut: April 26, 1884 (St. Louis, Union Association)
- Final game: June 27, 1901 (Washington, American Association)
- Lifetime batting average (17 seasons): .262
- Stole more than 20 bases seven times and hit over .300 four times
- League-leading second baseman (by fielding average) three times: 1890 Players' League: .942; 1892 National League: .951; 1899 National League: .962
- Played on five championship winning teams: 1884 St. Louis (Union Association), 1888 Des Moines (Western Association), 1890 Boston (Players' League), 1891 Boston (National League), 1896 Baltimore (National League)
- Played in 4 different major leagues: National League, American League, Players' League, Union Association
- Played for the team with the best ever winning percentage: St. Louis, 1884 (94–19, .832)
- Captained and managed the team with the worst ever winning percentage: Cleveland, 1899 (20–134, .132)
- Voted "Most Popular Ball Player" in 1893 by readers of *The Sporting News*
- Spouse: Mary Ellen McGrath (1868–1937)
- Children: Catherine Marie (1887–1953), Thomas (1891–1954), Joseph Francis (1893–1956), Clarence Patrick (1894–1968), Marguerite (1896–1969), John Richard (1897–1920), Estelle (1899–1982), Richard T. (1904–1964), Dorothy (1905–1905)

Appendices

Appendix A: Joe Quinn, Career Statistics

Major League Batting Statistics

Year	Age	Team	LG	G	PA	AB	R	H	2B	3B	HR	RBI	SB	BB	SO	BA	OBP	SLG	OPS	OPS+	TB	HBP	SH	Pos
1884	21	SLM	UA	103	438	429	74	116	21	1	0			9		.270	.285	.324	.609	105	139			*3/O6
1885	22	SLM	NL	97	352	343	27	73	8	2	0	15	12	9	38	.213	.233	.248	.481	57	85			O53
1886	23	SLM	NL	75	279	271	33	63	11	3	1	21	12	8	31	.232	.254	.306	.561	76	83	0		O4/356
1888	25	BSN	NL	38	158	156	19	47	8	3	4	29	24	2	5	.301	.310	.468	.778	142	73			4
1889	26	BSN	NL	112	474	444	57	116	13	5	2	69	24	25	21	.261	.308	.327	.635	74	145	5		*4
1890	27	BOS	PL	130	555	509	87	153	19	8	7	82	29	44	24	.301	.359	.411	.769	102	209	2		64/5
1891	28	BSN	NL	124	542	508	70	122	8	10	3	63	24	28	28	.24	.288	.313	.601	69	159	6		*4
1892	29	BSN	NL	143	574	532	63	116	14	1	1	59	17	35	40	.218	.275	.254	.529	54	135	7		*4
1893	30	STL	NL	135	584	547	68	126	18	6	0	71	24	33	7	.23	.279	.285	.564	50	156	4		*4
1894	31	STL	NL	106	443	405	59	116	18	1	4	61	25	24	8	.286	.328	.365	.693	67	148	1	13	*4
1895	32	STL	NL	135	602	547	86	172	19	9	3	76	22	37	7	.314	.36	.399	.759	96	218	2	16	*4
1896	33	STL	NL	48	209	191	19	40	6	1	1	17	8	9	5	.209	.252	.267	.519	39	51	2	7	4
1896	33	BLN	NL	24	89	82	22	27	1	1	0	5	6	6	1	.329	.375	.366	.741	94	30	0	1	/4O56
1897	34	BLN	NL	75	304	285	33	74	11	4	1	45	12	13	10	.260	.299	.337	.636	68	96	3	3	564/O3
1898	35	BLN	NL	12	34	32	5	8	1	0	0	5	0	1	0	.250	.273	.281	.554	57	9	0	1	/54O
1898	35	STL	NL	103	411	375	35	94	10	5	0	36	13	24	31	.251	.301	.304	.605	72	114	3	9	46/O
1899	36	CLV	NL	147	640	615	73	176	24	6	0	72	22	21	10	.286	.312	.345	.657	89	212	2	2	*4
1900	37	STL	NL	22	90	80	12	21	2	0	1	11	4	10	2	.263	.344	.325	.669	86	26	0	0	4/65
1900	37	CIN	NL	74	290	266	18	73	5	2	0	25	7	16	16	.274	.316	.308	.624	74	82	0	8	4
1901	38	WSH	AL	66	284	266	33	67	11	2	2	34	7	11	10	.252	.287	.331	.618	72	88	2	5	4
17 Yrs				1769	7352	6883	893	1800	228	70	30	796	268	365	294	.262	.302	.328	.631	76	2258	39	65	

Minor League Batting Statistics

Year	Age	Team	LG	G	PA	AB	R	H	2B	3B	HR	RBI	SB	BB	SO	BA	OBP	SLG
1887	24	DUL	NWL	94		435	87	162	37	6	11		46			.372		.561
1888	25	DM	WA	77		340	64	105	16	5	3		40			.309		
1902	39	DM	WL	135		532	66	147	21	5	2		18			.276		.346
1903	40	DM	WL	127		535	56	150	29	3	3		19			.280		.363
				433		1842	273	564	103	19	19		123			.310		.423

Glossary of Terms

LG	League played in
G	Games played
PA	Plate appearances
AB	At-bats
R	Runs scored
H	Hits
2B	Doubles hit
3B	Triples hit
HR	Home runs hit
RBI	Runs batted in
SB	Stolen bases
BB	Walks (base on balls)
SO	Strikeouts
BA	Batting average
OBP	On-base percentage
SLG	Slugging average
OPS	On-base + slugging percentage
OPS+	Normalized OPS
TB	Total bases
HBP	Hit by pitch
SH	Sacrifice hits
Pos	Positions played

PA Includes at-bats, walks, hit-by-pitch, sacrifice flies, and sacrifice hits

OPS (Total bases/at-bats)

OPS+ Adjusted for league and park

* indicates played more than ⅔ of games, / indicates fewer than 10 games

Appendix A: Joe Quinn, Career Statistics

Major League Fielding Statistics*

Year	Team	LG	Age	Pos	G	Ch	PO	A	E	DP	Fld%
1884	SLM	UA	21	1B	100	1128	1033	33	62	55	.945
1884	SLM	UA	21	OF	3	6	5	0	1	0	.833
1884	SLM	UA	21	SS	1	5	1	3	1	0	.800
1885	SLM	NL	22	OF	57	104	83	8	13	0	.875
1885	SLM	NL	22	3B	31	116	33	64	19	1	.836
1885	SLM	NL	22	1B	11	120	113	4	3	3	.975
1886	SLM	NL	23	OF	48	114	89	13	12	1	.895
1886	SLM	NL	23	2B	15	79	33	32	14	3	.823
1886	SLM	NL	23	1B	7	77	72	1	4	8	.948
1886	SLM	NL	23	3B	4	15	5	8	2	0	.867
1886	SLM	NL	23	SS	2	3	0	1	2	1	.333
1888	BSN	NL	25	2B	38	232	97	115	20	11	.914
1889	BSN	NL	26	SS	63	272	67	167	38	19	.860
1889	BSN	NL	26	2B	47	269	105	144	20	17	.926
1889	BSN	NL	26	3B	2	6	2	3	1	0	.833
1890	BOS	PL	27	2B	130	877	431	395	51	70	.942
1891	BSN	NL	28	2B	124	681	275	364	42	44	.938
1892	BSN	NL	29	2B	143	822	356	426	40	75	.951
1893	STL	NL	30	2B	135	764	354	366	44	63	.942
1894	STL	NL	31	2B	106	714	341	339	34	74	.952
1895	STL	NL	32	2B	135	801	363	394	44	63	.945
1896	STL	NL	33	2B	48	271	92	167	12	7	.956
1896	BLN	NL	33	2B	8	41	18	21	2	3	.951
1896	BLN	NL	33	OF	8	8	7	0	1	0	.875
1896	BLN	NL	33	3B	5	21	4	16	1	0	.952
1896	BLN	NL	33	SS	1	4	2	2	0	0	1.000
1897	BLN	NL	34	3B	37	129	41	81	7	6	.946
1897	BLN	NL	34	SS	21	116	56	57	3	10	.974
1897	BLN	NL	34	2B	11	64	24	36	4	3	.938
1897	BLN	NL	34	OF	6	8	7	1	0	0	1.000
1897	BLN	NL	34	1B	2	16	14	1	1	2	.938
1898	BLN	NL	35	3B	8	28	12	13	3	1	.893
1898	BLN	NL	35	2B	1	7	3	3	1	0	.857
1898	STL	NL	35	2B	62	343	139	191	13	19	.962
1898	STL	NL	35	SS	41	246	79	149	18	11	.927
1898	STL	NL	35	OF	1	2	2	0	0	0	1.000
1899	CLV	NL	36	2B	147	821	350	440	31	61	.962
1900	STL	NL	37	2B	14	60	26	30	4	3	.933
1900	STL	NL	37	SS	6	33	17	13	3	1	.909
1900	STL	NL	37	3B	1	4	1	3	0	0	1.000
1900	CIN	NL	37	2B	74	340	154	169	17	24	.950
1901	WSH	AL	38	2B	66	351	158	177	16	17	.954
17 Seasons					1771	10118	5064	4450	604	676	.940

* No minor league fielding statistics available

Glossary of Terms

LG	League
Age	Age at the start of the season
Pos	Position played
G	Games in this position
Ch	Defensive chances Putouts + Assists + Errors
PO	Putouts

A   Assists
E   Errors committed
DP   Double-plays turned
Fld%   Fielding percentage   Putouts + Assists/Chances

Career Managerial Statistics

Year	Age	Team	LG	G	W	L	W-L %
1887	24	Duluth	NWL	exact statistics unknown			
1895	32	St. Louis	NL	136	39	92	0.298
1899	36	Cleveland	NL	154	20	134	0.130
1902	39	Des Moines	WL	137	54	83	0.394
1903	40	Des Moines	WL	131	55	76	0.420

Appendix B: Sabermetric Comparison of Nineteenth-Century Second Basemen

In his 1940 obituary in *The Sporting News*, Joe Quinn was rated one of the nineteenth century's "Big Four" second basemen alongside Fred Pfeffer, Fred Dunlap, and Hall of Famer Bid McPhee. The following table provides common sabermetric Player Value ratings for each. See **Glossary** on facing page.

Player		G	PA	Rbat	Rbaser	Rfield	RAA	WAA	Rrep	RAR	WAR	oWAR	dWAR	OPS+	TPR
Quinn	*Lifetime*	**1769.0**	**7352.0**	**−227.0**	**−7.0**	**−5.0**	**−214.0**	**−18.9**	**231.0**	**17.0**	**4.6**	**5.3**	**1.8**	**76.0**	**−27.4**
	Average			−11.4	−0.4	−0.3	−10.7	−1.0	11.6	0.9	0.2	0.3	0.1	77.2	
	Maximum			7.0	1.0	12.0	8.0	0.8	22.0	16.0	1.6	2.0	1.4	142.0	
	Minimum			−42.0	−2.0	−16.0	−46.0	−3.7	0.0	−26.0	−1.7	−1.2	−1.3	39.0	
Pfeffer	*Lifetime*	**1671.0**	**7128.0**	**−75.0**	**16.0**	**48.0**	**26.0**	**2.1**	**236.0**	**262.0**	**26.2**	**23.1**	**7.1**	**94.0**	**21.8**
	Average			−4.5	1.0	2.8	1.6	0.1	13.9	15.5	1.5	1.4	0.4	83.4	
	Maximum			27.0	4.0	15.0	44.0	3.9	20.0	60.0	5.6	4.4	1.5	153.0	
	Minimum			−22.0	−1.0	−8.0	−19.0	−1.4	1.0	−8.0	−0.6	−0.3	−0.4	6.0	
McPhee	*Lifetime*	**2138.0**	**9429.0**	**101.0**	**12.0**	**154.0**	**306.0**	**25.3**	**266.0**	**571.0**	**52.7**	**40.1**	**16.3**	**107.0**	**40.1**
	Average			5.6	0.6	8.6	16.8	1.4	14.8	31.8	2.9	2.2	0.9	105.6	
	Maximum			22.0	4.0	19.0	38.0	3.0	21.0	58.0	5.2	4.5	1.8	129.0	
	Minimum			−6.0	−2.0	0.0	−5.0	−0.5	7.0	5.0	0.6	0.4	0.1	84.0	
Dunlap	*Lifetime*	**965.0**	**4264.0**	**168.0**	**−1.0**	**80.0**	**265.0**	**23.6**	**124.0**	**389.0**	**36.8**	**30.1**	**8.9**	**134.0**	**27.4**
	Average			11.9	−0.1	5.7	19.0	1.7	8.9	27.8	2.6	2.1	0.6	122.6	
	Maximum			75.0	1.0	14.0	87.0	7.7	17.0	87.0	7.8	6.6	1.5	256.0	
	Minimum			−12.0	−1.0	−2.0	−5.0	−0.5	0.0	−3.0	−0.3	−0.1	−0.2	48.0	

* "Obituary: Joe Quinn" (1940). *The Sporting News* (St. Louis, Missouri). Thursday, November 21, p. 8.

Glossary

Yrs	Years	Years active in major league baseball
G	Games played	
PA	Plate appearances	
Rbat	Runs batting	Number of runs better or worse than average as a hitter
Rbaser	Runs from baserunning	Number of runs better or worse than average from all baserunning events
RAA	Runs better than average	Number of runs better than the average league player
WAA	Wins above average	Wins added by the player above the league average player
Rrep	Runs from replacement level	Number of runs the player is better than a replacement player obtained from a team with a .294 winning percentage.
RAR	Runs above replacement level	Number of runs this player is better than a replacement player
WAR	Wins above replacement	Number of wins added to the team above what a replacement player would contribute. The average Hall of Fame second baseman (of which there are 19) has a career WAR of 69.5.
oWAR	Offensive wins above replacement	The same statistic as WAR but with fielding values excluded
dWAR	Defensive wins above replacement	Defensive wins calculated using only the defensive statistics
OPS+	Normalized on-base and slugging percentage	Adjusted for ballpark and league. Direct measure of hitting power and ability to get on base.
TPR	Total Player Rating	Combines offensive and defensive production, assigns events such as doubles, stolen bases, and walks a value in runs. Babe Ruth leads the lifetime TPR rankings on 107.7, followed by Nap Lajoie with 94.4.

* "Baseball-Reference.Com" (2013). Sports Reference LLC. [cited August 20, 2013]. Available from: http://www.baseball-reference.com/.

Appendix C: Australian-born Major League Baseball Players, 1884–2013*

Player	Born In	Date of Birth	Debut Year	Final Year
Joe Quinn	Ipswich, Australia	24/12/1862	1884	1901
Craig Shipley	Parramatta, Australia	1/7/1963	1986	1998
Dave Nilsson	Brisbane, Australia	12/14/1969	1992	1999
Mark Ettles	Perth, Australia	10/30/1966	1993	1993
Mark Hutton	South Adelaide, Australia	2/6/1970	1993	1998
Graeme Lloyd	Victoria, Australia	4/9/1967	1993	2003
Shayne Bennett	Adelaide, Australia	4/10/1972	1997	1999
Trent Durrington	Sydney, Australia	8/27/1975	1999	2005
Jeff Williams	Canberra, Australia	6/6/1972	1999	2002
Cameron Cairncross	Queensland, Australia	5/11/1972	2000	2000
Luke Prokopec	Blackwood, Australia	2/23/1978	2000	2002
Grant Balfour	Sydney, Australia	12/30/1977	2001	Active
Damian Moss	Darlinghurst, Australia	11/24/1976	2001	2004
Brad Thomas	Sydney, Australia	10/12/1977	2001	Active
John Stephens	Sydney, Australia	11/15/1979	2002	2002
Travis Blackley	Melbourne, Australia	11/4/1982	2004	Active
Justin Huber	Melbourne, Australia	7/1/1982	2005	2009
Chris Oxspring	Ipswich, Australia	5/13/1977	2005	2005
Glenn Williams	Gosford, Australia	7/18/1977	2005	2005
Peter Moylan	Western Australia, Australia	12/2/1978	2006	Active
Ryan Rowland-Smith	Sydney, Australia	1/26/1983	2007	Active
Rich Thompson	Hornsby, Australia	7/1/1984	2007	Active
Brad Harman	Melbourne, Australia	11/19/1985	2008	Active
Trent Oeltjen	Sydney, Australia	2/28/1983	2009	Active
Luke Hughes	Perth, Australia	8/2/1984	2010	2012
Liam Hendriks	Perth, Australia	2/10/1989	2011	Active
Shane Lindsay	Melbourne, Australia	1/25/1985	2011	Active
Josh Spence	Victoria, Australia	1/22/1988	2011	Active

* "Major League Baseball Players Born in Australia" (2013). Baseball Almanac. [cited August 30, 2013]. Available from: http://www.baseball-almanac.com/players/birthplace.php?loc=Australia.

Chapter Notes

Introduction

1. W.J. Monaghan, "One of Baseball's Great" (1933), *St. Louis Globe-Democrat*, Sunday, November 26, pp. 6, 14.
2. S. Bradbury and G. Smart (2005), *Steven Bradbury: Last Man Standing* (Docklands, VIC: Geoff Slattery Publishing).
3. D. Young (2011), *Rebound Strong: Hope and Strength for Life's Toughest Challenges* (Round Rock, TX: Wind Runner Press), p. 317.
4. From the 1914 poem "For the Fallen," written by British poet Laurence Binyon in tribute to Allied soldiers killed during the opening days of World War I. The poem is now an integral part of Remembrance Day and ANZAC Day services in Australia. From: Binyon, L. (1917), *For the Fallen and Other Poems* (London: Hodder & Stoughton).
5. D. Dezen (2013), "Abf Announces 2013 Hall of Fame Inductees [Press Release: March 14, 2013]," Australian Baseball Federation [cited May 3, 2013]. Available from: http://www.baseball.com.au/default.asp?Page=92259&MenuID=Website+Administration%2F17%2F20%2CEdit+Main+Menu%2F2084%2F0.
6. J. Thorn, P. Palmer, and D. Reuther (2001), *Total Baseball* (Kingston, NY: Total Sports), p. 879.
7. Born and raised in Parramatta, Sydney, Shipley came to the United States in 1982 and played three seasons with the University of Alabama, hitting a home run in his first at-bat as a freshman. He signed with the Dodgers as a free agent in 1984 and hit .309 with Albuquerque in the Pacific Coast League before his call-up. His first game was against the San Diego Padres. Facing left-hander Mark Thurmond in the second inning, Shipley grounded out to second base, but then drove in Alex Trevino for the game's first run: "Aussie in the Dodgers' Diamond" (1986), *The Canberra Times*, Tuesday, June 24, p. 20.
8. Quinn was born on December 24, 1862, and Shipley on January 7, 1963. Shipley made his debut with the Dodgers on June 22, 1986, and Quinn on April 26, 1884. From: "Craig Shipley (Player Page)" (2013), Baseball-Reference.com [cited June 29, 2013]. Available from: http://www.baseball-reference.com/players/s/shiplcr01.shtml; "Joe Quinn (Player Page)" (2013), Baseball-Reference.com [cited January 9, 2013]. Available from: http://www.baseball-reference.com/players/q/quinnjo02.shtml.
9. J. Kavanagh and N.L. Macht (1999), *Uncle Robbie* (Cleveland, OH: Society for American Baseball Research), p. 31.
10. C. Shipley (2013), personal communication. "The Place of Joe Quinn in Australian Baseball History [Unpublished interview transcript]." To: R. Nicholls. (July 25).
11. "Historical Events for Year 1884" (2013), History-Orb.com [cited March 3, 2013]. Available from: http://www.historyorb.com/events/date/1884.
12. "The Speed of Bicycles" (1884), *Evening Critic* (Washington, DC), Thursday, October 30, p. 1.
13. C.F. Pardon (1984), *The Australians in England: A Complete Record of the Cricket Tour of 1884* (London: J.W. McKenzie).
14. B. Dabscheck (1995). "Australian Baseballers Form a Team of Their Own," *Sporting Traditions* 12 (1): pp. 61–101.
15. American diggers are popularly believed to have played on the Victorian goldfields as early as the 1850s; ironically, baseball was taking over in popularity from cricket in America around the same time: J. Clark (2003), *A History of Australian Baseball: Time and Game* (Lincoln: University of Nebraska Press), p. 5.
16. B. Dabscheck (1998), "Australian Baseball's Second Unsuccessful Attempt to Establish a Players' Association," *Sporting Traditions* 14 (2): pp. 87–89.
17. B. Mitchell (1997), "Baseball in Australia. Two Tours and the Beginnings of Baseball in Australia," *Sporting Traditions* 13 (1): pp. 2–24.
18. "'Swaggies, Tuckerbags and Jumbucks'—What the Words Mean" (2011), Who'll come a-Waltzing Matilda with me? National Exhibition, National Library of Australia [cited June 29, 2013]. Available from: http://pandora.nla.gov.au/pan/34755/20110606-1326/www.nla.gov.au/epubs/waltzingmatilda/3-Meanings.html.
19. Monaghan, "One of Baseball's Great."
20. Ibid.
21. Ty Cobb, "the Georgia Peach," has modern baseball's highest career batting average at .366, or 36.6 hits per 100 at bats, meaning even he effectively "failed" in 63.4 percent of his at-bats. "Ty Cobb (Player Page)" (2013), Baseball-Reference.com [cited June 29, 2013]. Available from: http://www.baseball-reference.com/players/c/cobbty01.shtml.
22. "J. Quinn" (1893), *The Sporting News*, Monday, February 11, p. 1.
23. B.M. Nash and A. Zullo (1985), *Baseball Hall of Shame* (New York: Pocket Books), pp. 12–13.
24. Twister, "The Australian Baseballers—An Eastern Welcome" (1897), *The Argus* (Melbourne), Friday, July 23, p. 6.
25. K.R. Arnold (2011), *Anti-Immigration in the United States: A Historical Encyclopedia* (Santa Barbara, CA: Greenwood Press), p. 5.
26. J. Zoss and J.S. Bowman (1989), *Diamonds in the Rough: The Untold History of Baseball* (New York: Macmillan), p. 66.

27. D. Farrington, "Half a Century through Joe Quinn's Eyes: Union Star Recalls Birth of *The Sporting News*" (1936), *The Sporting News*, Saturday, May 21, p. 9B.

Chapter 1

1. J.J. Putman (1981), "A New Day for Ireland," *National Geographic* 159 (4): pp. 442–469.
2. "Daily Life in Ipswich" (2011), City of Ipswich, Ipswich, QLD, p. 14.
3. "Classified Advertising" (1862), *Queensland Courier* (Brisbane, QLD), Wednesday, December 24, p. 1.
4. T.A. Coghlan, ed. (2011), *Labour and Industry in Australia: From the First Settlement in 1788 to the Establishment of the Commonwealth in 1901*, Vol. 2 (New York: Cambridge University Press), p. 48.
5. "Commercial Intelligence" (1862), *The Argus* (Melbourne), Tuesday, April 15, p. 4.
6. Despite his lineage, which can be traced back to King David, Joseph earned his living as a *tekton*, or worker of wood, stone, and bricks. From: L.B. Perrotta (2000). *Saint Joseph: His Life and His Role in the Church Today* (Huntingdon: Our Sunday Visitor), p. 32, 111.
7. R. Patrick and H. Patrick (1989), *Exiles Undaunted: The Irish Rebels Kevin and Eva O'Doherty* (St. Lucia: University of Queensland Press), p. 30.
8. O'Doherty became a prominent citizen in Queensland, instrumental in the establishment of the Royal Brisbane Hospital, Brisbane Grammar School, and St. Stephen's Catholic Cathedral, and serving in both houses of the Queensland Parliament before his death in 1905: Patrick and Patrick, *Exiles Undaunted*.
9. R. Broome (2010), *Aboriginal Australians: A History since 1788*, 4th ed. (Crows Nest: Allen & Unwin), p. 5.
10. T. Flannery (2000), *The Explorers: Stories of Discovery and Adventure from the Australian Frontier* (New York: Grove Press), p. 17.
11. A. Frost (2012), *Botany Bay: The Real Story* (Collingwood: Black Inc.), p. 150.
12. R. Fisher (2009), *Boosting Brisbane: Imprinting the Colonial Capital of Queensland* (Salisbury: Boolarong Press), p. 66.
13. "Ipswich Heritage Trails—Rivers of Ipswich Then & Now (Ipswich City Council)" (2011), Ipswich, QLD.
14. After the murder of two members of a surveying party near Mt. Lindesay in May 1840, three Aboriginal men were apprehended and tried for the crimes. In July 1841, the two surviving Aborigines were hanged from a beam from an upper window of the windmill: B. Roberts (1991), *Stories of the Southside* (Archerfield, QLD: Aussie Books), p. 63.
15. "Our Strange Past: Few Tears for Captain Logan" (1951), *The Mail* (Adelaide, SA), Saturday, December 15, p. 6S.
16. The Jagera, Yuggera and Ugarapul peoples: R. Evans (2008), *A History of Queensland* (New York: Cambridge University Press), p. 57.
17. A wild dog native to Australia: L.K. Corbett and F. Knight (2001), *The Dingo in Australian and Asia* (Sydney: UNSW Press).
18. G.C. Ingleton (1952). *True Patriots All: Or, News from Early Australia, as Told in a Collection of Broadsides* (Sydney: Angus & Robertson), p. 64.
19. S. Bennett (1865), *The History of Australian Discovery and Colonisation* (London: Hanson and Bennett), p. 553.
20. K. Suter (2008), "The Continuing Plight of Australia's Indigenous Peoples," *Contemporary Review* 290 (1690): pp. 349–360.
21. R. Fotheringham "Inside the Killing Fields of Queensland" (2010), *The Australian* (Melbourne), Wednesday, October 6, p. 12.
22. R. Ørsted-Jensen (2011), *Frontier History Revisited—Colonial Queensland and the "History War"* (Brisbane, QLD: Lux Mundi Publishing), p. 21.
23. H. Haenke (1976), "Thorn, George (1806–1876)," Australian Dictionary of Biography [cited July 6, 2013]. Available from: http://adb.anu.edu.au/biography/thorn-george-4719.
24. Some specimens of the slow-growing and long-lived *Xanthorrhoea* still survive in Ipswich's Queens Park, itself dating back to 1864: "Ipswich" (1864), *Brisbane Courier* (Brisbane, QLD), Wednesday, August 24, p. 1.
25. A legendary creature with origins in Aboriginal folklore, the *bunyip* is thought to inhabit Australian waterways, particularly the small oxbow lakes known as *billabongs*. While its physical characteristics have never been precisely documented, it is generally accepted to have a malevolent presence and is still much dreaded in some indigenous cultures: R. Holden (2001), *Bunyips: Australia's Folklore of Fear* (Canberra: National Library of Australia).
26. "Cattle and Sheep" (1848), *Sydney Morning Herald*, Wednesday, February 2, p. 4.
27. J. Verne (1872), *Around the World in Eighty Days* (London: Lord, Dean & Son).
28. From records of the ship *Matoaka*: "Matoaka [Passenger List]: Online Microfilm of Shipping Lists" (2012), New South Wales Government State Records [cited July 7, 2012]. Available from: http://www.records.nsw.gov.au.
29. S. Lewis (1837) *A Topographical Dictionary of Ireland* (London: S. Lewis), p. 135.
30. M. Comerford (1886), *Colllections Relating to the Dioceses of Kildare and Leighlin* (Dublin: James Duffy and Sons). Available from: http://www.archive.org/stream/collectionskild00comeuoft/collectionskild00comeuoft_djvu.txt.
31. "Griffith's Valuation: Primary Valuation of Tenements: Parish of Killabban" (1847–1864), Ask About Ireland [cited June 29, 2013]. Available from: http://www.askaboutireland.ie/griffith-valuation/.
32. Ibid.
33. The passenger list of the *Matoaka* indicated Patrick Quinn could neither read nor write: "Matoaka [Passenger List]."
34. J. Judge (1981), "The Travail of Ireland," *National Geographic* 159 (4): pp. 432–441.
35. The scheme brought over 18,000 British immigrants a year to Australia between 1831 and 1860: C. Price (1987), "Chapter 1: Immigration and Ethnic Origin," in *Australians: Historical Statistics*, ed. W. Vamplew (Broadway, New South Wales, Australia: Fairfax, Syme & Weldon Associates), pp. 2–22.
36. "Labour Markets" (1855), *Sydney Morning Herald*, Saturday, May 19, p. 5.
37. The goals of the party included restriction of office-holding to native-born Americans, promotion of Bible reading in public schools, extending the waiting period for citizenship from five to 21 years, and "usage of every means in our power to diminish foreign influences." They insisted they were not bigots but attempting to protect the country from "men of immoral character ... ignorant of our laws and institutions." From: D.H. Bennett (1988), *The Party of Fear: From Nativist Movements to the New Right in American History* (Chapel Hill: University of North Carolina Press), pp. 53–60.
38. Of the extent of the depopulation which has taken

place, some estimate may be formed by the present high wages farmers are compelled to pay for laborers during the present spring. In this town and the vicinity, where before now men could be got to work for from 8d. to 1s. a day, the price ranges now from 1s. to 1s. 6d . "Ireland (Saturday, April 14, 1855)," *The Spectator*, London [cited July 6, 2013]. Available from: http://archive.spectator.co.uk/article/14th-april-1855/4/ireland.

39. "Matoaka [Passenger List]."

40. "Imports" (1855) *Sydney Morning Herald*, Friday, May 18, p. 4; "Shipping—Arrivals" (1855), *Sydney Morning Herald*, Friday, May 18, p. 4.

41. "Shipping News—The Matoaka" (1860), *Lyttelton Times*, December 8, p. 4.

42. B. Groom and W. Wickman (1982), *Sydney, the 1850s: The Lost Collection* (Sydney, NSW: University of Sydney), p. 13.

43. "Bucks and Brummels": slang term for the upper class, especially those fastidious about their appearance. The term is credited to George Bryan Brummell (1778–1840), an English fashion icon and close friend of King George IV. Brummell was variously known as "Buck" and "Beau" during his school years, and after inheriting a fortune from his father in 1799, became a well-known society figure famous for his immaculate dress. Britannica-online (2012). "Beau Brummell (English Dandy)," *Encyclopædia Britannica* [cited July 7, 2013]. Available from: http://www.britannica.com/EBchecked/topic/82094/Beau-Brummell.

44. L.H. Turnbull (2008), "Sydney in 1858," *Dictionary of Sydney* [cited May 14, 2013]. Available from: http://www.dictionaryofsydney.org/entry/entry/sydney_in_1858.

45. "Labour Markets."

46. *Votes & Proceedings*, Vol. 2: *Register of Quartz Vein Applications* (1852), Sydney: New South Wales Parliament (Legislative Council), p. 200.

47. The hotel was relocated to the nearby larger town of Moruya in 1859, but its original site on Broulee Island is now heritage-listed: *State of the Environment Report: Places on Heritage Registers in Eurobodalla Shire, June 2004* (2004), Office of the Commissioner for Sustainability and the Environment, Canberra [cited July 7, 2013]. Available from: http://www.envcomm.act.gov.au/soe/soe2004/Eurobodalla/heritage1.htm.

48. "Country Intelligence" (1841), *Sydney Gazette and New South Wales Advertiser* (Sydney), Tuesday, February 9, p. 2.

49. "Araluen—Historic Gold Ghost Town in the Heart of the Southern Tablelands" (2004), *Sydney Morning Herald*, Sunday, February 8, pp. 16, 34.

50. H. Ryan (2013), Personal communication. *"Research Enquiry [Moruya District History Society]."* To: R. Nicholls (March 2, 2013).

51. "Australia Birth Index, 1788–1922: Patrick F. Quin" (2010), Ancestry.com [cited July 1, 2012]. Available from: www.ancestry.com.

52. "Braidwood [from Our Correspondent]" (1858), *Sydney Morning Herald*, Saturday, May 15, p. 6.

53. While records of the marriage in Broulee are lost, the union was recorded on Joe Quinn's 1862 Queensland birth certificate (no. 1863/C451). "Family History Research" (2013), Queensland Government: Births, Deaths, Marriages and Divorces [cited July 7, 2013]. Available from: http://www.qld.gov.au/law/births-deaths-marriages-and-divorces/family-history-research/.

54. Catherine's surname has been reported with various spellings, including McAfie, McCafie, McCaffery, and McCaffrey, all derivations of McCafferty. The name is derived from the Irish surname MacEachmharcaigh, formed from the words for 'steed' and 'rider.'" From: E. MacLysaght (1991), *Irish Families: Their Names, Arms and Origins* (Dublin: Irish Academic Press) p. 70.

55. "1821 Fermanagh Census (Derryvolin Parish)" (2012), Ireland Genealogy Projects [cited December 20, 2012]. Available from: http://www.igp-web.com/fermanagh/Links.htm#Census.

56. C. Woodham-Smith (1962), *The Great Hunger: Ireland 1845–1849* (London: H. Hamilton), pp. 146–148.

57. Caddie McCaffrey is listed as "single" and 15 years of age in the Enniskillen admissions register. She was the only person admitted on December 7, 1846: V. Sage (2009), "Enniskillen Workhouse Register: Dec 1845–July 1847," Ireland Genealogy Projects [cited December 12, 2012]. Available from: http://www.igp-web.com/fermanagh/Donated.htm.

58. The 1834 Poor Law Amendment Act put an end to government relief for the able-bodied pauper. However, during the six years of the Great Famine in Ireland (1846–1852), lords who could collect no rent either sold out cheaply or resorted to mass evictions and destruction and burning of cottages. Many workhouses were therefore forced to accept the able poor due to the sheer volume of the homeless and destitute. From: P. Higginbotham (2011), "The New Poor Law," The Workhouse: the story of an institution [cited December 10, 2012]. Available from: www.workhouses.org.uk/poorlaws/newpoorlaw.shtml.

59. V. Sage.

60. P. Higginbotham (2011), "Enniskillen, Co. Fermanagh," The Workhouse: the story of an institution [cited December 10, 2012]. Available from: http://www.workhouses.org.uk/Enniskillen/.

61. J. O'Connor (1995), *The Workhouses of Ireland: The Fate of Ireland's Poor* (Dublin: Anvil Books), pp. 129–130.

62. N. Longmate (2003), *The Workhouse: A Social History* (London: Random House UK), p. 254.

63. According to the log of the *Telegraph*: "Telegraph [Passenger List]: Online Microfilm of Shipping Lists" (2012), New South Wales Government State Records [cited December 28, 2012]. Available from: http://www.records.nsw.gov.au.

64. The town, in the south of modern-day Northern Ireland, is perhaps most famous for the Battle of Newtownbutler in 1689. A Williamite force of fewer than 1,000 Enniskillen soldiers captured and killed 3,000 of James II's troops after they had become lost in an unmarked bog: D.P. Graham (2011), *Enniskillen and the Battle of Newtownbutler, 1689* (Farnham: Pike & Shot Society).

65. From the ship's passenger list: "Telegraph [Passenger List]."

66. "Abuses in the Immigration Department" (1853), *Empire* (Sydney), Saturday, October 1, p. 5.

67. "The Single Female Immigrants by the Ship Telegraph" (1853), *Sydney Morning Herald*, Saturday, September 24, p. 4.

68. NLA (1974), *New National Australian Encyclopaedia* (Sydney: National Literary Association), p. 98.

69. Waddell and ex-convict Hicken announced their discovery in a letter to the Colonial Secretary on August 1, 1851, describing an "extensive gold find in the bed of the Moruya River": "News from the Interior [from Our Correspondent]: Gold at the Moruya" (1851), *Sydney Morning Herald*, Tuesday, October 14, p. 3. Hicken was killed on the goldfields just 7 years later when, while riding home from Braidwood to Araluen late one night, his horse stumbled, pitching him into a pit dug by prospectors close to the road. The six-foot fall was fatal to Hicken, who was just 37 years old: "Braidwood [from Our Correspondent]" (1858), *Sydney Morning Herald*, Saturday, May 15, p. 6.

70. Gold was mined in Araluen until the end of the century, but after the removal of the shallow alluvial gold, dredges were employed from 1899 until cessation of operations in 1939. B. McGowan (2000), *The Golden South: A History of the Araluen, Bell's Creek and Major's Creek Gold Fields* (Canberra: Barry McGowan), p. 32.

71. "News from the Interior [from Our Correspondent]: Gold at the Moruya" (1851). Labor markets in 1855 reported the average annual salary of a farm laborer was 30–40 pounds: "Labour Markets" (1855).

72. "The Southern Gold Fields [from Our Correspondent]" (1856), *Sydney Morning Herald*, Saturday, July 5, p. 3.

73. P. Stiskin (1893), *Moruya: The First 150 Years* (Moruya, NSW: Moruya and District Historical Society), p. 28.

74. Stiskin, p. 30.

75. "Araluen [from Our Correspondent]" (1857), *Sydney Morning Herald*, Tuesday, July 7, p. 5.

76. "The Late Floods" (1860), *Empire* (Sydney), Friday, February 17, p. 2.

77. "Country News" (1860), *Sydney Morning Herald*, Tuesday, February 7, p. 3.

78. "The Late Floods."

79. "The Floods" (1860), *Sydney Morning Herald*, Monday, February 20, p. 3.

80. "The Floods."

81. "The Late Floods."

82. "The Late Floods."

83. "February Floods" (1910), *Braidwood Dispatch and Mining Journal* (Braidwood, NSW), Wednesday, February 16, p. 2.

84. "The Floods."

85. "The Floods [Araluen]" (1860), *Sydney Morning Herald*, Saturday, February 18, p. 8.

86. R. Flanagan (1862), *The History of New South Wales: With an Account of Van Diemen's Land (Tasmania), New Zealand, Port Phillip (Victoria), Moreton Bay, and Other Australasian Settlements: Comprising a Complete View of the Progress and Prospects of Gold Mining in Australia/the Whole Compiled from Official and Other Authentic and Original Sources by Roderick Flanagan* (London: Sampson Low, Son), p. 464.

87. Putman, pp. 442–469.

88. The colony of Queensland was declared in 1859, prior to which time it had been part of the original Australian colony of New South Wales. From: CBCS (1910), *Official Year Book of the Commonwealth of Australia*, No. 3: 1910 (Canberra: Australian Bureau of Statistics/Commonwealth Bureau of Statistics), p. 20.

89. W.H. De Puy (1908), *The World-Wide Encyclopedia and Gazetteer* (New York: The Christian Herald), p. 3479.

90. Fisher, p. 220.

91. "Classified Advertising" (1862), *Queensland Courier* (Brisbane, QLD), Wednesday, December 24, p. 1.

92. Ibid.

93. "Progress of the Moreton Bay Tramway Company" (1861), *The Courier* (Brisbane, QLD), Monday, September 16, pp. 4, 5.

94. "Supreme Court, Brisbane. In the Insolvent Estate of the Moreton Bay Tramway Company" (1863), *Queensland Times, Ipswich Herald & General Advertiser* (Brisbane), Tuesday, February 17, p. 3.

95. "50 Years Ago: Cotton Concern" (1951), *Sunday Mail* (Brisbane, QLD), Sunday, March 11, p. 9.

96. "Queensland" (1864), *Sydney Morning Herald*, Tuesday, July 12, p. 5.

97. G. Hallam (1994), "Life and Death on the Ipswich-Toowoomba Railway: Gibbons and Fountains Camps 1865–67," in: *Brisbane: Cemeteries as Sources* (History Group Papers No. 13), ed. R. Fisher and B. Shaw (Brisbane, QLD), pp. 22–34.

98. "Municipal Council" (1864), *Queensland Times, Ipswich Herald & General Advertiser* (Brisbane, QLD). Tuesday, July 12, p. 3.

99. "Ipswich" (1865), *Queensland Times, Ipswich Herald & General Advertiser* (Brisbane, QLD), Thursday, January 12, p. 3.

100. "Bremer River Works" (1864), *Brisbane Courier* (Brisbane, QLD), Saturday, December 17, p. 5.

101. "Local and General News" (1864), *Brisbane Courier* (Brisbane, QLD), Friday, August 19, p. 3.

102. "Opening of the First Railway in Queensland (from Our Special Reporter)" (1865), *Brisbane Courier* (Brisbane, QLD), Tuesday, August 1, pp. 2, 3.

103. Originally called Googabilla (meaning "honey") by the Ugarapul people, the area was renamed Bigges Camp by the Europeans when the railway line was constructed from Ipswich to this area. At the opening of the line in 1865, Governor Bowen suggested that the name be Latinized from Bigges Camp (which sounded rather too like "Big Scamp") to Grand (*big*) Chester (*camp*). From: "Place Names Origins" (2011), City of Ipswich, Ipswich, QLD.

104. Fisher, p. 82.

Chapter 2

1. Swag (Australian slang): a blanket usually carried by itinerant workers with their belongings rolled inside.

2. J.C. Foley (1957), *Droughts in Australia: Review of Records from Earliest Years of Settlement to 1955* (Melbourne: Director of Meteorology), p. 5.

3. "Ipswich" (1864), *The Darling Downs Gazette and General Advertiser* (Toowoomba, QLD), Thursday, November 24, p. 4.

4. "Telegraphic" (1866), *Brisbane Courier* (Brisbane, QLD), Wednesday, April 11, p. 2.

5. A term adopted from the English slang term for canal builders, who were commonly known during the nineteenth century as "navigators": G. Hallam, "Life and Death on the Ipswich-Toowoomba Railway."

6. "The Unemployed Railway Navvies" (1866), *Darling Downs Gazette and General Advertiser* (Toowoomba, QLD), Saturday, September 8, p. 3.

7. "Waltzing Matilda: A National Anthem?"

8. H.H. Pearce (1971), *On the Origins of Waltzing Matilda (Expression, Lyric, Melody)* (Melbourne: Hawthorn Press), p. 13.

9. M. Richardson (2006), *Once a Jolly Swagman: The Ballad of Waltzing Matilda* (Melbourne: Melbourne University Press), p. 44.

10. "Supreme Court: Thursday, November 22: Criminal Sittings before His Honor Mr. Justice Lutwyche. Riot: Regina V. Hayes, Parker and Murray" (1866), *Brisbane Courier* (Brisbane, QLD), Friday, November 23, p. 2.

11. M. Campbell (1997), *The Kingdom of the Ryans: The Irish in Southwest New South Wales 1816–1890* (Sydney, NSW: University of New South Wales), p. 64.

12. C. Chisholm (2004), *Female Immigration Considered: In a Brief Assessment of the Sydney Immigrants' Home* (Sydney, NSW: Sydney University Press), p. 35.

13. W.A. Bayley (1965), *History of Campbelltown, New South Wales*. 2nd ed. (Campbelltown, NSW: Campbelltown Municipal Council), pp. 68–114.

14. Ibid.

15. O. MacDonagh and W.F. Mandle (1986), *Ireland*

and Irish-Australia: Studies in Cultural and Political History (Dublin: Routledge, Kegan & Paul), p. 197.

16. "Obituary: The Rev. Father J.P. Roche" (1880), *Australian Town and Country Journal* (Sydney), Saturday, November 20, p. 13.

17. "Obituary: Joe Quinn" (1940), *The Sporting News*, Thursday, November 21, p. 8; Twister, "The Australian Baseballers—An Eastern Welcome" (1897), *The Argus* (Melbourne), Friday, July 23, p. 6.

18. J. McGill, K. Richardson, and V. Fowler (1995). *Campbelltown's Streets and Suburbs: How and Why They Got Their Names* (Campbelltown, NSW: Campbelltown & Airds Historical Society).

19. C. Liston (1988), *Campbelltown: The Bicentennial History* (Sydney: Allen & Unwin), p. 50.

20. Bayley.

21. J.F. Godl (1993), "The Ghost of Frederick Fisher," *Journal of the Royal Australian Historical Society* 27: pp. 6–7.

22. K. Gelder and R. Weaver (2007), *The Anthology of Colonial Australian Gothic Fiction* (Melbourne: Melbourne University Press), p. 11–31.

23. Bayley.

24. C. Pratten and R. Irving (1994), "Quandong: The Old Catholic School House Campbelltown. Conservation Plan," Heritage Conservation Consultants, Balmain, NSW [cited July 14, 2013]. Available from: http://www.westernsydneylibraries.nsw.gov.au/campbelltown/education.html

25. The Crown Lands Alienation Act and Crown Lands Occupation Act were intended to allow lower-income families to acquire land and simultaneously promote more intensive agriculture at the expense of large pastoral leases. The resulting grab for land by selectors and profiteers generated widespread discontent, with the 1883 Morris and Ranken inquiry reporting large-scale rorting (or "dummying") of the system: M. Clark and M. Cathcart (1993), *History of Australia* (Melbourne: Melbourne University Publishing), pp. 357–385.

26. The mining sector was one of the few exceptions: the 1862 Coalfields Regulation Act prohibited any person aged under 13 from being employed in a colliery: M. Brown (2010), *Australia's Worst Disasters* (Sydney: Hachette Australia), p. 12.

27. M. Murray (1993), "Children's Work in Rural New South Wales in the 1870s," *Journal of the Royal Australian Historical Society* 79 (3–4): pp. 226–244.

28. Ibid.

29. Victoria introduced legislation to provide free secular education in 1872; it was not until 1880 that Henry Parkes's Public Education Act committed New South Wales schools to free, compulsory and secular education: Clark and Cathcart, p. 333.

30. Pratten and Irving.

31. Bayley, pp. 68–114.

32. P. Begg (2005), *Mary Celeste: The Greatest Mystery of the Sea* (London: Pearson Educaton Limited).

33. "Stuart's Diary" (1863), *Sydney Morning Herald*, Tuesday, January 13, p. 3.

34. "Exploration Westward" (1872), *South Australian Register* (Adelaide, SA), Thursday, December 5, p. 3.

35. "Opening of the Great Southern Railway Extension" (1869), *Empire* (Sydney), Saturday, May 29, p. 3.

36. Bayley, pp. 68–114.

37. Ibid.

38. "Destructive Storm of Hail and Ice" (1861), *Sydney Morning Herald*, Saturday, December 14, p. 6.

39. "Distress in the Agricultural Districts" (1864), *Sydney Morning Herald*, NSW). Wednesday, March 9, p. 5.

40. A. Thornton, "Windmills Were an Important Part of Wheatgrowing in the Early Days of N.S.W." (1953), *The Land* (Sydney), Friday, April 17, p. 20.

41. C. Liston (1988), *Campbelltown: The Bicentennial History* (Sydney: Allen & Unwin), p. 56.

42. "The Public Health Act of England" (1849), *Sydney Morning Herald*, Friday, September 14, p. 2.

43. F. Walker, "Campbelltown: Forthcoming Centenary" (1920), *Sydney Morning Herald*, Tuesday, November 30, p. 8.

44. While the logs of these passenger ships do not record the names of steerage passengers, the year of the Quinns' arrival is recorded in the 1900 United States census: Joseph J. Quinn (image no. 00620): "United States Census: City of St. Louis, Missouri—Division of St. Louis City" (1900), United States Census Office [cited November 11, 2012]. Available from: www.familysearch.org.

45. H. Lawson (2004), *In the Days When the World Was Wide* (Whitefish, MT: Kessinger), p. 14.

46. J.P. Byrne, P. Coleman, and J. King (2008), *Ireland and the Americas: Culture, Politics, and History*, Vol. 2 (Santa Barbara, CA: ABC-CLIO), p. 451.

47. H. Arden (1981), "Iowa, America's Middle Earth," *National Geographic* 159 (6): pp. 603–629.

48. M. Mulrooney (2003), *Fleeing the Famine: North America and Irish Refugees, 1845–1851* (Santa Barbara, CA: Praeger), p. 124.

49. H.L. Calkin (1964), "The Irish in Iowa," *Palimpsest* 45 (2): p. 33–97.

50. Ibid.

51. Byrne, Coleman, and King, p.450.

52. V. Deloria and R.J. DeMallie (1999), *Documents of American Indian Diplomacy: Treaties, Agreements, and Conventions, 1775–1979* (Legal History of North America) (Tulsa: University of Oklahoma Press), p. 1210.

53. F.T. Oldt and P.J. Quigley (1911). *History of Dubuque County, Iowa; Being a General Survey of Dubuque County History, Including a History of the City of Dubuque and Special Account of Districts Throughout the County, from the Earliest Settlement to the Present Time* (Chicago: Goodspeed Historical Association), p. 19.

54. G.A. Ludvigson and J.A. Dockal (2011), "Lead and Zinc Mining in the Dubuque Area," Iowa Geological & Water Survey, Iowa Department of Natural Resources [cited March 8, 2013]. Available from: http://www.igsb.uiowa.edu/browse/leadzinc/leadzinc.htm.

55. Pryor & Co. (1877). *Pryor & Co's Dubuque City Directory 1877–8: Comprising an Alphabetical List of Citizens, a Classified Business Directory, Lists of City and County Officers, Churches, Schools, Societies, Streets and Wards* (Dubuque, IA: Pryor).

Chapter 3

1. Quinn's profession, and that of his father, was listed as miner in the 1880 United States Federal Census. Patrick was listed as a laborer in the Dubuque city directories between 1875 and 1880, but in the 1881 edition, his occupation was first shown as "miner": C.E. Marble (1881), *Marble's Dubuque City Directory* (Dubuque, IA: Chas. A. Marble).

2. D. Hudson, M. Bergman, and L. Horton (2009), *The Biographical Dictionary of Iowa* (Iowa City: University of Iowa Press), pp. 139–140.

3. G.A. Ludvigson and J.A. Dockal (2011), "Lead and Zinc Mining in the Dubuque Area," Iowa Geological & Water Survey, Iowa Department of Natural Resources [cited March 8, 2013]. Available from: http://www.igsb.uiowa.edu/browse/leadzinc/leadzinc.htm.

4. "Iowa Census Record Information Online" (2013), The Records Project [cited July 25, 2013]. Available from: http://recordsproject.com/census/iowa.asp.

5. G.M. Bakken (2011), *The Mining Law of 1872: Past, Politics, and Prospects* (Albuquerque: University of New Mexico Press), pp. 8–16.

6. The Upper Mississippi Valley includes part of Illinois, Iowa, southeast Minnesota and southwest Wisconsin. A. Williams (1885), *Mineral Resources of the United States 1883–84* (Washington: U.S. Geological Survey, Department of the Interior), pp. 474.

7. J. Emsley (2011), *Nature's Building Blocks: An A–Z Guide to the Elements* (Oxford, UK: Oxford University Press), p. 502.

8. "History of Zinc" (2013), International Zinc Association [cited March 30, 2013]. Available from: http://www.zinc.org/basics/history_of_zinc.

9. H.F. Bain (1906), *U.S. Geological Survey Bulletin: Zinc and Lead Deposits of the Upper Mississippi Valley* (Washington: U.S. Government Printing Office), p. 57.

10. "Zinc Production—From Ore to Metal" (2013), International Zinc Association [cited March 30, 2013]. Available from: http://www.zinc.org/basics/zinc_production.

11. C. Ervin Brown and J.W. Whitlow (1960), *Geology of Parts of the Upper Mississippi Valley Zinc-Lead District: Geology of the Dubuque South Quadrangle Iowa-Illinois*, Geological Survey Bulletin 1123-A (Washington: U.S. Government Printing Office), p. 55.

12. A. Atkins (2003), *Harvest of Grief: Grasshopper Plagues and Public Assistance in Minnesota, 1873–78* (Minneapolis: Minnesota Historical Society Press), p. 13.

13. M.J. Pfeifer (2006), *Rough Justice: Lynchings and American Society 1874–1947* (Champaign: University of Illinois Press).

14. F.T. Oldt and P.J. Quigley (1911), *History of Dubuque County, Iowa; Being a General Survey of Dubuque County History, Including a History of the City of Dubuque and Special Account of Districts Throughout the County, from the Earliest Settlement to the Present Time* (Chicago: Goodspeed Historical Association), p. 29.

15. "Obituary: Joe Quinn" (1940), *The Sporting News*, Thursday, November 21, p. 8.

16. Oldt and Quigley, p. 20.

17. Sphalerite ((ZnFe)S) is a mineral that is the chief ore of zinc. It consists largely of zinc sulfide in crystalline form but almost always contains variable quantities of iron: Emsley, p. 77.

18. Located on modern-day University Avenue in central Dubuque. J.L. Shaffer and J.T. Tigges (2000), *Dubuque, Iowa: Then and Now (Images of America Series)* (Chicago: Arcadia Publishing), p. 34.

19. J.F. Witt (2006), *The Accidental Republic: Crippled Workingmen, Destitute Widows, and the Remaking of American Law* (Boston: Harvard University Press), pp. 113–115.

20. G.E. Sherard (2007), "Mining Accidents Index: Iowa Mining Accidents 1893–1895 & 1906–1921," Denver Public Library Digital Collections [cited July 12, 2013]. Available from: http://digital.denverlibrary.org/cdm/ref/collection/p16079coll16/id/3342.

21. "Occupational Safety and Health Guidelines for Zinc Oxide" (2012), United States Department of Labor—Occupational Safety & Health Administration (OSHA) [cited March 11, 2013]. Available from: http://www.osha.gov/SLTC/healthguidelines/zincoxide/recognition.html.

22. While data from U.S. lead and zinc mining were collected in the 1870, 1880, and 1890 censuses, differences in the scope of enquiry and method of reporting the results render the 1902 census the most complete and accurate data for mining rates of pay: W.A. Steuart (1905), *Special Report: Mines and Quarries* Steuart (Washington: Department of Commerce and Labor, Bureau of the Census), pp. 445, 449.

23. S. Martelle (2007), *Blood Passion: The Ludlow Massacre and Class War in the American West* (New Brunswick, NJ: Rutgers University Press), p. 18.

24. Steuart, p. 450.

25. M. Swenson, "Analysis of Baseball," Poetry Foundation [cited March 10, 2013]. Available from: http://www.poetryfoundation.org/poem/177796.

26. Patrick Quinn Jr. (record no. 00049), "United States Census, 1880," FamilySearch.org: The Church of Jesus Christ of Latter-day Saints [cited March 10, 2013]. Available from: https://familysearch.org/pal:/MM9.1.1/MD2C-RC4.

27. "P.F. Quinn's Social Quadrille Band," *Encyclopedia Dubuque*, Carnegie-Stout Public Library [cited March 9, 2013]. Available from: http://www.encyclopediadubuque.org/index.php?title=P._F._QUINN%27S_SOCIAL_QUADRILLE_BAND.

28. Quinn was particularly fond of Irish songs, his favorite a ballad called "That Old Red Shawl My Mother Wore," which in later life he would often perform in public: "St. Louis Sayings" (1895), *The Sporting Life*, Saturday, December 28, p. 7.

29. D. Farrington, p. 9B.

30. J. Clark, p. 12.

31. Zoss and Bowman, p. 63.

32. Ibid., p. 65.

33. J. Charlton (1991), *The Baseball Chronology: The Complete History of the Most Important Events in the Game of Baseball* (New York: Macmillan), p. 83.

34. "The Dubuque 9 for 1880" (1880), *Dubuque Herald* (Dubuque, IA), Sunday, March 7, p. 4.

35. W. Goldstein (1989), *Playing for Keeps: A History of Early Baseball* (Ithaca, New York: Cornell University Press), p. 18.

36. A.H. Spink (1911; reprinted April 2000), *The National Game*, 2nd ed. (Carbondale: Southern Illinois University Press), p. xlii.

37. Ibid.

38. H. Seymour and D.S. Mills (1960), *Baseball: The Early Years* (New York: Oxford University Press), p. 102.

39. M. Benson (1989), *Ballparks of North America* (Jefferson, NC: McFarland), p. 138.

40. J.T. Tigges and J.L. Shaffer (2000), *Dubuque: The 19th Century* (Chicago: Arcadia Publishing), p. 6.

41. Spink, p. 152.

42. Spink, p. 294.

43. "Thought He Used Fake Baseball" (1912), *Washington Times*, Sunday, February 4, p. 14.

44. At Sullivan's invitation, the White Stockings arrived in Dubuque on July 29, 1879. Some 2,000 fans jammed the local park (despite vastly inflated ticket prices) to see the visitors win the first contest 8–1, the *Dubuque Herald* mourning a "comedy of errors" which handed the visitors four unearned runs in the sixth inning. Anson's men returned a week later, on August 4, although ticket sales were far slower for Radbourn's 1–0 triumph: B. Cooper (2005), "Dubuque—Chicago, 1879," *The National Pastime (Society for American Baseball Research)* 25: pp. 112–116.

45. Charlton, p. 101.

46. "Chicago Cubs (Team History & Encyclopedia)" (2013), Baseball-Reference.com. [cited July 24, 2013]. Available from: http://www.baseball-reference.com/teams/CHC/.

47. B. McKenna (2012), "Old Hoss Radbourn," Society for American Baseball Research (SABR) BioProject [cited December 1, 2012]. Available from: http://sabr.org/bioproj/person/83bf739e.

48. "Old Hoss Radbourn (Player Page)" (2013), Baseball-Reference.com [cited December 2, 2012]. Available from: http://www.baseball-reference.com/players/r/radboch01.shtml.
49. M. Davis (1953), *The Lore and Legends of Baseball* (New York: Lantern Press), p. 121.
50. Such accidents were not uncommon. In 1879, the same year as Hoss joined the Dubuque Rabbits, his brother William shot himself in the left side and in both hands while on a hunting trip: McKenna, "Old Hoss Radbourn."
51. "Old Hoss Radbourn (Player Page)," Baseball-Reference.com.
52. Spink, p. 365.
53. The pair shared a room at the college and later married two sisters from Dubuque: B. Cooper, "Dubuque—Chicago, 1879."
54. Von der Ahe's 1882 Browns were the forerunners of today's St. Louis Cardinals, joining the National League in 1892; the team was briefly known as the Perfectos in 1899 before assuming the modern Cardinals mantle in 1900: J.D. Cash (2002), *Before They Were Cardinals—Major League Baseball in Nineteenth-Century St. Louis* (St. Louis: University of Missouri Press).
55. Spink, p. 176.
56. Spink, p. 178.
57. "St. Louis Cardinals (Team History & Encyclopedia)" (2013), Baseball-Reference.com [cited July 24, 2013]. Available from: http://www.baseball-reference.com/teams/STL/.
58. G.W. Axelson, G. Mitchem, and M. McGee (2003), *Commy: The Life Story of Charles A. Comiskey* (Jefferson, NC: McFarland).
59. "The Dubuque 9 for 1880," p. 4.
60. D. Pajot (2009), *The Rise of Milwaukee Baseball: The Cream City from Midwestern Outpost to the Major Leagues, 1859–1901* (Jefferson, NC: McFarland), p. 106.
61. It was 1888 before Dubuque rejoined professional baseball in the Central Interstate League: "1884 St. Louis Maroons (Batting, Pitching & Fielding Statistics)" (2013), Baseball-Reference.com [cited August 7, 2013]. Available from: http://www.baseball-reference.com/teams/SLM/1884.shtml.
62. D. Farrington, p. 9B.
63. Spink, p. 394.
64. R. Smith (1970), *Baseball* (New York: Simon & Schuster), p. 68.
65. D. Nemec (2006), *The Great Encyclopedia of Nineteenth-Century Major League Baseball* (Tuscaloosa: University of Alabama Press), p. 220.
66. Spink, p. 11
67. Goldstein, p. 98.
68. Spink, p. 14.
69. Goldstein, p. 149.
70. D.M. Pearson (1993) *Baseball in 1889: Players Vs. Owners* (Bowling Green, OH: Bowling Green State University Popular Press), p. 92.
71. Seymour and Mills, p. 112.
72. Blacklist: expulsion from a club or league without pay: Seymour and Mills, p. 130.
73. Nemec, p. 178.
74. Spink, p. 26.
75. Seymour and Mills, p. 149.
76. "From St. Louis" (1884), *The Sporting Life*, Wednesday, January 9.
77. W.A. Borst (1980), *Baseball Through a Knothole: A St. Louis History* (St. Louis: Krank Press), p. 34.
78. Nemec, p. 284.
79. J.S. Gross (1986), "Wilmington Quicksteps: Glory to Oblivion," Baseball Research Journal. Society for American Baseball Research [cited July 4, 2013]. Available from: http://research.sabr.org/journals/wilmington-quicksteps-glory-to-oblivion.
80. Mullane had pitched 35 winning games for the 1883 St. Louis Browns to 35 victories before jumping to the crosstown St. Louis Union Association outfit for 1884, despite the Browns' retaining the rights to his services under the reserve clause. Threatened with blacklisting, Mullane jumped back, but was then sold to the expansion Toledo Blue Stockings as punishment. The Browns did attempt to reclaim Mullane after the 1884 season, but before the Browns could re-sign him, Mullane signed with Cincinnati. B. James and R. Neyer (2004), *The Neyer/James Guide to Pitchers: An Historical Compendium of Pitching, Pitchers, and Pitches* (New York: Simon & Schuster), p. 65.
81. Spink, p. 367.
82. Goldstein, p. 127.
83. "Baseball News" (1883), *St. Louis Globe-Democrat*, Sunday, December 30, p. 6.
84. Farrington, p. 9B.
85. Williams, pp. 478–480.
86. "Notes and Comments," (1885), *The Sporting Life*, Wednesday, April 22, p. 7.

Chapter 4

1. The blaze destroyed almost every building within a two-square-mile area fronting the Levee, and caused explosions which left at least 4 people dead and hundreds homeless. At least 23 steamboats were completely destroyed, a loss of stock and cargo estimated at almost $520,000. From: "Tremendous Conflagration!! In St. Louis, 23 Steamboats Burned! Several Squares in Ashes, Loss of Life!!" (1848), *Glasgow Weekly Times* (Glasgow, MO), Thursday, May 24, p. 2.
2. "Tonnage for Selected U.S. Ports in 2008" (2008), U.S. Army Corps of Engineers Navigation Data Center, Waterborne Commerce Statistics Center, New Orleans, LA [cited July 28, 2013]. Available from: http://www.navigationdatacenter.us/wcsc/portton08.htm.
3. M. Twain (1968), *Life on the Mississippi* (New York: Dodd Mead), p. 73.
4. "American Fact Finder" (2013), United States Census Bureau—U.S. Department of Commerce, [cited July 28, 2013]. Available from: http://factfinder2.census.gov/faces/nav/jsf/pages/index.xhtml.
5. C. van Ravensway (1991), *Saint Louis: An Informal History of the City and Its People, 1764–1865* (St. Louis: Missouri History Museum), p. 356.
6. Spink, p. 38.
7. Spink, p. 361.
8. Spink, p. 38.
9. Cash, p. 11.
10. Cash, p. 44.
11. Spink, p. 47.
12. "St. Louis Cardinals (Team History & Encyclopedia)" (2013), Baseball-Reference.com [cited July 24, 2013]. Available from: http://www.baseball-reference.com/teams/STL/.
13. "The Base-Ball Union: Work of the Philadelphia Convention—Players' Engagements" (1883), *New York Times*, Thursday, December 20, p. 5.
14. B. James (2010), *The New Bill James Historical Baseball Abstract* (New York: Simon & Schuster), p. 32.
15. Cash, p. 78.
16. "Restraining Order Granted" (1884), *Sedalia Weekly Bazoo* (Sedalia, MO), Tuesday, May 13, p. 1.

17. Spink, p. xiv.
18. Farrington, p. 9B.
19. J.T. Hetrick (1999), *Chris Von Der Ahe and the St. Louis Browns* (Lanham, MD: Scarecrow), p. 28.
20. M. Eisenbath and S. Musial (1999), *The Cardinals Encyclopedia* (Philadelphia: Temple University Press), p. 419
21. M. Benson (1989), *Ballparks of North America* (Jefferson, NC: McFarland), p. 349.
22. J.M. Thomas (2012), "Union Base Ball Park (St. Louis)," Society for American Baseball Research (SABR) BioProject [cited July 28, 2013]. Available from: http://sabr.org/bioproj/park/d9c10c59.
23. J.M. Thomas (2012), "Henry V. Lucas," Society for American Baseball Research (SABR) BioProject [cited June 13, 2012]. Available from: http://sabr.org/bioproj/person/20cd29bd.
24. "1884 St. Louis Maroons (Batting, Pitching & Fielding Statistics)" (2013), Baseball-Reference.com [cited August 7, 2013]. Available from: http://www.baseball-reference.com/teams/SLM/1884.shtml.
25. Charlton, p. 54.
26. "Rum-Crazed Frank Larkin" (1883), *The Sun* (New York), Wednesday, April 25, p. 1.
27. Charlton, p. 55.
28. "Washington Whispers" (1890), *The Sporting Life*, Wednesday, September 6, p. 13.
29. "Base Ball" (1884), *The Sporting Life*, Wednesday, September 3, p. 4.
30. "Iowa Items" (1884), *Omaha Daily Bee*, Tuesday, April 15, p. 7.
31. Seymour and Mills, p. 91.
32. Taylor, ironically, was another product of the Dubuque baseball proving grounds— he played for the club in its inaugural year of 1879 alongside Comiskey and Radbourn: "Billy Taylor (Minor League Player Page)" (2013), Baseball-Reference.com [cited July 24, 2013]. Available from: http://www.baseball-reference.com/minors/player.cgi?id=taylor001bil.
33. "Just Think of It!" (1884), *St. Louis Republican*, Monday, April 21, p. 3.
34. "Sporting: The Altoonas Again Defeated by Our Union Club" (1884), *St. Louis Republican*, Sunday, April 27, p. 3.
35. "1884 St. Louis Maroons (Schedule, Box Scores and Splits)" (2013), Baseball-Reference.com [cited July 30, 2013]. Available from: http://www.baseball-reference.com/teams/SLM/1884-schedule-scores.shtml.
36. "The King Batters" (1884), *St. Louis Republican*, Monday, May 5, p. 6.
37. "Altoona Mountain City (Team History & Encyclopedia)" (2013), Baseball-Reference.com [cited July 28, 2013]. Available from: http://www.baseball-reference.com/teams/ALT/.
38. D. Fischer, J. Buckley, and J. Gigliotti (2007), *Obsessed with...Baseball: Test Your Knowledge of America's Pastime* (San Francisco: Chronicle Books), p. 140.
39. Slang term for being relegated to the bench.
40. "St. Louis 20, Baltimore 6" (1884), *Baltimore American*, Friday, May 16, p. 3.
41. Nemec, p. 935.
42. Charlton, p. 54.
43. "Yearly League Leaders and Records for Home Runs" (2013), Baseball-Reference.com [cited July 28, 2013]. Available from: http://www.baseball-reference.com/leaders/HR_leagues.shtml.
44. Spink, p. 26.
45. P. Dickson (2011), *The Dickson Baseball Dictionary*, 3rd ed. (New York: W.W. Norton), p. 812.

46. M. Motto (2000), personal communication, "Re: Joe Quinn" (e-mail) To: R. Nicholls, Wednesday, May 31.
47. By the 1940s, the first reports of oral cancer among tobacco chewers emerged, and many players switched to cigarettes or, in the 1970s, "smokeless tobacco." R.N. Golden (2010), *The Truth About Smoking* (New York: Infobase Publishing), p. 165.
48. "Base Ball Briefs" (1899), *St. Paul Globe*, Sunday, September 17, p. 10.
49. "The King Batters,", p. 6; "St. Louis Unions 16; Bostons, 4" (1884), *Boston Globe*, Friday, May 23, p. 8.
50. Spink, p. 198.
51. Ibid.
52. Ibid.
53. Ibid., p. 367.
54. "The First Defeat" (1884), *St. Louis Republican*, Sunday, May 25, p. 3.
55. "Close Games All Around" (1884), *Boston Globe* (supplement), Friday, July 18, p. 1.
56. "1884 St. Louis Maroons (Schedule, Box Scores and Splits)" (2013), Baseball-Reference.com [cited July 30, 2013]. Available from: http://www.baseball-reference.com/teams/SLM/1884-schedule-scores.shtml.
57. "Base Ball" (1884), *St. Louis Globe-Democrat*, Monday, June 23, p. 4.
58. In 1884, Sullivan managed the St. Louis team to 35 wins and just 4 losses before Lucas dispatched him to take on the struggling Kansas City outfit, Fred Dunlap taking over control of the St. Louis nine. However, even the genial Irishman couldn't drag the Cowboys beyond a paltry 13–46 return, and they would finish the season in eleventh place, winning just 16 of their 79 games: Cash, p. 81.
59. "Base Ball" (1884), *St. Louis Globe-Democrat*, Monday, June 23, p. 4.
60. Benson, p. 22.
61. "Many Games of Ball" (1884), *Baltimore American*, Saturday, July 5, p. 4.
62. "Standings and Games on Sunday, October 19, 1884" (2013), Baseball-Reference.com [cited August 15, 2013]. Available from: http://www.baseball-reference.com/games/standings.cgi?date=1884-10-19.
63. "Billy Taylor (Player Page)" (2013), Baseball-Reference.com [cited August 15, 2013]. Available from: http://www.baseball-reference.com/players/t/taylobi01.shtml.
64. "1884 St. Louis Maroons (Batting, Pitching & Fielding Statistics)" (2013), Baseball-Reference.com. [cited August 7, 2013]. Available from: http://www.baseball-reference.com/teams/SLM/1884.shtml.
65. D. Hubbard and R.A. Johnson (2008). *The Heavenly Twins of Boston Baseball: A Dual Biography of Hugh Duffy and Tommy McCarthy* (Jefferson, NC: McFarland), p. 25.
66. "Close Games All Around," p. 1.
67. C. Carter (1983), *The Sporting News Official Baseball Record Book* (St. Louis, MO: The Sporting News), p. 278.
68. "Obituary: Joe Quinn."
69. L. Spatz (2012), *Historical Dictionary of Baseball* (Lanham, MD: Scarecrow Press), p. 332.
70. A.J. Reach (1987), *Spalding Baseball Guide and Official League Book for 1885: A Complete Hand Book of the National Game of Base Ball* (St. Louis, MO: Horton), p. 30.
71. Their win-loss record at August 5 was 57–9, with Baltimore second and Cincinnati third, 12 wins behind: "Standings and Games on Tuesday, August 5, 1884" (2013), Baseball-Reference.com [cited August 15, 2013]. Available from: http://www.baseball-reference.com/games/standings.cgi?date=1884-08-05.

72. A.S. John (2006), *Made to Be Broken: The 50 Greatest Records and Streaks in Sports* (Chicago: Triumph Books), p. 106.
73. Charlton, p. 56.
74. McKenna, "Old Hoss Radbourn."
75. "St. Louis 15, Philadelphia 1" (1884), *Philadelphia Record*, Friday, June 27, p. 4.
76. "Base Ball" (1884), *The Sporting Life*, Wednesday, September 3, p. 4.
77. "Many Games of Ball," p. 4.
78. F. Vaccaro (2012), "Hugh Daily," SABR Baseball Biography Project, Society for American Baseball Research [cited August 15, 2013]. Available from: http://sabr.org/bioproj/person/8d8c99e4.
79. "Billy Taylor (Player Page)" (2013), Baseball-Reference.com [cited August 15, 2013]. Available from: http://www.baseball-reference.com/players/t/taylobi01.shtml.
80. Zoss and Bowman, p. 292.
81. "Record of the Game" (1884), *St. Louis Globe-Democrat*, Friday, August 22, p. 6.
82. "The Maroons Downed" (1884), *St. Louis Republican*, Saturday, October 25, p. 4.
83. "The Plucky Unions Get Away with the Dandy Team from St. Louis" (1884), *Boston Globe*, Wednesday, September 24, p. 4.
84. Spink, p. 28.
85. "Shut Out" (1884), *St. Louis Republican*, Monday, October 20, p. 6.
86. "Sporting: The Louisville Team Given a Fearful Drubbing at Union Park" (1884), *St. Louis Republican*, Sunday, October 26, p. 14.
87. Dunlap led the Union in the following offensive categories: Batting average (.412), On-Base Percentage (.448), Slugging Percentage (.621), Runs Scored (160), Hits (185), Total Bases (279), Home Runs (13), Runs Created (125), Extra Base Hits (60), Times on Base (214), Offensive Winning Percentage (.918), At-Bats per Home Run (34.5): "1884 Union Association Batting Leaders" (2013), Baseball-Reference.com [cited July 30, 2013]. Available from: http://www.baseball-reference.com/leagues/UA/1884-batting-leaders.shtml. Defensive categories: Total Assists (302), Putouts as 2B (341), Assists as 2B (300), Double Plays as 2B (54), Range factor/game as 2B (6.41), Fielding Percentage as 2B (.926): "1884 Union Association Fielding Leaders" (2013), Baseball-Reference.com [cited July 30, 2013]. Available from: http://www.baseball-reference.com/leagues/UA/1884-fielding-leaders.shtml.
88. "1884 Union Association Fielding Leaders" (2013), Baseball-Reference.com [cited July 30, 2013]. Available from: http://www.baseball-reference.com/leagues/UA/1884-fielding-leaders.shtml.
89. "1884 Union Association Pitching Leaders" (2013), Baseball-Reference.com [cited July 30, 2013]. Available from: http://www.baseball-reference.com/leagues/UA/1884-pitching-leaders.shtml.
90. Calculated retrospectively as Earned Run Average, which was not adopted as an official baseball statistic until 1911. "1884 Union Association Pitching Leaders" (2013), Baseball-Reference.com [cited July 30, 2013]. Available from: http://www.baseball-reference.com/leagues/UA/1884-pitching-leaders.shtml.
91. "News of the Players" (1884), *The Sporting Life*, Wednesday, November 19, p. 3.
92. "Joe Quinn (Player Page)" (2013), Baseball-Reference.com [cited January 9, 2013]. Available from: http://www.baseball-reference.com/players/q/quinnjo02.shtml.
93. Joseph Quinn in household of Patrick Quinn (image no. 00019). "Iowa State Census" (1885), FamilySearch.org: The Church of Jesus Christ of Latter-day Saints [cited November 11, 2012]. Available from: http://familysearch.org.

Chapter 5

1. "A Startling Story: Mr. Lucas to Desert Union Association" (1884), *The Sporting Life*, Wednesday, December 17, p. 1.
2. "Association Meets" (1884), *The Sporting Life*, Wednesday, October 2, p. 2.
3. "Standings and Games on Monday, September 14, 1885" (2013), Baseball-Reference.com [cited August 3, 2013]. Available from: http://www.baseball-reference.com/games/standings.cgi?date=1885-09-14.
4. "Base Ball" (1884), *The Sporting Life*, Wednesday, December 3, p. 2.
5. H. Turkin and S.C. Thompson (1979), *The Official Encyclopedia of Baseball* (New York: A.S. Barnes), pp. 16–23.
6. D.Q. Voigt (2010), *American Baseball: From Gentleman's Sport to the Commissioner System* (University Park: Pennsylvania State University Press), p. 136.
7. Cash, p. 100.
8. Spink, p. 26.
9. James, pp. 24–31.
10. "Base Ball" (1885), *The Sporting Life*, Wednesday, April 22, p. 7.
11. Seymour and Mills, p. 149.
12. J.N. Primm (1998), *Lion of the Valley: St. Louis, Missouri, 1764–1980* (St. Louis: Missouri Historical Society Press), p. 192.
13. "At Work" (1885), *The Sporting Life*, Wednesday, April 15, p. 4.
14. "Active Work at St. Louis" (1885), *The Sporting Life*, Wednesday, April 22, p. 4.
15. "Lucas Triumphant—The League Surrenders to the Millionaire" (1885), *The Sporting Life*, Wednesday, April 22, p. 3.
16. D. Schlossberg (1983), *The Baseball Catalog* (Middle Village, NY: Jonathan David Publishers), p. 10.
17. "At Work" (1885), *The Sporting Life*, Wednesday, April 15, p. 4.
18. "Active Work at St. Louis" (1885), *The Sporting Life*, Wednesday, April 22, p. 4.
19. "Victory for Lucas" (1885), *Boston Globe*, Tuesday, May 12, p. 5.
20. "Games Played May 11" (1885), *The Sporting Life*, Wednesday, May 20, p. 4.
21. "Lucas Triumphant—The League Surrenders to the Millionaire" (1885), *The Sporting Life*, Wednesday April 22, p. 3.
22. "The National League—The Record" (1885), *The Sporting Life*, Wednesday, June 3, p. 3.
23. Spink, pp. 395–404.
24. "The National League—The Record," p. 3.
25. Benson, p. 350.
26. "Sporting Matters—St. Louis Again Defeated by the Chicago Team" (1885), *Chicago Tribune*, Wednesday, June 10, p. 6.
27. D.L. Fleitz (2005), *Cap Anson: The Grand Old Man of Baseball* (Jefferson, NC: McFarland), p. 310.
28. H. Zinn (2003), *A People's History of the United States: 1492–Present* (New York: HarperCollins), pp. 370–390.
29. C. Gunderson (2004), *The Dred Scott Decision* (Edina, MN: Abdo).

30. Zoss and Bowman, pp. 130–135.
31. A. Rust (1992), *Get That Nigger Off the Field: An Oral History of Black Ballplayers from the Negro Leagues to the Present* (Brooklyn: Book Mail Services), p. 14.
32. B. Dabscheck (1995), "Australian Baseballers Form a Team of Their Own," *Sporting Traditions* 12 (1): pp. 61–101.
33. "Games Played June 20" (1885), *The Sporting Life*, Wednesday, June 24, p. 3.
34. "Lewis Expelled by Lucas" (1885), *Boston Globe*, Saturday, June 20, p. 8.
35. "From the Mound City" (1885), *The Sporting Life*, Wednesday, July 1, p. 5.
36. Seymour and Mills, p. 329.
37. Zoss and Bowman, p. 197.
38. "Games Played July 10" (1885), *The Sporting Life*, Wednesday, July 15, p. 2.
39. Hetrick, p. 42.
40. "Games Played July 30/July 31" (1885), *The Sporting Life*, Wednesday, August 2, p. 2.
41. "Base Ball" (1884), *The Sporting Life*, Wednesday, August 26, p. 5.
42. "1885 St. Louis Maroons (Schedule, Box Scores and Splits)" (2013), Baseball-Reference.com [cited August 19, 2013]. Available from: http://www.baseball-reference.com/teams/SLM/1885-schedule-scores.shtml.
43. 'Standings and Games on Monday, September 14, 1885" (2013), Baseball-Reference.com [cited August 3, 2013]. Available from: http://www.baseball-reference.com/games/standings.cgi?date=1885-09-14.
44. Spink, p. 96.
45. Ibid., p.271.
46. "Fred Dunlap (Player Page)" (2013), Baseball-Reference.com [cited August 15, 2013]. Available from: http://www.baseball-reference.com/players/d/dunlafr01.shtml.
47. Spink, p. 170.
48. D. Nemec and S. Flatow (2008). *This Day in Baseball: A Day-by-Day Record of the Events That Shaped the Game* (Lanham, MD: Taylor Trade), p. 157.
49. "A Complete Change of Heart" (1885), *The Sporting Life*, Wednesday, October 14, p. 1.
50. "Egyptian Healy (Player Page)" (2013), Baseball-Reference.com [cited August 3, 2013]. Available from: http://www.baseball-reference.com/players/h/healyjo01.shtml.
51. "Sporting Affairs—Chicago Beaten by St. Louis in a Ridiculously Easy Manner," (1885), *Chicago Tribune*, Thursday, September 10, p. 6.
52. "From the Mound City: The St. Louis Club's New Manager—Reasons for the Change, Etc." (1885), *The Sporting Life*, Wednesday, September 16, p. 4.
53. "Joe Quinn (Player Page)" (2013), Baseball-Reference.com [cited January 9, 2013]. Available from: http://www.baseball-reference.com/players/q/quinnjo02.shtml.
54. "From the Mound City: The St. Louis Club's New Manager," p. 4.
55. "1885 National League Pitching Leaders" (2013), Baseball-Reference.com [cited July 30, 2013]. Available from: http://www.baseball-reference.com/leagues/NL/1885-pitching-leaders.shtml.
56. M. Davis (1953), *The Lore and Legends of Baseball* (New York: Lantern Press), p. 79.
57. C.J. Gibson and E. Lennon (1999). "Historical Census Statistics on the Foreign-Born Population of the United States: 1850–1990," U.S. Bureau of the Census [cited August 19, 2013]. Available from: http://www.census.gov/population/www/documentation/twps0029/twps0029.html.

58. D.A. Lossos (2004), *Irish St. Louis* (Chicago: Arcadia Publishing), p. 27.
59. E. Diamond (1989), "Kerry Patch: Irish Immigrant Life in St. Louis," *Gateway Heritage* (Fall 1989): pp. 23–30.
60. Lossos, p. 27.
61. J.M. McGuire, "Tales of the Kerry Patch" (1986), *St. Louis Post-Dispatch*, Monday, March 17, p. 6D.
62. Diamond, pp. 23–30.
63. J.M. O'Toole (1981), "*My God, What a Life!*" (St. Louis: O'Toole), p. 13.
64. Spink, p. 116.
65. Ibid.
66. D.B. Gould (1886), *Gould's St. Louis Directory for 1885 (for the Year Ending April 1st, 1886)* (St. Louis, MO: Gould Directory), p. 116.
67. "Playing Great Ball" (1890), *Pittsburg Dispatch*, Monday, September 8, p. 6.
68. Seymour and Mills, pp. 332–333.
69. "Funeral Homes/Parlours/Chapels/Undertakers" (2002), St. Louis Public Library [cited August 20, 2013]. Available from: http://www.slpl.lib.mo.us/libsrc/funeral.htm.
70. Farrington, p. 9B.
71. *Encyclopædia Britannica* (1998), "Embalming" (Chicago: Encyclopædia Britannica), p. 468.
72. L. Ajmani (2009), *Embalming: Principles and Legal Aspects* (New Delhi: Jaypee Brothers, Medical Publishers), p. 32.
73. R. Mayer (2011), *Embalming: History, Theory, and Practice*, 5th ed. (New York: McGraw-Hill Professional), p. 492.
74. R.N. Ratnaike (2003), "Acute and Chronic Arsenic Toxicity," *Postgraduate Medical Journal* 79 (933): pp. 391–396.
75. "Forty Years Ago..." (1884), *Omaha Daily Bee*, Tuesday, April 15, p. 7.
76. "Base Ball" (1885), *Daily Evening Bulletin* (Maysville, KY), Friday, October 30, p. 4.
77. J.L. Konefes and M.K. McGee, "Old Cemeteries, Arsenic, and Health Safety," Embalming [cited December 1, 1999]. Available from: http://waterindustry.org/arsenic-3.htm.
78. From the Twelfth United States census, 1900: City of St. Louis: 20th Ward: McGrath family. "United States Census: City of St. Louis, Missouri—Division of St. Louis City, 1900" (2012). United States Census Office [cited November 11, 2012]. Available from: www.familysearch.org.
79. Spink, p. lxiii.
80. After 126 years in print, evolving from its early newspaper format through to a glossy magazine, *The Sporting News* became a digital publication at the end of December 2012. The St. Louis office was closed and operations relocated to Charlotte, NC. D. Gould (2012), "History Shared, History Removed: *The Sporting News* Roots in St. Louis," *St. Louis Post-Dispatch* [cited August 20, 2013]. Available from: http://bit.ly/S4MzOs.
81. Spink, p. lxiii.
82. Farrington, p. 9B.
83. Schmelz remains the only manager in major league history to wear a full beard. Davis, p. 240.
84. "Base Ball" (1885), *Daily Evening Bulletin* (Maysville, KY), Friday, October 30, p. 4.
85. "The Opening Championship Games, April 29" (1886), *The Sporting Life*, Wednesday, May 5, p. 4.
86. "History of Zinc" (2013), International Zinc Association [cited March 30, 2013]. Available from: http://www.zinc.org/basics/history_of_zinc.
87. Seymour and Mills, p. 204.
88. Turkin and Thompson, p. 108.

89. Nemec, p. 378.
90. Jerry Denny (Player Page)." (2013). Baseball-Reference.com. [cited August 15, 2013]. Available from: http://www.baseball-reference.com/players/d/dennyje01.shtml.
91. "Alex Mckinnon (Player Page)" (2013), Baseball-Reference.com [cited August 15, 2013]. Available from: http://www.baseball-reference.com/players/m/mckinal01.shtml.
92. "Jack Glasscock (Player Page)" (2013), Baseball-Reference.com [cited August 15, 2013]. Available from: http://www.baseball-reference.com/players/g/glassja01.shtml.
93. "1886 St. Louis Maroons (Batting, Pitching & Fielding Statistics)" (2013), Baseball-Reference.com [cited August 7, 2013]. Available from: http://www.baseball-reference.com/teams/SLM/1886.shtml.
94. S. Gietschier, S. and *Sporting News* (2005), *Complete Baseball Record Book, 2005 Edition* (St. Louis: The Sporting News), p. 79.
95. "How a Georgia Pig Won the Pennant for Chicago in 1886" (1911), *El Paso Herald*, Saturday, February 4, p.22.
96. "What They Have Done" (1886), *The Sporting Life*, Wednesday, July 7, p. 2.
97. Gietschier, p. 21.
98. "Games Played Monday August 16" (1886), *The Sporting Life*, Wednesday, August 25, p. 2.
99. M. Eisenbath and S. Musial (1999), *The Cardinals Encyclopedia* (Philadelphia: Temple University Press), p. 12.
100. Charlton, p. 64.
101. Spink, p. 26.
102. "Standings and Games on Saturday, October 9, 1886" (2013), Baseball-Reference.com [cited August 20, 2013]. Available from: http://www.baseball-reference.com/games/standings.cgi?date=1886-10-09.
103. "How a Georgia Pig Won the Pennant," p. 22.
104. "1886 Chicago White Stockings (Batting, Pitching & Fielding Statistics)" (2013). Baseball-Reference.com [cited August 20, 2013]. Available from: http://www.baseball-reference.com/teams/CHC/1886.shtml.
105. "Baseball Stories by Joe Quinn; Outlook for the Cardinals in 1906" (1905), *St. Louis Republican*, Sunday, December 10, p. 6.
106. D. Stevens (1998), *Baseball's Radical for All Seasons: A Biography of John Montgomery Ward* (Lanham, MD: Scarecrow Press), p. 154.
107. Bats with one flat side were permitted in major league baseball between 1885 and 1893. Such bats were primarily useful in bunting, although the original intent of the design was to decrease the incidence of foul tips. P. Dickson (2011), *The Dickson Baseball Dictionary*, 3rd ed. (New York: W.W. Norton), p. 330.
108. B. Hill (2000), *Crack of the Bat: The Louisville Slugger Story* (Champaign, IL: Sports Publishing), p. 8.
109. "From the Mound City" (1886), *The Sporting Life*, Wednesday, March 24, p. 8.
110. "Joe Quinn in the Outfield" (1888), *The Sporting News*, Thursday, April 12, p. 5.
111. D.A. Kistemaker, H. Faber, and P.J. Beek (2009), "Catching Fly Balls: A Simulation Study of the Chapman Strategy," *Human Movement Science* 28 (2): pp. 236–249.
112. "Joe Quinn (Player Page)" (2013), Baseball-Reference.com [cited January 9, 2013]. Available from: http://www.baseball-reference.com/players/q/quinnjo02.shtml.
113. Seymour and Mills, p. 90.
114. B.G. Rader (2008), *Baseball: A History of America's Game*, 3rd ed. (Urbana: University of Illinois Press), p. 66.
115. Pearson, p. 68.
116. "Late News: Wholesale Engagement of Players" (1886), *The Sporting Life*, Wednesday, November 3, p. 1.
117. "Wray's Column: With 4 Champions" (1940), *St. Louis Post-Dispatch*, Wednesday, November 13, p. 8.
118. Thomas, "Henry V. Lucas."
119. "Successful Ball Players: Some of the Men Who Have Laid up Snug Fortunes" (1888), *St. Paul Daily Globe*, Sunday, December 16, p. 6.
120. "Never Broke" (1895), *The Sporting Life*, Wednesday, August 3, p. 6.
121. Seymour and Mills, p. 332.
122. "St. Louis Screed" (1886), *The Sporting Life*, Wednesday, October 27, p. 2.
123. "From St. Louis" (1886), *The Sporting Life*, Wednesday, October 6, p. 4.
124. Joe probably picked up the nickname from the McGrath family, who, according to Quinn's granddaughter Mary Catherine Butler, first bestowed it upon their eldest daughter: M. Motto (2000), Personal communication. "Re: Joe Quinn" [e-mail]." To: R. Nicholls, Wednesday, May 31.
125. D.B. Gould (1888), *Gould's St. Louis Directory for 1887 (for the Year Ending April 1st, 1888)* (St. Louis, MO: Gould Directory).

Chapter 6

1. Charlton, p. 67.
2. J. Saccoman (2012), "John Brush," Society for American Baseball Research (SABR) BioProject [cited August 21, 2013]. Available from: http://sabr.org/bioproj/person/a46ef165.
3. "Doom of Baseball: How It Is Being Sounded by the Mismanagement of Puffed up Managers" (1899), *St. Paul Globe*, Sunday, May 14, p. 10.
4. "Baseball Rule Change Timeline" (2011), Baseball Almanac [cited August 20, 2013]. Available from: http://www.baseball-almanac.com/rulechng.shtml.
5. "Baseball Stories by Joe Quinn," p. 6.
6. D.L. Fleitz (2009), *The Irish in Baseball: An Early History* (Jefferson, NC: McFarland), pp. 20–21.
7. S.R. Fox (1998), *Big Leagues: Professional Baseball, Football, and Basketball in National Memory* (Lincoln: University of Nebraska Press), p. 163.
8. "Jerry Denny (Player Page)" (2013), Baseball-Reference.com [cited August 15, 2013]. Available from: http://www.baseball-reference.com/players/d/dennyje01.shtml.
9. Charlton, p. 67.
10. H.W. Rosenberg (2004), *Cap Anson 2: The Theatrical and Kingly Mike Kelly: U.S. Team Sport's First Media Sensation and Baseball's Original Casey at the Bat* (Arlington, VA: Tile Books), pp. 109–122.
11. "Alex Mckinnon (Player Page)" (2013), Baseball-Reference.com [cited August 15, 2013]. Available from: http://www.baseball-reference.com/players/m/mckinal01.shtml.
12. "1887 Detroit Wolverines (Batting, Pitching & Fielding Statistics)" (2013), Baseball-Reference.com [cited August 7, 2013]. Available from: http://www.baseball-reference.com/teams/DTN/1887.shtml.
13. "Jack Glasscock (Player Page)" (2013), Baseball-Reference.com [cited August 15, 2013]. Available from: http://www.baseball-reference.com/players/g/glassja01.shtml.
14. Spink, p. 250.
15. "1887 St. Louis Browns (Schedule, Box Scores and Splits)" (2013), Baseball-Reference.com [cited August 19,

2013]. Available from: http://www.baseball-reference.com/teams/STL/1887-schedule-scores.shtml.
16. Charlton, pp. 67–73.
17. Ibid., p. 68.
18. "Base Ball Uniforms" (1887), *The Sun* (New York), Sunday, June 12, p.10.
19. "The Outlook for the Indianapolis Club" (1887), *The Sun* (New York), Sunday, June 12, p. 10.
20. D. Nemec (1994), *The Beer and Whiskey League: The Illustrated History of the American Association—Baseball's Renegade Major League* (New York: Lyons and Burford), p. 85.
21. "Rotunda Riff-Raff: Some Men Who Were Visitors in St. Paul Yesterday" (1887), *St. Paul Daily Globe*, Friday, May 13, p. 4.
22. Ibid.
23. "Joe Quinn" (1887), *Indianapolis Herald*, Wednesday, June 15, p. 3.
24. "The World of Sports" (1887), *Duluth Weekly Tribune* (Duluth, MN), June 3.
25. W. Akin, "Jack Glasscock," SABR Baseball Biography Project [cited April 3, 2013]. Available from: http://sabr.org/bioproj/person/0bcddad0.
26. "The Outlook for the Indianapolis Club" (1887), *The Sun* (New York), Sunday, June 12, p. 10.
27. "Indianapolis: The Causes of Ill Success on the Recent Trip—Comment on the Team Collectively and Individually" (1887), *The Sporting Life*, Wednesday, September 14, p. 1.
28. "Joe Quinn," *Indianapolis Herald*, p. 3.
29. "The World of Sports," *Duluth Weekly Tribune*, June 3.
30. Ibid.
31. "The Outlook for the Indianapolis Club," *The Sun*, p. 10; "Joe Quinn," *Indianapolis Herald*, p. 3.
32. *State & County Quickfacts: Duluth (City)*, *Minnesota* (2013), United States Census Bureau—U.S. Department of Commerce [cited April 3, 2013]. Available from: http://quickfacts.census.gov/qfd/states/27/2717000.html. pages.
33. "Injury to Stock" (1887), *St. Paul Daily Globe*, Friday, February 4, p. 4.
34. A. Bush (2012), "Duluth's First Pro Baseball Team: 1886 Champions," Zenith City: celebrating historic Duluth, western Lake Superior, and Minnesota's arrowhead [cited March 31, 2013]. Available from: http://zenithcity.com/duluths-first-pro-baseball-team-1886-champions/.
35. Ibid.
36. "Standings and Games on Saturday, October 9, 1886" (2013), Baseball-Reference.com [cited August 20, 2013]. Available from: http://www.baseball-reference.com/games/standings.cgi?date=1886-10-09.
37. B. McKenna, "Mark Baldwin," SABR Baseball Biography Project [cited April 4, 2013]. Available from: http://sabr.org/bioproj/person/41f65388.
38. "1886 Chicago White Stockings (Batting, Pitching & Fielding Statistics)" (2013), Baseball-Reference.com [cited August 20, 2013]. Available from: http://www.baseball-reference.com/teams/CHC/1886.shtml.
39. *Sporting News* (2006), *The Complete Baseball Record & Fact Book* (St. Louis, MO: Sporting News), p. 71.
40. Bush.
41. "Had a Sunday See-Saw" (1887), *St. Paul Daily Globe*, Monday, June 20, p. 5.
42. "Duluth the Victor" (1887), *Duluth Daily News* (Duluth, MN), June 1, p. 1.
43. "Joe Quinn (Player Page): Minor League Statistics" (2013), Baseball-Reference.com [cited April 2, 2013]. Available from: http://www.baseball-reference.com/minors/player.cgi?id=quinn-003jos.
44. Spink, p. 203.
45. "Joe Quinn (Player Page): Minor League Statistics."
46. Babe Ruth reportedly began his career using a 54-oz. bat and used a 40-oz. bat to hit a record 60 home runs in 1927. Ty Cobb and Joe DiMaggio both used 42-oz. bats. Other Hall of Fame hitters, such as Ted Williams and Stan Musial, used far lighter bats, just 31 to 33 oz.: S. Ashley (1990), "Getting Good Wood (or Aluminum) on the Ball," *Mechanical Engineering* 112 (10): pp. 40–47.
47. "West Hotel: The Only Fire-Proof Hotel in Minneapolis" (1887), *St. Paul Daily Globe*, Sunday, May 22, p. 3.
48. "Five Fires" (1887), *St. Paul Daily Globe*, Friday, May 13, p. 4.
49. "To Enjoy the Great Day" (1887), *St. Paul Daily Globe*, Monday, July 4, p. 3.
50. "Best Teeth" (1887), *St. Paul Daily Globe*, Sunday, May 22, p. 3.
51. "Games Played July 4" (1887), *The Sporting Life*, Wednesday, July 13, p. 6.
52. "The Spalding Trophy" (1887), *St. Paul Daily Globe*, Sunday, July 24.
53. "Must Have First Place" (1887), *St. Paul Daily Globe*, Wednesday, July 13, p. 4.
54. "The Golden Gate Pitcher" (1887), *St. Paul Daily Globe*, Thursday, July 14, p. 4.
55. Born of the temperance movement, the Pittsburgh society was formed in 1887 to protest the conduct of drinking, gambling, gaming, and trading on Sundays, "never proposing to reform anyone but solely to enforce the law and leave the reformation of the inmates to those societies whose particular province it may be." See: M.H. Frisch and D.J. Valkowitz (1983), *Working Class America: Essays on Labor, Community, and American Society* (Urbana: University of Illinois Press), p. 125.
56. "Death in the Sun's Rays" (1887), *St. Paul Daily Globe*, Monday, July 18, p. 1.
57. "The Zenith City Team Goes Down in One of the Most Hotly-Contested Games of the Season" (1887), *St. Paul Daily Globe*, Monday, July 18.
58. "St. Paul Is Now on Even Terms with Milwaukee" (1887), *St. Paul Daily Globe*, Monday, July 18.
59. "Des Moines Scores a Ninth Successive Victory by Doing up the Men from Duluth" (1887), *St. Paul Daily Globe*, Sunday, July 24.
60. "Boston's Latest: Joe Quinn, Their New Second Baseman, and His Record" (1888), *Wichita Daily Eagle*, Tuesday, October 16, p. 7.
61. "Duluth Club Changes" (1887), *St. Paul Daily Globe*, Sunday, July 31, p. 1.
62. "The Duluth Team" (1887), *St. Paul Daily Globe*, Thursday, August 2, p. 5.
63. "Games Played August 1" (1887), *The Sporting Life*, Wednesday, August 10, p. 6.
64. "Games Played August 6" (1887), *The Sporting Life*, Wednesday, August 17, p. 6.
65. "Duluth's New Manager" (1887), *The Sporting Life*, Wednesday, August 31, p. 7.
66. Eisenbath and Musial, p. 13.
67. Seymour and Mills, p. 211.
68. "Minneapolis Drops on the Duluth Twirlers with Great Emphasis" (1887), *St. Paul Daily Globe*, Wednesday, August 24, p. 5.
69. "Games Played August 24" (1887), *The Sporting Life*, Wednesday, September 7, p. 6.
70. "Minneapolis Hammers the Ball in a Most Heartless Manner" (1887), *St. Paul Daily Globe*, Sunday, August 28.
71. "Full of Sharp Work" (1887), *St. Paul Daily Globe*, Thursday, September 1, p. 5.

72. "St. Paul in the Van" (1887), *St. Paul Daily Globe*, Monday, September 8, p. 5.
73. "Oshkosh Leads by Defeating Duluth Twice" (1887), *St. Paul Daily Globe*, Wednesday, September 14, p. 5.
74. "A Protested Game" (1887), *St. Paul Daily Globe*, Tuesday, September 15, p. 5.
75. "He Was Wild" (1887), *St. Paul Daily Globe*, Saturday, September 17, p. 5.
76. Mira Becherer, "United States Census: City of St. Louis, Missouri—Division of St. Louis City, 1940" (2012). United States Census Office [cited August 20, 2013]. Available from: www.familysearch.org.
77. "Northwestern League: The Record" (1887), *The Sporting Life*, Wednesday, October 12, p. 5.
78. "Pyle Was Pounded" (1887), *St. Paul Daily Globe*, Sunday, October 2, p. 5.
79. "A Case of Kellogg" (1887), *St. Paul Daily Globe*, Wednesday, October 5, p. 5.
80. "Games Played October 6" (1887) *The Sporting Life*, Wednesday, October 18, p. 6.
81. "Northwestern League: The Record" (1887), *The Sporting Life*, Wednesday, October 12, p. 5.
82. "Will Duluth Drop Out?" (1887), *St. Paul Daily Globe*, Wednesday, October 5, p. 5.
83. "Duluth Will Stay" (1887), *St. Paul Daily Globe*, Wednesday, October 19, p. 1.
84. "Sports, Limited" (1888), *St. Paul Daily Globe*, Wednesday, February 8, p. 5.
85. "A Talk with Joe Quinn" (1887), *The Sporting Life*, Wednesday, November 23, p. 3.
86. Earle was a genuine journeyman, playing for 13 different minor league teams between 1886 and 1906: "Billy Earle (Minor League Player Page)" (2013), Baseball-Reference.com [cited August 21, 2013]. Available from: http://www.baseball-reference.com/minors/player.cgi?id=earle-001bil.
87. As the first club to have formally accepted his services, the St. Paul Apostles eventually signed Earle for the 1888 season: "Too Often Signed" (1887), *St. Paul Daily Globe*, Friday, October 18, p. 4.
88. "Duluth Very Eager" (1888), *St. Paul Daily Globe*, Thursday, January 19, p. 5.
89. "Sports, Limited" (1888), *St. Paul Daily Globe*, Wednesday, February 8, p. 5.
90. Professional baseball was resurrected in Duluth in 1891 when Jay Anderson bought the St. Paul franchise from the Western Association and relocated it to Minnesota: Bush, "Duluth's First Pro Baseball Team: 1886 Champions."
91. Charlton, p. 73.
92. "Base Ball: From the Hub" (1886), *The Sporting Life*, Wednesday, June 9, p. 8.
93. "Des Moines Gets Him" (1888), *St. Paul Daily Globe*, Saturday, January 7, p. 5.
94. "Sporting Notes" (1888), *Boston Globe*, Friday, January 6, p. 6.
95. H. Sheumaker and S.T. Wajda (2008), *Material Culture in America: Understanding Everyday Life* (Santa Barbara, CA: ABC-CLIO), pp. 309–310.
96. H. Schechter (2009), *The Whole Death Catalog: A Lively Guide to the Bitter End* (New York: Ballantine), pp. 100–101.
97. "U.S Corn for Grain: Acreage, Yield & Production" (2010), Corn Refiners Association [cited March 31, 2013]. Available from: http://www.corn.org/publications/statistics/u-s-corn-production/.
98. H. Arden (1981), " Iowa, America's Middle Earth," *National Geographic* 159 (6): pp. 603–629.

99. R.W. Frazer (1965), *Forts of the West: Military Forts and Presidios, and Posts Commonly Called Forts, West of the Mississippi River to 1898* (Norman: University of Oklahoma Press), pp. 48–50. For details of the 1851 flood, see C.S. McCue and R. Playle (2007), *Des Moines* (Chicago: Arcadia Publishing), pp. 73–77.
100. "The Base Ball Outlook" (1888), *Omaha Daily Bee*, Monday, April 16, p. 2.
101. "Joe Quinn Chats" (1888), *St. Paul Daily Globe*, Saturday, January 28, p. 4.
102. "The Base Ball Outlook," p. 2.
103. "Des Moines Gets Him," p. 5.
104. "1888 Des Moines Prohibitionists (Batting, Pitching and Fielding Statistics)" (2013), Baseball-Reference.com [cited May 30, 2013]. Available from: http://www.baseball-reference.com/minors/team.cgi?id=8f208be7.
105. "Flashes from the Diamond" (1888), *Omaha Daily Bee*, Thursday, December 20, p. 2.
106. D. Heldt (2011), "U.I. Archaeologists Find 7,000-Year-Old Site in Des Moines," *The Gazette* (online): Cedar Rapids, IA [cited August 22, 2013]. Available from: http://thegazette.com/2011/08/18/ui-archaeologists-find-7000-year-old-site-in-des-moines/.
107. McCue and Playle, pp. 73–77.
108. "The Base Ball Outlook," p. 2.
109. "Boston's Latest: Joe Quinn, Their New Second Baseman, and His Record" (1888), *Wichita Daily Eagle*, Tuesday, October 16, p. 7.
110. "Spasmodic Sprague" (1888), *St. Paul Daily Globe*, Sunday, August 12, p. 6.
111. "Frank Selee (Manager Page)" (2013), Baseball-Reference.com [cited May 22, 2013]. Available from: http://www.baseball-reference.com/managers/seleefr99.shtml.
112. "Boston's Latest: Joe Quinn," p. 7.
113. "Money Well Spent: How the Boston Management Is Increasing Its Funds" (1887), *St. Paul Daily Globe*, Saturday, June 25, p. 4.
114. Ibid.
115. "Hunting for Talent" (1888), *St. Paul Daily Globe*, Sunday, August 12, p. 6.
116. "Boston's Latest: Joe Quinn," p. 7.
117. Ibid.
118. "The Current Opinion: In Europe Undoubtedly Tending Warward" (1888), *Evening Bulletin* (Maysville, KY), Tuesday, August 28, p. 1.

Chapter 7

1. The salary outlay for the Boston club was $38,000 in 1886, and the costs of travel and park maintenance approximately $27,000. Total receipts for the season were "in the neighborhood of $100,000," rendering the club a profit of about $35,000. From: "Money Well Spent," p. 4.
2. "From the Bostons" (1889), *Pittsburg Dispatch*, Sunday, June 16, p. 15.
3. "Billy Klusman (Player Page)" (2013), Baseball-Reference.com [cited April 24, 2013]. Available from: http://www.baseball-reference.com/players/k/klusmbi01.shtml.
4. Klusman achieved this feat on July 17, 1888, hitting both off Detroit's Ed Beatin. From: "Games Played Tuesday, July 17" (1888), *The Sporting Life*, Wednesday, July 25, p. 2.
5. "Billy Klusman (Br Bullpen)" (2013), Baseball-Reference.com [cited April 26, 2013]. Available from: http://www.baseball-reference.com/bullpen/Billy_Klusman.
6. "1888 Boston Beaneaters (Batting, Pitching & Fielding Statistics)" (2013), Baseball-Reference.com [cited May

15, 2013]. Available from: http://www.baseball-reference.com/teams/BSN/1888.shtml.

7. *Harper's Weekly* of May 16, 1885, listed "the nine men universally acknowledged as the most expert players in their respective positions in the field." Their all-star team included future Hall of Famers King Kelly (right field), Charles "Hoss" Radbourn (pitcher), Buck Ewing (catcher), John Montgomery Ward ("best base runner"), and Burdock at second base. From: K. Torres (2012), "Jack Burdock," SABR Baseball Biography Project, Society for American Baseball Research [cited May 5, 2013]. Available from: http://sabr.org/bioproj/person/834f6239.

8. He had made his professional debut in 1872, the year Quinn arrived in America, with the Brooklyn Atlantics. From: Torres, "Jack Burdock."

9. "The price of his release has not been made public, but it is well known that it was not less than $4,000. The Boston management is to be praised for its liberality and perseverance in bringing to a close this negotiation, which ranks with those that secured Clarkson and Kelly." From: "Boston's Latest: Joe Quinn," p. 7.

10. "The Des Moines people refused to listen to any overtures, and would not think of allowing Quinn to go until they were compelled to do so through financial reasons." From: "Boston's Latest: Joe Quinn," p. 7.

11. D. Pajot (2009), *The Rise of Milwaukee Baseball: The Cream City from Midwestern Outpost to the Major Leagues, 1859–1901* (Jefferson, NC: McFarland), p. 144.

12. "Sparks from the Diamond" (1888), *Omaha Daily Bee*, Sunday, September 30, p. 7.

13. "Spasmodic Sprague," p. 6.

14. Des Moines' debt was estimated at about $2,000 in August 1888. Clubs such as Chicago and Milwaukee were almost $5,000 in arrears. From: Pajot, p. 148.

15. "1888 Des Moines Prohibitionists (Batting, Pitching and Fielding Statistics)."

16. "Sporting Notes" (1888), *Evening Bulletin* (Maysville, KY), Tuesday, August 28, p. 1.

17. "Hunting for Talent," p. 6.

18. Ibid.

19. Ten days' notice was a standard in the nineteenth century for released or traded players; the *Boston Globe* announced Quinn's arrival on August 26. From: "Joe Quinn Signs" (1888), *Boston Globe*, Tuesday, August 26, p. 4.

20. Ibid.

21. "Three Straight Games: Record Gained by the New-Yorks in Boston" (1888), *New York Times*, Tuesday, August 5, p. 5.

22. Kelly's release was purchased on February 14, 1887: "King Kelly (Player Page): Transactions" (2013), Baseball-Reference.com [cited June 1, 2013]. Available from: http://www.baseball-reference.com/players/k/kellyki01.shtml#trans.] Clarkson's was purchased on April 3, 1888: "John Clarkson (Player Page): Transactions" (2013), Baseball-Reference.com [cited June 1, 2013]. Available from: http://www.baseball-reference.com/players/c/clarkjo01.shtml#trans.]

23. "Their Fiftieth Victory: The New-Yorks Scored It in Boston Yesterday" (1888), *New York Times*, Sunday, August 3, p. 5.

24. "Three Straight Games," p. 5.

25. "Their Fiftieth Victory," p. 5.

26. "The New Yorks Win Again: They Defeat the Bostons Nine to Six" (1888), *New York Times*, Monday, August 4, p. 5; "Three Straight Games," p. 5.

27. "1888 Boston Beaneaters (Schedule, Box Scores and Splits)" (2013), Baseball-Reference.com. [cited April 14, 2013]. Available from: http://www.baseball-reference.com/teams/BSN/1888-schedule-scores.shtml.

28. Ibid.

29. "Better for the Batter" (1888), *Boston Globe*, Wednesday, August 27, p. 8.

30. Triple Crown winner Tim Keefe was the National League's leading pitcher in 1888, with 35 wins (.745 win-loss percentage), 335 strikeouts, and a 1.74 Earned Run Average. From: "Tim Keefe (Player Page)" (2013), Baseball-Reference.com [cited June 1, 2013]. Available from: http://www.baseball-reference.com/players/k/keefeti01.shtml.

31. "Baseball Stories by Joe Quinn," p. 6.

32. "Won by a Home-Run Hit" (1888), *New York Times*, Saturday, August 30, p. 7.

33. On August 27, Boston defeated the Giants 4–2 in New York on the back of a grand-slam home run hit by Brown, whom the *New York Times* described as "known as a short hitter of the bunting order who depends on his speed as a runner." After Brown's winning blow, the paper sniffed, "In every respect the hit was a very lucky one. It was the first hit Brown had made in the game, and the only home-run hit he has ever made against the New-York Club." From: "Brown's One Home Run: It Won a Game from the Giants Yesterday" (1888), *New York Times*, Thursday August 28, p.8.

34. "Won by a Home-Run Hit," p. 7.

35. "Joe Quinn (Player Page): Minor League Statistics."

36. "New-York Did Not Score: But the Bostons Made Two Runs and Won" (1888), *New York Times*, Friday, August 29, p. 8.

37. Ibid.

38. "Won by a Home-Run Hit."

39. Ibid.

40. C. Bevis (2012) "Tim Keefe." SABR Baseball Biography Project. Society for American Baseball Research [cited June 15, 2013]. Available from: http://sabr.org/bioproj/person/6f1dd1b1.

41. "Won by a Home-Run Hit."

42. M. Chipp (1980), "Inside the Park Home Runs," Society for American Baseball Research: Research Journals Archive (Vol. 9) [cited April 30, 2013]. Available from: http://research.sabr.org/journals/inside-the-park-home-runs.

43. "Won by a Home-Run Hit."

44. Ibid.

45. "Four Straight Defeats" (1888), *New York Times*, Sunday, August 31, p. 6.

46. Ibid.

47. Ibid.

48. Ibid.

49. "Sparks from the Diamond," p. 7.

50. Spink, p. 266.

51. "Baseball Stories by Joe Quinn," p. 6.

52. The sale of the "king of the field" was announced in the *New York Sun*, which marveled at "the extent to which managers must go to strengthen their clubs": "The Base Ball Conundrum" (1887), *New York Sun*, Sunday, February 20, p. 7.

53. P.M. Gordon (2012), "King Kelly," SABR Baseball Biography Project, Society for American Baseball Research [cited June 20, 2013]. Available from: http://sabr.org/bioproj/person/ffc40dac.

54. Ibid.

55. Pearson, p. 59.

56. "Startling Intelligence" (1887), *St. Paul Daily Globe*, Thursday, October 20, p. 4.

57. The production ran from March 12, 1888, until April 1889, and starred Elsie Leslie and Tommy Russell. From: "Little Lord Fauntleroy" (2012), Internet Broadway Database [cited June 11, 2013]. Available from: http://ibdb.com/production.php?id=5718.

58. M. Motto (2000), personal communication, "Re: Joe Quinn" [e-mail]. To: R. Nicholls, Wednesday, May 31.
59. F.H. Burnett (1993), *Little Lord Fauntleroy* (Boston, MA: David R. Godine), p. 34.
60. Spink, p. 103.
61. "Baseball Stories by Joe Quinn; Outlook for the Cardinals in 1906." (1905). *The St. Louis Republic* (St. Louis, MO). Sunday December 10, p.6.
62. C. Cunningham and R. Roberts (2011), *Before the Curse: The Chicago Cubs' Glory Years, 1870–1945* (Champaign: University of Illinois Press), p. 56.
63. Gordon, "King Kelly."
64. "Baseball Stories by Joe Quinn," p. 6.
65. D. Okrent and S. Wulf (1989), *Baseball Anecdotes* (New York: Oxford University Press), p. 16.
66. "Baseball Stories by Joe Quinn," p. 6.
67. "Joe Quinn (Player Page)" (2013), Baseball-Reference.com [cited January 9, 2013]. Available from: http://www.baseball-reference.com/players/q/quinnjo02.shtml.
68. "Boston's Latest: Joe Quinn," p. 7.
69. "Flashes from the Diamond" (1888), *Omaha Daily Bee*, Thursday, December 20, p. 2.
70. Pajot, p. 150.
71. Ibid.
72. "Western Association (Br Bullpen)" (2013), Baseball-Reference.com [cited May 10, 2013]. Available from: http://www.baseball-reference.com/bullpen/Western_Association.
73. MILB.com (2013), "Iowa Cubs History (Iowacubs.Com)," Minor League Baseball [cited June 10, 2013]. Available from: http://www.milb.com/content/page.jsp?sid=t451&ymd=20100319&content_id=8838460&vkey=team4.
74. "Western Association (Br Bullpen)."
75. "The Great Scheme: The Plans of the Brotherhood Given in Detail" (1889), *The Sporting News*, Saturday, September 28, p. 3.
76. Pearson, p. 7.
77. Goldstein, p. 151.
78. "Dust of the Diamond" (1889), *St. Paul Daily Globe*, Sunday, February 24, p. 6.
79. "The St. Louis Man Who Makes Osculation a Fine Art: A St. Louis Sensation" (1889), *Omaha Daily Bee*, Tuesday, February 19, p. 5.
80. "This Girl Liked the Kisser" (1889), *Omaha Daily Bee*, Tuesday, February 19, p. 5.
81. "The St. Louis Man Who Makes Osculation a Fine Art," p. 5.
82. Posters advertising the tour announced it as "Spalding's Australian Base Ball Tour" and prominently featured the Australian coat of arms. From: M. Lamster (2006), *Spalding's World Tour: The Epic Adventure That Took Baseball round the Globe—and Made It America's Game* (New York: Public Affairs), p. 44.
83. "Sparks from the Diamond," p. 7.
84. D.L. Fleitz (2005), *Cap Anson: The Grand Old Man of Baseball* (Jefferson, NC: McFarland), p. 53.
85. Lamster, p. 43.
86. Zoss and Bowman, p. 400.
87. Clark, p. 14.
88. Lamster, p. 178.
89. Clark, p. 17.
90. Ibid., p. 21.
91. "On the Fly" (1883), *The Sporting Life*, Monday, July 30, p. 7.
92. "Splinters from the Bats" (1888), *Wichita Daily Eagle*, Sunday, May 6, p. 6.
93. Rader, p. 64.
94. Goldstein, p. 18.
95. "Quinn's Proposal" (1895), *The Sporting Life*, Saturday, November 2, p. 3.
96. "Boston, March 29" (1889), *The Sun* (New York), Saturday, March 30, p. 6.
97. "Boston Lines" (1889), *The Sporting News*, Friday, April 12, p. 3.
98. Rosenberg, p. 308.
99. Morrill was the National League's leading first baseman in 1883 and 1888 and his fifteen-year major league tenure yielded a batting average of .260. From: "John Morrill (Player Page)" (2013), Baseball-Reference.com [cited June 2, 2013]. Available from: http://www.baseball-reference.com/players/m/morrijo01.shtml.
100. Morrill never resurrected his career, playing only one season with the Senators (and batting a dreadful .185) and appearing in two games for Boston's Players' League team in 1890 before his distinguished career sank into ashes. From: "John Morrill (Player Page)."
101. "The Diamond Field: What's the Matter with Kelly, the $10,000 Beauty?" (1889), *Salt Lake Herald*, Sunday, May 19, p. 14.
102. Spink, p. 103.
103. "Joe Quinn in the Outfield" (1888), *The Sporting News*, Thursday, April 12, p. 5.
104. Benson, p. 256.
105. "Special Correspondence of the Dispatch, Boston, August 24, 1889" (1889), *Pittsburg Dispatch*, Monday, August 26, p. 6.
106. "Done by the Umpire" (1887), *St. Paul Daily Globe*, Saturday, August 13, p. 5.
107. Welch's achievement came on August 28, 1884, as part of a 10–2 win over Cleveland. From: "Hall of Famers: Welch, Mickey" (2012), National Baseball Hall of Fame and Museum, Cooperstown, NY [cited June 16, 2013]. Available from: http://baseballhall.org/hof/welch-mickey, and "1884 New York Giants (Schedule, Box Scores and Splits)" (2013), Baseball-Reference.com [cited June 16, 2013]. Available from: http://www.baseball-reference.com/teams/NYG/1884-schedule-scores.shtml.
108. Pearson, p. 10.
109. Seymour and Mills, p. 277.
110. "Baseball Stories by Joe Quinn," p. 6.
111. Common advice to an outfielder having trouble catching the ball. From: Dickson, p. 678.
112. "Quinn as an Outfielder" (1888), *St. Paul Daily Globe*, Sunday, December 16, p. 6.
113. "Baseball" (1888), *Daily Times* (Richmond, VA), Monday, August 6, p. 4.
114. "Hardy Richardson (Player Page)" (2013), Baseball-Reference.com [cited June 1, 2013]. Available from: http://www.baseball-reference.com/players/r/richaha01.shtml.
115. "Quinn as an Outfielder," p. 6.
116. "Joe Quinn in the Outfield," p. 5.
117. "Diamond Dashes" (1888), *St. Paul Daily Globe*, Sunday, December 16, p. 6.
118. "Baseball Stories by Joe Quinn," p. 6.
119. "Tim Keefe (Player Page)" (2013), Baseball-Reference.com [cited June 1, 2013]. Available from: http://www.baseball-reference.com/players/k/keefeti01.shtml.
120. "1889 Boston Beaneaters (Schedule, Box Scores and Splits)" (2013), Baseball-Reference.com [cited May 30, 2013]. Available from: http://www.baseball-reference.com/teams/BSN/1889-schedule-scores.shtml.
121. "How the Struggle Goes On" (1889), *Pittsburg Dispatch*, Sunday, June 16, p. 15.
122. Ibid.
123. Pearson, p. 58.
124. Spink, p. 91.

125. "Charlie Bennett's Misfortune" (1894), *Wichita Daily Eagle*, Monday, January 11, p. 1.
126. S. Ferkovich (2012), "Bennett Park (Detroit)," SABR Baseball Biography Project, Society for American Baseball Research [cited May 20, 2013]. Available from: http://sabr.org/bioproj/park/336604.
127. Spink, p. 126.
128. B. McKenna (2012), "Dickey Pearce," SABR Baseball Biography Project, Society for American Baseball Research [cited June 5, 2013]. Available from: http://sabr.org/bioproj/person/db8ea477.
129. "Flashes from the Diamond" (1889), *Omaha Daily Bee*, Sunday, August 4, p. 9.
130. "From the Bostons" (1889), *Pittsburg Dispatch*, Sunday, June 16, p. 15.
131. "Joe Quinn" (1889), *The Sporting News*, Saturday, June 22, p. 5.
132. Seymour and Mills, p. 201.
133. Ibid.
134. "Joe Quinn" (1889), *The Sporting News*, Saturday, June 22, p. 5. It was a sentiment Quinn also expressed to the *Sporting Life* on two occasions: "Joe Quinn" (1888), Wednesday, December 5, p. 5; and "Joe Quinn, of the Bostons" (1889), Wednesday, August 14, p. 5.
135. Poet and essayist Oliver Wendell Holmes is commonly believed to have christened Boston "the Hub of the Universe." What he actually said was, "Boston State-house is the hub of the solar system." L.M. Legarde and D. Northrup (1995), *Frommer's 96 New England* (New York: Macmillan), p. 55.
136. "Joe Quinn, of the Bostons," p.5.
137. "Flashes from the Diamond," August 4, p. 9.
138. "Joe Quinn, of the Bostons," p. 5. In 1890, Molly Quinn and baby Mira would join Joe in Boston in July, remaining there for the rest of the season: "News, Notes and Comment" (1890), *The Sporting Life*, Wednesday, July 5.
139. Such was the belief in this ancient superstition that New York manager John McGraw once paid a truck driver to deliberately drive past his park with a load of empty barrels just as his players were arriving. The ruse worked and the Giants won four games in a row before the driver balked because he hadn't been paid for his services. From: M. Davis, p. 165.
140. Pearson, p. 96.
141. "1889 Boston Beaneaters (Schedule, Box Scores and Splits)."
142. "Joe Quinn (Player Page)" (2013), Baseball-Reference.com [cited January 9, 2013]. Available from: http://www.baseball-reference.com/players/q/quinnjo02.shtml.
143. "Gossip from Boston: Charley Foley Tells of the Bean Eaters' Great Financial Success" (1889), *Pittsburg Dispatch*, Monday, September 9, p. 6.
144. Pearson, p. 43.
145. "Base Ball Brotherhood" (1887), *St. Paul Daily Globe*, Wednesday, August 24, p. 5.
146. Stevens, p. 49.
147. Stevens, p. 39.
148. Spink, p. 234.
149. "Flashes from the Diamond" (1890), *Omaha Sunday Bee*, Sunday, March 16, p. 1.
150. D.A. Sullivan (1995), *Early Innings: A Documentary History of Baseball, 1825–1908* (Ann Arbor: University of Michigan Press), p. 197.
151. Pearson, p. 75.
152. Ibid.
153. Dickson, p. 140.
154. Pearson, p. 92.
155. King Kelly's salary was $4,000 and Hoss Radbourn's $4,800 in 1886. From: "Money Well Spent," p. 4.
156. Pearson, p. 29.
157. Seymour and Mills, p. 225.
158. Ibid.
159. Spink, p. 28.
160. "Hub Pick-Ups" (1889), *The Sporting Life*, Wednesday, July 17, p. 5.
161. "1889 Boston Beaneaters (Schedule, Box Scores and Splits)."
162. "The Latest Scheme: A New Organization to Sign All the National League Players" (1889), *Pittsburg Dispatch*, Monday, September 9, p. 6.
163. "Other Games" (1889), *Evening Star* (Washington, DC), Friday, August 16, p. 8.
164. Pearson, p. 120.
165. Ibid.
166. "Special Correspondence of the Dispatch, Boston, August 24, 1889" (1889), *Pittsburg Dispatch*, Monday, August 26, p. 6.
167. "Standings and Games on Thursday, August 22, 1889" (2013), Baseball-Reference.com [cited June 16, 2013]. Available from: http://www.baseball-reference.com/games/standings.cgi?date=1889-08-22.
168. "Gossip from Boston: Charley Foley," p. 6.
169. Pearson, p. 105.
170. Okrent and Wulf, p. 16.
171. "Baseball Stories by Joe Quinn," p. 6.
172. "An Exciting Scene" (1889), *Pittsburg Dispatch*, Tuesday, August 27, p. 6.
173. "One Victory for Boston" (1889), *New York Times*, August 30, p. 5.
174. Pearson, p. 157.
175. "One Victory for Boston," p. 5.
176. "Lost or Stolen!" (1889), *Boston Globe*, August 30, p. 5.
177. "Gossip from Boston: Charley Foley," p. 6.
178. Ibid.
179. Ibid.
180. Ibid.
181. The Bachelors' Club was a gentlemen's club located in the historic Jamaica Plain neighborhood of Boston, with meetings held at the John A. Andrew Hall on Washington Street. From "Local Lines" (1885), *Boston Daily Globe*, November 12, p. 1; City of Boston (2010), "Jamaica Plain: Exploring Boston's Neighborhoods," Boston Landmarks Commission, Boston, MA [cited June 22, 2013]. Available from: www.cityofboston.gov/images_documents/Jamaica_Plain_brochure_tcm3-19120.pdf. 6 pages.
182. "Joe Quinn Gets a Bat" (1889), *Boston Daily Globe*, Friday, September 13, p. 8.
183. "What an Escape!" (1889), *Boston Globe*, Saturday, September 14, p. 5.
184. Pearson, p. 137.
185. "Stole a March" (1889), *Boston Globe*, September 13, p. 5.
186. "What an Escape!," p. 5.
187. "Gossip from Boston: Charley Foley," p. 6.
188. "Standings and Games on Thursday, September 19, 1889" (2013), Baseball-Reference.com [cited June 17, 2013]. Available from: http://www.baseball-reference.com/games/standings.cgi?date=1889-09-19.
189. "Nothing but Praise for the Globe" (1889), *Boston Globe*, Monday, October 7, p. 5.
190. Pearson, p. 147.
191. "Sure of the Pennant: New Yorkers Think Their Club Will Beat the Bostons Out" (1889), *Pittsburg Dispatch*, Monday, September 9, p. 6.
192. "Peppermint Drops" (1889), *Omaha Daily Bee*, Sunday, July 28, p. 9.
193. "Joe Hornung (B.R. Bullpen)" (2013), Baseball-

Reference.com [cited April 4, 2013]. Available from: http://www.baseball-reference.com/bullpen/Joe_Hornung.

194. Pearson, p. 136.

195. "The Great Scheme: The Plans of the Brotherhood Given in Detail" (1889), *The Sporting News*, Saturday, September 28, p. 3.

196. Stevens, p. 91.

197. George Wright was the star shortstop of baseball's first professional team, the 1869 Cincinnati Red Stockings, for whom he batted an amazing .633, including 49 home runs in 57 games. He then captained the Boston Red Stockings to four straight National Association pennants between 1872 and 1875, led Boston to National League pennants in 1877 and 1878, and in 1879 led Providence to the city's first league championship. From: "Hall of Famers: Wright, George" (2012), National Baseball Hall of Fame and Museum, Cooperstown, NY [cited June 18, 2013]. Available from: http://baseballhall.org/hof/wright-george.

198. "The Great Scheme," p. 3.

199. Spink, p. 26.

200. "The Brotherhood" (1889), *The Sporting News*, Saturday, September 21, p. 1.

201. "The Great Scheme," p. 3. "*The Sporting News* is the only sporting paper in America not controlled by the League bosses," the paper boasted. "Quite naturally, then, it is the only one to stand by the players in their fight for right and liberty." From: "Caught on the Fly" (1889), *The Sporting News*, Sunday, October 6, p. 5.

202. "The Brotherhood," p. 1.

203. "Chaff from Chicago" (1889), *The Sporting News*, Saturday, September 21, p. 1.

204. "The Latest Scheme: A New Organization to Sign All the National League Players" (1889), *Pittsburg Dispatch*, Monday, September 9, p. 6.

205. A.J. Reach (1989 reprint), *Reach Baseball Guide 1890* (St. Louis: Horton, p 10).

206. "1889 Boston Beaneaters (Schedule, Box Scores and Splits)."

207. "Standings and Games on Monday, September 30, 1889" (2013), Baseball-Reference.com [cited June 17, 2013]. Available from: www.baseball-reference.com/games/standings.cgi?year=1889&month=9&day=30&submit=Submit+Date.

208. "Mike Kelly Disgraced: He Assaults Umpire Mcquaid and Is Dragged Away by Policemen" (1889), *Pittsburg Dispatch*, Thursday, October 3, p. 6.

209. Ibid.

210. Pearson, p. 152.

211. "New-York Holds the Lead: Today's Games Will Decide the Championship" (1889), *New York Times*, October 5, p. 6.

212. New York had won the pennant for the second consecutive year and would also defend their World Series title, taking the best-of-eleven series in nine games over the Brooklyn Bridegrooms. From: Pearson, p. 182.

213. Pearson, p. 154.

214. Reach (1989), p. 78.

215. "1889 Boston Beaneaters (Schedule, Box Scores and Splits)."

216. "1889 National League Standard Pitching" (2013), Baseball-Reference.com [cited May 31, 2013]. Available from: http://www.baseball-reference.com/leagues/NL/1889-standard-pitching.shtml.

217. "1889 National League Standard Batting" (2013), Baseball-Reference.com [cited May 31, 2013]. Available from: http://www.baseball-reference.com/leagues/NL/1889-standard-batting.shtml.

218. "Joe Quinn (Player Page)" (2013), Baseball-Reference.com [cited January 9, 2013]. Available from: http://www.baseball-reference.com/players/q/quinnjo02.shtml.

219. "1889 National League Shortstop" (2013), Baseball-Reference.com [cited May 31, 2013]. Available from: http://www.baseball-reference.com/leagues/NL/1889-specialpos_ss-fielding.shtml.

220. Pearson, p. 155.

221. "The Same Old Story" (1889), *The Sporting Life*, Friday, August 16, p. 7.

222. Pearson, p. 155.

223. "Baldwin at Work in St. Louis" (1889), *Pittsburg Dispatch*, Tuesday, November 26, p. 6.

224. Ibid.

225. "Facts" (1889), *The Sporting Life*, Wednesday, November 6, p. 3.

226. "News, Notes and Comment," *The Sporting Life*, Wednesday, December 11, p. 5.

227. "J. Quinn" (1893), *The Sporting News*, Monday, February 11, p. 1.

Chapter 8

1. W.I. Harris, "An Equal Fight: W I. Harris Writes of the Coming Baseball Battle" (1890), *Wichita Daily Eagle*, Tuesday, February 25, p. 2.

2. Ibid.

3. Spink, pp. 28–29.

4. Spink, p. 173.

5. D.Q. Voigt (2010) *American Baseball: From Gentleman's Sport to the Commissioner System* (University Park: Pennsylvania State University Press), p. 210.

6. J.T. Hetrick (1999), *Chris Von Der Ahe and the St. Louis Browns* (Lanham, MD: Scarecrow), p. 119.

7. "Base Ball Briefs" (1890), *St. Paul Daily Globe*, Sunday, May 4, p. 6.

8. Pearson, pp. 65–75.

9. Pearson, p. 199.

10. "News by Wire: The League Accused of Tampering with Players" (1890), *The Sporting Life*, Wednesday, August 2, p. 1.

11. "To Deal with the Contract Breakers" (1890), *Ft. Worth Gazette*, Friday, March 28, p. 5.

12. The League had sought injunctions against "jumpers" including Ward, Buck Ewing, and George Hallman, but the courts ruled an absence of mutuality in the contracts prevented the league from restraining them: W.B. Gould (2011), *Bargaining with Baseball: Labor Relations in an Age of Prosperous Turmoil* (Jefferson, NC: McFarland), pp. 59–61.

13. Spink, p. 28.

14. Charlton, p. 83.

15. The two-umpire system was not formally adopted in professional baseball until 1911. Zoss and Bowman, p. 292.

16. "Echoes of the Game" (1890), *Boston Globe*, Tuesday, May 27, p. 5.

17. "The Boys Arrive at Savannah" (1890), *The World–Evening Edition* (New York), Tuesday, March 18, p. 1.

18. "Boston Leaguers Report" (1890), *The World–Evening Edition* (New York), Tuesday, March 18, p. 1.

19. "The Boston Players' League club claims to have made money enough from the exhibition games to pay for the new grounds": "Base Ball Briefs" (1890), *St. Paul Daily Globe*, Sunday, May 4, p. 6. The park was subsequently used by three different leagues—the Players' League in 1890, the Boston franchise of the American Association in 1891, and the National League in 1894. Benson, p. 40.

20. "Base Ball Briefs," p. 6.
21. "Players' League News Notes" (1890), *The Sporting Life*, Wednesday, April 19, p. 9.
22. Charlton, p. 106.
23. R.P. Gelzheiser (2006), *Labor and Capital in 19th Century Baseball* (Jefferson, NC: McFarland), p. 28.
24. "'Twas a Beauty" (1890), *Boston Sunday Globe*, Sunday, April 20, p. 4.
25. "Players League" (1890), *St. Paul Daily Globe*, Sunday, May 4, p. 6.
26. "Joe Quinn (Player Page)" (2013), Baseball-Reference.com [cited January 9, 2013]. Available from: http://www.baseball-reference.com/players/q/quinnjo02.shtml.
27. "Base Ball Briefs" (1890), *St. Paul Daily Globe*, Sunday, May 4, p. 6.
28. "1890 Boston Reds (Batting, Pitching & Fielding Statistics)" (2013), Baseball-Reference.com [cited August 23, 2013]. Available from: http://www.baseball-reference.com/teams/BOS/1890.shtml.
29. Spink, p. 394.
30. "Joe Quinn, the Champion Second Baseman" (1890), *Boston Globe*, Saturday, October 11, p. 7.
31. Charlton, p. 67.
32. The sprinter Stovey also led the league with 97 stolen bases, almost 20 more than his nearest rival and teammate Tom Brown (79): Charlton, p. 85.
33. The league's leading hurler was Chicago's Silver King, with an ERA of 2.69 and 30 wins from 53 complete games, including 4 shutouts: "1890 Players League Pitching Leaders" (2013), Baseball-Reference.com [cited August 23, 2013]. Available from: http://www.baseball-reference.com/leagues/PL/1890-pitching-leaders.shtml.
34. Nemec and Flatow, p. 86.
35. "Games Played Saturday, July 26" (1890), *The Sporting Life*, Wednesday, August 26, p. 3.
36. "Games Played Friday, July 12" (1890), *The Sporting Life*, Wednesday, July 19, p. 3.
37. Voigt, p. 166.
38. "Some 'Figgers'" (1890), *The Sporting Life*, Wednesday, June 14, p. 5.
39. C. Einstein (1968), *The Third Fireside Book of Baseball* (New York: Simon & Schuster), p. 410.
40. J. Hawking (2012), *Strikeout: Baseball, Broadway and the Brotherhood in the 19th Century* (Santa Fe, NM: Sunstone Press), pp. 210–212.
41. "Still Scheming." (1890). *The Sporting Life*, Wednesday, October 25, p. 1.
42. R.F. Burk (2001), *Never Just a Game: Players, Owners, and American Baseball to 1920* (Chapel Hill: University of North Carolina Press), p. 111.
43. "Chicago Gleanings" (1890), *The Sporting Life*, Wednesday, November 15, p. 3; "Trouble in New York" (1890), *The Sporting Life*, Wednesday, November 22, p. 1.
44. Spink, pp. 30–31.
45. L. Lowenfish and R.W. Creamer (2010), *The Imperfect Diamond: A History of Baseball's Labor Wars* (Lincoln: University of Nebraska Press), p. 51.
46. F.H. Brunell (1890), *1890 Players' National League Baseball Guide* (Chicago: F.H. Brunell).
47. Rader, p. 68.
48. "News, Notes and Comment" (1890), *The Sporting Life*, Wednesday, December 13.
49. Society for American Baseball Research (1999), "A Review of Baseball History," *The National Pastime* 19: pp. 81–82.
50. Spink, p. 29.
51. B. Dabscheck (2012), "A Primer on Australian Player Associations," *Economic and Labour Relations Review* 23 (3). Online only: http://www.freepatentsonline.com/article/Economic-Labour-Relations-Review/305080849.html. Accessed April 9, 2013
52. Clark, pp. 60–74, 116–124.
53. B. Dabscheck (1995), "Australian Baseballers Form a Team of Their Own," *Sporting Traditions* 12 (1): pp. 61–101.
54. Ibid.
55. *Household Income Survey Shows Effect of Life Cycle. From: Income Distribution, Australia, 1996–97* (Cat. No. 6523.0) (1998), Australian Bureau of Statistics, Canberra, ACT [cited 2013, May 30]; Available from: http://www.abs.gov.au/ausstats/abs@.nsf/mediareleasesbytitle/C68FDE8DCA48ABCECA2568A9001362A0?OpenDocument.
56. *Rent and Sales Report: Rent (June Quarter 2012), Sales (March Quarter 2012)* (2012). New South Wales Government: Housing Analysis and Research Branch, Sydney, NSW [cited May 30, 2013]. Available from: www.housing.nsw.gov.au (Quick Links).
57. P. Slade (1998), *Player Unions in Australian Professional Sport*, Conference on Globalisation and Regionalism: Employment Relations Issues in the Asia Pacific [Proceedings], Wollongong, NSW: University of Wollongong, pp. 301–312.
58. Dabscheck, "Australian Baseball's Second Unsuccessful Attempt," pp. 87–89.
59. Major League players on Australian rosters are exempt from the salary cap and in 1996-7 received a stipend of $1,000 per month plus a use of car: Dabscheck, "Australian Baseballers Form a Team of Their Own," pp. 61–101.
60. Ibid.
61. Ibid.
62. Dabscheck, "Australian Baseball's Second Unsuccessful Attempt," pp. 87–89.
63. Slade, pp. 301–312.

Chapter 9

1. "Digging Their Graves: League Worthies Now Start to Wreck the Association" (1891), *Pittsburg Dispatch*, Thursday, February 19, p. 1.
2. Nemec, *Great Encyclopedia*, p. 570.
3. S.A. Riess (2006), *Encyclopedia of Major League Baseball Clubs* (Westport, CT: Greenwood), p. 405.
4. "Base Ball: The Childs Case" (1891), *The Sporting Life*, Wednesday, April 25, p. 6.
5. "Quinn Signs" (1891), *Boston Globe*, Friday, February 20, p. 1.
6. "A Word with the Players" (1891), *The Sporting Life*, Wednesday, February 28, p. 3.
7. Where the Boston American Association club would be based in 1891: Benson, p. 40.
8. "A Pair of Wreckers: Kelly and Irwin Get on the Road with a Deal of Bluff" (1891), *Pittsburg Dispatch*, Thursday, February 19, p. 1.
9. "Kelly on His Travels" (1891), *St. Paul Daily Globe*, Thursday, February 19, p. 6.
10. "A Talk with Hanlon" (1891), *Pittsburg Dispatch*, Thursday, February 19, p. 1.
11. A contract whose terms would remain unsurpassed until 1914, when Ty Cobb signed a two-year, $30,000 deal with Detroit in the American League: M. Haupert (2011), "Baseball's Major Salary Milestones," Society for American Baseball Research [cited March 5, 2013]. Available from: http://sabr.org/research/baseball-s-major-salary-milestones.
12. Davis, p. 157.
13. The park remained the home of National League

baseball in Boston until 1915. The steep majestic double-decked grandstand featured six spires on the wooden pavilion roof until it burned in 1894. Benson, p. 40.

14. Spink, p. 280.
15. Pearson, pp. 196–197.
16. McKenna, "Old Hoss Radbourn."
17. B. McKenna (2012), "John Clarkson," Society for American Baseball Research (SABR) BioProject [cited December 10, 2012]. Available from: http://sabr.org/bioproj/person/47feb015.
18. Nichols was inducted into the Baseball Hall of Fame in 1949. "Kid Nichols (Player Page)" (2013), Baseball-Reference.com [cited June 1, 2013]. Available from: http://www.baseball-reference.com/players/n/nichoki01.shtml.
19. "Grand Send Off" (1891), *Boston Globe*, Thursday, April 23, p. 11.
20. "Cap Anson (Player Page)" (2013), Baseball-Reference.com[cited May 20, 2013]. Available from: http://www.baseball-reference.com/players/a/ansonca01.shtml.
21. Charlton, p. 89.
22. "Played in Hard Luck" (1891), *Boston Globe*, Saturday, August 8, p. 5.
23. Spink, p. 370.
24. "Inks in the Box" (1896), *St. Paul Globe*, Sunday, July 12, p. 10.
25. "Tim Hurst's Methods" (1900), *St. Paul Globe*, Thursday, October 11, p. 5.
26. Davis, p. 224.
27. Zoss and Bowman, p. 292.
28. Turkin and Thompson.
29. Farrington, p. 9B.
30. "Chit Chat of the Ball Players" (1892), *Omaha Daily Bee*, Sunday, September 18, p. 19.
31. Farrington, p. 9B.
32. "1891 Boston Beaneaters (Batting, Pitching & Fielding Statistics)" (2013), Baseball-Reference.com [cited August 17, 2013]. Available from: http://www.baseball-reference.com/teams/BSN/1891.shtml.
33. Charlton, p. 89.
34. "News, Gossip and Comment" (1891), *The Sporting Life*, Saturday, August 15, p. 2.
35. "A Very Good Trip" (1891), *Pittsburg Dispatch*, Sunday, September 20, p. 6.
36. "Once More Exciting: The Teams in the League Race Making a Lively Wind-Up" (1891), *Pittsburg Dispatch*, Sunday, September 20, p. 6.
37. R. Berger (2012), "Amos Rusie," SABR Baseball Biography Project, Society for American Baseball Research [cited August 24, 2013]. Available from: http://sabr.org/bioproj/person/b7d42c08.
38. "Games Played Wednesday, August 17" (1891), *The Sporting Life*, Saturday, September 12, p. 3.
39. R.M. Gorman and D. Weeks (2011), "Death at the Ballpark: A Comprehensive Study of Game-Related Fatalities, 1862–2007" [cited August 24, 2013]. Available from: http://www.deathattheballpark.com/fatalities.html.
40. "It Smacks of a Combination" (1891), *Chicago Tribune*, Thursday, October 1, p. 1.
41. "Kid Nichols (Player Page)" (2013), Baseball-Reference.com [cited June 1, 2013]. Available from: http://www.baseball-reference.com/players/n/nichoki01.shtml.
42. Nemec, *Great Encyclopedia*, pp. 570–576.
43. "Wray's Column: With 4 Champions" (1940), *St. Louis Post-Dispatch*, Wednesday, November 13, p. 8.
44. "News, Gossip, Editorial Comment" (1884), *The Sporting Life*, Wednesday, December 12, p. 2.
45. A.G. Evans (1997), *Fanatic Heart: A Life of John Boyle O'Reilly, 1844–1890* (Nedlands, WA: University of Western Australia Press).

46. "South West Attractions: John Boyle O'Reilly" (2013) [cited August 24, 2013]. Available from: http://www.southwestattractions.com.au/john-boyle-oreilly.html.
47. "National League Meeting" (1892), *Chicago Tribune*, Wednesday, March 2, p. 7.
48. Fleitz, *The Irish in Baseball*, p. 96.
49. "The Diamond" (1892), *Pittsburg Dispatch*, Wednesday, April 20, p. 8.
50. Ibid.
51. "Long's Tumble" (1892), *Boston Globe*, Thursday, April 14, p. 5.
52. A dispatch from St. Louis claimed Von der Ahe had signed Quinn for 1892, but the *Sporting Life* dismissed the news as "nonsense," exclaiming, "Joe Quinn has re-signed for 1892 with Boston, and doesn't belong to the contract-breaking ilk": "News, Gossip, Editorial Comment" (1891), *The Sporting Life*, Saturday, November 7, p. 2. However, the rumors persisted well into July, with Louisville papers hinting, "Boston may have another second baseman soon": "Editorial Views, News, Comment" (1892), *The Sporting Life*, Saturday, July 16, p. 2.
53. "Top Notchers" (1892), *Boston Globe*, Monday, June 6, p. 12.
54. 'Editorial Views, News, Comment," p. 2.
55. "History of the Kidney Punch" (1951), *Montreal Gazette*, Friday, June 29, p. 20.
56. "The Australian Won" (1892), *Pittsburg Dispatch*, Wednesday, April 20, p. 8.
57. M. Appel (1999), *Slide, Kelly, Slide: The Wild Life and Times of Mike "King" Kelly, Baseball's First Superstar* (Lanham, MD: Scarecrow Press), p. 167.
58. "In New Uniforms" (1892), *Boston Globe*, Tuesday, July 12, p. 5.
59. "Kid Nichols (Player Page)" (2013), Baseball-Reference.com [cited June 1, 2013]. Available from: http://www.baseball-reference.com/players/n/nichoki01.shtml.
60. "Club Weakened" (1892), *Boston Globe*, Tuesday, September 20, p. 5.
61. "Jack Stivetts (Player Page)" (2013), Baseball-Reference.com [cited August 24, 2013]. Available from: http://www.baseball-reference.com/players/s/stiveja01.shtml.
62. Zoss and Bowman, p. 209.
63. "Standings and Games on Thursday, September 29, 1892" (2013), Baseball-Reference.com [cited August 24, 2013]. Available from: http://www.baseball-reference.com/games/standings.cgi?date=1892-09-29.
64. "The Worst Game in Years" (1892), *Evening Star* (Washington, DC.), Friday, September 30, p. 10.
65. Charlton, p. 94.
66. "Season Closed" (1892), *Boston Globe*, Sunday, October 16, p. 6.
67. Nemec, *Great Encyclopedia*, pp. 217–607.
68. D. Jones (2012), "Jesse Burkett," SABR Baseball Biography Project, Society for American Baseball Research [cited August 24, 2013]. Available from: http://sabr.org/bioproj/person/53d6808e.
69. P. Wynn (1995), *Baseball's First Stars* (Phoenix, AZ: Society for American Baseball Research), p. 130.
70. "Bostons Score One—The Clevelands Downed in Another Rattling Good Exhibition, Errors Lost the Contest" (1892), *Pittsburg Dispatch*, Wednesday, October 19, p. 9.
71. G. Waggoner, K. Moloney, and H. Howard (2000), *Spitters, Beanballs, and the Incredible Shrinking Strike Zone: The Stories Behind the Rules of Baseball* (Chicago: Triumph Books), p. 118.
72. "Baseball Stories by Joe Quinn," p. 6.

73. "Why Boston Won" (1892), *Boston Sunday Globe*, Sunday, October 30, p. 23.
74. B. Solomon (1997), *The Baseball Timeline: The Day-by-Day History of Baseball, from Valley Forge to the Present Day* (New York: Avon Books), p. 75.
75. "Looking out for '93" (1892), *The Sporting News*, Saturday, October 15, p. 3.
76. "Editorial News, Views, and Comment" (1892), *The Sporting News*, Saturday, June 25, p. 2.
77. "Looking out for '93," p. 3.
78. "The Diamond" (1892), *Pittsburg Dispatch*, Wednesday, October 19, p. 9.
79. "Farrell Won't Sign" (1892), *Pittsburg Dispatch*, Monday, December 5, p. 6.
80. "Looking out for '93," p. 3.
81. "Will Probably Be Called" (1892), *The Sporting Life*, Saturday, October 15, p. 1.

Chapter 10

1. V. Geist (1998), *Buffalo Nation: History and Legend of the North American Bison* (Stillwater, MN: Voyageur Press).
2. Charlton, p. 64.
3. Spink, p. 177.
4. Farrington, p. 9B.
5. Zoss and Bowman, p. 68.
6. Hetrick, *Chris Von Der Ahe*, p. 55.
7. Davis, p. 242.
8. Ibid., p. 79.
9. G. Lipsitz (1991), *The Sidewalks of St. Louis: Places, People, and Politics in an American City* (St. Louis: University of Missouri Press), p. 58.
10. Cash, pp. 190–194.
11. Seymour and Mills, p. 192.
12. "Troubles of Chris Von Der Ahe" (1915), *Washington Post*, Sunday, August 8, p. 3.
13. Hetrick, *Chris Von Der Ahe*, p. 150.
14. Charlton, p. 75.
15. "A Tribute to Watkins" (1892), *The Sporting Life*, Saturday, December 24, p. 4.
16. "The Baseball Outlook in St. Louis" (1893), *The Sun* (New York), Thursday, March 16, p. 4.
17. "Caruthers Set Adrift" (1893), *New York Daily Tribune*, Friday, March 17, p. 5.
18. Monaghan, pp. 6, 14.
19. "J. Quinn" (1893), *The Sporting News*, Monday, February 11, p. 1.
20. G. Elston (2006), *A Stitch in Time* (Houston, TX: Halcyon Press), p. 30.
21. St. Louis City Directory 1893–1894: *United States City Directories, 1882–1901. Saint Louis, Mo.* [Microform] (1990) (Research Publications: Woodbridge, CT).
22. "An Anonymous Letter" (1893), *The Sporting News*, Saturday, February 11, p. 5.
23. "The Baseball Outlook in St. Louis" (1893), *The Sun* (New York), Thursday, March 16, p. 4.
24. W. Akin (2012), "Jack Glasscock," SABR Baseball Biography Project [cited April 3, 2013]. Available from: http://sabr.org/bioproj/person/0bcddad0.
25. "The Value of Peitz" (1893), *The Sporting Life*, Saturday, April 1, p. 4.
26. "Ted Breitenstein (Player Page)" (2013), Baseball-Reference.com [cited June 29, 2013]. Available from: http://www.baseball-reference.com/bullpen/Ted_Breitenstein.
27. Eisenbath and Musial, p. 259.
28. "Their Probable Positions" (1893), *The Sun* (New York), Saturday, April 5, p. 4.

29. "St. Louis 3–Louisville 1" (1893), *The Sun* (New York), Saturday, April 29, p. 8.
30. "St. Louis Siftings—The Dedication of a New Park a Social Event" (1893), *The Sporting Life*, Saturday, May 6, p. 3.
31. The St. Louis Empires and Unions played on Old Sportsman's Park in 1858, and the old Browns adopted it as home in 1876. When the park fell into disuse after the failure of St. Louis's first attempt at maintaining a National League franchise, Al Spink helped organized the Sportsman's Park and Club Association that refurbished the park and lent its name to the facility. Von der Ahe took possession of the Browns and the park in 1882, and when his lease expired in October 1893, it was returned to its owners, the John Dunn estate, and turned into building lots. From: Benson, pp. 348–349.
32. *New Sportsman's Park Official Score Book* (1893) (St. Louis, MO: Great West), pp. 1–20.
33. The site of New Sportsman's Park at 2901 N. Grand Blvd now hosts the Herbert Hoover Boys & Girls Club. The original site now forms part of the club playing fields: J.M. Thomas (2012), "Robison Field (St. Louis)," Society for American Baseball Research (SABR) BioProject [cited July 28, 2013]. Available from: http://sabr.org/bioproj/park/88929e79.
34. *New Sportsman's Park Official Score Book*, pp. 1–20.
35. Charlton, p. 96.
36. "Baseball" (1893), *Salt Lake Herald*, Sunday, June 4, p. 13.
37. "1893 St. Louis Browns (Schedule, Box Scores and Splits)" (2013), Baseball-Reference.com [cited August 19, 2013]. Available from: http://www.baseball-reference.com/teams/STL/1893-schedule-scores.shtml.
38. "Their Probable Positions," p. 4.
39. "Standings and Games on Sunday, July 2, 1892" (2013), Baseball-Reference.com [cited August 24, 2013]. Available from: http://www.baseball-reference.com/games/standings.cgi?date=1893-07-02.
40. Charlton, p. 97.
41. "A Chance Given Mr. Sharrott" (1893), *New York Times*, Tuesday, August 8, p. 6.
42. P. Morris (2006), *A Game of Inches: The Stories Behind the Innovations That Shaped Baseball: The Game on the Field* (Chicago: Ivan R. Dee), p. 308.
43. Charlton, p. 98.
44. "Flashes from the Diamond" (1895), *Omaha Daily Bee*, Saturday, January 26, p. 4.
45. Charlton, p. 103.
46. Farrington, p. 9B.
47. "Connie Mack (Player Page)" (2013), Baseball-Reference.com [cited August 25, 2013]. Available from: http://www.baseball-reference.com/players/m/mackco01.shtml.
48. Home teams supplied the umpire with balls one by one and Mack kept spares on ice until an hour before the game to let the cover warm up: Seymour and Mills, p. 187.
49. "Connie Mack (Manager Page)" (2013), Baseball-Reference.com [cited August 25, 2013]. Available from: http://www.baseball-reference.com/managers/mackco01.shtml.
50. N.L. Macht (2007), *Connie Mack and the Early Years of Baseball* (Lincoln: University of Nebraska Press), p. 72.
51. Joseph Francis Quinn, Joe's second son, was born on August 10, 1893.
52. "An Anonymous Letter" (1893), *The Sporting News*, Saturday, February 11, p. 5.
53. "1893 St. Louis Browns (Batting, Pitching & Fielding Statistics)" (2013), Baseball-Reference.com [cited Au-

gust 17, 2013]. Available from: http://www.baseball-reference.com/teams/STL/1893.shtml.

54. "Captain Joe Quinn—Business Cares Affected His Last Playing Season" (1893), *The Sporting News*, Saturday, October 21, p. 1.

55. "St. Louis Siftings—Waterlooed Browns Homecoming from the East" (1893), *The Sporting Life*, Saturday, September 16, p. 11.

56. "Obituary: Joe Quinn" (1940), *The Sporting News*, Thursday, November 21, p. 8.

57. "J. Quinn" (1893), *The Sporting News*, Monday, February 11, p. 1.

58. *The Sporting Life* reported, "Capt. Joe Quinn has sold his livery stable business. Joe has a nice competence, and is of that steady, thrifty character that gives him the reputation of being one of the really substantial members of the profession": "St. Louis Siftings—Rumors as to the Make-up of the '94 Team" (1894), *The Sporting Life*, Saturday, October 21, p. 5.

59. "1893 St. Louis Browns (Batting, Pitching & Fielding Statistics)".

60. "Baseball-Reference.Com" (2013), Sports Reference LLC [cited August 20, 2013]. Available from: http://www.baseball-reference.com/.

61. "1893 St. Louis Browns (Batting, Pitching & Fielding Statistics)".

62. "Editorial News, Views, and Comment" (1893), *The Sporting Life*, Saturday, September 9, p. 2.

63. "St. Louis Siftings—The Browns as Seen from the Small End of the Opera Glass" (1893), *The Sporting Life*, Saturday, September 2, p. 3.

64. Farrington, p. 9B.

65. "Mt. Sterling Club Disbands" (1894), *Sterling Advocate* (Mount Sterling, KY), Tuesday, September 4, p. 1.

66. Farrington, p. 9B.

67. K.R. Arnold (2011), *Anti-Immigration in the United States: A Historical Encyclopedia* (Santa Barbara, CA: Greenwood), pp. 4–6.

68. B. McKenna (2007), *Early Exits: The Premature Endings of Baseball Careers* (Lanham, MD: Scarecrow Press), p. 43.

69. "The Players at Work" (1893), *The Sporting Life*, Saturday, March 31, p. 6.

70. "Boss Von Der Ahe" (1893), *The Sporting Life*, Saturday, March 31, p. 6.

71. "St. Louis Siftings" (1894), *The Sporting Life*, Saturday, August 4, p. 4.

72. "Toledo Badly Beaten" (1895), *The Sporting Life*, Wednesday, April 4, p. 6.

73. "A St. Louis Victory" (1894), *The Sporting Life*, Wednesday, April 21, p. 5.

74. "Started: The League Championship Season" (1894), *The Sporting News*, Saturday, April 21, p. 4.

75. "League-Association" (1894), *The Sporting News*, Saturday, April 28, p. 4.

76. "St. Louis Siftings—Ready for the Great Fight of 1894" (1894), *The Sporting Life*, Saturday, April 21, p. 6.

77. "Bones Ely (Player Page)" (2013), Baseball-Reference.com [cited August 15, 2013]. Available from: http://www.baseball-reference.com/players/e/elybo01.shtml.

78. "St. Louis Siftings—Ready for the Great Fight of 1894," p. 6.

79. "1894 Chicago Colts (Batting, Pitching & Fielding Statistics)" (2013), Baseball-Reference.com [cited August 7, 2013]. Available from: http://www.baseball-reference.com/teams/CHC/1894.shtml.

80. "1894 St. Louis Browns (Schedule, Box Scores and Splits)" (2013), Baseball-Reference.com [cited August 17, 2013]. Available from: http://www.baseball-reference.com/teams/STL/1894-schedule-scores.shtml.

81. "St. Louis Siftings—The Gratifying Showing of the Browns" (1894), *The Sporting Life*, Saturday, May 5, p. 8.

82. "League Association" (1894), *The Sporting News*, Saturday, May 5, p. 6.

83. "Chris' Slick Scheme" (1894), *The Sporting Life*, Saturday, May 26, p. 6.

84. Charlton, pp. 99, 101.

85. "National League: No Striking Changes in the Championship Race: Games Played May 10" (1894), *The Sporting Life*, Saturday, May 19, p. 4.

86. "League-Association" (1894), *The Sporting News*, Saturday, May 19, p. 6.

87. The current mark (at 2013) stands at 19, set by the Los Angeles Dodgers' Shawn Green on May 23, 2002: Society for American Baseball Research (2007), *The Sabr Baseball List & Record Book: Baseball's Most Fascinating Records and Unusual Statistics* (New York: Scribner), p. 70.

88. D.L. Porter (2000), *Biographical Dictionary of American Sports*, Volume 2: *Baseball* (Westport, CT: Greenwood Press), p. 904.

89. Charlton, p. 103.

90. Fleitz, *The Irish in Baseball*, p. 89.

91. The Black Sox scandal broke during the 1919 World Series, which the Chicago White Sox lost to the Cincinnati Reds amid accusations that eight of the White Sox had deliberately thrown matches at the behest of gambling syndicates. While the players were eventually cleared of any wrongdoing, they were all banned for life from professional baseball. Gleason was not implicated in the scandal and continued to manage the White Sox until 1923 under owner Charlie Comiskey. D. Lindner (2012), "Kid Gleason," SABR Baseball Biography Project, Society for American Baseball Research [cited August 15, 2013]. Available from: http://sabr.org/bioproj/person/632ed912.

92. "1894 St. Louis Browns (Schedule, Box Scores and Splits)."

93. "Again the Giants Failed" (1894), *New York Times*, Thursday, August 2, p. 6.

94. "Standings and Games on Friday, June 1, 1894" (2013), Baseball-Reference.com [cited August 20, 2013]. Available from: http://www.baseball-reference.com/games/standings.cgi?date=1894-06-01.

95. "Back to Form" (1894), *Boston Sunday Globe*, Sunday, June 10, p. 7; "Boston Second" (1894), *Boston Sunday Globe*, Sunday, June 10, p. 7.

96. R. Kerr (2011), *Roger Connor: Home Run King of 19th Century Baseball* (Jefferson, NC: McFarland), pp. 127–128.

97. "St. Louis Siftings" (1894), *The Sporting Life*, Saturday, June 30, p. 5.

98. "With the Baltimores" (1894), *Baltimore Sun*, Saturday, June 30, p. 6.

99. "Home-Run Jennings" (1894), *Baltimore Sun*, Friday, June 15, p. 6.

100. "Three from the Browns" (1894), *Baltimore Sun*, Monday, June 18, p. 6.

101. "St. Louis Siftings" (1894), *The Sporting Life*, Saturday, June 30, p. 5.

102. "An Alleged New Regime at Sportsmens' Park" (1894), *The Sporting Life*, Saturday, July 7, p. 10.

103. "Divided the Honors—The Browns and the Washingtons Each Took a Game" (1894), *St. Louis Globe-Democrat*, Thursday, July 5.

104. "Games Played July 4" (1894), *The Sporting Life*, Saturday, July 14, p. 3.

105. "St. Louis Siftings" (1894), *The Sporting Life*, Saturday, July 14, p. 6.

106. "On Top of the Heap" (1894), *Baltimore Sun*, Monday, July 16, p. 6.

107. Sweeney would be remembered for two remarkable records: he struck out 19 Boston batters in a game in 1884, a feat only bettered by Roger Clemens who struck out 20 in 1986. Sweeney remains the only pitcher to have given up seven home runs in a game, on June 12, 1886, with the St. Louis Maroons. "Charlie Sweeney (Player Page)" (2013), Baseball-Reference.com [cited June 29, 2013]. Available from: http://www.baseball-reference.com/players/s/sweench01.shtml.

108. "Out of Sight" (1894), *Boston Globe*, Tuesday, July 31, p. 5.

109. "St. Louis 6, Louisville 4" (1894), *Boston Daily Globe*, Saturday, July 28, p. 3; "Louisville 8, St. Louis 4" (1894), *Boston Daily Globe*, Sunday, July 29, p. 7.

110. "League-Association" (1894), *The Sporting News*, Saturday, August 4, p. 5.

111. "St. Louis Siftings" (1894), *The Sporting Life*, Saturday, August 4, p. 4.

112. Ibid.

113. "A Bad State of Affairs among the Browns" (1894), *The Sporting Life*, Saturday, August, 11, p. 5.

114. "Von Der Ahe's Woe" (1894), *The Sporting Life*, Saturday, August 25, p. 1.

115. Hetrick, *Chris Von Der Ahe*, p. 160.

116. "A Bad State of Affairs among the Browns."

117. "A New King Lear" (1894), *The Sporting Life*, Saturday, August 18, p. 2.

118. Hetrick, *Chris Von Der Ahe*, p. 245.

119. "1894 St. Louis Browns (Schedule, Box Scores and Splits)."

120. "Champions Tired" (1894), *Boston Daily Globe*, Wednesday, August 29, p. 2.

121. "Forfeited the Game" (1894), *Washington Post*, Thursday, September 6, p. 6.

122. "'Der Boss' and 'Theo'" (1894), *The Sporting Life*, Saturday, September 22, p. 2.

123. S. Thornley (2000), *Land of the Giants: New York's Polo Grounds* (Philadelphia: Temple University Press), p. 155.

124. "The Browns Disbanded—Chris Von Der Ahe Arrested for Assault—Meeting of the Directors Etc." (1894), *The Sporting Life*, Saturday, October 13, p. 2.

125. "1894 National League Fielding Leaders" (2013), Baseball-Reference.com [cited August 20, 2013]. Available from: http://www.baseball-reference.com/leagues/NL/1894-fielding-leaders.shtml.

126. "Baseball Stories by Joe Quinn," p. 6.

127. Ibid.

128. M. Appel (1999), *Slide, Kelly, Slide: The Wild Life and Times of Mike "King" Kelly, Baseball's First Superstar* (Lanham, MD: Scarecrow Press), p. 187.

129. Spink, p. 104.

130. The song "Slide, Kelly, Slide!" by George Gaskin, became the first baseball song to feature in the popular music charts in January 1892: G. Elston, (2006), *A Stitch in Time* (Houston: Halcyon Press), p. 7.

Chapter 11

1. C.S. Littleton (2005), *Gods, Goddesses, and Mythology*, Vol. 10 (New York: Marshall Cavendish), p. 1307.

2. "Wray's Column: With 4 Champions" (1940), *St. Louis Post-Dispatch*, Wednesday, November 13, p. 8.

3. Former second baseman Fred Pfeffer was also implicated and suspended. R.F. Burk (2001), *Never Just a Game: Players, Owners, and American Baseball to 1920* (Chapel Hill: University of North Carolina Press), p. 126.

4. "1894 National League Team Statistics and Standings" (2013), Baseball-Reference.com [cited August 20, 2013]. Available from: http://www.baseball-reference.com/leagues/NL/1894.shtml.

5. "Al Buckenberger (Manager Page)" (2013), Baseball-Reference.com [cited August 2, 2013]. Available from: http://www.baseball-reference.com/managers/buckeal99.shtml.

6. "Mr. Von Der Ahe in a Very Hopeful Mood" (1896). *The Sporting Life*, Saturday, April 6, p. 7.

7. "The Browns All Right Despite Their Poor Start" (1896), *The Sporting Life*, Saturday, April 27, p. 10.

8. "A Wail of Distress from the Mound City" (1896), *The Sporting Life*, Saturday, May 4, p. 4.

9. "Chris' Hoodoo" (1895), *The Sporting Life*, Saturday, May 11, p. 5.

10. "Mercer Knocked Out" (1895), *Washington Post*, Saturday, May 4, p. 4.

11. "League-Association" (1895), *The Sporting News*, Saturday, May 18, p. 6.

12. "The Big League Race" (1895), *The Sporting Life*, Saturday, June 8, pp. 10–11.

13. "Baseball: Personal" (1895), *The Sporting Life*, Saturday, June 8, p. 4.

14. "Eight in Eighth" (1895), *Boston Daily Globe*, Thursday, May 9, p. 5.

15. "The Browns Little Benefitted by Their Trip" (1895), *The Sporting Life*, Saturday, April 20, p. 7.

16. "League-Association" (1895), *The Sporting News*, Saturday, August 10, p. 3.

17. "Change in the St. Louis Team" (1895), *Los Angeles Herald*, Tuesday, June 25, p. 2; "News Briefly Reported" (1895), *New Ulm Review* (New Ulm, MN), Wednesday, June 26; "The National Game" (1895), *The Courier* (Lincoln, NE), Saturday, June 29, p. 9.

18. "Released by Von Der Ahe" (1895), *San Francisco Call*, Monday, June 24, p. 2.

19. "Baseball Notes" (1895), *Washington Times*, Monday, July 1, p. 3.

20. "The Facts About Manager Buckenberger's Release" (1895), *The Sporting Life*, Saturday, July 6, p. 10.

21. Ibid.

22. "League-Association" (1895), *The Sporting News*, Saturday, August 10, p. 3.

23. "Baseball Notes" (1895), *Washington Times*, Monday, July 1, p. 3.

24. "Diamond Dust" (1896), *Morning Times* (Washington, DC), Saturday, June 13, p. 3.

25. "J. Quinn" (1893), *The Sporting News*, Monday, February 11, p. 1.

26. l. Durocher and E. Linn (2009), *Nice Guys Finish Last* (Chicago: University of Chicago Press).

27. "Late News by Wire: Von Der Ahe and Day" (1895), *The Sporting Life*, Saturday, June 29, p. 2.

28. "Von Der Ahe Discusses His Players" (1894), *The Sporting Life*, Saturday, December 8, p. 3.

29. "League-Association" (1895), *The Sporting Life*, Saturday, July 6, p. 3.

30. "Obituary: Joe Quinn" (1940), *The Sporting News*, Thursday, November 21, p. 8.

31. "Chatter with the Ball Cranks" (1895), *Omaha Daily Bee*, Sunday, August 25, p. 16.

32. Connie Mack had arrived from Pittsburgh on July 7, checked anonymously into a hotel, and pleaded on his knees with Von der Ahe to sell Breitenstein to the Pirates for $10,000, and the trio of Quinn, Ely, and Peitz for a further $25,000. The offer was rejected, as had been a $5,000

offer for Breit from Baltimore on June 15: "The Browns in a Rather Crippled Condition" (1895), *The Sporting Life*, Saturday, July 13, p. 10.
33. Hetrick, *Chris Von Der Ahe*, p. 171.
34. "The Browns in a Rather Crippled Condition" (1895).
35. "St. Louis Sayings" (1895), *The Sporting Life*, Saturday, July 27, p. 10.
36. "How Fred Ely Queered His Own Game" (1895), *The Sporting Life*, Saturday, December 28, p. 7.
37. "The Browns in a Rather Crippled Condition."
38. "Joe Otten (Player Page)" (2013), Baseball-Reference.com [cited August 20, 2013]. Available from: http://www.baseball-reference.com/players/o/ottenjo01.shtml.
39. "St. Louis Sayings: Von Der Ahe Saves Baseball in the West" (1895), *The Sporting Life*, Saturday, July 20, p. 11.
40. Ibid.
41. "Joe Quinn Exalted" (1895), *The Sporting News*, Saturday, July 27, p. 4.
42. "1895 St. Louis Browns (Schedule, Box Scores and Splits)" (2013), Baseball-Reference.com [cited August 18, 2013]. Available from: http://www.baseball-reference.com/teams/STL/1895-schedule-scores.shtml.
43. "The Big League Race" (1895), *The Sporting Life*, Saturday, August 10, p. 4.
44. P. Morris (2012), "Billy Kinloch," Society for American Baseball Research (SABR) BioProject [cited August 20, 2013]. Available from: http://sabr.org/bioproj/person/e961c4c9.
45. "Battle Begun: Last Sectional Trip of the Season On" (1895), *The Sporting News*, Saturday, August 24, p. 4.
46. "The Browns in a State of Demoralization" (1895), *The Sporting Life*, Saturday, August 10, p. 11.
47. "League-Association" (1895), *The Sporting News*, Saturday, August 10, p. 3.
48. P. Morris (2013), *Cracking Baseball's Cold Cases: Filling in the Facts About 17 Mystery Major Leaguers* (Jefferson, NC: McFarland), p.43.
49. Ibid., pp. 46–48.
50. Hetrick, *Chris Von Der Ahe*, pp. 169, 245.
51. Eisenbath and Musial, p. 396.
52. D. Rosensweig (2005), *Retro Ball Parks: Instant History, Baseball, and the New American City* (Knoxville, TN: University of Tennessee Press), p. 81.
53. "St. Louis Sayings: Another Change in the Browns' Management" (1895), *The Sporting Life*, Saturday, August 17, p. 10.
54. "Palaver of the Ball Players" (1895), *Omaha Daily Bee*, Sunday, November 17, p. 23.
55. "Standings and Games on Monday, September 2, 1895" (2013), Baseball-Reference.com [cited August 30, 2013]. Available from: http://www.baseball-reference.com/games/standings.cgi?date=1895-09-02.
56. "St. Louis Sayings: Von Der Ahe Stuck on the Young Blood Theory" (1895), *The Sporting Life*, Saturday, August 24, p. 9.
57. "Eagle Baseball Notes" (1895), *Wichita Daily Eagle*, Saturday, September 28, p. 3.
58. "League-Association" (1895), *The Sporting News*, Saturday, August 10, p. 3.
59. "Baseball Notes" (1895), *St. Louis Globe-Democrat*, Monday, September 23, p. 6.
60. "Inks in the Box" (1896), *St. Paul Globe*, Sunday, July 12, p. 10.
61. "Quinn's Proposal" (1895), *The Sporting Life*, Saturday, November 2, p. 3.
62. "O'Connell and Biddy Moriarty" (1857), *The Argus* (Melbourne), Tuesday, October 13, p. 7.
63. Formed in 1842 and named for Revolutionary War hero William Jasper, Capt. John Foley's Irish Jasper Greens was one of Savannah's dominant volunteer militia companies, and the only one from Savannah accepted for service in the Mexican War. From T.G. Rodgers and R. Hook (2008), *Irish-American Units in the Civil War* (Oxford, UK: Osprey).
64. "Here and There" (1895), *The Sporting Life*, Saturday, June 8, p. 9.
65. "How Fred Ely Queered His Own Game."
66. M. Motto (2000), personal communication, "Re: Joe Quinn" [e-mail]. To: R. Nicholls (Wednesday, May 31).
67. "Palaver of the Ball Players."
68. Eisenbath and Musial, p. 20.
69. Hetrick, *Chris Von Der Ahe*, p.188.
70. "St. Louis Sayings: Royal Welcome Accorded the New Manager" (1896), *The Sporting Life*, Saturday, February 8, p. 3.
71. "How Fred Ely Queered His Own Game."
72. "One More St. Louis Brown Joins the Pirates" (1896), *The Sporting Life*, Saturday, January 11, p. 8.
73. "Ted Breitenstein (Player Page)" (2013), Baseball-Reference.com [cited June 29, 2013]. Available from: http://www.baseball-reference.com/bullpen/Ted_Breitenstein.
74. "Breitenstein Still Firm" (1896), *The Sporting Life*, Saturday, February 8, p. 3.
75. "Not Illiberal" (1896), *The Sporting Life*, Saturday, March 7, p. 2.
76. "Safe in St. Louis" (1896), *The Sporting Life*, Saturday, March 14, p. 1.
77. D. Randall (1976), *The First Modern Olympics* (Berkeley, CA: University of California Press).
78. R. Witt (2012), *A Lifetime of Training for Just Ten Seconds: Olympians in Their Own Words* (New York: Bloomsbury), p. 65.
79. P. Sweeney (2004), *Edwin Flack, the Lion of Athens: Australia's First Olympic Games Gold Medallist* (Australia: Peter Sweeney).
80. "Hall of Fame: Edwin Flack—Athletics" (2012), Sport Australia Hall of Fame [cited December 2, 2012]. Available from: http://www.sahof.org.au/hall-of-fame/member-profile/?memberID=380&memberType=legends.
81. "Edwin Flack—Our First Olympic Champion" (2013), City of Casey, VIC [cited March 9, 2013]. Available from: http://www.casey.vic.gov.au/olympic/.
82. G. Robertson (2013), personal communication re: Australian Baseball Hall of Fame Heritage Committee: Joe Quinn [telephone]. To: R. Nicholls (Friday, April 12).
83. W.N. Wilbert (2007), *The Arrival of the American League: Ban Johnson and the 1901 Challenge to National League Monopoly* (Jefferson, NC: McFarland), p. 41.
84. Charlton, p. 106.
85. D.L. Fleitz (2004), *Ghosts in the Gallery at Cooperstown: Sixteen Little-Known Members of the Hall of Fame* (Jefferson, NC: McFarland), p. 223.
86. "1896 St. Louis Browns (Schedule, Box Scores and Splits)" (2013), Baseball-Reference.com [cited August 21, 2013]. Available from: http://www.baseball-reference.com/teams/STL/1896-schedule-scores.shtml.
87. "Mr. Von Der Ahe Shakes Things up Lively" (1896), *The Sporting Life*, Saturday, May 16, p. 8.
88. Pearson, p. 110.
89. "Arlie Latham (Manager Page)" (2013), Baseball-Reference.com [cited August 15, 2013]. Available from: http://www.baseball-reference.com/managers/lathaar01.shtml.
90. "1896 St. Louis Browns (Batting, Pitching, & Fielding Statistics)" (2013), Baseball-Reference.com [cited August 21, 2013]. Available from: http://www.baseball-reference.com/teams/STL/1896.shtml.

91. "Gossip of the Country's Game" (1896), *St. Paul Globe*, Sunday, May 17, p. 3.
92. Ibid.
93. "Inks in the Box."
94. J. Curzon (1896), *The Great Cyclone at St. Louis and East St. Louis, May 27, 1896: Being a Full History of the Most Terrifying and Destructive Tornado in the History of the World* (Carbondale: Southern Illinois University Press).
95. "1896 St. Louis Browns (Schedule, Box Scores and Splits)."
96. "Browns' President Sued" (1896), *St. Paul Globe*, Thursday, September 17, p. 5.
97. "Joe Quinn (Player Page)" (2013). Baseball-Reference.com [cited January 9, 2013]. Available from: http://www.baseball-reference.com/players/q/quinnjo02.shtml.
98. "Joe Quinn Released: Der Cherman Pand Must Be Playing Madhouse Airs!" (1896), *New York World*, Wednesday, July 1, p. 3.
99. "The Great Race" (1896), *The Sporting Life*, Saturday, July 11, pp. 2–3.

Chapter 12

1. Monaghan, pp. 6, 14.
2. Farrington, p. 9B.
3. "Questions and Answers" *Omaha Daily Bee*, Sunday, August 25, p. 16.
4. Monaghan, pp. 6, 14.
5. On one occasion, the ball was apparently returned simultaneously to second base by the left- and center fielders; that game was forfeited to the opposition: P. Morris (2007), *Level Playing Fields: How the Groundskeeping Murphy Brothers Shaped Baseball* (Lincoln: University of Nebraska Press), pp. 35–37.
6. J.H. Bready (1998), *Baseball in Baltimore: The First Hundred Years* (Baltimore: Johns Hopkins University Press), p. 106.
7. "The Mound City Mad" (1893), *The Sporting Life*, Saturday, September 9, p. 1.
8. Kavanagh and Macht, pp. 25–26.
9. B. Solomon (1999), *Where They Ain't: The Fabled Life and Ultimely Death of the Original Baltimore Orioles, the Team That Gave Birth to Modern Baseball* (New York: Free Press), p. 5.
10. "Willie Keeler (Player Page)" (2013). Baseball-Reference.com [cited July 18, 2013]. Available from: http://www.baseball-reference.com/players/k/keelewi01.shtml.
11. Solomon, *Where They Ain't*, p. 118.
12. Spink, p. 246.
13. J. Smiles (2005), *"Ee-Yah": The Life and Times of Hughie Jennings, Baseball Hall of Famer* (Jefferson, NC: McFarland), pp. 71–79.
14. Kavanagh and Macht, p. 21.
15. Zoss and Bowman.
16. Kavanagh and Macht, p. 26.
17. Monaghan, pp. 6, 14.
18. C.C. Alexander (1995), *John McGraw* (Lincoln: University of Nebraska Press), p. 37.
19. Charlton, p. 99.
20. "Career Leaders & Records for Hit by Pitch" (2013), Baseball-Reference.com [cited August 30, 2013]. Available from: http://www.baseball-reference.com/leaders/HBP_career.shtml.
21. In 1898, Baltimore set an all-time record of 158 HBPs for the season—Jennings with 42, Dan McGann 48, and John McGraw 18. By August 1899, a movement was afoot to abolish the rule allowing a man a base for being hit by a pitched ball. See: "Notes of the National Game" (1899), *Evening Times* (Washington, DC), Thursday, August 3, p. 6.
22. Benson, p. 407.
23. "Crowds in League Cities: Catcher Kittridge Writes About the Patrons of the Game" (1896), *Evening Times* (Washington, DC), Friday, September 4, p. 3.
24. Apparently Quinn, instead of charging Chris Von der Ahe with meanness and unfairness, still had a good word for the St. Louis chief: "News and Comment" (1896), *The Sporting Life*, Saturday, July 18, p. 5.
25. Monaghan, pp. 6, 14.
26. "Baseball Stories by Joe Quinn," p. 6.
27. A high-risk play used to generate offensive momentum. Generally executed with runners on first and second or first and third bases, the maneuver relies on using a stolen base attempt to draw the opposing infielders out of position and the hitter driving the ball past them.
28. "Baseball Stories by Joe Quinn," p. 6.
29. "Whipped Again" (1896), *The Sun* (Baltimore, MD), Saturday, June 6, p. 6.
30. "Games Played Wednesday, June 3" (1896), *The Sporting Life*, Saturday, June 6, p. 3.
31. "Diamond Dust" (1896), *Morning Times* (Washington, DC), Thursday, July 9, p. 3.
32. "Gossip of the Country's Game."
33. "Diamond Dust," op. cit.
34. "Inks in the Box," p. 10.
35. Fleitz, *The Irish in Baseball*, p. 87.
36. "1896 St. Louis Browns (Batting, Pitching, & Fielding Statistics)."
37. Charlton, p. 118.
38. Kavanagh and Macht, p. 19.
39. "They Slugged the Ball" (1896), *Morning Times* (Washington, DC), Sunday, August 9, p. 7.
40. "Base Ball" (1896), *The Sporting Life*, Saturday, August 8, p. 5.
41. "Patsy Tebeau (Player Page)" (2013). Baseball-Reference.com [cited August 20, 2013]. Available from: http://www.baseball-reference.com/players/t/tebeapa01.shtml.
42. "1896 Baltimore Orioles (Schedule, Box Scores and Splits)" (2013). Baseball-Reference.com [cited August 19, 2013]. Available from: http://www.baseball-reference.com/teams/BLN/1896-schedule-scores.shtml.
43. "Between the Bases" (1896), *Evening Times* (Washington, DC), Friday, September 4, p. 3.
44. Ibid.
45. From the *Baltimore News*. In "Between the Bases," p. 3.
46. "1896 Baltimore Orioles (Schedule, Box Scores and Splits)."
47. Gietschier, p. 18.
48. The .698 win-loss percentage of the 1896 Orioles bettered their 1894 effort by 0.003; the team won the National League pennant in both years, in addition to their 1895 triumph. The franchise was born in 1882 and spent its first 9 seasons in the American Association before transferring to the National League. In 1899, the team franchise and that of the Brooklyn Superbas were co-owned by Baltimore owner Harry Van der Horst and Ned Hanlon. Most of the star Baltimores were shipped to Brooklyn and the denuded Orioles finished only fourth. They were one of four teams dropped by the National League as it downsized to 8 teams for the 1900 season. "Baltimore Orioles (Team History & Encyclopedia)" (2013), Baseball-Reference.com [cited August 21, 2013]. Available from: http://www.baseball-reference.com/teams/BLO/; M.L. Armour and D.R. Levitt (2004), *Paths to Glory: How Great Baseball*

Teams Got That Way (Washington, DC: Brassey's), pp. 12–17.
49. Smiles, p. 54.
50. "Base Ball Briefs" (1898), *St. Paul Globe*, Monday, July 4, p. 5.
51. "Latest News and Gossip of the Sporting World" (1909), *Fort Wayne Sentinel* (Fort Wayne, IN), Thursday, November 4, p. 8.
52. "One for the Temple Cup" (1896), *The Sun* (Baltimore, MD), Saturday, October 3, p. 6.
53. Spink, p. 119.
54. "Baltimore Bulletin: Echoes of the Series for the Temple Cup" (1896), *The Sporting Life*, Saturday, October 10, p. 6.
55. "Between the Bases," p. 3.
56. Ibid.
57. M.D. Peterson (1960), *The Jefferson Image in the American Mind* Peterson (New York: Oxford University Press), p. 79.
58. "Guests of a Cardinal" (1896), *Evening Times* (Washington, DC), Tuesday, September 15, p. 3.
59. Hetrick, *Chris Von Der Ahe*, p. 254.
60. Kavanagh, and Macht, p. 29.
61. Ibid., pp. 33–35.
62. Farrington, p. 9B.
63. "News and Comment" (1896), *The Sporting Life*, Saturday, July 18, p. 5.
64. "Where the Ball Players Are" (1896), *St. Paul Globe*, Sunday, November 8, p. 10.
65. "Diamond Dust" (1897), *Evening Times* (Washington, DC), Friday, March 12, p. 5.
66. "Clarke Had a Revolver, Drew the Weapon on Davis and Joyce on Saturday" (1897), *Evening Times* (Washington, DC), Monday, July 19, p. 6.
67. "Diamond Dust," op.cit., p.5.
68. Ibid.
69. A. Mott "Baltimore Bulletin" (1897), *The Sporting Life*, April 24.
70. Ibid.
71. M. Seidel (2002), *Streak: Joe Dimaggio and the Summer of '41* (Lincoln: University of Nebraska Press), pp. 164–165.
72. "The World of Base Ball" (1897), *The Sporting Life*, May 1.
73. "Baltimore Bulletin" (1897), *The Sporting Life*, May 15, p. 7.
74. Charlton, p. 111.
75. Nemec and Flatow, p. 88.
76. "Bill Joyce (Br Bullpen)" (2013), Baseball-Reference.com [cited August 21, 2013]. Available from: http://www.baseball-reference.com/bullpen/Bill_Joyce.
77. P. Morris (2006), *A Game of Inches: The Stories Behind the Innovations That Shaped Baseball: The Game on the Field* (Chicago: Ivan R. Dee), p. 409.
78. Charlton, p. 112.
79. "Diamond Dust" (1897), *Evening Times* (Washington, DC), Saturday, May 29, p. 3.
80. "The League Race: The Contest Becoming Close and Exciting" (1897), *The Sporting Life*, Saturday, May 29, p. 2.
81. "Maul Will Be an Oriole" (1897), *Evening Times* (Washington, DC), Saturday, May 29, p. 3.
82. "The League Race: The First Trip Favorable to the Eastern Teams" (1897), *The Sporting Life*, Saturday, June 5, p. 2.
83. "The World of Base Ball" (1897), *The Sporting Life*, June 5, p. 2.
84. "They Would Not Bunt" (1897), *The Sun* (Baltimore, MD), Monday, June 21, p. 6.
85. "Orioles on Top Again" (1897), *The Sun* (Baltimore, MD), Wednesday, June 23, p. 6.
86. "Games Played Tuesday, July 6" (1897), *The Sporting Life*, Saturday July 10, p. 3.
87. "Joe Quinn's Blood Poisoned" (1897), *Morning Times* (Washington, DC), Saturday, July 17, p. 6.
88. "Injured Ball Players. Fifty-Nine Men of the 214 Listed Players Have Been Disabled Thus Far This Season" (1897), *Evening Times* (Washington, DC), Monday, July 19, p. 6.
89. Mitchell, pp. 2–24.
90. Clark, *History of Australian Baseball*.
91. "Baseball Notes" (1897), *Chronicle* (Adelaide, SA), Saturday, June 5, p. 31.
92. "Dingo Land Ball Players" (1897), *Morning Times* (Washington, DC), Wednesday, March 24, p. 3.
93. Clark, p. 35.
94. "The Australian Baseball Team—Further Particulars of the Tour" (1897), *South Australian Register* (Adelaide, SA), Friday, July 23, p. 7.
95. "Baseball Notes" (1897), *Chronicle* (Adelaide, SA), Saturday, June 5, p. 31.
96. Twister, p. 5.
97. Clark, *History of Australian Baseball*.
98. Mitchell, pp. 2–24.
99. Clark, *History of Australian Baseball*.
100. J.J. Evers and H.S. Fullerton (1910), *Touching Second: The Science of Baseball* (Kessinger Publishing).
101. Twister, "The Australian Base-Ballers."
102. "International Baseball—Australian in America" (1897), *The Chronicle* (Adelaide, SA), Saturday, July 31, p. 33.
103. F. Laver, "America's National Game—High Prices for Players" (1908), *The Argus* (Melbourne), Saturday, August 22, p. 9.
104. Corbett's baseball-related troubles coincided with a family tragedy in August 1898 in which his father shot his mother to death before turning the gun on himself. The murder-suicide put paid to Corbett's career until 1903, when he signed with the Los Angeles Angels of the Pacific Coast League: B. Lamb (2012), "Joe Corbett," SABR Baseball Biography Project, Society for American Baseball Research [cited August 10, 2013]. Available from: http://sabr.org/bioproj/person/bcebe2e6.
105. "Stranded Cricketers" (1913), *Cairns Post* (Cairns, QLD), Monday, August 18, p. 6.
106. Clark, *History of Australian Baseball*.
107. Dabscheck, "Australian Baseballers Form a Team of Their Own."
108. "Brilliant Ball Game" (1897), *The Sun* (Baltimore, MD), Tuesday, August 3, p. 6.
109. Charlton, p. 113.
110. "Notes of the Game" (1897), *Chicago Tribune*, Saturday, July 17, p. 6.
111. "Diamond Dust" (1897), *Morning Times* (Washington, DC), Sunday, September 5, p. 4.
112. "Browns Overwhelmed" (1897), *The Sun* (Baltimore, MD), Saturday, September 4, p. 6.
113. D. O'Brien (2012) "Rube Waddell," SABR Baseball Biography Project, Society for American Baseball Research [cited August 10, 2013]. Available from: http://sabr.org/bioproj/person/a5b2c2b4.
114. "Diamond Dust" (1897), *Evening Times* (Washington, DC), Wednesday, September 15, p. 6.
115. Ibid.
116. Smiles, pp. 79, 93, 161–162.
117. "Diamond Dust," op. cit., p. 6.
118. Zoss, and Bowman, p. 120
119. "Orioles Narrow Escape: The Colonels Give Them

a Hard Fight to the Finish" (1897), *Morning Times* (Washington, DC), Friday, September 10, p. 6.
    120. "Outplayed by Boston" (1897), *The Sun* (Baltimore, MD), Saturday, September 25, p. 6.
    121. Benson, p. 22.
    122. L. Reidenbaugh and *The Sporting News* (1997), *Cooperstown: Baseball's Hall of Fame—Revised* (New York: Random House Value Publishing).
    123. "Ended in Gloom" (1897), *The Sun* (Baltimore, MD), Monday, October 4, p. 6.
    124. Nemec and Flatow, p. 239.
    125. "Kings of Fielders" (1897), *St. Paul Globe*, Monday, October 25, p. 5.
    126. Ibid.

Chapter 13

    1. "Sporting World Gossip" (1898), *Evening Times* (Washington, DC), Wednesday, January 26, p. 9.
    2. "30+ Game Hitting Streaks" (2012), Baseball Almanac [cited August 28, 2013]. Available from: http://www.baseball-almanac.com/feats/feats-streak.shtml.
    3. "Hanlon on His New Men—Thinks De Montreville Is the Superior of Reitz" (1898), *The Times* (Washington, DC), Wednesday, January 12, p. 6.
    4. "League Changes" (1898), *The Sporting Life*, Saturday, June 11, p. 4.
    5. "United States Census: City of St. Louis, Missouri—Division of St. Louis City" (1900). United States Census Office [cited November 11, 2012]. Available from: www.familysearch.org.
    6. "Base Ball Gossip" (1898), *St. Paul Globe*, Thursday, February 24, p. 3.
    7. Putman, pp. 442–469.
    8. "St. Louis Sundries: Hopes Rather High Just Now in the Mound City" (1898), *The Sporting Life*, Saturday, March 26, p. 9.
    9. Hetrick, pp. 231–233.
    10. J. Snyder (2005), *Cubs Journal: Year by Year and Day by Day with the Chicago Cubs Since 1876* (Cincinnati: Emmis Books), p. 95.
    11. "Diamond Dust" (1898), *The Times* (Washington, DC), Monday, August 8, p. 6.
    12. "The League Race" (1898), *The Sporting Life*, Saturday, September 3, p. 3.
    13. L. Spatz (2004), *Bad Bill Dahlen: The Rollicking Life and Times of an Early Baseball Star* (Jefferson, NC: McFarland), p. 58. The twentieth century trio of Joe Tinker (shortstop), Johnny Evers (second base), and Frank Chance (first base) dominated the Chicago Cubs infield between 1903 and 1910, and are still widely considered among the greatest double-play combinations to have played the game: A. Ahrens (2007), *Chicago Cubs: Tinker to Evers to Chance* (Chicago: Arcadia Publishing).
    14. Less than two years later, at the age of 26, Taylor would be dead. His cause of death was acute nephritis (kidney failure), probably brought on by years of alcohol abuse: B. McKenna (2007), *Early Exits: The Premature Endings of Baseball Careers* (Lanham, MD: Scarecrow Press), p. 251.
    15. Hurst died of acute indigestion while attending a relative's funeral in 1915. He had already been in poor health, to the point that the *New York Times* ran a story in 1912 stating that he was ill from pneumonia and was not expected to recover. However, he was well enough to travel from his home on Long Island to Pennsylvania, where he passed away. "Tim Keefe (Umpire Page)" (2013), Baseball-Reference.com [cited August 2, 2013]. Available from: http://www.baseball-reference.com/bullpen/Tim_Hurst.

    16. S.A. Riess (2006) Riess, *Encyclopedia of Major League Baseball Clubs* (Westport, CT: Greenwood), p. 407.
    17. Hetrick, *Chris Von Der Ahe*, p. 230.
    18. J. Hamilton, "Quinn Was First Australian Player in Major Leagues" (1997), *Oneonta Star* (New York). Friday, October 10, p. 6.
    19. Solomon, p. 155–158.
    20. R. Worth (2013), *Baseball Team Names: A Worldwide Dictionary, 1869–2011* (Jefferson, NC: McFarland), p. 110.
    21. "1898 Cleveland Spiders (Schedule, Box Scores and Splits)" (2013), Baseball-Reference.com [cited August 1, 2013]. Available from: http://www.baseball-reference.com/teams/CLV/1898-schedule-scores.shtml.
    22. Spink, p. 170.
    23. Kavanagh and Macht, p. 22.
    24. Davis, p. 238.
    25. Snyder, p. 89.
    26. "1899 Cleveland Spiders (Batting, Pitching & Fielding Statistics)" (2013), Baseball-Reference.com [cited August 17, 2013]. Available from: http://www.baseball-reference.com/teams/CLV/1899.shtml.
    27. "Under Sunny Skies" (1899), *The Sporting News*, Saturday, April 8, p. 4.
    28. "National League" (1899), *The Sporting News*, Saturday, April 22, p. 3; "Overflow Crowds" (1899), *The Sporting News*, Saturday, April 22, p. 4.
    29. "The Farce Has Begun" (1899), *Cleveland Plain Dealer*, Sunday, April 16, p. 1.
    30. "Cy Young (Player Page)" (2013), Baseball-Reference.com [cited August 2, 2013]. Available from: http://www.baseball-reference.com/players/y/youngcy01.shtml.
    31. "Overflow Crowds," p. 4.
    32. "Kid Carsey (Player Page)" (2013), Baseball-Reference.com [cited August 2, 2013]. Available from: http://www.baseball-reference.com/players/c/carseki01.shtml.
    33. "Jack Stivetts (Player Page)" (2013), Baseball-Reference.com [cited August 24, 2013]. Available from: http://www.baseball-reference.com/players/s/stiveja01.shtml.
    34. "Games Played Saturday, April 22" (1899), *The Sporting Life*, Saturday, April 29, p. 3.
    35. "Robison's Bereavement" (1899), *The Sporting Life*, Saturday, May 6, p. 6.
    36. "National League" (1899), *The Sporting News*, Saturday, April 22, p. 3.
    37. "Are Rooting Now" (1899), *The Sporting News*, Saturday, May 13, p. 6.
    38. Charlton, p. 120.
    39. "1899 Cleveland Spiders (Schedule, Box Scores and Splits)" (2013), Baseball-Reference.com [cited August 12, 2013]. Available from: http://www.baseball-reference.com/teams/CLV/1899-schedule-scores.shtml.
    40. In 1898, just 75 fans showed up for one Cleveland-Orioles game, and by the end of the year, National League attendances had fallen from 2.3 million to fewer than 1.8 million through the effects of the war. Zoss and Bowman, p. 87.
    41. "Doom of Baseball: How It Is Being Sounded by the Mismanagement of Puffed up Managers" (1899), *St. Paul Globe*, Sunday, May 14, p. 10.
    42. Ibid.
    43. "The League Race: The Two Big B's Still at the Top Rung" (1899), *The Sporting Life*, Saturday, June 10, pp. 2, 3.
    44. Charlton, p. 120.
    45. "Standings and Games on Thursday, June 1, 1889"

(2013), Baseball-Reference.com [cited August 15, 2013]. Available from: http://www.baseball-reference.com/games/standings.cgi?date=1899-06-01.

46. This myth is thought to originate in early Christian mythology based on the belief Christ was crucified on a Friday, and that Friday itself was named after the Norse goddess of love, Frigg, who was declared a witch by early Christians. N. Compton (2013), *Why Sailors Can't Swim and Other Marvellous Maritime Curiosities* (New York: Bloomsbury), p. 27.

47. "1899 Cleveland Spiders (Schedule, Box Scores and Splits)."

48. Zoss and Bowman, p. 126.

49. D.L. Fleitz (2012), "Louis Soxalexis," SABR Baseball Biography Project, Society for American Baseball Research [cited August 15, 2013]. Available from: http://sabr.org/bioproj/person/2b1aea0a.

50. J. Shiffert (2006). *Base Ball in Philadelphia: A History of the Early Game, 1831–1900* (Jefferson, NC: McFarland), pp. 187–189.

51. "Gossip of the Diamond" (1899), *St. Paul Globe*, Tuesday, May 16, p. 5.

52. "Cleveland Chatter—Cross' Men Broke Even with the Eastern Clubs" (1899), *The Sporting Life*, Saturday, June 3, p. 4.

53. "News and Comments" (1899), *The Sporting Life*, Saturday, May 27, p. 5.

54. G. Robinson and C. Salzberg (1991), *On a Clear Day They Could See Seventh Place—Baseball's Worst Teams* (New York: Dell), p. 23.

55. "Cleveland Chatter" (1899), *The Sporting Life*, Saturday, June 17, p. 5.

56. "News and Comment" (1899), *The Sporting Life*, Saturday, June 17, p. 5.

57. "1899 Cleveland Spiders (Batting, Pitching & Fielding Statistics)" (2013), Baseball-Reference.com [cited August 17, 2013]. Available from: http://www.baseball-reference.com/teams/CLV/1899.shtml.

58. "The National League" (1899), *The Sporting News*, Saturday, June 17, p. 3.

59. "Cleveland Vs. New York at Cleveland, June 24" (1899), *The Sporting Life*, Saturday, July 1, p. 3.

60. H.A. Smith, I.L. Smith, and L. Hershfield (2000), *Low and Inside: A Book of Baseball Anecdotes, Oddities, and Curiosities* (New York: Doubleday), p. 42.

61. Robinson and Salzberg, p. 33.

62. Ibid., p. 35.

63. It was into the fall before normal streetcar operations resumed: "Streetcar Strike of 1899" (1999), *The Encyclopedia of Cleveland History* [cited June 2, 2013]. Available from: http://ech.cwru.edu/ech-cgi/article.pl?id=SSO1.

64. "A Revival of Interest in the Forest City" (1899), *The Sporting Life*, Saturday, July 8, p. 5.

65. "Games Played July 17" (1899), *The Sporting Life*, Saturday, July 22, p. 3.

66. Davis, p. 47.

67. "Gossip of the Diamond" (1899), *Evening Times* (Washington, DC), Saturday, August 12, p. 6.

68. "Gossip of the Diamond" (1899), *The Times* (Washington, DC), Wednesday, July 19, p. 6.

69. "Baseball Notes" (1899), *Deseret Evening News* (Salt Lake City), Tuesday, July 18, p. 5.

70. "Cupid Childs (Player Page)" (2013), Baseball-Reference.com [cited August 20, 2013]. Available from: http://www.baseball-reference.com/players/c/childcu01.shtml.

71. "Notes of the National Game" (1899), *Evening Times* (Washington, DC), Thursday, August 3, p. 6.

72. H. Chadwick (1899), *Spalding Official Base Ball Guide for 1899* (New York: American Sports Publishing), p. 145.

73. "News and Comment" (1899), *The Sporting Life*, Saturday, June 17, p. 5.

74. "Lose with Phyle Pitching" (1899), *Chicago Tribune*, Monday, August 7, p. 4.

75. "Nearer the Top" (1899), *Boston Globe*, Thursday, August 31, p. 4.

76. "Games Played August 31" (1899), *The Sporting Life*, Saturday, September 9, p. 2.

77. "On the Fly" (1899), *The Sporting News*, Saturday, October 14, p. 4.

78. "Base Ball Briefs" (1899), *St. Paul Globe*, Sunday, September 17, p. 10.

79. Ibid.

80. "Are Not Worrying" (1899), *The Sporting Life*, Saturday, October 7, p. 4.

81. J.T. Hetrick (1991), *Misfits!: The Cleveland Spiders in 1899: A Day-by-Day Narrative of Baseball Futility* (Jefferson, NC: McFarland).

82. "1899 Cleveland Spiders (Schedule, Box Scores and Splits)."

83. Morris, *Cracking Baseball's Cold Cases*, pp. 29–31.

84. J. Weeks (2012), *Cellar Dwellers: The Worst Teams in Baseball History* (Lanham, MD: Scarecrow Press), p. 22.

85. "Baseball Rule Change Timeline" (2011), Baseball Almanac [cited August 20, 2013]. Available from: http://www.baseball-almanac.com/rulechng.shtml.

86. Nemec, *Great Encyclopedia*, p. 802.

87. "1899 Cleveland Spiders (Batting, Pitching & Fielding Statistics)."

88. Benson, p. 106.

89. "1899 Cleveland Spiders (Batting, Pitching & Fielding Statistics)."

90. John McGraw's 23-year-old wife Minnie died on August 31 following surgery for appendicitis. Her funeral, with Ned Hanlon, Willie Keeler, Joe Kelley, and Hughie Jennings as pallbearers, was one of the largest in Baltimore history: Solomon, p. 172.

91. Riess, *Touching Base*, p. 63.

92. The percentage of balls in play converted into outs. Cleveland's record of .610 was far behind leaders Boston (.699): "1899 National League Team Statistics and Standings" (2013), Baseball-Reference.com [cited August 20, 2013]. Available from: http://www.baseball-reference.com/leagues/NL/1899.shtml.

93. "Joe Quinn (Player Page)" (2013), Baseball-Reference.com [cited January 9, 2013]. Available from: http://www.baseball-reference.com/players/q/quinnjo02.shtml.

Chapter 14

1. D.L. Barnhill (1999), *At Home on the Earth: Becoming Native to Our Place: A Multicultural Anthology* (Berkeley: University of California Press), p. 85.

2. J. Kent (2002), *America in 1900* (Armonk, NY: M.E. Sharpe), pp. 86–88.

3. Cited in: Charlton, p. 124.

4. "(No Title)" (1901), *St. Paul Globe*, Friday, April 12, p. 3.

5. The year of Quinn's naturalization was recorded in the 1910 United States Census: "United States Census: City of St. Louis, Missouri—Division of St. Louis City" (1910), United States Census Office [cited November 12, 2012]. Available from: www.familysearch.org.

6. "What Are the Benefits and Responsibilities of Citizenship?" (2013), U.S. Citizenship and Immigration Serv-

ices [cited August 15, 2013]. Available from: www.uscis.gov/files/article/chapter2.pdf.

7. Patsy Tebeau and Patsy Donovan were both 35 years old, Lave Cross 34, and Cy Young 33: "1900 St. Louis Cardinals (Batting, Pitching & Fielding Statistics)" (2013), Baseball-Reference.com [cited August 17, 2013]. Available from: http://www.baseball-reference.com/teams/STL/1900.shtml.

8. "Donlin and Dillard Walloped the Ball" (1900), *St. Louis Republic*, Thursday, April 5, p. 4.

9. Ibid.

10. Morris, *A Game of Inches*, p. 304.

11. "Donlin and Dillard Walloped the Ball," p. 4.

12. Ibid.

13. "St. Louis Club Improves as Season Progresses" (1900), *St. Louis Republic*, Sunday, May 6, p. 4.

14. "The League Race: The Eight Teams Now in the Fight for Honors" (1900), *The Sporting Life*, Saturday, April 28, p. 2.

15. "Runs Scored Team Records" (2011), Baseball Almanac [cited August 20, 2013]. Available from: http://www.baseball-almanac.com/recbooks/rb_runs2.shtml.

16. "The League Race: The Eight Teams," p. 2.

17. "American League: The Championship Season Now Under Way" (1900), *The Sporting Life*, Saturday, April 28, p. 6.

18. "1900 St. Louis Cardinals (Schedule, Box Scores and Splits)" (2013), Baseball-Reference.com [cited August 17, 2013]. Available from: http://www.baseball-reference.com/teams/STL/1900-schedule-scores.shtml.

19. "St. Louis Gets McGraw" (1900), *San Francisco Call*, Wednesday, May 9, p. 4.

20. F. Lieb (1955), *The Baltimore Orioles: The History of a Colorful Team in Baltimore and St. Louis* (New York: Putnam), p. 90.

21. "McGraw and Robinson Arrive" (1900), *St. Louis Republic*, Wednesday, May 9, p. 6.

22. Lieb, p. 91.

23. "Strike Stops Ball Games" (1900), *St. Louis Republic*, Wednesday, May 9, p. 6.

24. S.L. Piott (2011), *Daily Life in the Progressive Era* (Santa Barbara, CA: ABC-CLIO), pp. 137–139; "Attempt Will Be Made to Operate System Today" (1900), *St. Louis Republic*, Wednesday, May 9, pp. 1, 2.; "Inquest on Riot Victims Today" (1900), *St. Louis Republic*, Tuesday, June 12, pp. 1, 2.

25. "McGraw Erred, Young Weakened" (1900), *St. Louis Republic*, Sunday, May 13, p. 9.

26. "The League Race: The Inter-Sectional Battle Is Now On" (1900), *The Sporting Life*, Saturday, May 19, p. 2.

27. "1900 St. Louis Cardinals (Schedule, Box Scores and Splits)."

28. "Strike Stops Ball Games."

29. "Strike Stops Ball Games."

30. "Baseball Gossip" (1900), *St. Louis Republic*, Friday, June 15, p. 6.

31. "Weyhing Was Not Given Any Support" (1900), *St. Louis Republic*, Friday, June 15, p. 6.

32. "St. Louis Smiles over the Unexpected Triumps in Brooklyn" (1900), *The Sporting Life*, Saturday, June 9, p. 4.

33. "The League Race: The Contestants Gradually Becoming Bunched" (1900), *The Sporting Life*, Saturday, June 16, pp. 2, 3.

34. "St. Louis Sad over the Persistent Bad Luck of the Cardinals" (1900), *The Sporting Life*, Saturday, June 16, p. 5.

35. "Joe Quinn (Player Page)" (2013), Baseball-Reference.com [cited January 9, 2013]. Available from: http://www.baseball-reference.com/players/q/quinnjo02.shtml.

36. "Baseball Gossip" (1900), *St. Louis Republic*, Friday, June 15, p. 6.

37. In: "Players Released by St. Louis Achieve Success" (1900), *St. Louis Republic*, Sunday, June 17, p. 5.

38. "Boosts for Quinn" (1900), *St. Louis Republic*, Friday, June 15, p. 6.

39. "Baseball Gossip" (1900), *Cincinnati Enquirer*, Saturday, June 16, p. 3.

40. "Standings and Games on Saturday, June 16, 1900" (2013), Baseball-Reference.com [cited August 15, 2013]. Available from: http://www.baseball-reference.com/games/standings.cgi?date=1900-06-16.

41. In: "Joe Quinn May Join the Bostons as Utility Infielder" (1900), *St. Louis Republic*, Friday, June 15, p. 6.

42. J. Keenan (2012), "Cupid Childs," Society for American Baseball Research (SABR) BioProject [cited August 3, 2013]. Available from: http://sabr.org/bioproj/person/d373e248.

43. "Chicago Wants Quinn" (1900), *St. Louis Republic*, Saturday, June 16, p. 5.

44. In: "Boosts for Quinn," p. 6.

45. "St. Louis Sad over the Persistent Bad Luck of the Cardinals," p. 5.

46. "Batted" (1900), *Cincinnati Enquirer*, Sunday, June 17, p. 10.

47. "Quinn Goes to Cincinnati" (1900), *St. Louis Republic*, Sunday, June 17, p. 10.

48. "St. Louis Lost in Eleven Innings" (1900), *St. Louis Republic*, Sunday, June 17, p. 10.

49. "Base-Ball Riot" (1886), *Cincinnati Enquirer*, Monday, July 12, p. 8.

50. Charlton, p. 64.

51. The other fatal ballpark collapse occurred at Philadelphia's Baker Bowl in 1903, a tragedy in which 12 people died and more than 200 were injured: Elston, p. 174.

52. Benson, p. 100.

53. "Quinn Started Winning Rally: 'Old Reliable' Led the Reds in a Batting Rally Which Defeated St. Louis" (1900), *St. Louis Republic*, Wednesday, June 27, p. 7.

54. Ibid.

55. "Baseball Gossip" (1900), *St. Louis Republic*, Wednesday, June 27, p. 7.

56. "Mulford's Musings" (1900), *The Sporting Life*, Saturday, August 11, p. 5.

57. "Tebeau Resigns and Mcgraw Succeeds Him" (1900), *St. Louis Republic*, Monday, August 20, p. 8.

58. "Peculiar Status of John Mcgraw: Insists He Is Not Manager of the St. Louis Club, yet Admits He Will Fulfil Manager's Duties" (1900), *St. Louis Republic*, Tuesday, August 21, p. 5.

59. "Baseball Gossip" (1900), *Cincinnati Enquirer*, Friday, July 6, p. 5.

60. "1900 Cincinnati Reds (Schedule, Box Scores and Splits)" (2013), Baseball-Reference.com [cited August 17, 2013]. Available from: http://www.baseball-reference.com/teams/CIN/1900-schedule-scores.shtml.

61. "The League Race: The Eastern Teams Badly Mauled in the West" (1900), *The Sporting Life*, Saturday, July 14, p. 2.

62. W.N. Wilbert (2013), *The Shutout in Major League Baseball: A History* (Jefferson, NC: McFarland), p. 37.

63. "The League Race: The West Fairly Tramples on the East for Once" (1900), *The Sporting Life*, Saturday, July 21, p. 2.

64. Charlton, p. 126.

65. "Tim Hurst's Methods" (1900), *St. Paul Globe*, Thursday, October 11, p. 5.

66. "Luck with the Champions" (1900), *The Sun* (New York), Sunday, July 22, p. 8.

67. "Deceptive Shoots Slaughtered" (1900), *St. Louis Wilbert*, Tuesday, August 21, p. 5.
68. Ibid.
69. "1900 Cincinnati Reds (Schedule, Box Scores and Splits)."
70. Gietschier, p. 108.
71. "Double Victory for Allen's Men" (1900), *Cincinnati Enquirer*, Tuesday, October 9, p. 4.
72. "Exposed at Last" (1900), *The Sporting Life*, Saturday, September 22, p. 7.
73. R.A. Mayer (2008), *Christy Mathewson: A Game-by-Game Profile of a Legendary Pitcher* (Jefferson, NC: McFarland), pp. 16–20.
74. "Amos Rusie (Player Page)" (2013), Baseball-Reference.com [cited June 1, 2013]. Available from: http://www.baseball-reference.com/players/r/rusieam01.shtml.
75. "Christy Mathewson (Player Page)" (2013), Baseball-Reference.com [cited June 1, 2013]. Available from: http://www.baseball-reference.com/players/m/mathech01.shtml.
76. "The Passing of Quinn" (1900), *The Sporting Life*, Wednesday, September 29, p. 7.
77. "Robisons Mortgage St. Louis Ball Club" (1900), *St. Louis Republic*, Tuesday, November 20, p. 7.
78. "Gossip of the Ball Players" (1900), *St. Louis Republic*, Tuesday, November 20, p. 7.
79. Seymour and Mills, p. 308.
80. Spink, p. 22.
81. Armour and Levitt, p. 41.
82. W.N. Wilbert (2007), *The Arrival of the American League: Ban Johnson and the 1901 Challenge to National League Monopoly* (Jefferson, NC: McFarland), p. 13.
83. Ibid., p.44.
84. Charlton, p. 124.
85. Seymour and Mills, pp. 309–301.
86. Wilbert, *Arrival of the American League*, p. 28.
87. "Johnson Defies Big League" (1900), *St. Louis Republic*, Tuesday, November 20, p. 7.
88. "St. Louis Men for St. Louis Ball Team" (1901), *St. Louis Republic*, Sunday, February 3, p. 11.
89. Ibid.
90. "Gossip of the Green Diamond" (1901), *St. Louis Republic*, Monday, April 8.
91. "News of the Baseball Field" (1901), *St. Louis Republic*, Thursday, April 11, p. 6.
92. Joe Quinn's Baseball Reference "Transactions" page states he jumped from Cincinnati to Washington before the 1901 season, which is incorrect as Quinn was out of contract with the Reds at the time. "Joe Quinn (Transactions)" (2013), Baseball-Reference.com [cited January 9, 2013]. Available from: http://www.baseball-reference.com/players/q/quinnjo02.shtml.
93. "News of the Baseball Field" (1901), *St. Louis Republic*, Thursday, April 11, p. 6.
94. "Sports Big and Small" (1901), *St. Paul Globe*, Thursday, November 14, p. 5.
95. Wilbert, *Arrival of the American League*, p. 75.
96. "In the Baseball World: Manning's Players Rapidly Rounding into Shape" (1901), *The Times* (Washington, DC), Monday, April 15, p. 3.
97. Benson, p. 408.
98. "Senators Arrive Home" (1901), *The Times* (Washington), Sunday, April 21, p. 9.
99. Ibid.
100. Ibid.
101. "In the Baseball World: The Orioles Win Their First Game from Washington" (1901), *The Times* (Washington, DC). Thursday, May 2, p. 5.
102. Ibid.
103. Ibid.
104. "Pete Loos (Player Page)" (2013), Baseball-Reference.com [cited August 2, 2013]. Available from: http://www.baseball-reference.com/players/l/loospe01.shtml.
105. "In the Baseball World: Washington Wins from Boston in First Inning" (1901), *The Times* (Washington, DC), Sunday, May 12, p. 9.
106. "Dale Gear (Player Page)" (2013), Baseball-Reference.com [cited August 2, 2013]. Available from: http://www.baseball-reference.com/players/g/gearda01.shtml.
107. "1901 Washington Senators (Schedule, Box Scores and Splits)" (2013), Baseball-Reference.com [cited August 12, 2013]. Available from: http://www.baseball-reference.com/teams/WSH/1901-schedule-scores.shtml.
108. "American League: The Expanded Organization's First Campaign" (1901), *The Sporting Life*, Saturday, June 1, p. 6.
109. "In the Baseball World: Senators Redeem Themselves by Shutting out Milwaukee" (1901), *The Times* (Washington), Sunday, June 2, p. 8.
110. "In the Baseball World: Lee's Masterful Pitching Too Much for Chicago" (1901), *The Times* (Washington, DC), Sunday, June 9, p. 8.
111. "In the Baseball World: Washington Makes a Wonderful Rally in the Eighth" (1901), *The Times* (Washington), Tuesday, June 11, p. 3.
112. "In the Baseball World" (1901), *The Times* (Washington, DC), Monday, June 17, p. 3.
113. "1901 Washington Senators (Schedule, Box Scores and Splits)."
114. "In the Baseball World" (1901), *Evening Times* (Washington, DC), Thursday, June 20, p. 6.
115. Charlton, p. 131.
116. "Notes About the Big and Little Ball Tossers" (1902), *St. Paul Globe*, Monday, April 7, p. 5.
117. "1901 Washington Senators (Batting, Pitching & Fielding Statistics)." (2013). Baseball-Reference.com. [cited August 17, 2013]. Available from: http://www.baseball-reference.com/teams/WSH/1901.shtml.
118. W. Akin (2012), "Win Mercer," SABR Baseball Biography Project [cited August 3, 2013]. Available from: http://sabr.org/bioproj/person/a128b34b.
119. "May Do a Double-Header Today" (1901), *St. Louis Republic*, Thursday, September 12, p. 7.
120. "Baseball Hits and Runs" (1902), *The Times* (Washington), Sunday, February 2, p. 7.
121. "Baseball Gossip" (1901), *St. Paul Globe*, Monday, December 30, p. 5.
122. "Western All Right" (1902), *Salt Lake Herald*, Sunday, March 9, p. 4.
123. "Notes About the Big and Little Ball Tossers" (1902), *St. Paul Globe*, Monday, April 7, p. 5.
124. "Patrick Quinn Is Dead" (1902), *Dubuque Telegraph-Herald*, Saturday, April 12, p. 3.
125. "St. Columbkille's History" (2013), St. Columbkille Catholic Church, Dubuque, IA [cited August 28, 2013]. Available from: http://stcolumbkille.net/about/about-us/st-columbkilles-history/.
126. "Joe Quinn (Minor League Player Page)" (2013), Baseball-Reference.com [cited April 2, 2013]. Available from: http://www.baseball-reference.com/minors/player.cgi?id=quinn-003jos.
127. "Tom Barry (Player Page)" (2013), Baseball-Reference.com [cited August 29, 2013]. Available from: http://www.baseball-reference.com/players/b/barryto01.shtml.
128. "Personal Comment on Men and Things in the

Field of Sports" (1904), *Washington Times*, Saturday, October 15, p. 8.

129. "1902 Des Moines Midgets" (2013), Baseball-Reference.com [cited August 12, 2013]. Available from: http://www.baseball-reference.com/minors/team.cgi?id=7b148e3d.

130. A.J. Reach (1902), *Reach's Official American League Base Ball Guide for 1902* (Philadelphia: A.J. Reach), p. 232.

131. "Baseball Gossip" (1902), *Evening Times* (Washington, DC), Thursday, May 1, p. 6.

132. "Baseball Yarns" (1906), *Salt Lake Herald*, Monday, January 8, p. 7.

133. H.C. Frankenfield (1904), *The Floods of the Spring of 1903, in the Mississippi Watershed* (Washington, DC: Weather Bureau), pp. 49–51.

134. D. Pajot (2011), *Baseball's Heartland War, 1902–1903: The Western League and American Association Vie for Turf, Players and Profits* (Jefferson, NC: McFarland), p. 174.

135. Pajot, *Baseball's Heartland War*, p. 199.

136. C.H. Myrick (1903), Myrick personal communication, "Re: Joe Quinn." To: A. Herrmann. (Friday, August 28).

137. "Historical Events for Year 1903" (2013), HistoryOrb.com [cited March 5, 2013]. Available from: http://www.historyorb.com/events/date/1903.

138. Spink, p. 266.

139. Farrington, p. 9B.

140. Speculation remains as to the "accidental" nature of Delahanty's death, occurring as it did just months before the team's corrupt owners organized the first World Series: J. Casway (2006), *Ed Delahanty in the Emerald Age of Baseball* (Notre Dame, IN: University of Notre Dame Press).

141. Goldstein, p. 44.

Chapter 15

1. Eight players from the Chicago White Sox were charged with deliberately losing games during the 1919 World Series in exchange for payments from gambling syndicates. While all eight were eventually acquitted, the lifetime bans from baseball imposed on each were never lifted: D.A. Nathan (2005), *Saying It's So: A Cultural History of the Black Sox Scandal* (Urbana: University of Illinois Press).

2. Zoss and Bowman, pp. 89–93.

3. "Personal Comment on Men and Things in the Field of Sports" (1905), *Washington Times*, Monday, December 25, p. 8.

4. "Current Sporting Gossip" (1905), *The Sun* (New York), Sunday, February 26, p. 8.

5. On 10 November, Second Army advanced on German positions, already in disorder and retreating. Word did not reach the units advancing until after eleven-hundred hours on 11 November, making it one of the last units to fight to the very conclusion of the war. "Chicago Calumets Beat Local Kcs" (1905), *St. Louis Republic*, Wednesday, July 5, p. 11.

6. "United States Census: City of St. Louis, Missouri—Division of St. Louis City" (1920). United States Census Office [cited November 12, 2012]. Available from: www.familysearch.org.

7. While McGrath & Quinn is listed in the 1902 St. Louis City Directory under both Undertakers and Livery Stables, the 1910–11 and 1919–20 directories list Joseph J. Quinn only as Undertakers: *Gould's Blue Book for the City of St. Louis, 1903: Alphabetically Arranged and Classified by Streets, Also a List of the Most Prominent Citizens in Alton, St. Charles and Carlinville: Also a Complete List of Club Members with Their Business Locations* (1902–03) (St. Louis, MO: Gould Directory Co.); St. Louis City Directory 1910–11 and 1919–20 in "United States City Directories, 1882–1901: Saint Louis, Mo. [Microform]" (1990), Research Publications, Woodbridge, CT.

8. I.D. Wyatt and D.E. Hecker (2006), "Occupational Changes During the 20th Century," *Monthly Labor Review* (March 2006): pp. 35–58.

9. Clarence's physical description, occupation, and enlistment details are listed on his service card: Missouri State Archives Digital Heritage Project: "Soldiers' Records: War of 1912—World War I" (2013), Missouri Digital Heritage [cited April 27, 2013]. Available from: http://www.sos.mo.gov/archives/soldiers/default.asp#soldsearch.

10. The 7th Infantry Division was born in the latter years of World War I, activated in December 1917 and deployed to Europe shortly afterward: B. Gardener and B. Stahura (1997), *Seventh Infantry Division: 1917–1992. World War I, World War II, Korea, and Panamanian Invasion* (Nashville, TN: Turner), pp. 6–10.

11. "Soldiers' Records: War of 1812—World War I: Quinn, Joseph F" (2013), Missouri Digital Heritage [cited April 27, 2013]. Available from: http://www.sos.mo.gov/archives/soldiers/details.asp?id=A104512&conflict=World%20War%20I&txtName=jos&selConflict=All&txtUnit=&rbBranch=&offset=12375.

12. E.T. Fell (1927), *History of the Seventh Division, United States Army, 1917–1919* (Philadelphia: H. Moore), p. 145.

13. A salient is a projection of the main battlefield which falls into enemy territory. Fell, p. 150.

14. The design of the red and black divisional logo gave rise to the "Hourglass" nickname: "History of the 7th Infantry Division" (2003), Fort Carson United States Military [cited August 28, 2013]. Available from: http://www.carson.army.mil/UNITS/F7ID/F7ID_Historylong.htm.

15. "Soldiers' Records: War of 1812—World War I: Quinn, Clarence P." (2013), Missouri Digital Heritage [cited April 27, 2013]. Available from: http://www.sos.mo.gov/archives/soldiers/details.asp?id=A104496&conflict=World%20War%20I&txtName=quinn,%20clarence&selConflict=World%20War%20I&txtUnit=&rbBranch=.

16. D. Killingray and H. Phillips (2003), *The Spanish Influenza Pandemic of 1918–1919: New Perspectives* (Oxford, UK: Routledge), pp. 101–103.

17. Ibid., pp. 173–177.

18. R. Collier (1974), *The Plague of the Spanish Lady* (New York: Atheneum), p. 305.

19. T. Brookes and A.P.H. Association (2005). *A Warning Shot: Influenza and the 2004 Flu Vaccine Shortage* (Washington, DC: American Public Health Association), p. 2.

20. I. Starr (1976), "Influenza in 1918: Recollections of the Epidemic in Philadelphia" *Annals of Internal Medicine* 85: pp. 516–518.

21. N. Ahmed et al. (2006), *Biology of Disease* (New York: Taylor & Francis), p. 29.

22. Margaret McGrath. Date of death: December 5, 1918, St. Louis City. Certificate number: 48907. "Missouri Death Certificates, 1910–1962" (2013), Missouri Digital Heritage [cited April 28, 2013]. Available from: http://www.sos.mo.gov/archives/resources/deathcertificates/advanced.asp.

23. "1919 New York Giants (Batting, Pitching & Fielding Statistics)" (2013), Baseball-Reference.com [cited August 7, 2013]. Available from: http://www.baseball-reference.com/teams/NYG/1919.shtml.

24. Youngs's kidney disorder ended his career in 1926

and caused his premature death in 1927. "Hall of Famers: Youngs, Ross" (2012), National Baseball Hall of Fame and Museum, Cooperstown, NY [cited August 7, 2013]. Available from: http://baseballhall.org/hof/youngs-ross.

25. Grant is commonly believed to have been the only active major league player killed in combat during World War I. However, one-gamers Bun Troy and Alex Burr were both killed in France in 1918. T. Simon (2012), "Eddie Grant," Society for American Baseball Research (SABR) BioProject [cited August 7, 2013]. Available from: http://sabr.org/bioproj/person/0d10da81.

26. Spink, p. 281.

27. Farrington, p. 9B.

28. The death certificate of John R. Quinn lists his profession as "undertaker": "Missouri Death Certificates, 1910–1962" (2013), Missouri Digital Heritage [cited April 28, 2013]. Available from: http://www.sos.mo.gov/archives/resources/deathcertificates/advanced.asp.

29. John R. Quinn: "Missouri Death Certificates, 1910–1962" (2013). Missouri Digital Heritage [cited April 28, 2013]. Available from: http://www.sos.mo.gov/archives/resources/deathcertificates/advanced.asp.

30. "Section and Lot Report for Calvary Cemetery" (1988), Catholic Cemeteries of the Archdiocese of St. Louis [cited May 17, 2000]. Available from: http://archstl.org/cemeteries/content/view/91/233/.

31. "Quinn, John R." (1920), *St. Louis Post-Dispatch*, Saturday, February 7, p. 7.

32. T. Hesemann (2000), personal communication, "Re: Joe Quinn—Australian Born Major League Ball Player Reply [Email]." To: R. Nicholls (Thursday, April 20).

33. Monaghan, p. 6, 14.

34. Farrington, p. 9B.

35. T. Hesemann (2013), personal communication, "Re: Joe Quinn—Australian Baseball Hall of Fame [Email]." To: R. Nicholls (Friday, August 9).

36. St. Louis City Directory 1930–31: "United States City Directories, 1882–1901: Saint Louis, Mo. [Microform]" (1990), Research Publications, Woodbridge, CT.

37. Mary Ellen Quinn: "Missouri Death Certificates, 1910–1962" (2013). Missouri Digital Heritage [cited April 28, 2013]. Available from: http://www.sos.mo.gov/archives/resources/deathcertificates/advanced.asp; "Death Notice—Mary E. Quinn (Nee Mcgrath)" (1937), *St. Louis Globe-Democrat*, December 14, p. 5C.

38. On October 12, 1900, Quinn and Thomas McGrath purchased adjacent plots at Calvary Cemetery in St. Louis (section 012, Lot 0834 and Lot 0835 respectively). The Quinn family plot contains the graves of Joe and Molly Quinn, three unnamed infants, Dorothy Quinn, and Scotty Quinn. McGrath's plot was used for burial of Thomas and his wife Margaret, and three of their children: Lydia, Catherine, and John. "Section and Lot Report for Calvary Cemetery" (1988), Catholic Cemeteries of the Archdiocese of St. Louis [cited May 17, 2000]. Available from: http://archstl.org/cemeteries/content/view/91/233/.

39. The St. Louis City Directory 1939–40 still lists Joseph J. Quinn among the city's funeral directors: from "United States City Directories, 1882–1901: Saint Louis, Mo. [Microform]" (1990), Research Publications, Woodbridge, CT.

40. MedlinePlus (2013), "Myocarditis," U.S. National Library of Medicine/National Institutes of Health [cited April 29, 2013]. Available from: http://www.nlm.nih.gov/medlineplus/ency/article/000149.htm.

41. "Obituary: Joe Quinn" (1940), *The Sporting News*, Thursday, November 21, p. 8.

42. McGuire, p. 6D.

Epilogue

1. "Triple Crown of Baseball" (2013), Baseball Almanac [cited August 31, 2013]. Available from: http://www.baseball-almanac.com/awards/aw_triph.shtml.

2. "The Sporting Mill: St. Louis Daguerrotypes No. 105" (1937), *St. Louis Daily Globe-Democrat*, Sunday, November 28, p. 16.

3. C. Shipley (2013), personal communication, "The Place of Joe Quinn in Australian Baseball History [unpublished interview transcript]." To: R. Nicholls (July 25).

4. Hamilton, p. 6.: This statistic, which assigns events such as doubles, stolen bases, and walks a value in runs, does distinguish Quinn uncomfortably from his three cohorts in the Big Four. An annual TPR of between 3 and 6 is considered an excellent season. Babe Ruth leads the lifetime TPR rankings on 107.7, followed by Nap Lajoie with 94.4. Hall of Famer McPhee had a lifetime TPR of 40.1 (averaging 2.5 per season), which places him in the top 50 players ever. Dunlap (27.4) and Pfeffer (21.8) are both in the top 200 all-time, but Quinn's lifetime rating doesn't even make the top 500, his blue-collar habit of hitting for average and early years often spent out of position in the field costing him dearly.

5. Monaghan, pp. 6, 14.

Bibliography

"30+ Game Hitting Streaks" (2012). Baseball Almanac [cited August 28, 2013]. Available from: http://www.baseball-almanac.com/feats/feats-streak.shtml.

"50 Years Ago: Cotton Concern" (1951). *Sunday Mail* (Brisbane, QLD). Sunday. March 11, p. 9.

"1821 Fermanagh Census (Derryvolin Parish)" (2012). Ireland Genealogy Projects [cited December 20, 2012]. Available from: http://www.igp-web.com/fermanagh/Links.htm#Census.

"1884 New York Giants (Schedule, Box Scores and Splits)" (2013). Baseball-Reference.com [cited June 16, 2013]. Available from: http://www.baseball-reference.com/teams/NYG/1884-schedule-scores.shtml.

"1884 St. Louis Maroons (Batting, Pitching & Fielding Statistics)" (2013). Baseball-Reference.com [cited August 7, 2013]. Available from: http://www.baseball-reference.com/teams/SLM/1884.shtml.

"1884 St. Louis Maroons (Schedule, Box Scores and Splits)" (2013). Baseball-Reference.com [cited July 30, 2013]. Available from: http://www.baseball-reference.com/teams/SLM/1884-schedule-scores.shtml.

"1884 Union Association Batting Leaders" (2013). Baseball-Reference.com [cited July 30, 2013]. Available from: http://www.baseball-reference.com/leagues/UA/1884-batting-leaders.shtml.

"1884 Union Association Fielding Leaders" (2013). Baseball-Reference.com [cited July 30, 2013]. Available from: http://www.baseball-reference.com/leagues/UA/1884-fielding-leaders.shtml.

"1884 Union Association Pitching Leaders" (2013). Baseball-Reference.com [cited July 30, 2013]. Available from: http://www.baseball-reference.com/leagues/UA/1884-pitching-leaders.shtml.

"1885 National League Pitching Leaders" (2013). Baseball-Reference.com [cited July 30, 2013]. Available from: http://www.baseball-reference.com/leagues/NL/1885-pitching-leaders.shtml.

"1885 St. Louis Maroons (Schedule, Box Scores and Splits)" (2013). Baseball-Reference.com [cited August 19, 2013]. Available from: http://www.baseball-reference.com/teams/SLM/1885-schedule-scores.shtml.

"1886 Chicago White Stockings (Batting, Pitching & Fielding Statistics)" (2013). Baseball-Reference.com [cited August 20, 2013]. Available from: http://www.baseball-reference.com/teams/CHC/1886.shtml.

"1886 St. Louis Maroons (Batting, Pitching & Fielding Statistics)" (2013). Baseball-Reference.com [cited August 7, 2013]. Available from: http://www.baseball-reference.com/teams/SLM/1886.shtml.

"1887 Detroit Wolverines (Batting, Pitching & Fielding Statistics)" (2013). Baseball-Reference.com [cited August 7, 2013]. Available from: http://www.baseball-reference.com/teams/DTN/1887.shtml.

"1887 St. Louis Browns (Schedule, Box Scores and Splits)" (2013). Baseball-Reference.com. [cited August 19, 2013]. Available from: http://www.baseball-reference.com/teams/STL/1887-schedule-scores.shtml.

"1888 Boston Beaneaters (Batting, Pitching & Fielding Statistics)" (2013). Baseball-Reference.com. [cited May 15, 2013]. Available from: http://www.baseball-reference.com/teams/BSN/1888.shtml.

"1888 Boston Beaneaters (Schedule, Box Scores and Splits)" (2013). Baseball-Reference.com [cited April 14, 2013]. Available from: http://www.baseball-reference.com/teams/BSN/1888-schedule-scores.shtml.

"1888 Des Moines Prohibitionists (Batting, Pitching and Fielding Statistics)" (2013). Baseball-Reference.com [cited May 30, 2013]. Available from: http://www.baseball-reference.com/minors/team.cgi?id=8f208be7.

"1889 Boston Beaneaters (Schedule, Box Scores and Splits)" (2013). Baseball-Reference.com [cited May 30, 2013]. Available from: http://www.baseball-reference.com/teams/BSN/1889-schedule-scores.shtml.

"1889 National League Shortstop" (2013). Baseball-Reference.com [cited May 31, 2013]. Available from: http://www.baseball-reference.com/leagues/NL/1889-specialpos_ss-fielding.shtml.

"1889 National League Standard Batting" (2013). Baseball-Reference.com [cited May 31, 2013]. Available from: http://www.baseball-reference.com/leagues/NL/1889-standard-batting.shtml.

"1889 National League Standard Pitching" (2013). Baseball-Reference.com [cited May 31, 2013]. Available from: http://www.baseball-reference.com/leagues/NL/1889-standard-pitching.shtml.

"1890 Boston Reds (Batting, Pitching & Fielding Statistics)" (2013). Baseball-Reference.com [cited August 23, 2013]. Available from: http://www.baseball-reference.com/teams/BOS/1890.shtml.

"1890 Players League Pitching Leaders" (2013). Baseball-Reference.com [cited August 23, 2013]. Available from: http://www.baseball-reference.com/leagues/PL/1890-pitching-leaders.shtml.

"1891 Boston Beaneaters (Batting, Pitching & Fielding Statistics)" (2013). Baseball-Reference.com [cited August 17, 2013]. Available from: http://www.baseball-reference.com/teams/BSN/1891.shtml.

"1893 St. Louis Browns (Batting, Pitching & Fielding Statistics)" (2013). Baseball-Reference.com [cited August 17, 2013]. Available from: http://www.baseball-reference.com/teams/STL/1893.shtml.

"1893 St. Louis Browns (Schedule, Box Scores and Splits)" (2013). Baseball-Reference.com [cited August 19, 2013]. Available from: http://www.baseball-reference.com/teams/STL/1893-schedule-scores.shtml.

"1894 Chicago Colts (Batting, Pitching & Fielding Statistics)" (2013). Baseball-Reference.com [cited August 7, 2013]. Available from: http://www.baseball-reference.com/teams/CHC/1894.shtml.

"1894 National League Fielding Leaders" (2013). Baseball-Reference.com [cited August 20, 2013]. Available from: http://www.baseball-reference.com/leagues/NL/1894-fielding-leaders.shtml.

"1894 National League Team Statistics and Standings" (2013). Baseball-Reference.com [cited August 20, 2013]. Available from: http://www.baseball-reference.com/leagues/NL/1894.shtml.

"1894 St. Louis Browns (Schedule, Box Scores and Splits)" (2013). Baseball-Reference.com [cited August 17, 2013]. Available from: http://www.baseball-reference.com/teams/STL/1894-schedule-scores.shtml.

"1895 St. Louis Browns (Schedule, Box Scores and Splits)" (2013). Baseball-Reference.com [cited August 18, 2013]. Available from: http://www.baseball-reference.com/teams/STL/1895-schedule-scores.shtml.

"1896 Baltimore Orioles (Schedule, Box Scores and Splits)" (2013). Baseball-Reference.com [cited August 19, 2013]. Available from: http://www.baseball-reference.com/teams/BLN/1896-schedule-scores.shtml.

"1896 St. Louis Browns (Batting, Pitching, & Fielding Statistics)" (2013). Baseball-Reference.com [cited August 21, 2013]. Available from: http://www.baseball-reference.com/teams/STL/1896.shtml.

"1896 St. Louis Browns (Schedule, Box Scores and Splits)" (2013). Baseball-Reference.com [cited August 21, 2013]. Available from: http://www.baseball-reference.com/teams/STL/1896-schedule-scores.shtml.

"1898 Cleveland Spiders (Schedule, Box Scores and Splits)" (2013). Baseball-Reference.com [cited August 1, 2013]. Available from: http://www.baseball-reference.com/teams/CLV/1898-schedule-scores.shtml.

"1899 Cleveland Spiders (Batting, Pitching & Fielding Statistics)" (2013). Baseball-Reference.com. [cited August 17, 2013]. Available from: http://www.baseball-reference.com/teams/CLV/1899.shtml.

"1899 Cleveland Spiders (Schedule, Box Scores and Splits)" (2013). Baseball-Reference.com [cited August 12, 2013]. Available from: http://www.baseball-reference.com/teams/CLV/1899-schedule-scores.shtml.

"1899 National League Team Statistics and Standings" (2013). Baseball-Reference.com [cited August 20, 2013]. Available from: http://www.baseball-reference.com/leagues/NL/1899.shtml.

"1900 Cincinnati Reds (Schedule, Box Scores and Splits)" (2013). Baseball-Reference.com [cited August 17, 2013]. Available from: http://www.baseball-reference.com/teams/CIN/1900-schedule-scores.shtml.

"1900 St. Louis Cardinals (Batting, Pitching & Fielding Statistics)" (2013). Baseball-Reference.com [cited August 17, 2013]. Available from: http://www.baseball-reference.com/teams/STL/1900.shtml.

"1900 St. Louis Cardinals (Schedule, Box Scores and Splits)" (2013). Baseball-Reference.com [cited August 17, 2013]. Available from: http://www.baseball-reference.com/teams/STL/1900-schedule-scores.shtml.

"1901 Washington Senators (Batting, Pitching & Fielding Statistics)" (2013). Baseball-Reference.com [cited August 17, 2013]. Available from: http://www.baseball-reference.com/teams/WSH/1901.shtml.

"1901 Washington Senators (Schedule, Box Scores and Splits)" (2013). Baseball-Reference.com [cited August 12, 2013]. Available from: http://www.baseball-reference.com/teams/WSH/1901-schedule-scores.shtml.

"1902 Des Moines Midgets" (2013). Baseball-Reference.com [cited August 12, 2013]. Available from: http://www.baseball-reference.com/minors/team.cgi?id=7b148e3d.

"1919 New York Giants (Batting, Pitching & Fielding Statistics)" (2013). Baseball-Reference.com [cited August 7, 2013]. Available from: http://www.baseball-reference.com/teams/NYG/1919.shtml.

"Abuses in the Immigration Department" (1853). *Empire* (Sydney, NSW). Saturday, October 1, p. 5.

"Active Work at St. Louis" (1885). *The Sporting Life*, Wednesday, April 22, p. 4.

"Again the Giants Failed" (1894). *New York Times*, Thursday, August 2, p. 6.

Ahmed, N., et al. (2006). *Biology of Disease*. New York: Taylor & Francis.

Ahrens, A. (2007). *Chicago Cubs: Tinker to Evers to Chance*. Chicago: Arcadia.

Ajmani, L. (2009). *Embalming: Principles and Legal Aspects*. New Delhi: Jaypee Brothers, Medical Publishers.

Akin, W. (2012). "Jack Glasscock." SABR Baseball Biography Project [cited April 3, 2013]. Available from: http://sabr.org/bioproj/person/0bcddad0.

_____. (2012). "Win Mercer." SABR Baseball Biography Project [cited August 3, 2013]. Available from: http://sabr.org/bioproj/person/a128b34b.

"Al Buckenberger (Manager Page)" (2013). Baseball-Reference.com [cited August 2, 2013]. Available from: http://www.baseball-reference.com/managers/buckeal99.shtml.

"Alex Mckinnon (Player Page)" (2013). Baseball-Reference.com [cited August 15, 2013]. Available from: http://www.baseball-reference.com/players/m/mckinal01.shtml.

Alexander, C.C. (1995). *John McGraw*. Lincoln: University of Nebraska Press.

"An Alleged New Regime at Sportsman's Park" (1894). *The Sporting Life*, Saturday, July 7, p. 10.

"Altoona Mountain City (Team History & Encyclopedia)" (2013). Baseball-Reference.com [cited July 28, 2013]. Available from: http://www.baseball-reference.com/teams/ALT/.

"American Fact Finder" (2013). United States Census Bureau—U.S. Department of Commerce [cited July 28, 2013]. Available from: http://factfinder2.census.gov/faces/nav/jsf/pages/index.xhtml.

"American League: The Championship Season Now under Way" (1900). *The Sporting Life*, Saturday, April 28, p. 6.

"American League: The Expanded Organization's First Campaign" (1901). *The Sporting Life*, Saturday, June 1, p. 6.

"Amos Rusie (Player Page)" (2013). Baseball-Reference.com [cited June 1, 2013]. Available from: http://www.baseball-reference.com/players/r/rusieam01.shtml.

"An Anonymous Letter" (1893). *The Sporting News*, Saturday, February 11, p. 5.

Appel, M. (1999). *Slide, Kelly, Slide: The Wild Life and Times of Mike "King" Kelly, Baseball's First Superstar*. Lanham, MD: Scarecrow Press.

"Araluen [from Our Correspondent]" (1857). *Sydney Morning Herald*, Tuesday, July 7, p. 5.

"Araluen—Historic Gold Ghost Town in the Heart of the Southern Tablelands" (2004). *Sydney Morning Herald*, Sunday, February 8, p. 16.

Arden, H. (1981). "Iowa, America's Middle Earth." *National Geographic* 159 (6): pp. 603–629.

"Are Not Worrying" (1899). *The Sporting Life*, Saturday, October 7, p. 4.

"Are Rooting Now" (1899). *The Sporting News*, Saturday, May 13, p. 6.

"Arlie Latham (Manager Page)" (2013). Baseball-Reference.com [cited August 15, 2013]. Available from: http://www.baseball-reference.com/managers/lathaar01.shtml.

Armour, M.L., and D.R. Levitt (2004). *Paths to Glory: How Great Baseball Teams Got That Way*. Washington, DC: Brassey's.

Arnold, K.R. (2011). *Anti-Immigration in the United States: A Historical Encyclopedia*. Santa Barbara, CA: Greenwood Press.

Ashley, S. (1990). "Getting Good Wood (or Aluminum) on the Ball." *Mechanical Engineering* 112 (10): pp. 40–47.

"Association Meets" (1884). *The Sporting Life*, Wednesday, October 2, p. 2.

"At Work" (1885). *The Sporting Life*, Wednesday, April 15, p. 4.

Atkins, A. (2003). *Harvest of Grief: Grasshopper Plagues and Public Assistance in Minnesota, 1873–78*. Minneapolis: Minnesota Historical Society Press.

"Attempt Will Be Made to Operate System Today" (1900). *The Republic* (St. Louis, MO), Wednesday, May 9, pp. 1, 2.

"Aussie in the Dodgers' Diamond" (1986). *Canberra Times*, Tuesday, June 24, p. 20.

"Australia Birth Index, 1787–1922: Patrick F. Quin" (2010). Ancestry.com [cited July 1, 2012]. Available from: www.ancestry.com.

"The Australian Baseball Team—Further Particulars of the Tour" (1897). *South Australian Register* (Adelaide, SA), Friday, July 23, p. 7.

"The Australian Won" (1892). *Pittsburg Dispatch*, Wednesday, April 20, p. 8.

Axelson, G.W., G. Mitchem, and M. McGee (2003). *Commy: The Life Story of Charles A. Comiskey*. Jefferson, NC: McFarland.

"Back to Form" (1894). *Boston Sunday Globe*, Sunday, June 10, p. 7.

"A Bad State of Affairs among the Browns" (1894). *The Sporting Life*, Saturday, August 11, p. 5.

Bain, H.F. (1906). *U.S. Geological Survey Bulletin: Zinc and Lead Deposits of the Upper Mississippi Valley*. Washington, D.C.: U.S. Government Printing Office.

Bakken, G.M. (2011). *The Mining Law of 1872: Past, Politics, and Prospects*. Albuquerque: University of New Mexico Press.

"Baldwin at Work in St. Louis" (1889). *Pittsburg Dispatch*, Tuesday, November 26, p. 6.

Ballparks of America.

"Baltimore Bulletin" (1897). *The Sporting Life*, May 15, p. 7.

"Baltimore Bulletin: Echoes of the Series for the Temple Cup" (1896). *The Sporting Life*, Saturday, October 10, p. 6.

"Baltimore Orioles (Team History & Encyclopedia)" (2013). Baseball-Reference.com [cited August 21, 2013]. Available from: http://www.baseball-reference.com/teams/BLO/.

Barnhill, D.L. (1999). *At Home on the Earth: Becoming Native to Our Place : A Multicultural Anthology*. Berkeley: University of California Press.

"Base Ball" (1884). *St. Louis Globe-Democrat*, Monday, June 23, p. 4.

"Base Ball" (1884). *The Sporting Life*, Wednesday, February 20, p. 4; Wednesday, August 26, p. 5; Wednesday, December 3, p. 2.

"Base Ball" (1885). *Daily Evening Bulletin* (Maysville, KY), Friday, October 30, p. 4.

"Base Ball" (1885). *The Sporting Life*, Wednesday, April 22, p. 7.

"Base Ball" (1896). *The Sporting Life*, Saturday, August 8, p. 5.

"Base Ball Briefs" (1890). *St. Paul Daily Globe*, Sunday, May 4, p. 6.

"Base Ball Briefs" (1898). *St. Paul Globe*, Monday, July 4, p. 5.

"Base Ball Briefs" (1899). *St. Paul Globe*, Sunday, September 17, p. 10.

"Base Ball Brotherhood" (1887). *St. Paul Daily Globe*, Wednesday, August 24, p. 5.

"The Base Ball Conundrum" (1887). *New York Sun*, Sunday, February 20, p. 7.

"Base Ball: From the Hub" (1886). *The Sporting Life*, Wednesday, June 9, p. 8.

"Base Ball Gossip" (1898). *St. Paul Globe*, Thursday, February 24, p. 3.

"Base-Ball Riot" (1886). *Cincinnati Enquirer*, Monday, July 12, p. 8.

"Base Ball Uniforms" (1887). *The Sun* (New York), Sunday, June 12, p. 10.

"Base Ball: The Childs Case" (1891). *The Sporting Life*, Wednesday, April 25, p. 6.

"The Base Ball Outlook" (1888). *Omaha Daily Bee*, Monday, April 16, p. 2.

"Baseball" (1893). *Salt Lake Herald*, Sunday, June 4, p. 13.

"Baseball" (1888). *Daily Times* (Richmond, VA), Monday, August 6, p. 4.

"Baseball-Reference.Com" (2013). Sports Reference LLC [cited August 20, 2013]. Available from: http://www.baseball-reference.com/.

"Baseball Gossip" (1900). *The Republic* (St. Louis, MO), Wednesday, June 27, p. 7; Friday, June 15, p. 6.

"Baseball Gossip" (1900). *Cincinnati Enquirer*, Saturday, June 16, p. 3; Friday July 6, p. 5.

"Baseball Gossip" (1901). *St. Paul Globe*, Monday, December 30, p. 5.

"Baseball Gossip" (1902). *Evening Times* (Washington, DC), Thursday, May 1, p. 6.

"Baseball Hits and Runs" (1902). *Washington Times*, Sunday, February 2, p. 7.

"Baseball News" (1883). *St. Louis Globe-Democrat*, Sunday, December 30, p. 6.

"Baseball Notes" (1895). *Washington Times*, Monday, July 1, p. 3.

"Baseball Notes" (1895). *St. Louis Globe-Democrat*, Monday, September 23, p. 6.

"Baseball Notes" (1897). *The Chronicle* (Adelaide, SA), Saturday, June 5, p. 31.

"Baseball Notes" (1899). *Deseret Evening News* (Salt Lake City, UT), Tuesday, July 18, p. 5.

"The Baseball Outlook in St. Louis" (1893). *The Sun* (New York), Thursday, March 16, p. 4.

"Baseball: Personal" (1895). *The Sporting Life*, Saturday, June 8, p. 4.

"Baseball Rule Change Timeline" (2011). Baseball Almanac [cited August 20, 2013]. Available from: http://www.baseball-almanac.com/rulechng.shtml.

"Baseball Stories by Joe Quinn; Outlook for the Cardinals in 1906" (1905). *St. Louis Republic*, Sunday, December 10, p. 6.

"The Base-Ball Union: Work of the Philadelphia Convention—Players' Engagements" (1883). *New York Times*, Thursday, December 20, p. 5.

"Baseball Yarns" (1906). *Salt Lake Herald*, Monday, January 8, p. 7.

"Batted" (1900). *Cincinnati Enquirer*, Sunday, June 17, p. 10.

"Battle Begun: Last Sectional Trip of the Season On" (1895). *The Sporting News*, Saturday, August 24, p. 4.

Bayley, W.A. (1965). *History of Campbelltown, New South Wales*. 2nd ed. Campbelltown, NSW: Campbelltown Municipal Council.

Begg, P. (2005). *Mary Celeste: The Greatest Mystery of the Sea*. London: Pearson Education.

Bennett, D.H. (1988). *The Party of Fear: From Nativist Movements to the New Right in American History*. Chapel Hill: University of North Carolina Press.

Bennett, S. (1865). *The History of Australian Discovery and Colonisation*. London: Hanson and Bennett.

Benson, M. (1989). *Ballparks of North America*. Jefferson, NC: McFarland.

Berger, R. (2012). "Amos Rusie." SABR Baseball Biography Project. Society for American Baseball Research [cited August 24, 2013]. Available from: http://sabr.org/bioproj/person/b7d42c08.

"Best Teeth" (1887). *St. Paul Daily Globe*, Sunday, May 22, p. 3.

"Better for the Batter" (1888). *Boston Globe*, Wednesday, August 27, p. 8.

"Between the Bases" (1896). *Evening Times* (Washington, DC), Friday, September 4, p. 3.

Bevis, C. (2012). "Tim Keefe." SABR Baseball Biography Project. Society for American Baseball Research [cited June 15, 2013]. Available from: http://sabr.org/bioproj/person/6f1dd1b1.

"The Big League Race" (1895). *The Sporting Life*, Saturday, June 8, pp. 10–11; August 10, p. 4.

"Bill Joyce (Br Bullpen)" (2013). Baseball-Reference.com [cited August 21, 2013]. Available from: http://www.baseball-reference.com/bullpen/Bill_Joyce.

"Billy Earle (Minor League Player Page)" (2013). Baseball-Reference.com [cited August 21, 2013]. Available from: http://www.baseball-reference.com/minors/player.cgi?id=earle-001bil.

"Billy Klusman (Br Bullpen)" (2013). Baseball-Reference.com [cited April 26, 2013]. Available from: http://www.baseball-reference.com/bullpen/Billy_Klusman.

"Billy Klusman (Player Page)" (2013). Baseball-Reference.com [cited April 24, 2013]. Available from: http://www.baseball-reference.com/players/k/klusmbi01.shtml.

"Billy Taylor (Minor League Player Page)" (2013). Baseball-Reference.com [cited July 24, 2013]. Available from: http://www.baseball-reference.com/minors/player.cgi?id=taylor001bil.

"Billy Taylor (Player Page)" (2013). Baseball-Reference.com [cited August 15, 2013]. Available from: http://www.baseball-reference.com/players/t/taylobi01.shtml.

Binyon, L. (1917). *For the Fallen and Other Poems*. London: Hodder & Stoughton.

"Bones Ely (Player Page)" (2013). Baseball-Reference.com [cited August 15, 2013]. Available from: http://www.baseball-reference.com/players/e/elybo01.shtml.

"Boosts for Quinn" (1900). *The Republic* (St. Louis, MO), Friday, June 15, p. 6.

Borst, W.A. (1980). *Baseball Through a Knothole: A St. Louis History*. St. Louis: Krank Press.

"Boss Von Der Ahe" (1893). *The Sporting Life*, Saturday, March 31, p .6.

"Boston Leaguers Report" (1890). *The World—Evening Edition* (New York), Tuesday, March 18, p. 1.

"Boston Lines" (1889). *The Sporting News*, Friday, April 12, p. 3.

"Boston, March 29" (1889). *The Sun* (New York), Saturday, March 30, p. 6.

"Boston Second" (1894). *Boston Sunday Globe*, Sunday, June 10, p. 7.

"Boston's Latest: Joe Quinn, Their New Second Baseman, and His Record" (1888). *Wichita Daily Eagle*, Tuesday, October 16, p. 7.

"Bostons Score One—The Clevelands Downed in Another Rattling Good Exhibition, Errors Lost the Contest" (1892). *Pittsburg Dispatch*, Wednesday, October 19, p. 9.

"The Boys Arrive at Savannah" (1890). *The World—Evening Edition* (New York), Tuesday, March 18, p. 1.

Bradbury, S., and G. Smart. (2005). *Steven Bradbury: Last Man Standing*. Docklands, VIC: Geoff Slattery.

"Braidwood [from Our Correspondent]" (1858). *Sydney Morning Herald*, Saturday, May 15, p. 6.

Bready, J.H. (1998). *Baseball in Baltimore: The First Hundred Years*. Baltimore: Johns Hopkins University Press.

"Breitenstein Still Firm" (1896). *The Sporting Life*, Saturday, February 8, p. 3.

"Bremer River Works" (1864). *Brisbane Courier* (Brisbane, QLD), Saturday, December 17, p. 5.

"Brilliant Ball Game" (1897). *The Sun* (Baltimore), Tuesday, August 3, p. 6.

Britannica-online (2012). "Beau Brummell (English Dandy)." *Encyclopædia Britannica* [cited July 7, 2013]. Available from: http://www.britannica.com/EBchecked/topic/82094/Beau-Brummell.

Brookes, T., and A.P.H. Association. (2005). *A Warning Shot: Influenza and the 2004 Flu Vaccine Shortage*. Washington, DC: American Public Health Association.

Broome, R. (2010). *Aboriginal Australians: A History since 1788*. 4th ed. Crows Nest: Allen & Unwin.

"The Brotherhood" (1889). *The Sporting News*, Saturday, September 21, p. 1.

"The Browns All Right Despite Their Poor Start" (1896). *The Sporting Life*, Saturday, April 27, p. 10.

"The Browns Disbanded—Chris Von Der Ahe Arrested for Assault—Meeting of the Directors Etc." (1894). *The Sporting Life*, Saturday, October 13, p. 2.

"The Browns in a Rather Crippled Condition" (1895). *The Sporting Life*, Saturday, July 13, p. 10.

"The Browns in a State of Demoralization" (1895). *The Sporting Life*, Saturday, August 10, p. 11.

"The Browns Little Benefitted by Their Trip" (1895). *The Sporting Life*, Saturday, April 20, p. 7.

"Brown's One Home Run: It Won a Game from the Giants Yesterday" (1888). *New York Times*, Thursday, August 28, p. 8.

Brown, M. (2010). *Australia's Worst Disasters*. Sydney: Hachette Australia.

"Browns Overwhelmed" (1897). *The Sun* (Baltimore), Saturday, September 4, p. 6.

"Browns' President Sued" (1896). *St. Paul Globe*, Thursday, September 17, p. 5.

Brunell, F.H. (1890). *1890 Players' National League Baseball Guide*. Chicago: F.H. Brunell.

Burk, R.F. (2001). *Never Just a Game: Players, Owners, and American Baseball to 1920*. Chapel Hill: University of North Carolina Press.

Burnett, F.H. (1993). *Little Lord Fauntleroy*. Boston, MA: David R. Godine.

Bush, A. (2012). "Duluth's First Pro Baseball Team: 1886 Champions." Zenith City: celebrating historic Duluth, western Lake Superior, and Minnesota's arrowhead [cited March 31, 2013]. Available from: http://zenithcity.com/duluths-first-pro-baseball-team-1886-champions/.

Byrne, J.P., P. Coleman, and J. King (2008). *Ireland and the*

Americas: Culture, Politics, and History. Vol. 2. Santa Barbara, CA: ABC-CLIO.

Calkin, H.L. (1964). "The Irish in Iowa." *Palimpsest* 45 (2): pp. 33–97.

Campbell, M. (1997). *The Kingdom of the Ryans: The Irish in Southwest New South Wales 1816–1890.* Sydney: University of New South Wales.

"Cap Anson (Player Page)" (2013). Baseball-Reference.com [cited May 20, 2013]. Available from: http://www.baseball-reference.com/players/a/ansonca01.shtml.

"Captain Joe Quinn—Business Cares Affected His Last Playing Season" (1893). *The Sporting News,* Saturday, October 21, p. 1.

"Career Leaders & Records for Hit by Pitch" (2013). Baseball-Reference.com [cited August 30, 2013]. Available from: http://www.baseball-reference.com/leaders/HBP_career.shtml.

Carter, C. (1983). *The Sporting News Official Baseball Record Book.* St. Louis, MO: The Sporting News.

"Caruthers Set Adrift" (1893). *New York Daily Tribune,* Friday, March 17, p. 5.

"A Case of Kellogg" (1887). *St. Paul Daily Globe,* Wednesday, October 5, p. 5.

Cash, J.D. (2002). *Before They Were Cardinals—Major League Baseball in Nineteenth-Century St. Louis.* St. Louis: University of Missouri Press.

Casway, J. (2006). *Ed Delahanty in the Emerald Age of Baseball.* Notre Dame, IN: University of Notre Dame Press.

"Cattle and Sheep" (1848). *Sydney Morning Herald,* Wednesday, February 2, p. 4.

"Caught on the Fly" (1889). *The Sporting News,* Sunday, October 6, p. 5.

CBCS (1910). *Official Year Book of the Commonwealth of Australia No. 3—1910.* Canberra: Australian Bureau of Statistics/Commonwealth Bureau of Statistics.

Chadwick, H. (1899). *Spalding Official Base Ball Guide for 1899.* New York: American Sports Publishing.

"Chaff from Chicago" (1889). *The Sporting News,* Saturday, September 21, p. 1.

"Champions Tired" (1894). *Boston Daily Globe,* Wednesday, August 29, p. 2.

"A Chance Given Mr. Sharrott" (1893). *New York Times,* Tuesday, August 8, p. 6.

"Change in the St. Louis Team" (1895). *Los Angeles Herald,* Tuesday, June 25, p. 2.

"Charlie Bennett's Misfortune" (1894). *Wichita Daily Eagle,* Monday, January 11, p. 1.

"Charlie Sweeney (Player Page)" (2013). Baseball-Reference.com [cited June 29, 2013]. Available from: http://www.baseball-reference.com/players/s/sweench01.shtml.

Charlton, J. (1991). *The Baseball Chronology: The Complete History of the Most Important Events in the Game of Baseball.* New York: Macmillan.

"Chatter with the Ball Cranks" (1895). *Omaha Daily Bee,* Sunday, August 25, p. 16.

"Chicago Calumets Beat Local Kcs" (1905). *St. Louis Republic,* Wednesday, July 5, p. 11.

"Chicago Cubs (Team History & Encyclopedia)" (2013). Baseball-Reference.com [cited July 24, 2013]. Available from: http://www.baseball-reference.com/teams/CHC/.

"Chicago Gleanings" (1890). *The Sporting Life,* Wednesday, November 15, p. 3.

"Chicago Wants Quinn" (1900). *St. Louis Republic,* Saturday, June 16, p. 5.

Chipp, M. (1980). "Inside the Park Home Runs" Society for American Baseball Research: Research Journals Archive (Vol. 9) [cited April 30, 2013]. Available from: http://research.sabr.org/journals/inside-the-park-home-runs.

Chisholm, C. (2004). *Female Immigration Considered: In a Brief Assessment of the Sydney Immigrants' Home.* Sydney: Sydney University Press.

"Chit Chat of the Ball Players" (1892). *Omaha Daily Bee,* Sunday, September 18, p. 19.

"Chris' Hoodoo" (1895). *The Sporting Life,* Saturday, May 11, p. 5.

"Chris' Slick Scheme" (1894). *The Sporting Life,* Saturday, May 26, p. 6.

"Christy Mathewson (Player Page)" (2013). Baseball-Reference.com [cited June 1, 2013]. Available from: http://www.baseball-reference.com/players/m/mathech01.shtml.

City of Boston (2010). *"Jamaica Plain: Exploring Boston's Neighborhoods."* Boston Landmarks Commission, Boston, MA [cited June 22, 2013]. Available from: www.cityofboston.gov/images_documents/Jamaica_Plain_brochure_tcm3-19120.pdf.

Clark, J. (2003). *A History of Australian Baseball: Time and Game.* Lincoln: University of Nebraska Press.

Clark, M., and M. Cathcart (1993). *History of Australia.* Melbourne: Melbourne University Publishing.

"Clarke Had a Revolver, Drew the Weapon on Davis and Joyce on Saturday" (1897). *Evening Times* (Washington, DC), Monday, July 19, p. 6.

"Classified Advertising" (1862). *Queensland Courier* (Brisbane, QLD), Wednesday, December 24, p. 1.

"Cleveland Chatter" (1899). *The Sporting Life,* Saturday, June 17, p. 5.

"Cleveland Chatter—Cross' Men Broke Even with the Eastern Clubs" (1899). *The Sporting Life,* Saturday, June 3, p. 4.

"Cleveland Vs. New York at Cleveland, June 24" (1899). *The Sporting Life,* Saturday, July 1, p. 3.

"Close Games All Around" (1884). *Boston Globe,* Friday, July 18, p. 1.

"Club Weakened" (1892). *Boston Globe,* Tuesday, September 20, p. 5.

Coghlan, T.A., ed. (2011). *Labour and Industry in Australia: From the First Settlement in 1788 to the Establishment of the Commonwealth in 1901.* Vol. 2. New York: Cambridge University Press.

Collier, R. (1974). *The Plague of the Spanish Lady.* New York: Atheneum.

Comerford, M. (1886). "Collections Relating to the Dioceses of Kildare and Leighlin." James Duffy and Sons, Dublin. Available from: http://www.archive.org/stream/collectionskild00comeuoft/collectionskild00comeuoft_djvu.txt.

"Commercial Intelligence" (1862). *The Argus* (Melbourne), Tuesday, April 15, p. 4.

"A Complete Change of Heart" (1885). *The Sporting Life,* Wednesday, October 14, p. 1.

Compton, N. (2013). *Why Sailors Can't Swim and Other Marvellous Maritime Curiosities.* New York: Bloomsbury.

"Connie Mack (Manager Page)" (2013). Baseball-Reference.com [cited August 25, 2013]. Available from: http://www.baseball-reference.com/managers/mackco01.shtml.

"Connie Mack (Player Page)" (2013). Baseball-Reference.com [cited August 25, 2013]. Available from: http://www.baseball-reference.com/players/m/mackco01.shtml.

Cooper, B. (2005). "Dubuque—Chicago, 1879" *The National Pastime (Society for American Baseball Research)* 25: pp. 112–116.

Corbett, L.K., and F. Knight (2001). *The Dingo in Australian and Asia.* Sydney: University of New South Wales Press.

"Country Intelligence" (1841). *Sydney Gazette and New South Wales Advertiser*, Tuesday, February 9, p. 2.

"Country News" (1860). *Sydney Morning Herald*, Tuesday, February 7, p. 3.

"Craig Shipley (Player Page)" (2013). Baseball-Reference.com [cited June 29, 2013]. Available from: http://www.baseball-reference.com/players/s/shiplcr01.shtml.

"Crowds in League Cities: Catcher Kittridge Writes About the Patrons of the Game" (1896). *Evening Times* (Washington, DC), Friday, September 4, p. 3.

Cunningham, C., and R. Roberts (2011). *Before the Curse: The Chicago Cubs' Glory Years, 1870–1945*. Champaign: University of Illinois Press. p. 56.

"Cupid Childs (Player Page)" (2013). Baseball-Reference.com [cited August 20, 2013]. Available from: http://www.baseball-reference.com/players/c/childcu01.shtml.

"The Current Opinion: In Europe Undoubtedly Tending Warward" (1888). *Evening Bulletin* (Maysville, KY), Tuesday, August 28, p. 1.

"Current Sporting Gossip" (1905). *The Sun* (New York), Sunday, February 26, p. 8.

Curzon, J. (1896). *The Great Cyclone at St. Louis and East St. Louis, May 27, 1896: Being a Full History of the Most Terrifying and Destructive Tornado in the History of the World*. Carbondale: Southern Illinois University Press.

"Cy Young (Player Page)" (2013). Baseball-Reference.com [cited August 2, 2013]. Available from: http://www.baseball-reference.com/players/y/youngcy01.shtml.

Dabscheck, B. (1995). "Australian Baseballers Form a Team of Their Own." *Sporting Traditions* 12 (1): pp. 61–101.

_____. (1998). "Australian Baseball's Second Unsuccessful Attempt to Establish a Players' Association." *Sporting Traditions* 14 (2): pp. 87–89.

_____. (2012). "A Primer on Australian Player Associations." *Economic and Labour Relations Review* 23 (3). Online only: http://www.freepatentsonline.com/article/Economic-Labour-Relations-Review/305080849.html.

"Dale Gear (Player Page)" (2013). Baseball-Reference.com [cited August 2, 2013]. Available from: http://www.baseball-reference.com/players/g/gearda01.shtml.

Davis, M. (1953). *The Lore and Legends of Baseball*. New York: Lantern Press.

Deane, W. (1989). *Total Baseball*. Baseball Ink. J. Thorn and P. Palmer Warner Books.

"Death in the Sun's Rays" (1887). *St. Paul Daily Globe*, Monday, July 18, p. 1.

"Death Notice—Mary E. Quinn (Nee Mcgrath)" (1937). *St. Louis Globe-Democrat*, December 14, p. 5C.

"Deceptive Shoots Slaughtered" (1900). *St. Louis Republic*, Tuesday, August 21, p. 5.

Deloria, V., and R.J. DeMallie (1999). *Documents of American Indian Diplomacy: Treaties, Agreements, and Conventions, 1775–1979 (Legal History of North America)*. Tulsa: University of Oklahoma Press.

De Puy, W.H. (1908). *The World-Wide Encyclopedia and Gazetteer*. New York: The Christian Herald.

"'Der Boss' and 'Theo'" (1894). *The Sporting Life*, Saturday, September 22, p. 2.

"Des Moines Gets Him" (1888). *St. Paul Daily Globe*, Saturday, January 7, p. 5.

"Des Moines Scores a Ninth Successive Victory by Doing up the Men from Duluth" (1887). *St. Paul Daily Globe*, Sunday, July 24.

"Destructive Storm of Hail and Ice" (1861). *Sydney Morning Herald*, Saturday, December 14, p. 6.

Dezen, D. (2013). "ABF Announces 2013 Hall of Fame Inductees [Press Release: March 14, 2013]." Australian Baseball Federation [cited May 3, 2013]. Available from: http://www.baseball.com.au/default.asp?Page=92259&MenuID=Website+Administration%2F17%2F20%2CEdit+Main+Menu%2F2084%2F0.

"The Diamond" (1892). *Pittsburg Dispatch*, Wednesday, October 19, p. 9.

"The Diamond" (1892). *Pittsburg Dispatch*, Wednesday, April 20, p. 8.

"Diamond Dashes" (1888). *St. Paul Daily Globe*, Sunday, December 16, p. 6.

"Diamond Dust" (1897). *Evening Times* (Washington, DC), Saturday, May 29, p. 3; Wednesday, September 15, p. 6; Friday, March 12, p. 5.

"Diamond Dust" (1896). *Morning Times* (Washington, DC), Saturday, June 13, p. 3.

"Diamond Dust" (1897). *Morning Times* (Washington, DC), Sunday, September 5, p. 4; Wednesday, March 24, p. 3.

"Diamond Dust" (1898). *The Times* (Washington, DC), Monday, August 8, p. 6.

Diamond, E. (1989). "Kerry Patch: Irish Immigrant Life in St. Louis." *Gateway Heritage* (Fall 1989): pp. 23–30.

"The Diamond Field: What's the Matter with Kelly, the $10,000 Beauty?" (1889). *Salt Lake Herald*, Sunday, May 19, p. 14.

Dickson, P. (2011). *The Dickson Baseball Dictionary*, 3rd ed. New York: W.W. Norton.

"Digging Their Graves: League Worthies Now Start to Wreck the Association" (1891). *Pittsburg Dispatch*, Thursday, February 19, p. 1.

"Dingo Land Ball Players" (1897). *Morning Times* (Washington, DC), Wednesday, March 24, p. 3.

"Distress in the Agricultural Districts" (1864). *Sydney Morning Herald*, Wednesday, March 9, p. 5.

"Divided the Honors—The Browns and the Washingtons Each Took a Game" (1894). *St. Louis Globe-Democrat*, Thursday, July 5.

"Done by the Umpire" (1887). *St. Paul Daily Globe*, Saturday, August 13, p. 5.

"Donlin and Dillard Walloped the Ball" (1900). *St. Louis Republic*, Thursday, April 5, p. 4.

"Doom of Baseball: How It Is Being Sounded by the Mismanagement of Puffed up Managers" (1899). *St. Paul Globe*, Sunday, May 14, p. 10.

"Double Victory for Allen's Men" (1900). *Cincinnati Enquirer*, Tuesday, October 9, p. 4.

"The Dubuque 9 for 1880" (1880). *Dubuque Herald*, Sunday, March 7, p. 4.

"Duluth Club Changes" (1887). *St. Paul Daily Globe*, Sunday, July 31, p. 1.

"The Duluth Team" (1887). *St. Paul Daily Globe*, Thursday, August 2, p. 5.

"Duluth the Victor" (1887). *Duluth Daily News*, June 1, p. 1.

"Duluth Very Eager" (1888). *St. Paul Daily Globe*, Thursday, January 19, p. 5.

"Duluth Will Stay" (1887). *St. Paul Daily Globe*, Wednesday, October 19, p. 1.

"Duluth's New Manager" (1887). *The Sporting Life*, Wednesday, August 31, p. 7.

Durocher, L., and E. Linn (2009). *Nice Guys Finish Last*. Chicago: University of Chicago Press.

"Dust of the Diamond" (1889). *St. Paul Daily Globe*, Sunday, February 24, p. 6.

"Eagle Baseball Notes" (1895). *Wichita Daily Eagle*, Saturday, September 28, p. 3.

"Echoes of the Game" (1890). *Boston Globe*, Tuesday May 27, p. 5.

"Editorial News, Views, and Comment" (1892). *The Sporting News*, Saturday, June 25, p. 2; Saturday, July 16, p. 2.

"Editorial News, Views, and Comment" (1893). *The Sporting News*, Saturday, September 9, p. 2.

"Edwin Flack—Our First Olympic Champion" (2013). City of Casey, Victoria, Australia [cited March 9, 2013]. Available from: http://www.casey.vic.gov.au/olympic/.

"Egyptian Healy (Player Page)" (2013). Baseball-Reference.com [cited August 3, 2013]. Available from: http://www.baseball-reference.com/players/h/healyjo01.shtml.

"Eight in Eighth" (1895). *Boston Daily Globe*, Thursday, May 9, p. 5.

Einstein, C. (1968). *The Third Fireside Book of Baseball*. New York: Simon & Schuster.

Eisenbath, M., and S. Musial (1999). *The Cardinals Encyclopedia*. Philadelphia: Temple University Press.

Elston, G. (2006). *A Stitch in Time*. Houston, TX: Halcyon Press.

Emsley, J. (2011). *Nature's Building Blocks: An A–Z Guide to the Elements*. Oxford, UK: Oxford University Press.

Encyclopædia Britannica (1998). "Embalming." Chicago: Encyclopædia Britannica.

"Ended in Gloom" (1897). *The Sun* (Baltimore), Monday, October 4, p. 6.

Ervin Brown, C., and J.W. Whitlow (1960). *Geology of Parts of the Upper Mississippi Valley Zinc-Lead District: Geology of the Dubuque South Quadrangle Iowa-Illinois*. Geological Survey Bulletin 1123-A. Washington, DC: U.S. Government Printing Office.

Evans, A.G. (1997). *Fanatic Heart: A Life of John Boyle O'Reilly, 1844–1890*. Nedlands: University of Western Australia Press.

Evans, R. (2008). *A History of Queensland*. New York: Cambridge University Press.

Evers, J.J., and H.S. Fullerton (1910). *Touching Second: The Science of Baseball*. Chicago: Reilly & Britton.

"An Exciting Scene" (1889). *Pittsburg Dispatch*, Tuesday, August 27, p. 6.

"Exploration Westward" (1872). *South Australian Register* (Adelaide, SA), Thursday, December 5, p. 3.

"Exposed at Last" (1900). *The Sporting Life*, Saturday, September 22, p. 7.

"Facts" (1889). *The Sporting Life*, Wednesday, November 6, p. 3.

"The Facts About Manager Buckenberger's Release" (1895). *The Sporting Life*, Saturday, July 6, p. 10.

"Family History Research" (2013). Queensland Government: Births, Deaths, Marriages and Divorces [cited July 7, 2013]. Available from: http://www.qld.gov.au/law/births-deaths-marriages-and-divorces/family-history-research/.

"The Farce Has Begun" (1899). *Cleveland Plain Dealer*, Sunday, April 16, p. 1.

"Farrell Won't Sign" (1892). *Pittsburg Dispatch*, Monday December 5, p. 6.

Farrington, D. "Half a Century through Joe Quinn's Eyes: Union Star Recalls Birth of *The Sporting News*" (1936). *The Sporting News*, Saturday, May 21 p. 9B.

"February Floods" (1910). *Braidwood Dispatch and Mining Journal* (Braidwood, NSW), Wednesday February 16, p. 2.

Fell, E.T. (1927). *History of the Seventh Division, United States Army, 1917–1919*. Philadelphia: H. Moore.

Ferkovich, S. (2012). "Bennett Park (Detroit)." SABR Baseball Biography Project. Society for American Baseball Research [cited May 20, 2013]. Available from: http://sabr.org/bioproj/park/336604.

"The First Defeat" (1884). *St. Louis Republican*, Sunday, May 25, p. 3.

Fischer, D., J. Buckley, and J. Gigliotti (2007). *Obsessed with...Baseball: Test Your Knowledge of America's Pastime*. San Francisco: Chronicle Books.

Fisher, R. (2009). *Boosting Brisbane: Imprinting the Colonial Capital of Queensland*. Salisbury: Boolarong Press.

"Five Fires" (1887). *St. Paul Daily Globe*, Friday, May 13, p. 4.

Flanagan, R. (1862). *The History of New South Wales: With an Account of Van Diemen's Land (Tasmania), New Zealand, Port Phillip (Victoria), Moreton Bay, and Other Australasian Settlements: Comprising a Complete View of the Progress and Prospects of Gold Mining in Australia/the Whole Compiled from Official and Other Authentic and Original Sources by Roderick Flanagan*. London: Sampson Low, Son.

Flannery, T. (2000). *The Explorers: Stories of Discovery and Adventure from the Australian Frontier*. New York: Grove Press.

"Flashes from the Diamond" (1888). *Omaha Daily Bee*, Thursday, December 20, p. 2.

"Flashes from the Diamond" (1889). *Omaha Daily Bee*, Sunday, August 4, p. 9.

"Flashes from the Diamond" (1890). *Omaha Daily Bee*, Sunday, March 16, p. 1.

"Flashes from the Diamond" (1895). *Omaha Daily Bee*, Saturday, January 26, p. 4.

Fleitz, D.L. (2005). *Cap Anson: The Grand Old Man of Baseball*. Jefferson, NC: McFarland.

_____. (2004). *Ghosts in the Gallery at Cooperstown: Sixteen Little-Known Members of the Hall of Fame*. Jefferson, NC: McFarland.

_____. (2009). *The Irish in Baseball: An Early History*. Jefferson, NC: McFarland.

_____. (2012). "Louis Soxalexis." SABR Baseball Biography Project. Society for American Baseball Research [cited August 15, 2013]. Available from: http://sabr.org/bioproj/person/2b1aea0a.

"The Floods" (1860). *Sydney Morning Herald*, Monday, February 20, p. 3.

"The Floods [Araluen]" (1860). *Sydney Morning Herald*, Saturday, February 18, p. 8.

Foley, J.C. (1957). *Droughts in Australia: Review of Records from Earliest Years of Settlement to 1955*. Melbourne: Director of Meteorology.

"Forfeited the Game" (1894). *Washington Post*, Thursday, September 6, p. 6.

"Forty Years Ago..." (1884). *Omaha Daily Bee*, Tuesday, April 15, p. 7.

Fotheringham, R. (2010). "Inside the Killing Fields of Queensland." *The Australian* (Melbourne), Wednesday, October 6, p. 12.

"Four Straight Defeats" (1888). *New York Times*, Sunday, August 31, p. 6.

Fox, S.R. (1998). *Big Leagues: Professional Baseball, Football, and Basketball in National Memory*. Lincoln: University of Nebraska Press.

"Frank Selee (Manager Page)" (2013). Baseball-Reference.com [cited May 22, 2013]. Available from: http://www.baseball-reference.com/managers/seleefr99.shtml.

Frankenfield, H.C. (1904). *The Floods of the Spring of 1903, in the Mississippi Watershed*. Washington, DC: Weather Bureau.

Frazer, R.W. (1965). *Forts of the West: Military Forts and Presidios, and Posts Commonly Called Forts, West of the Mississippi River to 1898*. Norman: University of Oklahoma Press.

"Fred Dunlap (Player Page)" (2013). Baseball-Reference.com [cited August 15, 2013]. Available from: http://www.baseball-reference.com/players/d/dunlafr01.shtml.

Frisch, M.H., and D.J. Valkowitz. (1983). *Working Class America: Essays on Labor, Community, and American Society*. Urbana: University of Illinois Press.

"From St. Louis" (1884). *The Sporting Life*, Wednesday, January 9.

"From St. Louis" (1886). *The Sporting Life*, Wednesday, October 6, p. 4.

"From the Bostons" (1889). *Pittsburg Dispatch*, Sunday, June 16, p. 15.

"From the Mound City" (1885). *The Sporting Life*, Wednesday, July 1, p. 5.

"From the Mound City" (1886). *The Sporting Life*, Wednesday, March 24, p.8.

"From the Mound City: The St. Louis Club's New Manager—Reasons for the Change, Etc." (1885). *The Sporting Life*, Wednesday, September 16, p. 4.

Frost, A. (2012). *Botany Bay: The Real Story*. Collingwood, Australia: Black Inc.

"Full of Sharp Work" (1887). *St. Paul Daily Globe*, Thursday, September 1, p. 5.

"Funeral Homes/Parlours/Chapels/Undertakers" (2002). St. Louis Public Library [cited August 20, 2013]. Available from: http://www.slpl.lib.mo.us/libsrc/funeral.htm.

"Games Played August 1" (1887). *The Sporting Life*, Wednesday, August 10, p. 6.

"Games Played August 6" (1887). *The Sporting Life*, Wednesday, August 17, p. 6.

"Games Played August 24" (1887). *The Sporting Life*, Wednesday, September 7, p. 6.

"Games Played August 31" (1899). *The Sporting Life*, Saturday, September 9, p. 2.

"Games Played Friday, July 12" (1890). *The Sporting Life*, Wednesday, July 19, p. 3.

"Games Played July 4" (1887). *The Sporting Life*, Wednesday, July 13, p. 6.

"Games Played July 4" (1894). *The Sporting Life*, Saturday, July 14, p. 3.

"Games Played July 10" (1885). *The Sporting Life*, Wednesday, July 15, p. 2.

"Games Played July 17" (1899). *The Sporting Life*, Saturday, July 22, p. 3.

"Games Played July 30/July 31" (1885). *The Sporting Life*, Wednesday, August 2, p. 2.

"Games Played June 20" (1885). *The Sporting Life*, Wednesday, June 24, p. 3.

"Games Played May 11" (1885). *The Sporting Life*, Wednesday, May 20, p. 4.

"Games Played Monday, August 16" (1886). *The Sporting Life*, Wednesday, August 25, p. 2.

"Games Played October 6" (1887). *The Sporting Life*, Wednesday, October 18, p. 6.

"Games Played Saturday, April 22" (1899). *The Sporting Life*, Saturday, April 29, p. 3.

"Games Played Saturday, July 26" (1890). *The Sporting Life*, Wednesday, August 26, p. 3.

"Games Played Tuesday, July 6" (1897). *The Sporting Life*, Saturday, July 10, p. 3.

"Games Played Tuesday, July 17" (1888). *The Sporting Life*, Wednesday, July 25, p. 2.

"Games Played Wednesday, June 3" (1896). *The Sporting Life*, Saturday, June 6, p. 3.

"Games Played Wednesday, August 17" (1891). *The Sporting Life*, Saturday, September 12, p. 3.

Gardener, B., and B. Stahura (1997). *Seventh Infantry Division: 1917–1992. World War I, World War II, Korea, and Panamanian Invasion*. Nashville: Turner.

Geist, V. (1998). *Buffalo Nation: History and Legend of the North American Bison*. Stillwater, MN: Voyageur Press.

Gelder, K., and R. Weaver (2007). *The Anthology of Colonial Australian Gothic Fiction*. Melbourne: Melbourne University Press.

Gelzheiser, R.P. (2006). *Labor and Capital in 19th Century Baseball*. Jefferson, NC: McFarland.

Gibson, C.J., and E. Lennon (1999). "Historical Census Statistics on the Foreign-Born Population of the United States: 1850–1990." U.S. Bureau of the Census [cited August 19, 2013]. Available from: http://www.census.gov/population/www/documentation/twps0029/twps0029.html.

Gietschier, S., and *Sporting News* (2005). *Complete Baseball Record Book, 2005 Edition*. St. Louis: The Sporting News.

Godl, J.F. (1993). "The Ghost of Frederick Fisher." *Journal of the Royal Australian Historical Society* 27: pp. 6–7.

"The Golden Gate Pitcher" (1887). *St. Paul Daily Globe*, Thursday, July 14, p. 4.

Golden, R.N. (2010). *The Truth About Smoking*. New York: Infobase Publishing.

Goldstein, W. (1989). *Playing for Keeps: A History of Early Baseball*. Ithaca, NY: Cornell University Press.

Gordon, P.M. (2012). "King Kelly." SABR Baseball Biography Project. Society for American Baseball Research. [cited June 20, 2013]. Available from: http://sabr.org/bioproj/person/ffc40dac.

Gorman, R.M., and D. Weeks (2011). "Death at the Ballpark: A Comprehensive Study of Game-Related Fatalities, 1862–2007" [cited August 24, 2013]. Available from: http://www.deathattheballpark.com/fatalities.html.

"Gossip from Boston: Charley Foley Tells of the Bean Eaters' Great Financial Success" (1889). *Pittsburg Dispatch*, Monday, September 9, p. 6.

"Gossip of the Ball Players" (1900). *St. Louis Republic*, Tuesday, November 20, p. 7.

"Gossip of the Country's Game" (1896). *St. Paul Globe*, Sunday, May 17, p. 3.

"Gossip of the Diamond" (1899). *Washington Times*, Wednesday, July 19, p. 6.

"Gossip of the Diamond" (1899). *St. Paul Globe*, Tuesday, May 16, p. 5.

"Gossip of the Diamond" (1899). *Evening Times* (Washington, DC), Saturday, August 12, p. 6.

"Gossip of the Green Diamond" (1901). *St. Louis Republic*, Monday, April 8.

Gould, D. (2012). "History Shared, History Removed: *The Sporting News* Roots in St. Louis." *St. Louis Post-Dispatch* [cited August 20, 2013]. Available from: http://bit.ly/S4MzOs.

Gould, D.B. (1886). *Gould's St. Louis Directory for 1885 (for the Year Ending April 1st, 1886)*. St. Louis Gould Directory Co.

Gould, D.B. (1888). *Gould's St. Louis Directory for 1887 (for the Year Ending April 1st, 1888)*. St. Louis: Gould Directory Co.

Gould, W.B. (2011). *Bargaining with Baseball: Labor Relations in an Age of Prosperous Turmoil*. Jefferson, NC: McFarland.

Gould's Blue Book for the City of St. Louis, 1903: Alphabetically Arranged and Classified by Streets, Also a List of the Most Prominent Citizens in Alton, St. Charles and Carlinville: Also a Complete List of Club Members with Their Business Locations (1902–03). St. Louis: Gould Directory Co.

Graham, D.P. (2011). *Enniskillen and the Battle of Newtownbutler, 1689*. Farnham: Pike & Shot Society.

"Grand Send Off" (1891). *Boston Globe*, Thursday, April 23, p. 11.

"The Great Race" (1896). *The Sporting Life*, Saturday, July 11, pp. 2–3.

"The Great Scheme: The Plans of the Brotherhood Given

in Detail" (1889). *The Sporting News*, Saturday, September 28, p. 3.

"Griffith's Valuation: Primary Valuation of Tenements: Parish of Killabban" (1847–1864). Ask About Ireland [cited June 29, 2013]. Available from: http://www.askaboutireland.ie/griffith-valuation/.

Groom, B., and W. Wickman (1982). *Sydney, the 1850s: The Lost Collection*. Sydney: University of Sydney.

Gross, J.S. (1986). "Wilmington Quicksteps: Glory to Oblivion." Baseball Research Journal. Society for American Baseball Research [cited July 4, 2013]. Available from: http://research.sabr.org/journals/wilmington-quicksteps-glory-to-oblivion.

"Guests of a Cardinal" (1896). *Evening Times* (Washington, DC), Tuesday, September 15, p. 3.

Gunderson, C. (2004). *The Dred Scott Decision*. Edina, MN: Abdo Publishing.

"Had a Sunday See-Saw" (1887). *St. Paul Daily Globe*, Monday, June 20, p. 5.

Haenke, H. (1976). "Thorn, George (1806–1876)." Australian Dictionary of Biography [cited July 6, 2013]. Available from: http://adb.anu.edu.au/biography/thorn-george-4719.

"Hall of Fame: Edwin Flack—Athletics" (2012). Sport Australia Hall of Fame [cited December 2, 2012]. Available from: http://www.sahof.org.au/hall-of-fame/member-profile/?memberID=380&memberType=legends.

"Hall of Famers: Welch, Mickey" (2012). National Baseball Hall of Fame and Museum, Cooperstown, NY [cited June 16, 2013]. Available from: http://baseballhall.org/hof/welch-mickey.

"Hall of Famers: Wright, George" (2012). National Baseball Hall of Fame and Museum, Cooperstown, NY [cited June 18, 2013]. Available from: http://baseballhall.org/hof/wright-george.

"Hall of Famers: Youngs, Ross" (2012). National Baseball Hall of Fame and Museum, Cooperstown, NY [cited August 7, 2013]. Available from: http://baseballhall.org/hof/youngs-ross.

Hallam, G. (1994). "*Life and Death on the Ipswich-Toowoomba Railway: Gibbons and Fountains Camps 1865–67*." In *Brisbane: Cemeteries as Sources* (History Group Papers, No. 13). Ed. by R. Fisher and B. Shaw. Brisbane, QLD. pp. 22–34.

Hamilton, J. "Quinn Was First Australian Player in Major Leagues" (1997). *Oneonta Star* (New York), Friday, October 10, p. 6.

"Hanlon on His New Men—Thinks De Montreville Is the Superior of Reitz" (1898). *Washington Times*, Wednesday, January 12, p. 6.

"Hardy Richardson (Player Page)" (2013). Baseball-Reference.com [cited June 1, 2013]. Available from: http://www.baseball-reference.com/players/r/richaha01.shtml.

Harris, W.I. "An Equal Fight: W I. Harris Writes of the Coming Baseball Battle" (1890). *Wichita Daily Eagle*, Tuesday, February 25, p. 2.

Haupert, M. (2011). "Baseball's Major Salary Milestones." Society for American Baseball Research [cited March 5, 2013]. Available from: http://sabr.org/research/baseballs-major-salary-milestones.

Hawking, J. (2012). *Strikeout: Baseball, Broadway and the Brotherhood in the 19th Century*. Santa Fe, NM: Sunstone Press.

"He Was Wild" (1887). *St. Paul Daily Globe*, Saturday, September 17, p. 5.

Heldt, D. (2011). "U.I. Archaeologists Find 7,000-Year-Old Site in Des Moines." *The Gazette* (online): Cedar Rapids, IA [cited August 22, 2013]. Available from: http://thegazette.com/2011/08/18/ui-archaeologists-find-7000-year-old-site-in-des-moines/.

"Here and There" (1895). *The Sporting Life*, Saturday, June 8, p. 9.

Hetrick, J.T. (1999). *Chris Von Der Ahe and the St. Louis Browns*. Lanham, MD: Scarecrow.

_____. (1991). *Misfits!: The Cleveland Spiders in 1899: A Day-by-Day Narrative of Baseball Futility*. Jefferson, NC.: McFarland.

Higginbotham, P. (2011). "Enniskillen, Co. Fermanagh." The Workhouse: the story of an institution [cited December 10, 2012]. Available from: http://www.workhouses.org.uk/Enniskillen/.

_____. (2011). "The New Poor Law." The Workhouse: the story of an institution [cited December 10, 2012]. Available from: www.workhouses.org.uk/poorlaws/newpoorlaw.shtml.

Hill, B. (2000). *Crack of the Bat: The Louisville Slugger Story*. Champaign, IL: Sports Pub.

"Historical Events for Year 1884" (2013). HistoryOrb.com [cited March 3, 2013]. Available from: http://www.historyorb.com/events/date/1884.

"Historical Events for Year 1903" (2013). HistoryOrb.com [cited March 5, 2013]. Available from: http://www.historyorb.com/events/date/1903.

"History of the 7th Infantry Division" (2003). Fort Carson United States Military [cited August 28, 2013]. Available from: http://www.carson.army.mil/UNITS/F7ID/F7ID_Historylong.htm.

"History of the Kidney Punch" (1951). *Montreal Gazette*, Friday, June 29, p. 20.

"History of Zinc" (2013). International Zinc Association [cited March 30, 2013]. Available from: http://www.zinc.org/basics/history_of_zinc.

Holden, R. (2001). *Bunyips: Australia's Folklore of Fear*. Canberra: National Library of Australia.

"Home-Run Jennings" (1894). *Baltimore Sun*, Friday, June 15, p. 6.

Household Income Survey Shows Effect of Life Cycle. From: Income Distribution, Australia, 1996–97 (Cat. No. 6523.0) (1998). Australian Bureau of Statistics, Canberra, ACT [cited 2013, May 30]. Available from: http://www.abs.gov.au/ausstats/abs@.nsf/mediareleasesbytitle/C68FDE8DCA48ABCECA2568A9001362A0?OpenDocument.

"How a Georgia Pig Won the Pennant for Chicago in 1886" (1911). *El Paso Herald*, Saturday, February 4, p. 22.

"How Fred Ely Queered His Own Game" (1895). *The Sporting Life*, Saturday, December 28, p. 7.

"How the Struggle Goes On" (1889). *Pittsburg Dispatch*, Sunday, June 16, p. 15.

"Hub Pick-Ups" (1889). *The Sporting Life*, Wednesday, July 17, p. 5.

Hubbard, D., and R.A. Johnson (2008). *The Heavenly Twins of Boston Baseball: A Dual Biography of Hugh Duffy and Tommy McCarthy*. Jefferson, NC: McFarland.

Hudson, D., M. Bergman, and L. Horton (2009). *The Biographical Dictionary of Iowa*. Iowa City: University of Iowa Press.

"Hunting for Talent" (1888). *St. Paul Daily Globe*, Sunday, August 12, p. 6.

"Imports" (1855). *Sydney Morning Herald*, Friday, May 18, p. 4.

"In New Uniforms" (1892). *Boston Globe*, Tuesday, July 12, p. 5.

"In the Baseball World" (1901). *Evening Times* (Washington, DC), Thursday, June 20, p. 6.

"In the Baseball World" (1901). *Washington Times*, Monday, June 17, p. 3.

"In the Baseball World: Lee's Masterful Pitching Too Much for Chicago" (1901). *Washington Times*, Sunday, June 9, p. 8.

"In the Baseball World: Manning's Players Rapidly Rounding into Shape" (1901). *Washington Times*, Monday, April 15, p. 3.

"In the Baseball World: Senators Redeem Themselves by Shutting out Milwaukee" (1901). *Washington Times*, Sunday, June 2, p. 8.

"In the Baseball World: The Orioles Defeat the Senators by Heavy Batting" (1901). *Washington Times*, Friday, May 3, p. 5.

"In the Baseball World: The Orioles Win Their First Game from Washington" (1901). *Washington Times*, Thursday, May 2, p. 5.

"In the Baseball World: Washington Makes a Wonderful Rally in the Eighth" (1901). *Washington Times*, Tuesday, June 11, p. 3.

"In the Baseball World: Washington Wins from Boston in First Inning" (1901). *Washington Times*, Sunday, May 12, p. 9.

"Indianapolis: The Causes of Ill Success on the Recent Trip—Comment on the Team Collectively and Individually" (1887). *The Sporting Life*, Wednesday, September 14, p. 1.

Ingleton, G.C. (1952). *True Patriots All: Or, News from Early Australia, as Told in a Collection of Broadsides*. Sydney: Angus & Robertson.

"Injured Ball Players. Fifty-Nine Men of the 214 Listed Players Have Been Disabled Thus Far This Season" (1897). *Evening Times* (Washington, DC), Monday, July 19, p. 6.

"Injury to Stock" (1887). *St. Paul Daily Globe*, Friday, February 4, p. 4.

"Inks in the Box" (1896). *St. Paul Globe*, Sunday, July 12, p. 10.

"Inquest on Riot Victims Today" (1900). *St. Louis Republic*, Tuesday, June 12, pp.1, 2.

"International Baseball—Australian in America" (1897). *The Chronicle* (Adelaide, SA.). Saturday, July 31, p. 33.

"Iowa Census Record Information Online" (2013). The Records Project [cited July 25, 2013]. Available from: http://recordsproject.com/census/iowa.asp.

"Iowa Items" (1884). *Omaha Daily Bee*, Tuesday April 15, p. 7.

"Iowa State Census" (1885). FamilySearch.org: The Church of Jesus Christ of Latter-day Saints [cited November 11, 2012]. Available from: http://familysearch.org.

"Ipswich" (1864). *Brisbane Courier* (Brisbane, QLD), Wednesday, August 24, p. 1.

"Ipswich" (1864). *Darling Downs Gazette and General Advertiser* (Toowoomba, QLD), Thursday, November 24, p. 4.

"Ipswich" (1865). *Queensland Times, Ipswich Herald & General Advertiser* (Brisbane, QLD), Thursday, January 12, p. 3.

"Ipswich Heritage Trails—Rivers of Ipswich Then & Now (Ipswich City Council)" (2011). Ipswich, QLD.

"Ireland (Saturday, April 14, 1855)" (1855). London: *The Spectator* [cited July 6, 2013]. Available from: http://archive.spectator.co.uk/article/14th-april-1855/4/ireland.

"It Smacks of a Combination" (1891). *Chicago Tribune*, Thursday, October 1, p. 1.

"J. Quinn" (1893). *The Sporting News*, Monday, February 11, p. 1.

"Jack Glasscock (Player Page)" (2013). Baseball-Reference.com [cited August 15, 2013]. Available from: http://www.baseball-reference.com/players/g/glassja01.shtml.

"Jack Stivetts (Player Page)" (2013). Baseball-Reference.com [cited August 24, 2013]. Available from: http://www.baseball-reference.com/players/s/stiveja01.shtml.

James, B. (2010). *The New Bill James Historical Baseball Abstract*. New York: Simon & Schuster.

James, B., and R. Neyer (2004). *The Neyer/James Guide to Pitchers: An Historical Compendium of Pitching, Pitchers, and Pitches*. New York: Simon & Schuster.

"Jerry Denny (Player Page)" (2013). Baseball-Reference.com [cited August 15, 2013]. Available from: http://www.baseball-reference.com/players/d/dennyje01.shtml.

"Joe Hornung (B.R. Bullpen)" (2013). Baseball-Reference.com [cited April 4, 2013]. Available from: http://www.baseball-reference.com/bullpen/Joe_Hornung.

"Joe Otten (Player Page)" (2013). Baseball-Reference.com [cited August 20, 2013]. Available from: http://www.baseball-reference.com/players/o/ottenjo01.shtml.

"Joe Quinn" (1887). *Indianapolis Herald*, Wednesday, June 15, p. 3.

"Joe Quinn" (1888). *The Sporting Life*, Wednesday, December 5, p. 5.

"Joe Quinn" (1889). *The Sporting News*, Saturday, June 22, p. 5.

"Joe Quinn Chats" (1888). *St. Paul Daily Globe*, Saturday, January 28, p. 4.

"Joe Quinn Exalted" (1895). *The Sporting News*, Saturday, July 27, p. 4.

"Joe Quinn Gets a Bat" (1889). *Boston Daily Glove*, Friday, September 13, p. 8.

"Joe Quinn in the Outfield" (1888). *The Sporting News*, Thursday, April 12, p. 5.

"Joe Quinn May Join the Bostons as Utility Infielder" (1900). *St. Louis Republic*, Friday, June 15, p. 6.

"Joe Quinn (Minor League Player Page)" (2013). Baseball-Reference.com [cited April 2, 2013]. Available from: http://www.baseball-reference.com/minors/player.cgi?id=quinn-003jos.

"Joe Quinn, of the Bostons" (1889). *The Sporting Life*, Wednesday, August 14, p. 5.

"Joe Quinn (Player Page)" (2013). Baseball-Reference.com [cited January 9, 2013]. Available from: http://www.baseball-reference.com/players/q/quinnjo02.shtml.

"Joe Quinn (Player Page): Minor League Statistics" (2013). Baseball-Reference.com [cited April 2, 2013]. Available from: http://www.baseball-/reference.com/minors/player.cgi?id=quinn-003jos.

"Joe Quinn Released: Der Cherman Pand Must Be Playing Madhouse Airs!" (1896). *New York World*, Wednesday, July 1, p. 3.

"Joe Quinn Signs" (1888). *Boston Globe*, Tuesday, August 26, p. 4.

"Joe Quinn, the Champion Second Baseman" (1890). Boston *Globe*, Saturday, October 11, p. 7.

"Joe Quinn (Transactions)" (2013). Baseball-Reference.com [cited January 9, 2013]. Available from: http://www.baseball-reference.com/players/q/quinnjo02.shtml.

"Joe Quinn's Blood Poisoned" (1897). *Morning Times* (Washington, DC), Saturday, July 17, p. 6.

John, A.S. (2006). *Made to Be Broken: The 50 Greatest Records and Streaks in Sports*. Chicago: Triumph Books.

"John Clarkson (Player Page): Transactions" (2013). Baseball-Reference.com [cited June 1, 2013]. Available from: http://www.baseball-reference.com/players/c/clarkjo01.shtml#trans.

"John Morrill (Player Page)" (2013). Baseball-Reference.com [cited June 2, 2013]. Available from: http://www.baseball-reference.com/players/m/morrijo01.shtml.

"Johnson Defies Big League" (1900). *St. Louis Republic*, Tuesday, November 20, p. 7.

Jones, D. (2012). "Jesse Burkett." SABR Baseball Biography Project. Society for American Baseball Research [cited August 24, 2013]. Available from: http://sabr.org/bioproj/person/53d6808e.

Judge, J. (1981). "The Travail of Ireland." *National Geographic* 159 (4): pp. 432–441.

"Just Think of It!" (1884). *St. Louis Republic*, Monday, April 21, p. 3.

Kavanagh, J., and N.L. Macht (1999). *Uncle Robbie*. Cleveland, OH: Society for American Baseball Research.

Keenan, J. (2012). "Cupid Childs." Society for American Baseball Research (SABR) BioProject [cited August 3, 2013]. Available from: http://sabr.org/bioproj/person/d373e248.

"Kelly on His Travels" (1891). *St. Paul Daily Globe*, Thursday, February 19, p. 6.

Kent, J. (2002). *America in 1900*. Armonk, NY: M.E. Sharpe.

Kerr, R. (2011). *Roger Connor: Home Run King of 19th Century Baseball*. Jefferson, NC: McFarland.

"Kid Carsey (Player Page)" (2013). Baseball-Reference.com [cited August 2, 2013]. Available from: http://www.baseball-reference.com/players/c/carseki01.shtml.

"Kid Nichols (Player Page)" (2013). Baseball-Reference.com [cited June 1, 2013]. Available from: http://www.baseball-reference.com/players/n/nichoki01.shtml.

Killingray, D., and H. Phillips (2003). *The Spanish Influenza Pandemic of 1918-1919: New Perspectives*. Oxford, UK: Routledge.

"The King Batters" (1884). *St. Louis Republican*, Monday, May 5, p. 6.

"King Kelly (Player Page): Transactions" (2013). Baseball-Reference.com [cited June 1, 2013]. Available from: http://www.baseball-reference.com/players/k/kellyki01.shtml#trans.

"Kings of Fielders" (1897). *St. Paul Globe*, Monday, October 25, p. 5.

Kistemaker, D.A., H. Faber, and P.J. Beek (2009). "Catching Fly Balls: A Simulation Study of the Chapman Strategy." *Human Movement Science* 28 (2): pp. 236–249.

Konefes, J.L., and M.K. McGee. "Old Cemeteries, Arsenic, and Health Safety." Embalming [cited December 1, 1999]. Available from: http://waterindustry.org/arsenic-3.htm.

"Labour Markets" (1855). *Sydney Morning Herald*, Saturday, May 19, p. 5.

Lamb, B. (2012). "Joe Corbett." SABR Baseball Biography Project. Society for American Baseball Research [cited August 10, 2013]. Available from: http://sabr.org/bioproj/person/bcebe2e6.

Lamster, M. (2006). *Spalding's World Tour: The Epic Adventure That Took Baseball around the Globe—and Made It America's Game*. New York: Public Affairs.

"The Late Floods" (1860). *Empire* (Sydney), Friday, February 17, p. 2.

"Late News by Wire: Von Der Ahe and Day" (1895). *The Sporting Life*, Saturday, June 29, p. 2.

"Late News: Wholesale Engagement of Players" (1886). *The Sporting Life*, Wednesday, November 3, p. 1.

"Latest News and Gossip of the Sporting World" (1909). *Fort Wayne Sentinel*, Thursday, November 4, p. 8.

"The Latest Scheme: A New Organization to Sign All the National League Players" (1889). *Pittsburg Dispatch*, Monday, September 9, p. 6.

Laver, F. "America's National Game—High Prices for Players" (1908). *The Argus* (Melbourne), Saturday, August 22, p. 9.

Lawson, H. (2004). *In the Days When the World Was Wide*. Whitefish, MT: Kessinger.

"League-Association." (1895). *The Sporting Life*, Saturday, July 6, p. 3.

"League-Association" (1894). *The Sporting News*, Saturday, April 28, p. 4; Saturday, May 5, p. 6; Saturday, May 19, p. 6; Saturday, August 4, p. 5.

"League-Association" (1895). *The Sporting News*, Saturday, May 18, p. 6; Saturday, July 6, p. 3.

"League Changes" (1898). *The Sporting Life*, Saturday, June 11, p. 4.

"The League Race" (1898). *The Sporting Life*, Saturday, September 3, p. 3.

"The League Race: The Contest Becoming Close and Exciting" (1897). *The Sporting Life*, Saturday, May 29, p. 2.

"The League Race: The Contestants Gradually Becoming Bunched" (1900). *The Sporting Life*, Saturday, June 16, pp. 2, 3.

"The League Race: The Eastern Teams Badly Mauled in the West" (1900). *The Sporting Life*, Saturday, July 14, p. 2.

"The League Race: The Eight Teams Now in the Fight for Honors" (1900). *The Sporting Life*, Saturday, April 28, p. 2.

"The League Race: The First Trip Favorable to the Eastern Teams" (1897). *The Sporting Life*, Saturday, June 5, p. 2.

"The League Race: The Inter-Sectional Battle Is Now On" (1900). *The Sporting Life*, Saturday, May 19, p. 2.

"The League Race: The Two Big B's Still at the Top Rung" (1899). *The Sporting Life*, Saturday, June 10, pp. 2, 3.

"The League Race: The West Fairly Tramples on the East for Once" (1900). *The Sporting Life*, Saturday July 21, p. 2.

Legarde, L.M., and D. Northrup (1995). *Frommer's 96 New England*. New York: Macmillan.

"Lewis Expelled by Lucas" (1885). *Boston Globe*, Saturday, June 20, p. 8.

Lewis, S. (1837). *A Topographical Dictionary of Ireland*. London: S. Lewis & Co.

Lieb, F. (1955). *The Baltimore Orioles: The History of a Colorful Team in Baltimore and St. Louis*. New York: Putnam.

Lindner, D. (2012). "Kid Gleason." SABR Baseball Biography Project. Society for American Baseball Research [cited August 15, 2013]. Available from: http://sabr.org/bioproj/person/632ed912.

Lipsitz, G. (1991). *The Sidewalks of St. Louis: Places, People, and Politics in an American City*. St. Louis: University of Missouri Press.

Liston, C. (1988). *Campbelltown: The Bicentennial History*. Sydney: Allen & Unwin.

"Little Lord Fauntleroy" (2012). Internet Broadway Database [cited June 11, 2013]. Available from: http://ibdb.com/production.php?id=5718.

Littleton, C.S. (2005). *Gods, Goddesses, and Mythology*. Vol. 10. New York: Marshall Cavendish.

"Local and General News" (1864). *Brisbane Courier*, Friday, August 19, p. 3.

"Local Lines" (1885). *Boston Daily Globe*, November, 12, p. 1.

"Long's Tumble" (1892). *Boston Globe*, Thursday, April 14, p. 5.

Longmate, N. (2003). *The Workhouse: A Social History*. London: Random House UK.

"Looking out for '93" (1892). *The Sporting News*, Saturday, October 15, p. 3.

"Lose with Phyle Pitching" (1899). *Chicago Tribune*, Monday, August 7, p. 4.

Lossos, D.A. (2004). *Irish St. Louis*. Chicago: Arcadia Publishing.

"Lost or Stolen!" (1889). *Boston Globe*, August 30, p. 5.
"Louisville 8, St. Louis 4" (1894). *Boston Daily Globe*, Sunday, July 29, p. 7.
Lowenfish, L., and R.W. Creamer (2010). *The Imperfect Diamond: A History of Baseball's Labor Wars*. Lincoln: University of Nebraska Press.
"Lucas Triumphant—The League Surrenders to the Millionaire" (1885). *The Sporting Life*, Wednesday, April 22, p. 3.
"Luck with the Champions" (1900). *The Sun* (New York), Sunday, July 22, p. 8.
Ludvigson, G.A., and J.A. Dockal (2011). "Lead and Zinc Mining in the Dubuque Area." Iowa Geological & Water Survey. Iowa Department of Natural Resources [cited March 8, 2013]. Available from: http://www.igsb.uiowa.edu/browse/leadzinc/leadzinc.htm.
McCue, C.S., and R. Playle. (2007). *Des Moines*. Chicago: Arcadia Publishing.
MacDonagh, O., and W.F. Mandle (1986). *Ireland and Irish-Australia: Studies in Cultural and Political History*. Dublin: Routledge, Kegan & Paul.
McGill, J., K. Richardson, and V. Fowler (1995). *Campbelltown's Streets and Suburbs: How and Why They Got Their Names*. Campbelltown, NSW: Campbelltown & Airds Historical Society.
McGowan, B. (2000). *The Golden South: A History of the Araluen, Bell's Creek and Major's Creek Gold Fields*. Canberra: Barry McGowan.
"McGraw and Robinson Arrive" (1900). *St. Louis Republic*, Wednesday, May 9, p. 6.
"McGraw Erred, Young Weakened" (1900). *St. Louis Republic*, Sunday, May 13, p. 9.
McGuire, J.M. "Tales of the Kerry Patch" (1986). *St. Louis Post-Dispatch*, Monday, March 17, p. 6D.
Macht, N.L. (2007). *Connie Mack and the Early Years of Baseball*. Lincoln: University of Nebraska Press.
McKenna, B. (2012). "Dickey Pearce." SABR Baseball Biography Project. Society for American Baseball Research [cited June 5, 2013]. Available from: http://sabr.org/bioproj/person/db8ea477.
McKenna, B. (2007). *Early Exits: The Premature Endings of Baseball Careers*. Lanham, MD: Scarecrow Press.
_____. (2012). "John Clarkson." Society for American Baseball Research (SABR) BioProject [cited December 10, 2012]. Available from: http://sabr.org/bioproj/person/47feb015.
_____. "Mark Baldwin." SABR Baseball Biography Project [cited April 4, 2013]. Available from: http://sabr.org/bioproj/person/41f65388.
_____. (2012). "Old Hoss Radbourn." Society for American Baseball Research (SABR) BioProject [cited December 1, 2012]. Available from: http://sabr.org/bioproj/person/83bf739e.
MacLysaght, E. (1991). *Irish Families: Their Names, Arms and Origins*. Dublin: Irish Academic Press.
"Major League Baseball Players Born in Australia" (2013). Baseball Almanac [cited August 30, 2013]. Available from: http://www.baseball-almanac.com/players/birthplace.php?loc=Australia.
"Many Games of Ball" (1884). *Baltimore American*, Saturday, July 5, p. 4.
Marble, C.E. (1881). *Marble's Dubuque City Directory*. Dubuque, IA: Chas. A. Marble.
"The Maroons Downed" (1884). *St. Louis Republican*, Saturday, October 25, p. 4.
Martelle, S. (2007). *Blood Passion: The Ludlow Massacre and Class War in the American West*. New Brunswick, NJ: Rutgers University Press.
"Matoaka [Passenger List]: Online Microfilm of Shipping Lists" (2012). New South Wales Government State Records [cited July 7, 2012]. Available from: http://www.records.nsw.gov.au.
"Maul Will Be an Oriole" (1897). *Evening Times* (Washington, DC), Saturday, May 29, p. 3.
"May Do a Double-Header Today" (1901). *St. Louis Republic*, Thursday, September 12, p. 7.
Mayer, R. (2011). *Embalming: History, Theory, and Practice*. 5th ed. New York: McGraw-Hill Professional.
Mayer, R.A. (2008). *Christy Mathewson: A Game-by-Game Profile of a Legendary Pitcher*. Jefferson, NC: McFarland.
MedlinePlus (2013). "Myocarditis." U.S. National Library of Medicine/National Institutes of Health [cited April 29, 2013]. Available from: http://www.nlm.nih.gov/medlineplus/ency/article/000149.htm.
"Mercer Knocked Out" (1895). *Washington Post*, Saturday, May 4, p. 4.
"Mike Kelly Disgraced: He Assaults Umpire Mcquaid and Is Dragged Away by Policemen" (1889). *Pittsburg Dispatch*, Thursday, October 3, p. 6.
MILB.com (2013). "Iowa Cubs History (Iowacubs.Com)." Minor League Baseball [cited June 10, 2013]. Available from: http://www.milb.com/content/page.jsp?sid=t451&ymd=20100319&content_id=8838460&vkey=team4.
"Minneapolis Drops on the Duluth Twirlers with Great Emphasis" (1887). *St. Paul Daily Globe*, Wednesday, August 24, p. 5.
"Minneapolis Hammers the Ball in a Most Heartless Manner" (1887). *St. Paul Daily Globe*, Sunday, August 28.
"Missouri Death Certificates, 1910–1962" (2013). Missouri Digital Heritage [cited April 28, 2013]. Available from: http://www.sos.mo.gov/archives/resources/death certificates/advanced.asp.
Mitchell, B. (1997). "Baseball in Australia. Two Tours and the Beginnings of Baseball in Australia." *Sporting Traditions* 13 (1): pp. 2–24.
Monaghan, W.J. "One of Baseball's Great" (1933). *St. Louis Globe-Democrat*, Sunday, November 26, pp. 6, 14.
"Money Well Spent: How the Boston Management Is Increasing Its Funds" (1887). *St. Paul Daily Globe*, Saturday, June 25, p. 4.
Morris, P. (2012). "Billy Kinloch." Society for American Baseball Research (SABR) BioProject [cited August 20, 2013]. Available from: http://sabr.org/bioproj/person/e961c4c9.
Morris, P. (2013). *Cracking Baseball's Cold Cases: Filling in the Facts About 17 Mystery Major Leaguers*. Jefferson, NC: McFarland.
_____. (2006). *A Game of Inches: The Stories Behind the Innovations That Shaped Baseball: The Game on the Field*. Chicago: Ivan R. Dee.
_____. (2007). *Level Playing Fields: How the Groundskeeping Murphy Brothers Shaped Baseball*. Lincoln: University of Nebraska Press.
Mott, A. "Baltimore Bulletin" (1897). *The Sporting Life*, April 24.
"The Mound City Mad" (1893). *The Sporting Life*, Saturday, September 9, p. 1.
"Mr. Von Der Ahe in a Very Hopeful Mood" (1896). *The Sporting Life*, Saturday, April 6, p. 7.
"Mr. Von Der Ahe Shakes Things up Lively" (1896). *The Sporting Life*, Saturday, May 16, p. 8.
"Mt. Sterling Club Disbands" (1894). *Sterling Advocate* (Mount Sterling, KY), Tuesday, September 4, p. 1.
"Mulford's Musings" (1900). *The Sporting Life*, Saturday, August 11, p. 5.
Mulrooney, M. (2003). *Fleeing the Famine: North America and Irish Refugees, 1845–1851*. Santa Barbara, CA: Praeger.

"Municipal Council" (1864). *Queensland Times, Ipswich Herald & General Advertiser* (Brisbane, QLD), Tuesday, July 12, p. 3.

Murray, M. (1993). "Children's Work in Rural New South Wales in the 1870s." *Journal of the Royal Australian Historical Society* 79 (3–4): pp. 226–244.

"Must Have First Place" (1887). *St. Paul Daily Globe*, Wednesday, July 13, p. 4.

Nash, B.M., and A. Zullo (1985). *Baseball Hall of Shame*. New York: Pocket Books.

Nathan, D.A. (2005). *Saying It's So: A Cultural History of the Black Sox Scandal*. Urbana: University of Illinois Press.

"The National Game" (1895). *Lincoln Courier*, Saturday, June 29, p. 9.

"The National League" (1899). *The Sporting News*, Saturday June 17, p. 3.

"The National League—The Record" (1885). *The Sporting Life*, Wednesday, June 10, p. 3.

"National League" (1899). *The Sporting News*, Saturday, May 6, p. 3.

"National League Meeting" (1892). *Chicago Tribune*, Wednesday, March 2, p. 7.

"National League: No Striking Changes in the Championship Race: Games Played May 10" (1894). *The Sporting Life*, Saturday, May 19, p. 4.

"Nearer the Top" (1899). *Boston Globe*, Thursday, August 31, p. 4.

Nemec, D. (1994). *The Beer and Whiskey League: The Illustrated History of the American Association—Baseball's Renegade Major League*. New York: Lyons and Burford, p. 85.

_____. (2006). *The Great Encyclopedia of Nineteenth-Century Major League Baseball*. Tuscaloosa: University of Alabama Press.

Nemec, D., and S. Flatow (2008). *This Day in Baseball: A Day-by-Day Record of the Events That Shaped the Game*. Lanham, MD: Taylor Trade.

"Never Broke" (1895). *The Sporting Life*, Wednesday, August 3, p. 6.

"A New King Lear" (1894). *The Sporting Life*, Saturday, August 18, p. 2.

New National Australian Encyclopaedia (1974). Sydney: National Literary Association.

New Sportsman's Park Official Score Book (1893). St. Louis, MO: Great West.

"New-York Did Not Score: But the Bostons Made Two Runs and Won" (1888). *New York Times*, Friday, August 29, p. 8.

"New-York Holds the Lead: Today's Games Will Decide the Championship" (1889). *New York Times*, October 5, p. 6.

"The New Yorks Win Again: They Defeat the Bostons Nine to Six" (1888). *New York Times*, Monday, August 4, p. 5.

"News and Comment" (1896). *The Sporting Life*, Saturday, October 5, p. 5.

"News and Comments" (1899). *The Sporting Life*, Saturday, May 27, p. 5; Saturday, June 17, p. 5.

"News Briefly Reported" (1895). *New Ulm Review* (New Ulm, MN), Wednesday, June 26.

"News by Wire: The League Accused of Tampering with Players" (1890). *The Sporting Life*, Wednesday, August 2, p. 1.

"News from the Interior [from Our Correspondent]: Gold at the Moruya" (1851). *Sydney Morning Herald*, Tuesday, October 14, p. 3.

"News, Gossip and Comment" (1891). *The Sporting Life*, Saturday, August 15, p. 2.

"News, Gossip, Editorial Comment" (1884). *The Sporting Life*, Wednesday, December 12, p. 2.

"News, Gossip, Editorial Comment" (1891). *The Sporting Life*, Saturday, November 7, p. 2.

"News, Notes and Comment" (1890). *The Sporting Life*, Wednesday, July 5; Wednesday, December 13.

"News of the Baseball Field" (1901). *St Louis Republic*, Thursday, April 11, p. 6.

"News of the Players" (1884). *The Sporting Life*, Wednesday, November 19, p. 3.

"(No title)" (1901). *St. Paul Globe*, Friday, April 12, p. 3.

"Northwestern League: The Record" (1887). *The Sporting Life*, Wednesday, October 12, p. 5.

"Not Illiberal" (1896). *The Sporting Life*, Saturday, March 7, p. 2.

"Notes About the Big and Little Ball Tossers" (1902). *St. Paul Globe*, Monday, April 7, p. 5.

"Notes and Comments" (1885). *The Sporting Life*, Wednesday, April 22, p. 7.

"Notes of the Game" (1897). *Chicago Tribune*, Saturday, July 17, p. 6.

"Notes of the National Game" (1899). *Evening Times* (Washington, DC), Thursday, August 3, p. 6.

"Nothing but Praise for the Globe" (1889). *Boston Globe*, Monday, October 7, p. 5.

"Obituary: Joe Quinn" (1940). *The Sporting News*, Thursday, November 21, p. 8.

"Obituary: The Rev. Father J.P. Roche" (1880). *Australian Town and Country Journal* (Sydney), Saturday, November 20, p. 13.

O'Brien, D. (2012). "Rube Waddell." SABR Baseball Biography Project. Society for American Baseball Research [cited August 10, 2013]. Available from: http://sabr.org/bioproj/person/a5b2c2b4.

"O'Connell and Biddy Moriarty" (1857). *The Argus* (Melbourne), Tuesday, October 13, p. 7.

O'Connor, J. (1995). *The Workhouses of Ireland: The Fate of Ireland's Poor*. Dublin: Anvil Books.

O'Toole, J.M. (1981). *"My God, What a Life!"* St. Louis: O'Toole.

"Occupational Safety and Health Guidelines for Zinc Oxide" (2012). United States Department of Labor—Occupational Safety & Health Administration (OSHA) [cited March 11, 2013]. Available from: http://www.osha.gov/SLTC/healthguidelines/zincoxide/recognition.html.

Okrent, D., and S. Wulf (1989). *Baseball Anecdotes*. New York: Oxford University Press.

"Old Hoss Radbourn (Player Page)" (2013). Baseball-Reference.com [cited December 2, 2012]. Available from: http://www.baseball-reference.com/players/r/radboch01.shtml.

Oldt, F.T., and P.J. Quigley (1911). *History of Dubuque County, Iowa; Being a General Survey of Dubuque County History, Including a History of the City of Dubuque and Special Account of Districts Throughout the County, from the Earliest Settlement to the Present Time*. Chicago: Goodspeed Historical Association.

"On the Fly" (1883). *The Sporting Life*, Monday, July 30, p. 7.

"On the Fly" (1899). *The Sporting News*, Saturday, October 14, p. 4.

"On Top of the Heap" (1894). *Baltimore Sun*, Monday, July 16, p. 6.

"Once More Exciting: The Teams in the League Race Making a Lively Wind-Up" (1891). *Pittsburg Dispatch*, Sunday, September 20, p. 6.

"One for the Temple Cup" (1896). *The Sun* (Baltimore), Saturday, October 3, p. 6.

"One More St. Louis Brown Joins the Pirates" (1896). *The Sporting Life*, Saturday, January 11, p. 8.
"One Victory for Boston" (1889). *New York Times*, August 30, p. 5.
"The Opening Championship Games, April 29" (1886). *The Sporting Life*, Wednesday, May 5, p. 4.
"Opening of the First Railway in Queensland (from Our Special Reporter)" (1865). *Brisbane Courier* (Brisbane, QLD), Tuesday, August 1, pp. 2, 3.
"Opening of the Great Southern Railway Extension" (1869). *Empire* (Sydney), Saturday, May 29, p. 3.
"Orioles Narrow Escape: The Colonels Give Them a Hard Fight to the Finish" (1897). *Morning Times* (Washington, DC), Friday, September 10, p. 6.
"Orioles on Top Again" (1897). *The Sun* (Baltimore), Wednesday, June 23, p. 6.
Ørsted-Jensen, R. (2011). *Frontier History Revisited—Colonial Queensland and the "History War."* Brisbane, QLD: Lux Mundi Publishing.
"Oshkosh Leads by Defeating Duluth Twice" (1887). *St. Paul Daily Globe*, Wednesday, September 14, p. 5.
"Other Games" (1889). *Evening Star* (Washington, DC), Friday, August 16, p. 8.
"Our Strange Past: Few Tears for Captain Logan" (1951). *The Mail* (Adelaide, SA), Saturday, December 15, p. 6S.
"The Outlook for the Indianapolis Club" (1887). *The Sun* (New York), Sunday, June 12, p. 10.
"Out of Sight" (1894). *Boston Globe*, Tuesday, July 31, p. 5.
"Outplayed by Boston" (1897). *The Sun* (Baltimore), Saturday, September 25, p. 6.
"Overflow Crowds" (1899). *The Sporting News*, Saturday, April 22, p. 4.
"P.F. Quinn's Social Quadrille Band" *Encyclopedia Dubuque*. Carnegie-Stout Public Library [cited March 9, 2013]. Available from: http://www.encyclopediadubuque.org/index.php?title=P._F._QUINN%27S_SOCIAL_QUADRILLE_BAND.
"A Pair of Wreckers: Kelly and Irwin Get on the Road with a Deal of Bluff" (1891). *Pittsburg Dispatch*, Thursday, February 19, p. 1.
Pajot, D. (2011). *Baseball's Heartland War, 1902–1903: The Western League and American Association Vie for Turf, Players and Profits*. Jefferson, NC: McFarland.
_____. (2009). *The Rise of Milwaukee Baseball: The Cream City from Midwestern Outpost to the Major Leagues, 1859–1901*. Jefferson, NC: McFarland.
"Palaver of the Ball Players" (1895). *Omaha Daily Bee*, Sunday, November 17, p. 23.
Pardon, C.F. (1984). *The Australians in England: A Complete Record of the Cricket Tour of 1884*. London: J.W. McKenzie.
"The Passing of Quinn" (1900). *The Sporting Life*, Wednesday, September 29, p. 7.
"Patrick Quinn Is Dead" (1902). *Dubuque Telegraph-Herald*, Saturday, April 12, p. 3.
Patrick, R., and H. Patrick (1989). *Exiles Undaunted: The Irish Rebels Kevin and Eva O'Doherty*. St. Lucia: University of Queensland Press.
"Patsy Tebeau (Player Page)" (2013). Baseball-Reference.com [cited August 20, 2013]. Available from: http://www.baseball-reference.com/players/t/tebeapa01.shtml.
Pearce, H.H. (1971). *On the Origins of Waltzing Matilda (Expression, Lyric, Melody)*. Melbourne: Hawthorn Press.
Pearson, D.M. (1993). *Baseball in 1889: Players Vs. Owners*. Bowling Green, OH: Bowling Green State University Popular Press.
"Peculiar Status of John McGraw: Insists He Is Not Manager of the St. Louis Club, yet Admits He Will Fulfill Manager's Duties" (1900). *St. Louis Republic*, Tuesday, August 21, p. 5.
"Peppermint Drops" (1889). *Omaha Daily Bee*, Sunday, July 28, p. 9.
Perrotta, L.B. (2000). *Saint Joseph: His Life and His Role in the Church Today*. Huntingdon: Our Sunday Visitor.
"Personal Comment on Men and Things in the Field of Sports" (1904). *Washington Times*, Saturday, October 15, p. 8.
"Personal Comment on Men and Things in the Field of Sports" (1905). *Washington Times*, Monday, December 25, p. 8.
"Pete Loos (Player Page)" (2013). Baseball-Reference.com [cited August 2, 2013]. Available from: http://www.baseball-reference.com/players/l/loospe01.shtml.
Peterson, M.D. (1960). *The Jefferson Image in the American Mind*. New York: Oxford University Press.
Pfeifer, M.J. (2006). *Rough Justice: Lynchings and American Society 1874–1947*. Champaign: University of Illinois Press.
Piott, S.L. (2011). *Daily Life in the Progressive Era*. Santa Barbara, CA: ABC-CLIO.
"Place Names Origins" (2011). City of Ipswich, QLD.
"Played in Hard Luck" (1891). *Boston Globe*, Saturday, August 8, p. 5.
"The Players at Work" (1893). *The Sporting Life*, Saturday, March 31, p. 6.
"Players League" (1890). *St. Paul Daily Globe*, Sunday, May 4, p. 6.
"Players' League News Notes" (1890). *The Sporting Life*, Wednesday, April 19, p. 9.
"Players Released by St. Louis Achieve Success" (1900). *St. Louis Republic*, Sunday, June 17, p. 5.
"Playing Great Ball" (1890). *Pittsburg Dispatch*, Monday, September 8, p. 6.
"The Plucky Unions Get Away with the Dandy Team from St. Louis" (1884). *Boston Globe*, Wednesday, September 24, p. 4.
Porter, D.L. (2000). *Biographical Dictionary of American Sports*. Vol. 2: *Baseball, G–P*. Westport, CT: Greenwood Press.
Pratten, C., and R. Irving (1994). "Quandong: The Old Catholic School House Campbelltown. Conservation Plan." Heritage Conservation Consultants, Balmain, NSW [cited July 14, 2013]. Available from: http://www.westernsydneylibraries.nsw.gov.au/campbelltown/education.html
Price, C. (1987). "Chapter 1: Immigration and Ethnic Origin." In *Australians: Historical Statistics*. Ed. W. Vamplew. Broadway, NSW, Australia: Fairfax, Syme & Weldon Associates, pp. 2–22.
Primm, J.N. (1998). *Lion of the Valley: St. Louis, Missouri, 1764–1980*. St. Louis: Missouri Historical Society Press.
"Progress of the Moreton Bay Tramway Company" (1861). *The Courier* (Brisbane, QLD), Monday, September 16, pp. 4, 5.
"A Protested Game" (1887). *St. Paul Daily Globe*, Tuesday, September 15, p. 5.
Pryor & Co's Dubuque City Directory 1877–8: Comprising an Alphabetical List of Citizens, a Classified Business Directory, Lists of City and County Officers, Churches, Schools, Societies, Streets and Wards. Dubuque, IA: Pryor.
"The Public Health Act of England" (1849). *Sydney Morning Herald*, Friday, September 14, p. 2.
Putman, J.J. (1981). "A New Day for Ireland." *National Geographic* 159 (4): pp. 442–469.
"Pyle Was Pounded" (1887). *St. Paul Daily Globe*, Sunday, October 2, p. 5.

"Queensland" (1864). *Sydney Morning Herald*, Tuesday, July 12, p. 5.
"Questions and Answers" (1895). *Omaha Daily Bee*, Sunday, August 25, p. 16.
"Quinn as an Outfielder" (1888). *St. Paul Daily Globe*, Sunday, December 16, p. 6.
"Quinn Goes to Cincinnati" (1900). *St. Louis Republic*, Sunday, June 17, p. 10.
"Quinn Signs" (1891). *Boston Globe*, Friday, February 20, p. 1.
"Quinn Started Winning Rally: 'Old Reliable' Led the Reds in a Batting Rally Which Defeated St. Louis" (1900). *St. Louis Republic*, Wednesday, June 27, p. 7.
"Quinn, John R" (1920). *St. Louis Post-Dispatch*, Saturday, February 7, p. 7.
"Quinn's Proposal" (1895). *The Sporting Life*, Saturday, November 2, p. 3.
Rader, B.G. (2008). *Baseball: A History of America's Game*. 3rd ed. Urbana: University of Illinois Press.
Randall, D. (1976). *The First Modern Olympics*. Berkeley: University of California Press.
Ratnaike, R.N. (2003). "Acute and Chronic Arsenic Toxicity" *Postgraduate Medical Journal* 79 (933): pp. 391–396.
Reach, A.J. (1989, reprint). *Reach Baseball Guide 1890*. St. Louis: Horton Publishing.
_____. (1902). *Reach's Official American League Base Ball Guide for 1902*. Philadelphia: A.J. Reach Co.
_____. (1987, reprint). *Spalding Baseball Guide and Official League Book for 1885: A Complete Hand Book of the National Game of Base Ball*. St. Louis: Horton Publishing.
"Record of the Game" (1884). *St. Louis Globe-Democrat*, Friday, August 22, p. 6.
Reidenbaugh, L., and *The Sporting News* (1997). *Cooperstown: Baseball's Hall of Fame—Revised*. New York: Random House Value Publishing.
"Released by Von Der Ahe" (1895). *San Francisco Call*, Monday, June 24, p. 2.
Rent and Sales Report: Rent (June Quarter 2012), Sales (March Quarter 2012) (2012). New South Wales Government: Housing Analysis and Research Branch, Sydney, NSW [cited May 30, 2013]. Available from: www.housing.nsw.gov.au (Quick Links).
"Restraining Order Granted" (1884). *Sedalia Weekly Bazoo* (Sedalia, MO), Tuesday, May 13, p. 1.
"A Revival of Interest in the Forest City" (1899). *The Sporting Life*, Saturday, July 8, p. 5.
Richardson, M. (2006). *Once a Jolly Swagman: The Ballad of Waltzing Matilda*. Melbourne: Melbourne University Press.
Riess, S.A. (2006). *Encyclopedia of Major League Baseball Clubs*. Westport, CT: Greenwood Publishing Group.
_____. (1999). *Touching Base: Professional Baseball and American Culture in the Progressive Era*. Westport, CT: Greenwood Press.
Roberts, B. (1991). *Stories of the Southside*. Archerfield, QLD: Aussie Books.
Robinson, G., and C. Salzberg (1991). *On a Clear Day They Could See Seventh Place—Baseball's Worst Teams*. New York: Dell Publishing.
"Robison's Bereavement" (1899). *The Sporting Life*, Saturday, May 6, p. 6.
"Robisons Mortgage St. Louis Ball Club" (1900). *St. Louis Republic*, Tuesday, November 20, p. 7.
Rodgers, T.G., and R. Hook (2008). *Irish-American Units in the Civil War*. Oxford, UK: Osprey.
Rosenberg, H.W. (2004). *Cap Anson 2: The Theatrical and Kingly Mike Kelly: U.S. Team Sport's First Media Sensation and Baseball's Original Casey at the Bat*. Arlington, VA: Tile Books.
Rosensweig, D. (2005). *Retro Ball Parks: Instant History, Baseball, and the New American City*. Knoxville: University of Tennessee Press.
"Rotunda Riff-Raff: Some Men Who Were Visitors in St. Paul Yesterday" (1887). *St. Paul Daily Globe*, Friday, May 13, p. 4.
"Rum-Crazed Frank Larkin" (1883). *The Sun* (New York), Wednesday, April 25, p. 1.
"Runs Scored Team Records" (2011). Baseball Almanac [cited August 20, 2013]. Available from: http://www.baseball-almanac.com/recbooks/rb_runs2.shtml.
Rust, A. (1992). *Get That Nigger Off the Field: An Oral History of Black Ballplayers from the Negro Leagues to the Present*. Brooklyn: Book Mail Services.
Saccoman, J. (2012). "John Brush." Society for American Baseball Research (SABR) BioProject [cited August 21, 2013]. Available from: http://sabr.org/bioproj/person/a46ef165.
"Safe in St. Louis" (1896). *The Sporting Life*, Saturday, March 14, p. 1.
Sage, V. (2009). "Enniskillen Workhouse Register: Dec 1845–July 1847." Ireland Genealogy Projects [cited December 12, 2012]. Available from: http://www.igp-web.com/fermanagh/Donated.htm.
"St. Louis 3–Louisville 1" (1893). *The Sun* (New York), Saturday, April 29, p. 8.
"St. Louis 6, Louisville 4" (1894). *Boston Daily Globe*, Saturday, July 28, p. 3.
"St. Louis 15, Philadelphia 1" (1884). *Philadelphia Record*, Friday, June 27, p. 4.
"St. Louis 20, Baltimore 6" (1884). *Baltimore American*, Friday, May 16, p. 3.
"St. Louis Cardinals (Team History & Encyclopedia)" (2013). Baseball-Reference.com [cited July 24, 2013]. Available from: http://www.baseball-reference.com/teams/STL/.
St. Louis City Directory (1885–86). St. Louis: R.L. Polk.
"St. Louis Club Improves as Season Progresses" (1900). *St. Republic*, Sunday, May 6, p. 4.
"St. Louis Gets McGraw" (1900). *San Francisco Call*, Wednesday, May 9, p. 4.
"St. Louis Lost in Eleven Innings" (1900). *St. Louis Republic*, Sunday, June 17, p. 10.
"The St. Louis Man Who Makes Osculation a Fine Art: A St. Louis Sensation" (1889). *Omaha Daily Bee*, Tuesday, February 19, p. 5.
"St. Louis Men for St. Louis Ball Team" (1901). *St. Louis Republic*, Sunday, February 3, p. 11.
"St. Louis Sad over the Persistent Bad Luck of the Cardinals" (1900). *The Sporting Life*, Saturday, June 16, p. 5.
"St. Louis Sayings" (1895). *The Sporting Life*, Saturday, December 28, p. 7.
"St. Louis Sayings" (1895). *The Sporting Life*, Saturday, July 27, p. 10.
"St. Louis Sayings: Another Change in the Browns' Management" (1895). *The Sporting Life*, Saturday, August 17, p. 10.
"St. Louis Sayings: Royal Welcome Accorded the New Manager" (1896). *The Sporting Life*, Saturday, February 8, p. 3.
"St. Louis Sayings: Von Der Ahe Saves Baseball in the West" (1895). *The Sporting Life*, Saturday, July 20, p. 11.
"St. Louis Sayings: Von Der Ahe Stuck on the Young Blood Theory" (1895). *The Sporting Life*, Saturday, August 24, p. 9.
"St. Louis Screed" (1886). *The Sporting Life*, Wednesday, October 27, p. 2.
"St. Louis Siftings" (1894). *The Sporting Life*, Saturday, June 30, p. 5; Saturday, July 14, p. 6.; Saturday, August 4, p. 4.

"St. Louis Siftings—Ready for the Great Fight of 1894" (1894). *The Sporting Life*, Saturday, April 21, p. 6.

"St. Louis Siftings—Rumors as to the Make-up of the '94 Team" (1894). *The Sporting Life*, Saturday, October 21, p. 5.

"St. Louis Siftings—The Browns as Seen from the Small End of the Opera Glass" (1893). *The Sporting Life*, Saturday, September 2, p. 3.

"St. Louis Siftings—The Dedication of a New Park a Social Event" (1893). *The Sporting Life*, Saturday, May 6, p. 3.

"St. Louis Siftings—The Gratifying Showing of the Browns" (1894). *The Sporting Life*, Saturday, May 5, p. 8.

"St. Louis Siftings—Waterlooed Browns Homecoming from the East" (1893). *The Sporting Life*, Saturday, September 16, p. 11.

"St. Louis Smiles over the Unexpected Triumphs in Brooklyn" (1900). *The Sporting Life*, Saturday June 9, p. 4.

"St. Louis Sundries: Hopes Rather High Just Now in the Mound City" (1898). *The Sporting Life*, Saturday, March 26, p. 9.

"St. Louis Unions 16; Bostons, 4" (1884). *Boston Globe*, Friday, May 23, p. 8.

"A St. Louis Victory" (1894). *The Sporting Life*, Wednesday, April 21, p. 5.

"St. Paul in the Van" (1887). *St. Paul Daily Globe*, Monday, September 8, p. 5.

"St. Paul Is Now on Even Terms with Milwaukee" (1887). *St. Paul Daily Globe*, Monday, July 18.

"The Same Old Story" (1889). *The Sporting Life*, Friday, August 16, p. 7.

Schechter, H. (2009). *The Whole Death Catalog: A Lively Guide to the Bitter End*. New York: Ballantine Books.

Schlossberg, D. (1983). *The Baseball Catalog*. Middle Village, NY: Jonathan David Publishers.

"Season Closed." (1892). *Boston Globe*, Sunday, October 16, p. 6.

"Section and Lot Report for Calvary Cemetery" (1988). Catholic Cemeteries of the Archdiocese of St. Louis [cited May 17, 2000]. Available from: http://archstl.org/cemeteries/content/view/91/233/.

Seidel, M. (2002). *Streak: Joe DiMaggio and the Summer of '41*. Lincoln: University of Nebraska Press.

"Senators Arrive Home" (1901). *Washington Times*, Sunday, April 21, p. 9.

Seymour, H., and D.S. Mills (1960). *Baseball: The Early Years*. New York: Oxford University Press.

Shaffer, J.L., and J.T. Tigges (2000). *Dubuque, Iowa: Then and Now (Images of America Series)*. Chicago: Arcadia Publishing.

Sherard, G.E. (2007). "Mining Accidents Index: Iowa Mining Accidents 1893–1895 & 1906–1921." Denver Public Library Digital Collections [cited July 12, 2013]. Available from: http://digital.denverlibrary.org/cdm/ref/collection/p16079coll16/id/3342.

Sheumaker, H., and S.T. Wajda (2008). *Material Culture in America: Understanding Everyday Life*. Santa Barbara, CA: ABC-CLIO.

Shiffert, J. (2006). *Base Ball in Philadelphia: A History of the Early Game, 1831–1900*. Jefferson, NC: McFarland.

"Shipping—Arrivals" (1855). *Sydney Morning Herald*, Friday, May 18, p. 4.

"Shipping News—The Matoaka" (1860). *Lyttelton Times*, December 8, p. 4.

"Shut Out" (1884). *St. Louis Republican*, Monday, October 20, p. 6.

Simon, T. (2012). "Eddie Grant." Society for American Baseball Research (SABR) BioProject [cited August 7, 2013]. Available from: http://sabr.org/bioproj/person/0d10da81.

"The Single Female Immigrants by the Ship Telegraph" (1853). *Sydney Morning Herald*, Saturday, 24 September, p. 4.

Slade, P. (1998). *Player Unions in Australian Professional Sport*. Conference on Globalization and Regionalism: Employment Relations Issues in the Asia Pacific [Proceedings]. Wollongong, NSW: University of Wollongong, pp.301–312.

Smiles, J. (2005). *"Ee-Yah": The Life and Times of Hughie Jennings, Baseball Hall of Famer*. Jefferson, NC: McFarland.

Smith, H.A., I.L. Smith, and L. Hershfield (2000). *Low and Inside: A Book of Baseball Anecdotes, Oddities, and Curiosities*. New York: Doubleday.

Smith, R. (1970). *Baseball*. New York: Simon & Schuster.

Snyder, J. (2005). *Cubs Journal: Year by Year and Day by Day with the Chicago Cubs since 1876*. Cincinnati: Emmis Books.

Society for American Baseball Research (1999). "A Review of Baseball History." *The National Pastime* 19: pp. 81–82.

Society for American Baseball Research (2007). *The Sabr Baseball List & Record Book: Baseball's Most Fascinating Records and Unusual Statistics*. New York: Scribner.

"Soldiers' Records: War of 1812—World War I: Quinn, Clarence P." (2013). Missouri Digital Heritage [cited April 27, 2013]. Available from: http://www.sos.mo.gov/archives/soldiers/details.asp?id=A104496&conflict=World%20War%20I&txtName=quinn,%20clarence&selConflict=World%20War%20I&txtUnit=&rbBranch=.

"Soldiers' Records: War of 1812–World War I: Quinn, Joseph F." (2013). Missouri Digital Heritage [cited April 27, 2013]. Available from: http://www.sos.mo.gov/archives/soldiers/details.asp?id=A104512&conflict=World%20War%20I&txtName=jos&selConflict=All&txtUnit=&rbBranch=&offset=12375.

Solomon, B. (1997). *The Baseball Timeline: The Day-by-Day History of Baseball, from Valley Forge to the Present Day*. New York: Avon Books.

_____. (1999). *Where They Ain't: The Fabled Life and Untimely Death of the Original Baltimore Orioles, the Team That Gave Birth to Modern Baseball*. New York: Free Press.

"Some 'Figgers'" (1890). *The Sporting Life*, Wednesday, June 14, p. 5.

"South West Attractions: John Boyle O'Reilly" (2013), [cited August 24, 2013]. Available from: http://www.southwestattractions.com.au/john-boyle-oreilly.html.

"The Southern Gold Fields [from Our Correspondent]" (1856). *Sydney Morning Herald*, Saturday, July 5, p. 3.

"The Spalding Trophy" (1887). *St. Paul Daily Globe*, Sunday, July 24.

"Sparks from the Diamond" (1888). *Omaha Daily Bee*, Sunday, September 30, p. 7.

"Spasmodic Sprague" (1888). *St. Paul Daily Globe*, Sunday, August 12, p. 6.

Spatz, L. (2004). *Bad Bill Dahlen: The Rollicking Life and Times of an Early Baseball Star*. Jefferson, NC: McFarland.

_____. (2012). *Historical Dictionary of Baseball*. Lanham, MD: Scarecrow Press.

"Special Correspondence of the Dispatch, Boston, August 24, 1889" (1889). *Pittsburg Dispatch*, Monday, August 26, p. 6.

"The Speed of Bicycles" (1884). *Evening Critic* (Washington, DC), Thursday, October 30, p. 1.

Spink, A.H. (1911, reprinted April 2000). *The National Game*. 2nd ed. Carbondale: Southern Illinois University Press.

"Splinters from the Bats" (1888). *Wichita Daily Eagle*, Sunday, May 6, p. 6.

"Sporting Affairs—Chicago Beaten by St. Louis in a Ridiculously Easy Manner" (1885). *Chicago Tribune*, Thursday, September 10, p. 6.

"Sporting Matters—St. Louis Again Defeated by the Chicago Team" (1885). *Chicago Tribune*, Wednesday, June 10, p. 6.

"The Sporting Mill: St. Louis Daguerreotypes No. 105" (1937). *St. Louis Daily Globe-Democrat*, Sunday, November 28, p. 16.

Sporting News (2006). *The Complete Daguerreotypes & Fact Book*. St. Louis: The Sporting News.

"Sporting Notes" (1888). *Boston Globe*, Friday, January 6, p. 6.

"Sporting Notes" (1888). *Evening Bulletin* (Maysville, KY), Tuesday, August 28, p. 1.

"Sporting: The Altoonas Again Defeated by Our Union Club" (1884). *St. Louis Republican*, Sunday, April 27, p. 3.

"Sporting: The Louisville Team Given a Fearful Drubbing at Union Park" (1884). *St. Louis Republican*, Sunday, October 26, p. 14.

"Sporting World Gossip" (1898). *Evening Times* (Washington, DC), Wednesday, January 26, p. 9.

"Sports Big and Small" (1901). *St. Paul Globe*, Thursday, November 14, p. 5.

"Sports, Limited" (1888). *St. Paul Daily Globe*, Wednesday, February 8, p. 5.

"St. Columbkille's History" (2013). St. Columbkille Catholic Church, Dubuque, IA [cited August 28, 2013]. Available from: http://stcolumbkille.net/about/about-us/st-columbkilles-history/.

"Standings and Games on Tuesday, August 5, 1884" (2013). Baseball-Reference.com [cited August 15, 2013]. Available from: http://www.baseball-reference.com/games/standings.cgi?date=1884-08-05.

"Standings and Games on Sunday, October 19, 1884" (2013). Baseball-Reference.com [cited August 15, 2013]. Available from: http://www.baseball-reference.com/games/standings.cgi?date=1884-10-19.

"Standings and Games on Monday, September 14, 1885" (2013). Baseball-Reference.com [cited August 3, 2013]. Available from: http://www.baseball-reference.com/games/standings.cgi?date=1885-09-14.

"Standings and Games on Saturday, October 9, 1886" (2013). Baseball-Reference.com [cited August 20, 2013]. Available from: http://www.baseball-reference.com/games/standings.cgi?date=1886-10-09.

"Standings and Games on Thursday, June 1, 1889" (2013). Baseball-Reference.com [cited August 15, 2013]. Available from: http://www.baseball-Reference.com/games/standings.cgi?date=1899-06-01.

"Standings and Games on Thursday, August 22, 1889" (2013). Baseball-Reference.com [cited June 16, 2013]. Available from: http://www.baseball-reference.com/games/standings.cgi?date=1889-08-22.

"Standings and Games on Thursday, September 19, 1889" (2013). Baseball-Reference.com [cited June 17, 2013]. Available from: http://www.baseball-reference.com/games/standings.cgi?date=1889-09-19.

"Standings and Games on Monday, September 30, 1889" (2013). Baseball-Reference.com [cited June 17, 2013]. Available from: www.baseball-reference.com/games/standings.cgi?year=1889&month=9&day=30&submit=Submit+Date.

"Standings and Games on Sunday, July 2, 1892" (2013). Baseball-Reference.com [cited August 24, 2013]. Available from: http://www.baseball-reference.com/games/standings.cgi?date=1893-07-02.

"Standings and Games on Thursday, September 29, 1892" (2013). Baseball-Reference.com [cited August 24, 2013]. Available from: http://www.baseball-reference.com/games/standings.cgi?date=1892-09-29.

"Standings and Games on Friday, June 1, 1894" (2013). Baseball-Reference.com [cited August 20, 2013]. Available from: http://www.baseball-reference.com/games/standings.cgi?date=1894-06-01.

"Standings and Games on Monday, September 2, 1895" (2013). Baseball-Reference.com [cited August 30, 2013]. Available from: http://www.baseball-reference.com/games/standings.cgi?date=1895-09-02.

"Standings and Games on Saturday, June 16, 1900" (2013). Baseball-Reference.com [cited August 15, 2013]. Available from: http://www.baseball-reference.com/games/standings.cgi?date=1900-06-16.

Starr, I. (1976). "Influenza in 1918: Recollections of the Epidemic in Philadelphia." *Annals of Internal Medicine* 85: pp. 516–518.

"Started: The League Championship Season" (1894). *The Sporting News*, Saturday, April 21, p. 4.

"Startling Intelligence" (1887). *St. Paul Daily Globe*, Thursday, October 20, p. 4.

"A Startling Story: Mr. Lucas to Desert Union Association" (1884). *The Sporting Life*, Wednesday, December 17, p. 1.

State & County Quickfacts: Duluth (City), Minnesota (2013). United States Census Bureau—U.S. Department of Commerce [cited April 3, 2013]. Available from: http://quickfacts.census.gov/qfd/states/27/2717000.html.

State of the Environment Report: Places on Heritage Registers in Eurobodalla Shire, June 2004 (2004). Office of the Commissioner for Sustainability and the Environment, Canberra [cited July 7, 2013]. Available from: http://www.envcomm.act.gov.au/soe/soe2004/Eurobodalla/heritage1.htm.

Steuart, W.A. (1905). *Special Report: Mines and Quarries*. Washington: Department of Commerce and Labor (Bureau of the Census).

Stevens, D. (1998). *Baseball's Radical for All Seasons: A Biography of John Montgomery Ward*. Lanham, MD: Scarecrow Press.

"Still Scheming" (1890). *The Sporting Life*, Wednesday, October 25, p. 1.

Stiskin, P. (1893). *Moruya: The First 150 Years*. Moruya, NSW: Moruya and District Historical Society.

"Stole a March" (1889). *Boston Globe*, September 13, p. 5.

"Stranded Cricketers" (1913). *Cairns Post* (Cairns, QLD), Monday, August 18, p. 6.

"Streetcar Strike of 1899" (1999). *Encyclopedia of Cleveland History* [cited June 2, 2013]. Available from: http://ech.cwru.edu/ech-cgi/article.pl?id=SSO1.

"Strike Stops Ball Games" (1900). *St. Louis Republic*, Wednesday, May 9, p. 6.

"Stuart's Diary" (1863). *Sydney Morning Herald*, Tuesday, January 13, p. 3.

"Successful Ball Players: Some of the Men Who Have Laid up Snug Fortunes" (1888). *St. Paul Daily Globe*, Sunday, December 16, p. 6.

Sullivan, D.A. (1995). *Early Innings: A Documentary History of Baseball, 1825–1908*. Ann Arbor, MI: University of Michigan.

"Supreme Court, Brisbane. In the Insolvent Estate of the Moreton Bay Tramway Company" (1863). *Queensland Times, Ipswich Herald & General Advertiser* (Brisbane), Tuesday, February 17, p. 3.

"Supreme Court: Thursday, November 22: Criminal Sittings before His Honor Mr. Justice Lutwyche. Riot: Regina V. Hayes, Parker and Murray" (1866). *Brisbane Courier* (Brisbane, QLD), Friday, November 23, p. 2.

"Sure of the Pennant: New Yorkers Think Their Club Will Beat the Bostons Out" (1889). *Pittsburg Dispatch*, Monday, September 9, p. 6.

Suter, K. (2008). "The Continuing Plight of Australia's Indigenous Peoples." *Contemporary Review* 290 (1690): pp. 349–360.

"'Swaggies, Tuckerbags and Jumbucks'—What the Words Mean" (2011). Who'll come a-Waltzing Matilda with me? National Exhibition. National Library of Australia [cited June 29, 2013]. Available from: http://pandora.nla.gov.au/pan/34755/20110606-1326/www.nla.gov.au/epubs/waltzingmatilda/3-Meanings.html.

Sweeney, P. (2004). *Edwin Flack, the Lion of Athens: Australia's First Olympic Games Gold Medallist*. Australia: Peter Sweeney.

Swenson, M. "Analysis of Baseball." Poetry Foundation [cited March 10, 2013]. Available from: http://www.poetryfoundation.org/poem/177796.

"A Talk with Hanlon" (1891). *Pittsburg Dispatch*, Thursday, February 19, p. 1.

"A Talk with Joe Quinn" (1887). *The Sporting Life*, Wednesday, November 23, p. 3.

"Tebeau Resigns and McGraw Succeeds Him" (1900). *St. Louis Republic*, Monday, August 20, p. 8.

"Ted Breitenstein (Player Page)" (2013). Baseball-Reference.com [cited June 29, 2013]. Available from: http://www.baseball-reference.com/bullpen/Ted_Breitenstein.

"Telegraph [Passenger List]: Online Microfilm of Shipping Lists" (2012). New South Wales Government State Records [cited December 28, 2012]. Available from: http://www.records.nsw.gov.au.

"Telegraphic" (1866). *Brisbane Courier* (Brisbane, QLD), Wednesday, April 11, p. 2.

"Their Fiftieth Victory: The New-Yorks Scored It in Boston Yesterday" (1888). *New York Times*, Sunday, August 3, p. 5.

"Their Probable Positions" (1893). *The Sun* (New York), Saturday, April 5, p. 4.

"They Slugged the Ball" (1896). *Morning Times* (Washington, DC), Sunday, August 9, p. 7.

"They Would Not Bunt" (1897). *The Sun* (Baltimore), Monday, June 21, p. 6.

"This Girl Liked the Kisser" (1889). *Omaha Daily Bee*, Tuesday, February 19, p. 5.

Thomas, J.M. (2012). "Henry V. Lucas." Society for American Baseball Research (SABR) BioProject [cited June 13, 2012]. Available from: http://sabr.org/bioproj/person/20cd29bd.

_____. (2012). "Robison Field (St. Louis)." Society for American Baseball Research (SABR) BioProject [cited July 28, 2013]. Available from: http://sabr.org/bioproj/park/88929e79.

_____. (2012). "Union Base Ball Park (St. Louis)." Society for American Baseball Research (SABR) BioProject [cited July 28, 2013]. Available from: http://sabr.org/bioproj/park/d9c10c59.

Thorn, J., P. Palmer, and D. Reuther (2001). *Total Baseball*. Kingston, NY: Total Sports.

Thornley, S. (2000). *Land of the Giants: New York's Polo Grounds*. Philadelphia: Temple University Press.

Thornton, A. "Windmills Were an Important Part of Wheatgrowing in the Early Days of N.S.W." (1953). *The Land* (Sydney), Friday, April 17, p. 20.

"Thought He Used Fake Baseball" (1912). *Washington Times*, Sunday, February 4, p. 14.

"Three from the Browns" (1894). *Baltimore Sun*, Monday, June 18, p. 6.

"Three Straight Games: Record Gained by the New-Yorks in Boston" (1888). *New York Times*, Tuesday August 5, p. 5.

Tigges, J.T., and J.L. Shaffer (2000). *Dubuque: The 19th Century*. Chicago: Arcadia Publishing.

"Tim Hurst's Methods" (1900). *St. Paul Globe*, Thursday, October 11, p. 5.

"Tim Keefe (Player Page)" (2013). Baseball-Reference.com [cited June 1, 2013]. Available from: http://www.baseball-reference.com/players/k/keefeti01.shtml.

"Tim Keefe (Umpire Page)" (2013). Baseball-Reference.com [cited August 2, 2013]. Available from: http://www.baseball-reference.com/bullpen/Tim_Hurst.

"To Deal with the Contract Breakers" (1890). *Ft. Worth Gazette*, Friday, March 28, p. 5.

"To Enjoy the Great Day" (1887). *St. Paul Daily Globe*, Monday, July 4, p. 3.

"Toledo Badly Beaten" (1895). *The Sporting Life*, Wednesday, April 4, p. 6.

"Tom Barry (Player Page)" (2013). Baseball-Reference.com [cited August 29, 2013]. Available from: http://www.baseball-reference.com/players/b/barryto01.shtml.

"Tonnage for Selected U.S. Ports in 2008" (2008). U.S. Army Corps of Engineers Navigation Data Center. Waterborne Commerce Statistics Center, New Orleans, LA [cited July 28, 2013]. Available from: http://www.navigationdatacenter.us/wcsc/portton08.htm.

"Too Often Signed" (1887). *St. Paul Daily Globe*, Friday, October 18, p. 4.

"Top Notchers" (1892). *Boston Globe*, Monday, June 6, p. 12.

Torres, K. (2012). "Jack Burdock." SABR Baseball Biography Project. Society for American Baseball Research [cited May 5, 2013]. Available from: http://sabr.org/bioproj/person/834f6239.

"Tremendous Conflagration!! In St. Louis, 23 Steamboats Burned! Several Squares in Ashes, Loss of Life!!" (1848). *Glasgow Weekly Times* (Glasgow, MO), Thursday, May 24, p. 2.

"A Tribute to Watkins" (1892). *The Sporting Life*, Saturday, December 24, p. 4.

"Triple Crown of Baseball" (2013). Baseball Almanac [cited August 31, 2013]. Available from: http://www.baseball-almanac.com/awards/aw_triph.shtml.

"Trouble in New York" (1890). *The Sporting Life*, Wednesday, November 22, p. 1.

"Troubles of Chris Von Der Ahe" (1915). *Washington Post*, Sunday, August 8, p. 3.

Turkin, H., and S.C. Thompson (1979). *The Official Encyclopedia of Baseball*. New York: A.S. Barnes.

Turnbull, L.H. (2008). "Sydney in 1858." Dictionary of Sydney [cited May 14, 2013]. Available from: http://www.dictionaryofsydney.org/entry/entry/sydney_in_1858.

Twain, M. (1968). *Life on the Mississippi*. New York: Dodd Mead.

"'Twas a Beauty" (1890). *Boston Sunday Globe*, Sunday, April 20, p. 4.

Twister. "The Australian Baseballers—An Eastern Welcome" (1897). *The Argus* (Melbourne), Friday July 23, p. 6.

"Ty Cobb (Player Page)" (2013). Baseball-Reference.com [cited June 29, 2013]. Available from: http://www.baseball-reference.com/players/c/cobbty01.shtml.

"Under Sunny Skies" (1899). *The Sporting News*, Saturday, April 8, p. 4.

"The Unemployed Railway Navvies" (1866). *The Darling Downs Gazette and General Advertiser* (Toowoomba, QLD), Saturday, September 8, p. 3.

"United States Census" (1880). FamilySearch.org: The Church of Jesus Christ of Latter-day Saints [cited March

10, 2013]. Available from: https://familysearch.org/pal:/MM9.1.1/MD2C-RC4.

"United States Census: City of St. Louis, Missouri—Division of St. Louis City" (1900). United States Census Office [cited November 12, 2012]. Available from: www.familysearch.org.

"United States Census: City of St. Louis, Missouri—Division of St. Louis City" (1910). United States Census Office [cited November 11, 2012]. Available from: www.familysearch.org.

"United States Census: City of St. Louis, Missouri—Division of St. Louis City" (1920). United States Census Office [cited November 12, 2012]. Available from: www.familysearch.org.

"United States Census: City of St. Louis, Missouri—Division of St. Louis City" (1940). United States Census Office [cited August 20, 2013]. Available from: www.familysearch.org.

"United States City Directories, 1882–1901. Saint Louis, MO [Microform]" (1990). Research Publications [Woodbridge, CT].

"U.S. Corn for Grain: Acreage, Yield & Production" (2010). Corn Refiners Association [cited March 31, 2013]. Available from: http://www.corn.org/publications/statistics/u-s-corn-production/.

Vaccaro, F. (2012). "Hugh Daily." SABR Baseball Biography Project. Society for American Baseball Research [cited August 15, 2013]. Available from: http://sabr.org/bioproj/person/8d8c99e4.

"The Value of Peitz" (1893). *The Sporting Life*, Saturday, April 1, p. 4.

Van Ravenswaay, C. (1991). *Saint Louis: An Informal History of the City and Its People, 1764–1865*. St. Louis: Missouri History Museum.

Verne, J. (1872). *Around the World in Eighty Days*. London: Lord, Dean & Son.

"A Very Good Trip" (1891). *Pittsburg Dispatch*, Sunday, September 20, p. 6.

"Victory for Lucas" (1885). *Boston Globe*, Tuesday, May 12, p. 5.

Voigt, D.Q. (2010). *American Baseball: From Gentleman's Sport to the Commissioner System*. University Park: Pennsylvania State University Press.

"Von Der Ahe Discusses His Players" (1894). *The Sporting Life*, Saturday, December 8, p. 3.

"Von Der Ahe's Woe" (1894). *The Sporting Life*, Saturday, August 25, p. 1.

Votes & Proceedings, Vol. 2: *Register of Quartz Vein Applications* (1852). Sydney: New South Wales Parliament (Legislative Council).

Waggoner, G., K. Moloney, and H. Howard (2000). *Spitters, Beanballs, and the Incredible Shrinking Strike Zone: The Stories Behind the Rules of Baseball*. Chicago: Triumph Books.

"A Wail of Distress from the Mound City" (1896). *The Sporting Life*, Saturday, May 4, p. 4.

Walker, F. "Campbelltown: Forthcoming Centenary" (1920). *Sydney Morning Herald*, Tuesday, November 30, p. 8.

"Waltzing Matilda: A National Anthem?" (2011). "Who'll come a-Waltzing Matilda with me?" National Exhibition. National Library of Australia [cited June 6, 2013]. Available from: bit.ly/1cquyCH.

"Washington Whispers" (1890). *The Sporting Life*, Wednesday, September 6, p. 13.

Weeks, J. (2012). *Cellar Dwellers: The Worst Teams in Baseball History*. Lanham, MD: Scarecrow Press.

"West Hotel: The Only Fire-Proof Hotel in Minneapolis" (1887). *St. Paul Daily Globe*, Sunday, May 22, p. 3.

"Western All Right" (1902). *Salt Lake*, Sunday, March 9, p. 4.

"Western Association (Br Bullpen)" (2013). Baseball-Reference.com [cited May 10, 2013]. Available from: http://www.baseball-reference.com/bullpen/Western_Association.

"Weyhing Was Not Given Any Support" (1900). *St. Louis Republic*, Friday, June 15, p. 6.

"What an Escape!" (1889). *Boston Globe*, Saturday, September 14, p. 5.

"What Are the Benefits and Responsibilities of Citizenship?" (2013). U.S. Citizenship and Immigration Services [cited August 15, 2013]. Available from: www.uscis.gov/files/article/chapter2.pdf.

"What They Have Done" (1886). *The Sporting Life*, Wednesday, July 7, p. 2.

"Where the Ball Players Are" (1896). *St. Paul Globe*, Sunday, November 8, p. 10.

"Whipped Again" (1896). *The Sun* (Baltimore), Saturday, June 6, p. 6.

"Why Boston Won" (1892). *Boston Sunday Globe*, Sunday, October 30, p. 23.

Wilbert, W.N. (2007). *The Arrival of the American League: Ban Johnson and the 1901 Challenge to National League Monopoly*. Jefferson, NC: McFarland.

_____. (2013). *The Shutout in Major League Baseball: A History*. Jefferson, NC: McFarland.

"Will Duluth Drop Out?" (1887). *St. Paul Daily Globe*, Wednesday, October 5, p. 5.

"Will Probably Be Called" (1892). *The Sporting Life*, Saturday, October 15, p. 1.

Williams, A. (1885). *Mineral Resources of the United States 1883–84*. Washington: U.S. Geological Survey, Department of the Interior.

"Willie Keeler (Player Page)" (2013). Baseball-Reference.com [cited July 18, 2013]. Available from: http://www.baseball-reference.com/players/k/keelewi01.shtml.

"With the Baltimores" (1894). *Baltimore Sun*, Saturday, June 30, p. 6.

Witt, J.F. (2006). *The Accidental Republic: Crippled Workingmen, Destitute Widows, and the Remaking of American Law*. Boston: Harvard University Press.

Witt, R. (2012). *A Lifetime of Training for Just Ten Seconds: Olympians in Their Own Words*. New York: Bloomsbury Publishing.

"Won by a Home-Run Hit" (1888). *New York Times*, Saturday, August 30, p. 7.

Woodham-Smith, C. (1962). *The Great Hunger: Ireland 1845–1849*. London: H. Hamilton.

"A Word with the Players" (1891). *The Sporting Life*, Wednesday, February 28, p. 3.

"The World of Base Ball" (1897). *The Sporting Life*, May 1; June 5, p.2.

"The World of Sports" (1887). *Duluth Weekly Tribune*, June 3.

"The Worst Game in Years" (1892). *Evening Star* (Washington, DC), Friday, September 30, p. 10.

Worth, R. (2013). *Baseball Team Names: A Worldwide Dictionary, 1869–2011*. Jefferson, NC: McFarland, p. 110.

"Wray's Column: With 4 Champions" (1940). *St. Louis Post-Dispatch*, Wednesday, November 13, p. 8.

Wyatt, I.D., and D.E. Hecker (2006). "Occupational Changes During the 20th Century." *Monthly Labor Review* (March 2006): pp. 35–58.

Wynn, P. (1995). *Baseball's First Stars*. Phoenix, AZ: Society for American Baseball Research.

"Yearly League Leaders and Records for Home Runs" (2013). Baseball-Reference.com [cited July 28, 2013].

Available from: http://www.baseball-reference.com/leaders/HR_leagues.shtml.

Young, D. (2011). *Rebound Strong: Hope and Strength for Life's Toughest Challenges*. Round Rock, TX: Wind Runner Press.

"The Zenith City Team Goes Down in One of the Most Hotly-Contested Games of the Season" (1887). *St. Paul Daily Globe*, Monday, July 18.

"Zinc Production—from Ore to Metal" (2013). International Zinc Association [cited March 30, 2013]. Available from: http://www.zinc.org/basics/zinc_production.

Zinn, H. (2003). *A People's History of the United States: 1492–Present*. New York: HarperCollins.

Zoss, J., and J.S. Bowman (1989). *Diamonds in the Rough: The Untold History of Baseball*. New York: Macmillan.

Index

Numbers in ***bold italics*** indicate pages with photographs.

Adcock, Joe 145
admission price 44, 74, 79, 120
Ake, John 78–79, 82, 85
alcohol 42, 44, 46, 53, 57, 62, 71, 75, 89, 120, 125, 138, 148, 151, 155, 158, 162, 166–167, 171, 185, 195
Alien Contract Labor Law 143
American Association 43–46, 51–52, 54, 56–57, 60–62, 65, 67–68, 71, 73–74, 77, 80, 83, 85, 87, 89, 100, 114, 116, 119, 122–123, 126, 128, 130–131, 135–137, 152, 158, 199, 219
American Federation of Labor 115
American League 126, 140, 162, 192, 199–204, 213–214, 219
American League Park 201
An Gorta Mor see Ireland, potato famine
Anderson, Jay 78–80, 83–85
Anson, Adrian Constantine (Cap) 3, 42–43, 60, 64–65, 69, 73–74, 77, 93, 97, 100, 104, 111, 114–115, 119, 125, 129–130, 140, 144, 173–174, 176, 199, 217
Araluen Valley see Australia
Arlington, Lizzie 130
Assisted Immigrant Scheme 12–13, 17
Australia 1–3, 5, 7–17, 20–39, 79, 97, 100, 120–122, 128–129, 151, 155, 158, 161–162, 173, 190, 218, 219; Araluen Valley 13–14, 17, ***18***, ***19***, 20; Broulee 13–14, 17, ***18***, ***19***, 20; Campbelltown 5, 20, ***28***, ***29***, 30, ***31***, 32, ***33***, 171, 175; convict history 8–11, ***21***, 29–30, 128; drought 3, 26–28, 32–33; Ipswich 3, 7–8, ***9***, 10, ***11***, 20, ***21***, ***22***, ***23***, ***24***, ***25***, 26, 27, 30, 228; railways 20–28, 32; Sydney 2, 8–10, 12, ***13***, 17, 20–21, ***28***, 33, 39, 47, 97, 121, 162, 174, 218
Australia, baseball in: Australian Baseball Federation 120, 162; Australian Baseball Hall of Fame 1, 162, 218; Australian Baseball League 120–121, 176; Australian-born major league players 2, 218, 228; Claxton Shield 3, 120; competition with cricket 3, 32, 39, 161, 174, 176; 1897 United States tour 3, 5, 173–176; history 3, 65, 97, ***98***, 105, 120–121, 162, 173–174, ***175***, 176, 218, 228; player associations 120–121; *see also* World Tour (Spalding, 1887–1888)
automobiles 206, 210

Baldwin, Charles (Lady) 73, 77, 119
Baldwin, Mark (Fido) 79–80, 113
balk 64, 94, 188
Baltimore 2, 5, 148, 150–152, 154, 159, 164–179
Barnie, Bill 152
Barry, Tom 205
base-running 5, 53, 94–95, 117, 164, 166, 172, 193, 197
Baseball Hall of Fame 3, 4, 38, 40, ***41***, 42–44, 72, 77, 89, ***93***, 97, 105, 109, ***111***, ***112***, 114, ***118***, 119, 123, 125, 128, 130–131, ***139***, 140, 143–144, 146, 156, 164–165, 170–171, 177, 184, 198, 202, 205, 207, 212, 216–217, 226–227
Bassett, Charley 78
Bates, Frank 185–186
beanball see Hit By Pitch
Becherer, Catherine Marie see Quinn, Catherine Marie
Becker, Edward C. 181
beer see alcohol
Belair Lot 56
Bennett, Charlie 101, 103–105, 108, 111, 117, 129–130, 137, 192
bicycles 2, 129
Bierbauer, Lou 118, 131
Biggio, Craig 166
Bignell, George 80
Billings, James B. 100, 106–107, 122
Black Sox 43, 146, 209, 249n91
blacklist 45–46, 51, 62–63, 96, 105, 116, 152, 156

Boston Congress Street Grounds 117, 123; National League 64, 66, 68, 73–74, 77–78, 80, 86, 88–113, 120, 123, ***124***, 125, 127–131, ***132***, 133, 138, 141, 146, 148, 150–151, 153, 157, 162–163, 165–166, 168–169, 172, 176, 177–178, 183–184, 186, 189, 192, 194–195, 198, 200–206, 219; Players League 109–110, 114–117, ***118***, 119–120; South End Grounds ***102***, ***103***, 117, 123, 127; Union Association 46, 54–59, 61
Boyle, Henry 57–58, 60, 62–64, 66–67, 71–72, 76
Breitenstein, Theodore (Ted) 138, 141–150, 153–158, 160–161, 173, 184, 194–195, 200–201
Brodie, Walter (Steve) 138–139, 165, 171, 184
Brotherhood of Base Ball Players 96, 105–106, 109–110, 112–117, 119–120, 122–123, 125
Broulee see Australia
Brouthers, Dan 60, 72, 77, 89, 99, 103, 105, ***111***, 114, ***118***, 123, 137, 164
Brown, Bill 145
Brown, Tom 89, 91, 108, 116, 159
Browning, Pete 97, 122
Brunell, F.H. 120
Brush, John T. 61, 76, 78–79, 105, 119, 181, 195, 198
Buckenberger, Al 152–156, 205
Buckley, Dick 127, 145–147, 149, 171
Burdock, Jack 89
Burkett, Jesse 131–132, 139, 141, 145, 167, 169–170, 181, 191–192
Butler, Mary Catherine 55, 93, 160

Campbelltown see Australia
Carrick, Bill 202–204
Carroll, Cliff 133, 136, 139
Carsey, Wilfred (Kid) 166, 182–183, 186
Caruthers, Bob 73, 137

281

Index

Cassidy, Pete 55, 117
Chadwick, Henry 116, 201, 207
Chamberlain, Icebox 145
Chapman, Ray 166
cheating 5, 66, 107, 164–165, 198
child labor 31–32, 38
Childs, Clarence (Cupid) 145, 170, 187, 195, 201
Chisholm, Caroline *29*
Cincinnati 195–199
Clarke, Fred 171, 173, 183, 205
Clarke, Josh (Pepper) 205
Clarkson, Arthur (Dad) 141, 146–147, 149–150, 154
Clarkson, John 68, 73, 86, 89–90, 92, 101, 104, 107–110, *111*, *112*, 116–117, 123, 125, 130–131
Classification Rule 105–106, 110, 116
Clements, Jack 182, 185
Cleveland, Grover 97
Cleveland Spiders 4, 106, 125, 131, 139, 144–145, 158, 167–170, 179–181, *182*, 183–189; street-car strike 186
Cobb, Ty 169, 209
Colliflower, Harry 186
Collins, Eddie 126
Comiskey, Charles 3, *40*, *41*, 43, 44, 51, 73, 75, 77, 97, 105, 114, 117, 135–137, 181, 184, 199, 217
Conant, William 100, 110, 112
Connor, Roger 91, 114, 127, 139, 146, 149, 153–154, 156, 159, 162–163
Cooley, Dick (Duff) 146–147, 149, 153, 157, 161, 163
Corbett, Joe 171, 176
Corcoran, Tommy 198
cricket 3, 32, 39, 81, 121, 161, 174, 176
Crimean War 12
Crooks, Jack 140–141
Cross, Lave 182, 185, 194
crowd violence 59, 66, 107, 145, 166, 170
Cushman, Ed 87

Dahlen, Bill 144, 180, 193
Daily, Hugh (One Arm) 53, 58, 65
Daley, Bill 106–107, 123
Dawson, George 129
Day, John B. 119, 155, 158
Delahanty, Ed 105, 116, 118, 141, 160, 207
DeMontreville, Gene 179, 193–194
Denny, Jerry 72, 76
Des Moines 81–90, 92, *95*, 96, 155, 201, 205–206, 219, 225
Diddlebock, Harry 61, 160–162
DiMaggio, Joe 172
Dixwell, Arthur 92, 107
Dolan, Tom 52, 59, 62, 67, 69, 72
Donlin, Mike 126, 187
Donnelly, Jim 168, 171
Donovan, Patsy 192, 195
Dowd, Tommy 146, 153, 158, 161–163, 168, 182, 202

Doyle, Jack 171–173, 177, 197
Dubuque 3, 34, *35*, 38–40, *50*, 60, 75, 205; mining 34, *35*, 37–39, 60
Dubuque, Julien 34, *35*, 37
Dubuque Rabbits *40*, *41*, 42–43, 47, 49, 51, 53, 54, 69, *112*
Duffy, Hugh 105, 128–129, 131, 141, 177, 205–206
Duluth 78–87, 90, 113, 115, 225
Dunlap, Fred 4, 44, 46–47, 51–67, 71–77, 80, 86–87, 114, 137, 226

Earle, Billy 78, 84–85
Ehret, Red 153, 156, 158, 160, 173
Ely, William (Bones) 143–144, 146, 148–150, 153–154, 156–157, 160–161, 191
embalming *see* undertaking
Esper, Duke 148, 171
Ewing, Buck 3, 90–91, 97, 101, 103, 105, 107, 114, 117, 154

Farrar, Sid 107
Farrell, Duke 172
Fisher's Ghost 30
Flack, Edwin 161–162
Foley, Charles 104, 107–108
Foulkrod, Frank 82, 84
Frisch, Frankie 213, 217
Fruin, Jeremiah 50

Gaffney, John 148
Gallagher, Jack 129
gambling 44–45, 52, 66, 70, 75, 96, 135, 158, 162, 199, 204
Ganzel, Charlie 128
Garrett, Robert 161
Gear, Dale 202–204
Gilks, Bob 108
Glasscock, Jack 58, 62, 64, 71–72, 76, 78, 108, 111, 116, 138, 141, 144–147, 150, 201
Gleason, Jack 42, 46–47, 51, 57, 59, 62, 67
Gleason, William (Kid) 42, 46–47, 51, 116, 141–142
goldfields 3, 13–14, 17, *18*, *19*, 20, 32, 37, 97, 120
Gompers, Samuel 115
Goold, James 29
Gore, George 64–65, 107, 125
Gorry, Patrick 137, 141
Grant, Eddie 212
Gruber, Henry 110
Gruner, G.A. 180–181

Hahn, Frank (Noodles) 197
Hanlon, Ned 97, 103, 105–106, 114, 123, 137, 159, 164–168, 170–171, 176–181, 184, 193, 197–198, 200
Harley, Dick 182–183, 191
Hart, James Aristotle 100, 106–107, 109–111, 128, 151, 195
Hawley, Pink 144, 146–147, 149–150, 153, 158
Healy, John (Egyptian) 67, 72, 76
Hecker, Guy 73
Heidrick, Emmet 192, 195
Heilbroner, Louis 196

Hemming, George 127, 166, 171
Hesemann, June 213, *214*
Higgins, Bill 89, 91
Hill, Bill 186
Hit By Pitch (HBP) 166–167, 180, 193, 203, 222
Hoffer, Bill 170, 173, 203, 205
Hogan, Bob 100
Holacher, Charles 82
Holliday, Bug 87
Hornsby, Rogers 169, 209, 213, 217
Hornung, Joe 101, 109
Hoy, Dummy 114, 119, 203
Hughey, Jim (Coldwater) 182, 186–187, 191
Hulbert, William A. 44
Hunt, Ron 166
Hurst, Timothy 126–127, 169–170, 180, 197
Hutchinson, Bill 127

immigration 5, 12, *13*, 17, *18*, 29, 34, 49, 51, 68, 93, 143, 190
The Importance of Being Earnest 185
inside baseball 213
International Baseball Federation 120, 176
Ipswich *see* Australia
Ireland: Arles (Queens County) 11; Derryvullan (County Fermanagh) 14; Enniskillen Workhouse 14, *15*, 16; potato famine 8, 14–15, 29, 34, 49, 93, 205

Jack the Kisser 96–97
Jennings, Hugh 38, 44, 147, 164–169, 173, 175, 177–178, 180–181
Johnson, Albert 106, 109–110, 115, 119
Johnson, Bancroft B. 162, 195, 199–210, 209
Johnston, Dick 89, 91, 105, 107, 111–112, 117
Jones, Bert 191, 196
Joyce, Bill 171–172

Keefe, Tim 64, 67, 90–92, 101, 105, 107, 110, 114, *115*
Keeler, Willie 141, 164–165, 167–168, 172–173, 177–178, 181
Keister, Bill 192, 194–195, 201
Kelley, Joe 164–165, 167–168, 173, 181
Kellogg, Nate 80, 84
Kelly, Michael (King) 4, 64, 69, 73–74, 76–77, 86, 88–90, 92, *93*, *94*, 95, 97, 99, 100–101, 104–108, 110, *111*, 112, 114, 116–117, *118*, 123, 125–126, 128–129, 132, 151, 217
Kerry Patch *see* St. Louis
Killen, Frank 143, 167, 173
Kinloch, Billy 157, 159
Kittridge, Malachi 167
Klusman, Billy 89–90
Knight, Lon 103
Knights of Columbus 209–210
Kolb, Eddie 188

Index

Ladies' Days 66
Lajoie, Nap 55, 190, 193–194, 201–203, 227
Latham, Arlie 69, 114, 159–160, 162, 164, 184
Lee, Wyatt (Watty) 202–204
Little Lord Fauntleroy 93
livery stables 69, 137, 142–143, 155, 161, 210
Loftus, Tom 42, 47, 63, 181, 195, 199
Logan, Patrick 8–10
Long, Herman 125, 127, 129–130, 145, 201, 206
Loos, Pete 202
Lowe, Bobby (Link) 117, 130, *132*, 133, 137, 145–146, 153, 104–195
Lucas, Henry V. 46–47, 50–53, 55–59, 61–64, 67, 71–76
Lucas, William 78–79, 82

Mack, Connie 105, 114, 119, *139*, 140, 144, 152, 160, 166, 195, 200
Madden, Kid 104, 107–112
Manning, Jimmy 201–202, 204
Mason, Ernie 149
Mathewson, Christy 198, 212
Matoaka 12
McAleer, Jimmy 131, 199
McCaffrey, Catherine *see* Quinn, Catherine (Caddie)
McCarthy, Tommy 57, 93, 128–129
McCormick, Jim 60, 73
McFarland, Ed 160–161, 163
McGill, Willie 119
McGillicuddy, Cornelius *see* Mack, Connie
McGrath, Margaret 179, *212*
McGrath, Mary Ellen *see* Quinn, Mary Ellen
McGrath, Thomas 4, *69*, 70–71, 75, 179, 210, 212, 214
McGraw, John 69, 77, 164, *165*, 166–168, 171–173, 177, 189, 192–196, 200, 202, 212, 217
McGraw, Minnie 189
McKinnon, Alex 64, 67, 71–72
McMahon, Sadie 147, 166, 168, 171
McPhee, Bid 55, 73, 97, 131, *139*, 151, 162, 226
Medwick, Joe (Ducky) 217–218
Mercer, Win 203–204
Miller, George (Doggie) 143–149, 153, 155–160
Morrill, John 90–91, 100
Morris, Ed 77
Morton, Charlie 85, 87
Most Popular Ball-player in America (award) 4, 142, 219
Mott, Albert 172
Muir, George W. 188
Mullane, Tony 46, 51, 53, 139
Munson, George 149
Murphy, Morg' 117, 123, 160
Murphy, Thomas J. 165
Musgrove, Harry 174
Mutrie, Jim 110
Myrick, C.H. 206

Nash, Billy 105, 117, 123, 129
National Agreement 45–46, 51, 63, 65, 106, 120, 122, 200
National Association of Professional Base Ball Players 44
National League 3, 40–42, 44–46, 51, 53–55, 57–58, 61–64, 67–68, 71, 74–77, 86, 88–95, 97, 101, 105–106, 109–117, 119–120, 122–126, 128, 131–132, 136, 140–141, 147–148, 150, 152–153, 155–158, 161–162, 164–165, 170, 173–174, 179–185, 188–189, 192, 194–195, 198–202, 212–214, 217, 219
New York Giants 64, 90–92, 100–101, 106–108, 110–111, 125, 127–128, 138, 146, 150–151, 155–156, 158, 165, 167, 172, 181, 197–198, 212
Nichols, Kid 117, 125, 128–131, 146, 178, 201, 205
night baseball 76
Nimick, William A. 116
Nops, Jerry 171–172, 197
Northwestern League 40, 43, 45, 78–81, 84, 87

O'Connor, Jack 113
O'Doherty, Kevin Izod 8, *9*
off-season 69, 138, 159
Olympic Games 161–162
O'Neill, Tip 77
O'Reilly, John Boyle 128
Otten, John 156

Parrott, Tom 160
Patten, Case 203–204
Pearce, Dickey 104
Peitz, Henry (Heinie) 138, 145, 148–149, 153–154, 156–158, 160, 173, 184, 194–196
Pfeffer, Fred 55, 97, 118, 151, 226
Phelan, Lew 158–159
Phillips, Bill 197
Players' League 106, 112, 114–120, 122–123, 125, 140, 158, 164, 200, 219
Polo Grounds 92, 100, 105, 107, 125, 198
Pond, Arlie (Doc) 69, 166, 173

Quinn, Catherine (Caddie) *14*, *15*, 16–17, *18*, *19*, 20, 28, 38, 55, 205
Quinn, Catherine Marie 55, 75, 85, *215*, *216*
Quinn, Clarence Patrick 151, 210, *211*, 214
Quinn, Dorothy *213*
Quinn, Estelle 189, 212–213, *215*, *216*
Quinn, John Richard (Scotty) 165, 178, 212–214
Quinn, Joseph James: baseball debut 39, 43–44; birth 3, 7–8; death 214; fielding awards 117–118, 131, 189; immigration to United States 32–34; major league debut 54; manager 82–85, 154–158, 185–189; marriage 75; miner 38–39, 60; minor leagues 78–88, 205–207; naturalization 5, 190; Players' League plot 96, 109; professional signing 47; retirement 207; testimonials 4, 108, 128, 142, 195, 219; undertaker 69–71, 75, 93, 142, 155, 159, 161, 169, 172–173, 184–185, 187, 191, 195–197, 199, 201–204, 207, 209–210, 213, 218
Quinn, Joseph, Jr. 210, *211*, 212, 214
Quinn, Marguerite *215*, *216*
Quinn, Mary 11
Quinn, Mary Ellen (Molly) 69, 71, 75, 84, 86, 97, 179, 212, 213, 214, *215*
Quinn, Patrick, Jr. 17, 30, 38–39
Quinn, Patrick, Sr. 7–8, 11–14, 17, 18–23, 27–28, 30–34, 38–39, 205
Quinn, Richard 213
Quinn, Thomas 11

Radbourn, Charles (Ol' Hoss) 3, *41*, 42–43, 54, 58, 60, 66, 87, 89, 97, 101, 104–110, *111*, *112*, 114, 117, *118*, 125
Reitz, Heinie 151, 167–168, 170, 172, 177, 179, 194
reserve clause 45–46, 51, 61–62, 71, 84, 96, 105–106, 110, 115–116, 120–121, 160–161, 192, 200
revolving 45–46
Richardson, Hardie 60, 72–73, 92, 101, 107–108, 110–111, 117, 123, 137
Ricks, John 147–148
Robinson, Wilbert 2, 69, 170, 171, 173, 192, 193, 195, 200
Robison, Frank de Haas 181, *182*, 183–188, 192, 194, 196, 199
Robison, Matthew Stanley 181, *182*, 184–188, 192, 194, 199
Rowe, Dave 44, 46, 52–53, 58, 60, 62, 67
Rowe, Jack 72, 103, 106
rule changes 141, 166, 188
Rusie, Amos 127, 146, 177, 185, 198
Ryan, Jimmy 144, 177

St. George's Ground 100
St. Louis: baseball history 49–51; Kerry Patch 68–69, 104, 137, 214–215; street-car strike 192–193; tornado (1896) 163
St. Louis Browns 4, 42–43, 46, 51–52, 62–63, 67–69, 73–75, 77, 83, 86, 93, 115, 122–123, 130, 135–150, 152–163, 165, 167, 169, 173, 177, 179–183, 203, 209, 213
St. Louis Maroons 52–53, 56, 58–60, 63–68, 71–76, 78, 87, 138, 148
salaries 45–47, 51, 55, 74–75, 77, 78–79, 85–86, 88, 90, 95, 101, 105–106, 109, 116, 120–122, 133, 136–137, 146–147, 149, 151, 154, 156, 158, 161, 168, 176, 188, 192, 200; *see also* classification rule
Schmelz, Gustavus Heinrich 71, 86

Index

Schmit, Fred (Crazy) 186, 188
Schreckengost, Ossee 185, 190
Selee, Frank 88, 90, 117, 123–125, 127–129, 132, 178, 195
Shafer, Orator 51, 53–54, 56, 60, 62, 65, 67, 87
Shaw, Frederick (Dupee) 57, 59
Shipley, Craig 2, 218, 228
Shugart, Frank 145, 147, 155, 157, 203
Simpson, Harry 97
Smith, Elmer 139, 145
Smith, Pop 107
Soden, Arthur 100, 181
Sowders, Bill 91
Soxalexis, Lou 185, 190
Spalding, Albert G. 3, 5, 44–46, 57, 65, 77, 81, 97, *98*, 99–100, 105–106, 109, 116, 119, 135, 162, 173–176, 181, 187
Spanish influenza *165*, 210–212
Spink, Alfred Henry 40, 42–44, 46, 51, 55, 65, 69, 71, 96, 101, 104–106, 109, 115–116, 120, 123, 136, 141, 149, 158, 165, 170, 188, 199–200, 206
Sportsman's Park 50, 52, 138, 140, 146, 152, 154, 158–161, 172, 180–181, 214
spring training 40, 53, 74, 97, *99*, 100, 121, 129, 152–153, 159–161, 164, 166, 171, 191, 209
Staley, Harry 111, 129, 131, 157–158
Stenzel, Jake 173, 179
Stern, Aaron 119
Stivetts, Jack 128–131, 183, 186
Stovey, Harry 118, 127, 129, 153
Sudhoff, Willie 182–183, 185, 194
Sullivan, Marty 78
Sullivan, Ted 40–43, 46–47, 51–53, 55–56, 61, 97, 114, 126, 135–136, 160, 199

Sunday baseball 44, 53, 62, 75, 83, 89, 120, 162, 180, 195–196
superstitions 105, 184
Sutcliffe, Cy 110
Sweeney, Charlie 46, 52, 58–60, 62–64, 66–67, 72, 148
syndicate baseball 181, 184, 189, 192

Taylor, Billy 53–54, 56–57, 59–60, 75–76
Tebeau, Oliver Wendell (Patsy) 108, 169–170, 177, 181, 187, 191–192, 194–196
Telegraph 16–17
Temple Cup 150, 168–170, 178–179, 181, 212
Thompson, Sam 77, 107, 137, 153, 160
Thornton, Walter 180
Tiernan, Mike 78, 92, 107
Tucker, Tommy 130, 166
Twitchell, Larry 106

umpires 57, 59, 66, 73, 93, 94, 100–101, *102–103*, 107, 110, 116, 123, 126, 131, 142, 144, 147–148, 150–151, 154, 164, 166, 168–169, 172–173, 175–178, 180–181, 184, 186–187, 195, 197, 203, 218; *see also* Gaffney, John; Hurst, Timothy
Union Association 41, 46, 51–57, 60–62, 67, 80, 86, 219

Vandeventer Lot 63, 65, 72
Van Haltren, George 77
Vaughn, Harry 138, 145
Virtue, Jake 145
Von der Ahe, Chris 51, 62–63, 67–68, 73, 77, 83, 86, 115, 122, 135–141, 143–163, 167–168, 172, 177, 179–182, 184, 199, 217
Von der Ahe, Eddie 147, 149

Waddell, Rube 177, 190
walkabout 190, 207
Wallace, Bobby 170, 181, 187, 191–192, 1941–195
Waltzing Matilda 3, 27–28
Ward, John Montgomery 45, 69, 90–93, 97, 105–109, 112, 114, *115*, 116–117, 119–120, 123
Washington 46, 54, 56–57, 61, 78, 100, 106, 108, 128–130, 140, 147, 149–153, 167–169, 172–184, 186–188, 200–203, *204*, 205, 219
Watkins, William H. (Bill) 73, 133, 137–138, 140, 143, 165
Welch, Mickey 66–67, 83, 101, 107
Werden, Perry 52, 59, 138, 141, 143, 145, 149
Western Association 84–87, 89, *95*, 120, 219
Western League 61, 96, 162, 180, 195, 199, 205–206
Weyhing, Gus 100
White, Deacon 72, 106, 119, 137
workhouse, Enniskillen *see* Ireland
World Series 43, 58, 77, 93, 131, 133, 136, *139*, 140, 164
World Tour (1888) 3, 65, *98*, 105, 162, *175*
World War I 209–210, *211*; *see also* Quinn, Clarence; Quinn, Joseph, Jr.
Woulfe, Jimmy 53

Young, Denton (Cy) 125, 131, 144–145, 168, 170, 181, 183, 191–193, 197, 202
Young, Nicholas 62, 152, 167, 174
Youngs, Ross (Pep) 212

Zimmerman, Heinie 212

www.ingramcontent.com/pod-product-compliance
Lightning Source LLC
Chambersburg PA
CBHW080935020526
44116CB00034B/2728